HISTORY OF THE OTTOMAN EMPIRE AND MODERN TURKEY

Volume I: Empire of the Gazis: The Rise and Decline of the Ottoman Empire, 1280–1808

HISTORY OF THE OTTOMAN EMPIRE AND MODERN TURKEY

Volume I: Empire of the Gazis: The Rise and Decline of the Ottoman Empire, 1280–1808

STANFORD SHAW

Professor of History
University of California, Los Angeles

CAMBRIDGE UNIVERSITY PRESS

Cambridge
London   New York   Melbourne

Published by the Syndics of the Cambridge University Press
The Pitt Building, Trumpington Street, Cambridge CB2 1RP
Bentley House, 200 Euston Road, London NW1 2DB
32 East 57th Street, New York, NY 10022, USA
296 Beaconsfield Parade, Middle Park, Melbourne 3206, Australia

First published 1976

Printed in the United States of America
Typeset by The Heffernan Press, Inc., Worcester, Mass.
Printed and bound by The Colonial Press, Inc., Clinton, Mass.

Library of Congress Cataloging in Publication Data

Shaw, Stanford Jay.

History of the Ottoman Empire and Modern Turkey.

Bibliography: p.

Includes index.

Contents: v. 1. Empire of the Gazis: the rise and decline of the
Ottoman Empire, 1280–1808.
1. Turkey – History – Ottoman Empire, 1288–1918.
2. Turkey – History – 1918–1960.
3. Turkey – History – 1960–   I. Title.

DR440.S5   956.1   76-9179

ISBN 0 521 21280 4 hardcovers

ISBN 0 521 2916 31 paperback

CONTENTS

v

PREFACE

The story of Ottoman history is a complicated and complex one. It involves not only the Ottoman dynasty itself but also the many peoples who operated and ruled the empire and were ruled by it – the Turks, the Arabs, the Serbs, the Greeks, the Armenians, the Jews, the Bulgars, the Hungarians, the Albanians, and many others. It constitutes the history of the major religious groups among the subjects, the Muslims, the Jews, and the Christians. It takes into account relations between the Ottomans and their neighbors in Europe and Asia, complicated stories of wars, conquests, diplomacy, and territorial losses that much later were called the Eastern Question. It includes the history of the political, administrative, and social institutions incorporated into this multinational and multicultural empire. It demands discussion of the rise and fall, the birth, efflorescence, and decline of the empire.

To undertake such a task requires considerable choice and selection. The work has been divided into two volumes. This, the first, discusses the Ottoman Empire from its foundations through its apogee in the sixteenth century and subsequent decline until the beginning of the nineteenth century. Its companion volume, *Reform, Revolution, and Republic: The Rise of Modern Turkey, 1808–1975*, will continue the story through the major reform efforts made during the nineteenth century to save the empire, its collapse as a consequence of World War I, and the birth of the Republic of Turkey in the subsequent half-century. The main themes of Ottoman history such as the evolution of central institutions and leadership, foreign relations, and social and economic change, have been emphasized, while provincial developments are included mainly to demonstrate specific issues or problems faced by the empire. Of course, Ottoman history has been discussed many times before, and in considerable detail, but always from the European perspective, through the light of European prejudice, and largely on the basis of European sources. Based on both Ottoman and European sources, this work attempts to balance the picture without introducing the distortions that have previously characterized much of the West's view of the Ottomans.

A book on Ottoman history confronts unusual difficulties regarding transliteration and place names. Because the Ottoman language was written in the Arabic script, scholars have been forced to adapt various methods of transliterating it into Western languages, usually based on their own native tongues. Modern Turkey has complicated matters by developing its own method of spelling, which in some instances is quite different from that used in the West. In addition, Europe has tended to retain the older classical place names in preference to those used by the Ottomans, while the different nationalities that have emerged from the empire in modern times also have assigned names of their own to former Ottoman cities and provinces. Any effort to present all the variants would complicate an already complicated text. Reciting all the Greek and Latin names alone would distort a half-millennium of history. To simplify matters as much as possible, therefore, this text has adapted the standard modern Turkish spellings and place names except when their European forms are unusually familiar to the English-speaking reader. The variants of these names will be found in the index along with a glossary of technical terms and important individuals discussed in the book. Terms have been translated according to their original significance in the Ottoman administrative framework; the often misleading modern literary meanings sometimes given in dictionaries have been avoided.

This work is the product of almost 20 years of research in the Ottoman archives as well as other collections in Europe and the United States. I would like to express my most sincere gratitude to the directors and staffs of the following archives and libraries: in Istanbul the Prime Minister's Archives (Baş Vekâlet Arşivi), in particular Midhat Sertoğlu, Rauf Tuncay, Turgut Işıksal, and Ziya Eşrefoğlu; the Topkapı Palace Museum archives and library, especially Haluk Sehsuvaroğlu, Hayrullah Örs, Kemal Çiğ, and Ismail Hakkı Uzunçarşılı; the Istanbul Municipal Library, Istanbul University Library, Istanbul Archaeological Museum Library, Süleymaniye Library, Bayezit General Library, and Hakkı Tarık Us Library; in Ankara the Turkish National Library (Milli Kütüphane) and the Library of the Turkish Historical Society; the British Museum, the Public Record Office, and the Commonwealth Relations Office in London; the Haus- Hof- und Staats-Archiv and the Austrian National Library in Vienna; the Bibliothèque Nationale, Archives Nationales, Archives du Ministère de la Guerre (Chateau de Vincennes), and Archives du Ministère des Affairs Étrangères (Quai d'Orsay), Paris; the Harry Elkins Widener Library, Harvard University; and the University Research Library, University of California, Los Angeles.

I would like to pay tribute to my teachers, colleagues, and friends who have contributed to this volume in one way or another: Ömer Lutfi Barkan (University of Istanbul), Hamilton A. R. Gibb (Oxford University and Harvard University), Tibor Halasi-Kun (Columbia University). Halil Inalcık (Ankara University and the University of Chicago), Bernard Lewis (University of London and Princeton University), Gustav E. von Grunebaum (University of California, Los Angeles), T. Cuyler Young (Princeton), and Paul Wittek (University of London). My research would not have been possible without the generous assistance of the Ford Foundation, the Rockefeller Foundation, the Guggenheim Foundation, the Social Sciences Research Council, the National Endowment for the Humanities, the American Research Institute in Turkey, and the Research Committee of the Academic Senate, University of California, Los Angeles.

I would like to express particular gratitude to my wife, Ezel Kural Shaw, who has critically revised many sections of this work, particularly those dealing with Ottoman institutions, society, and culture, and whose analytic mind and knowledge of Ottoman history have made significant contributions in its preparation.

STANFORD J. SHAW

Los Angeles, California
August 1976

ABBREVIATIONS

Adıvar, *Ilim*	Abdülhak Adnan-Adıvar, *Osmanlı Türklerinde Ilim*, Istanbul, 1943.
AHR	*American Historical Review*
Aktepe, *Patrona Isyanı*	M. Münir Aktepe, *Patrona Isyam (1730)*, Istanbul, 1958.
Anderson	M. S. Anderson, *The Eastern Question, 1774–1923*, London, 1966.
Ata	Tayyarzade Ahmet Ata, *Tarih-i Ata*, 5 vols., Istanbul, 1291–3/1874–6.
Benedikt	Heinrich Benedikt, *Der Pascha-Graf Alexander von Bonneval 1675–1747*, Graz-Köln, 1959.
Berkes	Niyazi Berkes, *The Development of Secularization in Turkey*, Montreal, 1964.
BSOAS	*Bulletin of the School of Oriental and African Studies.*
BVA	Başvekâlet Arşivi, also called the Başbakanlık Arşivi. The Prime Minister's Archives, Istanbul. For information on the collections cited see S. J. Shaw, "Archival Sources for Ottoman History: The Archives of Turkey," JAOS, 80 (1960), 1–12.
Cahen	Claude Cahen, *Pre-Ottoman Turkey*, London, 1968.
Cevdet¹	Ahmet Cevdet Paşa, *Tarih-i Cevdet*, 1st ed., 12 vols., Istanbul, 1270–1301/1858–83.
Cevdet²	Ahmet Cevdet Paşa, *Tarih-i Cevdet: Tertib-i Cedid*, 2nd ed., 12 vols., Istanbul, 1303/1885–6.
Çelebizade Asım	Küçükçelebizade Ismail Asım, *Tarih-i Celebizade, Asım, Raşit tarihine zeyil*, Istanbul, 1282/1865–6.
Danişmend	Ismail Hami Denişmend, *Izahlı Osmanlı Tarihi kronolojisi*, 4 vols., Istanbul, 1947–61; repr. in 5 vols., Istanbul, 1971–2.
de Testa	Baron Ignatz de Testa, ed., *Recueil des traités de la Porte Ottoman avec les puissances étrangères depuis 1536*, 11 vols., Paris, 1864–1911.
EI¹	*Encyclopaedia of Islam*, ed. Th. Houtsma et al., 4 vols., and Supplement, Leiden, 1931–38.
EI²	*Encyclopaedia of Islam: New Edition*, ed. H.A.R. Gibb, B. Lewis, et al., Leiden, 1960 to date.
Enveri	Trabzoni Sadullah Enveri, *Tarih-i Enveri*, TKS ms. Hazine 5994.

Ergin, *Belediye*	Osman Nuri Ergin, *Mecelle-i Umur-u Belediye,* 5 vols., Istanbul, 1912–17.
Ergin, *Maarif*	Osman Nuri Ergin, *Türkiye Maarif Tarihi,* 5 vols., Istanbul, 1939–43.
Evliya Çelebi	Evliya Çelebi, *Seyahatname,* Istanbul, 10 vols., 1896–1938.
Fisher	Alan Fisher, *The Russian Annexation of the Crimea, 1772–1783,* Cambridge, 1970.
Gibb and Bowen	H. A. R. Gibb and H. Bowen, *Islamic Society and the West: A Study of the Impact of Western Civilization on Moslem Culture in the Near East,* vol. I in 2 parts, London and New York, 1950–7.
Gibb, *Ottoman Poetry*	E. J. W. Gibb, *A History of Ottoman Poetry,* 6 vols., London, 1900–1909.
Holt, *Egypt and the Fertile Crescent*	P. Holt, *Egypt and the Fertile Crescent, 1516–1922,* London and Ithaca, 1966.
Hurewitz, *Diplomacy*	J. C. Hurewitz, *Diplomacy in the Near and Middle East: A Documentary Analysis,* 2 vols., Princeton, N.J., 1956.
IJMES	*International Journal of Middle East Studies,* ed. S. J. Shaw, 1970 to date.
IA	Türkiye Cumhuriyeti, Maarif Vekâleti, *Islam Ansiklopedisi,* Istanbul and Ankara, 1940 to date.
Inalcık, "Bursa"	Halil Inalcık, "Bursa and the Commerce of the Levant," JESHO, 3 (1960), 131–47.
Inalcık, "Methods"	Halil Inalcık, "Ottoman Methods of Conquest," *Studia Islamica, 2* (1954), 103–29.
Iorga	N. Iorga, *Geschichte des Osmanischen Reiches,* 5 vols., Gotha, 1908–13, repr. 1962.
JAOS	*Journal of the American Oriental Society.*
JESHO	*Journal of the Economic and Social History of the Orient.*
JRAS	*Journal of the Royal Asiatic Society.*
JRCAS	*Journal of the Royal Central Asian Society.*
Kâtip Çelebi, *Fezleke*	Mustafa b. Abdullah Kâtip Çelebi, Hacı Halife, *Fezleke-i Kâtip Çelebi,* Istanbul, 2 vols., 1286–7/1869–70.
Kâtip Çelebi, *Düstur*	Mustafa b. Abdullah Kâtip Çelebi, Hacı Halife, *Düstur ül-amel li-Islah al-Halel,* Istanbul, 1280/1863.
Kâtip Çelebi, *Balance*	Mustafa b. Abdullah Kâtip Çelebi, Hacı Halife, *The Balance of Truth,* tr. Geoffrey Lewis, London, 1957.
Koçi Bey	Mustafa Koçi Bey, *Nizam-i Devlete müteallik Göriceli Koçi Beyin . . . Murad-i Rabiyaya verdiği Risaledir,* Istanbul, 1277/1860–1.
Lewis	Bernard Lewis, *The Emergence of Modern Turkey,* 1st ed., London and New York, 1961; 2nd ed., 1968.
Muahedat Mecmuası	Mesut Paşa, ed., *Muahedat Mecmuası,* 5 vols., Istanbul, 1292–8/1876–82.
Mehmet Halife, *Tarih-i Gilmani*	Mehmet Halife, *Tarih-i Gilmani,* Istanbul, 1340.
Naima	Mustafa Naima, *Ravzat ul-Hüseyin fi hûlâsat ul-ahbar ul-hafikin. Tarih-i Naima;* 1st ed., 2 vols., Istanbul, 1147; 2nd ed., 6 vols., Istanbul, 1280. Partly tr. as *Annals of the Turkish*

Empire from 1591 to 1659 of the Christian Era, by C. Fraser, London, 1832.

Noradounghian | Gabriel Noradounghian, ed., *Recueil d'actes internationaux de l'Empire Ottoman,* 4 vols., Paris, 1897–1903.

Pakalın | Mehmet Zeki Pakalın, *Osmanlı Tarih Deyimleri ve Terimleri Sözlüğü,* 3 vols., Istanbul, 1946–55.

Raşit | Mehmet Raşit, *Raşit Tarihi,* 5 vols., Istanbul, 1867.

REI | *Revue des Etudes Islamiques.*

Shaw, *French Revolution* | Stanford J. Shaw, *Ottoman Egypt in the Age of the French Revolution,* Cambridge, 1964.

Shaw, *Between Old and New* | Stanford J. Shaw, *Between Old and New: The Ottoman Empire Under Sultan Selim III, 1789–1807,* Cambridge, Mass., 1971.

Shaw, "Archival Materials" | Stanford J. Shaw, "Ottoman Archival Materials for the Nineteenth and Early Twentieth Centuries: The Archives of Istanbul," IJMES, 6 (1975), 94–114.

Shaw, *Financial* | Stanford J. Shaw, *The Financial and Administrative Organization and Development of Ottoman Egypt, 1517–1798,* Princeton, N. J., 1962.

Silâhdar | Fındıklılı Silâhdar Mehmet Ağa, *Silâhdar Tarihi,* 2 vols., Istanbul, 1928; 2nd ed., Ankara, 1947.

Suphi | Mehmet Suphi, Mustafa Sami, and Hüseyin Şakir, *Tarih-i Suphi, Sami ve Şakir,* Istanbul, 1783.

Thomas, *Naima* | Lewis V. Thomas, *A Study of Naima,* New York, 1972.

TKS | Topkapı Saray Museum and Archives, Istanbul.

TM | *Türkiyat Mecmuası,* Istanbul.

TV | *Tarih Vesikaları*

TOEM | *Tarih-i Osmani Encümeni Mecmuası.*

TTEM | *Türk Tarih Encümeni Mecmuası.*

Uzunçarşılı, *Beylik* | Ismail Hakkı Uzunçarşılı, *Anadolu beylikleri ve Akkoyunlu, Karakoyunlu devletleri,* Ankara, 1937; 2nd ed., Ankara, 1969.

Uzunçarşılı, *Çandarlı* | Ismail Hakkı Uzunçarşılı, *Çandarlı Vezir Ailesi,* Ankara, 1974.

Uzunçarşılı, *Ilmiye* | Ismail Hakkı Uzunçarşılı, *Osmanlı Devletinin Ilmiye Teşkilâtı,* Ankara, 1965.

Uzunçarşılı, *Kapukulu* | Ismail Hakkı Uzunçarşılı, *Osmanli Devleti Teşkilâtından Kapukulu Ocakları,* 2 vols., Ankara, 1943–4.

Uzunçarşılı, *Merkez* | Ismail Hakkı Uzunçarşılı, *Osmanlı Devletinin Merkez ve Bahriye Teşkilatı,* Ankara, 1948.

Uzunçarşılı, OT | Ismail Hakkı Uzunçarşılı, *Osmanlı Tarihi,* 4 vols., Ankara, 1947–59.

Uzunçarşılı, *Saray* | Ismail Hakkı Uzunçarşılı, *Osmanlı Devletinin Saray Teşkilâtı,* Ankara, 1945.

Vasıf | Ahmet Vasıf Efendi, *Tarih-i Vasıf,* 2 vols., Cairo, 1830 (for years 1753–74 only; subsequent vols. only in ms. form:
vol. I (1188/1774–1198/1784), TKS Hazine 1406;
vol. II (1197/1783–1202/1788), Istanbul Archaeological Museum, ms. 355;

vol. III (1203/1788–1309/1794), Istanbul University Library, ms. TY 5980;

vol. IV (1209/1794–1214/1799), Istanbul University Library, ms. TY 5979;

vol. V (1214/1799–1217/1802), Istanbul University Library, ms. TY 6012;

vol. VI (1217/1802–1219/1804), Millet Library, Istanbul, Ali Emiri ms. 609.

von Hammer, GOR   Joseph von Hammer-Purgstall, *Geschichte des Osmanischen Reiches,* 10 vols., Pest, 1827–35; repr. Graz, 1963.

von Hammer,   Joseph von Hammer-Purgstall, *Des Osmanischen Reiches*
Staatsverwaltung   *Staatsverwaltung* . . . , 2 vols., Vienna, 1815; repr., Hildesheim, 1963.

ZDMG   *Zeitschrift der Deutschen Morgenländischen Gesellschaft.*

Zinkeisen   Johann Wilhelm Zinkeisen, *Geschichte des Osmanischen Reiches in Europa,* 7 vols., Hamburg, 1840, Gotha, 1854–63; repr. Darmstadt, 1963.

NOTE ON PRONUNCIATION

The modern standard Turkish spelling system has been employed in this book with only a few exceptions. The Latin letters used in this system are pronounced about the same as their English equivalents, with the following exceptions:

Letter	English pronunciation
c	j
ç	ch
ğ	lengthens preceding vowel; thus *ağa* is pronounced a–a
ı	like the *a* in *serial* or *io* in *cushion*
j	zh
ö	like the German ö
ş	sh
ü	like the German ü
v	lighter than English v

The modern Turkish tendency to change the final Ottoman letters d and b into t and p has been followed, thus Murat, Mahmut, and *kitap,* but these letters return to d and b when followed by vowels, as Mahmudu and *kitabı.* Arabic terms used in Ottoman Turkish have been given their Turkish pronunciations and spellings, thus *mültezim* and *mütevelli* rather than *multazim* and *mutawalli.*

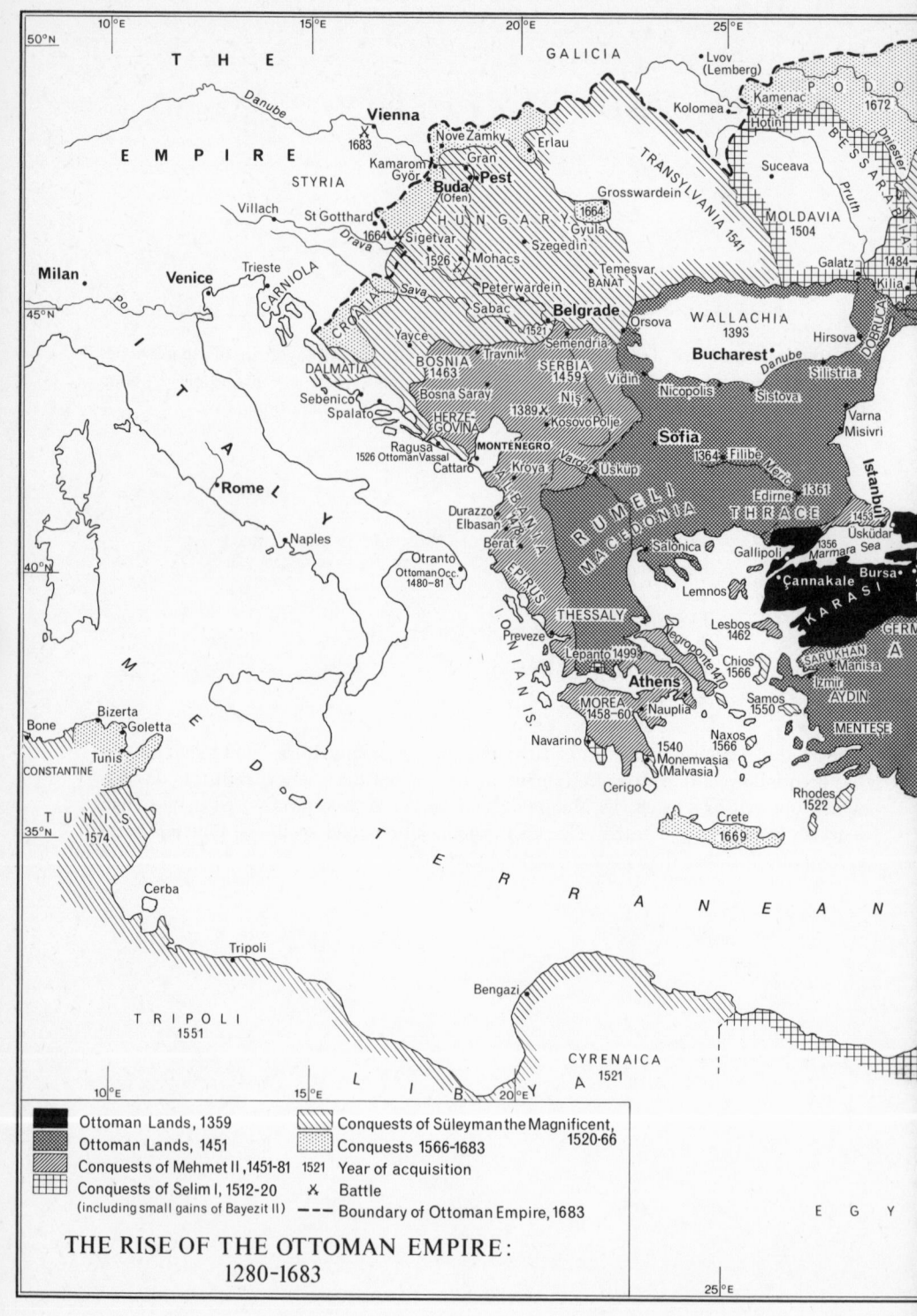

THE RISE OF THE OTTOMAN EMPIRE:
1280-1683

Ottoman Lands, 1359
Ottoman Lands, 1451
Conquests of Mehmet II, 1451-81
Conquests of Selim I, 1512-20
(including small gains of Bayezit II)
Conquests of Süleyman the Magnificent, 1520-66
Conquests 1566-1683
1521 Year of acquisition
✗ Battle
--- Boundary of Ottoman Empire, 1683

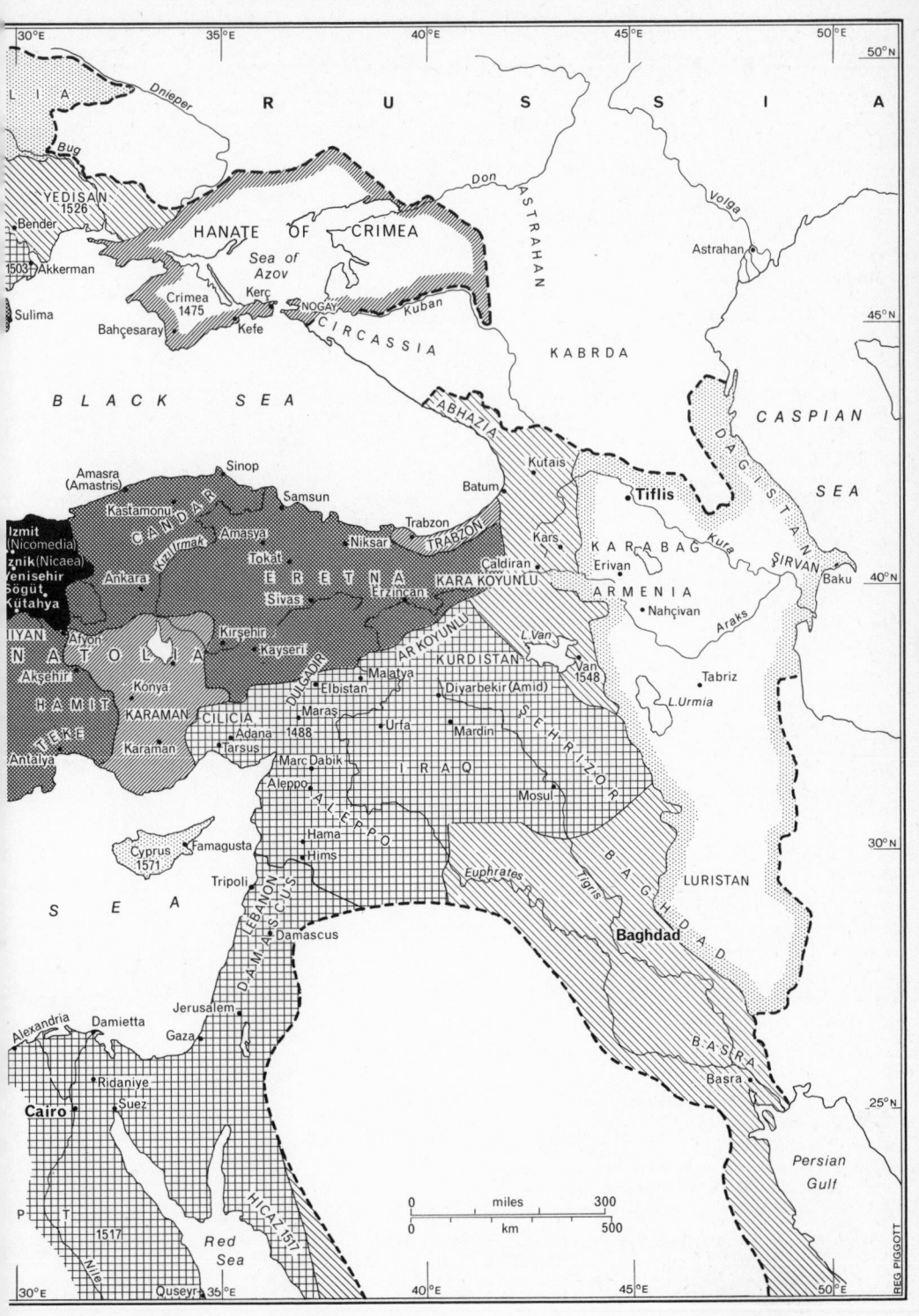

30°E · 35°E · 40°E · 45°E · 50°E · 50°N

LIA · R U S S I A · A

Dnieper

Bug

YEDISAN
1526

Bender

1503 Akkerman

Sulima

HANATE OF CRIMEA

Sea of Azov

Kerç

Crimea
1475

Bahçesaray

Kefe

NOGAY

Don

ASTRAHAN

Kuban

CIRCASSIA

KABRDA

Volga

Astrahan

CASPIAN

45°N

B L A C K   S E A

ABHAZIA

Kutais

Batum

Tiflis

SEA

DAGISTAN

ŞIRVAN

Baku

40°N

Amasra
(Amastris)

Sinop

Samsun

Kastamonu

CANDAR

Kızılırmak

Amasya

Trabzon

Niksar

TRABZON

Kars

Çaldıran

KARA KOYUNLU

KARABAG

Erivan

ARMENIA

Kura

Araks

Nahçivan

Tabriz

L.Urmia

Tokat

Ankara

ERETNA

Sıvas

Erzincan

Izmit
(Nicomedia)

znik(Nicaea)

Yenisehir

Söğüt

Kütahya

Kırşehir

Kayseri

AK KOYUNLU

L.Van

Van
1548

IIYAN

A N A T O L I A

Afyon

Akşehir

HAMIT

TEKE

Antalya

KARAMAN

Konya

Karaman

CILICIA

Adana

Tarsus

DULCADIR

1488

Maraş

Elbistan

Malatya

KURDISTAN

Diyarbekir (Amid)

Urfa

Mardin

SEHRIZOR

Marc Dabik

Aleppo

ALEPPO

Hama

Hıms

Mosul

I R A Q

Cyprus
1571

Famagusta

Tripoli

S E A

LEBANON

DAMASCUS

Damascus

Euphrates

Tigris

BAGHDAD

Baghdad

LURISTAN

30°N

Jerusalem

Gaza

Alexandria

Damietta

Cairo

Ridaniye

Suez

HICAZ 1517

Nile

Red
Sea

1517

Quseyr

35°E

P   T

BASRA

Basra

Persian
Gulf

25°N

miles
0   300

km
0   500

30°E · 40°E · 45°E · 50°E

REG PIGGOTT

PART ONE

RISE OF THE OTTOMAN EMPIRE, 1280–1566

The rise of the Ottoman dynasty to rule much of Europe and Asia is one of the most remarkable stories in history. In the thirteenth century the Ottomans ruled only one of a number of Turkoman principalities that ringed the decadent Byzantine state in western Anatolia. Within two centuries they had established an empire that encompassed not only the former Byzantine lands of Southeastern Europe and Anatolia but also Hungary and the Arab world, and that empire was to endure into modern times. Who were the Ottomans? Where did they come from? How did they establish their rule? And what was the result for both them and the people whom they came to dominate?

1

The Turks in History

Before examining the rise of the Ottoman Empire we must try to find out who the Ottomans were and how they came to western Anatolia in the first place.

Turkish Origins

The Ottomans descended from the mass of nomads who roamed in the area of the Altai Mountains, east of the Eurasian steppes and south of the Yenisei River and Lake Baikal in lands that today are part of Outer Mongolia. These Altaic nomads had a primitive, mobile civilization based on tribal organization, customs, and social sanctions without the formal organs of government and laws characteristic of more advanced societies. Their livelihood came mainly from raising flocks and taking what they could from their weaker neighbors. Temporary leadership was entrusted to *hans*, but the scope of their authority was limited to searching for pastures and to military activities and did not extend to relations among individuals within the tribes or among the tribes themselves. Their Shamanistic beliefs involved worship of the elements of nature through a series of totems and spirits considered to have special powers that could affect man for both good and evil. Man himself was helpless in the face of their power but could secure protection through the intercession of shamans, priests with special power to control and use the spirits. It was a simple religion of

1

fear in which the dark elements of nature as interpreted by the shamans rather than the moral considerations of higher religions were the accepted determinants of right and wrong, and the nomadic way was considered the ideal of human existence.

Beginning in the second century before Christ, changing political, military, and climatic conditions in the Altaic homeland sent successive nomadic waves against the settled civilizations located on the borders of the steppes. Those who moved to the south and west toward eastern Europe, the Middle East, and Central Asia came to be known as Oğuz among themselves and, in general, as Turkomans or Turks to those whom they attacked. They swept the settled peoples out of the way and destroyed towns and fields in the process of seeking out fodder and shelter for themselves and their flocks. Then they passed on, allowing the settled peoples who survived to restore their homes and former activities. Thus in most places such incursions left no permanent changes in ethnic or economic patterns. But in those lands where the Turkomans chose to establish their pastures and to remain more permanently, centuries-old systems of agriculture and trade were replaced by pastoral economies and the Turks largely supplanted the settled ethnic elements that preceded them.

For the most part the great mountain ranges of the Hindu Kush, the Elborz, and the Caucasus provided the Middle East with a natural defense line against these incursions. But this line was broken in the northeast in the lands lying between the Hindu Kush and the Aral Sea, bounded in the north by the Jaxartes river and in the south by the Oxus and known generally as Transoxania, the land across the Oxus. Here a natural road led directly from the steppes into Iran. Transoxania was the staging area for the great nomadic invasions of the Middle East. Through here the nomadic waves were funneled, and it was here where the states and empires that ruled the Middle East had to organize their defenses to protect civilization from disruption and destruction.

Up to the eleventh century the great Middle Eastern empires were largely successful in this endeavor. The Oğuz nomads bounced off the northeastern defense tier of Middle Eastern civilization and moved north and west into areas of less resistance in what is today Russia and Eastern Europe. The different waves of migration were exemplified by the Huns in the fifth century and later the Avars, the Magyars, the Bulgars, the Hazars, who ruled an empire that stretched well into the Caucasus and the Crimea between the seventh and tenth centuries, and the Pechenegs, who ruled east of the Caucasus as well as in Bessarabia and Moldavia and all the way to the eastern Carpathians in the ninth century.

The Göktürk Empire

Most of the nomads moved on to the west when they were unable to penetrate the Oxus defense line, but a few settled along the borders of the Middle East, were assimilated and civilized by its antecedent culture, and eventually became its revivers and defenders against the continued attacks of their uncivilized brethren. This stage of assimilation lasted as long as the Middle East defense line held under the leadership of the Abbasid Empire of Baghdad from the seventh century to the beginning of the eleventh century. Its first manifestation was the earliest known Turkish political entity, the Göktürk Empire, which lasted from 552 to 744, extending from the Black Sea across Asia along the northern borders of Mongolia and China almost to the Pacific Ocean. This empire was in fact little more than a confederation of nomadic tribes with a level of civilization mainly reflecting that of its components. The great difference between it and what preceded was the subordination of the tribes and their temporary *han*s to a kind of central authority that was left in the hands of a dynasty of tribal chiefs. The empire had no real capital, boundaries, or laws beyond the decrees of the Göktürk chiefs. The rulers had no permanent residence – only summer and winter quarters where they camped while searching for grazing lands for their flocks. The people continued to practice the rites of Shamanism as they had done in the past. Their culture advanced just beyond the use of stone clubs and arrows to a point where they began to tip their weapons with metal. The significance of this empire was its manifestation of the first evidence of some kind of contact between the nomads and the settled civilizations to the south, namely, the outlines of state organization and the idea of dynasty.

Soon after its inception the Göktürk Empire was divided into two parts, the eastern and western empires, both of which accepted the nominal suzerainty of the rulers of northern China in the seventh century. In 682 the western group, centered in the Semirechye, regained its independence and preserved it until 744, leaving the earliest inscriptions in the Turkish language to have survived into modern times, found on the Orhon and Yenisei rivers in Central Asia. It traded actively with its civilized neighbors and for a time entered a military alliance with Byzantium against the Sassanids of Iran.

For three centuries after the final collapse of the western Göktürk empire in the mid-eighth century, the areas of its dominions in Transoxania were partitioned among its constituent tribes and other newly arrived Altaic nomads including the Oğuz in Transoxania and the Karluks, who dominated the area from the Jaxartes to the northeast and were the immediate neighbors of the Arabs. The Uygurs lived on the upper basin of the Yenisei from about 745 to 940, after which they were displaced by the Kirgiz, while the Kipchaks took over the area from the Irtush down to the Jaxartes from the late ninth to the twelfth centuries. None of these ever achieved the extent or permanency of the Göktürk Empire, but all evidenced the results of contact with the advanced Islamic civilization to the south. Thus for three centuries two cultures came into contact along the Oxus river; the traditional Middle Eastern settled civilization embodied in the Muslim empires of Iran and Iraq and the nomadic civilization of the Göktürks and their successors. What were the principal means of contact, and what were the results?

The first and most obvious means was military conflict as the nomads continued their efforts to cross south of the Oxus and raid the settled areas and the Muslims developed an active defense policy by penetrating Transoxania and establishing forts and walls maintained by a military guard system. Along this frontier both sides developed colonies of permanent guards who on the Muslim side were called gazis, fighters for the faith against the infidels. On both sides of the frontier these groups came to live the same kind of borderline existence, adopting each other's weapons, tactics, and ways of life and gradually forming a common military frontier society, more similar to each other than to the societies from which they came and which they defended.

A second means of contact was provided by trade and commerce. The Göktürk Empire and its successors lay across international caravan routes between the old civilized centers of Europe and the East. While the initial nomadic conquests disrupted these routes, the Göktürks and their successors later found that they could benefit more by allowing and even encouraging the passage of caravans through their territory, collecting from them in return the clothing, utensils, and weapons developed in the civilized countries. This, in turn, pushed the Göktürks closer to the settled civilization of their neighbors.

The third means of contact and transmission was that provided by the missionary activity undertaken by the settled states to convert and "civilize" the heathen nomads. Zoroastrians came from Sassanian Iran, Manicheans from Soghdia, Buddhists from China, and Muslims from Iran and Iraq. The latter were not sent by the orthodox Muslim states themselves, as there never was an official policy to force or even encourage conversions of large groups of non-Muslims. It was the more zealous and energetic sufi mystics of Iran who sent active missionaries across the Oxus. Therefore, the nomads were exposed and converted mainly to the more heterodox forms of Islam, a fact of considerable importance later on when their leaders assumed control of the orthodox Islamic states. The missionaries sometimes traveled with the nomads but more often established colonies to diffuse their beliefs. Conversion meant more than mere changes in one's religious beliefs. It brought an acceptance of the entire civilizations that the new religions represented, in particular of their moral codes, especially the abandonment of the fierce practices associated with Shamanism, and replacement of the nomadic and warrior life with a more settled existence. The Turks adopted the written alphabets of the missionaries for their own language, leaving Turkish inscriptions. Since the missionaries were willing to reconcile their teachings with old nomadic beliefs and practices, the religions and manners practiced by these nomads in the name of Christianity or Islam or Buddhism were often far removed from those of the settled lands.

Nomads also came to civilized centers to sell animal products and to buy some of the artifacts of civilization. Many came in the employ of caravans and as slaves, bodyguards, or members of the armies of the later Abbasid caliphs, subsequently rising to powerful positions in the Abbasid government and army in the tenth century. Some ultimately established their own dynasties in the borderlands of the declining Abbasid Empire, as did the Karahanids, who took over Transoxania from the mid-tenth century until the beginning of the thirteenth century; the Gaznevids, who built an empire in Horasan, southern Iraq, and Afghanistan at about the same time; and the Great Seljuks, who took over the heartland of Islamic civilization as guardians of the caliphs from the eleventh to the thirteenth centuries. Each of these Turkish dynasties revived and reinvigorated Islam, defending it from their uncivilized brothers still flowing from the steppes, but each lasted for only a short time before breaking up, leaving the Middle East in an increasing state of anarchy as well as in danger of new and ever more destructive nomadic invasions from the north and the east.

The Great Seljuks and Their Successors

Most important in terms of their influence over the Ottomans were the Seljuks, a group of Oğuz warriors that apparently entered the Middle East in the tenth century. The Seljuks rose originally as mercenary guards in the service of the Karahanids. Later they acted to defend towns in Horasan and Transoxania against nomads and military adventurers. And, finally, they assumed the role of protectors of the later Abbasid caliphs of Baghdad against threats to their dominions. In 1055 the real founder of the Seljuk dynasty, Tuğrul Bey, forced the Abbasid caliph to make him protector of orthodox Islam and to recognize him as sultan, or temporal ruler. The Seljuks were not the first military protectors of the powerless later caliphs, but they were the first to complete the process of regularizing and institutionalizing the relationship.

With northern Iran entirely under Seljuk control and Iraq professing submission, the Seljuks were confronted with the problem of consolidating their rule and restoring order and prosperity in the Middle East while providing their nomadic vassals with the booty and grazing lands they demanded. Were the Seljuks still leaders of nomadic Turkomans, or were they now rulers and protectors of the civilization they had conquered? It was the latter role that came to dominate, leading to conflicts between the Seljuk rulers and their nomadic commanders and followers, who were dissatisfied with the restrictions imposed on them to save the settled populations of the area. The Seljuk leader, as sultan, assumed most of the caliph's authority to legislate and rule in matters concerning administrative, military, and secular questions not directly regulated in the Muslim law. The caliph remained more as a spiritual leader with the power to regulate matters of personal behavior and individual relationships. As temporal rulers of the Islamic state the Seljuks took over, restored, and elaborated the traditional Perso-Islamic administrative apparatus developed in late Abbasid times, relying largely on Persian ministers who emphasized their own culture, reviving the Persian language and largely eliminating Arabic in government and culture alike, using Persians in most of the administrative positions of the empire, even those in areas inhabited mainly by Arabs.

In return for caliphal recognition the Seljuks became champions of orthodoxy in the Islamic world and leaders of the movement to eradicate the political, military, and religious influence of Shiism. Shias were routed out of administrative positions and replaced by orthodox officials. To provide the latter in sufficient quality and numbers the Muslim educational system was reorganized and centered in the mosque schools and higher *medrese* schools, which strengthened the orthodox religious institution. The sufi mystic movement, which was fulfilling the popular need for a more personal religion, was reconciled with the interpretations of the orthodox establishment. The sufi orders now were recognized as orthodox and spread all over the empire to counteract the efforts of the heterodox Shias to capture the masses.

What was to be done with the Turkoman nomads who were driving out the settled populations of eastern Iran and Azerbaijan to the northwest and establishing their own pastoral economy? As long as the nomads formed the main element of the Seljuk army, their demands for booty and fodder could not be entirely ignored. But controlling them was very difficult. The Seljuk solution provided the key to the sultans' success in maintaining power and organizing their administration. They first used their position as sultans to institute a new regular salaried army of *mamluk* slaves brought from the highlands of the Caucasus and of prisoners taken in the conquests. Once the new army gave the Seljuks a sufficient military alternative to the Turkomans, they solved the remainder of their problem by using it to drive the Turkomans out of Iran and Iraq into the territories of their enemies.

But these solutions created a new financial problem. How were the bureaucrats and soldiers to be paid? Clearly, the booty that had satisfied the nomads could no longer be relied on. But the state was not yet strong enough to establish direct rule and levy sufficient taxes to meet its obligations. The solution was a system of indirect revenue assignment (*ikta*), developed originally in Iran by the Buyids as a means of tax collection and now used also as the primary unit of administration. The essential premise of the system was the idea that all wealth (though not necessarily all property) belonged to the ruler. To exploit it he acted not through salaried officials of state, but rather by superimposing the *ikta* units, each of which gave its possessor the right to administer a source of wealth and to collect its revenues. Officers of the new army and officials of the administration were given these *iktas* in return for performing their duties, thus as the equivalent of a salary. This relieved the treasury of the problem of finding money to pay its soldiers and civil servants and also gave the *ikta* holders an interest in preserving the prosperity of agriculture and trade. They could no longer ravage the land and move on as the nomads had done in the past.

With the new army and bureaucracy organized and financed, the Turkomans could be and were pushed out of the settled areas of Iran and Iraq as rapidly as possible. At the end of the eleventh century the Seljuks actually seem to have wanted the nomads to move against the Fatimids in Egypt as a further means of ending the heterodox threat against Islamic orthodoxy. But the more natural road for the Turkomans was to the north and west. The plateaus of Iran and Iraq running into the highlands of eastern Anatolia seem to have been far more convenient conduits to pastures than were the mountains of southwestern Iran and the deserts of Syria and Sinai. In addition, the Byzantine and Armenian states in Anatolia appeared to be much weaker and offered the prospect of much more booty than did that of the Fatimids. The Seljuks opposed the Turkoman pushes into Anatolia because of their own efforts to ally with the first Crusaders and even with the Byzantines against the Fatimids, and they made little effort to follow up the early Turkoman onslaughts with formal occupation. Eventually, however, the momentum of the Turkomans carried the Seljuks along.

Indeed, times were propitious for a Seljuk move into Anatolia. The Christian defenses there were extremely weak. The regular Byzantine army was weakened by internal political dissension and military revolts. The Armenian vassal chiefs who defended much of the southeastern frontier also were fighting among themselves and generally were unwilling to accept Byzantine direction. Moreover, the Byzantine defense system consisted of a few large garrisons stationed in widely separated forts, and it was not too difficult for the nomads to slip past them. The Christians relied mainly on heavy armor, pikes, and axes and found it almost impossible to compete successfully with the mobile nomadic cavalrymen who used the bow and arrow with deadly effectiveness. And, finally, Byzantine economic policy and religious strife left the populace largely unwilling to support the efforts of their masters against invaders, whoever they might be.

The Turkoman raids began in 1048, pillaging Armenia, Erzurum, and Trabzon to the north and the valley of the Murat Su to the south. The Seljuk sultan Tuğrul Bey led a campaign into the same areas in 1054 while the Turkomans raided farther and farther west each year. The centralizing policies of Sultan Alp Arslan (1063–1072) caused more Turkomans to flee Seljuk rule in Iran. Since most of them entered Anatolia in flight, they were willing to hire themselves out as mercenaries, helping Armenian and Byzantine feudal nobles and princes against each other as well as against Turkoman raids, but this situation made the Christians even more vulnerable.

As soon as Alp Arslan settled his position in Iraq, he undertook a new campaign (1065) in eastern Anatolia to consolidate his control over the frontier Turkomans as well as the Christian princes in the area. Byzantine efforts to stop the invasion by raiding along the upper Euphrates into Syria were beaten back (1068–1069) while the nomads raided farther and farther into western Anatolia. Alp Arslan still hoped to make a truce with the Byzantines so that he could concentrate against the Fatimids; but when he heard that Emperor Romanus Diogenus was leading a new offensive to the east, he moved north for a direct confrontation with the Byzantine army, the first time that the Turks had risked such a battle. The two armies came together at Manzikert, north of Lake Van (August 19, 1071), where one of the great momentous battles of history took place. Turkish maneuverability and superiority with the bow and arrow, combined with dissension in the Byzantine army, caused the latter to flee while the emperor was captured. Because Alp Arslan still considered the Fatimids as his primary objective, he did not use the victory to make further organized attacks into Anatolia. But whether he intended it or not, the victory destroyed the old Byzantine border defense system and organized resistance against the Turkomans, opening the gates for the latter to enter in increasing numbers as they sought to evade the organized governmental controls being extended by the Seljuks. The Turkomans, therefore, stepped up the attack, devastating agriculture and trade and paralyzing Byzantine administration. Within a few years all of Byzantine Anatolia east of Cappadocia was occupied by the nomads except for a few forts in the Taurus mountains and Trabzon, on the Black Sea, which was to hold out for centuries. Continued Byzantine internal disputes and feudal anarchy also enabled the Turkomans to raid westward all the way to Iznik (Nicaea) and the Bosporus, though here they were unable to settle down to the extent that they had in the east.

At this point some of the Turkomans were led by their own *han*s. Others submitted to the authority of individual Seljuk princes, military commanders, and others who sought to make their fortunes on the western frontiers rather than accepting the authority of the sultan in Iraq. Some of these established their own small states and left them to heirs, thus founding their own dynasties. In Cilicia one of these, Süleyman, son of Tuğrul's cousin Kutlumuş, led a group of Turkomans that helped several Byzantine emperors and princes and in return was recognized as ruler of much of south-central Anatolia, forming the base of the Seljuk Empire of Rum, which later rose to dominate most of Turkoman Anatolia.

While Anatolia was gradually transformed into a Turkish dominion, the Great Seljuk Empire, now centered at Isfahan, reached its peak. Alp Arslan was killed a year after Manzikert during a campaign against the Karahanids and was succeeded by his son Malikşah (1072–1092), whose reign inaugurated the decline. Because of his youth the new sultan had to rely heavily on his father's trusted chief minister, Nizam ul-Mülk. The establishment of the Seljuks of Rum posed a threat to Malikşah, who responded by establishing his dominion in northern Syria and reaching the Mediterranean. With the help of the Byzantines he also extended his power into Anatolia, gaining the allegiance of most of the Turkomans against the Rum Seljuks, who were left in control of only a few areas of central and eastern Anatolia from their capital, Konya.

These activities prevented Nizam ul-Mülk from consolidating the Seljuk Empire as he had hoped to do. The Fatimids remained in Egypt and southern Syria and extended their disruptive Shia missionary activities throughout the sultan's dominions. The Seljuks also were undermined by the activities of a new Shia movement that arose within their own boundaries, that of the Ismaili Assassins founded by Hasan al-Sabbah from his fortified center at Alamut, south of the Caspian Sea. He began a successful campaign of assassination and terror against political and religious leaders of the Seljuk state. In addition, the Seljuks were weakened by the old nomadic idea that rule had to be shared among all members of the ruling dynasty. The sultan gave large provinces to members of his family, and they began to create their own armies and treasuries. Malikşah also compensated his *mamluk* officers with similar feudal estates where they built autonomous power and thus prepared for the day when a weakening of the central authority would enable them to establish independent states. Finally, divisions between the orthodox establishment of the sultans and the heterodox Turkoman tribes became increasingly serious. Alp Arslan had solved this problem by pushing the tribes into Anatolia. But this outlet was cut off when the Seljuks of Rum rose in Cilicia along with petty Armenian states and the Crusaders in northern Syria. The Turkomans, therefore, now remained in the Great

Seljuk possessions, continuing their attacks on the settled populations and resisting Nizam ul-Mülk's effort to strengthen orthodoxy as the basis of the Seljuk Empire. As long as Maliksah and Nizam ul-Mülk lived, these disruptive tensions were controlled. But with their deaths in 1092 anarchy and dissolution soon followed. The Middle East fell into a new era of anarchy and foreign invasion that lasted through most of the twelfth and thirteenth centuries. In the east the Great Seljuks were replaced by a number of small Turkoman states, some ruled by tribal chiefs with nomadic armies, others by Seljuk princes under the tutelage and domination of military chiefs appointed as regents (*atabegs*) by the decaying sultanate. In Anatolia the Seljuks of Rum managed to extend their rule though they were cut off from their Iraqi homeland by the arrival in 1099 of the Crusaders, who established their own kingdoms in Cilicia and at Antioch and Edessa. The last Great Seljuk ruler was Sultan Sancar, son of Maliksah, who gained control (1096) of the province of Horasan, in the northeast, shortly after the death of his father. To him fell the task of defending the Middle East against the Mongol hordes that now threatened it from Transoxania, but after his death in 1157 there was little left to stand in their way. At the same time, a strong and able caliph, al-Nasir (1180–1225), rose in Baghdad. Ending the last ties with the Seljuks, al-Nasir suppressed many of the independent Turkomans in Iraq and established direct caliphal rule once again, even getting the Assassins of Alamut to refrain from their terroristic policies in return for recognition of their autonomy. He also continued the Seljuks' work of reviving Islamic orthodoxy through the sufi mystic orders, using the *futuwwah* brotherhoods originally formed by lower-class artisans in the large cities as guilds and mutual-aid organizations, absorbing them into the sufi system, giving them religious ideals into which they could channel their energies, and making them into a kind of chivalric society and an instrument through which Islamic society could revitalize itself in the age of political disruption.

With the death of al-Nasir and the extinction of the Great Seljuk line the Middle East fell mostly to two new Mongol invaders from the east. In the mid- and late twelfth century most of the Mongols were driven out of northern China. Those Mongols who fled westward formed the Kara Hitay Empire, which took much of Transoxania in the late twelfth century in succession to the Seljuks. Other Mongols stayed in China, forming confederations and alliances against the continued attacks of their enemies from north and south. In 1205 the united Mongol confederation came under the leadership of one Temugin, who took the title Genghis Han (Great Han) to manifest his claim and ambition of uniting all the Mongols and, perhaps, all the Altaic peoples under his leadership. Between 1206 and 1215 he incorporated most of the Asian steppes between northern China and Transoxania into his empire, in the process adding large numbers of Turkomans to his army while building a society devoted almost entirely to war. He next aimed at moving back into China, but when he was unable to establish a peaceful relationship with the Hvarezmsahs who had displaced both the Great Seljuks and the Kara Hitays in Transoxania, he responded with an attack that overwhelmed the Middle East in a relatively short time. In the end the invasion was stopped not by the Middle East's military defenses, but rather by periodic crises within the Mongol Empire caused by the deaths of Genghis Han and his successors. In 1242 the Mongols defeated the Seljuks of Rum and forced them to recognize the Mongol Great Han as suzerain. After a temporary retreat in 1252 the Mongol prince Hulagu returned to take Iraq, ravaging Baghdad and killing the last Abbasid caliph (1258) before going on into Syria. In response to the Mongol threat Egypt fell under the Mamluk slave dynasty (1250–1517), which defeated Hulagu's garrisons at Ayn Calut (1260) and in Syria and Palestine, thus marking the high point of Mongol expansion but leaving them in control of the rest of the Middle East as well as of Central Asia and northern China in one of the greatest empires the world has ever known. Soon afterward the Great Mongol Empire itself broke into sections divided among the relatives of the last Great Han.[1] The one in Iran, Iraq, and Anatolia founded by Hulagu took the name Ilhanid (provincial *han*) and lasted from the mid-thirteenth century to the beginning of the fourteenth century. The Ilhanids restored relative order and security in the area. They continued and extended the ethnic and economic changes begun by the Seljuks, driving out the settled natives in the northern parts of the Middle East and replacing them with pastoral nomads, most of who were Turkomans rather than Mongols. While including substantial Christian and Muslim elements, they were mainly Buddhist and they allowed relative freedom to all the major religious groups. Eventually, however, they converted to Shia Islam and thereafter assumed the Seljuk role of reviving and spreading Islam. Militarily, the Ilhanids used Iran and Iraq as bases for new attacks against the Mamluks (1250–1517) of Egypt and Syria and defended Middle Eastern civilization against the non-Muslim Mongol Çağatay hordes that tried to follow them in from the north. Politically, the Ilhanids joined the Mamluks in restoring internal unity in the Middle East, but the same nomadic concept of dynasty and rule that had caused previous Turkish empires to break up eventually caused the Mongols also to decline and collapse after less than a century of rule, leaving the Middle East again in anarchy. The question was whether it would again be subjected to a destructive invasion from the outside. In the end it was not. A new empire emerged from within the Middle East, this time not from the heartlands of the old Islamic caliphates but from the frontier in western Anatolia settled by the Ottomans at the end of the thirteenth century. How did thirteenth-century Anatolian society and institutions contribute to the development of the Ottoman Empire and its rescue of the Middle East?

Anatolia in the Twelfth and Thirteenth Centuries

In the transitional stage from Byzantine to Turkish hegemony, Anatolia combined elements of the High Islamic civilization of the great caliphates with the radically different hybrid culture peculiar to border provinces (*uc*) or marches.[2] The authority of the sultan was represented by an emir, or commander of the frontier province, who was both an administrative and a military commander and often was a member of one of the leading families of Konya. In contrast to this official organization, on the local level the real centers of power in the marches were the Turkoman tribes. The commanders, called beys, led the struggle against the infidel and were therefore gazis, or fighters for the faith of Islam. Despite Seljuk claims to the contrary, these march beys were independent of the Seljuk march emirs except for whatever personal bonds of loyalty might have existed.

The march provinces were mixed ethnically and religiously. Here were not only nomads but also city dwellers of many races and religions driven from the turmoil in the East, men and women who came in search of new lives on the frontiers of Islam. While nomadic warriors lived on the borderlands, the towns in the area were influenced by both Byzantine and High Islamic civilization, became cultural centers, and served as capitals for leaders who tried to establish some kind of stable control over the tribes. Thus within the marches there developed the same sort of conflict between High Islamic settled civilization and anarchial nomadic society that was found in the older lands of Islam. The heterodox forms of Islam popular among the nomads, and especially mystic Sufism, became the most important and widespread popular religion in Turkish Anatolia. The Turkomans brought with them mystic leaders whom the Great Seljuks were happy to get rid of because of their influence over the people. All over Anatolia these leaders were able to establish their orders and extend them into confederations that, with the related artisan guilds, came to comprise a strong and vital substructure of society that cushioned the mass of the people against the political and military turmoil of the time. Turkish Anatolia took over and partly reflected a living Christian culture and tradition. While some Christians were displaced or killed in the course of the Turkish occupation of Anatolia, most remained in their places, preserving their old traditions and religions, and some converted to Islam and mixed racially and culturally with the invaders. Their ways of living and governing were adopted by the nomads as part of the process of settling down. Some Turkoman mystic orders even occupied Christian holy places, creating the spectacle of Christians and Muslims worshiping at the same shrine side by side.

Turkish Anatolia was not, however, merely Byzantium with an Islamic and Turkish veneer. The basic institutions of government and society under the Seljuks of Rum were those developed in the old Islamic caliphates, as revitalized and transmitted by the Great Seljuks. The Turkomans also retained the practices and traditions of statecraft and warfare developed from the time of the Göktürk Empire in Central Asia. In the long run these Islamic and Turkish elements came to predominate in the new amalgam of civilization that emerged in Turkish Anatolia.[3]

The Turkoman Principalities

Many of the Turkoman beys and their followers not only fought the infidel but also mixed into the struggles then endemic within the Seljuk empire of Rum, sometimes using the booty of conquest to build their own independent principalities as the Seljuks and then the Mongols weakened. One of the earliest of the Turkoman leaders in western Anatolia was Menteşe Bey, a gazi leader in the southwestern coastal marches who raided the Byzantine coasts. To the northeast the powerful Germiyan dynasty was founded around Kütahya in 1286, and it attracted large numbers of Turkomans by leading their resistance to Mongol rule. The Germiyan commanders sent into the valleys of the Menderes (Meander) and Gediz (Hermon) rivers as far as the Aegean coast were so successful against the Byzantines that they were able to establish their own independent principalities. Thus rose the dynasty of Aydın, originally established around Smyrna (Izmir), which under the founder's second son, Umur Bey, became a major sea power by building a fleet that raided the coast of Byzantine Thrace and at times intervened as mercenaries in the Byzantine struggles for the throne. Around 1313 other Germiyan commanders established the Saruhan dynasty in northern Lydia with its capital at Magnesia (Manisa). Saruhan also became an Aegean sea power and regularly engaged in battle the dukes of Naxos and the Genoese islands in the area. The last principality established by the Germiyan commanders was that of Karesi, which built a sizable state in Mysia with its capital at Paleocastro (Balıkesir), including Pergamum (Bergama), the coastal districts of Edremit and Çanakkale, and the entire Marmara coastal area as far as the Dardanelles, though it did not develop such a naval presence in the Aegean as did Aydın and Saruhan.[4]

Compared with the Aydın, Saruhan, and Karaman principalities, the Ottoman (Osmanlı) principality established by Osman and his descendants seemed, at first, to have no advantage over several others of its size. Establishing themselves in northern Phrygia along the frontiers of Bithynia between Dorylaem (Eskişehir) and Nicaea (Iznik) in the pasture stretching from the slopes of the Domaniç mountain northeast to Söğüt, extending subsequently through the passes leading westward from the central Anatolian plateau into the plains of Bithynia, the Ottomans made a quiet entry into history.

The Byzantine Resistance

While Turkoman threat increased, the Byzantine Empire, weakened by longstanding internal problems, was unable to resist. There were endemic struggles for power between the bureaucrats and the landed gentry, which dominated the army, and between the latter and the free peasants. There were economic difficulties involving the debasement of the coinage, overtaxation, and wasteful spending by the rulers and governors. The Byzantine collapse at the Battle of Manzikert (1071) and the temporary Turkoman occupation of most of Anatolia in the following decade were early symptoms of decline. Though the Byzantines were able to push the Turkomans back from western Anatolia (1081–1143), the Latin control of Constantinople (1204–1261) and Byzantine efforts to regain their capital disrupted their defenses against the Turkomans. With the restoration of Byzantine rule over Constantinople, imperial interest in Anatolia waned, making it difficult for the Byzantine feudal holders to coordinate their resistance against the advancing Turkomans.

Notes to Chapter 1

1 These included the Mongol Empire of China; that of the Golden Horde in what today is Russia; the Çağatay dynasty in Turkistan; and the Mongol Empire of the Middle East, the Ilhanid.

2 Among the most important was the one that lay along the Byzantine border in the west from the Gulf of Makri to Kastamonu. There was also the "Principality of the Ruler of the Shores" (*Emareti-i malik al-sevahil*) in Cilicia, directed mainly against the kingdom of Little Armenia (1080–1375), formed by the refugees who had fled southward following Manzikert, and also against the Latin principalities of Antioch and Cyprus. Finally, the third march province faced the frontiers of the Byzantine principality of Trabzon and included Samsun and Bafra in the east and Kastamonu and Sinop in the west.

3 For a detailed account of the civilization of pre-Ottoman Anatolia see Cahen.

4 Along the southern Anatolian coast east of Menteşe lay the principality of Hamit, with its capital at Agrıdır, which included Antalya. Eşref was centered at Beyşehir and included Philadelphia (Akşehir) and Seydişehir until it was absorbed by Hamit in 1325. The most powerful of all the principalities was Karaman, which after originating at Lârende in the lower Taurus mountains early in the thirteenth century gradually came to rule all of southeastern Anatolia, including the areas of Ermenak and the eastern Antalya area as far as the Kargı river. In the late thirteenth century it extended into central Anatolia and was twice defeated by the Ilhanids before capturing Konya and making it the capital of its state in succession to the Seljuks.

Finally, along the southern shores of the Black Sea from Trabzon, still under Byzantine control, west to the Bosporus and the Sea of Marmara were several smaller principalities. There were Canik, in the area of Samsun, the Emir oğulları in Kotyora (Ordu) and Kerasus (Giresun), the Tavşan oğulları in Phazemon (Merzifon) and Havza; the Tacuddin oğulları in Themisyra (Terme) and Çarşamba; the Candar dynasty, with its capital at Kastamonu, founded by a member of the Karaman dynasty, which later extended along the Black Sea coast to include Sinop and inland to Gangra (Çankırı); and Umur Han, based at Göynük and extending to Taraklı and Mudurnu.

2

The First Ottoman Empire, 1280–1413

The first century of Ottoman existence was their heroic age. Living largely in the saddle as leaders of the gazis, the founders of the dynasty were no more than commanders of Turkish tribes organized primarily to raid and conquer the infidel territory around them. With the collapse of Byzantine resistance, the Ottomans found it far easier to expand in western Anatolia and across the Dardanelles into Southeastern Europe than to move against their more powerful Muslim and Turkish neighbors. Advancing rapidly through Thrace and Macedonia, the Ottomans took much of Bulgaria, northern Greece, Bosnia, and Serbia as far as the Danube, developing a system of rule by which the native Christian princes retained their positions and lands in return for acknowledging Ottoman suzerainty and providing soldiers and money. The Ottomans were successful at this time because as gazis fighting the infidel they attracted into their service thousands of nomads fleeing into Anatolia from the Mongols. The early Ottoman leaders also were members and sometimes leaders of the urban *ahi* brotherhoods that were organized so as to bring help and relief to the people when the defenses of the centralized state failed. While there were other Turkoman gazi leaders in Anatolia, the Ottomans were in direct contact with the Byzantines and could best exploit the latter's weakness and thus attract the manpower that enabled them to conquer and rule the Christian lands across the Straits in Europe.

The first Ottoman Empire was, then, based on both religious and economic motives. Its followers sought to extend the dominion of Islam and to secure booty. But when the last ruler of the period tried to use the wealth and power gained by European conquests to capture the Turkish and Muslim East, he brought on himself and his state the onslaught of a new nomadic hoard, led by Tamerlane, who defeated the Ottoman army, broke up the empire, and reduced the Ottomans to equal status with the other restored Turkoman principalities. The first period of Ottoman history and, in fact, the first Ottoman Empire thus ended in an Interregnum (1402–1413) in which the different elements of Ottoman society struggled for power, with chaos again enveloping the entire area.

Ottoman Origins and the Age of the Gazis, 1250–1389

The rise of the Ottomans was closely connected with events in the principality of the western emir of the marches, which faced Byzantium from its capital at Kastamonu. Beginning in 1284 it was ruled by Yavlak Arslan, son of the Seljuk minister Hüsamuddin Çoban, from whose name the principality came to be called that of the "sons of Çoban," or Çobanoğulları. Disputes in the Ilhanid state after the death of Argun Han and the election of Gaihatu (July 22, 1291) led the Seljuk military com-

12

mander in the marches, Kılıç Arslan, brother of the Seljuk sultan Mesut, to revolt against his brother. Yavlak Arslan and his son Ali cooperated with the combined Mongol and Seljuk armies, defeated Kılıç Arslan, and used the prestige gained from these victories to become independent. Ali penetrated Byzantine territories to the west as far as the Sakarya river. He then maintained his power by cooperating with the Byzantines, more or less becoming their mercenary march commander against the other Turkoman gazis and the Mongols. The role abandoned by Ali as leader of the gazis in the western marches was taken up by Osman Bey, founder of the Ottoman dynasty. Who was he? How and why did his dynasty emerge at this time?

The problem of Ottoman origins has preoccupied students of history, but because of both the absence of contemporary source materials and conflicting accounts written subsequent to the events there seems to be no basis for a definitive statement. The traditional account relates that the ancestor of the dynasty was one Süleyman Şah, leader of the Kayı tribe of Turkomans, who ruled the small area of Mâhân in northeastern Iran in the late twelfth century. He is said to have fled from the Mongol invasion in the early thirteenth century along with thousands of other Turkomans trying to avoid death or enslavement at the hands of the new conquerors coming from Central Asia. It is believed that he drowned while crossing the Euphrates into Syria, after which his family divided; two sons led most of the family back to Horasan to enter Mongol service while one son, Ertuğrul, led part of it westward into Anatolia.

Ertuğrul is considered to have been the founder of the Ottoman dynasty in Anatolia. Supposedly, he brought some 400 followers into the service of the Seljuks of Rum as auxiliaries against both the Byzantines and the Mongols as the latter began pressing through Iraq into eastern Anatolia. In return for this service, according to legend, the Seljuk sultan gave Ertuğrul lands in the marches of western Anatolia, two small districts, Söğüt and Domaniç, in northern Phrygia on the borders of the Byzantine province of Bithynia. When Ertuğrul died (c. 1280), this dominion and his leadership of his portion of the Kayı tribe passed to his son Osman.

There are many variations to this story, the most important of which, deriving from recently discovered thirteenth-century accounts, indicate that the ancestors of the Ottomans entered Anatolia not in the thirteenth century in flight from the Mongols but in the eleventh century among the Turkomans who spread into the subcontinent following the Battle of Manzikert. According to this information, the Ottomans' ancestors for two centuries were no more than rootless nomads who sold their services to the highest bidders, leaving their claimed connection with the Seljuks very questionable. Further, it was considerably afterward, after the Ottomans had built an empire, that they spread the idea that their ancestors had entered Anatolia as military commanders in Seljuk service rather than as common nomads, to enhance their own claims to rule. Whatever the truth of these stories, the fact remains that Osman, founder of the Ottoman dynasty, was born at Söğüt, in northeastern Anatolia, around 1258 and inherited his patrimony on the borders of Bithynia some time before 1280 just as the emir of the marches was abandoning his struggle with the Byzantines.

Osman I, 1280–1324

Osman's contributions seem to have been limited to establishing the dynasty and beginning the policy of developing it primarily at Byzantine expense while avoiding conflict with the more powerful Turkoman neighbors until the state was strong enough to deal with them. His initial advances were through the passes leading from the barren areas of northern Phrygia near Dorylaeum (Eskişehir) to the more fertile plains of Bithynia and against the Christian feudatories to the north. In imitation of the policy of the Seljuks, Osman divided his border areas into three principalities, each commanded by an *uc* bey, facing respectively the Black Sea to the north, Nicomedia (Izmit), and Nicaea (Iznik). Most of his initial advances were made by the leaders of these principalities at the expense of the feudal Byzantine nobles, some of whom were defeated in battle, others being absorbed peacefully by purchase contracts, marriage alliances, and the like. His real conquests began about 1300 when the final collapse of the Seljuks enabled him to occupy the key forts of Eskişehir and Karacahisar, which commanded the passes leading from the central Anatolian plateau into the plains of Bithynia. He captured the first significant city in his dominion, Yenişehir, which became the Ottoman capital, beginning the process of transforming his followers from a nomadic to a more settled existence. Osman and his warriors then overran the plains from Inegöl eastward to the Sakarya river, including the forts of Bilecik and Yarhisar, thus severing land communications between Bursa, Byzantine capital of Bithynia, and Nicaea and leaving the Byzantines in the area able to communicate with Constantinople only by sea via Mudanya and other smaller ports along the coast of the Sea of Marmara. As the Seljuk dynasty declined and disappeared, the Ottomans, like the other Turkoman dynasties in Anatolia, seem to have accepted the suzerainty of the Ilhanids, sending regular payments of tribute and at times fighting men as well, though Mongol concentration in the east left Osman and his followers free from any direct control or subjugation.

Following the establishment of the Ottoman principality at Yenişehir Osman spent the remainder of his reign expanding in two directions, northward up the Sakarya river toward the Black Sea and southwest toward the Sea of Marmara, achieving his objectives in both areas by 1308. He thus isolated the last important Byzantine city in the area, Bursa, which stood at the foot of Mount Uludağ (Olympus). It was still well fortified, and as long as the Byzantines were able to keep open their lines of communication to the sea, they continued to receive needed supplies from Constantinople and were able to hold out long after the territories around Bursa fell to the Ottomans. But when Osman took the port of Mudanya, Bursa's last connection with the outside world was broken (1321). Its ability to hold out for another five years against overwhelming odds is a tribute to its defenders. But it finally fell on April 6, 1326, to an army led by Osman's son Orhan, who by this time was his father's principal lieutenant for both the state and the army.

The capture of Bursa was an important step forward for the Ottomans. Their dominion changed from a nomadic border principality to a real state with a capital, boundaries, and settled population and with the means to develop a regular army to defend and expand the state as well as an administration to rule it. Byzantine political factions in Constantinople now began to turn to the Ottomans for help. Ottoman leaders became supporters of competing Byzantine emperors and notables and regularly sent forces as mercenaries to Constantinople and Thrace; their eyes were opened to both the extent of Byzantine weakness and the opportunities for conquest at Byzantine expense. The Ottomans had already become independent of the Ilhanids in all but name. But with the acquisition of Bursa even these last nominal ties came to an end as Orhan began to display the traditional Middle Eastern manifestations of rule – minting coins and having the public Friday prayers recited in his name alone.

Orhan Gazi, 1324–1359

The basic Ottoman policy of conquest as developed by Osman, with the Ottomans acting both as emirs of the marches, leading the gazi Turkomans against the infidels, and as agents of the *ahi* guilds to restore political unity and order to Anatolia, remained unchanged under his successors in the fourteenth century. After Osman's death Orhan's succession was confirmed by the *ahi*s, while continued attacks on the infidels assured the support of the gazis. In the newly conquered areas, Orhan created in turn endowments (*vakıf*) to finance and support the activities of the *ahi* brotherhoods as well as the Sufi mystic orders, which encouraged the nomads to accept Ottoman leadership. Orhan institutionalized the policies of conquest begun by his father, emphasizing expansion against the infidel, avoiding hostilities against his more powerful Muslim Turkoman neighbors, and limiting expansion in their territories to that which could be gained by peaceful means. Orhan's army and government at this time were led and staffed mainly by members of the leading Anatolian Turkoman families who like their gazi followers served the Ottomans to secure fame and booty through conquests in the lands of the infidel. Although a few Christians and Christian converts entered Ottoman service at this time, it was only much later, following the major conquests in Europe, that their numbers became significant enough to influence Ottoman development.

Shortly after his accession, Orhan moved toward the Sea of Marmara. This led to a major Byzantine expedition personally commanded by Emperor Andronicus III (1328–1341), but it was routed at Maltepe (Pelecanon) in 1328. The emperor fled back to Constantinople, and Byzantium abandoned further efforts to organize military resistance in Anatolia or even to supply the remaining Byzantine cities there. Orhan then took most of the Nicaean peninsula and the coasts of the gulf of Nicomedia as far as Yalova on the south, including the towns of Gebze and Eskihisar, isolating and taking Nicaea itself on March 2, 1331, without resistance.

During the next six years, Orhan occupied most of the remaining Byzantine lands in northwestern Anatolia with little difficulty, climaxing his efforts by taking the trade center of Izmit (Nicomedia) in 1337 after a six-year siege and Üsküdar (Scutari) a year later. These made the Ottoman state one of the strongest Turkoman principalities in the area and reinforced its position as leader of the fight against the infidel. Trabzon, in northeastern Anatolia, still remained Byzantine though it had been independent of Constantinople since the Fourth Crusade. Byzantium retained direct control over the coastal strip of western Anatolia from Sile, on the Black Sea, to Üsküdar, and the city of Amastris in Paphlagonia, but these were too isolated and scattered to offer any serious resistance to the Ottomans.

Orhan also strengthened his position by securing Umur Han's territory around Göynük, on the Sea of Marmara, as well as the entire principality of Karesi, to the west, taking advantage of internal divisions, allying with one faction and then the other, and receiving land from each party as a reward (1345). The acquisition of Karesi was particularly important, perhaps more so than the victories against the Byzantines, since it brought the Ottomans all the way to Çanakkale, across the Dardanelles from the Gallipoli Peninsula, completed their control of the southern coast of the Sea of Marmara, and enabled them to move across the Dardanelles into Europe whenever the opportunity arose. Orhan thus was in a position where he could mix into Byzantine quarrels and actually raid or occupy Byzantine lands. Another important result was the entry into Orhan's service of men who were to become some of the dynasty's leading military and administrative figures in subsequent years, including a number of Turkish commanders and the Byzantine convert Evrenos Bey. The Ottoman state now included four provinces: (1) the original principality, including Söğüt and Eskişehir; (2) the province of Hüdavendigâr (Domain of the Monarch), which incorporated Bursa and Iznik and was ruled as Orhan's personal possession; (3) Koca Eli, which included Izmit; and (4) the former principality of Karesi, which included Balıkesir (Palaeocastro) and Bergama (Pergamum).

Only now did Orhan turn his primary attention to Europe. After the death of Emperor Andronicus III (1341), John VI Cantacuzene attempted to take full possession of the Byzantine throne from the coemperor John V Paleologues, using Serbian and Turkish mercenary assistance, the latter mainly from Aydın, which in return was allowed to ravage Macedonia and take considerable booty. After Umur Bey's death (1344) Aydın disintegrated rapidly and Cantacuzene turned to Orhan for help as soon as the latter's acquisition of Çanakkale put him in position to respond. In 1346 Orhan led some 5500 soldiers into Thrace and conquered the coastal region of the Black Sea north of Istanbul from Anne of Savoy, mother of John V, enabling Cantacuzene to take the throne. In return the new emperor gave his daughter Theodora to Orhan as his bride and allowed Orhan's men to ravage and raid Gallipoli and Thrace without opposition. This was accomplished primarily between 1345 and 1348 by Orhan's son Süleyman, who was thereby appointed first ruler of the Ottoman marches, as Osman had been for the Seljuks a half-century before.

Up to this point Orhan had done no more than Umur Bey of Aydın, helping Cantacuzene and raiding Byzantine territory in return. But he now went one step further: He used the permission to enter Byzantine territory as a wedge not only to raid but also to make permanent conquests. In 1349 when the Serbian Stefan Duşan (1331–1355) took Salonica from the Byzantines, Orhan, at Cantacuzene's request, sent Süleyman Paşa with 20,000 men to regain it. With the help of the Byzantine fleet Süleyman forced the Serbs back and so regained Salonica for the Byzantines. Soon after, however, Cantacuzene again began to attack John V, again with Orhan's assistance, routing an allied Serbian and Bulgarian force called in by John V at Dimotica (1352). In return Cantacuzene gave the Ottomans the fort of Çimpe (Tzympe) on the Dardanelles as a base for future expeditions of the same kind. This gift stimulated a new phase in Orhan's conquests. Beginning in 1353 Süleyman Paşa advanced north from Çimpe, not only to raid in Thrace but also to capture and establish permanent Ottoman rule in a number of towns as far as Tekirdağ (Rodosto), using an alliance with Genoa (1354), which hoped to use the Ottomans to break the dominant commercial position of Venice within the Byzantine Empire.

Cantacuzene strongly protested Süleyman's conquests, arguing that the Ottomans had been permitted only to ravage and that Çimpe had been turned over as a temporary base. Orhan replied that while he would be willing to tell his son to leave Çimpe, he could not surrender Gallipoli or the conquered lands in Thrace, since by Muslim law infidel territories conquered by Muslim forces could not be so surrendered. An Ottoman tradition also relates that the Byzantine forts in Gallipoli, including Çimpe, were destroyed by an earthquake at this time (March 2, 1354), leading Süleyman to reply, to the emperor's protests, that he could not leave because the earthquake was a sign of God's will that the Turks should remain. Gallipoli, then, became the first permanent Ottoman base in Europe, from which the initial Ottoman raids into and conquests of the Balkans were made in subsequent years.

Süleyman mounted a series of new raids into Thrace, reaching Çorlu, Lüleburgaz, Malkara, and Tekirdağ, which were ravaged and then made into advanced bases for ever more distant Turkish raids. Cantacuzene attempted to get the help of the Serbs and Bulgars against his rebellious Ottoman allies, but his role in bringing the latter into Europe enabled his rivals in Constantinople to force him from the throne (1355), leaving John V Paleologues in full control. The latter, however, was unable to do any better and in 1356 was forced to acknowledge all Orhan's European conquests in return for promises to allow food and other supplies to be brought to Constantinople. Orhan began to send large numbers of Turkoman nomads to Thrace to "Turkify" it and prevent any Christian effort to push the Turks out of Europe. Only now did Europe begin to become aware of the extent of the Turkish menace. There were the first stirrings of talk of a Christian Crusade against the Turks, though no immediate action was taken. Süleyman died because of an accident in 1358, and Orhan died two years later, so that there was no time for them to take further advantage of the situation. Orhan, however, did provide the base in Europe and the means and method for further conquests. He doubled the state that he had inherited and placed it in a position where it could and did become an empire under his successor.

Murat I, 1360–1389

With Orhan's eldest son, Süleyman, preceding him in death, succession fell to his second son, Murat, who earlier had replaced his brother in command of the Ottoman forces in Europe. Murat used the base left by his father in Gallipoli to conquer Thrace, Macedonia, Bulgaria, and Serbia; actually, therefore, he was the real builder of the first Ottoman Empire in Europe.

The situation here was quite favorable to further Ottoman expansion. Bulgaria and Byzantium were in advanced stages of decline. The Serbian empire built by Stefan Dušan had been falling apart since his death in 1355. The Latin principalities in Greece and the Morea were weakened by internal divisions. The Aegean Islands were ruled by Greek, Venetian, and Genoese dynasties as well as the Knights of Rhodes, who found it impossible to cooperate against the Ottomans.

In Europe Murat and his successors bypassed Constantinople as Orhan had done, leaving it to survive under Byzantine rule for almost a century longer while the Ottomans went beyond it into Europe. This was because however weak the Byzantines were, however meager their army and defenses, their heavy land and sea walls made it difficult for the Ottomans to overcome them. At this time the Ottoman army had some infantry, but its basis was still the Turkoman cavalry force. It was not ready to storm such a powerful fortified city as Constantinople.

Murat's first move was to extend Ottoman power in central Anatolia. He persuaded the autonomous *ahi* leaders of Ankara to transfer their allegiance from Germiyan to the Ottomans (1362) and at the same time eliminated the claim to his throne of his brother Halil, who was based near Ankara. Murat then culminated his expansion in Anatolia by capturing Gerede and the lands east as far as Tokat, along with one of the two Black Sea ports left under Byzantine rule, Heraclea Pontica (Karadeniz Ereğlisi), leaving the Byzantines with only Trabzon. Then he resumed his father's push into Europe and balanced Anatolia and Europe during the rest of his reign.

Murat's strategy in Europe demonstrated considerable knowledge of its strategic geography. His first objective was Edirne, which commanded the gap between the Balkan and Rhodope mountains formed by the Maritsa river. He planned to aim next at Sofia, which commanded the watershed between the valleys of the Maritsa and the Nisava; then the passes over the Balkan Mountains to Niş, which guarded the fork where the road from Salonica turned toward Belgrade in the north; Üsküp (Skopje),

which controlled the Morava-Vardar trough and the east–west road from Istanbul to
Albania; and, finally, in eastern Bulgaria he sought to capture Sliven, Karinova, and
Aydos, which controlled the passes over the eastern Balkan ranges. Against him the
Bulgars held the middle and upper Maritsa valley and the northeastern Balkan range,
including part of eastern Thrace. Serbia ruled the areas of Siroz (Serez) and Drama,
while Albania and northern Epirus were divided among Serbo-Albanian and Albanian states and Latin principalities that recognized the suzerainty of Naples or
Venice. Bosnia was semi-independent under Hungarian domination, while Ragusa
controlled most of the Dalmatian coast. Serbia was breaking up and unable to provide
significant military resistance. This left Hungary, which under the Anjou dynasty,
and in particular during the reign of Louis the Great (1342–1382), achieved considerable size and strength in central Europe, ruling from the mountains of Bohemia
through Moravia into Hungary itself, including Transylvania and extending to Wallachia, Moldavia, Bulgaria, and Croatia. Its chances were seemingly enhanced by the
weakness of Serbia following Duşan's death. It also was strengthened in the area by
its suzerainty over the feudal nobles of Croatia, who in turn had considerable influence in Bosnia, Slovenia, and parts of Dalmatia. But Hungary had internal problems.
Its Greek Orthodox subjects strongly resented the rule of a Catholic dynasty. The
feudal nobles were using every possible weapon to exploit the cultivators and increase
their power at the expense of the king, leading to quarrels that sapped much of the
nation's ability to organize Christian resistance against the Muslim invasion.

Murat already had begun to move into Thrace when he succeeded Süleyman as
commander of the Ottoman forces in Europe during Orhan's last years. But while
he had to go to Anatolia to take the throne and retake Ankara from Karaman, the
Byzantines regained most of the Thracian towns earlier taken by Orhan and made
some efforts to unite the Christians of the area against the Ottomans. Murat returned
to Europe as soon as his position in Anatolia was established and restored the Ottoman position in 1361 with the capture of Edirne (Adrianople), the capital of Byzantine Thrace and the second important city remaining to the empire. Murat now made
it his new capital, signifying his intention to concentrate on the gazi role of expanding
into Europe. Edirne's capture greatly facilitated this effort. The strongest fort between Constantinople and the Danube, it controlled the road leading from the Byzantine capital into the Balkan Mountains and was the center of Byzantine military and
administrative systems in the Balkans. The Ottomans could use it as a base to advance as well as to resist any effort to push them out of Europe.

Using his new strategic advantage, Murat took Filibe (Philippopolis/Plovdiv) in
1363, thus gaining control of the Maritsa valley, which supplied Constantinople with
much of its grain and rice as well as tax revenues. This also enabled him to isolate the
Bulgarians from the Greeks resisting his forces along the Aegean coast. Byzantium
was forced to accept some kind of subordination to the Ottomans and signed a treaty
with Murat (1363) confirming all the Ottoman conquests in Europe and promising
to refrain from plots with the Balkan princes in return for Murat's assurance that he
would not attack Constantinople and would provide it with needed food. Murat, therefore, was free to move ahead without worrying too much about the rear.

The Ottoman capture of Edirne also stimulated Serbia, Bosnia, and Hungary to
unite against the sultan. In 1364 they formed an allied army and marched toward the
Maritsa in the hope of pushing the Turks out of Europe before it was too late. However, Murat ambushed their camp on the Maritsa near Edirne in a battle known in
Turkish history as the "Rout of the Serbs" (*Sırp Sındığı*). Many soldiers and princes
were drowned as they tried to swim across the river to safety. Louis the Great of

Hungary was able to escape only with difficulty. This was the first of many Christian efforts at united action against the Ottomans, and the ease of his success encouraged Murat to attempt further advances. Europe also reacted with more widespread efforts to organize resistance, now led by the pope, who attempted to secure cooperation among the Byzantine emperor, the king of Hungary, and the rulers of a number of Italian city-states. The pope issued a bull formally proclaiming a Crusade against the Turks (December 25, 1366), but the only serious response came from Count Amadeus II of Savoy, who led a fleet that recaptured Gallipoli and then turned it over to the Byzantines (August 24, 1366). By this time, however, the Ottomans were too well established in Thrace for this setback to affect their position significantly. Murat responded with a program of mass immigration and settlement of Turkomans in the newly conquered Balkan territories to assure their control, rid Anatolia of sources of disruption, and gain their services as shock troops in areas where local resistance was especially strong. He also began a policy of settling many Christian peasants from the Balkans in Anatolia and the environs of Edirne to assure the obedience of their fellows back home.

The Ottomans followed the traditional Islamic policy of tolerance toward *zimmis*, or "people of the book," Christians, Jews, and others who accepted the same one God and who, therefore, had the right to protection of their lives, properties, and religions, as long as they accepted Muslim rule and paid the special head tax (*cizye*) in lieu of performing military service. A few Balkan Christians did convert to Islam to secure the benefits of membership in the state religion or because they were members of religious minority groups, such as the Bogomils of Bosnia, who had been persecuted under Christian rule and found the Ottoman conquest to be deliverance from oppression. But there was no major effort to enforce mass conversion if for no other reason than the desire to retain the head tax as a major source of treasury revenue. Only where cities or towns resisted conquest or their rulers refused to accept Ottoman suzerainty did the populations suffer enslavement and loss of property and homes to the conquerors or to Muslims resettled from Anatolia and elsewhere.

The victory of the *Sırp Sındığı* ended the first phase of Ottoman conquest in Bulgaria. Edirne and western Thrace were secured. The allied resistance had been smashed. The full length of the Maritsa was under Ottoman control. Byzantium had been reduced to vassalage. The capture of Filibe had opened the way to Serbia, and Hungarian influence in the Balkans had suffered a serious blow.

The second phase of Murat's Balkan conquests began in 1366 and continued to the end of his reign. He now developed a real plan of conquest. Like Osman and Orhan, he organized the frontier areas facing the infidel into march provinces but divided them into right, center, and left wings. The eastern frontier province, or right flank, was directed personally by Murat and gained control of the Thracian Black Sea coast, which had been taken over by the Bulgarian prince John Alexander (1355–1365) after Dusan's death. The Byzantines were thus cut off from their last land communications to Europe, leaving them to communicate only by sea, either through the Black Sea to the Principalities or through the Dardanelles, both of which were sometimes subject to Ottoman pressure and control. In response to this desperate situation, John V went to Rome (October 1369) in the hope of gaining papal assistance by converting to the Roman faith. The leaders of the Orthodox church repudiated this "conversion," however, deeming it only an individual act of the emperor without real significance. Far from gaining the needed help against the Turks, the emperor only divided his subjects further, and made it more difficult for them to resist.

The western front, or left flank, of the marches, located along the Aegean coast, was established with the aim of taking Macedonia with its capital, Salonica. Its commander was Evrenos Bey, originally a Byzantine feudal prince in Anatolia who had entered Ottoman service following the capture of Bursa, converted to Islam, and become a leading military commander under both Orhan and Murat. His main opponents on the left flank were the Bulgars, who resisted fairly well until the kingdom broke up after Alexander's death (1371), with disputes for succession among his sons. Evrenos first moved up the Maritsa and took Ipsala and Dimotica, then southwest through the Rhodope mountains, capturing Komotini (Gümülcine) on the Aegean in 1371. He went into western Thrace and the Macedonian lowlands (1371–1375), separating the Serbs and Bulgars, took Kavalla, Drama, Serez, and Salonica and sent raiders into Albania (1385), helping some of the local notables against others as well as against the Bosnians and Venetians, who were trying to take the coastal ports. Murat then invaded central Bulgaria, captured Sofia, and compelled Şişman to accept Ottoman suzerainty (1376), cementing the arrangement by marrying the latter's daughter Tamara. The new Byzantine emperor Andronicus IV Palaeologus finally was forced to renew the ties of vassalage, surrendering to Murat the fort of Gallipoli, which had been turned back to him by the Latin Crusaders of Amadeus of Savoy less than a decade earlier.

These successes in central Bulgaria and the plains of Macedonia and Thrace opened the way for Kara Timurtaş, the commander of the center frontier army, to undertake a campaign through the Vardar valley into the Balkan mountain ranges to the north and west between 1385 and 1389. Starting from Samakov, Timurtaş took the major forts at Monastir and Prilep in western Bulgaria, routing an allied Serbian-Bulgarian army at Çirmen, on the Maritsa between Edirne and Svilengrad (Mustafa Paşa). He then advanced into southern Serbia, captured Niş (1386), forced the Serbian prince Lazar to accept Ottoman suzerainty and pay tribute, and then went on to take most of southern Serbia and raid well into Bosnia (1386–1388).

But every advance took the Ottomans farther from their center of power and closer to that of their enemies. While Prince Lazar initially accepted Ottoman suzerainty, Timurtaş's continued successes alarmed him with the fear that the Ottomans might attempt to eliminate him altogether. Hence he allied with Duşan's other heirs in Serbia and with the king of Bosnia. Taking advantage of Ottoman diversions against Karaman in Anatolia, the allies routed Timurtaş at Ploşnik, on the Morava (1388), forcing the latter to abandon southern Serbia and move all the way back to Niş. This was the first major Christian victory over the Turks. Lazar gained tremendous prestige, enabling him to form a Balkan union including Serbs, Bulgarians, Bosnians, Wallachians, and even some Albanians, many of whom had previously accepted Ottoman suzerainty when they thought the Turks could not be stopped.

Murat, however, was able to smash the Bulgarians soon afterward and force Şişman to accept his suzerainty once again, thus detaching the largest Balkan contingent from Lazar's army. Despite this setback Lazar moved ahead and formed his army, including some soldiers from as far away as Bosnia, Hungary, and Poland, countries that were just beginning to realize the danger posed by the Turks. To meet the threat Murat attempted to bring his various forces, including vassal units from Bulgaria and Byzantium, into a united army. But while preparing to meet the Balkan Union, he was forced to send the bulk of his army into Anatolia to face a number of increasingly dangerous rivals.

The situation in Anatolia was extremely complicated. First among Murat's enemies was the principality established at Sivas, on the central plateau, by Kadi Burhaneddin, who used his position as chief vezir of the Eretna Turkoman principality to take it for himself. To the southeast was the state formed by the White Sheep (*Ak Koyunlu*) Turkomans, who were extending their power from Erzincan and Diyarbekir, in eastern Anatolia, into Azerbaijan, in northwestern Iran. And to the south was Karaman, the strongest Turkoman principality in central Anatolia, which since its origins at Larende in the Taurus had extended well into Cilicia, beating back the Mamluks and making vassals out of the rulers of Little Armenia before advancing into central Anatolia and transferring its capital to Konya, center of the old Seljuk empire of Rum. In reaction to these threats Murat initially continued his father's policy of advancing in Anatolia only by peaceful means. He married his son Bayezit to the daughter of the ruler of the Turkoman principality of Germiyan, acquiring as her dowry the whole half of the principality nearest Karaman including Kütahya. He then persuaded the rulers of Hamit to sell him most of its territories bordering Karaman, including the lake area of Beyşehir and Akşehir and the capital Eğridir, with both Hamit and Germiyan thus being limited to the western portions of their territory, as far away from Karaman as possible.

These acquisitions brought the Ottomans into the Taurus Mountains. Karaman in turn was alarmed, particularly since the advance into Iran of a new Central Asian conqueror, Tamerlane, flooded Anatolia with a third great wave of Turkoman nomads, most of who joined Murat's army because of the opportunities for booty in Europe. Apparently also to divert Murat from the Balkan Union, Venice, Serbia, and the pope encouraged Karaman to attack the Ottomans. In response Karaman occupied most of the lands that Murat had bought from Hamit. To maintain his prestige in Anatolia and to settle his rear Murat was then forced to rush away from the danger posed by Lazar. Fearing that the Turkomans who formed the bulk of his army might not support him against another Turkoman principality, he brought a force composed mainly of vassal forces sent by the Bulgarian princes, thus using Christian auxiliaries to attack a Muslim Turkoman state. Murat finally won, regained his territories in Hamit, and established his influence throughout much of Anatolia. It is said that the Ottomans first used cannons and muskets at this time against Karaman and with such success that Murat brought them into Europe and used them with considerable effect against Lazar's Christian armies. As Murat returned to the west, he captured the valleys of the Köprü Su and Mangat Çay from the principality of Teke. This connected his new possessions with the Mediterranean and gave him access to them from the sea. The eastern front thus was under control again, and Murat was able to lead his army back to Europe in time to face the Balkan Union.

The decisive battle (1389) was fought at Kosova (Kossovo) west of Priştina and between Mitroviçe and Skopje in southern Serbia. Among the Balkan princes who accompanied Lazar were King Tvrtko of Bosnia, Vuk Brankoviç, son-in-law of Lazar, the Wallachian prince Mircea the Great, and George Castriotis, one of the princes of Albania. The Byzantine emperor John V did not participate, due less to his formal subjection to Murat than to his lack of direct communications with the Balkan forces and inability to reach them even if he had possessed an army capable of making a contribution. Murat took personal command of the Ottoman army and was accompanied by Constantine, Bulgarian prince of Köstendil, a number of lesser Serbian princes who were rivals of Lazar, and several Turkoman princes from Anatolia and their followers, particularly those of Saruhan, Aydın, Menteşe, Hamit, and Teke. The sources differ widely on the number of soldiers involved, but apparently the Balkan Union managed to gather about 100,000 men, while Murat had no more than 60,000 at best. In the battle itself Lazar and his forces gained the upper hand initially, but a last-minute defection by the forces led by Vuk Brankoviç seems to have turned the tide. Murat was killed, but his son Prince Bayezit assumed leadership and led the Ottomans to final victory. Some sources claim that the victory was in fact led by Murat and that he was assassinated shortly afterward. In any case, the Battle of Kosova was the first Ottoman success against a major allied European military force. It destroyed the last organized resistance in the Balkans south of the Danube, opened northern Serbia to Ottoman conquest, and left Hungary as the only important opponent in Southeastern Europe. It meant that Serbia, like Bulgaria, now was firmly under Ottoman control, although as before the Ottomans continued to establish their rule through vassal princes. Less than two decades after Murat had ascended the throne, a little more than 30 years after Orhan had crossed into Europe, the Ottomans had assured their rule in all of Southeastern Europe, with only the Principalities, Bosnia, Albania, and part of Greece remaining outside their control.

Ottoman Institutions and Society in the Fourteenth Century

Bayezit I's accession marked a fundamental break with the policies and traditions of Ottoman statecraft molded under Osman and maintained by both Orhan and Murat. To explain this change fully, its origins, implications, and results, we must first examine the development of Ottoman institutions during the fourteenth century under the first three rulers.

The Structure of Ottoman Government and Administration

The transformation of Osman's frontier principality into a state and then an empire altered the ruler's relation to his followers. As tribal leader, frontier bey, and then independent bey, the Ottoman leader carried the government and military command more or less in his saddle. The administration and army were composed of the same people, mostly members of the princely Turkoman families and of their nomadic followers along with a few Christian converts. In peace they collected taxes from the conquered areas; in war they led the fight against the enemy and took booty. The capital was wherever the bey and his commanders happened to be. All this time the Ottoman leader was still no more than a tribal chief, able to claim the loyalty of the clans and tribes that followed him only as long as he led them to good grazing land and booty. In the councils the leaders were all equals, and he was no more than first among them. Individual leaders and their followers could and did leave him when he failed to gain as much booty as they wished or for any other reason they deemed sufficient. Anyone who wished to approach the Ottoman leader could do so in camp or on the march without performing any special rituals or marks of obeisance. The authority of the bey extended only to those functions involved in his role as military leader of the allied clans. In all internal matters each tribe or clan was autonomous. Each settled matters of justice according to its own traditions and by its own leaders without any interference from the Ottomans. The Ottoman leader could intervene only in disputes between and among the clans, and then as a mediator. Most disputes were settled by tribal custom and law, with Muslim law and jurists having little influence regardless of the fact that the Ottomans and their followers professed to be gazis.

Under such a government what could territorial rule mean? Whatever administration existed in the early Ottoman territories was largely financial in scope. Each clan or tribe or family collected all the booty it could in the lands it conquered as part of the Ottoman army. It had the right to collect taxes afterward from the same territory as regularly as it could. It had neither the time nor the inclination to interfere with the producers of wealth in their possession of property or agricultural or trade operations as long as they paid their taxes. The only particular advantage given the Ottoman beys over their commanders in return for their function as leaders was the right to collect, as additional revenue, one-fifth of the booty acquired in battle, called the *pençik* (Pers. one-fifth). At this time the state treasury and the treasury of the ruler were the same, with only the *pençik* giving the leader's treasury more revenue than those of his followers. The bey had to meet whatever common expenses there were out of this treasury. Whatever common policies had to be decided were considered in the tribal council of elders. Here the bey had a strong voice but certainly not the only one. We might say that he was first among equals in a rough tribal democracy.

But as the Ottoman successes mounted and the territory under their rule expanded, particularly in Europe, the beys came to claim the title of sultan, enabling them to exercise full secular powers and to legislate in all areas not specifically covered by the Muslim religious law.[1] The simple tribal-type organization was inadequate when the principality expanded into an empire. The enemy was far from the lands already conquered and ruled by the Ottomans and their followers. There were different fronts, and, as we have seen, several armies had to be organized to deal with them. Inevitably, then, the administrative, financial, and legal functions at home had to be separated from the military ones. Taxes had to be collected to support the commanders and soldiers while they were away. The treasury of the sultan had to be separated from that of the state so that he would have a regular and assured income without being forced to support the administration out of his own pocket. As the state became large, therefore, the complexity of the tasks of governing and fighting at the same time made it imperative to develop out of the simple tribal structure separate institutions characteristic of an organized state. Under Orhan, and especially under Murat I, new institutions were introduced to meet the needs of the time.

As Ottoman governmental and military institutions evolved, there were a number of influences that determined their structure. The traditions left by the old Turkish dynasties of Central Asia had a pervasive though not necessarily dominant influence. These had already been significantly diluted in Iraq and Anatolia by the High Islamic civilization of the Abbasids and Seljuks. Nevertheless, thousands more nomads were entering Anatolia in flight from the Mongols and Tamerlane and bringing with them particularly Turkish forms of military organization, bureaucratic structure, and taxes – all of which became integral and essential parts of the Ottoman system. Another important source of tradition was Sunni (orthodox) Islam, developed by the classical empires of Islam and perpetuated and extended by the Seljuks. Sunni Islam became the state religion despite the dominant heterodox mystic traditions of the Turkomans. All the legal institutions, mosques, and schools as well as the *Şeriat* (religious law) were maintained and supported with an orthodox hierarchy of religious experts built up to promote and lead them. As we shall see presently, the most important elements in the structure of government, the vezirate, the *ikta* system of tax collection, and individual taxes also were adopted from classical Islam. Sufism, however, continued to be an influential intellectual and religious movement, particularly in the early centuries.

Finally, there was the Byzantine tradition. By assimilating a living Byzantine society in both Anatolia and Europe, the Ottomans inevitably inherited Byzantine ways of doing things – Byzantine fiefs, taxes, ceremonials, officials, and administrators. In many cases the veneer of High Islamic civilization was thrown over these institutions by giving them Muslim names, but the substance remained Byzantine, at least in the two centuries before the conquest of the Arab world gave High Islamic civilization a much more predominant role throughout the Ottoman Empire. Court ceremonial and central administrative practices were affected by Byzantine patterns. Beginning in Seljuk times and continuing into the fourteenth century, Byzantine and other Christian women were taken into the harems of Seljuk, Turkoman, and early Ottoman rulers. The mother of the Seljuk ruler Izzuddin II was the daughter of a Greek prince. Izzuddin II is said to have been secretly baptized and to have allowed strong Greek influence at his court. Orhan's wife Theodora, daughter of Cantacuzene, is said to have remained a Christian and to have provided help to the Christians of Bithynia while she was in the Ottoman court. Murat I and Bayezit I had Christian Greek mothers. Murat married the Bulgarian princess Tamara and the Byzantine princess Helena. Bayezit married Despina, daughter of the Serbian prince Lazar. All these women brought Christian advisers into the Ottoman court, influencing Ottoman court practice and ceremonial as it evolved in this crucial century. We shall see later how their influence changed Bayezit I from a gazi leader to an invader of the Muslim Turkoman principalities of Anatolia (see pp. 29–31).

The vassal Christian princes of the Balkans also sent contingents to the Ottoman army as well as advisers who helped develop Ottoman provincial and central administrative institutions. Since conversion was not yet a prerequisite for entering Ottoman service, many Christians served the sultans as officers, soldiers, and administrators.

It is extremely difficult to determine the exact extent of Turkish, Islamic, and Byzantine influence in the development of the institutions of the Ottoman Empire. The problem is complicated by limited source materials and also by the fact that the Islamic and Byzantine empires were similar in many ways and had been interacting for centuries before the Ottomans arrived, as had the Hellenistic and Persian cultures at an earlier time. They shared the traditional Middle Eastern characteristics of extreme heterogeneity in population and religion and, therefore, faced similar problems that had to be solved in similar ways.

There were, however, certain areas of Ottoman life where specific influences could be traced. We have indicated how Byzantine influence apparently was pervasive as Murat I and Bayezit I abandoned the simple tribal court of Osman and adopted the trappings of imperial rule. As sultans the Ottoman rulers began to isolate themselves. No longer approachable, they could be reached only through elaborate court ceremonies borrowed from the Byzantines and Persians. It seems that a number of court titles came from the Byzantines along with the Ottoman tendency, unique among the historic Turkish empires, to concentrate power in highly centralized institutions of government rather than to divide rule among members of the imperial family and high military officials. More than anything else this enabled the Ottomans to avoid the quick collapse characteristic of previous Turkish empires and to establish an extremely long-lived rule for their dynasty.

As a result of the increasing complexity of state and military functions and their isolation from the daily affairs of state, the sultans could no longer attend to the details of state. To secure needed help they had to delegate their civil and military duties to executive ministers to whom the Seljuk title vezir was given. Orhan, who first assumed his aged father's duties around 1320, was acting as a vezir. Since Orhan was a member of the ruling family, however, already designated as his father's heir, the real precedent was established when Orhan appointed a man outside his family, Alauddin Paşa, as vezir, with considerable power as his chief minister. Besides vezirs appointed as commanders and civil governors in the conquered provinces, other vezirs

were later created to handle financial and administrative duties. To give them authority all were given the rank of bey, with the old Turkish symbol of authority, the
horsetail, being assigned in varying numbers to indicate each one's rank and au-
thority.² Each vezir built up his own court or department to manifest his power and
enable him to accomplish his duties. The most important of these was the treasury of
state (Hazine-i Âmire), now separated from that of the ruler. The organization of
each department and the extent to which it relied on Islamic, Byzantine, or Turkish
traditions, to a certain extent depended on the background and leanings of its vezir
and his advisers at this formative stage.

State policy was discussed and determined by these vezirs in meetings referred to
by the Persian term Divan-ı Hümayun (Imperial Council). At first the divan was
normally chaired by the sultan, who made most of the final decisions. But as the
functions of state became more complex and the sultans isolated themselves even from
the vezirs, one of the latter was chosen to represent the sultan as head of the council
and coordinator of the other vezirs. This first minister, called sadr-ı azam by the
Ottomans and grand vezir in the west, became the chief executive officer of state
beginning about 1360.

Beneath the Divan-ı Hümayun, Ottoman provincial administration was so involved
with that of the military that the two must be discussed together. Originally, all the
soldiers in the Ottoman army were Turkoman horsemen, organized into clans and
tribes under tribal chiefs and heterodox religious leaders. They were almost entirely
cavalry, armed with bows, arrows, and spears. Those assigned to guard border areas
or to conquer or raid Christian lands were rewarded mainly with booty. Orhan, however, soon found that undisciplined soldiers were of little use in besieging and capturing fortified cities. While such nomads were useful in overwhelming enemies, their
desire for continued booty was incompatible with an effort to establish settled institutions in the conquered areas. The Seljuks had rid themselves of disruptive nomads by
sending them to the frontiers, and the Ottomans now began to do the same. But before
Orhan could dispense entirely with their military services he had to replace them with
some kind of new army. Therefore, he organized a separate army of soldiers who
entered his service in return for regular salaries rather than for booty or in fulfillment of religious objectives. Those organized as infantry were called yaya, while the
cavalrymen were called müsellems. The new army included both Christians and Muslim Turks, but as the Ottomans moved into the Balkans under Murat, the former
largely prevailed. As it increased in size and strength, the Ottoman leaders were able
to push the Turkomans to the frontier and to use them mainly as shock troops, with
the terms akıncı (raider) and deli (fanatic) being applied to them in place of gazi.
Now the latter went ahead of the regular Ottoman army to pulverize the opposition,
raiding far into enemy territory in Greece, Hungary, and even Austria in their
searches for booty. Also in the Balkans they were assigned to conquer the more inac-
cessible areas where the regular army could not go or be tied down for long periods of
time, particularly in the mountainous areas of Bosnia, Albania, and Montenegro. It
was only in such areas, therefore, where Christian resistance persisted for long periods of time, that large groups of Turkomans were brought in and settled, adding
new ethnic elements to the population. Elsewhere, where the Balkan rulers accepted
Ottoman rule with little or no resistance, there was little settlement of Turkish elements or disruption of the Christian populations. The Ottoman force became gazi
more in theory than practice as time went on.

Under Murat I the yayas and müsellems remained as the permanent Ottoman
army, though now largely compensated through provincial fiefs rather than salaries.

Murat, however, began to become dissatisfied with the quality of men who served the state for money alone and were in any case under the control of their commanders. Thus he began to organize a new military force composed of "slaves of the Porte" (*kapıkulları;* sing. *kapıkulu*). These men came to the ruler as his *pençik,* or one-fifth share, of booty captured from the enemy. Murat previously had collected the share in cash but now used it to build up an army directly under his control and command. When these youths came to the sultan, they were educated in the Turkish language, Islam, Arabic, and other characteristics of the Ottoman way. They then were given military training and organized as infantry, called *Yeni Çeri* ("New Force"), or Janissary corps, or as cavalry, called *Sipahis.* The *yayas* and *müsellems* were relegated more to rear-line duties, so that it was the *kapıkulları* rather than either the nomad or the salaried forces that led the conquests and were rewarded with lands in return for their efforts. It should be noted, however, that during the late fourteenth century while this process was taking place and new military forces were replacing the old, the Ottoman army was able to depend for much of its effectiveness on the contributions of the troops sent by their Balkan vassals.

In the areas where direct Ottoman rule was established, the old Seljuk *ikta* system, new generally called *mukata'a,* was applied (see pp. 5–6, 121). Portions of the conquered territories were cut into *mukata'as* to which the name timar (fief) was given. The existing tax structure as well as feudal practices developed under Byzantine rule were retained with little change. The timars were then assigned to the Ottoman military commanders as rewards for their service and also to make them governors of the new districts and provinces. Aside from their administrative duties, timar holders had to feed, train, and supply soldiers to the army, when needed, with the state treasury thus being relieved of this obligation as well. The *yayas* and *müsellems* originally were paid salaries by the treasury, but once their commanders secured timars, they assumed these payments, and the same system was applied to the cavalry branches of the *kapıkulları* as they were organized.

For both military and administrative purposes, then, the timar holders were grouped into units called *alay* (regiment), commanded by *alay* beys, and then into larger units called *sancak* or *liva* (standard, banner), commanded by *sancak* beys. At the top were the governors, called *beylerbeyis* (beys of beys), who ruled the provinces (*eyalets*). Within this structure the individual timar holders performed all the duties of local administration, making sure that the land was cultivated and that the merchants engaged in trade and commerce so that taxable revenues were produced, and then assessing, levying, and collecting taxes and keeping order and security. In each *sancak* the Muslim religious judges (kadis) cared for matters of municipal and local administration as well as justice with the help of police chiefs (*subaşıs*) appointed by the *sancak* beys. Thus both the military and religious elements of the Ottoman Ruling Class cooperated to rule and enforce justice.

The most important Ottoman *sancak* in the fourteenth century was that of Hüdavendigâr, including the first capital Bursa, which was put under the personal governorship of the ruler. The kadi of Bursa, therefore, was considered as the most important judicial official of the empire, had a place on the Imperial Council, and appointed all the other kadis. The administrative structure of authority remained intact when the ruler led the timariots to war, thus completing the combination of military and administrative roles in the Ottoman system.

Since the conquered European provinces were organized in the timar system and given to the Turkish notables who commanded the Ottoman armies, it was inevitable that they should develop extensive estates with revenues in excess of those remaining to the rulers. It also was inevitable that the men in the army should obey those who paid their salaries, the timar holders, rather than the rulers. As a result, as the fourteenth century continued, the power and influence of the Turkish notables increased considerably in relation to that of the rulers. This process culminated late in the century when a Turkoman notable family, the Çandarlı, obtained the post of grand vezir, manifesting the power of the oligarchy that they led and represented.

Aside from timars some conquered lands were given as private property (*mülk*) or developed into the religious foundations or endowments known as *vakıf* (pl. *evkaf*). The former were granted mainly in the border areas to provide for the gazi leaders and to encourage the settlement of Turkomans brought from the east to fight the infidels. The latter were founded to promote the development of Islamic religious institutions in the conquered lands and to provide public services such as baths, fountains, hotels, and the maintenance of streets and water supplies. Most revenues in the conquered lands remained in the hands of the Turkish notables, who thus monopolized power in both the state and the army as the century continued.

Murat I sought to counteract the power of the notables by developing the Christian vassal soldiers and converted *kapıkulları* as his personal troops, independent of the regular army. In addition, he took over the Seljuk system of training youthful slaves as *gulâms* (foreign youths) and instituted the new practice of *devşirme* (literally a "gathering" of youths), periodic conscription of Christian boys in the Balkans, with the best being entered into the army and palace (on the development of the *devşirme* system and class, see pp. 113–114). The Turkish notables, however, continued to lead the conquering armies and receive most of the fruits; thus they supported further conquests while the slave forces and Christian advisers at court tried to convince the rulers to turn toward conquests in Muslim Turkish Anatolia, which would not strengthen their rivals as much. Here we see the background of tensions that would eventually tear the Ottoman state asunder and bring a tragic and sudden end to Bayezit I's reign early in the fifteenth century.

Ottoman Society in the Fourteenth Century

What was the effect of Ottoman expansion on the mass of the people who composed Ottoman society? During the conquests, the rapid movement of armies and nomads through settled areas inevitably diminished the original populations – not only from death in battle but also from famine, plagues, and mass movements away from the fighting. But for the most part the conquered people remained where they were. Where Turkomans were settled in the Balkan areas of greatest resistance as well as in the major military centers such as Edirne (Adrianople), Filibe (Philippopolis), Sofia, Salonica, Terhala, Larissa, and Skopje, there was Turkish influence, but these remained as colonies among a mass of people who continued to be predominantly Christian.

As a result the conquered provinces witnessed a considerable survival of Christian traditions. Transmission occurred most in those areas not taken up by the nomadic Turks such as agriculture, trade, and maritime life. Byzantine scribal traditions were influential at first, but later these and other areas of government and life were submerged by the legacy of the old Islamic empires. Since Islamic law was well developed and since the Christians and Jews in any case were permitted to retain their own legal traditions under Ottoman rule, there was little borrowing here. In the arts and crafts both the settled Christian peoples and the Muslims entering from the Middle East had strongly developed and long-lived traditions that survived side by side under the Ottomans, with considerable intermixture and mutual enrichment.[3]

In the area of religion, while formal Islamic institutions had little need to accept Byzantine influence, heterodox mystic Islam always found room to absorb elements from other religions it encountered. Just as the pagan Turks of Central Asia had brought Shamanistic elements into Islam, in Ottoman Anatolia Christian religious practices and beliefs entered Islam through the conversion of Christians as well as through observation and social assimilation. Mystic Muslim worshipers adopted the cults of a number of Christian saints, equating them with their own Muslim saints – St. George and St. Theodore with Khidr Elias, St. Nicholas with Sarı Saltuk, St. Charalampos with Haccı Bektaş, and so forth. Apparently, the Muslims were also influenced by the Christian practices of baptism and animal sacrifice, while Turkish traditions seem to have prevailed over those of both Byzantium and classical Islam in the areas of food, entertainment, and the forms of folk entertainments.[4]

Collapse of the First Ottoman Empire: Bayezit I (1389–1402) and the Interregnum (1402–1413)

In spite of elements of social and cultural fusion in the fourteenth century, political tensions between government and society and within the Ruling Class remained unresolved. The dynastic crisis that followed the brief reign of Bayezit I precipitated a collapse and a period of confusion in which no single leader ruled the empire, the so-called Interregnum (*Fetret*). What were its main causes? How did the lands of the empire develop during its course? How was it brought to an end? And how did this in turn influence Ottoman development in the fifteenth century?

Ottoman Dynastic Quarrels

The manner in which Bayezit came to power determined what followed. Of Murat I's surviving sons, Bayezit and Yakup, the latter was the elder and tended to represent the Turkoman notables in the struggles for power within the Ottoman court; Bayezit, the son of a Greek woman, was the candidate of the new Christian and convert elements brought to the fore by Murat. In the end Bayezit was able to secure the throne at Kosova not because of the power of his supporters per se (most of the army at that time was dominated by the Turkoman notables through the Çandarlı family), but rather simply because he was on the scene while Yakup was in Anatolia recruiting Turkomans. Bayezit's supporters among the Christian vassals in Murat's camp had him confirmed as ruler before the Turkoman notables knew that Murat was dead, concealing this fact until they could assassinate Yakup, thereby leaving the latter's supporters with a *fait accompli*. The Çandarlı and other notables accepted Bayezit's accession because he was the last surviving male member of the Ottoman dynasty. The leaders of the Turkoman principalities in Anatolia had accepted Murat's primacy because of his successes in Europe; but they retained considerable independent power, and now they resisted Bayezit because of his sympathies for the Christian elements in Ottoman life against the older gazi tradition.

While Bayezit was busy in Europe, the Turkoman principalities surviving in southwestern Anatolia joined with Karaman and Kadi Burhaneddin, who held much of central Anatolia and had a strong influence among the Turkoman nomads in the east, in an alliance against the Ottomans, regaining much of the territory turned over to Murat by the rulers of Germiyan and Hamit, including Beyşehir and Kırşehir. It was in response to this threat as well as because of the influence of the Christian elements in his court that Bayezit turned most of his attention to the east for the remainder of his reign and largely abandoned the gazi traditions of his predecessors.

Ottoman Dominion in Europe

But how was Bayezit to gain the strength needed to overcome the powerful Anatolian beys? His predecessors had avoided them not only because of the gazi tradition but also because they were more powerful. Bayezit reversed this policy, deciding to quiet his rear by attacking and destroying the beys rather than by temporizing with them. To accomplish this he turned to Europe. Instead of using Kosova as a tool to conquer Serbia from Duşan's son Lazar, he agreed to allow Lazar to remain in power in return for token tribute and military assistance in Anatolia. The new arrangement was sealed with Bayezit's marriage to Lazar's daughter Maria Despina, which led to a new influx of Christian advisers into the Ottoman court and its Byzantinization and Christianization in the next few years. So that the remaining European princes would not use an extended campaign in Anatolia to attack his European possessions, Bayezit revived the old march organization. He also sent his border commanders on large-scale raids into Bosnia, which was falling into feudal division and weakness following the death of Tvrtko I (1353–1391), and into Wallachia, securing the vassalage of both for the first time in 1391. Ensuing raids into the remaining Christian states north of the Danube kept them in a perpetual state of disturbance and thus paved the way for subsequent conquests when the Ottomans were ready.

Bayezit completed the conquest of the Macedonian highlands by taking Skopje, settling the Vardar valley with thousands of Turkomans to constitute a new frontier base for invasions to the west and north and also to guard against a possible effort by Lazar or the other vassal princes while the Ottoman army was busy in Anatolia. Bayezit also guarded himself against the possibility of Serbian treachery by recognizing a rival Serbian prince, Vuk Branković, as ruler of Priştina, allowing the latter's son and successor George Branković (1398–1457) to struggle with Lazar for the right to dominate the whole country. Skopje now was occupied by Turkomans from Saruhan. Paşa Yiğit Bey, their leader, led them into Albania, taking Scutari, Dulcigno, and Kroya (1393–1395), while Venice took Alessio, Durazzo, and Drivasto from the Balsa family in return for subsidies and help against the Ottomans. Thus began the Ottoman-Venetian rivalry in Albania and the Adriatic area that was to lead to several wars before the Ottomans prevailed. In the conquered portions of Albania Bayezit made vassals of the local rulers in return for help against the Venetians and in Anatolia. Direct rule was established only where the native princes resisted this kind of settlement, beginning with the regions of Premedi and Korce, which now supplied large contingents to the sultan's army.

Back in Thrace Bayezit also began the process of "Turkifying" Edirne, building mosques, schools, and houses, settling Turkomans in the environs, and establishing a regular administration. He also ringed Constantinople with a series of forts and ended all Byzantine rule outside the walls of the city. Bayezit's last move before leaving for Anatolia was to receive representatives of Ragusa and Genoa, accepting their professions of vassalage and payments of tribute in return for permission for them to continue to trade in his dominions. These grants were in essence the first Capitulations (see pp. 97–98), since the foreign merchants concerned were placed under the direct jurisdiction of their consular representatives, thus beginning the system of foreign extraterritoriality that was to have such an important effect on subsequent Ottoman economic development.

Development of the Ottoman Slave System

Bayezit, like Murat I, tried to make himself independent of the old Turkish aristocracy and the older Ottoman army by developing the new slave force as his personal bodyguards and, subsequently, as his army. Murat had begun the practice of conscripting young Christians through the *devşirme* system (see p. 114). Bayezit extended the system on a far larger scale, developing also various institutions to train them as Ottomans and soldiers. In addition, he employed them not only in the army but also for the first time in the administration, much to the displeasure of the older Turkish notables as well as the frontier gazi leaders, who clearly saw this new element as a major rival to their power.[5]

Bayezit's Initial Anatolian Campaigns

Bayezit now was ready to use the power gained through European conquests to conquer the Turko-Islamic world. Anatolia at this time remained under the suzerainty of the Ilhanids, but they had almost no power to enforce their rule. Whatever central authority there was lay in the hands of Kadi Burhaneddin, who in 1365 succeeded the last Ilhanids in the north and the central plateau, with the capital at Sivas, while Karaman, which had risen in the 1320s, used Ilhanid decline to take Konya and most of the southeast. Karaman considered itself to be the legal heir of the Seljuks as suzerain over the other Turkoman principalities, so that it bitterly opposed the Ottoman claims to rule that were based primarily on the success of their gazi advances in Europe. Forceable expansion into Muslim areas, however, could have imperiled the Ottoman reputation as gazis, an important consideration indeed, since most of the Ottoman soldiers still were Muslims and Turks attracted to their service. Thus annexations achieved through all kinds of pressures and threats were presented as legitimate and honorable by the Ottomans, while Karaman criticized even peaceful acquisitions as a direct affront to Islam. Beginning with Bayezit, whenever the Ottomans did wage war with Karaman or any other Muslim state, they secured legal rulings (*fetvas*) from the ulema justifying their acts, charging that such wars were not only legal but also mandatory against those who had attacked in the rear while the Ottomans were fighting the infidels and annexing their territory.

Bayezit marched against Karaman with an army composed primarily of Serbian and Byzantine vassal troops because he feared that his Muslim Turkomans would resent an attack on their brothers. First he overcame Karaman's smaller allies – Saruhan, Aydın, and Menteşe – in a single campaign during the summer and fall of 1390. Karaman responded by allying with Kadi Burhaneddin and the remaining Turkoman principalities. Despite this resistance Bayezit was able to push on into central Anatolia in the fall and winter of 1390, overwhelming most of the remaining principalities, including Hamit, Teke, and Germiyan, taking Akşehir and Niğde as well as Konya and Beyşehri from Karaman. At this point, however, he accepted Karaman's peace proposals (1391) because of the fear that further advances would antagonize his Turkoman followers even more and cause them to ally with Kadi Burhaneddin. Karaman accepted the Ottoman conquests in western Anatolia to its own territory, with the Çarşanba Suyu river, located in the plain of Konya, becoming the new boundary between the two states. This freed Bayezit to move north against the Isfendiyar principality of Kastamonu, which had been giving refuge to many of the Turkoman princes whom he had displaced. He conquered both Sinop and Kastamonu and placed Isfendiyar under his suzerainty. Bayezit thus conquered most of western and central Anatolia and put down the resistance led by Karaman and Kadi Burhaneddin. But as long as he could not eliminate these rivals, the possibility of new trouble prevented him from becoming too active in Europe.

New Campaigns in Europe

Only a short time intervened between Bayezit's first and second campaigns in Anatolia. His return to Europe in the winter of 1390 came after reports that Emperor John V had used his absence to repair the walls and towers of Constantinople. Bayezit forced the emperor to destroy the additions. But John V died soon afterward, and his son Manuel began to resist Ottoman suzerainty, refusing Bayezit's demands for increased tribute and the establishment of a Muslim quarter in Constantinople. A series of minor Ottoman sieges of Constantinople followed almost yearly until Manuel accepted the new demands, agreeing to turn several hundred houses over to establish a Turkish quarter in his capital, with a Muslim religious court and mosque in the section of the city that later came to be known as Sirkeci; he also permitted the stationing of 6000 Turkish garrison troops along the northern shores of the Golden Horn in territory previously held by the Genoese and increased his payments of tribute to the sultan, including a tax of one-tenth of all his revenues from the orchards immediately outside the city.

The conquest of Macedonia had opened the way for a push into the plains of Thessaly, which Evrenos had taken beginning in 1392. Larissa was captured and transformed into the provincial capital of Yenişehir, with the entire province being organized as a single timar given to Evrenos in return for his leading the Ottoman forces farther into central Greece and the Morea. Evrenos then pressured the Latin states in Greece at Athens, Achaea, and Salona and the Venetian colonies at Modon and Koron, in the Morea, partly at the request of the Byzantine despot Theodóros, youngest son of John V. Using these successes, Evrenos partly occupied the Morea. Large-scale raids also were launched to the north, into Bosnia and Hungary, to gain booty and keep the Turkomans happy.

With Byzantium, Bulgaria, and Serbia accepting Ottoman suzerainty, the strongest independent European state able to resist the advance was, indeed, Hungary, whose direct rule extended southward to Dalmatia and to Belgrade and whose suzerainty was still accepted by the princes of Wallachia and Moldavia. Under King Sigismund (1387–1437) efforts were made to stir Christendom against the Turk, but the leaders of western Europe were preoccupied with their own problems. Hungary also was undermined by internal divisions between the feudal barons and the central government and between the Orthodox peasants and the Catholic nobles and rulers. Nevertheless, Sigismund did what he could, and in fact his capture of Nicopolis and move into Bulgaria caused Bayezit to return from his first Anatolian campaign. The latter regained Nicopolis late in 1392 and eliminated his Bulgarian vassal Şişman, who had just agreed to join the Hungarians, taking the Bulgarian capital of Tirnovo (July 17, 1393) and most of the rest of the country except for the Dobruca and Vidin, which remained under minor Bulgarian princes. Direct rule in Bulgaria thus brought the Ottomans into immediate contact with Hungary. At the same time, Bayezit was commencing a new policy of renouncing the older Ottoman system of ruling through vassal princes and replacing it with a new method of direct conquest and rule. He was too busy in Anatolia afterward to extend this new policy, but it was taken up and completed by his fifteenth-century successors.

New Ottoman Advances in Anatolia and the Rise of Tamerlane

Constant threats against his dominions kept Bayezit moving back and forth between Anatolia and Europe, gaining for him the name *Yıldırım* (thunderbolt) because of the rapidity of his marches. In 1393–1394 he advanced into Anatolia due to the rising power of Kadi Burhaneddin and the fear that the powerful Tatar invader of Iran, Tamerlane, might invade from the east. Indeed, after Bayezit returned to Europe, the Turkoman princes left outside his control had organized a new resistance movement against the Ottomans and asked for Tamerlane's assistance. In reaction Bayezit returned to Bursa to mass his forces. Kadi Burhaneddin expanded, captured Amasya, Niğde, and Kayseri, and reached the Black Sea coast in 1393. Bayezit had to respond to maintain his prestige. Therefore, he advanced toward Amasya. Kadi Burhaneddin retreated to Sivas because he realized that he could not defeat the Ottomans in open battle. Most of the Turkomans who had joined him now returned to their former Ottoman subjection. To reinforce his restored hegemony Bayezit organized the new province of Anadolu (Anatolia), creating a second position of *beylerbeyi* to administer it and lead its army on the model of the *beylerbeylik* of Rumeli created earlier by Orhan, with the the conquered areas again being organized into timars under his control. As had occurred along the Danube, this victory eliminated the buffers that had previously sheltered the Ottomans from more powerful enemies in the east, exposing them to the threat of Tamerlane.

Known as Timur the lame (Timurlenk) in the East, Tamerlane was born in April 1336 at Keş (today called Şehr-i Sebz), south of Samarcand in Transoxania, to a member of the Çagatay dynasty left in control of the area by Genghis Han. Tamerlane rose to power in the 1360s as the final victor in the struggles for power among various members of the declining Çagatay dynasty. Rule of Transoxania was completed with the conquest of the Hvarizm Empire, with capital at Hiva (1379), after which he eliminated the last Çagatays in Mongolia (1381–1389) south of the Altai Mountains. He began to move into eastern Iran in 1381, reducing the dynasties that had risen after the decline of the Ilhanids, crossed the Taurus Mountains into Anatolia and the Caucasus in 1386, razing Kars, attacking the Georgian capital of Tiflis, and conquering the western part of Armenia. He then returned to western Iran in 1387 and took Shiraz, Isfahan, and Kirman, massacring thousands and taking huge quantities of booty. He had to return to Transoxania to meet a new threat from the Kıpçaks, and while he was absent, a number of native Iranian dynasties regained their possessions. But he returned to eliminate them all once again in the spring of 1393 and then went on to take Baghdad and the rest of western Iraq the next year.

In the winter of 1394 Tamerlane crossed the Tigris into Mesopotamia, thus posing a threat to the Mamluks in Syria as well as to the Ottomans. It was at this time that he received appeals for assistance from the Turkoman princes displaced by Bayezit who asked for help against the "Christian-inspired" Ottoman ruler. Tamerlane probably would not have responded to these appeals had he not in any case been fearful of the rise of a powerful Ottoman empire at his rear at a time when he was planning to achieve his primary ambition of invading and ravaging India. In any case, with Tamerlane in Mesopotamia the Mamluk sultan Barkuk gathered an army in Syria to defend his empire against a possible invasion, asking for the cooperation of Bayezit and Kadi Burhaneddin against the invader. With the Ottomans the more immediate threat, however, it was Tamerlane's help that was accepted by Karaman and the other principalities, and so the invasion began. After crossing the Tigris, Tamerlane captured Urfa, Mardin, Mosul, and Diyarbekir from the last of the Black Sheep and Artukid Turkomans in the spring of 1394. In reaction Bayezit, Barkuk, and Kadi Burhaneddin exchanged messages of mutual support. No practical result ensued, however, since Tamerlane became involved in Central Asia in the Caucasus and with his first invasion of India (1398), giving a new breathing spell to Anatolia as well as Iraq.

The Crusade of Nicopolis

With Tamerlane diverted and Karaman and Kadi Burhaneddin fighting over possession of the territories between them, Ottoman domination in Anatolia seemed assured. Bayezit, therefore, was able to turn back to Europe to meet new dangers caused by renewed Byzantine appeals for help from the West, by the advance of Venice into Macedonia (where Salonica was sold to Venice by Byzantium), and in Albania, where Ottoman penetration by land was countered by Venetian penetration by sea. In 1393 Venice and Hungary made a new agreement against the Turks, and Manuel II asked for help from Europe. In response Bayezit supported John VII against the latter and began the second Ottoman siege of the Byzantine capital (1395).

The immediate threat to the Ottomans in Europe was the arrival of a new European Crusade army, involving the major states of the West as well as those most immediately threatened by the Ottoman advance. Responding to appeals, Pope Boniface IX stimulated a Crusade. Crusaders came to Buda from England, Scotland, Poland, Bohemia, Austria, Italy, and Switzerland as well as from the lands of Southeastern Europe more directly threatened by the Ottomans. In the spring of 1396 Sigismund led a large Crusader force through Serbia, crossing the Danube at Nicopolis and then capturing the Danubian towns of Vidin and Orsova, massacring all the Muslims they could find. When Nicopolis, the last major Danubian defense point still under Ottoman control, was put under siege, there seemed little hope for the small Ottoman garrison defending it. But Bayezit brought together contingents from Anatolia and routed the attackers (September 25, 1396), with thousands of knights and their leaders being either killed on the battlefield or drowned as they attempted to cross the Danube. Thousands more were taken prisoner, including nobles from all over Europe, who were freed only after the payment of heavy ransom.

The Ottoman victory over the Crusaders at Nicopolis increased European fear of the Ottomans while adding to Ottoman prestige throughout the Islamic world. Significantly, Bayezit was designated as sultan, or civil ruler of Islam. In response thousands more Muslims began to flood into Anatolia and to enter Bayezit's service, including not only the Turkoman nomads but also many of those who had formed the backbone of governmental and economic life in Iran, Iraq, and Transoxania and who were fleeing the anarchy that followed the collapse of the Ilhanids and the invasion of Tamerlane. These elements gave Bayezit and his successors a new source of manpower with which they could rule as well as conquer an empire.

Bayezit now faced the crucial decision of his reign: Should he take advantage of the victory at Nicopolis to move farther into Europe? It would have been the logical thing to do if he was to carry on the gazi tradition, and this course was urged on him by the Turkoman notables led by the Çandarlı family. On the other hand his Christian advisers urged him to leave Europe alone so as not to provide the Turkish notables with new conquests and wealth and instead to return to Anatolia to eliminate the Turkoman principalities that had survived so long as threats to his rear.

Bayezit retired to Edirne to make up his mind. Meanwhile Ottoman forces raided into Wallachia, Hungary, Bosnia, and Styria and occupied the last independent Bulgarian state at Vidin. The latter was then organized along with Silistria and Nicopolis into a new frontier district to center the gazi activities directed against Hungary and Wallachia (1396). Albania was invaded once again, with Işkodra (Scutari), Kroya, Berat, and Kastoria falling under the sultan's direct control, while the Buşatlı family, which ruled the north, accepted his suzerainty. Constantinople was put under siege for the third time (1396–1397), and Anadolu Hisarı (the Anatolian fort) was built on the Bosporus to control Byzantine access to the Black Sea. But the siege was pushed only half-heartedly, perhaps because the Ottomans still lacked sufficient siege equipment but more likely because of the pleas of the sultan's Christian advisers that actual conquest of the city might stimulate a more powerful European Crusade effort than could be resisted. Finally, Bayezit agreed to abandon the siege in return for an increased tribute from and agreement by the emperor that all his successors should be confirmed by the sultan. Bayezit then moved to his last, fateful, campaign in Anatolia.

Bayezit's Last Anatolian Campaigns

While Bayezit was busy in Europe Alauddin Ali Bey, prince of Karaman, in an effort to regain his losses to the Ottomans, took Ankara, capital of the Ottoman *beylerbeylik* of Anatolia, and then advanced through Germiyan toward the old Ottoman capital of Bursa. Bayezit brought together his Rumeli and Anatolian armies at Bursa and moved toward Konya with such a large force that Alauddin Ali surrendered all the prisoners and booty he had taken and proposed peace. Bayezit, however, refused the overture and attacked and routed the Karamanid ruler at the plain of Akçay (1397), executing him shortly after the battle. Resolved to eliminate Karaman altogether, Bayezit occupied the principality's eastern territories around Larende/Karaman as well as Konya and its environs. In 1398 he advanced along the Black Sea coast, reaching the borders of Byzantine Trabzon, with only the Genoese colony at Amisus (Kara Samsun), east of Samsun, remaining out of his control. These conquests put Bayezit in control of all the lands to the north, west, and southwest of the Kadi Burhaneddin state. The latter still was quite large – including Sivas, Kayseri, Tokat, Niksar, and Kırşehir and encompassing much of central Anatolia – but with the death of Kadi Burhaneddin in 1398 internal divisions compelled the notables of the state to accept Bayezit's suzerainty in return for help against attacks mounted by the White Sheep Turkomans in the East. Bayezit not only helped against the latter but occupied the entire Kadi Burhaneddin state, establishing it as a new frontier province. The Ottomans thus were brought into direct contact with Mamluk territory from Malatya to Cilicia.

For a short time in 1399 Bayezit seems to have returned to Europe to direct the construction of the new Turkish quarter in Constantinople, which was settled by Turks from Göynük and Taraklı. But following the death of the Mamluk sultan Barkuk (June 1399) and his replacement by an unexperienced youth, Nasruddin Farac, and also the news that Tamerlane was involved in a major invasion of India, Bayezit resumed his conquests in the East. His immediate objective was the Mamluk vassal state of Dulgadır, which had ruled the area around Maraş and Elbistan since early in the fourteenth century and used Mamluk help to expand against the Armenians of Cilicia. Apparently fearing the effect a further advance against Muslims and Turkomans would have on his Turkoman forces, Bayezit's army seems to have been composed primarily of vassal troops, particularly those sent from Serbia. With the Mamluks in disarray following Barkuk's death, Bayezit had little trouble annexing the principality (August–September 1399). He then took most of Cilicia from the Mamluks and moved on to the east of the Euphrates, reestablishing the unity of Turkish Anatolia.

In the spring of 1400 Tamerlane restored his rule in Azerbaijan and eastern Iraq and forced the Christian king of Georgia to accept his suzerainty. It was just at this time that Bayezit took Erzincan and Kemah from Mutahherten Bey, who earlier had accepted Tamerlane's suzerainty and protection, making a clash inevitable. When Tamerlane came to Pasinler, near Erzurum, he was joined by a number of Turkoman princes driven from their lands by the Ottomans, all asking for his help to regain their power. It should be noted that they came to Tamerlane after he had entered Anatolia. It seems likely, therefore, that his decision was made more because of his own fear of Ottoman power than on the basis of their appeals.

Tamerlane moved to Sivas, the old Kadi Burhaneddin capital captured by Bayezit only a short time before, taking it (August 27, 1400) and slaughtering all the defenders, Muslim and non-Muslim alike. He then moved to solidify his position in the south, advancing into Mamluk Syria and capturing Malatya, Ayntap, Aleppo (October 1400), and Damascus (December 1400), routing the Mamluk army several times and massacring thousands as he went. While Tamerlane was in the south, Bayezit moved back into eastern Anatolia and retook Sivas and Erzincan, seeking to gain a strategic advantage before the conqueror returned. In the spring of 1402 the two armies maneuvered for advantage. Tamerlane assembled a large new army in Georgia, then entered Anatolia via Erzurum and Kemah, moving to Kayseri and then Ankara, which he put under siege, trying to lure Bayezit into battle while at the same time gaining the support of most of the Turkomans by restoring the lands of their beys as he took them from the Ottomans. Tamerlane also seems to have gained a strategic advantage by advancing from Sivas to Ankara via the well-watered northern route, thus compelling Bayezit to seek water and other supplies from the less well supplied south as best he could. The decisive battle finally took place at the plain of Çubuk, outside Ankara, on July 27, 1402. The sources vary widely as to the size of the two armies, but all agree that Tamerlane's force was larger. The battle lasted about 14 hours. Bayezit seems to have done well at first, but the betrayal of some of his Turkoman auxiliaries and, according to some, of his Serbian vassal forces finally turned the tide. The Ottoman army was routed. Bayezit fell captive and Tamerlane won the day.

The Interregnum, 1402–1413

Tamerlane's invasion was so successful because the Ottoman Empire built during the fourteenth century contained important seeds of instability, particularly the vassal system, which left Christian princes in a position to assert their independence whenever the central authority was troubled or weak. Bayezit's army collapsed so easily because by abandoning the gazi tradition that had brought success to his predecessors he alienated the officers and soldiers who had led the previous conquests, especially since the Eastern conquests offered nowhere the kind of booty and estates found in Europe. It was problems such as these that Bayezit's heirs had to face and solve during the Interregnum if the empire was to be restored.

Following the battle of Ankara Tamerlane remained in Anatolia about eight months (July 1402–March 1403), moving around to establish his overall authority and restore the old Turkoman principalities, while ravaging the Ottoman lands for the booty demanded by his men. In the process he killed thousands, destroyed mosques and schools, burned town and field alike, and sent thousands more into slavery. Bayezit himself, and most likely his sons Musa and Mustafa, remained as captives in the conqueror's suite until the former sultan died, at Akşehir, on March 9, 1403. Tamerlane himself returned to the East and died at Otrar on February 18, 1405, while planning a new expedition to China.

The political make-up of Anatolia as left by Tamerlane was not too dissimilar to that at the end of Murat I's reign. The Conqueror in fact did little more than eliminate the additions made by Bayezit, with the exception that the Ottoman corridor opened by Murat I from Ankara to the Mediterranean was now replaced by one from Ankara northeast to the Black Sea near Trabzon, with Tamerlane substituting his suzerainty for that of the Ilhanids. The Karamanid prince Mehmet was put at the head of an enlarged state encompassing one-third of Anatolia, including the eastern parts of Hamit and Germiyan and towns such as Kayseri, Isparta, Antalya, and Alaiye as well as the former Karaman possessions. Tamerlane apparently did this in order to give Karaman the strength it needed to resist any effort to restore Ottoman power in the area, declaring it to be the "emir of the marches," leader of all the other principalities, including the Ottomans, against the infidels. Beyond Karaman Tamerlane restored only those principalities that Bayezit had conquered, although even this was difficult, since many of the former ruling families had been absorbed into the Ottoman system.

Even the Ottomans had a place in the new order. Prince Süleyman was recognized as Ottoman ruler in Europe from his capital at Edirne. Of Bayezit's other sons, Isa Çelebi ruled at Balıkesir and Bursa and Mehmet Çelebi at Amasya, both acknowledging Tamerlane's suzerainty. The Ottomans thus retained control of all the territories of the empire as it existed before Bayezit, but their prestige had declined enormously and it was not at all clear whether the empire as it was could be retained. Some Europeans thought that if they had united to form a new Crusader force, they might have pushed the Ottomans out of Europe, but the situation was not that simple. Only Bayezit's expeditionary force had been destroyed along with many of the newly formed *kapıkulları*. But the feudal army in Europe and the gazis remained intact, largely under Süleyman's leadership, along with most of the chief ministers and commanders. Nor was Europe in any position to take advantage of the Ottomans' situation. Serbia remained dependent on Süleyman. Sigismund of Hungary was preoccupied with efforts to advance into central Europe, and his absence in turn strengthened the Hungarian feudal nobles. Without united Hungarian support any Crusader attack would probably have met the same fate as that of Nicopolis.

The Ottoman problem was not one of rebuilding defenses against a European counterattack. It was, rather, one of restoring united leadership, reasserting rule throughout Anatolia, and, most importantly, establishing the organization of state and society on firmer bases than those that had allowed Bayezit's Anatolian empire and his army to crumble so easily in the face of Tamerlane.

The internal politics of the Interregnum were very complicated, and here we can only discuss what led to the final conclusion. Most of the events centered on the struggle for power between the Turkish notables and their descendants, who wanted to restore the gazi tradition and the primacy of the High Islamic institutions of the Seljuks, and the survivors of the *kapıkulları* and the Christian advisers, who proposed opposite policies in order to retain their newly found position. As Bayezit's sons fought for power, they gained the support of one or another of these groups, with the alliances changing rapidly as the groups changed their estimates of which prince had the best chance of leading them to victory. Süleyman first was raised to the throne in Edirne by the Turkish notables led by the Çandarlı. But he began to base his support on the *kapıkulu* and Christian elements in the state, establishing close contacts with Emperor Manuel II and with the Christian vassals, whom he promised autonomy in return. He was recognized as Ottoman ruler by Tamerlane, since he was the only contender not attempting to restore the patrimony in Anatolia. The other brothers, Musa, Isa, and Mehmet, on the other hand, were building their power entirely in Anatolia. They were trying to create new Turkoman armies by emphasizing the old gazi tradition against the infidel. Since their policies corresponded more with the desires of the Turkish notables than did that of Süleyman, it was not long before the Çandarlı and their associates abandoned him for the younger sons, though it was difficult for them to agree on a single candidate. Throughout the entire period the Ottoman frontiers remained almost unchanged except for the territories taken by Tamerlane and those surrendered by Süleyman in return for Christian support. In neither Europe nor Asia did the enemies of the Ottomans make any real effort to take advantage of Ottoman division by cooperating among themselves.

The rivalries for power among the Ottoman princes in Anatolia surfaced initially in the winter of 1403 while Tamerlane was still on the scene. First to act was Mehmet Çelebi, who tried to claim the family patrimony from Bursa but was dissuaded because of Tamerlane's support of his brother Musa. Mehmet instead accepted the invitation of a number of notables from his old *sancak* of Amasya, who wanted his leadership to drive out Kara Devletşah, one of Tamerlane's lieutenants who had been established there. Mehmet accomplished this and took over Amasya in the latter's place (1403). He soon extended his influence to the neighboring towns of Sivas, Tokat, and Niksar, which had been ravaged by Tamerlane. Success bred success, as victory after victory enabled him to attract large numbers of his father's former supporters, so that within a year after Ankara he had a large Turkoman army ready and able to take on all enemies.

Musa had been the only one of Bayezit's sons to stay with his father in captivity. This gave him the opportunity to gain the Conqueror's favor, while Isa established himself at Balıkesir. The first clash between the Ottoman princes came near Karesi, with Musa emerging victorious as the ruler of the area between Bursa and Karesi. Soon afterward, however, Isa turned the tables and took the territory of Musa, who fled to refuge in Germiyan.

In the meantime Süleyman, the eldest son, was fairly secure in Edirne with the support of the Christian elements. Serbia was now ruled by Stephen, son of Lazar (1389–1427), but his eventual successor, George Branković, was just beginning to extend his power in southern Serbia. Süleyman was not unhappy to see the two Serbian princes fight one another, and he used the situation to increase his influence over both. At the same time, he had ambitions to regain his father's Anatolian dominions and to restore the Ottoman Empire by eliminating his brothers. He secured Byzantine financial and military help in return for a number of territorial concessions, including Salonica, much of southern Macedonia, the Morea, and part of coastal Thrace, the towns closest to Constantinople along the Sea of Marmara and the Black Sea. The Byzantine tribute also was ended, a high price indeed for Christian help against his own brothers. Similar agreements were made with Stephen of Serbia and with the Italian maritime states (June 3, 1403), with each receiving increased trade concessions from Süleyman in return for its help. In response Mehmet, Musa, and Isa accepted Tamerlane's suzerainty, promising payments of tribute and military assistance in return for support against the "agent of the infidels" in Edirne.

Back in Anatolia Çelebi Mehmet soon moved to the fore. After taking much of the central plateau from the Turkomans left there by Tamerlane, he routed Isa, adding Bursa and Balıkesir to his rapidly expanding state and then overrunning Saruhan. As soon as he retook Bursa, Mehmet had himself proclaimed sultan by the local religious leaders and began to mint coins in his own name, mentioning that of Tamerlane as suzerain. Isa fled first to Constantinople and then to Süleyman to seek refuge. To the Byzantine emperor he seemed an ideal weapon to keep the Ottomans divided; to Süleyman he was a convenient instrument against Mehmet. So with Byzantine support Süleyman sent Isa back to Anatolia at the head of a large army to raise popular opposition to Mehmet and recapture Bursa (1404). Isa fled to the East and was heard of no more, while his allies, the smaller Aegean principalities, were forced to accept Mehmet's suzerainty. Mehmet and Süleyman, therefore, ruled supreme in the Anatolian and European portions of the empire, and it appeared that this division might remain permanent (1405).

Süleyman, however, still wanted to rule the whole empire. Thus he led his own army into Anatolia against his brother and went on to take Ankara, thereby dividing Mehmet's possessions and coming close to total victory. The Turkoman chiefs united (spring 1406) in fear that a triumph by Süleyman would end their independence. But they were unable to subordinate their jealousies and individual ambitions to the common cause; the alliance broke up, and Süleyman was left in a position where he could defeat his rivals one at a time. When Mehmet tried to take Bursa to surprise Süleyman from the rear, the latter surprised and defeated him at Yenişehir forcing him to return to Amasya (1406). In a last desperate effort to stop Süleyman, Mehmet formed an alliance with Karaman. In 1409 Mehmet also tried a new tactic, sending Musa Çelebi to Europe in an effort to take over Süleyman's possessions there while he was absent. Apparently, Mehmet managed to get for Musa the support of Wallachia and of Stephen of Serbia, who feared that Süleyman would become too strong and threaten his own independence. In Wallachia Musa married the prince's daughter, built an army of Turks, Vlachs, Serbs, and Bulgars, and moved toward Edirne. Süleyman immediately returned to Europe, enabling Çelebi Mehmet to reoccupy the remainder of western Anatolia. Süleyman's early victories were reversed when Musa won the support of the gazi raiding chiefs who feared that Süleyman's triumph would end their ability to advance into Europe, and defeated and killed Süleyman (February 17, 1411).

Süleyman's European empire now came under the rule of his far more energetic and able brother Musa, who threw off his allegiance to Mehmet and became every bit as threatening as Süleyman had been. Musa declared himself sultan and had coins minted in his name. With Çandarlı Ibrahim as grand vezir, the old Ottoman court and institutions were reestablished and the gazi frontier raids revived under the direction of one of their leaders, Mihaloğlu, who became *beylerbeyi* of Rumeli. The old frontier element thus triumphed in the areas under Musa's rule. The *kapıkulları* were suppressed, and the estates again went to the Turkish notables and the frontier beys. And efforts were made to attract the masses by appointing as Şeyhulislam one of the leading Muslim jurists and mystic philosophers of the time, Bedreddin-i Simavni, a controversial figure whose teachings were regarded as heretical by the conservative Muslims.[6] He attracted large numbers of followers among the common people, Muslim and Christian alike, with doctrines demanding the division of all wealth equally among the people and an end to all differences among the peoples of different religions in the area. These became the official doctrines of Musa's regime.

To satisfy the frontier leaders who had supported him Musa punished Serbia and Byzantium for their support of Süleyman. Vigorously condemning the latter's surrender of territories once ruled by Muslims, he moved to regain them in the name of Islam, capturing large areas of southern Serbia, including the silver-mining center of Novo Brdo as well as the forts of Pravadi and Köprü, while Mihaloğlu and his raiders ravaged sections of Macedonia. When Manuel refused Musa's demands to surrender the territories turned over to him and to pay tribute in arrears, the fifth Ottoman siege of Constantinople was begun (1411–1412), with Musa regaining all the territories previously returned to the Byzantines with the exception of Salonica.

However, Musa's activist policies concealed internal problems that soon unhinged the bases of his support. He began to resent the wealth and power gained by the gazi chiefs through booty and timars, and he turned to the *kapıkulları*, transferring positions and timars to them while ordering the gazis to stop their raids into Christian territory. At the same time, Bedreddin's doctrines, while appealing to the impoverished masses, were abhorrent to the orthodox religious leaders and Turkish notables alike, so that the latter began to plot to eliminate the regime as rapidly as possible. Mihaloğlu broke with Musa, leading raids into Macedonia on his own and keeping all the resulting booty and timars for himself and his followers. The conservative religious leaders openly criticized Bedreddin as a heretic and demanded again that Musa remove him. The Çandarlı ministers entered into secret negotiations with Emperor Manuel and with Çelebi Mehmet with the object of putting the latter on the throne (March 1412), promising Manuel that the newly conquered territories would be restored if Mehmet won.

After obtaining Manuel's consent, Mehmet landed in Rumeli with his army but was routed by Musa and managed to escape only with ships provided by the Byzantines. Mehmet returned to Anatolia but continued to plot against Musa, expanding the base of his support by promising to restore more territories to both Serbia and Byzantium. This time he was more successful. Landing on the Black Sea coast north of Constantinople and advancing toward Edirne, he smashed Musa's army at Viza, near Filibe. With most of his supporters fleeing at the last minute because of Çandarlı intrigues, Musa fled but was captured and killed at Samakov, south of Sofia (July 10, 1413).

Thus was ended the great division in the house of Osman. With the support of the Turkish notables and the Byzantine elements in Ottoman society, as well as that of all his immediate neighbors, Mehmet had reunited the possessions of his father. It is interesting to note, therefore, that in the end those states most threatened by the Ottomans, far from taking advantage of Ottoman division after the Battle of Ankara, actually worked to bring the Interregnum to an end for their own immediate advantage. The Ottoman Empire emerged from the long decade of crisis in full control of all the important strategic points in Southeastern Europe, Edirne, Sofia, and Üsküp in the west and Sliven, Karınova, and Aydos in the eastern Balkan ranges, with only Niş going to Serbia in return for its help to Mehmet.

Notes to Chapter 2

1 While it is claimed that the title was granted by the shadow Abbasid caliph maintained by the Mamluks in Cairo following the Mongol capture of Baghdad in 1258, this is unlikely, since the Mamluks themselves claimed the title and were bitter rivals of the Ottomans for supremacy in the Muslim world. More likely, the title came simply in con-

sequence of the tremendous prestige gained by the Ottomans as a result of their conquests and rule of Christian territory.

2 At this time the regular beys were given one horsetail, the rank held by the Ottoman rulers themselves when they were only beys and not sultans; the *beylerbeyi*s two; the chief vezir three; and the sultan four.

3 S. Vryonis, "The Byzantine Legacy and Ottoman Forms," *Dumbarton Oaks Papers,* nos. 23–24, Washington, D.C., 1969–1970, p. 280.

4 S. Vryonis, *The Decline of Medieval Hellenism in Asia Minor and the Process of Islamization from the Eleventh Through the Fifteenth Century,* Berkeley, Calif., 1971.

5 Halil Inalcık, "Ghûlam," EI², II, 1085–1086.

6 Bedreddin-i Simavni had entered Anatolia from Iran in the suite of Tamerlane's conquest. While he had avoided the Conqueror's effort to get him to gain popular support for the new regime, he had undertaken his own missionary work throughout Anatolia and Rumeli, building his own mystic order, at least partly with the help of the beys of Germiyan and Karaman, who hoped to use him against the Ottomans. Originally a sufi, he gradually developed heretical syncretic ideas that made him anathema to the orthodox doctors, rejecting the basic Muslim ideas of the Day of Judgment and the Hereafter and leaning more toward radical forms of pantheism.

3

Restoration of the Ottoman Empire, 1413–1481

With the triumph of Mehmet over his brothers a new period of Ottoman imperialism was begun. The boundaries of Bayezit's empire were restored and even expanded and the internal bases of the state were reorganized to prevent the kind of weakness that had made the defeat of Ankara and its aftermath possible.

Mehmet I, 1413–1420

Mehmet I had won in the end because he gained the support of not only Byzantium but also the more important gazi frontier leaders and Turkoman notables. To conciliate the religious leaders whose support had enabled him to triumph, Şeyh Bedreddin was dismissed and sent into exile with his family, while his replacement was nominated by the conservative ulema. His supporters among the gazi leaders, including Mihaloğlu Mehmet Bey, were exiled to Anatolia even though they abandoned him at the last minute. In accordance with the agreement with Manuel all the Byzantine territories around Constantinople and Salonica regained by Musa were restored, despite the objections of the Turkoman notables and others, and peace agreements were made with the Balkan Christian states as well as with Venice and Genoa to gain the time needed to restore Ottoman strength.

This did not prevent Mehmet from moving to eliminate from the Ottoman court the Byzantine and Christian influences that had led Bayezit to abandon the gazi tradition. The Byzantine women and advisers were driven out of the palace. Greek was replaced by Turkish and Persian as languages of administration. Emphasis was placed on the dynasty's Turkish past, and historians were subsidized to stress this in the process of writing its history. The connections of the dynasty with the *ahi* guilds were restored, and the *kapıkulları* were suppressed, deprived of their timars, and dismissed from their positions. With the *kapıkulları* out of the way the feudal cavalry, still the military arm of the nobility, resumed its former role at the center of the Ottoman army. With the Christian and slave elements largely eliminated and the gazi leaders in eclipse, Mehmet fell under the control of the Turkish notables, led by the Çandarlı family, which had arranged his triumph over Musa. The basic policy propounded by the Çandarlıs at this time was abandonment of Bayezit's eastern ambitions and resumption of the gazi raids, with the thousands of nomads left in Anatolia after the collapse of Tamerlane's empire being sent to the western frontiers to provide the necessary manpower. Restoration of the gazi tradition also implied a return to the policy of avoiding conflicts with the Anatolian principalities, but this was difficult to do because of the aggressive policies of Karaman, Aydın and Candar, which were by far the strongest among them.

Initial Campaigns in Anatolia

Ottoman rule in Anatolia at this time was limited to a large strip of territory stretching west to east across the northern part of the plateau from the Aegean to Erzincan, including Bursa, Izmit, Eskişehir, Ankara, and Sivas. The Candaroğlu controlled much of the southeastern shore of the Black Sea, including Kastamonu and Samsun. The rest of eastern Anatolia was divided between the White Sheep, whose center was in Azerbaijan, and the Black Sheep Turkomans (who ruled as far west as Şebin Karahisar and Koyluhisar), who had been brought in by Tamerlane, while the Dulgadir maintained their state centered in Maraş and Elbistan and extended their territories westward to include the southern parts of Kayseri and Sivas. Trabzon remained under Byzantine control. Malatya was under the Mamluks, while the White Sheep and Black Sheep disputed the lands between it and Divrigi and Erzincan. Saruhan, Germiyan, Aydın, and Menteşe divided the southwest; Hamit, the Eşrefoğulları, and Karaman ruled the rest of south-central and eastern Anatolia. Karaman continued to press its claim to rule the entire Seljuk heritage, including large areas under Ottoman rule. Also Cüneyt Bey of Aydın, previously an ally of Musa, tried to take his old capital of Izmir as well as the Aegean coastal regions.

To consolidate his position Mehmet initiated a series of rapid campaigns through Anatolia early in his reign. In 1414 he forced Menteşe to accept his suzerainty and regained Izmir, partly with the help of the Genoese fleets stationed on the Aegean Islands. He followed this with two rapid campaigns against Karaman in 1414 and 1415, conquering most of the areas that Bayezit had taken from it before 1402 and Tamerlane had restored, including the districts of Akşehir, Beyşehir, and Hamit – all in the name of rescuing the Muslim states from Karaman's conquest.

European Campaigns

Mehmet then was diverted for a time by problems in Europe. The Albanian notables had used the Interregnum to massacre most of the Ottoman garrisons left in the country. Mehmet restored his position here by capturing Kroya (Akçahisar), in the central mountains, and Valona (Avlonya), on the coast. These became major centers for further expansion and rule in the area. He also raided the Morea and restored his suzerainty over Mircea, prince of Wallachia (1386–1418), who had helped Musa. Mehmet then occupied Giurgiu (Yergöğü), a key Danubian fort controlling the route leading into the central Hungarian plain. He also undertook a series of raids into Transylvania and Hungary, whose King Sigismund (1386–1437) also nourished ambitions in the area, and completed the conquest of the Dobruca. Regular raids into Bosnia caused many of its feudal nobles to fall under Ottoman influence, leading Tvrtko II (1420–1423) to accept Ottoman suzerainty formally. Finally, the Ottomans fought a naval war with Venice over the raids of pirates based in the Aegean Islands. But Mehmet had only begun to build a fleet; thus his ships were routed near Gallipoli (May 29, 1416). In the end peace was arranged through the mediation of Manuel II, who got Venice to curb its pirates in return for additional commercial privileges in the Ottoman Empire.

Return to Anatolia

Mehmet's remaining military activities were confined to Anatolia, not as much by plan as in reaction to continued threats to Ottoman suzerainty there. The Isfendiyar dynasty of Candar took most of the neighboring principalities left by Tamerlane, including Kastamonu and Safranbolu, and then allied with Karaman in an effort to end Ottoman influence in Anatolia. Mehmet's rule in the east also was endangered by the advances of the Black Sheep Turkomans, who took the areas of Erzurum, Erzincan, and then Şebin Karahisar. To this double threat Mehmet responded first by eliminating Candar and putting its territories under direct control. Most of its Turkoman soldiers were settled in Bulgaria, near Filibe (Plovdiv) at a place that came to be called Tatar Pazarı (Tatar Market) (1418). This began a new policy of large-scale settlement of Turkish nomads in the Balkans both to end their threats in Anatolia and to establish them as permanent garrisons to maintain Ottoman rule in the area.

The Revolts of Bedreddin, Dede Sultan, and the False Mustafa

Further expansion of Ottoman power in the east was, however, interrupted by a series of major new revolts in the west that brought a confused conclusion to Mehmet's reign. Inspiration for the uprisings came from Şeyh Bedreddin, Musa's chief kadi and spiritual adviser, whom Mehmet had exiled to Iznik. Bedreddin had already achieved considerable mass following, and the economic consequences of the long series of military actions added to his popularity among the impoverished. Bedreddin now worked to rebuild his order throughout the empire, sending out preachers to spread his message and organize secret cells of supporters. He fled from Iznik in fear of Mehmet I and went to Samsun in the hope of getting Candar support. The latter, however, recoiled from his radical doctrines and sent him to Rumeli in the hope that he would upset Ottoman stability there. He soon found a patron in Wallachia, now ruled by Mircea's son Mihail, who gave him the material support needed to raise a revolt among the discontented masses in the entire European part of the empire. He had wide success, particularly among the nomadic Turkomans recently settled there. Their heterodox beliefs were similar to his own, and, perhaps most important, they were unhappy with the relative lack of opportunities available to secure booty from raids into Christian territory.

While Bedreddin preached in Rumeli, his supporters raised several revolts in Anatolia. It seemed very likely that the popular protest might sweep the Ottomans out of Anatolia altogether. Only a full-scale military expedition organized and led by Grand Vezir Bayezit Paşa and the sultan's son Murat (later Murat II) finally suppressed the revolts. The leaders were executed, but the discontent remained. In the meantime, Bedreddin gathered thousands of followers at Deliorman, in the Dobruca, attracting all those who had lost their positions as a result of Musa's defeat, as well as many angered by Çelebi Mehmet's return of the lands promised to Byzantium and his recognition of the Christian vassals who had helped him regain power. To add to Mehmet's troubles he also was plagued by a parallel uprising led by a man named Mustafa Çelebi, who claimed to be the long lost son of Bayezit I and who had been imprisoned with his father by Tamerlane. Mustafa went to Thrace and then Thessaly, where he organized his own uprising, taking advantage of Mehmet's diversions first in Anatolia and then against Bedreddin to capture Edirne and declare himself sultan (1418). While Çelebi Mehmet led one army to fight this "Düzme Mustafa" (Mustafa the False), his grand vezir led another force to Deliorman against Bedreddin (spring 1419). The latter's followers melted away after learning of the defeat of their supporters in Anatolia, so that he was captured and executed with little difficulty. Mehmet then was able to unite his forces to rout Düzme Mustafa, who fled to refuge with the Byzantines while his movement was suppressed (1420).

Mehmet I's Final Conquests

Only after the revolts were suppressed could Mehmet achieve his final conquests. He annexed Aydın (1425) and Menteşe (1426), thus gaining control of western Anatolia, and then moved to the south, taking Teke and Antalya and bringing the entire western coast of Anatolia under Ottoman control. Since Germiyan had helped him during the Interregnum, he left it alone for a time, taking only its major communication centers of Kütahya and Afyon Karahisar. But its ruler finally bequeathed the principality to the Ottomans, completing Ottoman control of southwestern Anatolia (1428). When Mehmet died suddenly in 1421, his son Murat II succeeded to the throne.

Murat II, 1421–1451

Murat II became one of the great Ottoman sultans, the founder of Ottoman power in Europe and Asia. Building on the work of Çelebi Mehmet, Murat developed the institutions of state and army in such a way that his son and successor Mehmet II was able to make new conquests and establish a much greater empire in both the east and the west.

Internal Politics and Revolts

Before Murat could start rebuilding the empire, however, he first had to spend three years (1421–1423) fighting for his right to rule. He was only 17 years old at his accession, and the existence of four younger brothers provided an opportunity for his enemies to foment division within the Ottoman family. The Ottomans had already begun a policy of killing the brothers of the ruler to limit disputes for succession. But Çelebi Mehmet seems to have taken active measures before he died to avoid this, sending Prince Mustafa to Hamit to rule Anatolia and the younger princes Yusuf and Mahmut to Byzantine protection to assure their survival after their brother took power.

Murat hoped to keep peace to gain time to rebuild the state internally, but the Byzantines could not resist the temptation to use the False Mustafa, who was still in their hands, to weaken the empire as much as possible. Murat had Emperor Manuel return the princes, but the latter's son, made coemperor as John VIII (1421), also released the False Mustafa and his ally Cüneyt, sending them to Gallipoli (September 1421) in return for promises to restore Byzantine rule over it and Thessaly. Gallipoli fell to Mustafa with little opposition. Karaman used the occasion to occupy the old Hamit lands once again, while Menteşe, Aydın, and Saruhan threw off the bonds of vassalage.

Murat initially went to Bursa to build an army that would restore his position in Anatolia. The False Mustafa then crossed into Europe and marched toward Edirne. A great deal of his support came from (1) the frontier beys and their followers who hoped for new conquests in Europe and feared that Murat would continue his predecessor's policy of concentrating on Anatolian conquests and (2) the same disaffected masses that had been attracted to Bedreddin. When Grand Vezir Bayezit Paşa tried to rally Murat's feudal forces near Edirne, many of them also joined the rebel because of their dislike of the grand vezir, who was from the *kapıkulları*. With Murat in Anatolia and Mustafa in Europe, it seemed that the division of the empire developed during the Interregnum might become permanent. At this point, however, the main division was not between proponents and opponents of the gazi tradition. That tradition was accepted by all elements in the struggle for power. The conflict now was between the Turkish notables supporting the sultan, who wanted to establish centralized control of all parts of the empire, and the gazi frontier leaders and military commanders of Rumeli, supported by the Turkoman vassals of Anatolia, who wanted to be as independent as possible and supported Mustafa for that reason. Of course, Mustafa also had the support of Byzantium and the Christian vassals because of his promises of independence and reduced tribute payments. They also felt that they would benefit far more from the decentralized type of administration that he represented rather than the powerful, centralized kind of state that Murat, the Çandarlı ministers, and the Turkish notables espoused.

Mustafa made the same fatal mistake that had cost Bayezit I his throne, deciding to enter Anatolia to unite the empire under his rule. Apparently, this was done at the instigation of the Byzantines, who were happy to have him as far away as possible, and his ally Cüneyt Bey, who wanted help to regain his old family territories around Izmir. On the other hand, Mustafa's successes in Europe enabled Murat to receive some help from Serbia and the other Balkan princes who feared the reestablishment of Ottoman power under Mustafa's leadership. Mustafa marched toward Bursa, where Murat had been preparing his army. But the gazi commanders and others who had supported Mustafa because of his promises to resume the campaigns in Europe recoiled from his Anatolian adventure and went over to Murat. When the two armies met at Ulubat, then, the latter won easily. Mustafa fled back to Europe, closely followed by Murat, who obtained the boats needed to transport his men from the Genoese of Foça. Mustafa took his treasury and harem from Edirne and fled toward Wallachia, but he was captured and killed along the way, thus bringing his revolt to a sudden end.

Murat undertook the sixth Ottoman siege of Constantinople to punish the emperor for his support of the rebel (June 1422). The Byzantines put up a strong resistance and also encouraged new advances in Anatolia by Karaman and Germiyan as well as Murat's brother, Prince Mustafa, who had remained as governor of Hamit. The three formed an allied army that took Nicaea and put Bursa under siege (August 1422), again threatening Murat's empire. He therefore abandoned the siege of Constantinople and moved back to the East. Mustafa was joined by large numbers of Turkoman notables, who preferred his decentralizing policies, but the *ahi* guilds, whose Anatolian network had been a major factor in the initial Ottoman successes, continued to back Murat, helping his forces in Bursa to hold out until the sultan arrived from Istanbul, executed his brother, and restored his vassals to obedience (February 1423). The death of the Karamanid ruler Mehmet Bey during the siege of Antalya removed the other threat.

Murat used the rivalries within the Karaman ruling family to put his own choice, Mehmet Bey (1423–1426), on the throne. Hamit was again returned to the Ottomans, and Karaman accepted the sultan's suzerainty, with marriages being arranged to cement the ties of the two families further. Murat then concluded his Anatolian expedition by annexing the western Turkoman principalities, Aydın, Menteşe, and Teke. Karaman and Candar were left intact in the east, however, because any effort to annex them might attract a new invasion on the part of Tamerlane's successor in the east, Şahruh, who claimed suzerainty over all the territories once ruled by the Seljuks and Ilhanids.

Political Power in the Ottoman State

After his Anatolian problems were settled, Murat was free to establish himself and his dynasty in Edirne and to formulate new plans for conquest. First, however, he had to consolidate his own power, eliminate vassals, and achieve centralized control of the empire. He gave more money and timars to the Çandarlı ministers who supported this policy, broke down the power of the frontier gazi leaders, and restored the *kapıkulu* slaves to gain some independence from the feudal forces of Rumeli, whose support had proved so unreliable in the recent past. To build the power of the sultanate and make it more independent of the Çandarlı and the Turkish notables as well, he also began to develop his slaves as a major class in the Ottoman state, but under his control, to be used as his creatures against those who could contest his power. He used the *pençik* to secure strong young men from among those captured in war against the infidel. Murat also bought slaves in the Caucasus and elsewhere and resumed the *devşirme* system of recruitment originated by Bayezit I, restoring the latter's system of training to convert his slaves to Islam and make them Ottomans so that they could participate equally with the Turkish nobles in the Ottoman system. When he could, he built up their financial and political power by giving them newly conquered Balkan lands as fiefs and by appointing them to important military positions, although as before the Çandarlı were able to keep them out of the central administration. Conquest thus became a means of building Murat's slave family against the Turkish nobility. The latter, therefore, turned toward a policy of peace, advocating an end of the European conquests that were strengthening their rivals, while the increasingly powerful slaves became the war faction. With the two groups now largely equal in strength, Murat was able to balance them, accepting the demands of one group and then the other, keeping them in rivalry for his favor, and thereby achieving control over both in a system that was to become traditional in Ottoman politics during the next three centuries.

Murat set in motion factors that eventually were to assure the triumph of the slaves a century later. The *kapıkulu* men now became the basis of the Ottoman army and were divided into two services: (1) the *Sipahi* cavalry, supported mainly by feudal timars and under the control of the old Turkish nobility and (2) the Janissary infantry, supported by treasury salaries and hence more directly under the control of the central government. In addition a new *kapıkulu* force, the Cannon corps (*Topçu Ocağı*), was developed out of the old *yaya* infantry to use this most important new weapon of war. Murat's decision also to use the firearmed muskets then finding their place in world armories assured Ottoman military supremacy in Europe and Asia in the next century. The eventual triumph of the Janissary corps in the Ottoman political struggles was assured by its armament with the most modern weapons of the time, while the feudal cavalry was left with bows, arrows, and spears, which soon made it obsolete militarily though it remained important politically and administratively for some time through its control of the timar system.

Expansion and Settlement in Europe

Until Murat was in a position where his slave army could participate in the European conquests, and in consequence share in the spoils, he limited his European activities to largely defensive measures. In response to Wallachian raids across the Danube – apparently encouraged by Sigismund of Hungary – Murat sent his raiders into Wallachia (1422–1423) while continuing to besiege Constantinople. After Venice took Salonica from Byzantium (1423), Murat besieged it until its new defenders agreed to pay a substantial tribute (1424), while the Byzantines gave back all of Thessaly and Macedonia. Murat then stabilized his European relations in a series of peace treaties by which Byzantium, Serbia, Wallachia, and Hungary accepted Ottoman suzerainty and agreed to pay tribute in return for freedom from raids (1424).

New Campaigns in Anatolia

For the moment Anatolia provided the primary stage for Murat's military ambitions. He first overwhelmed Cüneyt Bey, who, in return for his desertion of Düzme Mustafa, had expanded the territory given him around Izmir to include much of Aydın. Murat got the Genoese fleets from Midilli (Mitilene) and Sakız (Chios) to sever Cüneyt's sea connections, thus depriving him of the supplies previously sent by Menteşe and Karaman, in return restoring the Genoese colonies along the Black Sea coast around Samsun. Once Cüneyt and his family were captured and executed (1426), the Ottomans were able to occupy Menteşe and Teke, thus assuring control of the Anatolian shores of the Aegean and providing a firm base for the development of a real naval establishment.

In the meantime, farther east the Mamluks of Egypt and Syria extended their influence into Cilicia, forcing the Karamanid Mehmet II to pay tribute and using him to undermine Ottoman influence to the north and west by supporting the independence movements of Turkoman leaders such as Cüneyt. Once the latter was out of the way, however, Murat encouraged dissension among the Karaman princes, finally putting the eldest son, Ibrahim Bey, on the throne (1426) in return for agreeing to transfer his allegiance from the Mamluks to the Ottomans. The same policy was followed to enable Murat to annex the territories of Germiyan on the death of its aged ruler Yakup II (1429), thus leaving all of Anatolia united once again under Ottoman domination. Murat, therefore, was finally able to return to Europe to face the opposition of two major opponents, Venice and Hungary.

The First Ottoman-Venetian War: Involvement of Serbia, Wallachia, and Hungary

Until this time the Ottomans and Venice had remained friendly for the most part. Venice wished to protect its commercial interests in the Ottoman dominions and the Black Sea area by maintaining good relations with the sultan, particularly since its Genoese rivals were seeking to use their friendship with Murat to squeeze it out. Venice had signed a trade agreement with Bayezit in 1388 and had stayed out of the Crusade of Kosova. But Ottoman expansion through Macedonia toward the Adriatic and into Greece toward the Aegean made it nervous and fearful of competition in an area that had been under Venetian influence for some time. Insofar as the Ottomans were concerned, as long as Venice dominated the Aegean sea passages, it could always threaten communications between Anatolia and Rumeli and prevent complete unification of these two major parts of the empire.

Venice sought to undermine Ottoman power in Macedonia by setting up another Ottoman prince claiming to be Mustafa, sending ships that helped him capture Kassandra and Kavalla and gain considerable support among the Turkomans in the area (1425). Murat wanted to conquer the remaining portions of Macedonia, including Salonica, and Venice's occupation of the city and support of Mustafa only deepened his conviction that he could not tolerate its control by a state stronger than Byzantium. Murat's advances into Albania, to the north, also increased the tension.

The result was the first Ottoman-Venetian war, which dragged on, with intervals, until 1430. The main reason for its length was the radically differing strategic situations of the adversaries. Venice, whose power was at sea, maintained its coastal bases with relatively small land forces. The Ottomans, whose main strength was on land, began to create their own fleet only after the recent advances in western Anatolia. Thus they had no way to contest Venice's power and consequent ability to supply its bases. Venice, moreover, was preoccupied with war against its opponents in Italy, led by Milan, so that it could use only a small part of its fleet against the Turks. Venice secured the support of Hungary on land, with Serbia and Wallachia becoming the principal scenes of its conflict with the armies of the sultan.

The Ottomans' conquest of Serbia up to the Danube and of Bulgaria south of the Balkan Mountains had, indeed, brought them into direct conflict with Hungary. The clash with Wallachia derived from its own internal weaknesses. It had been built into a strong and united principality under Mircea the Great (1386–1418), but struggles for succession following his death greatly weakened Wallachian ability to resist, with both the Hungarians and the Ottomans attempting to use the situation to their own advantage. In return for Ottoman assistance, and also in response to Ottoman raids, Lazar's son Stephen, the Serbian king, allowed Ottoman soldiers and raiders to cross Serbian territory on their way to a raiding expedition into Bosnia (1426), thus facilitating Ottoman conquests in that direction as well. Stephen's death (July 19, 1427), however, plunged Serbia into a half-century of dynastic quarrels very similar to the situation in Wallachia. Since he was childless, Stephen had arranged to leave the throne to his nephew George Branković, acknowledging Sigismund's suzerainty in return for Hungarian support. Murat responded by claiming Serbia for himself on the grounds of Bayezit I's marriage with Stephen's sister Olivera. Branković surrendered the great Danubian fort of Belgrade to Hungary in return for its help, thus making it the principal pillar of resistance to the Ottomans. Murat invaded Serbia again (1428) to enforce his claim, captured the Serbian capital of Kruševać (Alacahisar), and forced Branković to resume the old vassal ties, marrying another Serbian princess to cement the Ottoman position in the country.

The Hungarians, however, continued to resist in the north as well as in Wallachia. Sigismund organized a joint attack of Hungary, Wallachia, and Karaman against the Ottomans in Anatolia and Europe at the same time. Venice arranged for the Latins of Cyprus to help Karaman and also urged the remaining Turkoman princes of Anatolia as well as the Timurid ruler of Iran, Şahruh, ostensibly still suzerain of the Ottomans, to join the effort. Murat managed to convince the latter of his continued loyalty by refraining from a major push against Karaman. Şahruh's return to Afghanistan freed Murat to return to Europe, where he built a new fleet and finally captured Salonica (March 1, 1430) from the Venetians, thus completing his control of the major Aegean ports. Venice was forced to accept the Peace of Lapseki (July 1430), recognizing Ottoman control of Macedonia and paying a tribute to Murat in return for his acceptance of continued Venetian occupation of Lepanto and its other Adriatic bases and restoration of Venetian rights to sail through the Straits into the Black Sea. Murat now also was able to establish a similar tributary relationship with the commercial republic of Ragusa (Dubrovnik), which had escaped Venetian suzerainty in 1358.

With Venice now neutral in Albania and in fact occupied by a new war with Genoa, Murat was able to move ahead freely there, taking Janina (1431) and Serez (1433) and establishing direct Ottoman rule in central and southern Albania. But beginning in 1443 the native Albanian princes in the mountain areas began to mount a really united opposition, with secret Venetian help, under the leadership of George Castriotes (Skanderbeg), who was able to continue the resistance for another half-century. The Ottomans, however, were still supreme in the Balkans, ruling directly in parts of Albania and the Epirus and receiving tribute and military assistance from the rulers of Serbia, Bosnia, Wallachia, Ragusa, Venice, and Bulgaria as well as the Morea and Arta.

Under Hungarian stimulus, however, George Branković restored Serbian independence, building a new fort at Semendria to replace that of Belgrade. When the Wallachian prince continued to accept Ottoman vassalage, Sigismund arranged his replacement by Vlad Drakul I (1432–1446), who threw off Murat's suzerainty and joined an anti-Ottoman league (1434) with Branković and the Bosnian King Tvrtko. Murat was unable to respond because in 1435 Şahruh invaded Anatolia, moving largely against the Mamluk and Karaman positions in Cilicia. Murat did nothing at first, since he nominally accepted Timurid suzerainty. In fact, he moved to take advantage of the threat by allying with the Turkoman principality of Dulgadır and attacking Karaman from the north and west (1435–1437), occupying the province of Hamit and driving out the Karamanid ruler Ibrahim, who had been cooperating with the Mamluks. To avoid provoking the Timurids, however, Murat restored the Karaman principality and kept only the western portion of the Hamit state for the Ottoman Empire. This arrangement satisfied not only the Timurids but also the Mamluks, who had feared that complete Ottoman conquest of Karaman would threaten their own interests in Syria.

Internal Political Developments

The continued predominance of the Turkish nobility in Murat's palace was the main reason for this relatively passive policy in Europe and Anatolia. The Çandarlı emphasized a policy of peace and consolidation, fearing that large-scale conquests in either the East or West would expand the power of the *devşirme*. In fact, the only real counterweight to the power of the Turkish nobles at this time came not from the *kapıkulları*, but rather from the frontier raiding leaders. As in the time of Osman, the border beys now held their posts by heredity and commanded not only the *akıncıs* (raiders) and gazis but also the regular timar cavalry. In addition to raiding and keeping the enemy defenses upset, they scouted enemy territory to provide information for future Ottoman campaigns and, during campaigns, went in advance of the regular army to gain possession of strategic passes. They raided infidel lands almost continuously, even when official peace agreements were in force. Individual members of the *akıncı* forces were sometimes paid salaries by their beys and sometimes held timars within the latter's *sancaks*, but their main privilege was exemption from all local taxes as well as the right to keep booty captured in raids. They accepted the overall command of the *beylerbeyi* of Rumeli, who was usually a member of the *kapıkulu* and under the sultan's direct control. Therefore, the *akıncı* and *kapıkulu* forces cooperated in advocating an active policy of conquests into Europe. With the wealth thus obtained they constituted the main opposition to the Turkish nobility at court, at times encouraging and supporting opposition to the sultan by dissidents to secure a ruler who would give them a free hand to undertake the conquests that they wished. Consequently, as Murat entered the later years of his reign, the frontier beys joined many members of the *kapıkulu* in advocating the succession of his younger son Mehmet (later Mehmet II), whose martial spirit reflected their desires and interests.

The Çandarlı concentrated on the development of the institutions of government that they felt were necessary to consolidate the previous conquests. They set up a regular system to train all the sons of the ruling sultan so that whoever of them gained power would be capable of carrying on the work of his father in both government and military affairs. Learned doctors of Islam were brought to the court to train the princes in the religion and traditions of Islam. Each prince, now officially given the title of *çelebi*, was assigned from an early age to be governor, or *sancak* bey, of a large province or district. He was trained on the job by an experienced minister appointed as his tutor, called *atabeg* by the Seljuks and *lala* by the Ottomans. He built up his own provincial court, creating an Istanbul in miniature, occasionally even minting coins in his name and usually sending at least one son to live with the sultan as hostage for his good behavior. In campaigns the princes joined their father, becoming the commanders of the principal wings of the army, gaining military as well as administrative knowledge and experience.

New Conflicts with Europe

At the moment Murat's primary concern was the possibility of a new European Crusade effort. John VIII Paleologues had long attempted to negotiate a union of the churches of Constantinople and Rome to secure Western help against the infidel, although his people and religious leaders met this with considerable anti-Roman feeling. In November 1437 he left Constantinople and went to Rome to be brought into the Holy Roman church in the hope that this would bring general European assistance. In fact, a council called to meet in Florence proclaimed the union (July 6, 1439), but continued opposition in Constantinople left the union ineffective, with many preferring Islamic domination and toleration to the bigotry that Rome seemed to represent.

At times Murat did order new raids into Europe to satisfy the beys and their followers with new booty, thus to use them as counterweights against the Çandarlı and also to take advantage of any weakness within the states of his enemies whenever it appeared. The death of Sigismund (December 9, 1437) led to considerable internal dispute in Hungary, which Murat used to mount a sizable raiding expedition that destroyed the Danubian fort at Severin and put Sibiu under siege (1438). He invaded Serbia and captured Branković's fort at Semendria (1439) in order to weaken the Serbian-Hungarian connection. In the same way he used the internal anarchy in Bosnia that followed the death of Tvrtko II (1423), forcing both the Bosnian successors as well as the rulers of the now independent southern section of the country (now calling itself Herzegovina) to pay tribute. The new Hungarian king Ladislas, however, appointed as governor (*voyvoda*) of Transylvania one John Hunyadi, who in 1441 pushed the Ottomans out of Semendria and then routed them several times in Transylvania, not only giving Europe new encouragement to resist but also gaining for himself a reputation that soon would enable him to demonstrate his considerable military skills at the head of a new Crusade movement.

In all these advances into Europe Murat took advantage of the social, religious, and economic stresses that were rending society within the lands of his enemies. He was able to offer the downtrodden Balkan peasants what amounted to a social revolution, freedom from the tyranny of their feudal masters. Within the Balkan states struggles for power at the center had ended real central authority, allowing the feudal magnates to increase their power and subject the cultivators to increasingly tyrannical conditions of tax payments and forced labor. In contrast, whenever the Ottomans established direct administration, all land became the property of the sultan, the state established close control and supervision over the fief holders, and manorial dues and forced labor were abolished, the latter being replaced by an easily payable tax known as the plow tax (*çift resmi*). The Balkan masses, therefore, were at best lukewarm in support of the armies of their rulers, as well as those of the Crusaders, against the Muslims.

The Crusade of Varna and Its Aftermath, 1444

Agitation for a new Crusade against the Ottomans at the Council of Florence and later was led by Janaki Torzello, who traveled throughout Europe with the message that if a Christian fleet could block the Straits, the Ottomans would not be able to send reinforcements from Anatolia and no more than 80,000 men would be needed to drive the Turk from Europe and regain the Holy Land. After the council Murat demanded and received from the emperor assurances that Byzantium would never join any such effort (1442). At the same time, however, the emperor encouraged a new attack by Ibrahim of Karaman, forcing Murat to leave Rumeli just when he was needed to counter the effects of Hunyadi's victories. Murat drove Ibrahim back, but the news of Hunyadi's subsequent efforts again forced him to restore Karaman and leave it in peace despite the certainty of betrayal.

Hunyadi had suddenly risen as the great Hungarian national hero as a result of his victories over the Turks in 1442. His fame spread throughout Europe. People believed that they had found the leader who could, at long last, lead a successful Crusade. Stimulated by the pope, groups of Crusaders were organized in all the major countries of Europe. Joined by a Serbian force led by George Branković and a Hungarian army under King Ladislas, Hunyadi organized the Crusade at Ofen and then marched down the Morava, confident that with the sultan absent in Anatolia the Ottomans could offer little resistance (1443). Hunyadi captured Niş and most of southern Serbia, stimulating Scanderbeg and the Albanians to extend their resistance. The Crusaders then went over the Balkan Mountains into Bulgaria, taking Sofia and hoping to cross the mountains and reach the lowlands along the Maritsa river before winter closed in.

Murat returned rapidly from Anatolia at the news of the Crusader advance. His army in Rumeli was already dispersed. The border beys and many of the feudal commanders were using the defeats to advocate the immediate accession of his young son Mehmet. All Murat had with him was a force of his new *kapıkulu* infantry, the Janissary corps, which had returned with him from Karaman. Not able to match the Crusaders in numbers, he decided to try to stop them by holding one of the key Balkan passes, Kapulu Derbendi (Trayan gate), through which the enemy would have to pass to reach the lowlands. The Crusaders were victorious in their initial attack (December 24, 1443), but the approach of winter finally caused Hunyadi to abandon the expedition after slaughtering thousands of Muslim prisoners and to return to Hungary for the winter.

The Ottomans were in a critical situation. Now that they scented the possibility of victory, thousands more Crusaders flooded into Hungary and a new campaign was prepared. In Anatolia Karaman responded to the news by attacking once again. And while the Albanian revolt spread, the Byzantine despot Constantine of the Morea moved back into central Greece and occupied Athens and Thebes. In Edirne two years of warfare without the arrival of new booty left the treasury drained to the point where salaries could not be paid, creating considerable discontent on the part of soldiers and administrators alike. And, finally, the death of Murat's favorite son,

Alauddin Bey, depressed the sultan and made him unable to act decisively to meet the crisis. The grand vezir and Murat's Serbian wife, Mara, convinced him that peace was essential. Through the mediation of Branković an agreement was reached at Edirne (June 12, 1444). The reluctant Hunyadi and his partisans stipulated that Murat and most of his army return to Anatolia, a condition that was to make a subsequent violation of the agreement and the renewal of the Crusade that much easier. Branković made the greatest gains; he was given back all Serbian territory in return, thus essentially restoring the kingdom as it had been in 1427 at the death of Stefan Duşan. Murat also recognized the autonomy of Serbia and Wallachia, albeit under his suzerainty, and in return Ottoman rule in Bulgaria was accepted and a truce of 10 years established. Soon afterward a similar peace was reached with Karaman. Having achieved security for his state in both the East and the West, Murat renounced his throne in favor of Prince Mehmet (August 1444) and retired to Bursa, where he intended to pursue an ascetic existence for the remainder of his life. His retirement seems to have been the result of not only his longstanding depression following the death of his son Alauddin but also the opposition and partial desertion of his cause by the gazi and feudal leaders of Rumeli and the consequent defeats inflicted on him by Hunyadi. Since Mehmet, despite his youth, seemed to inspire general support, his accession might save Ottoman dominions in Europe from a renewed Crusade attack. Also, with Mehmet securely on the throne pretenders supported by the Byzantines and others would have no chance to contest the succession.

Murat's retirement and Mehmet's accession, however, unleashed new forces that threatened the Ottoman state. Mehmet's supporters, representing the *devşirme* as well as the gazi leaders of Rumeli, attempted to eliminate the Çandarlı and Turkish notables. Meanwhile, it seemed that the empire's remaining European possessions might be lost even without a Crusade, as the Albanian rebels spread southward while the new Greek despots of the Morea – Constantine Iragasis and Thomas Palaeologues, brothers of Emperor John VIII – crossed the Isthmus of Corinth and began to occupy Thessaly. And most threatening of all, a new Crusade army was gathering under the stimulus of the pope, who absolved the Christian signatories of the Peace of Edirne from their obligations to the Ottomans on the grounds that oaths taken with infidels were not binding. Ladislas in any case had signed the agreement only because of his immediate need to return to Poland, and as soon as his problems there were resolved, he was anxious to resume fighting and enjoy the fruits of victory. Under the same assumption Venice, which had previously avoided conflict with the Ottomans, joined Hungary and the pope in organizing the attack, which it hoped would enable it to regain Salonica and Gallipoli and thus cement its control of the Aegean and the Adriatic. But to be on the safe side its ships flew the banners of the pope and Burgundy rather than its own.

A large new Crusade army, with soldiers coming from all over Europe, was mobilized at Buda under the leadership of King Ladislas. Branković refused to provide Serbian support, however, since he was satisfied with his gains at Edirne. Thus he secretly notified the sultan of the new Crusade in the hope of being allowed to retain his possessions even if the Ottomans won. The Crusader army left Segedin on September 1, 1444, was joined at Orsova on the Danube by Hunyadi with a force of knights from Transylvania, and then marched west along the Danube toward Varna. The Rumeli commanders, who had supported Mehmet II for political reasons, now saw that this youth could hardly be counted on to organize and lead an army that could save their lands. So Çandarlı Halil and his supporters agreed to ask Murat to return to his throne and lead the resistance. Murat accepted the offer and with the help of several Genoese ships brought the Anatolian army back into Europe (October 1444). The opposing forces finally came together near Varna on November 10. While the Hungarian cavalry initially broke the Ottoman lines, the sultan was able to rally his forces. When the Janissaries captured and beheaded Ladislas, a rout began that ended in total Ottoman victory. Hunyadi was able to escape only with great difficulty, while thousands of knights were killed. European hopes for a Crusade victory were shattered. The fate of Byzantium was sealed. Ottoman prestige throughout the Muslim world was immensely enhanced, and once again Ottoman rule of Southeastern Europe was assured.

Murat still hoped to retire to Anatolia and leave the throne to Mehmet. But pressure applied by the Çandarlı and Turkish notables finally convinced him that Mehmet's continued rule at this point would lead only to the triumph of the *devşirme*. An uprising of the Janissaries in Edirne in support of Osman Çelebi, a claimant to the Ottoman throne, was used by Çandarlı Halil to get Murat back, again on the grounds that Mehmet lacked the authority and strength needed to defend the state. Murat, therefore, returned to the throne in August 1446 with the full support of the Turkish notables and the Janissaries. Apparently, Mehmet still held the title of sultan, and Zaganos Paşa and Şahabeddin Şahin Paşa were appointed as his tutors to prepare him for the day when he would resume power.

Campaigns in Europe

Murat spent his remaining years in a series of campaigns to stabilize Ottoman rule in Rumeli by suppressing the vassals who had revolted during the previous campaign. In 1446 he ravaged the Morea and forced its Byzantine despots to accept his suzerainty. He established direct Ottoman rule in most of mainland Greece, although Venice, Genoa, and the Byzantines continued to control a ring of ports and islands all the way from Corfu to Negroponte. Since a large number of Bulgarians had deserted him before the Battle of Izladi, Murat brought Bulgaria under direct Ottoman control, eliminating the remaining native princes and "Turkifying" and "Ottomanizing" it more than any other Balkan province. Large numbers of Turkish tribesmen were settled in the north and east, so that, in less than a century, they formed a majority of the population. The timar system was now fully applied, with most members of the old Bulgarian feudal classes being absorbed as Ottomans. Murat also undertook a major campaign against rebels in northern Albania in 1447, but the news that Hunyadi was advancing south with a new Crusade army forced him to abandon this effort without any success.

The Crusade of Kosova, 1448

Indeed, Hunyadi had been working to create a new Crusade army ever since his return to Buda. Upon the death of Ladislas, moreover, he was appointed regent for the former's infant son, thus strengthening his ability to take the lead in organizing a new effort against the Ottomans. Hunyadi then summoned Crusader knights from all Europe. With about 50,000 men he crossed the Danube into northern Serbia despite Branković's refusal to cooperate or help. As he marched south, he was joined by soldiers sent by Scanderbeg as well as from Wallachia. But Murat returned swiftly from Albania and intercepted the Crusaders as they headed for Macedonia, routing them at Kosova (October 17–20, 1448), where the Serbs had fallen to Bayezit I almost a century earlier. Ottoman rule south of the Danube again was assured. Murat then sent raiders into Wallachia and regained its vassalage.

Murat died of a stroke on February 5, 1451. To avoid new internal disputes he left a written will naming Mehmet as his successor and, with the assent of all the principal parties and ministers, appointing Çandarlı Halil as his guardian. Thus Murat arranged for an undisputed succession despite the vigorous party quarrels that had swirled around Mehmet's candidacy only a short time before. He had ended the threat of the Crusaders, but he left to his successor the task of sealing Ottoman unity through the final conquest of Constantinople.

4

The Apogee of Ottoman Power, 1451–1566

With the rise of Mehmet II, called "the Conqueror" (*Fatih*), the Ottomans began a new era of conquest that extended the empire's rule across the Danube and into central Europe as well as over the lands of the Islamic caliphates in the Middle East and through much of North Africa.

Conquest of a New Empire: The Reign of Mehmet II, 1451–1481

Upon his accession on February 18, 1451, Mehmet inherited an empire in far better condition than that which his father had come to rule three decades before. He was free to take the initiative without having to satisfy either internal or external pressures. It appears, however, that soon after his accession Mehmet and his principal advisers, Şahabeddin Şahin Paşa and Zaganos Paşa, decided that they needed a spectacular victory to fortify their political position against the Turkish nobility, which still wanted peace in order to prevent the *kapıkulu* and *devşirme* from using new conquests to build their power. Nothing could be more spectacular than the conquest of Constantinople. Arguing with some justice that Byzantium had sheltered Muslim claimants to the Ottoman throne to foment discord in the empire, Mehmet felt that as long as Byzantium held out, there would always be the possibility of new Crusade efforts to rescue it and complete unification of the empire would be impossible. Beyond these practical considerations there was the dream of establishing a world empire, with Constantinople as its natural center. For centuries Muslim hopes of world domination had been associated with the capture of the Byzantine capital. The ninth-century philosopher al-Kindi had expressed this feeling in his prophecy that the *Mahdi*, or "rightly-guided one" would return to "renew Islam and cause justice to triumph. He will conquer the Spanish peninsula and reach Rome and conquer it. He will travel to the East and conquer it. He will conquer Constantinople, and rule over the whole earth will be his."[1] The great Muslim historian Ibn Khaldûn related a tradition of the Prophet himself stating that: "He who will destroy the Byzantine emperor and will spend his treasures in God's behalf will be the expected [*Mahdi*] when he conquers Constantinople."[2] Constantinople was, indeed, the "Red Apple" (*Kızıl Elma*) of Muslim tradition.[3] Nourishing such dreams, Mehmet busied himself with plans for its conquest almost from the first moment of his accession. There were problems that had to be dealt with before the conquest could be undertaken. Even while acknowledging Mehmet's suzerainty, his vassals in Constantinople and the Balkans began to take advantage of his presumed inexperience. Karaman did the same in Anatolia, instigating the rise of anti-Ottoman claimants to power in the vassal Turkoman principalities. Mehmet also knew quite well that the Turkish nobility, led by Çandarlı Halil, opposed his plans for Constantinople.

55

Mehmet could not yet rid himself of the influential grand vezir, but he could and did remove the key to any deposition the opposition might plan by having his brother, the young prince Küçük Ahmet, killed. The act, condoned for reasons of state – that is, as a means of avoiding disputes that might rent the Islamic empire – established a precedent followed by Mehmet II's successors for over a century. Mehmet exiled his father's wife Mara back to Serbia along with most of her advisers, replacing them mainly with his own and putting them into key positions as rivals of the Çandarlı family.

Mehmet then moved to quiet his neighbors so that he could concentrate on Constantinople. Murat's peace treaties with Serbia and Wallachia were renewed. The situation with Karaman was more difficult, since it still ruled a large section of central and eastern Anatolia and most of Cilicia and used its influence to foment distrust of the Ottomans. Mehmet tried to eliminate the Karaman threat shortly after his accession, but when his army reached Akşehir, Ibrahim of Karaman agreed to restore the old boundaries, not to raid beyond them, and to give one of his daughters to Mehmet to cement the new relationship. Ishak Paşa was left as *beylerbeyi* of Anatolia, with the task of suppressing any revolts that might arise while the sultan was concentrating on Constantinople.

As a final step to solidify his own power, soon after returning to Edirne Mehmet moved boldly to take control of the Janissary corps from Çandarlı Halil. Using as pretext a Janissary uprising and demand for new bonus payments while returning from Anatolia, Mehmet replaced Halil's men as *ağa* (commander) of the corps and as infantry commanders with *devşirme* men, thus beginning the process by which the latter took over the corps. He then reorganized it to ensure that it would once again perform the function for which it had been originally created: to act as the personal guard and instrument of the sultan against all those who disputed his authority.

The Conquest of Constantinople

Çandarlı Halil continued to oppose the sultan's plans for an attack on Constantinople, but Mehmet went ahead. On his return from Karaman he built the fort of Rumeli Hisarı, 10 miles north of the city on the European side of the Bosporus, to gain control of the waterway and sever Byzantium's communications with the Black Sea as well as to assure the passage of Ottoman troops from Anatolia to Europe (January–August 1452). As soon as the new fort was completed, Mehmet demanded that Constantinople surrender, threatening a full-scale siege.

Byzantine efforts to secure European help were blunted by Çandarlı Halil, who renewed the old trade treaty with Venice, made a new agreement with Hungary (November 20, 1451), and generally signified Ottoman willingness to act reasonably with those states that did not actively oppose the attack. In the Imperial Council Çandarlı Halil and his colleagues continued to oppose the plans to conquer Constantinople, but the sultan prevailed with arguments stressing the gazi tradition and the Byzantine threat to the safety of the Ottoman state (September 1452).

The actual siege began in February 1453 when the first Ottoman forces sent from Edirne occupied the Byzantine seaports along the Sea of Marmara and huge cannons were dragged through Thrace to lead the attack on the city's great walls. In March the Ottoman armies of Anatolia crossed the Bosporus to the new Rumeli Hisarı, while an armada built in Gallipoli went through the Dardanelles into the Sea of Marmara and began to attack the city by sea. Within the city Mehmet's preparations were met with despair; religious and political division continued to undermine the defense effort, and very little new assistance came from outside. Byzantium's armed forces already had declined so much that there were hardly enough men left to man the vast wall defense system. Sections of the city were almost totally uninhabited. The Byzantines had little more to defend them than the walls, "Greek Fire," and a chain stretched across the mouth of the Golden Horn to prevent the entry of the Turkish fleet. Despite this the siege lasted for 54 days, from April 6 to May 29, 1453. On April 18 the Ottomans occupied all the islands in the Sea of Marmara outside the capital, which had been left undefended. Two days later four Latin ships and one Greek ship managed to evade the Ottoman blockade and bring large amounts of supplies to the defenders, considerably buoying their spirits. During the night of April 21–22, however, the Ottoman fleet, tired of its passive role in the Bosporus, managed to drag a number of boats over the Galata hill down into the Golden Horn, putting them in position to fire on the sea walls from the other side, thereby spreading the Byzantine defenders even more thinly. The Ottoman effort itself was hindered by Çandarlı Halil's continued opposition.

The final assault began on the night of May 28. In the end the defenders were simply worn down, isolated as they were from significant outside help. After two hours the huge Ottoman cannon tore large gaps in the walls between the modern Topkapı and the Yalıkapı, and the attackers flowed into the city. The Ottoman fleet broke the Byzantine chain and entered the Golden Horn, supplementing the land forces. The emperor apparently was killed while fighting on the city walls. Once within the city the Ottomans advanced slowly and methodically, clearing the streets of the remaining defenders. While Islamic law would have justified a full-scale sack and massacre of the city in view of its resistance, Mehmet kept his troops under firm control, killing only those Byzantines who actively resisted and doing all he could to keep the city intact so that it could be the center of his world empire. Many inhabitants and soldiers took refuge at the Genoese colony of Galata, across the Golden Horn, which had remained neutral during the siege. This violated its neutrality, but Zaganos made an agreement by which Galata was joined to the Ottoman Empire and its defenses torn down, in return for which its inhabitants were allowed to retain their holdings and gain freedom of religion and trade within the sultan's dominions. The people of Galata were to retain their properties, but they were to have no tax or customs privileges other than the exemption of their children from the *devşirme* tribute imposed in the Balkans.

Mehmet's conquest of Constantinople was not of major strategic importance, since the Ottomans had been able to bypass it as they advanced into Europe. Yet its capture deprived Europe of a base that, in the hands of an effective relief force, might have undermined the Ottoman defense system. Possession of the great commercial, administrative, and military center facilitated the assimilation, control, and defense of the sultan's conquests, while control of the waterways between the Black Sea and the Mediterranean established a stranglehold on European trade with the hinterlands to the north and east and provided considerable new revenue. The conquest made the Ottomans heirs to the imperial tradition as the conquered city once again became the capital of an extensive empire.

Organization of the Empire

With the prestige brought by the conquest of Constantinople, now called Istanbul by the Turks, Mehmet II moved ahead to become absolute ruler of a centralized empire, essentially the emperor of a restored Eastern Roman and caliphal empire, with worldwide implications. The first step was to remove the Turkish nobility as a dominating political force and to wipe out all members of the Ottoman family who had any aspirations for the throne. In any case, a move against the Turkish nobility and particularly the Çandarlı family had long been desired by Mehmet, who blamed Çandarlı Halil (with some justice) for his deposition in 1446 and for the latter's continued opposition to the conquest of Constantinople. On June 1, 1453, only two days after the conquest, Çandarlı Halil was dismissed as grand vezir on false charges of having received bribes from the Byzantines for opposing the attack. His property was confiscated, and he was imprisoned along with most members of his family. His replacement with Mehmet's close adviser Zaganos Paşa, member of the *devşirme* class, began a new tradition whereby the most important positions of the central government were reserved for the slaves of the sultan. Large-scale confiscations of timars and private properties soon reduced the power of the major Turkish families; they were awarded to *devşirme* members, who then accelerated their rise to power. The grand vezir now became the sultan's absolute representative in the processes of government, the only other member of the Ruling Class whose word had to be obeyed by all without question or appeal. He was entrusted with the imperial seal, which had to be applied to all state decrees, not only those of the sultan himself but also lesser regulations issued by other principal officials. The principal provincial officials also were put under the direct control of the grand vezir, who at the same time was given fiefs and revenues that made him the wealthiest Ottoman after the sultan.

Zaganos' power as grand vezir was further increased by his appointment as governor of Rumeli, which gave him control of the army in both the capital and Europe. Efforts were made to enlarge and strengthen the *kapıkulu* army, in particular the Janissary infantry and the *Topçu* Artillery corps. They were given the most modern fire weapons of the time, muskets and cannon, making them the most potent of the sultan's military forces. To assure Janissary loyalty Mehmet installed his own slaves as commanders and created new divisions of slaves not involved in the previous political conflicts, expanding the *devşirme* system of recruiting young Christians to provide the needed men. Thus with the support of the powerful and obedient grand vezir and the Janissary corps, Mehmet was able to gain autocratic authority over all his subjects.

This is not to say that the sultan left his supporters unchecked. His aim was to create a balance of forces so that no group would have sufficient power to control him. Therefore, some important administrative functions were withheld from the grand vezir and given to three other major officials, the *kazasker* (chief judge), *defterdar* (chief treasurer), and *nişancı* (chief scribe), who controlled the hierarchies of the religious, financial, and scribal administrations respectively. Nor did Mehmet wish to substitute *devşirme* domination for that of the Turkish nobility – thus he did not eliminate the latter. Many Turkish notable families kept their properties and were retained in positions, leaving them about equal to the *devşirme*. By balancing the Turkish aristocracy and the *devşirme,* Mehmet could play them off and hence assure himself of the loyalty and support of both. He reduced the power of the individual frontier beys by increasing their numbers while reducing the soldiers each could command in war and by placing them more directly under the command of the *beylerbeyi* of Rumeli than previously.

The sultan also sought the support of the Christian religious leaders. He assured the Greek Orthodox clergy that it would retain its religious freedom, both internally and against the possibility of union with Rome; he appointed the chief opponent of union,

Gennadius Scolarious, as patriarch, and gave him civil as well as religious authority over Orthodox Christians in the empire to assure his support of the new regime. Thus was created the *millet* system of autonomous self-government under religious leaders, later extended to the Armenians, the Jews, and the other major non-Muslim minorities. In return the *millet* leaders found their self-interest cemented to that of the sultan, since it was by his order that they were given more extensive power over their followers than had been the case in the Christian states that had previously dominated the area. The complete Ottoman conquest of Southeastern Europe once again united most of the Christians in the area, Greek and Slav alike, under the authority of the Greek patriarchate, making the church a particular beneficiary of the Ottoman expansion and further uniting the interests of patriarch and sultan.

Reconstruction of Istanbul

Mehmet's next move was to restore Istanbul to its former greatness. Much of the city's population and economic prosperity had disappeared long before the conquest – it had been left as a poor and largely depopulated city with about 60,000 to 70,000 inhabitants. Mehmet attempted to avoid as much pillage as possible immediately after the conquest, but many people fled in fear, leaving no more than 10,000 inhabitants by the time he turned to rebuilding the city. Mehmet's first task, therefore, was to repopulate Istanbul. Decrees were issued guaranteeing protection of the lives and properties of all inhabitants, regardless of religion, who recognized the sultan and paid taxes to him. Mehmet sought to make his capital a microcosm of all the races and religious elements in the empire, and when these encouragements in themselves were not sufficient to repopulate it fully, a policy of forced colonization was introduced to bring immigrants from Anatolia and the Balkans, with gifts of property being added to tax concessions to enable them to resume their occupations and restore the city's economic life. Muslims, Armenians, Jews, Greeks, Slavs, and others came from all parts of the empire. Many Jews were attracted from as far away as western Europe, where they were being subjected to a new wave of persecution at this time. Appeals were sent throughout the Muslim world for those of the faithful who wished to rise with the new capital of Islam. War prisoners were allowed to earn their freedom by working on road construction, while peasants from the Balkans were placed in and around the capital to tend orchards and fruit gardens and guard the flocks that would supply food for the capital. As a result, within a short time Istanbul once again thronged with humanity.

Efforts to repopulate the city were accompanied by construction work. Thousands of homes, bridges, markets, streets, walls, and factories had fallen into ruins during the later centuries of Byzantine rule. The basic public services no longer existed – water conduits had broken down, street pavings were in disrepair, and there was no regular sewage system. Mehmet immediately set to work to remedy these problems, and with tremendous vigor. Many of those who had participated in the conquest were assigned to construct or repair houses, markets, aqueducts, and roads. In 1455 Mehmet began to build the grand bazaar, or covered market, which was to become the center of Istanbul's commercial life for a half-millennium. The Conqueror's first palace, built at the center of the old city (where Bayezit Square and the University of Istanbul are located today), soon came to be known as the Old Palace. The new imperial residence, which under his successors became the center of the sultanate and the Ruling Class until the nineteenth century, was the Topkapı Palace, built at the high point of the city overlooking the Bosporus, the Sea of Marmara, and the Golden Horn. The monumental Fatih Mosque (Mosque of the Conqueror), built in the sultan's name, set the pattern for the numerous smaller religious and secular buildings that followed. As was the case in all the great empires of Islam, the religious foundations played a vital role in the growth of major cities, providing for the public services not considered to be within the scope of government. Public buildings such as schools, places of worship, fountains, hospitals, public baths, and hotels were constructed and maintained through religious endowment funds provided by the sultan, his family, the Ruling Class or rich subjects.

As a result of all these activities, by the close of Mehmet's reign Istanbul and its environs were inhabited by 16,324 households in all, perhaps 100,000 people (if one assumes conservatively about 4 to 5 persons per household), of whom approximately half were Muslims, one quarter Greek Orthodox, and the remainder Europeans, Jews, Armenians, and Gypsies.[4]

Economic Development

Mehmet developed the economic life of his empire to provide a pool of wealth that could be taxed to finance his military and political activities. Encouragement was given to the expansion of native industry by Muslim Turks as well as the Greek and Armenian subjects of the sultan, with the cotton industry rising in western Anatolia, mohair cloth in Ankara and Kastamonu, silk in Bursa and Istanbul, woolen cloth in Salonica and Istanbul, and footwear in Edirne. Mehmet also worked to expand international trade to and through his dominions, ending the privileged economic position given Europeans under the Byzantines so that native Ottoman merchants would be able to gain a share in this trade. During Mehmet's reign, Istanbul, Bursa, and Edirne resumed their former places as industrial and trade centers – all contributing to the general prosperity.

Economic development alone, however, was not sufficient to provide Mehmet with all the money needed to pay for the army, the buildings, and the new structure of government that he was creating. He resorted to increasingly radical economic measures to secure the funds, achieving his immediate objectives but in the process disturbing the economic expansion that he had sought to stimulate. He debased the coinage, withdrawing all outstanding coins on five different occasions and reissuing them with increased alloys of base metals. Basic and essential commodities such as salt, soap, and candles were made into monopolies and farmed out at high prices to private merchants, who increased the retail prices to compensate their costs and secure high profits at the expense of the masses. Mehmet also enforced his right to ownership of all wealth-producing property in the empire as part of his attributes of sovereignty. Lands and other property that had originally belonged to the state and were later transferred to private ownership or to foundations were now confiscated; property titles were investigated to ensure that only the most valid ones were left out of state control. Most of the lands secured for the state in this way were divided into timar fiefs and assigned to members of the *Sipahi* cavalry later in Mehmet's reign to restore at least partly some of the power of the Turkish aristocracy and thus counterbalance the growing power of the *devşirme*.[5]

Mehmet II's Aims of World Domination and Policies of Conquest

With the conquest of Constantinople the Muslim world acknowledged Mehmet as leader of the Holy War against Christianity. He now claimed superiority over all other Muslim rulers, including the neighboring Mamluk sultans, and demanded the right to replace the latter as leaders of the pilgrimage to the Holy Cities. He also emphasized Ottoman relationships with the old Turkish empires of Central Asia, encouraging the writing down of traditions showing that his family descended directly from Oğuz Han, thus countering the ambitions of his other principal rival in the East, Uzun Hasan, ruler of the White Sheep Turkomans of Iran, who, as we shall see, soon began to challenge his rule in eastern Anatolia.

Mehmet also began to see himself as heir not merely to eastern Rome but to a worldwide empire. Byzantine and Italian scholars surrounding him encouraged grandiose ideas of world dominion. After eliminating possible contenders for the Byzantine throne, he moved to regain all the lands previously ruled by his Byzantine predecessors between the Euphrates and the Danube. To further centralization he abandoned the vassal policies of the early Ottoman sultans and annexed most of the vassal territories, gaining the acquiesence of the Christian ruling families concerned by offering them the opportunity to rise high as Ottomans in the new empire. Only formal conversion to Islam and acceptance of Ottoman ways were expected as the price for membership in the *devşirme* class. To the mass of the people he offered an end to the feudal oppression of their former Christian masters, security of life and property, ties with the central administration through the timar system, and an opportunity to preserve their old traditions and ways as well as their religion through the *millet* system.

In developing his policies of conquest Mehmet basically followed the rules of Islamic law. The conquered people were left in possession of their lives and property under state protection in return for the payment of the special head tax (*cizye*) plus the regular taxes imposed on all producers of wealth whether Muslims or Christians. When he did encounter resistance, Mehmet used terror to achieve conquests, not only to overcome the particular enemy in question but also to break down resistance elsewhere and convince the mass of the people that they could attain peace and safety and avoid war only by accepting the sultan's invitation to join the empire and recognizing his rule.

As Mehmet eliminated the rulers of Southeastern Europe by force or persuasion, he imposed direct Ottoman administration, formalized by census taking, compilation of tax registers, and division of the lands into timars for tax purposes. Whenever mountainous terrain made it possible for Christians to hold out against Ottoman conquest, Turkomans from Anatolia were settled as permanent siege troops, eventually becoming integral parts of the settled populations in those areas. Before withdrawing from newly conquered territories, Mehmet organized the garrisons and administrations needed to safeguard them into what was by now the established Ottoman provincial system: The lands were subdivided into *sancak*s, sources of revenue were assigned as timars, and municipal duties were shared by the religious judges and police chiefs. In the Balkans the Christian peasants were left on their lands. Rather, it was their feudal masters who were affected mostly by the conquest, with both themselves and their holdings being absorbed into the Ottoman system. This process lessened the opposition of the military classes to Ottoman rule, since they were often allowed to retain their former lands in return for military service, only now as timars, without even the requirement of conversion to Islam during the fifteenth century. Similarly, in Anatolia the commanders and soldiers of the Turkoman principalities were mostly absorbed into the Ottoman army, retaining their old lands as timars. Finally, the resettlement policy used first to repopulate Istanbul was also developed to place loyal Muslims in the Balkans to watch over the conquered Christian population and to break up local resistance to Ottoman rule in Anatolia on the part of Turkoman dynasties and nomadic groups.

Legislation and the Legal System

One area of activity closely associated with the Roman-Byzantine heritage was codification. Mehmet II was the first Ottoman ruler to try to systematize and codify the different social and legal systems found in the conquered lands throughout the empire, incorporating specific practices into general patterns of government and society. In developing his centralized empire, Mehmet modified whatever contradicted his passion for control and then codified the results in a series of three codes of law (*kanunname*): The first, promulgated in 1453–1456, concerned the conditions and obligations of his subjects; the second, in 1477–1478, concerned the organization of the Ottoman state and Ruling Class; and the third, introduced late in his reign, concerned economic organization, landholding, and taxes. Thus the laws, practices, and traditions developed during the previous centuries were brought together and institutionalized, marking the initial stages of a process that culminated a half-century later during the reign of Süleyman the Magnificent (1520–1566).

While the law codes of Byzantine emperors such as Theodosius II (408–450), and Justinian (527–565) may have provided models for codification, Mehmet's legislative activity also was based on the traditions of the great Turkish and Mongol empires of Central Asia, as introduced into the Middle East by the Seljuks. It was the Seljuks who fully developed the institution of the sultan as the secular ruler in Islam, standing beside the caliph, who retained authority only in religious and personal matters. The result was a dual system of law, with the sultan legislating secular laws (*kanun*) in all those areas not covered in detail by the Islamic religious law. Mehmet II was the first Ottoman sultan to develop this right to legislate into full-fledged codes covering all aspects of government and society in a manner that previous Muslim rulers had never attempted or achieved.[6]

The Conquests of Mehmet II

What of the conquests themselves? The primary thrust of military advance throughout Mehmet's reign was against the infidel, in the gazi tradition, to prevent unified opposition from the Western world as well as to acquire new territories. Mehmet was able to detach the Italian commercial republics by granting them new trade privileges in his empire. In 1454 Venice was given the special right of paying only 2 percent ad valorem customs duties on goods entering and leaving the empire as well as that of having a commercial representative (called *baile/balyos*) living in Istanbul, in return for the payment of an annual tribute of 200,000 gold ducats. Genoa, its main rival, was given similar rights only in the Crimea and some of the Aegean Islands, again in return for tribute.

Contemplating future areas of expansion, Mehmet recognized the potential gains available in the north and the west. The northern hinterland of the Black Sea had become a political vacuum following the disintegration of the Golden Horde empire that for two centuries had controlled the lands from the steppes of the Ukraine to the valleys of the Don and the Volga. In the fourteenth century the Ukraine had been lost to the Polish-Lithuanian empire of the Jagellonians. By the mid-fifteenth century the Golden Horde had almost disappeared, with the steppes to the south falling under the Tatar Hans of Kazan after 1445, while the Crimea was controlled by a dynasty of Tatar Hans set up by the Jagellonians themselves in an effort to divide the Mongol remnants. Soon the Tatars became independent of the Poles and contacted Mehmet II. This led to an alliance between the Ottomans and the Crimean Tatars that proved advantageous to both.

In 1454 Mehmet made some efforts to conquer the Black Sea coast of Moldavia in order to cement the relationship with the Tatars. At this time, however, his primary interests were in the western Balkans, where autonomous but powerless Serbia constituted a channel through which the Hungarians or possible Crusader expeditions could march against him; similarly, the Byzantine despots of the Morea might be taken by Venice to provide a base for a new effort to displace the Ottomans in Europe. In response to these dangers Mehmet undertook a series of expeditions between 1454 and 1463 to extend his direct rule to the Danube and Aegean and thus establish a strong military defense line. Two campaigns in 1454 and 1455 smashed the Serbs. The Ottomans occupied the southern part of the country, secured direct connection with Macedonia from the north for the first time, and also gained control of the rich gold and silver mines of Novo Brdo, which thereafter provided much of the capital needed for the empire's economic expansion.

During the summer of 1456, Mehmet undertook his third Serbian campaign, this time in an effort to take Belgrade from the Hungarians, with Branković maintaining an uneasy neutrality although he allowed the expedition to pass through his territory. However, a six-week siege of the great Danubian base was unsuccessful, Hunyadi's arrival at the last minute with some 200 boats forcing the sultan to retire. This left the city in Hungarian hands for another half-century until it finally was taken by Süleyman the Magnificent.

Soon after the sultan returned to Istanbul, Branković died (December 24, 1456), leaving Serbia in a state of internal anarchy that contributed to its eclipse. Mehmet had a good claim to rule through Murat's marriage to Mara, but he was not able to act for some time because of pressing needs elsewhere. Encouraged by King Alfonso V of Naples, Scanderbeg tried to drive the Ottoman garrisons from Albania. Mehmet responded with expeditions that drove the Albanians back into the hills. In 1456 pirate activities based in the Genoese islands in the Aegean led him to mount a naval expedition that conquered Aynos (Enez), Imbros (Imroz), Lemnos (Limni), and Thasos (Taşöz). Intrigues between the two Byzantine despots of the Morea, brothers of the last emperor, Constantine, led to such internal strife that Mehmet conquered the northern part of the peninsula during the summer of 1458, adding Athens in January 1459 and the southern Morea in July 1460, thus ending the despotate and leaving Trabzon as the last relic of the Byzantine Empire. This meant that all Greece was under direct Ottoman control with the sole exception of the Morean ports of Koron, Modon, and Pylos, which were taken later under Bayezit II. Finally, in the summer of 1459 the Ottomans moved back into Serbia, drove out the Hungarian partisans, and occupied the entire country with the exception of Belgrade, ending its independence and incorporating the former feudal, legal, and financial systems with little change into the Ottoman administrative organization. In the meantime, Hungarian influence in Bosnia had greatly antagonized the large landholding nobles as well as many cultivators, many of whom had come to espouse the Bogomil heresy in reaction to Catholic oppression. The Bosnian king Stephen Thomas (1443–1461) managed to retain his throne with Hungarian assistance, secretly receiving papal support also by converting to Catholicism and taking measures to suppress "heretics" within his domains. Mehmet was not yet ready to conquer Bosnia completely, but he encouraged raiders to ravage north of the Danube into Hungary and southern Austria as well as along the Dalmatian and Istrian coasts.

By 1461 Mehmet's basic desire was to settle his problems in Europe so that he could concentrate on establishing control of Anatolia. With Serbia and Greece conquered, only Albania was causing real difficulty in the West. The death of Alfonso V in 1458 left Scanderbeg much more amenable, however, and he accepted a truce with the sultan (June 22, 1461) that enabled him to regain control of southern Albania and the Epirus in return for promises to refrain from further attacks on the Ottoman possessions in the north. There were also increasing problems in the Principalities. Moldavia was now ruled by the famous Stephen the Great (1457–1504), who built a sizable state, took the Danubian port of Kilia, and was intervening in Wallachian politics as a first step toward conquering the Black Sea coast and the Crimea. His conflict with the Ottomans at this time was limited to rivalry for control of the weak princes of Wallachia. Finally, Vlad IV Tepeş (the "Impaler") acknowledged Ottoman as well as Hungarian suzerainty and was recognized as prince of Wallachia. Mehmet promised to keep Ottoman raiders out as long as Stephen made no effort to enlarge his dominion in the area (1460).

With Wallachia neutralized, Mehmet was able to turn to Anatolia. The Black Sea coast, with the exception of Byzantine Trabzon, had been brought under Ottoman control by the early part of Mehmet's reign, but there were Muslim opponents in eastern and central Anatolia. After the collapse of the Timurid Empire, the Black Sheep had built a sizable empire in western Iran and northern Iraq, while the White Sheep, under the leadership of the notable Uzun Hasan (1453–1478) and with some Mamluk assistance, built their own dominion in western Iran and eastern Anatolia. Karaman again was extending its power in central Anatolia, fomenting revolts against the Ottomans. The Ottoman successes in the Balkans also frightened Venice and Genoa into encouraging these eastern ambitions in order to lessen the Ottoman threat against them. Mehmet, therefore, felt an urgency to complete his rule along the Black Sea coast to frustrate any advances that his enemies might make at European instigation. Beginning in April 1461, he used his newly built navy to join in land-sea attacks that successively overwhelmed the Genoese in Amasra, then Candar, the last Turkoman principality in the area, and, finally, Byzantine Trabzon itself. Uzun Hasan – not strong enough to meet the Ottomans alone – was forced to accept a separate peace at Erzincan (August 14, 1461). Karaman remained quiet, fearing that any overt act might draw the sultan's wrath against it. Mehmet established a new frontier province in the area under the command of the *beylerbeyi* of Anatolia, Gedik Ahmet Paşa, a Greek or Albanian *devşirme* convert, who established strong frontier garrisons to guard against the White Sheep and Karaman. As a result, the latter turned its attention more toward the Mamluk territories in Cilicia, particularly Adana and Tarsus, which it occupied for a time before losing them to a Mamluk counterattack. A civil war instigated by the Ottomans further debilitated Karaman's power after 1464.

Mehmet was distracted from his Anatolian campaigns by the raids of Vlad IV Tepeş into Ottoman territories in northern Bulgaria (1461–1462). He responded by invading and conquering Wallachia and annexing it to his empire (April–August 1462). Its autonomy soon was restored, however, under Vlad's brother, Radu IV the Handsome (1462–1479), who had grown up at the Ottoman court and was willing to pay tribute and accept the sultan's suzerainty in return for the throne. Another source of trouble was Venetian activity against the Ottomans. Fearing Ottoman expansion along the Adriatic, Venice got Scanderbeg to break his alliance with the sultan and to resume attacks on Ottoman garrisons in the north (February 1462). The new king of Bosnia, Stephen Tomasević (1461–1463), cooperated with Scanderbeg, throwing off Ottoman suzerainty and accepting Hungarian protection and occupation (1462). Mehmet responded by invading Albania, forcing Scanderbeg to sign a new peace and to abandon his conquests (April 27, 1463). This left the sultan free to deal with Bosnia, which he conquered during the remainder of the summer with the considerable help of the native Bogomils, who had been subjected to persecution during the recent Hungarian occupation. Only two northern Bosnian districts remained under Hungarian control at this time, being organized as *banats*, or Hungarian frontier provinces, ruled by a puppet king who claimed all Bosnia in the name of his master. Herzegovina, however, now accepted Ottoman suzerainty and eventual annexation, bringing the sultan even closer to the Adriatic.

War with Venice was therefore inevitable. Pope Pius II used the situation to join Venice and Hungary in an agreement against the Ottomans (September 12, 1463). If this new Crusade was to succeed, Venice would get the Morea and the Greek territories along the Adriatic; Scanderbeg would expand his Albanian state into Macedonia; Hungary would rule Bulgaria, Serbia, Bosnia, and Wallachia; and Constantinople and its environs would be returned to the surviving members of the Byzantine ruling house. Negotiations were also begun with Uzun Hasan, Karaman, and even the Crimean Tatars, who promised to attack the Ottomans in Anatolia at the same time that the Crusaders moved against Mehmet in Europe. Actual hostilities began in September 1463 when Venice seized a number of Aegean Islands as well as much of the Morea. Thus began an Ottoman-Venetian war that was not fully settled until 1479.

Pope Pius II now began to assemble a new Crusader army at Ancona. The Venetian fleet sailed to the mouth of the Dardanelles, capturing Lemnos and Tenedos (1464), preventing the Ottomans from sending supplies to the Morea, and threatening to attack Istanbul. In response a major new shipyard at Istanbul began to construct an entirely new fleet, while two powerful forts were built facing each other across the Dardanelles to keep the enemy out (1463–1464). The grand vezir then led a major expedition that retook the Morea, smashing the Venetian army (spring 1464). Not knowing how this would turn out, Mehmet had organized another new army at Istanbul. When he learned of the victory over Venice, he led it to Bosnia, driving the Hungarians back and beginning raids into Hungary but failing once again to take Belgrade. Mehmet thus effectively broke the back of the Crusade, and Pope Pius died in sorrow in Ancona soon afterward (August 15, 1464). Scanderbeg died in 1468, and the Ottoman conquest of Albania was completed shortly thereafter.

Mehmet led a major expedition to the east in the summer of 1468. Initially, its objective was declared to be either the White Sheep or the Mamluks who were occupying the Turkoman principality of Dulgadir, located at the headwaters of the Euphrates. But when Pir Ahmet of Karaman refused his suzerain's invitation to join the expedition against the latter, Mehmet conquered the western part of Karaman, centered at Konya. At first it seemed that Karaman was finally destroyed, but Pir Ahmet fled into the Taurus Mountains and organized the local tribes in resistance to the sultan, regaining most of the province as soon as Mehmet returned to deal with his problems in Europe. With the help of the Venetians as well as the White Sheep, he was able to carry the fight into Ottoman territory in a series of destructive attacks that reached well into central Anatolia (1470).

Mehmet's response was limited due to new difficulties in the West. In 1469 the Venetian fleet moved into the eastern Aegean, taking the islands of Lemnos and Imbros and ravaging the southern Anatolian coast in addition to landing supplies for Karaman. In response the next summer Mehmet led a naval force that took the island of Negroponte (Eğriboz), the principal Venetian naval base in the Aegean. While the pope and Venice tried to organize a new Crusade, Mehmet extended Ottoman rule in south-central Anatolia by a series of expeditions against Karaman. In the process, however, Mehmet's *devşirme* commander, Gedik Ahmet Paşa, so severely slaughtered the Turkoman nomads of the area that he stimulated a reaction that was to become a major source of division within the state during the next century.

The final conquest of Karaman brought the Ottomans into direct contact and conflict with the Mamluks and the White Sheep. The conflict with the Mamluks over the question of who should dominate Dulgadir was postponed, however, because of the outbreak of war between the Ottomans and Uzun Hasan, who saw his worst fears realized with the establishment of Ottoman rule along his entire western frontier. He considered himself legitimate successor to the Ilhanids and Timurids and claimed large portions of Anatolia as part of this heritage. He allied with Venice (1472), which promised to send arms and ammunition as well as experts to teach his men how to use them, threatening the Ottomans with a coordinated attack in the East and the West.

A Venetian fleet landed the promised equipment late in 1472 while an allied European fleet sailed into the Aegean. Uzun Hasan prepared by gathering around him all the Turkoman princes who had been deposed by Mehmet, promising to restore them in return for help in undermining Mehmet's resistance. A large White Sheep army advanced into central Anatolia, taking Sivas and Tokat and placing Ottoman Anatolia in danger. Mehmet, however, met the threat with his usual vigor. After preparing Istanbul to meet a possible Crusader naval attack and leaving the city under his 14-year-old son, Cem Sultan, he led a major army into Anatolia, beating back the efforts of the Crusaders to pass through the straits. After several ruses on both sides the combatants came together on the plain of Otluk Beli, near Erzurum. The onslaught of the Ottoman auxiliaries on the White Sheep flank carried the day before the two commanders were actually able to fight (August 11, 1472). Again realizing that he could not defeat the Ottomans in open combat, Uzun Hasan agreed to a peace treaty (August 24, 1473) and returned to Azerbaijan. Ottoman rule of Anatolia west of the Euphrates thus was assured. Uzun Hasan's ability to gain the support of the Anatolian Turkomans ended as soon as they saw he would not be able to support them against the sultan. Most of them now gave up their efforts to resist the rule of Istanbul. Uzun Hasan's alliances with Europeans also terminated when they realized he could do no more than divert the Ottomans. During the reign of his son Yakup (1479–1490), relations with the Ottomans remained quiet, with a wide territory of mountains forming a kind of no man's land between the two empires.

Internal Developments

Mehmet now was able to turn his attention back to Istanbul, where internal problems were sapping Ottoman ability to meet its enemies in Europe. The sultan's severe financial measures to pay for the campaigns, his new slave army, and the rebuilding of Istanbul and the other cities of the empire had caused repercussions. The forced population settlements, while providing those persons shifted with new homes and opportunities for trade and business, still created unhappiness. Also, many of the tax concessions given earlier to attract settlers to Istanbul later were withdrawn because of financial difficulties. And Mehmet's willingness to concede such privileges to non-Muslims as well as to appoint Byzantine notables to administrative positions created considerable dissatisfaction among the leading Turkish Muslim families, whose power and wealth had been reduced. Greeks rising through the slave class monopolized the office of grand vezir. Former Byzantine nobles and officials absorbed into the Ottoman system became administrators of tax farms and timars, much to the discontent of the Muslims who had to pay taxes to them. Greek businessmen were able to buy the monopolies that Mehmet had established over needed commodities to raise money, and the high prices they charged were also blamed on the sultan and his Christian slaves. Many of Mehmet's financial measures were in fact copied from the autocratic rulers of the time in Italy. But no matter who originated them, measures such as increasing the plow taxes on cultivators, imposing customs duties on trade within the empire, and confiscating the properties of the religious foundations created tremendous resentment as well as economic distress.

Beyond the apparent economic issues were manifestations of the continued conflict between the older Turkish aristocracy and Mehmet's new slave class. Though Mehmet at first had strengthened the *devşirme* to the detriment of the Turkish aristocracy, many of the measures taken after 1471, though introduced to meet the need for money, aimed at balancing the *devşirme* and the Turkish aristocracy in order to lessen the latter's ability to dominate the sultan. It was the Turkish aristocracy that was benefiting from the new conquests – hence it supported the sultan's aggressive policies in Europe. The *devşirme,* for the first time becoming the peace party, opposed them. As in earlier reigns, the political groups focused their rivalries and ambitions on the candidates for the throne. Cem Sultan, the more militant and active prince, was supported by the Turkish aristocracy, and the pacific Prince Bayezit became the candidate of the *devşirme*. Cem, therefore, advocated continued large-scale conquests in Europe regardless of the resulting financial and economic strains, while Bayezit opposed the sultan's financial policies and advocated peace in order to consolidate the empire already conquered. While Mehmet and Bayezit were campaigning against Uzun Hasan, Cem Sultan, left as regent in Istanbul, attempted to undo his father's financial policies and put himself on the throne on the pretext that there had been no news from the sultan for 40 days.

Cem's attempt was unsuccessful, and the *devşirme* ministers involved were executed by Mehmet soon after his return; but the incident stimulated and exacerbated the conflict between the groups and the princes and further undermined subsequent efforts to organize united attacks on the enemy.

New Wars in Europe: Conclusion of the War with Venice

Hungary's insistence on remaining in Belgrade and Ottoman construction of new forts along the Danube while supporting *Akıncı* raids into Hungarian territory presaged the approach of renewed conflict in Europe. Mathias Corvinus of Hungary got Stephen the Great of Moldavia to throw off Ottoman suzerainty and built a powerful military force to contest Ottoman rule in Wallachia. Hungarian ambitions in Moldavia led to a war with Stephen (1465–1467), but the latter won easily, taking the Danubian forts of Kilia and Ibrail (1465) and emerging as the major leader in the area, able to concentrate his efforts against the Ottomans without having to worry about his rear. Stephen then invaded Wallachia and replaced the Ottoman puppet Radu with his own man (1471). Another threat to Ottoman rule came from the principality of Muscovy, whose Prince Ivan III the Great (1462–1505) had married Zoe (Sophia) Paleologus, daughter of the last Byzantine despot of the Morea and niece of the last emperor. Accompanying the Byzantine princess were many Greek learned men and artists, who began the development of Muscovy as a center of Greek Orthodox culture. Ivan himself was busy gathering together the various parts of what was to become Russia, but as the result of the marriage, he and his successors considered themselves the legal heirs to the Eastern Roman Empire and attempted to make Moscow the new center of the Orthodox church as a demonstration of their aspirations. A third threat to Ottoman power came from the Jagellonians of Lithuania and Poland, now ruled by Casimir IV (1447–1492), whose dominions extended as far east as the Ukraine, bordering Moldavia to the north and across the Dniester to the Black Sea in the east. They allied with the Golden Horde, which ruled to the north. The *han* of the Crimean Tatars, Mengili Giray, while happy to accept the support of his Ottoman suzerain against these threats, was not pleased by Mehmet's efforts to extend Ottoman influence to the north shores of the Black Sea. In turn, then, he began to cooperate with Muscovy.

In spite of a conflict of interests, Stephen of Moldavia, the Jagellonians, Muscovy, the Golden Horde, and even the Crimean Tatars agreed on united action to prevent Ottoman domination of the Black Sea. In response Hadim Süleyman Paşa was sent from Albania through Serbia and Wallachia in the winter of 1475 to join the sultan in an attack on Moldavia. Because of illness, however, Mehmet was unable to bring his army from Istanbul, enabling Stephen to rout the Ottomans at Rakovitza (Racova) (January 17, 1475) with the help of Jagellonian and Hungarian troops. Mehmet was much more successful in the Crimea. He first used internal disputes in the Hanate family to replace Mengili Giray (1469–1475, 1478–1515) with his son Erminak Giray, who restored the tributory relationship and then cooperated with an Ottoman naval expedition in capturing all the remaining Genoese colonies along the northern shores of the Black Sea (June 1475). Mehmet then restored Mengili as a result of the intervention of the Crimean notables in Ottoman service, who said that Mengili would be better able to lead the Tatars against their enemies in the north. Mengili, in turn, accepted Ottoman suzerainty and agreed to provide military and financial support as needed. Thus Ottoman control of the Crimean Tatars was established. It was to continue for three centuries, providing the sultans with not only another base to control the Black Sea but also a regular supply of able fighting men. The power of the Crimean *han*s at this time was not extensive, hardly extending beyond the Crimea itself, but with Ottoman help they were at least able to avoid being absorbed by Muscovy, as happened to the other Tatar Hanates at the time. They remained the principal Ottoman buffers to keep the Russians away from the Black Sea for another two centuries.

The successes north of the Black Sea gave the sultan the added strategic advantage of being able to attack Stephen of Moldavia from north as well as south of the Black Sea. While the Tatars of Crimea diverted the Golden Horde, a joint attack occupied the shores of Bessarabia and took Akkerman, thus gaining control of the southern mouth of the Danube. Stephen tried to avoid open battle with the Ottomans by following a scorched-earth policy. But since Wallachian help to the sultan made this meaningless, he finally confronted the sultan at Valea Alba (Akdere) (July 17, 1476). Mehmet prevailed and ravaged Moldavia, but Stephen was able to escape and subsequently to resume his rule after the Ottomans returned home, although he lost his former prestige and ability to threaten the Ottomans.

The wars in the Principalities and north of the Black Sea ended just in time to enable Mehmet to face new threats to the West. Mathias Corvinus attacked the Ottoman fort at Semendria (1476), threatening the entire Danubian defense line, but Mehmet arrived from Moldavia, beating the Hungarians off with direct attacks and also by sending raiders into Dalmatia and Croatia. He then concentrated on Venice, hoping to force it to accept a peace by completing his conquest of Albania and thus gaining a firm foothold on the Adriatic. In 1477 Ottoman forces in Albania besieged the port of Lepanto (Inebahtı) and Scanderbeg's old capital of Kroya (Akçahisar), both of which were controlled by local Albanian leaders with Venetian assistance. The Venetian fleet responded with raids along the shores of western Anatolia, but this stopped when Mehmet sent the Bosnian raiders several times into northern Italy, causing havoc in the valleys opposite Venice (1477–1478). By the end of 1478 all of Albania was under direct Ottoman rule. It now was organized as a regular Ottoman province, and the economy was developed with the help of Jewish refugees from Spain who were settling here as well as at Salonica. Avlonya became an international port centering much of the trade between western Europe and the Ottoman Empire. Albanians also began to enter the Ottoman Ruling Class on a large scale, soon surpassing the Bosnians in influence and gaining a position of predominance far in excess of their numbers, a situation that was, in many ways, to continue until modern times. The Ottomans also moved into Montenegro (Crnagora/Karadağ), which had been established early in the fifteenth century in a revolt against Serbian rule in the mountains of the upper Zeta, sheltered by the coastal areas of Dalmatia under Venetian rule. Mehmet took the southern part of the country, while the Montenegrins moved their capital to Çetince, which became the center of their resistance.

Venice was clearly outflanked by Mehmet's conquests. A settlement was reached restoring Venetian commercial privileges in the Ottoman Empire and leaving it with sufficient power in the Adriatic to maintain its sea communications. Negotiations culminated with the signature of a peace treaty in Istanbul on June 25, 1479, ending the 16-year war. Venice agreed to surrender Işkodra (Scutari), the last major port it held in northern Albania, and to recognize Ottoman rule in Albania as well as Ottoman conquests of the Aegean Islands, thus giving the sultan full control of the northern Aegean except for the Sporades islands, which remained in Venetian hands, and Chios, still ruled by Genoa. In return Mehmet allowed Venice to retain a number of ports in Dalmatia along the Adriatic and its former possessions in the Morea with the exception of Argos. Venice agreed to pay an annual tribute in return for these possessions as well as for renewal of the right to trade freely in the sultan's dominions and to maintain its agent in Istanbul.

Mehmet's Final Campaigns

This victory over the strongest naval power in the eastern Mediterranean emboldened Mehmet to seek two more goals for his navy: (1) conquest of the island of Rhodes, considered the gateway to further advances toward the western Mediterranean, and (2) occupation of Italy, which seemed ripe for conquest due to the rivalries then endemic among Venice, Naples, and Milan as well as divisions caused by the political activities of the pope. Rhodes was the only major Aegean island not yet ruled by the Ottomans. It was controlled by the order of the Knights of St. John, which was originally founded in Jerusalem in 1070 and subsequently transferred to Cyprus (1292) and then to Rhodes (1306). After the Muslim reconquest of the Holy Land, the order had established itself as a fortified bastion against Islam, becoming the principal base for the pirates who raided Ottoman shipping in the Aegean and eastern Mediterranean and supported the various Crusader naval efforts in the environs.

Gedik Ahmet Paşa was now made *sancak* bey of Avlonya and commander of the Ottoman fleet in the Aegean with the task of organizing the campaigns against both Italy and Rhodes. His first fleet took the Greek islands of Cephalonia and Zanta and then put Rhodes under siege beginning on December 4, 1479, while another force sailed around southern Italy and landed at Otranto on August 11 to initiate the second phase of the campaign. Rome panicked, and the pope planned to flee northward along with most of the population of the city. At the same time, a new Crusade was called and support came from the Italian city-states, Hungary, and France. Gedik Ahmet returned to Rumeli in the winter of 1481 to raise additional forces and was there when the news arrived of the sultan's sudden death (May 3, 1481), as a result of which the siege of Rhodes was broken off. Gedik Ahmet's subsequent involvement in the conflicts for succession in Istanbul left the force at Otranto without leadership, so that it finally left for home on July 10, thus ending what might have been an entirely new area of Muslim expansion.

Consolidation of the Empire: Bayezit II, 1481–1512

The reign of Mehmet's son Bayezit II marked a period of transition from the old heroic age of the fourteenth and fifteenth centuries to the new age of grandeur. Mehmet II had made substantial conquests in the East and the West, restoring the empire of Bayezit I and adding to it. But he had left severe economic and social problems that had to be resolved if the empire was to be retained and new conquests made. Bayezit II's reign was a period of consolidation before conquests were resumed.

Reaction and Civil War

The tensions between the Turkish aristocracy and the *devşirme* and the rivalry of the two princes made some kind of conflict inevitable as soon as the old sultan was gone. That Mehmet recognized this eventuality was shown by his policy of stationing the two princes at equal distances from the capital so that after his death they could have the same chance to reach it and take his throne. Bayezit was governor of the Vilayet-i Rum, including the areas of Sivas, Tokat, and Amasya, and the younger Cem ruled the province of Karaman from his capital at Konya. It would appear that the sultan in fact supported Cem's claim to rule, due mainly to the latter's martial personality, much more like that of his father than was the sometimes ascetic and sometimes dissolute Bayezit, who hated violence and most of what his father represented. Those who had suffered from Mehmet's rigorous economic policies had long hoped for Bayezit's accession in the hope that further conquest would be abandoned until the resulting social and economic pressures were relieved. While the *devşirme* ministers sided with Bayezit, Cem was supported by the Turkish aristocracy, led by Karamani Mehmet Paşa, Mehmet's last grand vezir (see p. 67). When the sultan died, Karamani Mehmet tried to conceal the news long enough to inform Cem Sultan so that the latter could reach the capital and take the throne before Bayezit and his friends could do anything about it. He also ordered the Janissaries to new assignments in Anatolia, both to conceal the sultan's death from them and to prevent them from going to Istanbul to help Bayezit. But the plot was discovered. The Janissaries in the expeditionary army arranged for Bayezit to go to Istanbul to take the throne while sending agents who hindered Cem's efforts to reach the capital. Janissary military power thus assured the accession of Bayezit II as their candidate despite the wishes of the grand vezir and the Turkish aristocracy.

How much these events left Bayezit under the control of the *devşirme* is demonstrated by the fact that once he took the throne (May 21, 1481), he had to appoint its leader, Ishak Paşa, as the new grand vezir and to allow the Janissaries to execute Karamani Mehmet and his supporters and pillage their houses and property. Bayezit also was forced to increase the *kapıkulu* salaries considerably and to extend the practice begun by his father of paying them "tips" (*bahşiş*) at the accession of the sultan, a practice that would gradually impoverish his successors.

The new sultan was compelled to end his father's financial practices, in particular that of debasing the coinage. He restored all the private and foundation property confiscated in Mehmet's later years. *Devşirme* men were again placed in key positions, thus assuring for the moment their supremacy over members of the leading Turkish families, many of who went into hiding or fled to join Cem. The events of Bayezit's accession thus upset the carefully nurtured balance of forces developed by Mehmet and left the *devşirme* in firm control.

The Revolt of Cem Sultan

Cem, however, did not give up. By the time he learned of his father's death, it was too late for him to prevent Bayezit's accession. Thus he went to Bursa, summoned all his supporters along with those Turkomans and Muslims of Anatolia who had long resented *devşirme* rule in Istanbul, and declared himself sultan of Anatolia (May 28, 1481); he proposed division of the empire, with Bayezit ruling only in Europe. Bayezit rejected the proposal, of course, defending the continued unity of the Ottoman state, and received the support of Gedik Ahmet Paşa, who was in Anatolia at the time to recruit new troops for the Italian invasion and who was very popular among the Janissaries. In the end, the decisive battle between the two took place near Yenişehir (June 20, 1481). Bayezit's numerical supremacy, when combined with the powerful attack of the Janissaries, enabled him to carry the day. Cem and the remnants of his army were forced to flee, eventually taking refuge in the Mamluk Empire in the company of the last Karamanid prince, Kasım Bey.

Thus began a long period of exile. Cem's effort to depose Bayezit and regain the throne kept the sultan and his empire in apprehension until Cem's death 12 years later finally ended the threat. The fugitive prince initially was given some assistance by the Mamluks and built a small force at Aleppo (April 1482), where he was joined by a number of fugitive Turkoman princes and Anatolian feudal holders who had been dispossessed by Bayezit. In the meantime, Gedik Ahmet, Ishak Paşa, and the other *devşirme* ministers so dominated the new sultan that, in despair, he began to place members of the Turkish aristocracy in key positions and attempted to work through them to regain his power. When Cem's new expedition entered Ottoman territory in Cilicia (May 19, 1482), he found support from neither the *devşirme* nor the Turkish aristocracy, and after advancing near Ankara (June 8), he despaired of success and fled to Rhodes, where he was given refuge by the Knights.

Bayezit's last main opponent in Anatolia was neutralized when Kasım Bey surrendered and renounced all his claims to Karaman in return for an appointment as Ottoman governor of İçel, thus being absorbed into the Ottoman system in the same ways as many other Turkoman notables. Cem sailed to France (September 1, 1482), still under the protection of the Knights, who apparently were "persuaded" by the sultan's agents to remove him from the empire's immediate environs. Various negotiations followed with different Christian powers still hoping to use Cem against the sultan, finally leading to an agreement to send him to Pope Innocent VIII (1486), who was contemplating a new Crusade. When Charles VIII of France invaded Italy and occupied Rome, he captured Cem (January 27, 1495) and sent him to France, but on the way Cem fell ill and died in Naples (February 25, 1495), possibly as the result of poison given at Bayezit's instigation, though this has never really been proved.

Internal Problems

Aside from the threat of a Christian Crusade using Cem, there were other compelling factors that dissuaded Bayezit from undertaking foreign expeditions. Bayezit felt that the empire needed a period of repose in which to solve the problems left by his father. He also wanted to end serious military activities until he could reduce the domination achieved by the *devşirme* as a result of its role in bringing him to power and defeating Cem's initial threats. Toward this end the sultan used the unfounded rumor of complicity in Cem's revolt to secure Gedik Ahmet's dismissal (November 18, 1482) and that of Ishak Paşa as grand vezir as well, thus beginning a struggle, which would continue for much of the rest of his reign, to free himself of the *devşirme*.

The *devşirme,* however, still was very strong due to the revenues and positions given it during the previous reign. In fact, Ishak Paşa was followed by another *devşirme* grand vezir, Davut Paşa, the governor of Anatolia. But with the sultan now watchful and jealous of his authority the latter was not able to exercise as much control as his predecessors. To reduce the power of the *devşirme* Bayezit had to accomplish the opposite of what Mehmet II had done, namely, build up the Turkish leadership and the ulema by giving them positions and revenues. Therefore, he sought to conciliate his brother's major supporters, not only by restoring their confiscated properties but also by reviving the institutions of orthodox Islam, financing new mosques, supporting religious studies, and starting a new series of raids into infidel territory. By 1483 Bayezit had largely achieved control of the system, and Cem's death in 1495 freed him to pursue new conquests.

Balkan Problems

The first step in Bayezit's new aggressive policy was to send raiders from Serbia and Bosnia along the Dalmatian coast as far as Ragusa and across the Danube into Temesvar and other Hungarian territory. These raids secured much booty and led to the definitive conquest of Herzegovina (1483), but the coastal area of the Craina remained in Venetian hands.

For his initial field of operations Bayezit chose Wallachia, where Stephen the Great had inflicted serious defeats on Mehmet II, preventing the establishment of direct land communications around the Black Sea to the new Ottoman vassal in the Crimea. Bayezit also felt that possessing Moldavia would give him a strategic advantage when the war with Hungary was renewed and would enable him to control the mouths of the Danube to stop the Christian pirates who had been entering the Black Sea and raiding Ottoman shipping and coasts. The immediate pretext for the war was supplied by Stephen, who as soon as he had learned of Cem's revolt invaded Wallachia (June–July 1481) and then crossed the Danube and mounted a series of raids into Bulgaria, posing a major threat to the sultan's prestige and authority over all his European vassals. Bayezit replied by sending raiders into Moldavia and organizing a joint land-sea attack. Just before leaving Edirne, he made sure of the support of the ulema and frontier beys by laying the foundations for the new mosque bearing his name in that city as well as a *medrese,* a hospital, and other buildings on the Maritsa and by replacing the wooden Edirne covered market, which had burned down the previous year, with a new one of stone and brick. Nor did he fear intervention from Hungary, since Mathias Corvinus was still busy in central Europe, using a revolt of the nobility in Austria against the Habsburgs (1485) to conquer most of that country, including Vienna.

With vassal forces from Wallachia Bayezit crossed into Moldavia and captured Kilia, on the Danube (July 14, 1484), while a force of Crimean Tatars took Akkerman (Cetatea-Alba) in Bessarabia on the Dniester (August 3), thus achieving control of the western Black Sea shores as well as the mouths of the Danube and the Dniester. The Crimean leader Mengili Giray used the joint campaign with the Ottomans in Moldavia to take the entire northwest Black Sea coast from the Jagellonians, thus making himself a major power in the area. Moldavia and Hungary lost their entrepôts for the trade of central and northern Europe through the Black Sea, and this trade, and the prosperity of the lands depending on it, thus fell under Ottoman control. Stephen hastened to recognize Bayezit's suzerainty, and the sultan and his Crimean ally were content to return home without further conquests. Stephen soon afterward renounced these agreements and again tried to regain the forts in 1484 and again in 1486, but without success. Bayezit's advances in the area were finally recognized by Hungary and Poland in new treaties signed with the sultan in 1503, which officially recognized the vassal status of both Moldavia and Wallachia. Successes in Moldavia had brought the Ottomans in direct contact with Poland, but the incursions of the Crimean Tatars into Polish territory forced the Poles to concentrate on the Tatars, preventing direct conflict with the Ottomans.

War with the Mamluks

Bayezit preferred to keep out of war entirely at this time, but he was not able to avoid the troubles that had been building for some time with the Mamluks, rulers of Egypt and Syria. Longstanding rivalries over eastern Anatolia and the Holy Places – laid aside while Uzun Hasan and Karaman existed – were revived because of Mamluk assistance to Cem Sultan in the early stages of his revolt. In Cilicia Mehmet's annexation of Karaman had left Bayezit's empire in direct contact not only with the Mamluks but also with Dulgadir, which included the areas of Maraş and Elbistan. When the Mamluks attempted to remove Alauddevle of Dulgadir to secure a more friendly regime, he secured the assistance of the Ottoman governor of Kayseri, whose invasion of Mamluk territory led to the first Ottoman-Mamluk war (1485–1491). The war was no more than a series of skirmishes in which the Mamluks invariably won the initial encounters but were unable to follow up their victories because of internal financial and political problems. Neither side really used its main forces, and when large-scale famine and plague spread through Syria, the Mamluks offered peace, which Bayezit accepted (May 1491), leaving their territories approximately as they had been before. The Mamluks controlled the Cilician towns and the fort commanding the southern end of the Cilician gates, while the Ottomans held the main mountain passes. A new period of peace between the two empires ensued (1491–1516), although the old sources of disagreement remained to poison relations until the Ottoman conquest of the Mamluk Empire under Bayezit's successor.

Problems in Europe

The threat of a Crusade using Cem Sultan was eliminated in 1495, but new developments in Europe put the Ottomans in some danger. While Hungarian power was declining after the death of Mathias Corvinus, that of the Habsburg empire was rising under the leadership of Maximilian I, Holy Roman emperor since 1493. The Habsburgs had hoped to secure supremacy in central as well as eastern Europe as early as 1273, when Rudolph I became emperor, but they had been unable to achieve that objective during the next two centuries because they had concentrated on central Europe and the division of authority within the empire. At this time the Habsburgs ruled, or claimed to rule, Austria, Hungary, the Tyrol, Styria, Bohemia, and Carinthia as well as territories in the West, but each of these territories was under the control of different members of the family. Maximilian worked to establish more central control, hoping to achieve this at least partly by taking the lead in Christianity's fight against the Ottomans and, perhaps, gaining control of the lands of Southeastern Europe, including Istanbul.

Just as Bayezit renewed his peace with Poland (1490), the death of Mathias Corvinus without an heir led Maximilian to attempt to extend his control to Hungary. Bayezit, learning of this, decided to use Hungarian weakness to take Belgrade, hoping thereby to restore the prestige that had been damaged by the news of Mamluk victories in the East. As the Ottomans marched through Serbia, the Hungarian nobles, recalling Corvinus' efforts to reduce their powers, chose as king the weak ruler of Bohemia, Ladislas VII, thus putting their own selfish interests ahead of Hungary's need for the kind of strong leadership that the Habsburgs offered. Ladislas immediately rewarded the nobles by disbanding the central state apparatus as well as the mercenary army and frontier guard organization established by Corvinus, leaving the nobles free to suppress the peasants and town residents and gain control over him and the central government. Thus Hungarian ability to meet the Ottoman threat was dissipated.

Bayezit knew nothing of Hungary's politics. When he reached Sofia and learned of Ladislas' election, he merely assumed that this would end Hungarian divisiveness and make the capture of Belgrade impossible. To avoid personal defeat, then, he assigned the governor of Semendria, Hadım Süleyman Paşa, to lead a relatively minor attack on Belgrade while he sent the remainder of his forces on raids into Transylvania, Croatia, and Carinthia, a task greatly eased by the Austrian disbandment of Corvinus' frontier organization. Bayezit's abandonment of the expedition so angered the *devşirme* men who brought him to power, as well as the gazis and others, that they began once again to plot for his throne and to array themselves in support of his different sons, beginning a new period of internal political conflict.

A main reason for Bayezit's decision to give up the planned siege of Belgrade was the rise of new troubles with Poland over Moldavia and the Black Sea coast. Casimir's successor, the able and militant Jan Olbrecht (1492–1501), was elected by the notables because of his advocacy of an offensive policy against the Ottomans. Once he had consolidated his power in Poland, he made an alliance with Venice and with his brother Ladislas (king of Hungary) for a joint effort against the Ottomans (May 5, 1494). Stephen refused to join, fearing that Moldavia would be the main scene of any Ottoman-Polish war, but Olbrecht's consequent efforts to displace him led to a quarrel with Ladislas, who regarded Stephen as his vassal, thus effectively breaking up the recent alliance.

Olbrecht, therefore, tried to achieve his objectives without outside help. But lacking the necessary financial resources, he had to grant new privileges to the nobles in return (1496), leaving the Polish state more decentralized than before. He was able to raise an army, nevertheless, while Stephen secured Ottoman assurances of support in case of a Polish invasion of Moldavia. The Polish attack began in June 1497, a major effort to break the alliance of the Ottomans, the Crimean Tatars, Moldavia, and Moscow against the Jagellonians. But the Ottomans crossed into Bukovina and routed the Poles at Kozmin (October 26, 1497), raiding Poland as far as Lemberg (Lvov). Olbrecht's martial desires were curbed, and he made peace with

Moldavia (April 1499) and the Ottomans (September). As a result, the Crimean Tatars were left with a major empire, including the entire steppe north of the Crimea from the Dniester to the Volga, under the suzerainty of the sultan. This, however, subsequently led to an inevitable break with Muscovy, which would soon become a rival instead of an ally.

War with Venice

The conflicts in the Balkans, combined with the threat of Cem Sultan, had led Bayezit to sign a new treaty with Venice (January 6, 1482) by which its tribute to the sultan was ended and its privileges within the empire increased. However, the rivalries in the Adriatic, Albania, the Aegean, and the Morea continued to trouble relations. Venice was being encouraged by the pope to expand its power in northern Italy in return for Venetian help against the Ottomans. On the Ottoman side years of relative inactivity against the infidel had created some tension. Heterodox religious movements that had been dominant among the Turkomans in eastern Anatolia and served as outlets for political dissent began to spread into the cities and among the Janissaries. Bayezit hoped renewed warfare with Europe would direct attention elsewhere and inspire unity against the infidel.

The sultan, therefore, tried to provoke a war with Venice. In 1491 he expelled the Venetian *balyos*. In 1496, soon after Cem's death, Ottoman ports were closed to Venetian grain merchants, ostensibly because of a grain shortage in the empire but in fact to increase the pressure. The same year Ottoman forces from Albania occupied Montenegro, a Venetian protectorate. A Venetian passenger ship carrying Christian pilgrims to Jerusalem was captured by the Ottoman fleet (1497), and all aboard were killed or enslaved. Venice responded by building up its fleet in the Aegean, but this only further stimulated the sultan. Bayezit now moved to create a new fleet under the command of Kemal Reis, who since 1490 had led pirates in the western Mediterranean in raids against the coasts of France and Spain. New shipyards were built, new warships put into service, and thousands of Turkish and Greek sailors living along the coasts enlisted under his command.

Ottoman ships began to raid Venice's possessions in Dalmatia. When Venice in turn made an agreement with France, Bayezit used this as pretext for war and imprisoned all the Venetian residents in Istanbul (July 4, 1499). Within a short time a major Ottoman fleet was able to capture Lepanto (Inebahtı) in a joint land-sea assault (August 28, 1499), inflicting a blow on Venetian naval power in the Adriatic as well as the Aegean. Bayezit's fleet then captured the major Venetian ports in the Morea. Large-scale *akıncı* raids from Bosnia devastated Croatia and Dalmatia, again penetrating to the gates of Venice and capturing Durazzo (Draz) (August 14, 1501). Venice fell into financial difficulties and seemed unable to hold out much longer. Pope Alexander VI desperately tried to organize a new Crusade to save Venice, sending agents all over Europe, but Bayezit managed to detach Milan and Naples with commercial concessions at the expense of their rival, while peace agreements with Poland and Moldavia kept them out as well. A fairly large Crusader fleet did enter the Aegean in the summer of 1501, and its efforts to take the island of Lesbos, which commanded the Bosporus, alarmed the sultan. But in the end it was dispersed by a storm, and disputes among the allied commanders prevented them from taking united action against the Ottomans. Venice was ready for peace, since the war was proving far too costly, with the losses of its Levant markets and trade routes into the Black Sea worsening an already difficult financial situation. At the same time, new problems in the East, combined with uncertainty as to how Venice might be completely defeated, led Bayezit to agree to peace, which was signed in Istanbul (December 14, 1502) with Polish mediation.

While Venice retained ports in the Morea as well as Albania and had its trade privileges restored, the war was essentially a major Ottoman victory. It marked the emergence of the Ottoman Empire as a major Mediterranean naval power. The bases won from Venice gave it strategic locations that could be used for further advances, not only in the eastern Mediterranean but also in the West. The war and the concluding peace agreements also marked the entry of the Ottomans into European diplomacy as an increasingly important factor in the balance of power. The Ottomans had also become a major economic power by virtue of their control over the international trade routes passing through the eastern Mediterranean – Venice, for one, determined never again to become involved in war with the sultan, since this would harm its economic interests.

The peace of 1503 also sparked Ottoman interest in the western Mediterranean. As early as 1482, the Muslim Nasirids of Andalusia, the last Muslim dynasty in Spain, had asked for the help of the only gazi state against the advancing Christian forces of Aragon and Castille. Handicapped by Cem's revolt and uncertain of his naval strength, the sultan had to content himself with expressions of sympathy, with practical assistance being left to the Turkish pirates of North Africa. When Granada fell to the Spaniards in 1492 and the Muslim states in North Africa began to face the possibility of Christian invasions, the pressure for Ottoman intervention increased in the face of numerous appeals for help. Problems in the East still prevented Bayezit from sending assistance. But many of the Ottoman sea gazis, called pirates in the West, began to move to help their Muslim brothers while securing easy pickings from the Christians. Also, as the Ottoman fleet was built up, many of these "pirates" were drawn into Ottoman service, and under their influence it was not long before the Ottomans were ready to use their new naval power to begin operations in the West.

Internal Reforms

With the Venetian war ended, Bayezit withdrew from active direction, leaving power in the hands of the grand vezir and the men around him. This inaugurated a new phase in Ottoman affairs that culminated in the late sixteenth and seventeenth centuries when all power in the state was assumed by the ruling parties and the sultans were merely puppets in their hands. This did not happen under Bayezit II, however, because he was very successful in balancing the Turkish aristocracy and the *devşirme* and deferring to the interests of both so that neither would get the upper hand. Thus divisions were less over matters of state policy than simply the result of conflicting ambitions of the leaders of the two groups.

Bayezit now devoted himself mainly to religion, learning, and mystic contemplation. He encouraged the work of many learned men, including the historian Ibn Kemal (also called Kemal Paşazâde), who wrote a history of the Ottoman Empire, and the great Idris Bitlisi, who had been in White Sheep service at Tabriz and who now wrote his monumental *Hest Behişt*. Bayezit himself was a musician and poet. He gathered learned ulema and scientists in his court, while retaining many of the writers and thinkers of Mehmet II's court. But he lacked the spirit of thought and free inquiry of his father and fell under the influence of a group of fanatic Mollas, forerunners of the *Kadızadeler* (see p. 206). They persuaded him to restrict and even execute intellectuals who disagreed with them, causing many of the latter to flee.

This is not to say that Bayezit lost all interest in government. He had his vezirs build an orderly system of administration along the lines begun by Mehmet II, with tax farms and fiefs being made the principal units of government. Special attention was paid to regularizing the financial structure to provide for military campaigns without the desperate financial measures that had weakened the empire's economic structure under Mehmet. To provide financial reserves for future campaigns Bayezit increased the number of horsemen that timar holders had to provide in relation to the value of their holdings and developed a new household tax, called *avarız*, to build a war treasury to be retained intact until needed to pay for the special expenses of war. This also provided a precedent for subsequent rulers to extend the *rüsum* dues (see p. 120) far beyond the original *Şeriat* taxes, solely on the basis of the sultan's right to legislate. As a result of Bayezit's regularization of the administrative and financial systems, economic and commercial life developed tremendously and public revenues from these sources alone almost doubled during his reign. The population and size of the empire's great cities grew rapidly with vast public structures of various kinds adding to imperial grandeur. Bayezit also paid attention to arming his troops with more modern weapons and building a fleet that would reflect the newly won Ottoman supremacy in the Aegean. Thus were laid the bases for a fresh burst of conquest and splendor under his successors.

The Safavid Danger in the East

Bayezit was not given much time to enjoy his contemplations. As he became old and withdrawn, the unresolved tensions among the major political groups were manifested in his sons' struggles to succeed him. Added to this were the problems in the east, intensified by the rise of a new Iranian dynasty, the Safavids.

Originally founded by Şeyh Safiuddin (1252–1334) and bearing his name, the Safavid movement progressed from contemplative Sufism to militant Shia heresy in the mid-fifteenth century just when Murat II and Mehmet II were extending centralized Ottoman control to eastern Anatolia. Nomadic reaction and resistance provided the Safavids with a golden opportunity that they did not ignore. Gaining the military support of Uzun Hasan, the Safavids developed a distinctive red headgear – having 12 folds commemorating the 12 Shia imams – as the distinctive insignia of their followers, who thereafter were known as *Kızılbaş* ("red head"). Uzun Hasan's successors attempted to suppress the Safavids, leading at least partly to the collapse of their own state as well, but Ismail (1487–1524), one of the sons of the last Safavid leader, managed to escape into Iran with seven *Kızılbaş* tribes that enabled him to eliminate the small Iranian dynasts who had succeeded the White Sheep and the Timurids and to gain control of the entire country within a decade. While the dynasty had risen originally as the leader of a Sufi Turkoman movement, the transformation to Shia heterodoxy was completed in the early years of the sixteenth century as part of the process by which the masses of Iran were attracted to Ismail's leadership. Then, as later, religion in the Middle East served as a vehicle for the expression of political feelings and ambitions.

Ismail, determined to restore Safavid influence in Ottoman territory in eastern Anatolia, sent out hundreds of preachers who successfully spread his message among the nomads. The Ottomans correctly interpreted the heterodox religious message as a political threat and acted accordingly, opposing the Safavids not only because of the military danger but also because their religious message posed a basic challenge to the orthodox doctrines underpinning the authority of the classical Islamic dynasties since the time of the Abbasids.

Bayezit was reluctant to undertake an open attack against Ismail. Whether it was his own sympathy for the mystic message of the Safavid preachers, his desire to avoid war as much as possible, or simply his fear that the Safavid message might also seduce many members of his own army, Bayezit temporized. He entered into correspondence with Ismail in the hope of convincing him to end his heretical ways. During the winter of 1508–1509, Ismail actually conquered Baghdad and most of southwestern Iran and began large-scale massacres of Sunni Muslims and destruction of Sunni mosques and tombs; but Bayezit's only response was to ask Ismail to cease such practices. Bayezit appealed for help from the Mamluks, who did no more than to order their governor in Aleppo to resist such Safavid activity if they entered Cilicia, and from the Uzbeg Turkoman dynasty of Transoxania, which was just beginning to emerge as a major power and which responded with a series of attacks that were to preoccupy the Safavids for the remainder of Bayezit's reign.

Despite the Uzbeg attacks, however, the Safavid preachers continued their activities among the Anatolian Turkomans, particularly in the southwest, where the Safavid following had always been strong. One of the Safavids, Şah Kulu, was able to use widespread Turkoman resentment to lead a major revolt at Antalya in the spring of 1511, gaining the support of thousands of Ottoman soldiers sent to suppress it. Describing himself as the caliph (successor) to Ismail, Şah Kulu sent his own preachers around Anatolia; the more extreme of them called their leader the *Mahdi*, sent by God to save mankind, the Prophet, and even God himself. Ottoman resistance was hindered by the bitter rivalry for succession that was then developing between the sultan's two governors in the area, his sons Ahmet, governor at Amasya, and Korkut, governor of Antalya. Şah Kulu was able to move northward from Karaman, ravaging central Anatolia and defeating the Anatolian army of the Ottomans near Alaşehir (June 1511), opening the way for an attack on Bursa. It was only after most of central and southeastern Anatolia had fallen into rebel hands that Bayezit, increasingly withdrawn and ill, sent an army of 8000 Janissaries. Led by Grand Vezir Hadım Ali Paşa and in cooperation with Prince Ahmet, it finally routed the rebels near Kayseri (August 1511), turning an initial defeat into victory when Şah Kulu was accidentally killed by an arrow. Without its leader the movement quickly broke up. The surviving *Kızılbaş* forces fled back into Iran, but the Safavids remained in control of Iran, a continued source of trouble under Bayezit's successors.

The Struggle for Succession

Much of the reason for Bayezit's failure to suppress the Safavids more decisively and to follow up the victory at Kayseri was the rise of serious disputes for power and the right of succession among his sons. There were five adult sons at the time, each of who had been assigned as a provincial governor to provide him with the necessary administrative and military training. The eldest, Ahmet, was known as an able administrator and was well liked by the people. He favored his father's policies of peace and consolidation and had the support of most administrators as well as Bayezit but was bitterly opposed by the Janissary corps because of several defeats that it had suffered under his leadership in Anatolia. The main candidate of the ulema was Korkut, who had grown up in the court of his grandfather Mehmet II, was learned in the Islamic sciences as well as poetry and music, and shared his father's mystic and pacific proclivities. But Korkut had shown little military talent in dealing with the Şah Kulu revolt. Prince Selim – by far the most militant and warlike of the brothers – had the support of the Janissaries and the border beys along the frontiers in Europe but because of his hard and pitiless nature was opposed by his father and most men of state regardless of party. Şehinşah died in 1511 and Alemşah in 1512, leaving only three princes to fight for power in what turned out to be their father's last year.

For some time the struggle manifested itself primarily in competition to secure governorships as close as possible to Istanbul. In 1507 Bayezit showed his favor for Ahmet by sending him to govern at Amasya. Korkut went in anger to Egypt, ostensibly on his way to join the pilgrimage to the Holy Cities but in fact to secure Mamluk support for his claims. After the Mamluks abstained in fear of attracting an Ottoman attack, Korkut managed to secure his father's pardon, after which he returned to his post at Antalya (1511). He then asked for appointment to Aydın, which was closer to Istanbul, but Ahmet successfully opposed this. As a compromise, Korkut went to nearby Manisa instead. While his brothers fought in the more traditional ways, Selim followed a different policy to gain the throne, securing military support by leading the Janissaries in several successful expeditions into Georgia as well as the Safavid territories in eastern Anatolia following the Şah Kulu revolt.

In the course of this competition for the throne Selim secured the assistance of the Crimean Tatars and fought against his father twice in an effort to secure the succession. Finally, the Janissaries in Istanbul forced Bayezit to abdicate and put Selim on the throne on the grounds that he alone could save the empire from the Shia threat (April 25, 1512). Bayezit quickly left Istanbul, hoping to return to his birthplace at Demotica to spend his last years in ascetic contemplation, but he died en route (May 26, 1512), ostensibly of natural causes but perhaps as the result of medicines administered by his doctor at Selim's direction.

Thus while Bayezit had balanced the Turkish aristocracy and the *devşirme* for most of his reign, in the end the Janissary corps, though itself manned by the *devşirme*, managed to make itself into an independent political force that cooperated with the timariotes of Rumeli and the frontier beys of Serbia and Bosnia to secure the accession of their candidate, Selim. We shall see later how Selim in turn sought to throw off the dominance of his supporters so that he could rule as well as reign.[7]

Conquest of the East: The Reign of Selim I, 1512–1520

Selim I came to the throne with an ambition to restore Mehmet II's energetic policies of conquest and in fact to achieve Mehmet's goal of establishing a world empire. Since the major political groups in Ottoman society were divided and had opposed his accession, Selim was determined not to base his power on either and to rely instead on the Janissary corps, whose power in Istanbul had won him the throne. But how could he control the Janissary corps and make it his instrument rather than falling under those who had brought him to power, as had occurred early in the reigns of his father and grandfather? And how was he to gain the cooperation of the other political groups, which still manned most administrative and military positions in the state? His solution was twofold. On the one hand, he sought to control the opposition not by counterbalancing it, but rather by coercing it through the military power of the Janissaries. On the other hand, he sought to make the Janissaries the instrument of the sultan by conciliating them, enlarging their numbers to 35,000 men, increasing their salaries, paying high "accession tips," and, finally, by the more direct means of replacing their officers with his own slaves.

Challenges to the Throne

Selim's control of the government was assured within a few months after his accession. His next problem was to eliminate the challenge of his brothers. At first he sought this by conciliation, allowing Korkut to return to Manisa and offering Ahmet the governorship of Konya. The latter, however, wanted much more, declared himself sultan of Anatolia, and sent his own son Alauddin to capture Bursa, which was to be his capital (mid-June 1512). It was in reaction to this that Selim decided to cement his own power by eliminating not only all his brothers but also his nephews and, eventually, all his own sons except for his chosen successor, Süleyman.

Ahmet's revolt soon became far more dangerous than that of Cem Sultan ever had been. On June 18 Alauddin took Bursa and with a Turkoman army began to collect taxes and exact professions of loyalty from an ever-widening area of central and western Anatolia. But forced conscriptions and large-scale confiscations to support the revolt soon alienated the masses. Thus when Selim crossed into Anatolia with a large army, he received general support and was able to force Ahmet and his followers to flee to Cilicia (summer 1512).

Some of Ahmet's supporters wanted him to gain Safavid assistance, but Ahmet abhorred the Shia heresy and sought help from the Mamluks instead. While the negotiations proceeded from Ahmet's temporary capital at Amasya, Selim went through Anatolia killing all his nephews, thus extending the law of fratricide. Korkut was killed too. Ahmet was encouraged to attack by reports that Selim's ferocity toward his own relatives had alienated most of his support, but Selim routed the rebel forces at Yenişehir (April 15, 1513), executed Ahmet, and thus assured his rule without further challenge.

Preparations for Conquest

Selim's previous experience at Trabzon convinced him that his greatest problem was the Safavid threat. But as soon as he had defeated Ahmet, he went to Edirne first to make certain that the stable situation left in Europe by his predecessors would not be disturbed. Now he could concentrate on the East. He renewed the agreements with Venice and Hungary in particular, with increased concessions and trade privileges. Only the efforts of the Russian czar Basil III (1505–1533), Ivan III's successor, to establish good relations were rejected largely because of the objections of the Crimean *han*s, who were resisting Russian advances. Instead, a free hand was given the new Crimean *han* Mehmet Giray (1514–1523), who began strong raids into Russian as well as Polish territory and entered an alliance with the Kazan Hanate to protect the latter from Basil.

War with the Safavids

Selim thus was able to turn to the Safavids. Soon after his accession, Şah Ismail had been temporarily freed from his preoccupation with the Uzbegs and was ready again to support his partisans in Anatolia. Furthermore, the Mamluks, frightened by the Safavid threat to their possessions in Syria and the Holy Cities, concluded a formal alliance with the Ottomans against Ismail (1513), leaving Selim free to concentrate on the Safavids without worrying about the possibility of an attack on his southern flank. Even before the army marched, thousands of *Kızılbaş* followers in Anatolia were slaughtered in the first major campaign ever undertaken to stamp out Muslim heterodoxy in the East. As Selim brought his army through Anatolia in April and May 1514, he continued his ruthless attack on Ismail's followers – often using this as a pretext to eliminate all those who opposed his rule – thus bringing to culmination the centralizing policies begun by Mehmet II. He encountered a major supply problem when Dulgadir refused to help, fearing that an Ottoman victory over the Safavids would be followed by its own demise. Selim countered by shipping in supplies by sea through Trabzon, but the problem remained. The Janissaries already were unhappy because of the severe discipline that he was imposing as well as in consequence of Safavid propaganda. Selim sent away over half of the 140,000 men in his army to ease the supply problem as well as to remove the discontented and prevent the rise of new *Kızılbaş* disturbances as the army advanced.

As the Ottomans moved through Erzincan and Erzurum provinces to the upper reaches of the Euphrates, the Safavids avoided open battle, recognizing Selim's military supremacy and hoping to lure the sultan into northern Iran's mountainous areas, where the terrain and supply problems might well equalize the two forces. As they retreated, Ismail's commanders followed a scorched-earth policy to deprive the Ottomans of supplies that they desperately needed. Despite continued grumblings, Selim pressed onward, executing all the soldiers and commanders who demanded retreat. In mid-August the sultan finally decided to march directly toward Tabriz to force Şah Ismail into battle to defend his capital. Ismail might still have hung back had it not been for the pressure of the *Kızılbaş* tribes, which were angered by Ottoman accusations of cowardice and demanded battle so that they could save face. The climactic battle was finally fought in the valley of Çaldıran, half-way between Erzincan and Tabriz (August 23, 1514). Initial Ottoman defeat was followed by complete victory. Thousands of *Kızılbaş* tribesmen were killed, and the Şah himself, wounded and alone, was able to escape only with great difficulty. Both sides suffered heavy casualties, but only the Ottomans held together as an effective fighting force. Tabriz was occupied, and thousands of its leading merchants, artisans, and learned men were sent back to Istanbul. Nevertheless, Selim decided to evacuate the city, since he could not go on to eliminate the Safavids in the environs or arrange for supplies before winter came. He retired to Karabağ, in the Caucasus, the favorite wintering place of the normadic hordes of the Genghis Han and Tamerlane before him, hoping to return the following year to complete the conquest of Iran. But the resulting Safavid reoccupation of Tabriz, combined with continued problems of supplies and morale, finally forced the sultan to lead his army back into Anatolia. The onslaught of severe winter weather caused the deaths of thousands. The feudal *Sipahis* were demobilized during the retreat, making it certain that Selim would not be able to move quickly against the Safavids in the spring as he had originally planned to do (October 1514).

Selim finally reached Amasya on November 24. He sent most of the Janissaries back to Istanbul for the winter to avoid their constant pleas and bickering, but he prepared for a new spring campaign against the Safavids by sending the feudal army of Rumeli to winter at Ankara instead of having it return home and by stationing his cannon corps nearby at Şebin Karahısar. A delegation from Şah Ismail arrived with peace proposals, but it was imprisoned and the request rejected. On hearing of this the Janissary force that had been left in Amasya revolted once again (February 22, 1515); but since their fellows were mostly dispersed, they lacked the strength to prevail and were reprimanded. Grand Vezir Ahmet Paşa also was dismissed and executed because of his failure to keep the corps in line (March 4, 1515). Selim now made a full purge of the main Janissary commanders, appointing his own slaves in their place to make the corps once again into his instrument of power.

Though Şah Ismail's reoccupation of Tabriz and the rest of Azerbaijan nullified the territorial results of the victory at Çaldıran, the Ottoman victory did assure Ottoman control of Erzincan and Bayburt and lessened Safavid pressure in these areas. Ismail learned to avoid open conflict with the Ottomans. Through the remainder of the sixteenth century and much of the seventeenth century, whenever the Ottomans entered Azerbaijan, the Safavids resorted to a scorched-earth policy, counting on bad weather and supply shortages to force the enemy to relinquish its conquests. After Çaldıran, Ismail lost prestige within Iran, resulting in conflicts for power among the various groups that supported him, which lasted well into the reign of his son and successor, Tahmasp. It became difficult for the Safavids to concentrate on propaganda in Anatolia while Selim's ruthless suppression always hung over those who succumbed to the appeal. Selim's own inability to capitalize on the Çaldıran victory and the difficulties encountered during the campaign convinced him that before going after the Safavids again, he would have to purge dissenters in eastern Anatolia and eliminate the Mamluks, whose military presence in Syria was a threat even when they professed friendship.

The Conquest of Eastern Anatolia

To solidify Ottoman rule in eastern Anatolia Selim first organized a large new frontier province under the governorship of Bıyıklı Mehmet Paşa, who was charged with suppressing the remaining Safavid supporters and conquering the last areas of Anatolia outside Ottoman control. A major campaign took the fort of Kemah, located on a peak overlooking the Euphrates near Erzincan, which the *Kızılbaş* had used to threaten communications between Sivas and Erzurum. In reaction to this new Ottoman push, Dulgadır, the Mamluks, and the Safavids joined in a new alliance, but none dared to act openly, leaving Selim with an important new base for separate moves against the allies. First it was the turn of the smallest, Dulgadır. Selim used a dissident prince to undermine and defeat its army at Turna Dağ (June 12, 1515), after which the remaining members of the dynasty were either executed or absorbed into the Ottoman Ruling Class. Thus while the victory at Çaldıran had solidified Ottoman rule in eastern Anatolia generally, that at Turna Dağ gave the Ottomans final control of Cilicia and opened the way for a move against the Mamluks.

Selim then moved into Kurdistan, the area centered at Diyarbekir and stretching from Lake Urmiya to the Euphrates, partly in Azerbaijan and partly in Anatolia. The Sunni feudal Kurdish chiefs had accepted Safavid suzerainty but asserted their independence following the battle of Çaldıran. Selim realized that any effort to conquer them would have required considerably more military force than he could commit; thus he merely gave the Kurdish chiefs financial and military support, in return for which they switched their loyalty and began to spread pro-Ottoman and pro-Sunni propaganda throughout the area. In charge of this effort was Idris Bitlisi, once scribe for Uzun Hasan, who had been with Selim since Çaldıran and was very knowledgeable about Kurdish traditions and feelings. He now became governor of Kurdistan. Despite Safavid resistance, Bitlisi was able to capture Diyarbekir and Mardin, which then became the centers of the new province. While the vassal system had been abandoned elsewhere in the empire, it was retained here, with the Kurdish beys accepting the sultan's suzerainty and in return being appointed as hereditary governors of their own districts with full autonomy. Insofar as the Kurds were concerned, Safavid suzerainty was replaced by that of the Ottomans, with the local beys remaining as independent as they had been previously.

The conquests in eastern Anatolia enabled the sultan to control the main strategic passes leading from Anatolia into the Caucasus, Syria, and Iran, as well as to organize defense lines and mobilize attacks into these areas. Control of the international trade routes that brought the silks of Iran and other products of the East from Tabriz to Aleppo and to Bursa gave the Ottoman treasury important new sources of revenue and enabled Selim to cut off Iran's flourishing silk trade with the West whenever he wished. Finally, by controlling Mamluk access to their principal sources of slaves in the Caucasus, Selim could pressure them from different directions at this crucial time.

Internal Reforms

While Idris Bitlisi was busy in the East, Selim managed to spend some time in Istanbul – one of the rare occasions during his reign – attempting to carry on his father's work of reinvigorating the government and army. In the area of administration he concentrated on organizing the system of justice, introducing new codes of criminal law, and providing provincial judges and administrative officials with effective means of enforcing their judgments. Selim also worked to enlarge the trade of his empire, getting the Mamluk governor of Aleppo, Hayır Bey, to divert its international caravans north into Anatolia instead of south into Egypt, at the same time cutting off all trade from the Ottoman dominions into Iran and Egypt. Only when Selim was satisfied that these measures were successful did he finally leave Istanbul on his new eastern expedition.

Conquest of the Arab World

Now that Selim was ready to resume an aggressive policy in the east, he had to decide whom to attack: the still powerful Safavids or the fast-weakening Mamluks. The latter were suffering considerably from Portugese naval moves into the eastern seas. Beginning in 1502 Portugal had established itself in India and begun a naval campaign to compel all trade between it and Europe to use the all-water route around southern Africa, which it controlled. The capture of Socotra in the Gulf of Aden (1507) and of Hormuz on the Persian Gulf (1508) enabled it to enforce this blockade even more completely, causing a permanent crisis in Mamluk economy and the state budget. Şah Ismail, while not terribly anxious for Europeans to monopolize the Persian Gulf, which he had only just reached, was willing to help the Portugese by supplying their ships in return for their support against the Ottomans. Selim responded by sending guns, gunpowder, and some naval supplies to the Mamluks as well as shipwrights and seamen to help rebuild the Mamluk Red Sea fleet (January 1511). Despite this, however, the Mamluks feared – and with considerable justification – that Selim wished to preserve their empire only to keep it for himself; thus they maintained their neutrality in the Ottoman-Safavid conflict. Selim also had good strategic reasons for wanting to take Mamluk territory, since control of the ports of Cilicia would enable him to use a sea route, most likely from Istanbul to Payas, so that he could supply his subsequent expeditions against the Şafavids far more successfully than had been the case in the Çaldıran campaign.

As the Ottoman army moved through Anatolia in the spring of 1516, there was doubt in Cairo as to where it would go: again into Azerbaijan against the Safavids or into Syria. The Mamluks moved their main army across the Euphrates and into the Taurus in fear of the latter course, despite Selim's protestations to the contrary as well as the opposition of most of the leading Mamluk commanders and governors, who feared they might draw Selim into a battle for which they were not really prepared. Led by Hayır Bey, governor of Aleppo, who already had been in contact with Istanbul, many of the leading Mamluk officials secretly sent messages of support to Selim promising cooperation if he did invade Syria and asking for high positions and revenues in return. It would seem, in fact, that Selim had not yet decided where he should go. It was only after he learned that the Mamluk sultan al-Gawri was advancing into Anatolia that he decided that this immediate danger would have to come first while the Safavids waited.

Selim's army moved into Mamluk territory near Malatya on July 28, 1516. The Ottoman conquest of the Mamluk Empire then followed with amazing rapidity. Mamluk resistance was sapped by the desertion of many of their leading officials and by the disinclination of the Syrian population to support the losing side. The only major battle between the two sides came at Marc Dabik, near Aleppo (August 24, 1516), with Ottoman discipline, weapons, and tactics securing easy victory. Selim then swept quickly through the rest of Syria, taking Aleppo (August 28), Hama (September 19), and Damascus (September 27), in each case being welcomed by the local populations and governors. Al-Gawri died at Marc Dabik. While the Mamluks back in Cairo appointed a new sultan, Tuman Bay (October 11), his efforts to form a new army in Egypt met with only limited success. As Selim marched through Syria, he managed to conciliate the principal towns and provinces as well as the Bedouin tribal leaders and chiefs of the Muslim and non-Muslim religious groups. The Greek Orthodox had already been given their autonomous *millet* following the conquest of Constantinople, but the Armenian Gregorians were given their separate status only now in return for support against the Mamluks, with their patriarch promising loyalty and obedience to the sultan and his successors in return.[8]

The Ottoman army crossed the Sinai Peninsula with all its heavy equipment and cannon in only five days (January 11–16, 1517), a truly remarkable achievement. Tuman Bay led his new army in an effort to resist at Ridâniyye, which commanded the road coming from the Sinai to Cairo, but Selim outflanked the prepared Mamluk positions and overwhelmed them in a single day (January 22, 1517), with over 25,000 of the defenders being killed. Selim offered to pardon all the Mamluks who surrendered without resistance in the hope of taking Cairo intact as a fully functioning center of government and economic life (January 25, 1517). Tuman Bay and some of his commanders organized guerrilla resistance, however, so that the city was taken only after a vicious three-day battle, with the city partially wrecked and thousands killed as a result. In addition, the Mamluks continued their resistance in the Delta and Upper Egypt, and it was only some time later that Ottoman rule was fully established throughout the country. Tuman Bay himself was captured and executed on April 13, 1517, and afterward whatever Mamluk resistance remained was concentrated in Upper Egypt. With the Mamluk dynasty thus extinguished, Ottoman rule in Egypt was secure. As a matter of fact, it was only now that Selim received testaments of loyalty from the chiefs of the major bedouin tribes as well as from the şerif of Mecca (July 3), thus giving him control of the Holy Cities of Islam without the need of mounting a further expedition. In return, Selim's appointment of the şerif as governor of Cidde and Hicaz as well as of Mecca and Medina established a precedent for his successors.

Soon afterward, the Ottoman fleet arrived in Alexandria bringing the provisions

Selim needed to march his army back to Anatolia without having to live off the land in Egypt and Syria. The fleet was sent back to Istanbul with the caliph al-Mutawakkil and some 2000 leading Egyptian merchants, artisans, and religious leaders, thus beginning the process by which the leaders of the old centers of Islam were absorbed into the Ottoman system and traditional Islamic ways and culture were given renewed vigor. Men trained in the Arab and Persian civil services now entered Ottoman administration, influencing its structures and operations.

It was soon after the fleet returned to Istanbul, according to an old legend, that the caliph transferred his rights to Selim and his successors. This story seems to be supported by references in contemporary chronicles to Istanbul's and Edirne's being the "seat of the caliphate." But other contemporary evidence seems to refute the idea, if for no other reason than the Ottoman family did not fulfill the legal bonds of relationship with the family of the Prophet and also since al-Mutawakkil returned to Cairo and took up his caliphal duties there until 1543. The Ottomans did use the title caliph for a time after the conquest of the Arab world, but this was an old practice among Muslim rulers after they achieved something of distinction. It was in fact by the much more important titles of sultan and "Servant and Protector of the Holy Places" that Selim and his successors sought to be remembered – the idea of caliph being used only to emphasize their preeminence in the Islamic world and right to promote and defend the Muslim religion and law. By extending the gazi tradition, the Ottoman sultans came to stress their role as leaders and defenders of the entire Islamic world, thus using a new interpretation of the caliphate to establish Ottoman mastery over Islamic peoples. Real Ottoman claims to the caliphate were made only in the era of weakness, in the eighteenth century, particularly after the Treaty of Küçük Kaynarca, when Russia allowed the sultan to maintain certain religious rights in the Crimea as caliph of the Muslims, a claim that was recognized by the Russians although not by the Muslim doctors.

Selim thus made a major addition to the empire built by his ancestors. Using the new army built by Mehmet II and basing himself on the strategic and administrative foundations left by Mehmet and Bayezit II, he defeated the Safavids and extended the Ottoman Empire to include a significant part of the classical Islamic empires, with only Iran, part of Iraq, Horasan, and Transoxania remaining under Safavid rule.

Internal Reforms

With peace in both the east and the west Selim was able to spend some time in Istanbul building the state and army as bases for subsequent moves. The sultan enlarged the Janissary corps by expanding the *devşirme* recruitment system and by building a new school at Galata Saray to provide training for the young men brought into his palace, supplementing the cramped and inadequate quarters previously used at the Topkapı Palace and the imperial palace in Edirne. Magnificent new buildings were provided for the school on the heights of Galata, with a mosque, *medrese,* barracks, and kitchens. It was a center of Islamic life and the first large-scale Muslim settlement outside old Istanbul. An elaborate system of classification and training was established for the *devşirme* youths, with the best of them set aside for palace service and the rest sent subsequently to Anatolia for physical training before they entered the *kapıkulu* slave army.

Selim also completed the job of moving the Ottoman government to Istanbul from

Edirne, where many of the offices had remained long after the capital was moved. Scribes, soldiers, palace women, and the like, were transferred to the Topkapı Palace; when it became too crowded, a new small palace, the *Yalı Köşk,* was built on the shores of the Sea of Marmara between Sirkeci and Sarayburnu to provide the sultan and his chosen women with special solitude.

Major efforts were made to build a new and more powerful Ottoman fleet that could take advantage of Bayezit's victory over Venice to expand into the western Mediterranean against both the Spanish Habsburgs and France and also move to end the Portugese blockade in the eastern seas, which had seriously damaged the Arab world before the Ottoman conquest. A major new shipyard was built in the Golden Horn of Istanbul, at a place called Kasımpaşa, while the older shipyards at Gallipoli and Kadırga were rebuilt and expanded. In addition to the officers and shipwrights already at hand the leader of the Mamluk Red Sea fleet, Selman Reis, and his commanders and artisans were transported to Istanbul (May 1518); the Mediterranean and Black Sea shores were scoured for experienced seamen; and much of the booty of conquest coming from Egypt was poured into the building of ships and the training and organizing of men. By the end of Selim's reign, then, the Ottomans had a large, modern, and well-organized navy that caused increasing concern to all those having naval interests in the Mediterranean and the eastern seas. Use of the fleet, however, was left to Selim's successor, Süleyman the Magnificent.

Beginnings of the Celali Movement

The only major military concern to Selim in his last years was the rise of new difficulties among the Turkomans of eastern Anatolia, whose discontent remained long after the Safavids had ceased providing them with direct encouragement. The Turkomans resented the efforts of the central government to extend its control into the areas where they had roamed freely for so long. Their heterodox religious beliefs – at least partly an expression of their desire for political separatism – led them to oppose efforts to spread the institutions and beliefs of orthodox Islam, which now were made the basis of the Ottoman dynasty. The bloody manner in which Selim had suppressed the Safavid supporters added to the resentment and discontent. In 1519 a new nomad revolt broke out near Tokat, led by a man called Celal, a Safavid preacher who had escaped Selim's net and built a wide following while the sultan was in Egypt. Claiming to be the *Mahdi,* he also attracted cultivators and urban elements that were discontented with Selim's taxes. He took the name Şah Ismail and had considerable success until his army was attacked and destroyed by the Janissaries (April 24, 1519), with thousands slaughtered. Celal's name lived on, however, and movements of dissent in Anatolia in the next two centuries were called Celali revolts.

On July 18, 1520, Selim set out from Istanbul for Edirne. Historians are uncertain of his exact intentions. Some sources claim that he was planning an expedition against Hungary in revenge for its border raids; others that he merely wanted to plan a naval campaign against Cyprus or Rhodes or against a Crusader fleet that the pope was said to be preparing. Before he left, he had been complaining of pains in his back. When he reached the village of Sırt, near Çorlu, he could not go on. There he became increasingly ill and died on September 21, 1520, apparently of a carbuncle, although some sources indicate the plague or even cancer. Thus ended the meteoric career of one of the greatest conquerors in Islamic history.

The Peak of Ottoman Grandeur: Süleyman I the Magnificent, 1520–1566

No other prince of the house of Osman was able to take the throne with such advantages as those left to Süleyman I in 1520. There were no princes to dispute his right to rule, no one whom divergent political groups could use to secure their own power. Selim also left the Janissary corps to the new sultan as his instrument of power to control all elements of the Ruling Class to an extent never equaled before or after. The conquests of Bayezit II and Selim I left Süleyman in an unrivaled strategic position in both the east and the west. The Mamluks were gone. The Safavids and Venice were cowed; and while the rising Habsburg Empire was replacing Hungary as the main rival north of the Danube, its full strength had not yet been achieved. The powerful navy built during the previous quarter-century gave Süleyman a new weapon that he could use to fight his enemies at sea as well as on land. Selim's conquest of the lands of the old Islamic caliphate also left the new sultan with vast sources of revenue and with so much prestige in the Islamic world that he was, indeed, able to bring his empire to a peak of prosperity and grandeur that well justified the appellation of "the Magnificent" and the "Grand Turk" incarnate applied to him in Europe. Süleyman also brought to the throne a depth of experience as an administrator and a soldier sufficient not only to conquer but also to centralize, unify, and codify the administration of a state that had been molded out of many peoples, traditions, and civilizations. Known to his own people as *Kanuni*, the "Law Giver," he remained one of the greatest of all Ottoman military leaders, accompanying and leading his army on 13 major campaigns as well as numerous minor ones, spending over 10 years in the field, and, with an energy and intensity surpassed by few, conquering far beyond the boundaries left by his predecessors.

Internal Reforms

Süleyman began his reign with a campaign to secure justice and virtue in order to gain for himself the loyalty of those subjects alienated by his father's forceful policies. No more unpopular measure had been pursued by Selim than the one prohibiting trade with Iran – the Ottoman merchants suffered as much as their Persian counterparts. Now these prohibitions were ended, the goods that had been confiscated returned, and compensation paid. Artisans and intellectuals brought to Istanbul from Azerbaijan and Egypt were allowed to return to their homes if they wished, although liberal incentives ultimately induced most to remain. Süleyman attempted to build a system of justice to end the possibility of violent and arbitrary actions such as those of Selim and Mehmet II, and he substituted a new emphasis on protection for the lives, property, and honor of individuals regardless of religion. A day after taking the throne, he decreed that soldiers should pay for all provisions taken along the paths of their campaigns in Ottoman or enemy territory. Taxes were levied only according to the ability to pay, with the extra taxes and confiscations of his predecessors prohibited. The system of courts previously established was enlarged, and additional police and inspectors were charged with seeing that the court decrees and the laws were obeyed. The administration was reorganized, with officials admonished that violations of the rights of the subjects would be treated with severity. Dismissals came only for good reason, not because of the whims of the sultan and the higher officials of state. Only merit was to be considered in the appointment, assignment, and promotion of officials, and palace intervention in administrative affairs was to end. Hundreds of legal scholars and jurists were brought into the sultan's service. As the years went on, whether Süleyman was campaigning or in Istanbul, laws and law codes were issued that institutionalized and defined the structure of government as well as the rights and responsibilities of all members of the Ruling Class as well as the subjects of the sultan.

Alternating Campaigns and Internal Problems

Much of Süleyman's life, however, was devoted to a series of campaigns, partly forced on him and partly because of his desire to resume his father's work of building a world empire. One of Süleyman's greatest accomplishments in these campaigns was his success in avoiding conflict on different fronts in the same year. The army had feudal contingents that had to return to their fiefs in the winter to secure their revenues and replenish their men and equipment. Each campaign had to begin anew each spring from Istanbul, with the rare exception of those years when the sultan remained in the field during the winter so that he could begin the next year's march without having to undergo the long preliminary march from the capital to the frontier. In view of the need for beginning in Istanbul it would have been almost impossible for the sultan to fight in the east and the west during the same year. But because he held the initiative and since his enemies held him in such awe that they rarely chose to initiate conflict with the Ottomans on their own, this problem was avoided. This situation did mean, however, that he had to alternate his campaigns in the east and the west so that he could keep all his enemies off balance and not allow any of them to forget the brunt of his military might.

Süleyman's primary ambitions early in his reign were in Europe. But first he had to deal with several problems that arose soon after his accession. One was a revolt of the former Mamluks who had entered Selim's service in Syria, led by Canberdi al-Gazzâli, the governor of Damascus, who hoped to take Egypt and establish a restored Mamluk Empire while the new sultan was busy in the West. But while Damascus fell easily to the rebels, the Ottoman governor of Aleppo was able to organize the feudal forces of the areas and suppress the rebels by the end of 1527. To stabilize Ottoman rule in the area the old Mamluk administrative organizations and leaders were eliminated and replaced by the regular Ottoman feudal system, with the sole exception of Mount Lebanon, which was given special autonomous status under its feudal leaders.

The second problem to occupy Süleyman's attention was the island of Rhodes, a dangerous outpost of Christianity in an otherwise Ottoman sea. The pirates of Rhodes were capturing large numbers of ships bringing grain and gold from the new Arab provinces and carrying pilgrims to and from the Holy Cities, thus threatening the sultan's prestige as well as his pockets. Strategic as well as political reasons impelled Süleyman to neutralize Rhodes before moving into central Europe. A major expeditionary force mounted a prolonged siege during the summer of 1522. Pitted against the Ottomans were some 60,000 defenders manning one of the strongest forts known to the world at the time. Assault after assault was thrown back until Ottoman agents among the Jews and Muslim women enslaved by the Knights enabled the sultan's forces to break in and force a surrender (December 20, 1522). By its terms all inhabitants wishing to leave the island were allowed to go, and the Knights could take their weapons and other belongings. Those who remained were exempted from taxes for five years and given the same conditions of freedom of religion found elsewhere in the sultan's dominions. Thus in fact few inhabitants left. The Knights, however, were transported on papal ships to Malta, which they fortified and built into a new base of anti-Muslim operation in the heart of the central Mediterranean. With Rhodes in Ottoman hands, however, the eastern Mediterranean was now safe.

This settlement, however, was followed by a serious revolt in Egypt that prevented the sultan from moving to the West for some time. As in Syria, former Mamluks attempted to use the sultan's absence to make themselves independent. The situation in Egypt was somewhat different, though, because Hayır Bey, the former Mamluk who had been made the first Ottoman governor in the country, remained loyal to the sultan until his death in October 1522. It was only when he was eventually succeeded by an Ottoman official, Arnavut Ahmet Paşa (August 20, 1523), embittered over the sultan's failure to appoint him grand vezir, that the Mamluks found the leader they needed to coalesce into an open revolt. Within a short time Ahmet Paşa put his own men in command of the Janissary garrison left to represent the sultan's interest. Ottoman financial and administrative officers left there by Selim to check the governor's powers were replaced by Mamluks. The land tax revenues that had been administered by salaried Ottoman tax collectors for the benefit of the central treasury were transformed into fiefs and turned over to leading Mamluks. In January 1524 Arnavut Ahmet openly revolted against the sultan. He declared himself sultan of Egypt and had his name stamped on the new coins and mentioned in the Friday prayers. However, the Janissary garrison managed to hold out in the Cairo citadel. Within a short time Ahmet's tyrannical rule managed to alienate most of the people and notables of the country, leading to his assassination during a local uprising (1525) even before the Ottomans in Istanbul were able to react to the revolt.

Süleyman then sent Grand Vezir Ibrahim Paşa with a new expedition to Egypt to reorganize the administrative system to ensure that no similar revolt would be possible in the future. Ibrahim followed two policies: On one hand, he ruthlessly suppressed all those who had questioned the sultan's authority, including the last Mamluks, who were either executed or sent to serve elsewhere in the empire, and many of the bedouin tribes, which had sought to use the revolt to make themselves independent once again. On the other hand, Ibrahim worked to gain mass support for Ottoman rule by applying the same ideals of justice that Süleyman had insisted on elsewhere. Those whose properties had been confiscated during the conquest or revolt were compensated. The poor who had been imprisoned for debt were freed, their private debts being paid by the treasury. Buildings and irrigation systems destroyed during and after the conquest were rebuilt, and efforts were made to restore normal life and economic pursuits throughout the province. Tax concessions were made to induce the cultivators to return to the land and restore it to cultivation. Educational and charitable institutions were established and endowed out of the sultan's own possessions. And, finally, to prevent future revolts, Ibrahim introduced a complicated system of checks and balances to replace Selim's system of concentrating powers in the governor's hand. The entire province was made more or less the tax farm of the governor, who was required to deliver a fixed sum to Istanbul each year and allowed to keep the balance as profit for himself after paying for certain Ottoman obligations in the Holy Cities and for the annual pilgrimage from Egypt. As a check on him, the treasurer, the chief mufti, and the commander of the garrison were appointed by and responsible directly to Istanbul and were specifically enjoined to watch him as well as each other to make certain that the laws of the sultan and the rights of his subjects were not violated. To assure that most of Egypt's revenues would be sent to Istanbul in cash or kind, it was arranged that all the country's tax revenues, whether from agricultural or urban sources, would be collected by tax farmers rather than as fiefs, with the collectors being bound to deliver fixed annual sums to the treasury before retaining the balance as profit for themselves.

A number of Ottoman military corps, led by the Janissaries, were stationed thereafter in Egypt to garrison the country, but they were prohibited from holding or operating the tax farms. Thus they would be dependent on their treasury salaries and under its control. To ensure that there would be no locally based class that might rise to take over the province, it was further specified that no Egyptian who entered the Ottoman Ruling Class could serve in Egypt, that Mamluks who accepted the sultan's rule could enter his service but elsewhere in the empire, and that no Ottoman official could serve in the province for more than two years. The provincial structure established in Egypt by Ibrahim was so successful that it was extended to all other nonfeudal provinces of the empire in later years.

In the meantime, the rise of Ibrahim Paşa to the grand vezirate marked a fundamental change in the politics of the Ottoman Ruling Class. Frenk Ibrahim, as he was known, had come into the Ottoman system as a youth captured in a raid near his home at Parga, Italy, in the time of Bayezit II. His triumph over his Turkish predecessor, Piri Mehmet, marked the final triumph of the *devşirme* class over the old Turkish aristocracy. *Devşirme* men assumed a larger and larger proportion of the principal positions of state, whereas most members of the Turkish aristocracy were forced to retire to their estates in Anatolia, where they began to intrigue against the Istanbul government, contributing significantly to the Celali revolts that were to shake the dynasty later in the century. By this time, however, the old distinctions between the *devşirme* party and members of the old Turkish aristocracy and their descendants were modified because the Turks and Muslims serving the sultan now included in their number many descendents of *devşirme* men who because of intermixture with Turkish women and training had come to identify themselves with the opposition to the *devşirme*.

The *devşirme* – no longer challenged by the Turkish aristocracy – divided into political groupings formed by individual leaders to gain power and wealth for themselves rather than for their class. Just beginning to participate in the resulting power struggles were the sultan's mother, Hafsa Hatun, and other women in the harem, who began to promote the candidacy of their children and to work for influence over the sultan and in the government by cooperating with one or another of the political parties. It appears that Ibrahim's Paşa's triumph was the result of the intrigues of the party that he led jointly with Arnavut Ahmet Paşa and in cooperation with the sultan's wife Roxelana (Hürrem Sultan), a woman of Russian origin captured in Galicia by the Crimean Tatars. Hürrem Sultan contributed to the plot by exciting Süleyman's suspicions of the last Turkish grand vezir, Piri Mehmet, who as a result of his military victories had begun to dominate the young sultan. As we have seen, Ibrahim's triumph had been followed by Arnavut Ahmet's assignment to Egypt and subsequent revolt. If it marked anything, therefore, it was less the triumph of the *devşirme* as a class than the beginning of the process by which the Ottoman system came to be dominated by the political parties and the women of the harem. It also marked the beginning of the process by which the sultans increasingly relied on their chief ministers, who began to use their power for their own benefit rather than that of the sultans and the empire. Ibrahim was given additional positions and revenues, making him the second most powerful individual in the empire. His marriage to Hatice Sultan, daughter of Selim I, symbolized the prestige enjoyed by him and his successors, who tended to dominate the sultans in the middle years of the sixteenth century despite all the efforts of the latter to free themselves.

The First Hungarian Campaign

In Europe Süleyman's primary objective was Hungary. Initially an independent kingdom, then an autonomous vassal cooperating against the Habsburgs, it was finally annexed directly to the Ottoman Empire, bringing the Ottomans and the Habsburgs into direct contact. The kingdom of Hungary, ruled by Louis II, was sapped by a combination of royal incompetence and corruption, internal division over the family ties with the Habsburgs, and feudal appetites for control over both the king and the peasants. The smaller nobles, led by John Zapolya, prince of Transylvania, developed a national movement in opposition both to the crown and to Habsburg influence, while the oppressed peasants turned toward the new Protestant movement as a means of expressing their dissatisfaction with the establishment. The marriage of Louis II's sister Anna to Archduke Ferdinand I, brother of Emperor Charles V and his agent in Austria, gave the latter a claim to the Hungarian throne that before too long would place the Habsburgs in direct conflict with the Ottomans.

Süleyman's initial campaigns in Europe were directed toward eliminating the last Christian enclaves along the southern banks of the Drava and Danube, in Serbia and Bosnia, to pave the way for further conquests to the north. On August 8, 1520, the most important of these, the great fort of Belgrade, was taken by siege, breaching the Danube defense line of Christian Europe and bringing the last part of Serbia into Ottoman hands. Sabatz now became the center of a newly organized Muslim frontier province, with a group of *akıncıs* being stationed here to raid northward into Habsburg Austria. There Ferdinand organized his own frontier warrior society, getting the Croatians and Bosnians to ask for Habsburg occupation and support, with the sovereign rights of their rulers being preserved only formally. The pope attempted to secure general European support against the Ottomans, but Süleyman managed once again to detach Venice and Ragusa, giving them new trade privileges to keep their navies out of the Christian coalition. Christian unity against the Ottomans was further shattered by rivalry between the Habsburgs and France, then ruled by Francis I (1515–1547), with the anti-French alliances formed among the Habsburgs, the pope, and England impelling the French to seek Ottoman support. Francis I's defeat and capture by Charles V and subsequent surrender of his lands in Spain and Italy led France to cultivate the sultan's friendship and encourage Ottoman aggression against the Habsburgs from the south.

Because of internal diversions in the east, the initial Ottoman advance into Hungary was delayed until the spring of 1526. The Hungarians mobilized very slowly because of feudal unwillingness to strengthen the king and the defection of large number of Zapolya-led small notables, who feared that by fighting the Ottomans they would strengthen the Catholic and Habsburg elements in the country. The defenders challenged Süleyman's force at the plain of Mohacs, on the right bank of the Danube south of Buda (August 29, 1526). But Louis' poorly organized and scattered force was no match for the mightiest military force of the time, particularly the sultan's artillery. During the flight of the defeated army toward the Danube, the king and most of his men were killed. Buda and Pest fell 10 days later. The Ottomans occupied most of the country with the exception of the northern and western strips, which remained in Habsburgs hands. Süleyman, deciding not to attempt a full occupation and annexation because of competing demands for his attention in the East, accepted the offer of Zapolya and his associates to acknowledge Ottoman suzerainty and pay tribute if they were left in control of the country (September 24, 1526). Ottoman garrisons remained in only a few places but took over the remaining Hungarian possessions in Bosnia, making possible new raids into Habsburg territory in Croatia and Slavonia. Most of the Ottoman army, however, retired with the sultan, leaving Hungary under native rule.

Revolts in Anatolia, 1526–1528

In Anatolia the Turkomans were resisting the efforts of the governor, Ferhad Paşa, to establish direct control and end their autonomy. Local discontent was fanned by Safavid propaganda, which, though it had already ceased during Şah Ismail's later years, now was resumed under his son and successor, Tahmasp, who wanted to take advantage of the sultan's diversion in Hungary. In addition, the *devşirme* triumph in Istanbul and the consequent return to Anatolia of most members of the Turkish aristocracy gave the Celali movement a distinctly Turkish character, emphasizing resentment against *devşirme* domination in Istanbul. The first major Celali revolt came at Bozok, where the Turkoman nomads were led by a local sufi preacher, Baba Zünnûn, in resisting the efforts of the *sancak* bey to carry out a cadastral survey as the first step toward establishing a regular timar and tax system (August 28, 1526). This uprising was crushed by the local feudal forces, but a whole series of Celali uprisings followed in Cilicia and central Anatolia during the late months of 1526 and the early part of 1527. The most serious of these was led by Kalender Çelebi, who with the claim of being a descendant of Hacı Bektaş raised a large group of Turkoman rebels. He seems also to have attracted thousands of Turkomans from Elbistan who resented the suppression of the Dulgadır dynasty and also a number of non-Turkoman townsmen who were suffering from the misrule of Ferhad Paşa. It was this revolt in particular that caused the sultan to return. The initial Ottoman expedition against Kalender was routed at Gencefe (Karaçayır), with the governor of Karaman and leading *sancak* beys killed (June 8, 1527). It was only after Ibrahim undermined rebel support in the Elbistan area by restoring the lands of the surviving Dulgadır princes and promising full autonomy to the local Turkoman chiefs that the Ottomans were able to defeat and kill Kalender (June 22, 1527) and disperse his army.

The Second Hungarian Expedition, 1527–1529

In the meantime, however, the Habsburgs had upset the settlement left by Süleyman in Hungary. As soon as the Kalender revolt had been quelled, then, the sultan was forced into a new campaign. Zapolya had been chosen king of Hungary by a majority of the nobles at the Tokay diet (September 16, 1527). For the moment the Habsburgs did nothing, since Charles V was immersed in his second war in France (1527–1529), while Ferdinand was preoccupied with establishing his rights in Austria and Bohemia and resisting the spread of the Reformation. But the Hungarian nobles who supported the Habsburgs encouraged them to occupy the northern and western parts of Hungary while Zapolya was busy in Transylvania. The latter appealed for help from Sigismund I of Poland, but while the Polish country gentry sympathized with the Hungarian nationalists, the great nobles were divided, forcing Sigismund to temporize. This enabled Ferdinand to defeat Zapolya at Tokay (September 26, 1527) and occupy most of the country and then to be proclaimed king at the old Hungarian capital at Bratislava/Pressburg (December 17), although the Ottoman garrisons barred him from the south and Bosnia.

In reaction to the Habsburg invasion Zapolya made an agreement with the Otto-mans (February 28, 1528) by which he reacknowledged the sultan's suzerainty to secure a new invasion to drive Ferdinand out. Süleyman preferred to leave an autonomous Hungary under Zapolya's rule to act as a buffer against the Habsburgs rather than to commit the troops and resources that would be needed for direct occu-pation and control of the country. The result was the second Ottoman invasion of Hungary starting in the summer of 1528. With the Habsburgs preoccupied, Süley-man was able to reoccupy Buda (September 3, 1529) and the remainder of the coun-try with little difficulty. He then mounted the first Ottoman siege of Vienna (Septem-ber 27–October 15, 1529) in the hope of either capturing the Habsburg capital or at least so disrupting the Austrian military system that Ferdinand would be unable to threaten Hungary for some time to come. However, the season was too late. The attackers were unable to secure sufficient supplies and ammunition due to the early arrival of winter. Meanwhile, Charles was able to make peace with Francis at Cam-brai (August 3, 1529) and to send reinforcements. While the suburbs of Vienna were largely destroyed, the walls pierced in many places and the defenders suffering severely, Vienna held out even after Ferdinand and most of his court had fled. The Janissary corps – already unhappy because the sultan had not allowed it to ravage Buda – again became restless. Turkish raiders began going through the Alps into southern Germany, reaching Ratisbon in Bavaria and Brunn (Brno) in Bohemia. Europe was in a panic. If the sultan had held out only a little longer, his forces might well have broken into Vienna, where they could have remained for the winter before pushing onward. But the combination of difficulties finally convinced Süleyman to return to Istanbul for the winter. Therefore, the siege was broken off and Vienna saved for Christianity.

The first Ottoman effort to move into central Europe thus came to naught. Under existing conditions of supply and transport the Ottomans had reached the limit of viable expansion in the West from a winter base that had to be maintained in Istanbul due to the need to disperse the feudal troops so that they could exploit their fiefs, maintain themselves, and be prepared to meet the constant threat of military action in either the East or the West. But the siege of Vienna did have a number of important results. First, it secured Ottoman possession of Hungary as well as the new vassal relationship with Zapolya. Second, it left Austria and northern Hungary so ravaged that Ferdinand was incapable of launching a successful counterattack. Third, it did, therefore, enforce the status quo, with Habsburg rule continuing in the northern and western border areas of Hungary while the rest of the country remained under autonomous native rule, thus continuing to serve as a buffer between the super-powers to the north and the south.

The Third Hungarian Expedition, 1532

At this point neither side was anxious to resume the conflict. The Muslim threat to Vienna had shocked western Europe into advocating a new Crusade. Even Francis I promised to join Charles V in a joint campaign. But now it was Ferdinand who, through bitter experience, hesitated to act. Charles also cooled to the idea when he found that neither the pope nor Francis I would modify his claims in northern Italy to get the former's support. Hence the Habsburg leaders decided to concentrate on repairing their defenses and remedying the difficulties caused by the Reformation. Süleyman also wanted to refrain from campaigns so that he would have time to estab-lish the system of justice proposed at the time he took the throne. But Ferdinand's continued claims to be king of Hungary and a new Habsburg siege of Buda (December 23, 1530) convinced the sultan that he would have to undertake a new campaign, not only to restore the situation in Hungary but to destroy the German Empire and make it clear that the sultan of the Ottomans was the supreme ruler of all the world.

Unlike the 1529 expedition, then, which extended to the gates of Vienna only by chance, as the result of a last-minute decision following a quick victory in Hungary, the expedition of 1532 was specifically aimed at central Europe. Süleyman marched through Hungary in July and August, bringing together a massive force of almost 300,000 men. He crossed the Raab into Austria and sent out raiders in all directions in the hope of forcing the main Habsburg army into battle. However, he was unable to find it, and when the small fortress town of Guns (Koeszegh), on the Raab 100 kilometers southeast of Vienna, held out, his timetable was so set back that he finally decided to abandon the expedition without achieving its objective. Süleyman sent his raiders throughout Austria. They devastated widely in order to draw the Habsburgs out but without success; thus the sultan retired back into Hungary as winter came, sending his raiders down the Drava and into the Austrian frontier zone in Croatia and Slovenia before returning home.

The third Hungarian campaign thus had no immediate result. The Habsburgs were not defeated. Ferdinand was left in a position to reoccupy southern Austria as well as northern and western Hungary as soon as the sultan's army had left. The danger to Zapolya was not removed. At most, what Süleyman had done was to shock Austria and most of Europe by the depth of his penetration, causing Charles to make concessions to the Protestants in Germany to gain their support, a major factor in the subsequent survival and expansion of the Lutheran movement throughout western Europe. The campaign also convinced Süleyman that large-scale operations of this kind could not secure more territory for him under the existing conditions of transportation and warfare. He therefore agreed to a peace, mediated by Poland: Ferdinand recognized the sultan as "father and suzerain," accepted the grand vezir as "brother" and equal in rank, and abandoned his claims to rule in Hungary other than those border areas that he had occupied since the original Ottoman conquest. In return for these he agreed to pay a regular annual tribute to the sultan. Süleyman had achieved his basic aims in Hungary: he had not conquered and annexed it, but he had assured the rule of a friendly vassal who remained as a buffer against possible Habsburg expansion in the future (June 1533).

The peace of 1533 was followed by organization of new frontier garrisons on both sides, forming the basis of the relatively stable future frontier between the Ottomans and Habsburgs. On the Austrian side a vast chain of fortified villages, walls, blockhouses, and watchtowers was created and guarded by groups of hired mercenaries as well as permanent colonists settled under the supervision and control of Vienna rather than the less reliable local nobles. On the Ottomans' side frontier districts, called *derbent*s, were created, bringing to the Danube the system that had worked so well in earlier centuries of Muslim advance against the infidel world. Here the frontier was divided into *sancak* districts, each under the military and administrative control of a *sancak* bey. These in turn were divided into timars, whose holders used their revenues to maintain raiders as well as mounted *Sipahi* cavalrymen. Unlike the regular timar provinces, however, where the *Sipahi*s settled and administered the lands in their timars, here they stayed together in the main fortified towns – Buda, Temesvar, Belgrade, Gran, and so on – while the lands were administered and guarded by their hired mercenaries, often retired Janissaries and other soldiers who preferred to settle down in this way.

Conquest of Mesopotamia

The peace agreements made in 1533 left Süleyman relatively free of land engagements in Europe for almost a decade. This allowed him to deal with the Safavids and Anatolia once again, to build a new fleet to meet the challenges of the Portugese in the eastern seas and the Habsburgs in the western Mediterranean, and also to settle personally the political and administrative problems of his empire.

Most pressing was the long-postponed campaign against the Safavids, who had been stirring Turkoman uprisings in Anatolia even as Şah Tahmasp had been working to build his own central government in Iran. Though Kurdistan had been conquered after Çaldıran, central and southern Iraq, including Baghdad and Basra, had remained in Safavid hands, and efforts were being made to establish the Shia heresy in place of orthodox Islam in the lands that had been the heartland of the Abbasid caliphate. Orthodox doctors who refused to accept the new doctrines were executed and tombs and other orthodox Sunni shrines destroyed, including those of the venerated Abu Hanifa and Abd ul-Kadir Gilani. Leading Sunni scholars were killed and the main mosques converted to the Shia rites. While not extensive, some conversions did take place, and those remaining faithful to orthodoxy were subjected to persecution. As leader of the orthodox Muslim world Süleyman could not remain indifferent. In addition, there were new economic reasons for an attack. Safavid control of Iraq as well as Iran had hindered land trade between the Far East and Europe, while Portugese control of the eastern seas added to what had become a general blockade of all the old routes between the East and the West through a Middle East that was now under Ottoman control.

Within three months after the peace treaty with Austria was signed, Grand Vezir Ibrahim Paşa was heading toward Kurdistan in command of whatever army could be mobilized (October 1533), while the sultan remained behind to organize the rest of the army and bring it east as soon as possible. Ibrahim occupied the area between Erzurum and Lake Van as the first step toward a new invasion of Azerbaijan, allowing the local Kurdish beys to retain their autonomy. Süleyman, who hoped to gain glory by seeking out and defeating the Safavids, moved into central Iran, reaching Sultaniye (October 13). But Şah Tahmasp preferred to abandon territory in order to avoid battle. The sultan, fearing the result of pursuing the Persians in winter conditions, decided to concentrate instead on Iraq, where the climate was more favorable. Moving over the Zagros Mountains, he took Baghdad and the remainder of Iraq during November and December without meeting any significant resistance. As a matter of fact, as his army approached Baghdad, the Sunni religious leaders led the population in an uprising that massacred most of the Shia soldiers and religious leaders who had been persecuting them. For a time southern Iraq, including Basra, remained in the hands of a local Arab bedouin dynasty, but it too was finally conquered in 1538, thus fully extending Ottoman rule to the Persian Gulf. The danger of a Safavid push through Iraq into Syria had been ended. The lands of the old caliphate were fully incorporated into the sultan's dominions. Sunni orthodoxy here had been rescued from the danger of Shiism. Süleyman's supremacy in the world of Islam had been confirmed.

Süleyman spent the rest of the winter in Baghdad restoring the orthodox institutions that had been disrupted by the Safavids and establishing the regular Ottoman administrative and tax system in the newly conquered province. Though Azerbaijan changed hands a few times, Süleyman was unable to lure Tahmasp into open battle. He allowed the Safavids to reoccupy Azerbaijan, but before leaving the east, he organized the new province of Erzurum, beginning the process by which the areas previously left to the autonomous Turkoman and Kurdish chiefs and tribes were placed under more direct government control.

The great eastern expedition thus did not achieve definitive success against the Safavids. Kurdistan and most of Iraq had been added definitively to the empire, but the Safavids had not been defeated. Azerbaijan, parts of eastern Iraq, and the southern Caucasus remained under the Şah's control. The division of the lands of the old Abbasid caliphate between the east and the west and, thereby, the division of the Islamic world itself had in fact provided a boundary that was to survive to modern times. But Safavid military and religious prestige in Anatolia had waned, and Ottoman rule there had become secure enough for regular administration to be introduced. Again Süleyman was free to concentrate elsewhere.

Naval Conflict with the Habsburgs: The Rise of Hayruddin Barbarossa

Conflict between Islam and Christianity for control of the western Mediterranean in Ottoman times began in the sixteenth century. The Muslim domination of Spain that had made the entire sea a Muslim lake had ended during the early centuries of Ottoman rise. With Italy and Spain too divided and France diverted by the Hundred Years' War with England, there was for a time no dominating power. The European states that rose at the end of the fifteenth century made the first attempts to fill the vacuum. Spain was united by the marriage of the rulers of Aragon and Castille and strengthened by the conquest of the last Muslim possessions in Granada (1492). France's efforts to extend its power into northern Italy and its rivalry with Spain reflected the interests of both in the Mediterranean. In North Africa the so-called Moors – themselves refugees from Christian persecution in Spain – sought to gain vengeance by forming pirate fleets and attacking Christian ships and coasts. But in reaction to the pirate raids the Spanish took a number of strong points along the Moroccan and Algerian coasts and forced the local Muslim dynasty, the Hafsids, to accept their authority in Algiers and allow the establishment of a fortified naval base at the adjacent island of Peñon d'Argel.

In response to this new Christian aggression Muslim privateers who had been operating in the central and eastern Mediterranean turned to the rich booty now available in the west, beginning the process by which Ottoman power was extended to the area. Two of the most famous and successful privateers were Turkish brothers from the island of Midilli (Mytilene), Uruc Reis and Hızır Reis, who in 1502 settled at Goletta (Halk ul-Vad), the port of Tunis, and built a pirate empire. They gained the allegiance of most of the Moorish pirates of the area as the result of their successful raids on Christian shipping and coasts. For a time the brothers gained control of Algiers, but the Spanish allied with the local Arab dynasties and pushed them out. At that time Uruc Reis perished, but his brother subsequently emerged as the greatest Muslim naval hero of the time – called Hayruddin by the Muslims and Barbarossa, the Red-Bearded One, by those in Europe who dreaded the sight of his fleet. Hayruddin Barbarossa sought out Ottoman assistance just after Selim I's conquest of Egypt, gaining the permission of the sultan to recruit sailors in Anatolia and secure cannon and gunpowder to strengthen his fleet. In return Algiers would be annexed to the empire and Barbarossa recognized as its governor. Little was done to carry out the arrangement in Süleyman the Magnificent's early years because of the sultan's concentration on the eastern and western land campaigns. A new series of pirate raids finally enabled Hayruddin to regain Algiers and to add the island of Peñon d'Argel in 1529.

Charles V then gained the services of the great Genoese Admiral Andrea Dorea (who in fact had defeated the Habsburg fleets twice, in 1524 and 1528) and began building a major new fleet, settling the former Knights of Rhodes at Tripoli and Malta (1530) to provide bases for action in the eastern Mediterranean. Though the Ottomans had a fairly substantial fleet left from the time of Bayezit II – with several large shipyards at Istanbul and Gallipoli, harbors throughout the Aegean and eastern Mediterranean, and abundant timber and men with which to build and man the ships – Süleyman had allowed it to decline. It could not oppose Dorea, who ravaged the coasts of Greece, capturing the important ports of Lepanto and Koron in September 1532. Süleyman called on Barbarossa, who sailed eastward through the Mediterranean, routing a detachment of the Habsburg fleet near the Morea, and then went on to Istanbul, where the old arrangement that had been made with Selim was revised and extended. Barbarossa now became grand admiral (*kapudan paşa, kapudan-ı derya*) of the Ottomans (December 27, 1533) and began to build a new fleet to meet the Habsburgs. Algiers was officially annexed to the Ottoman Empire and its governorship set aside in perpetuity for the grand admiral, who was to use its revenues to maintain the ships and pay their officers and men. Hayruddin brought his own captains and sailors to form the nucleus of the new fleet and then led it out to fight the enemy just as Süleyman was campaigning in Azerbaijan and conquering Iraq. During the spring and summer of 1534, Koron and Lepanto were recaptured along with Tunis (April 2, 1534) and the coasts of southwestern Italy were ravaged to help the French against the Habsburgs. Thus was started a war between the Ottomans and the Habsburgs for control of the central Mediterranean. His base at Tunis enabled Hayruddin to attack Sicily and extend Ottoman naval power into the western Mediterranean on a large scale. Dorea replied by organizing a new Crusade fleet that recaptured Tunis (July 21, 1535), administering a severe blow to Ottoman hopes in the west.

It was in reaction to Dorea's counteroffensive that the Ottomans entered into a formal alliance with France for the first time. There are some indications that the French actually had encouraged Hayruddin to enter Süleyman's service in the hope that he would, indeed, divert the Habsburgs from the west. Now a French ambassador, Jean de la Forêt, reached the sultan as he was returning from Iraq to Azerbaijan in May 1535, conveying offers of joint action against the Habsburgs. A trade agreement, subsequently called the Capitulations, was reached (February 18, 1536) on the model of previous ones made with Venice and Genoa. It allowed French merchants in the sultan's dominions virtual freedom from Ottoman law while being subjected instead to the rule of the French representative in Istanbul in accordance with French law. In essence this made what came to be called the community of Franks in Istanbul a kind of *millet* and provided the model for privileges subsequently bestowed on other European nations wishing to share the trade of the Levant. Subjects of both signatories were given the right to travel and trade freely in the dominions of the other and to pay especially low customs duties on imports and exports. The French consuls were given the right to hear and judge all civil and criminal cases arising among and between French subjects in the sultan's dominions without interference by Ottoman officials or judges, although the latter were allowed to help enforce judgments if requested to do so. Civil cases involving Muslim Ottoman subjects did have to be tried in Ottoman courts according to Muslim law, but the defendants were allowed to have French consular representatives to advise them. In criminal cases French subjects were excused from being called before Ottoman judges but instead were referred to the grand vezir or his agent, in which case the testimonies of Ottoman and French subjects were given equal weight. This was unlike the situation in the Muslim courts, where the testimony of Muslims had to be given special credence. Soon afterward the trade agreement was followed by the signing of a military alliance providing for joint action against the Habsburgs, although this was kept secret, since neither side wanted publicity about its relationship with an infidel power.

The Execution of Ibrahim Paşa and Beginnings of the Sultanate of the Women

While an expeditionary force was being prepared to carry out the Ottoman side of the bargain, Süleyman began to feel the impact of new internal political problems, with the *devşirme* party, triumphant over the appointment of Ibrahim Paşa as grand vezir, breaking into small political groups whose primary purpose was to advance themselves regardless of the interests of the state. The first sign of this came immediately after the sultan's return to Istanbul, when he had Ibrahim Paşa strangled (March 14/15, 1536) and his property confiscated. The ostensible reasons were Ibrahim's advance into Azerbaijan in advance of the sultan's arrival, accusations that he had accepted bribes from the Safavids to frustrate a campaign from Baghdad into Iran and that he was attempting to use his command of the Ottoman army to make himself independent.

In fact the reasons for Ibrahim's fall were far more complicated. He had been the protégé of Süleyman's mother, Hafsa Hatun, and his position was seriously shaken by her death (March 19, 1534). Her position as queen mother (*valide sultan*) was assumed by the sultan's wife, Hürrem Sultan, who began to build her own harem party in alliance with Iskender Çelebi, one of Ibrahim's principal rivals. She aspired to control the Ottoman system and gain the right of succession for one of her four sons, for Mehmet, Cihangir, Selim, or Bayezit. She was opposed by Süleyman's older wife Gülbahar Hatun, who became active politically in support of her son Mustafa, the sultan's eldest; she had Ibrahim on her side. With the support of the French ambassador, who wanted a grand vezir more interested in western campaigns than Ibrahim was, Hürrem Sultan prevailed, convincing the sultan that Ibrahim had, indeed, betrayed him. The fall of Ibrahim thus not only marked the beginning of the ascendancy of the women of the harem but also that of the intrigues of foreign ambassadors in the Ottoman capital.

War in the Mediterranean

Soon both the French and the Ottomans moved to carry out the obligations of their alliance in a joint attack on Italy: the former by land from the north, the latter by sea from the south. A new front thus was opened against the Habsburgs, with the major scene of conflict between the two empires being transferred from land to sea. French armies advanced into northern Italy to take Milan and Genoa (April 1536). Barbarossa built a new fleet and began a series of raids against the Habsburg possessions in the western and central Mediterranean (summer 1536). He then returned to Istanbul to join the sultan in building a major expeditionary force, with Süleyman leading an army of 300,000 men out of Istanbul toward Albania, from where the fleet was to transport them to Italy. At this crucial point, however, with a mighty Ottoman armada poised off the Albanian coast to join France in an invasion of Italy, the sultan learned what many of his successors were to find out in later years: that infidel friends would abandon all agreements when it suited their interests in Europe to do so. Under papal pressure Charles V and Francis ended their conflict, so that Europe could unite against Islam. The French, therefore, retired from northern Italy, and the disappointed Süleyman diverted his force to relatively minor campaigns against Venetian bases along the coasts of Albania and Dalmatia (September 1537).

The only permanent results of the expedition were subsequently achieved by Hayruddin at sea. Frustrated by French betrayal in Italy, he moved into the Aegean Islands and transformed most of the islands into vassal principalities under Ottoman suzerainty, establishing full Ottoman naval supremacy in the Aegean (September–November 1537). The remaining Venetian islands in the area, including Crete, were ravaged the following summer, leaving Venice with very little to use as a naval base. The pope responded by organizing a second Holy League fleet, again under the direction of Dorea. It entered the Aegean only after the Ottoman fleet had already returned to Istanbul for the winter and was able to do no more than bombard (but not capture) the principal Ottoman port in Albania, Preveze, at the mouth of the Gulf of Arta south of Janina (August 13, 1538). When Hayruddin heard of this, he managed to bring a portion of his fleet back together again, sail into the Adriatic, and completely rout the allied fleet before Preveze (September 28, 1538). Quarrels among the different national commanders, particularly the Genoese and Venetians, added to Dorea's difficulties. Thus while he managed to bring his scattered fleet together again, he retired from the scene without attempting a further engagement.

Dorea and much of Europe considered the battle to be a stand-off, but the fact remains that the Ottomans were left in control of the Ionian and Aegean seas. Hayruddin's recent conquests of the adjacent islands were assured, as was the Ottoman naval dominance of the eastern Mediterranean won from Venice three decades earlier. After a few futile efforts to resist the Ottomans by itself, Venice signed a new peace treaty (October 20, 1540). It surrendered its last possessions in the Morea, acknowledging all of Hayruddin's Aegean conquests, and agreeing to pay a heavy war indemnity as well as an increased tribute in return for Ottoman recognition of its continued rule in Crete and Cyprus plus restoration of its trade privileges. The final blow thus was struck at the naval power of the Republic of Saint Mark. Now its prosperity depended on trading in the Ottoman dominions.

War in the Eastern Seas

While the Ottomans and Habsburgs fought in the Mediterranean, the Ottoman conquest of the Arab world also had put it in position to combat the Portugese dominance in the eastern seas. Portugese interest in a new route from Europe to the Far East had begun over a century ago when Prince Henry "the Navigator" had sent explorers to the coast of Africa. In 1488 Portugese navigators discovered the possibility of going around Africa via the Cape of Good Hope, and less than a decade later, in 1497, a fleet commanded by Vasco da Gama used the route to reach Calcutta. Portugal now developed and monopolized the route, establishing merchant bases at Cochin south of Calcutta in competition with Arab merchants from Egypt and Syria who were strongly entrenched at Calcutta itself. In 1502 the Portugese fleet blockaded the Red Sea and the Persian Gulf to force all trade between India and Europe to use the route that it controlled. While the Portugese push was largely economic in origin, there was also a decided religious emphasis, with the pope assigning it the task of encircling the world of Islam from the rear and helping restore Christianity in the Middle East and India while Spain did the same in the New World.

The Mamluks bore the brunt of the Portugese onslaught. Most seriously affected were the ports of Suez and Alexandria, entrepôts for the Rea Sea trade, and Basra, Aleppo, and Tripoli of Lebanon, centers of the commerce with the Persian Gulf.

The resulting financial and economic problems made it difficult for the Mamluks to build a fleet of their own. It was only after the Ottoman conquest that a major effort was made to counter the Portugese threat. While Grand Vezir Ibrahim Paşa was in Egypt, he revitalized the old Mamluk shipyard at Suez, creating a separate naval command for the Red Sea and financing it out of the Egyptian customs duties, most of which were assigned specifically to this purpose. The fleet was ready to act only in the 1530s when Süleyman's conquest of Iraq and, particularly, of Basra, was followed by the creation of another fleet there, thus providing the Ottomans with the opportunity for an enveloping push against the enemy. At about the same time, the sultan received an appeal for help from the Muslim ruler of Gucerat in western India against both the Portugese and the Mogols, who under Babur (d. 1530), one of Tamerlane's grandsons, had conquered much of northern and central India and were moving to the west. An Ottoman fleet was dispatched from Suez on June 13, 1538, under the command of Hadım Süleyman Paşa, governor of Egypt. While passing Aden and the Yemen he took advantage of local dynastic disputes to capture the coastal areas, providing the empire with important new advanced bases to defend the Red Sea area from future Christian incursions. This in fact was the most successful part of the expedition. When Hadım Süleyman's fleet reached Gucerat, the ruler who had invited Ottoman assistance had been replaced by a son who disavowed the request and in fact garrisoned the town with Portugese troops to prevent the Ottomans from landing. The resulting shortages, along with fears that a Portugese fleet would cut off their retreat, finally forced the Ottoman force to return to Egypt.

The Moldavian Campaign

While Ottoman fleets carried on the fight against Christianity in the east and the west, the sultan himself was undertaking new land campaigns into Europe. In 1538 he invaded Moldavia, whose native prince, Peter Rareş, had been inspired by the Habsburgs to throw off his bonds of vassalage. The prince fled into exile in Transylvania, and Süleyman occupied and ravaged the major cities of Moldavia, including the capital of Jassy (Yaş), and then revised the arrangement for the election of native princes, adding Ottoman confirmation to the election by the nobles. Süleyman also annexed southern Bessarabia between the Pruth and the Dniester, with a garrison of regular troops and raiders being maintained to watch over the sultan's vassals nearby. The new acquisition was organized as the *sancak* of Bucak, and the Moldavians agreed never to build forts or station troops along its boundaries so that the Ottoman troops could move where and when they wished without any resistance.

Internal Changes

From November 27, 1539, when he returned from Moldavia, until June 20, 1541, when he set out on a new expedition to Hungary, Süleyman spent almost two years in Istanbul in order to supervise personally the consolidation of his state. Since he intended to concentrate on administrative and cultural matters, he brought to the grand vezirate one of the ablest and most learned *devşirme* men in his court, second vezir Lütfi Paşa (d. 1562) a poet and juridical scholar as well as an able soldier and an administrator. Much of the work involved the codification of the administrative organization of the various provinces into laws (*kanuns*) and the adoption of measures to put those laws into force. In addition, a new general code of laws (*Kanunname*) was drawn up in Süleyman's name, building on previous codes and adding new sections based on experience in enforcing them. Whereas the *Kanunname* of Mehmet II had concentrated mainly on matters of state organization, that of Süleyman emphasized justice and finance, the two most acute problems left from the time of his father. The new code set down penalties for crimes of robbery, murder, and adultery as well as drunkenness and disorderly conduct. Sentences ranged from money fines, retribution in kind, and the cutting off of one's hands to execution. The *Kanunname* also established regulations for the timar holders, with their administrative and military duties being defined, the wages and duties of their *Sipahis* and foot soldiers assigned, and taxes on animals, cultivated patches, and gardens specified. The entire financial organization of the state, from the treasury down to the smallest tax collector, was systematized and institutionalized.

Lütfi Paşa also tried to solve a number of problems that had just begun to trouble the empire and that, subsequently, were to contribute to Ottoman decline. Firm rules were introduced to end harem intervention in the daily conduct of administrative affairs. Irregularities in the ports – involving the payment of bribes by foreign merchants in return for exemption from customs taxes and also the release of foreign slaves and other prisoners – were suppressed. Confiscation of property without compensation and imprisonment without trial were prohibited. Regulations were introduced to organize and provide for the rapidly expanding navy. The provincial administrative structure built by Mehmet II was tightened. Efforts were made to enforce the rules of appointment and promotion according to ability, and dismissal and demotion were only for just cause. Scribes and other bureaucrats were prohibited from using their power for the benefit of themselves and their friends, collecting illegal taxes, fees, or "tips," and engaging in private trade to supplement their state incomes. The idea of a balanced budget, with expenditures equaling anticipated income, was introduced into the Ottoman Empire, with particular efforts being made to keep military expenditures in line with available revenue. The grand vezir established a regular system to bring the details of each problem to the sultan and the Imperial Council, explaining all the ramifications and possible solutions and carefully recording each decision in a series of *mühimme* (important affairs) registers that, with few exceptions, continued to be the major records of official actions to the nineteenth century. Finally, to regularize and improve the supply operations of imperial campaigns particular attention was paid to placing supplies at major stops to await the army and to arranging compensation for provisions obtained from subjects living along the line of march.[9]

Lütfi Paşa also promoted a great deal of learned and scholarly activity, and he wrote a handbook for grand vezirs (see pp. 290–291). He finally fell (1541), however, to the same political parties and intrigues he had been trying to end, with parties led by Hayruddin Barbarossa and Selim I's daughter Şah Sultan finally securing his removal and replacement by the aged Hadım Süleyman Paşa, former governor of Egypt. The fall of Lütfi Paşa and the triumph of the parties signaled the beginning of decline in the Ottoman system.

Struggles with the Habsburgs

Conflicts with the Habsburgs occupied the sultan during much of the next six years. Relations with Ferdinand had been strained because of raids and counterraids across the boundary of the two empires in Bosnia and Croatia. John Zapolya, vassal king of Hungary, began to fear direct Ottoman occupation and hence made an agreement with Ferdinand at Grosswardein (Varadin, Varat) (February 1538) by which the childless Zapolya agreed to will all of Hungary to Ferdinand while the latter promised assistance against any possible Ottoman attack. But this Habsburg move clashed with the ambitions of Poland's Sigismund in Hungary, who subsequently arranged for the marriage of his daughter Isabella to Zapolya, resulting in the birth of a son and heir, Sigismund Janos. Zapolya then attempted to secure Polish mediation to nullify the agreement with Ferdinand to get the right of succession for his son, relying also on Ottoman assistance against any move to increase Habsburg power in the country.

Following Zapolya's death (August 22, 1540), Ferdinand, attempting to secure his own rights, declared Zapolya's subsequent marriage illegal according to the agreement and claimed that the child was not in fact a natural son. Habsburg troops invaded Hungary and occupied Pest, while Ferdinand's agents promised he would accept full Ottoman suzerainty if he was allowed to rule the country (November 7, 1540). Süleyman, however, was in no mood to permit an expansion of Habsburg power. In 1541 he led a major expeditionary force into Hungary, routing the Austrians. Deciding that it would be unwise to leave the country to the infant prince, he sent the latter with his mother to rule as vassal prince of Transylvania. Hungary was occupied and annexed to the Ottoman Empire and subsequently organized as the province of Buda. Ferdinand continued to control the highlands of the west and north as a tributary vassal, while a similar arrangement was made in Transylvania, which included the lowlands between the Danube and Tisza. Only the territory of Ofen, just north of the Danube, was put under direct Ottoman military control to provide a base against potential Habsburg attacks. The governor of Buda was given an unusually strong position to enable him to organize regular Ottoman administration and to react instantly to any Habsburg attack. Alone of the provincial governors he was given the rank of vezir, equal to the members of the Imperial Council. He also was given direct command of the border raiding forces as well as the urban garrisons – elsewhere such raiding forces were independent of the provincial authorities. He was given extraordinary powers to assign vacant timars, appoint the garrison commanders, and handle negotiations with foreign powers directly. His authority was limited only by Istanbul-appointed officials who handled financial, judicial, and religious tasks in his province. The Hungarian buffer thus was brought to an end.

The Habsburgs lost little time in attempting to reverse Süleyman's victories in Hungary. While Ferdinand had announced he would resume his payments of tribute to the sultan, he sought united German support for a new Crusade, giving significant concessions to the Protestant princes to secure their cooperation (January 14, 1542). A large new Crusade army was organized, with knights coming from all over Europe except France and Venice. France notified the sultan in enough time for him to reinforce Buda and enable its defenders to rout the attack (November 24, 1542). Süleyman followed with his fifth Hungarian campaign during the summer of 1543, capturing most of the remaining Habsburg forts in Hungary and Slavonia. While these conquests made it possible for the sultan to attack Vienna once again if he wished, the lessons of his previous efforts caused him to renounce such an idea and be content with clearing most of Hungary of the Habsburgs.

The Mediterranean Campaign of 1543

In the meantime, Barbarossa also led the Ottoman fleet in a campaign into the western Mediterranean, partly in response to French pleas for help against the Habsburgs. After ravaging the coasts of Italy and leaving Rome and Naples in a state of panic, the Ottomans sailed on to southern France, where they were given an elaborate welcome. By this time, however, new complaints about cooperation with the infidel led Francis I to abandon his earlier promises of cooperation against the Habsburgs in Italy. Hayruddin, therefore, occupied Toulon without permission (August 5, 1543) and compelled the local French authorities to provide some assistance in an unsuccessful effort to take Nice (August 20–September 8) before returning to the eastern Mediterranean, ravaging the coasts of Spain, France, and Italy as he went. Süleyman's disappointment at the French betrayal, combined with the signature of a new French-Habsburg peace at Crespy (September 18, 1544), led him to agree to a truce with the Habsburgs (November 10, 1545). It was concluded on the basis of uti possidetis, with the emperor recognizing the new Ottoman conquests and promising to pay tribute for the few areas of northern and western Hungary still under Habsburg control. Both sides again promised to refrain from raiding each other's territory. The truce was made into a permanent peace (June 13, 1547) following the death of Francis I, with added provisions extending commercial privileges to Habsburg merchants.

Internal Development

Peace with the Habsburgs enabled Süleyman to remain in Istanbul to concentrate on internal development for almost five years until he finally undertook a new expedition against Iran in 1548. Considerable attention was paid to the organization and hierarchy of the religious/cultural institution of the Ruling Class under the leadership of *Şeyhulislam* Ebu us-Suud Efendi (1490–1574), the leading jurisconsult of the time. The organizational regulations for the Ottoman ulema, set down on paper under Mehmet II, were put into practice fully. Regulations and procedures were added to assure that only the ablest and most learned men would be admitted to ulema ranks and that they would serve honestly and efficiently, without government interference, always emphasizing the sultan's desire to protect the rights of all his subjects. New standards of honesty and efficiency were introduced in courts all over the empire. But in developing the idea that the authority of the judges derived not from the religious law as such, but rather from their appointment by the sultan, Ebu us-Suud made it possible for later sultans and ministers less interested in justice to claim that the courts had to follow their will in applying the law, thus breaking down many of the standards that he and his master sought to make the basis of the Ottoman legal system.

Ebu us-Suud also made a collection of the practical applications of Islamic law in the sultan's dominions. Under his guidance Mehmet II's work of bringing together into law codes (*kanunname*) all the laws and regulations previously issued concerning the basic administrative, financial, military, and economic systems of the empire was largely completed. These were reconciled with the rules and principles of the religious law through a series of judicial opinions (*fetvas*), thus avoiding the hazards of dualism and justifying legislation according to the needs of the time. Ebu us-Suud himself drew up the famous *Kanunname-i Âl-i Osman* (Law Code of the House of Osman), with new regulations to punish violators of the law, organize the tax system, and establish a hierarchy among the various classes of rayas and soldiers. The legal and financial status of timar holders was clarified, with the timars being divided into three classes (*hass,* timar, and *zeamet*) according to the size of their revenues. Revisions were made in the law to allow state revenues to be given to religious foundations for religious and social purposes. The border, fortress, and other garrisons were given legal organization and regulation for the first time. The old Islamic regulations dividing conquered lands according to the manner in which they were conquered were replaced by a system wherein all such properties were made state (*miri*) holdings, subject to the same taxes. Cadastral surveys preceded their incorporation into the regular Ottoman financial and administrative system. Individuals living on state lands were allowed to possess as private property all movable property, their houses, and small gardens, with the right to buy and sell them as well as leave them to heirs. In provinces not divided into fiefs, mainly the newly conquered Arab territories, governors were required to assign the provincial taxes to tax farmers and to deliver a fixed annual revenue to the state treasury each year, keeping whatever surplus there was as profit for themselves. The circumstances under which the sultan could confiscate the properties of members of the Ruling Class were also set down. The latter received considerably more protection than they had in the past, although in the end as slaves of the sultan they were still subject to his absolute will in all matters.

Süleyman was just begining to experience the economic and social problems that were to disrupt the empire under his successors. During his reign alone, its population almost doubled, from 12 million to 22 million people. The amount of land put into cultivation was increasing at a much slower rate, resulting in problems of rural overpopulation, mass migration to the cities, urban unemployment, food shortages, and rising prices. Economic pressures were leading the timar holders, tax farmers, and other officials in the rural areas to restore many of the conditions of illegal taxation and forced labor that the Ottoman conquest had originally eliminated. And although Süleyman worked strenuously to prevent such misrule and punish those who were caught, the problem remained.

Much of the sultan's time and energy at this time was diverted to the increasing struggles for power among the various political groups. Hürrem Sultan had achieved success by securing the right of succession for her son Mehmet and the appointment of her allies to important positions in the government and the army. But the death of Mehmet led to a temporary eclipse of her influence. The right of succession was given to the eldest son, Mustafa, whose mother, Gülbahar Sultan, emerged as a power in her own right in alliance with the ulema and the Janissary corps as well as the powerful second minister Husrev Paşa, who was the power behind aged Grand Vezir Hadım Süleyman Paşa. Hürrem Sultan, however, fought back by arranging for the dismissal and exile of both Hadım Süleyman and Husrev on trumped-up charges of corruption, gaining the grand vezirate for her son-in-law, Damat Rüstem Paşa, and championing the cause of her incompetent son, Selim, who seemed to be the easiest prince to control. Rüstem's rise to power was another step toward decline.

Süleyman's Second Iranian Expedition

After Elkaz Mirza, Tahmasp's brother, had fled to refuge in Ottoman territory (1547), the sultan hoped to use Safavid dynastic quarrels to end the Shia threat and conquer at least the Caucasus and Azerbaijan. The palace parties supported the idea of an expedition, each for its own reasons. Mihrimah Sultan and Rüstem Paşa hoped that victory in Iran would enhance the prestige of Prince Bayezit, while Hürrem Sultan felt that her son Selim would become *kaimakam* (substitute) for the sultan in Istanbul and give her the opportunity to place her own men in key positions. Süleyman occupied Azerbaijan with no difficulty once again. Tahmasp followed the scorched-earth policy of his predecessor, then moved in to recapture the conquered areas as soon as the Ottoman army returned to Anatolia for the winter. The defection of Elkaz Mirza once he saw the Ottomans could not win easily and the sultan's own exhaustion and frustration finally caused him to return to Istanbul with little more to show for two years of campaigning than a few forts in Georgia and the newly captured fort of Van. The latter was organized as a separate province and established as a major fortified area against further Safavid penetration into Anatolia. The Safavid threat was thus blunted but certainly not eliminated.

The Transylvanian Campaign and the Rise of Mehmet Sokullu

Relations with the Habsburgs once again came to the fore at this time, with Transylvania becoming the main scene of action. Joining in the combat was Poland, where Sigismund I's son Sigismund II August (1548–1572), in response to the spread of Protestantism in his domains, allied with the Habsburgs (July 2, 1549) for joint action against all enemies, including those subjects who disputed their rule. This freed the Habsburgs to intervene in Transylvania without fear of Polish response. Here Süleyman had left an autonomous principality ruled by Zapolya's son, Sigismund Janos, under the influence of his mother, the Polish princess Isabella, and the regent Bishop Martinuzzi of Grosswardein. The latter attempted to increase his power by turning the crown of Transylvania over to Ferdinand and allowing him to occupy the province (July 19, 1551) in return for promises that he would be allowed to rule alone as the Habsburg governor. In response to the Habsburg occupation Süleyman sent a major expeditionary force commanded by the *beylerbeyi* of Rumeli, Mehmet Sokullu (1505–1579), himself a Christian *devşirme* boy from Bosnia. Thus began the rise to eminence and power of the minister who was to command Ottoman destinies for much of the remainder of the century. Mehmet Sokullu's initial campaign into the Banat of Temesvar during the summer of 1551 was unsuccessful, but the assassination of Martinuzzi (December 10, 1551) on the suspicion that he really was favoring the Ottomans cost the Habsburgs much of the popular and noble support that their initial occupation had gained. Now most preferred a restoration of the autonomy that they had received under the sultan's rule to Austrian occupation and misrule. As a result, during the summer of 1552 the Ottomans were able to capture Temesvar (July 26) and most of Transylvania, while Ferdinand retained only a few bases in the northern mountains. Although the war with the Habsburgs went on for another decade, there were no further changes of importance, with Sigismund Janos again ruling Transylvania under Ottoman suzerainty.

The Mediterranean War, 1551–1562

During the remainder of the war, there was much more action at sea than on land. The Ottoman fleet suffered a partial eclipse during Barbarossa's last years and immediately after his death when for political reasons its command was given to land commanders, first Mehmet Sokullu (1546–1550) and then Koca Sinan Paşa (1550–1554), whose main qualification was the fact that he was Rüstem's brother. The power of the grand admiral was reduced, with separate governors being appointed for Algiers and the fleet's revenues being limited to what the admiral could get from the *sancaks* of Gallipoli and Alexandria. Actual command of the fleet during this period was assumed by Turgut Reis (Dragut), who emerged as Barbarossa's most successful pupil and managed to maintain Ottoman dominance in the Mediterranean despite all the difficulties.

The new Mediterranean war opened in September 1550 when Charles V captured Mahdiye, in Tunis, and stimulated the Knights of Malta to undertake new acts of piracy against Ottoman shipping. Turgut responded by capturing Tripoli (August 15, 1551) but failed in an effort to take Malta. The Ottoman-French alliance had fallen into abeyance with the death of Francis I and the accession of Henri II (1547–1559), but the new French victories over the Habsburgs that followed emboldened the allies to formalize and publicize their alliance for the first time and to sign a new treaty (February 1, 1553) stipulating primarily naval cooperation against the Habsburgs. But fulfillment of the treaty was fitful and ineffective.

During the summer of 1553, Koca Sinan and Turgut jointly led a new fleet into the west, which, with the help of a French squadron, raided the coasts of Naples, Sicily, and Corsica. However, Sinan's jealousy of Turgut's emerging fame, combined with the intrigues of the Venetian representatives in Istanbul, who complained about Turgut's capture of several of their ships, led to his fall, while most of the fleet's best captains went back to their old careers as privateers (1553). The situation improved when Sinan (d. 1554) was replaced as grand admiral by the famous Piyale Paşa, a Croat who had been captured at the Battle of Mohacs and had served as Turgut's assistant for many years. Piyale rebuilt the fleet and appointed Turgut as governor of Tripoli, where the latter built his own provincial fleet as well as cooperating with the grand admiral in new actions against the enemy.

Peace with the Habsburgs

Habsburg interest in the Ottoman war waned as the emperor was diverted by the Reformation and by conflicts with his enemies in Europe. In 1555 Charles V abdicated after signing the Peace of Augsburg, despairing at his inability to stamp out Protestantism and restore the old Holy Roman Empire. The division of the Habsburg dominions between Philip II of Spain and Ferdinand, now elected emperor (1558–1564), further sapped Habsburg ability to mobilize Europe against the infidel and led to overtures for peace with France. A solution was reached at Cateau-Cambrésis (April 3, 1559), finally ending the struggle between the houses of Habsburg and Valois. Henri died soon afterward, and France for some time thereafter concentrated on its internal problems under the regency of Catherine de Medici (1519–1589), leaving Süleyman without major external encouragement for continued war against the Habsburgs. Within the Habsburg empire also the vast new wealth pouring into Philip's coffers in consequence of Spanish discoveries in the New World led to a general shift of emphasis to the west. Also, the German portion of the empire fell into relative obscurity and became preoccupied with its internal problems, leaving little time for new action against the Ottomans. Süleyman still hoped for new advances in northern Hungary, but increasing internal problems convinced the sultan to accept the Habsburg peace overtures. The new peace agreement (June 1, 1562) essentially restored that of 1547. While the land frontier was left in stalemate, the fleets of Algiers and Tripoli were once again free to ravage and raid without fear of opposition.

The Eastern Seas

Ottoman power in the eastern seas had risen considerably since the capture of Basra, Aden, and southern Yemen in the 1530s. Control of the Yemen had slowly spread inland, culminating in the capture of Sana in 1547 and the establishment of regular

Ottoman administration in the country, with coastal Zabid and inland Sana being organized into separate provinces. Meanwhile, the Ottoman Red Sea fleet was built into a major force, primarily under the leadership of the greatest of the sixteenth-century Ottoman naval heroes, Piri Reis (1465–1554), who originated as a Mediterranean pirate under Bayezit II, assisted in Selim's conquest of Egypt and in the Red Sea naval operations that followed, and in the process wrote the greatest Ottoman geographical compendium of the time, the *Kitab-ı Bahriye* (Book of the Sea). In 1547 Piri Reis was appointed grand admiral of the Indian Ocean fleet (*Hind Kapudan-ı Derya*) as well as admiral of the fleet of Egypt (*Mısır Kapudan-ı Derya*) as soon as those positions were separated from the governship of southern Yemen. The Portugese earlier had sent a major expedition into the Red Sea, raiding as far as Suez and taking Aden. Piri Reis now led his own campaign, which retook the latter (February 26, 1548), and then went on annual expeditions into the Indian Ocean. Although Basra, in southern Iraq, had acknowledged Ottoman suzerainty in 1539, its Arab bedouin rulers remained in power until 1547, when it was subjected to direct Ottoman control. It was only then, therefore, that a new Arab (Persian) Gulf fleet was built. The Arab chiefs along the Gulf reacted to the expansion of Ottoman power by cooperating with the Portugese, who established their own fort and garrison at Maskat and Hormuz and landed at Katif with the intention of blocking the development of Basra as an Ottoman naval base. In 1552, however, Piri Reis came with a large fleet and drove the Portugese from Maskat. After his death another pirate hero, Seydi Ali Reis, was appointed as the new captain of the Red Sea fleet, with the additional task of restoring Ottoman power in the Gulf (December 7, 1553). Seydi Ali rebuilt the Basra port and fleet but subsequently was routed by the Portugese off Hormuz (August 25, 1554), escaping only by fleeing all the way across the Indian Ocean to Diu. He returned home in an epic land journey through India, Afghanistan, Central Asia, and Iran (May 1557).

The Gulf remained largely closed to Ottoman shipping thereafter, but Ottoman control of the Red Sea, fortified by capture of the Red Sea ports in 1557, enabled Süleyman to restore much of the old international trade routes through Egypt, with the Portugese lacking the overall naval strength necessary to blockade the old routes completely. It was only in the seventeenth century and after, when they were replaced by the far stronger fleets of England and the Netherlands, that the old routes were finally closed and the Middle East was thrown into an economic depression from which it recovered only in modern times.

Economic and Financial Problems

The last decade of Süleyman's reign saw the beginnings of the economic and financial problems that were to stir discontent and even revolts during the remainder of the sixteenth century. Though Süleyman had largely counteracted the Portugese efforts to close the international trade routes through the Middle East, some of the damage was irreversible. Inflation was stimulated by population increases, while a shortage of precious metals led to debasement of the coinage. Most ironic was the fact that the shortage originally affected Europe and Iran far more than the Ottoman Empire, since the gold mines of Upper Egypt and the Sudan and the silver mines of Serbia provided it with all it needed. Eventually, however, the European shortage drove up the prices of gold and silver throughout the Continent so much that the Ottoman supply was largely drained. Adding to the problem was a tremendous increase in governmental expenditures during Süleyman's reign consequent on his creation of a vast new apparatus of government and a splendid court as well as his annual campaigns in Europe and Asia.

This led the sultan to create new and ever more burdensome taxes, generally called *tekalif-i divaniye* (taxes authorized by the Imperial Council), intended originally to provide temporary impositions for particular purposes but over time becoming permanent taxes. The cultivators in turn were forced to rely on moneylenders, who took full advantage of the situation, charging substantial interest rates that left the peasants with little or nothing for themselves from the product of their labor. Pressed by the demands of moneylenders and tax collectors alike, thousands of cultivators began to flee from their lands. Faced with inflation, timar holders with relatively fixed revenues could no longer afford to fulfill their military obigations. Feudal cavalrymen, unable to support themselves, began to form raiding bands that sought to maintain themselves by attacking those who remained on the lands as well as caravans and, at times, large urban centers. The countryside flooded into the cities, which lacked the political and economic organizations to meet the needs of their rapidly expanding populations, particularly since the flight from the land and the rise of provincial bands inevitably lessened the amount of available food.

Lacking any understanding of economics, the government sought to legislate surface solutions. A system of price controls was established to counter rising prices, but this only caused new shortages without remedying the situation. Needed funds were secured by raising taxes, confiscating the properties of the wealthiest merchants, and debasing the coinage. But these measures only further disturbed the economy, increased inflation, and made conditions more difficult than ever. Peasants who had fled to the cities were forceably returned to their lands without any effort to ameliorate the conditions that had forced them to flee. And, perhaps worst of all, to enforce these regulations and suppress manifestations of discontent the Janissary corps was spread throughout the empire as a provincial garrison army on a large scale, replacing the feudal forces that had traditionally been in charge of maintaining order and security in the areas under their control. The Janissaries had settled in the towns and villages originally only to suppress the provincial bandits, but as time went on they assumed all police powers. Not only were they unable to restore order, but they began to take over lands, property, and businesses in the localities where they were stationed, thus beginning the process by which the corps' discipline was ended and members largely abandoned their military pursuits for the more profitable life that was now opened for them.

Political Degeneration in Süleyman's Later Years

The last decade of Süleyman's reign was occupied by two major expeditions to the East led by the sultan himself despite his desire to remain at home. The expeditions were caused not only by renewed Safavid propagandizing and raids in eastern Anatolia but also by palace intrigues. Grand Vezir Rüstem Paşa frustrated the efforts of Prince Mustafa, governor of Amasya, to act effectively against the Safavid danger because the prestige the prince might gain would hurt Selim's chances to the throne. Rüstem and Hürrem Sultan also spread reports, not entirely without foundation, that Mustafa was gathering the support of the Anatolian *Sipahi*s, Turkomans, and bandits for a general uprising against *devşirme* misrule from Istanbul, with the objective of putting himself on the throne. Rüstem even forged a letter purporting to show that Mustafa was seeking Safavid support. In consequence, when Süleyman led a new expedition through Anatolia during the summer of 1553, ostensibly against the Safavids, he had Mustafa executed at Aktepe, near Konya (October 5), thus removing from the scene the ablest of the princes and dooming the empire to incompetent rule.

The sultan resumed the campaign against the Safavids the following summer, this time seeking to catch the retreating enemy by ravaging their territories in the Caucasus. The şah however withdrew into the mountains of Luristan, saving his army from destruction, although the Ottomans were able to capture and send back to Istanbul huge quantities of booty and prisoners. Frustrated by the lack of opportunity for a decisive victory, Süleyman finally signed a peace agreement at Amasya (May 29, 1555), which ended the long series of wars between the two empires for some time to come. Tahmasp acknowledged the Ottoman boundaries as they were, including the most recent conquests, and also promised to end his propaganda and raids. In return Süleyman gave permission for Persian pilgrims to go to the Holy Cities of Mecca and Medina as well as to the Shia holy places in Iraq. The frontier thus established ran across the mountains dividing eastern and western Georgia, through Armenia, and via the western slopes of the Zagros down to the Persian Gulf. Süleyman thereafter limited his interests in the East to maintaining good relations with the Uzbegs, encouraging their pressure to prevent Tahmasp from resuming his aggressions.

Another reason behind Süleyman's abandonment of the Persian campaign was the critical political situation at home. Mustafa's execution was criticized by the Janissaries and feudal holders of Anatolia, as well as by the bandit leaders, ever ready to use any weapon against the central government. Even as the sultan was returning to Istanbul in July 1555, the opposing forces coalesced into an open revolt against his authority in Rumeli. They were led by a man claiming to be the dead prince, who has come to be known in history as the second "false" (*düzme*) Mustafa. Claiming that he had, in fact, escaped the assassination effort and fled to Rumeli, Düzme Mustafa first raised the banner of revolt at Ereğli, gathering hundreds of timar holders, rebel cultivators, members of the ulema, and students of religion who were protesting *devşirme* rule in Istanbul. The rebels then crossed through Gallipoli into Rumeli, getting support from the feudal holders and also the border commanders, who apparently hoped that he would lead them in a new era of advancement into Christian territory. Mustafa built a substantial army in Macedonia, created his own government in exile with an *akıncı* leader as grand vezir, and attempted to capture Edirne, which he hoped to make the capital of his new state. He soon was able to capture most of Thrace and Macedonia as well as the Dobruca. The rapidity of his success and the popular support he received were significant testimonies to the depth of the empire's social and economic problems. His supporters began to seize the properties of government officials and wealthy rayas and raid government treasuries and storehouses, spreading the wealth among those most in need of it and thus, in certain respects, appealing to the same kind of "communistic" feeling that Bedreddin Simavni had used long before. Süleyman heard of the revolt only when he reached Bolu on his return from the East. But even before his detachments had arrived in Rumeli, Prince Bayezit managed to suppress the revolt and capture and execute its leader (August 18, 1555).

It appeared that Bayezit would be officially announced as crown prince in return for his role in suppressing the revolt. To prevent this, Mihrimah Sultan spread the report that the prince had in fact connived in the revolt to enhance his own image and that he had eliminated his protégé only after the rebel movement threatened to upset the internal structure of the empire. The sultan ordered Bayezit's execution, but Hürrem Sultan managed to save him, persuading Süleyman to appoint the prince instead as governor of Kütahya. The rebels were executed by the thousands, with those timar holders accused of involvement being dispossessed. Since the conditions that had contributed to Düzme Mustafa's early successes were not remedied, the social and economic unrest continued.

There were now only two princes left, Bayezit and Selim, the latter now ruling at Manisa. Sources differ on the exact political alignments. Both were children of Hürrem Sultan, and there are indications that she vacillated between the two. Selim was generally considered to be dissolute and slothful, while Bayezit was educated, reasonably active, capable, and was, therefore, favored by most of the soldiers and administrators. While the two princes built up their courts and armies in their respective capitals, there was no open conflict between them for some time because of their mother's influence. Violence, however, rapidly followed her death (March 16, 1558). The timar holders continued to advocate the cause of Bayezit, but the Janissaries gradually transferred their support to Selim, since they were suffering less from the economic problems of the time, dependent as they were on salaries rather than on direct tax collections. In addition, because Bayezit was capable and active in promoting his cause while Selim was indolent and inactive, preferring a kind of quiet diplomacy calculated to keep him in favor with his father, Süleyman seems to have begun to fear the former more than the latter and to act accordingly. He reassigned Bayezit to Amasya, to the east and far from Istanbul (September 6, 1558). Bayezit reacted by going to Ankara and began to raise an army against his brother. Süleyman attempted to calm both brothers, sending ministers to advise each. But the one sent to Selim was Sokullu Mehmet Paşa, thus giving him the services of the brilliant minister who subsequently was not only to secure the throne for him but also to dominate the state through much of the rest of the century.

With Selim's army composed primarily of Janissaries sent by his father and that of Bayezit attracting the discontented elements that had previously joined under Düzme Mustafa's leadership, the conflict between the princes emerged as a new duel for power between the old Turkish aristocracy, now represented by the Anatolian fief holders, and the *devşirme*. These distinctions were somewhat blurred, however, by the tendency of many of the fighting men on both sides to gravitate to the highest bidder regardless of which group he represented. But in the end with the men and supplies sent from Istanbul by the sultan as well as the order and discipline created by Sokullu Mehmet, Selim was able to create a far better army than that of Bayezit, which was composed of Turkoman nomads and feudal soldiers. The two armies clashed near Konya; Selim's won; and Bayezit fled to Iran, where he was eventually executed by Şah Tahmasp in return for substantial subsidies sent by Süleyman (February 12, 1560). Süleyman then appointed his sole surviving son, Selim, as his heir, while most of Bayezit's followers joined the mounting movement of rebellion in the countryside, which the Janissaries were able to control only with great difficulty during the remainder of his reign.

Süleyman's Last Years: The Siege of Malta and Expedition to Hungary

After returning from Iran in 1555, Süleyman left affairs of state almost entirely in the hands of the harem elements and the grand vezir. The new grand vezir, Sokullu Mehmet, managed to build his own power by marrying Selim's daughter Esma Sultan (September 25, 1561), creating a new harem-*devşirme* party that replaced the dominance of Hürrem Sultan and Rüstem and lasted for the next three decades.

Meanwhile, the conquest of the island of Sakız (April 14, 1566), last of the Dodecanese Islands in Genoese hands, strengthened the Ottoman naval position outside the Dardanelles and indicated continued Ottoman interest in the seas. On land, trouble mounted with the Habsburgs because of local raids and counterraids across the border and some Habsburg advances in Transylvania. Therefore, Sokullu convinced Süleyman of the need for a new expedition, with the sultan emerging to lead the army in person once again after a decade of retirement (1566). The principal aim of the expedition was the capture of Sigetvar, which could be used to defend the Ottoman-controlled areas of Hungary and Transylvania against further Habsburg raids. During the course of the march, the sultan fell increasingly ill – thus actual command was in the hands of his grand vezir. Sokullu's capture of Sigetvar (August 29) and the fort of Gyula (September 1), the last important Habsburg strong point in northern Hungary, immensely strengthened his prestige and influence at a crucial time. On September 7 Süleyman died after about a week's illness, apparently of the gout, although some sources indicate that it could have been dysentery, apoplexy, or angina. With his military prestige, Sokullu was able to keep the army in line until Selim II reached Istanbul and took the throne, thus assuring a peaceful succession despite all the difficulties of the previous decade.

Thus ended the reign of the man considered by some to be the greatest of the sultans. Coming to the throne with a base of wealth and power unequaled by any predecessor or successor, he added to the empire Hungary, Transylvania, Tripoli, Algiers, Iraq, Rhodes, eastern Anatolia from Van to Ardahan, part of Georgia, the most important Aegean Islands, Belgrade, and Cerbe. He successfully fought the Habsburgs in the Mediterranean and the Portugese in the eastern seas, making the empire a major naval power. Ottoman institutions reached their peak during his reign, and, as we shall see, there was considerable cultural accomplishment. But signs of trouble were also discernible. His reign saw the triumph of the *devşirme*, the retirement of the sultan from active direction of the government, the rise to power of the harem, a failure to deal with the economic and social problems that were causing major discontent, and consequent mass uprisings in Rumeli and Anatolia. All these were Süleyman's heritage to his successors in the century that followed.

Notes to Chapter 4

1 Quoted in Ibn Khaldûn, *The Muqaddimah: An Introduction to History*, tr. Franz Rosenthal, 3 vols., New York, 1958, II, 191.

2 *Muqaddimah*, II, 193.

3 M. Canard, "Les Expéditions des Arabes contre Constantinople dans l'histoire et dans la légende," *Journal asiatique*, 208 (1926), 105; and L. Massignon, "Textes relatifs à la prise de Constantinople," *Oriens*, 6 (1953), 10–17.

4 Census of Kadi Muhyi al-Din, TKS D9524; Ekrem Hakkı Ayverdi, *Fatih Devri Sonlarında Istanbul Mahalleleri, Şehrin Iskâm ve Nüfusu*, Ankara, 1968; idem, *Osmanlı Mimarisinde Fâtih Devri 855–886 (1451–1481)*, 2 vols., Istanbul, 1973–1974.

5 Bistra Cvetkova, "Sur Certaines Reformes du Régime Foncier au Temps de Mehmet II," JESHO, 6 (1963), 104–120.

6 Mustafa A. Mehmet, "De Certains Aspects de la Societe Ottomane à la lumière de la Legislation (Kanunname) de Sultan Mahomet II (1451–1481)," *Studia et Acta Orientalia*, 2 (1960), 127–160.

7 Çağatag Uluçay, "Yavuz Sultan Selim nasıl Padişah oldu?" *Tarih Dergisi*, VI/9 (Mart 1954), 59–90; VII/10 (Eylül 1954), 117–152.

8 TKS, E4312 (29).

9 M. Tayyip Gökbilgin, "Lütfi Paşa," IA, VII, 96–101; Lütfi Paşa, *Asafname*, Istanbul, 1326.

5

The Dynamics of Ottoman Society and Administration

While the Ottoman Empire reached its territorial peak in the sixteenth century, its social and administrative institutions assumed their classic forms and patterns. Therefore, the period of Süleyman the Magnificent provides a watershed for us to step aside from the confines imposed by individual reigns and examine the internal structure of the empire.

The Ottoman view of the purpose and structure of state and society appears to have come primarily from traditional Middle Eastern concepts developed by the Sassanids and introduced into the Islamic Middle Eastern civilization by the Persian bureaucrats in the service of the Abbasid caliphs. The philosophical basis of political organization was analyzed in the writings of Nizam ul-Mülk and al-Ghazzali, who emphasized justice and security for the subjects. The fifteenth-century Ottoman chronicler Mustafa Naima presented this view as a "Cycle of Equity." He pointed out that: (1) There could be no *mülk* (rule) or *devlet* (state) without the military; (2) maintaining the military required wealth; (3) wealth was garnered from the subjects; (4) the subjects could prosper only through justice; (5) without *mülk* and *devlet* there could be no justice.[1] Thus the production and the exploitation of wealth for purposes of supporting the ruler and the state and securing justice for the subjects were expressed as the basis of political organization and practice.

Accordingly, society was divided into two groups: the large mass of subjects, whose primary purpose in life was to produce wealth by engaging in industry, trade, and agriculture and to pay taxes to the ruler; and a small group of rulers, themselves neither producing wealth nor paying taxes, but rather acting as instruments of the sovereign in collecting his revenues and using them to support him and his family as well as themselves. The main purpose of the state was to (1) organize the exploitation of the wealth belonging to the ruler, (2) provide for the expansion and defense of this wealth, (3) keep order, and (4) promote Islam while permitting the practice of other religions within the ruler's dominions. Government was created and administration organized to carry out these functions, and the army was entrusted with the defense and expansion of the sources of wealth as well as the protection of the ruler and the state. To guide rulers, administrators, and soldiers, as well as subjects in carrying out their roles in society, the religion of Islam had to be maintained, protected, and promoted. All other functions were left to the subjects to deal with as they wished through their own instruments of organization, with the ruler's ultimate duty being that of ensuring their rights in return for their payment of taxes and protecting his flock (*reaya*, or rayas) against all injustice while leading them along the "straight and narrow path" of God's will.

The Ruling Class

Those involved in the governing of the state, members of the Ruling Class, were known as Ottomans (*Osmanlılar*) because they were in the service of the ruling dynasty or as military people (*askeri*) because of the essentially military nature of their functions in the first century of the empire. During the first three centuries of Ottoman rule, the Ruling Class was dominated, as we have seen, first by members of the Turkoman families who created the principalities ruling much of Anatolia following the decline of the Seljuks; later by the Muslim urban elite as well as members of the ruling classes of the Byzantine and classical Islamic empires who flooded into Ottoman service during the fourteenth and fifteenth centuries as the empire took their territories; and, finally, by those brought into the system through recruitment in the *devşirme* and through conversion as adults. Regardless of origin, to be a full member of the Ottoman Ruling Class, an individual had to (1) accept and practice the religion of Islam and the entire system of thought and action that was an integral part of it; (2) be loyal to the sultan and to the state established to carry out his sovereign duties and exploit his revenues; and (3) know and practice the complicated system of customs, behavior, and language forming the Ottoman way.

Persons lacking these qualifications were considered to belong to the Subject Class, the protected flock of the sultan. Its members were able to rise into the Ruling Class by acquiring and practicing these attributes, while those in the Ruling Class or their children could and did become rayas by failing to practice them. There was thus a system of social mobility based on the possession of certain definable and attainable attributes. While children of existing members of the Ruling Class found it relatively convenient to acquire the characteristics required to retain their fathers' social status, this was not automatic. It was accomplished by a long course of study in the various schools maintained by the Ruling Class to train new members and by apprenticeship in the departments of government. Ambition, ability, and good fortune determined who rose in the Ottoman system.

Recruitment and Training

How did this social mobility take place? Many Ottomans were themselves children of members of the Ruling Class, but as time went on even more came from the system of recruitment and training known as *devşirme*. Originally, the term *devşirme* had been applied to the process of collection of the ruler's *pençik* (Pers. one-fifth) right to a portion of the booty captured in warfare. This was taken in the form of young prisoners who were converted and trained before being formed into the ruler's personal bodyguard, the *Yeni Çeri* (Janissary) or "New Troop." The development of the *devşirme* into an institution for the periodic levy of Christian children to fill positions in the palace and administration took place most likely early in the reign of Bayezit I, with its general application coming later under Murat II and Mehmet II. Most Christian subjects outside Istanbul were liable to the levy, with agents going periodically through the provinces, conscripting the brightest subject youths for service to the sultan. Each group of recruited children was turned over to a *sürücü* ("driver"), who brought them to Istanbul or Bursa, with the rayas living along the road being compelled to pay special taxes to meet the costs of their transportation and maintenance. Those showing exceptional qualities were put into the group of novice boys (*Acemi oğlan*) who were trained as Inner Service boys (*İç oğlan*) for the imperial palace. The balance were sent to Turks (*Türk oğlanları*) to work for cultivators, mainly in Anatolia, who gave them physical as well as secular and religious training to become Muslims and full Ottomans in the military service of the *kapıkulu* army. The best of the latter, however, could also subsequently enter the palace service as members of the *Bostancı* (gardener) corps, which guarded the gates and cared for the grounds of the sultan's residences.

The *devşirme* levy normally was not applied to children in Istanbul or the other major cities of the empire. Nor were children of rural craftsmen recruited because of the fear that this would harm industry and trade. There is some evidence, however, that urban Christian and Muslim parents resorted to bribery or sending their children to the country to assure the advancement in life that *devşirme* recruitment could bring. Jews and Armenians seem to have been excluded entirely, perhaps because of arrangements made with their *millet* leaders or perhaps simply because most of them lived in towns. Exemptions also were given to rayas who served the sultan in some special way – as cultivators of his personal lands, laborers in gold or silver mines, or guards of major passes and road crossings. The only Muslims regularly included were those of Bosnia. Most of them had converted to Islam after the Ottoman conquest and had particularly requested inclusion of themselves and their descendants in the *devşirme* as part of their arrangement with Mehmet II. These were grouped together under the name *potor* and sent directly to the palace service rather than to the military.

The *İç oğlan*s in the Inner Service of the palace received schooling to prepare them for service in the highest positions of the empire. Their work for the sultan took relatively little time, and the remainder of their days was spent at religious instruction as well as training in weaponry and calligraphy. All had to learn how to read and write Arabic, Persian, and Ottoman Turkish, the Koran, and the various Muslim sciences. Specialized training was provided to prepare them to enter particular branches of the Ruling Class. The *İç oğlan*s were given considerable physical training, emphasizing sports like wrestling, archery, weight lifting, lance throwing, and horsemanship. They were subjected to strict discipline, isolated from the outside world as well as their families, and cut off from women under the guard of the white palace eunuchs. The *İç oğlan*s were subjected to a third selection process after four years of training. Those found most qualified were placed in the regular palace service, mainly in the sultan's personal treasury or kitchen, while the rest became officers of the *Sipah* or *Silâhtar* battalions of the *kapıkulu* cavalry, subsequently going on to service as soldiers or administrators in various parts of the empire. Most members of the Ruling Class in the sixteenth century also had their *gulâm* slaves, sometimes acquired through the *devşirme* system, sometimes through purchase or capture in war. They were given similar training and then "freed" for entry as full members of the Ruling Class or as subjects. Regardless of their ultimate role in life, such former slaves always considered themselves bound to their old masters, acting for mutual advantage whenever it was possible for them to do so.

It is easy to decry a system that required separation from one's family, home, and religion for advancement, but the practice should be evaluated in the context of sixteenth-century conditions and values. In Ottoman society, as in Europe at the time, religion was not merely an expression of individual or even group viewpoints of life and the position of man in relation to his maker but also a definition of human behavior and position in all aspects of life. Human beings thought, spoke, acted, carried on business, married, bought, sold, and inherited property, and died according to customs and practices that accorded with the dictates of their religions. Religion, therefore, had to be part of the process by which the individual's status and position were changed, and the *devşirme* and *gulâm* systems did no more than recognize and institutionalize this fact, thus making possible a fluid social structure in which talented people could rise to important positions in the service of the sultan.

The Ruling Class divided itself into four functional groups: the Palace Institution and the Scribal, the Military, and the Cultural or Religious institutions.

A. *The Palace Institution*

The Palace Institution provided leadership for the Ruling Class as a whole. Proximity to the ruler has traditionally enhanced the importance of individuals throughout Middle Eastern history. Those in the palace had the special power and authority not only to provide, educate, and maintain rulers – and also to ensure that there would always be at least one prince who would be able to rule when needed – but also to make the entire Ottoman system operate. The palace itself was divided structurally and symbolically between the isolated rear areas, the harem, and the Inner Section (*Enderun*), on the one hand, and the more accessible Outer Section (*Birun*), on the other.

The Harem. The ruler's harem remained relatively simple in structure and organization as long as the Ottomans maintained their simple tribal institutions. But with the expansion of the empire and the increasing prestige and wealth of the ruler – combined with the model provided by the hierarchical organization and ceremonials of the Byzantine court – the Ottoman harem became ever more elaborate and complex, particularly after it was moved to the Topkapı Palace by Hürrem Sultan late in Süleyman's reign.

The eunuchs who protected the harem were led by the *dar üs-saade ağası* (*ağa* of the Abode of Felicity), who in the sixteenth century was ranked below only the grand vezir and *şeyhulislam*. His influence stemmed from his power to provide access to and communication with the sultan and exploitation of harem rivalries and factions. Mainly white men from the Caucasus through most of the sixteenth century, the eunuchs were supplemented thereafter with black slaves from the Sudan and central Africa.

The Inner Service. Servants of the harem who comprised the Inner Service (*Enderun*) were housed in the adjacent inner section of the palace, which also provided the locale for official activities such as meetings of the Imperial Council, receptions for ambassadors, and so on, which brought the sultan into contact with persons from the outside service or from outside the palace.

Under the direction of the *dar üs-saade ağası* the Inner Service was divided into six departments in descending order of rank: The Privy Chamber (*Has Oda*) was the highest-ranking section because of its dual role of performing the general service of the sultan and of caring for the holy relics. It was usually in the in-between (*mâ beyin*) apartments between the walls of the harem and the third court. Its principal officials were the sultan's swordkeeper (*silâhtar ağa*), who handled all communications to and from the sultan, his valet (*çohadar ağa*), who directed the pages in his personal service, and his personal secretary (*sır kâtibi*). Second was the Treasury Chamber (*Hazine Odası*), divided into two sections: the Outer Treasury (*Dış Hazine*), which kept the financial archives and the fur cloaks and other robes of honor conferred on dignitaries and cared for revenues and expenditures outside the palace, and the Inner Treasury (*İç Hazine*), which cared for expenditures within the Inner Service and stored all the jewels, thrones, robes and other valuables of the

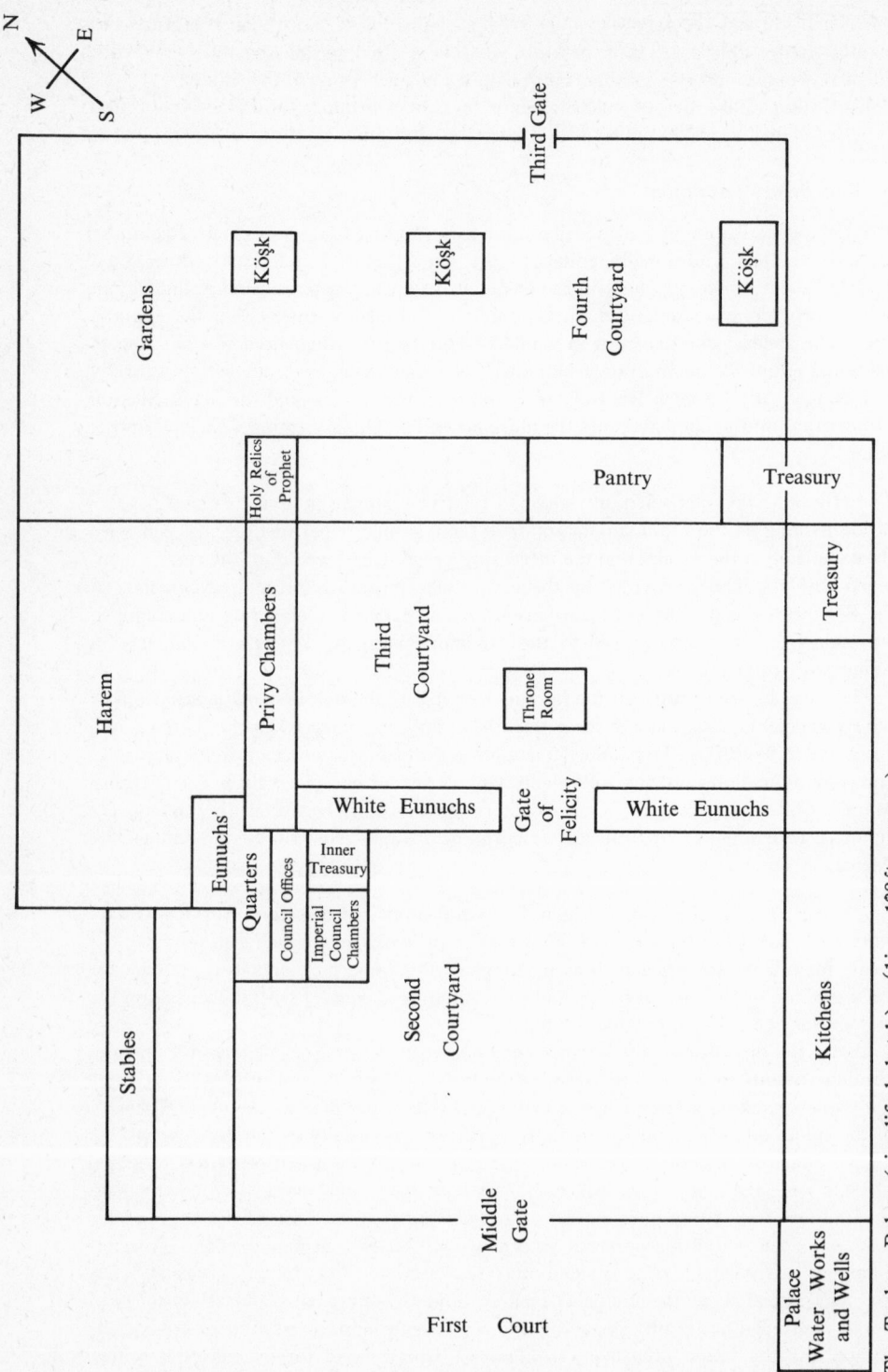

The Topkapı Palace (simplified sketch)   (1 in. = 188 ft. approx.)

sultan. Third was the Larder (*Kiler Odası*), responsible for meals. Fourth was the Campaign Chamber (*Seferli Odası*), created in 1635 to assume duties including "drum beating, folding turbans, head shaving and cleaning the royal clothes,"[2] important especially on campaigns. Fifth was the Falconry Department (*Doğancı Odası*), abolished in the middle of the seventeenth century. And sixth were the Large Chamber (*Büyük Oda*) and the Small Chamber (*Küçük Oda*), which organized the continued training and services of the *İç oğlan* pages.

Pages raised in the palace rose gradually in the Inner Service to the Privy Chamber, after which they were promoted either to positions in the Outer Service or to full membership in the Ruling Class, where, using their knowledge and experience, they assumed positions such as provincial governors, commanders, and grand vezirs.

The Outer Service (Birun). The second courtyard, or outer area (*Birun*), included servants of the sultan who were involved in affairs outside of as well as within the palace, in fact exercising the sultan's function of directing the army and administering the empire. Here there were five groups: (1) members of the ulema, including the sultan's teacher (*hoca*), in charge also of the education of the princes, his doctor (*hekim başı*), who also regulated other doctors throughout the empire, surgeon (*cerrah başı*), eye doctor (*kehhal başı*) and astrologer (*müneccim başı*), and the palace religious ritual leader (*hünkâr imamı*); (2) the *şehremini*, in charge of building and maintaining imperial palaces, supervising the construction and repair of public buildings and monuments in the capital through the chief architect (*mimar başı*), and maintaining the waterworks and water systems through the water supervisor (*su nazırı*); (3) the commissioner of the imperial kitchen (*matbah-ı âmire emini*), who supervised the preparation of food and provided supplies through the Imperial Pantry (*Kiler-i Âmire*) service; (4) the commissioner of the mint (*darphane emini*); and (5) the commissioner of grains (*arpa emini*), who provided grain and other supplies for the animals of the Imperial Stables (*Istabl-ı Âmire*) and who also cared for the animals of officials and ambassadors visiting the palace, working through the *emir-i ahor* in charge of the stables as well as caring for the carriages and wagons belonging to the sultan and members of his family.

The other officials of the Outer Service were divided into three groups. The first of these included officials of the imperial stirrup (*rikâb ağaları*) who because of their role of riding on both sides of the sultan in times of battle and in processions had special favor, such as the *ağa*s of the Janissary and other corps; the emir of the standard (*emir-i âlem*), who was in charge of storing and carrying the sultan's insignia of power and of transmitting messages between the sultan and foreign representatives; the chief gatekeeper (*kapıcı başı*), who supervised all the gatemen (*kapıcılar*) of the palace, in charge of guarding its gates, transmitting messages and orders, and executing the decisions of the Imperial Council, including the infliction of punishment through the bastinado; and the *çavuşlar*, directed by the *çavuş başı*, who acted as the messengers of the Imperial Council. The second group of *Birun* officials included the Gardener corps (*Bostancı Ocağı*), led by the *bostancı başı*, responsible for all the gardens of state, including those in the palace, and for policing the precincts of the palace itself as well as being charged with the organization and defense of the shoreline in Istanbul and the Sea of Marmara. The third group was composed of minor artisans, such as the tailors, furriers, cobblers, archers, and *peyk*s, who formed the sultan's personal bodyguard. The *Müteferrika* corps – composed primarily of the sons of vassal princes who were left in the sultan's service for training and as hostages for their fathers' good behavior – also belonged to this group.

All these officials and employees of the Inner and Outer services were formed into an extremely complex and highly regulated hierarchy. Their salaries and promotions were carefully determined by seniority, although this was sometimes modified by intervention of the sultan and close members of his family. They had to accompany the sultan on campaigns, during which each group was organized as a separate military force with specified military duties. Exceptional service was sometimes rewarded by assignments in the Ruling Class outside the palace, while most of the women of the palace who were not favored concubines of the sultan were ultimately given as wives to members of the Ruling Class as a sign of particular esteem.

B. *The Scribal Institution* (Kalemiye)

The most important single branch of the Ruling Class was that of the scribes (*kâtip;* pl. *küttâp*), or "men of the pen" (*ehl-i kalem*). Their institution had two branches, organized as the Imperial Council (*Divan-ı Hümayun*), in charge of correspondence and administration per se, and the Imperial Treasury (*Hazine-i Âmire*), which cared for finance and accounting. Within them departments were organized functionally, with the scribes also formed into a guild to perpetuate their arts and enforce professional standards. Each department was headed by a master (*hoca;* pl. *hâcegân*), operating through specialized foremen (*kalfa*) who directed the other scribes and supervised the training of apprentices (*şagirt*) and the examination of new candidates (*mülazım*) for membership in the guild as well as service in the department. Since all bureaucrats had to be trained in the traditional Islamic fields of knowledge, literature, history, geography, and the religious sciences, they received as much training from the ulema as they did from the scribes in their own department. The ulema achieved further influence in administration by sending many of their own to serve in the Scribal Institution. The relationship between the two was so close that members of both bore the common title *efendi,* and transfer between the two was far more frequent than it was with any of the other institutions of the Ruling Class. Members of the scribal guild served, of course, throughout the Ruling Class, but they were concentrated particularly in the Imperial Council and the Treasury.

The Imperial Council. The Imperial Council was from earliest times to the late seventeenth century the main central organ of Ottoman administration. It had four categories of members: (1) the vezirs, with rank of three horsetails, including the grand vezir and the governors of the more important provinces who were given the same rank and called *beylerbeyi;* (2) the scribes, represented by the treasurer and the *nişancı,* or head of the grand vezir's chancery. The *reis ul-küttap,* or chief of the council's scribes, and the chief translator (*baş tercüman*) were not formally members but attended the meetings and were allowed to participate in discussions and contribute information on special issues; (3) the military men, represented by the grand admiral and the *ağa,* or commander of the Janissary corps; and (4) the ulema, or religious and cultural class, represented by the judicial chiefs (*kazaskers*) of Rumeli and Anatolia as well as the *şeyhulislam.*

The work of the council was handled by its scribes under the *reis ul-küttap* in a number of departments: (1) the *Beylikçi,* or *Divan Kalemi* (directed by the *beylikçi,* the second most important scribal officer in the Imperial Council), which had the job of keeping the records of the council's deliberations and decisions and of drawing up official copies of those decisions in the form of decrees, proclamations, and treaties;

(2) the Appointments Department (*Tahvil Kalemi*), which recorded and issued orders for the appointment, dismissal, and transfer of all Ottomans of high rank as well as for all timars and *zeamets*, under the direction of the *tahvil kisedarı;* (3) the *Rüus*, or *Nişan Kalemi,* which under the *rüus kisedarı* did the same for all those in lower ranks; and (4) the *Âmedi Kalemi,* with the *âmedi* heading the personal secretarial staff of the grand vezir and the *reis ul-küttap,* in charge of transactions that involved the grand vezir's communications and contacts with foreign rulers, representatives, and merchants, making it the closest thing the Ottomans had to a foreign office until such a department was created in the nineteenth century. It should be noted that from the beginning of the office of the grand vezirate there was no special department for its holder other than the *âmedi* office in the Imperial Council. It was only much later (1654) that the grand vezirs began to build their own staff as a separate department of government, called *Paşakapısı* (Gate of the Paşa), or *Bab-ı Âli,* the Sublime Porte of European fame.

The Financial Institution (Maliye)

The scribes charged with the financial functions of the ruler conducted all activities connected with exploiting the wealth of the empire. Originally, during the first century of the empire, there had been little formal financial organization. The ruler had his personal treasury, and through his treasurer he collected the revenues that accrued from the *pençik* right to one-fifth of all booty. He collected also the revenues coming from lands left to his personal account as large royal holdings (*hass*). Since most revenues in the empire were alienated as timars to provide salaries for the sultan's soldiers and administrators, there was no need for a complicated central treasury. The payment of cash salaries to Janissaries and others led Grand Vezir Çandarlı Kara Halil Paşa (1368–1373) to develop such a treasury, with the revenues and expenditures of the sultan's treasury (*Hazine-i Hassa*) being separated from those of the state (*Hazine-i Âmire*).

Directing the entire financial structure was the *baş defterdar* (chief treasurer), entrusted with the additional duty of treasurer of Rumeli. Under him was the treasurer of Anatolia. Other treasurers were created subsequently to handle the financial affairs of provinces as they were conquered. The *defterdar* had been a relatively minor official during the empire's first century, with most financial matters being handled by the timar holders. But as he came to direct this complex organization, he became one of the major officials of the state, being authorized like the grand vezir and the judicial chiefs, to issue orders in his own name. Financial departments throughout the empire were organized according to a common kind of structure, which well demonstrated the elaborate system of bookkeeping that characterized Ottoman administration and reflected the Ottomans' particular concern for the effective exploitation of sources of wealth. Under the *defterdars* there were four types of departments. Of these, the *Defterhane* (Registry), headed by *defter emini*s (register commissioners), was in charge of basic records. It ran the *Icmal* (Summary) offices, which prepared the summary budgets of the individual provinces or the major treasury departments; the *Mufassal* (Detailed) offices, which kept itemized records of revenue sources and expenditures; and the *Ruzname* (Daybook) offices, which recorded payments. A second department, *Muhasebe* (Accounting), kept separate records of receipts, while a third, *Murakabe* (Auditing), audited the records of the other departments and kept the salary rolls of the army and of the palace service. The fourth department, the *Mevkufat* (Mortmain), was at first in charge only of recording property seized for the treasury but later also began to keep accounts of revenues and expenditures in kind.

The organization of the central treasury in Istanbul set the pattern for this distribution of function. The Imperial Treasury Department (*Hazine-i Âmire Dairesi*) recorded cash revenues, including the head tax from non-Muslims. Separate accounting offices for Rumeli and Anatolia recorded all revenues and expenditures of religious endowments founded by the sultans and their ministers. The Department of the Chief Treasurer (*Baş Defterdarlık Kalemi*) was in charge of the operation of ports and landing places along the Danube, regulated state monopolies such as salt, soap, and tobacco, and supervised the exploitation of gold, silver, and copper mines in Rumeli. The Mortmain Department kept a record of vacated holdings that reverted to the state, such as timars and tax farms. The fortresses accountant handled appointments and dismissals in forts all over the empire. After the sixteenth century these departments were expanded and modified according to need.

The Tax System. The Ottoman tax system, like its laws, was divided between those mentioned in and authorized by the Islamic law (*Şeriat*) and those decreed by the ruler on the basis of his sovereign right to legislate in secular matters not covered in the law. Most important of the *Şeriat* taxes were the tithe (*öşür;* pl. *âşâr*), the canonical one-tenth of the agricultural produce; the head tax (*cizye* or *harac*), collected from non-Muslims in three groups according to their ability to pay; the *zekât,* or alms, originally given by all pious Muslims directly in fulfillment of one of the basic requirements of their faith but later transformed into a tax collected by the state, at least ostensibly for the same pious purposes; the municipal tax (*ihtisap resmi*), collected by the market inspector (*muhtesip*) from all artisans and merchants as part of the licensing and regulating process; the sheep tax (*ağnam resmi*), which in addition to its strictly canonical charge on sheep included additional "customary" taxes added on all other animals; and the mines tax (*maden resmi*), which enabled the state to collect one-fifth of the yield of all privately owned mines.

The "sovereign prerogative" (*örfi*) taxes were also called taxes of the Imperial Council (*tekâlif-i divaniye*) because they were authorized by its decrees. These taxes (*rüsum*) varied widely throughout the empire and were often referred to as *âdat* (customary) because they included some pre-Ottoman local taxes. Of these, the *avarız* (household tax) was first imposed on villages and towns to meet extraordinary expenses such as providing for soldiers and functionaries visiting the area, campaign expenses, and emergency aid to neighboring areas that had suffered from natural calamities. Gradually, it developed into a regular tax. Another customary tax was the *çift resmi,* the basic tax paid by every Muslim and Christian subject in western Anatolia and Thrace in return for the right of cultivation of his *çift,* the basic unit of agricultural land, defined as the area that could be ploughed by a pair (*çift*) of oxen, with its exact size varying from 60 to 150 *dönüms* (1 *dönüm* being 940 square meters, or about ¼ acre) according to the fertility of the soil. In areas where the *çift resmi* was not imposed, the *ispenç resmi* (pasturage tax) was collected from Christian cultivators. Nomads paid pasturage fees to the holders of the *mukata'as* through which they passed. The *nüzûl bedeli* (alighting price) was levied in localities where officials passed while performing their duties. Numerous minor dues and fines were reminiscent of feudal practices. There were bridegroom taxes, fines paid to recover stray cattle, market taxes, customs duties levied on internal as well as external trade, and fees for using the public scales. Officials also received fees (*bahşiş*) from the subjects for the performance of their official duties.

The right to collect these taxes was considered by the Ottomans to be one of the most basic attributes of sovereignty. Indeed, the Ruling Class was created and maintained by the sultan largely for the very purpose of exercising this attribute. All such sources of revenue belonged to the sultan as his imperial possessions (*havass-ı hümayun*). He could and did sometimes alienate some of them permanently to individuals as private property (*mülk*) or in the form of endowments for religious purposes, or temporarily to individuals as fiefs (timars, *zeamets*, and *hasses*, according to size) in return for the performance of military or administrative duties other than those involved in collecting their taxes.

To carry out this function all sources of revenue in the imperial possessions were organized in units called *mukataʿa*, developed basically from the *iktas* of the earlier Islamic empires. The *mukataʿas* were further subdivided according to the extent to which the revenues of each went to the treasury or the holder. Those whose revenues went entirely to the treasury were called *emanets* (commissions), with their holders, the *emins* (commissioners), being compensated directly by treasury salary. These, however, were common only in the large cities, in administrative units involving the supervision of markets and the collection of customs duties where it was relatively easy for the treasury to supervise operations. Another practice was the assigning of *mukataʿas* as tax farms (*iltizam*) to holders (*mültezim*), who had to pay, in return, fixed annual sums to the treasury each year and were encouraged to be efficient by being allowed to keep the balance of their collections as personal profit. The exact opposite of the *emanet* was the timar, whose holder kept all the revenues in the holding in return for performing some other service for the sultan.

The Provincial Structure. So far we have discussed the institutions of the Ruling Class primarily at the central level of government. They were, however, also extended throughout the empire in administrative units formed on the provincial, district, and local levels.

The basic unit of provincial government in the Ottoman system was one inherited from the Seljuks, the *sancak* (Turkish; called *liva* in Arabic), literally, the "banner" of the ruler or administrator who was entitled to exercise all military and civil functions and powers with the Turkish title of bey. The original state of Osman consisted of his single *sancak*. Later other *sancaks* were created in Anatolia and Rumeli. The title of *beylerbeyi*, or "bey of beys," which at first was used to designate his principal military commander or adviser, subsequently came to signify the position of the civil ruler of the conquered territories in Rumeli as well as the commander of the Ottoman forces operating there. While the frontier districts were organized under the gazi leaders, they were allowed to retain their autonomy from the *beylerbeyi* so that they could better carry on their operations. A separate *beylerbeyi* for Anatolia, with his capital at Kütahya, was appointed at the end of the fourteenth century. He was always considered inferior in rank to the *beylerbeyi* of Rumeli, since large areas nominally under his control in the border areas were set aside for the ruler's sons, acting as *uc* beys over frontier *sancaks*, with the responsibility of warring against the enemies of the Ottomans, Muslim and Christian, while gaining the training and experience needed to serve as sultans if needed. Another reason for the superiority of the *beylerbeyi* of Rumeli was the fact that several leading figures held this post along with that of grand vezir, giving them the opportunity to dominate in the Imperial Council and ceremonies.

Additional *beylerbeyliks* were subsequently created in the border districts to defend the empire against its enemies. Beginning in the sixteenth century the term *vali* was used synonymously for *beylerbeyi* as governor, especially in the newer provinces, while vilayet became the standard term for "province."

The provinces were divided into *sancak*s and they in turn into districts (*kaza*s), towns, and villages. Governors were given the rank of two horsetails, the same as the vezirs, and bore the title *paşa*. They united both military and civilian functions. Officials appointed by the Ruling Class institutions in Istanbul to assist them were at first under their control but later were made more independent so as to balance their power and hinder efforts at revolt against the central authority. In most provinces the *divan efendisi* (council secretary) handled correspondence and records, and the treasurer (*mal defterdarı*) took care of provincial revenues and expenditures with the help of the timar *kethüdası* (timar lieutenant) and the timar *defterdarı* (timar treasurer). The provincial kadi (judge) supervised judicial and legal matters; the *tezkereci* was the governor's private secretary and was in charge of issuing all provincial orders and decrees; and a *subaşı* (police chief) was assigned to head the police in each major town or city, especially in the capital, which was invariably designated as the *sancak* of the governor, with its revenues being used to care for all governmental expenses in those provinces where all other revenues were assigned to timars. The Provincial Council (*Vilâyet Divanı*) had many of the same functions as the Imperial Council, including the right to issue orders, hear complaints, and punish infractions of the law by members of the Ruling Class.

There were two distinct types of provinces from the sixteenth century on. In the older timar provinces all the revenues were given out to the holders of timars, *zeamet*s, and *hass*es, with the governors and other officials being compensated from the revenues of the central *sancak* together with some revenues set aside especially for them. The timar holders accomplished all the duties of tax collection and maintaining order locally, under the supervision of the *sancak* holders. In the tax farm provinces that came into being in the sixteenth century, however, the governors essentially held each province as a tax farm. While obliged to deliver fixed annual sums to the central treasury as shipments (*irsâliye*), they were allowed to keep the balance of the tax collections as personal profit in addition to regular salaries (*salyâne*) paid them out of the central treasury. All the European provinces – with the exception of the autonomous Principalities of Wallachia, Moldavia, Transylvania, and the Crimea – were timar provinces, as was Anatolia, with the exception of a few border *sancak*s in the east. In the Arab world, parts of Aleppo, Tripoli of Syria, and Damascus were maintained in the same way, with their remaining portions as well as Egypt and North Africa being organized in the form of tax farms. In the tax farm provinces most of the duties of security, as well as tax assessment and collection, were arranged by officials of the government, with government expenses thus increasing in direct proportion to the revenues collected.

C. *The Military Institution* (Seyfiye)

Those Ottomans involved in protecting and expanding the empire, keeping order and security, assuring the proper exploitation of its resources, and protecting the organization and functions of the rest of the system were gathered together as the "Men of the Sword" (*Ehl-i Seyf*) in the Military Institution of the Ruling Class.

The Land Army. The Military Institution as such was basically divided into two groups the land army and the navy. The former was comprised of the "slaves of the porte" (*kapıkulu;* pl. *kapıkulları*) and the provincial forces.

1. *The* Kapıkulu *Army.* This was, essentially, the permanent standing central

army of the sultan. Originally manned by prisoners and mercenaries, Muslim and non-Muslim alike, later it was composed almost entirely of youths recruited through the *devşirme* system.

(*a*) *The Janissary Corps.* The Janissary infantry was the most important part of the *kapıkulu* army as it served as the military arm of the *devşirme* class. The corps was divided into 101 battalions (*orta*) commanded by officers called *çorbacıs* (literally "soup ladlers"). There also were the *segbans* (*seymens*, "keepers of the hounds"), with 34 battalions of from 40 to 70 men each, in charge of hunting and going to war with the sultan and acting as his personal guards at all times. Since they were closest to the sultan, the *segbans* provided most of the officers of the other corps. Selim I created a special new group of battalions, the *ağa bölüks* (commander units), which also served as the personal force of the Janissary commander (*ağa*), carrying out his increasingly multiple duties, which came to include keeping order in the capital, guarding the sultan, and forming the core of the army. Associated with the Janissaries was the *Bektaşi* mystic order. Its preachers served as the principal advisers of the Janissaries, maintaining the religious knowledge and practices of its men and serving as chaplains of its battalions. It was only in the late sixteenth century that the *Bektaşis* were officially attached to the corps through its ninety-ninth battalion, with their grand master appointed as its *çorbacı*.

The Janissary corps was supposed to maintain itself on a war basis at all times and be ready for instant action; therefore, its men were not allowed to marry and had to remain in their barracks and train regularly. Numbering no more than 30,000 men under Süleyman, they were not the largest group in the army, but because of their organization, training, and discipline, as well as their expert use of rifles, pikes, bows, and arrows, they formed the most important fighting force in the empire until well into the seventeenth century. When they were not campaigning, the Janissaries were charged with maintaining security in key points throughout the empire. In Istanbul they guarded the meetings of the Imperial Council and served as the city's police- and firemen, except at night and on Friday evenings, when their strict observance of their religious obligations left these duties to be performed by others. They also served in rotation as guards of the main gates of cities, towns, forts, and police stations around the empire and as provincial city police, normally for terms of nine months before returning to the Istanbul barracks. They were paid wages on a quarterly basis, with special bonuses for individuals in return for special or difficult service.

(*b*) *The Artillery Corps.* The bulkiness of the new weapons, such as cannon and guns using gunpowder, delayed their adoption for general use. The feudal cavalry resisted because its rapid movements were hindered, but the *kapıkulu* infantry, that is, the Janissaries, adopted them quickly and completely under Mehmet II. Under Bayezit II the defeats inflicted by the Mamluks in eastern Anatolia led the sultan to provide the Janissaries with hand weapons (harquebuses) and to develop more mobile cannon and effective shells than were available in the past so that they could be used in conjunction with the entire army and not only part of it. The *Cebeci* (Armorer) corps was in charge of making and providing the weapons used by the Janissaries and transporting them to where they were needed. The *Cebeci* men were also trained as infantrymen using hand guns and, as such, were charged with policing the districts of Istanbul around their barracks, opposite the Ayasofya in Istanbul. The corps was small and select, numbering no more than 625 men in 1574 and increasing rapidly only afterward as part of the general increase of corps membership and the collapse of standards and discipline that affected the army in the age of decline.

The Cannon corps (*Topçu Ocağı*) was organized under Murat II to manufacture and use cannons, came to its full strength as a result of Bayezit II's reforms, and thereafter supported both the Janissaries and the feudal forces in battles and sieges, in addition to guarding important forts and places. The corps was divided into two sections – foundry and firing – to carry out its functions. Its principal barracks and foundry were in the area of Istanbul known today as Tophane (Foundry), and additional branches of the corps were stationed and foundries built in different parts of the empire. Like the Janissary corps, the Cannon corps was divided into battalions and had about 1100 men in 1574 and 5000 in the seventeenth century. Since cannons and cannonballs slowed the march of the army, under Mehmet II a new Cannon-Wagon (*Top Arabacı*) corps was established to transport arms and ammunition during campaigns and also to manufacture and store the cannon wagons. Its factory was in the Tophane section, while its barracks were nearby in the Şehiremini district, with units also being stationed in forts and towns around the empire. Organized in 63 battalions, it had 400 men in 1574 and only 622 in the late seventeenth century. A special fleet of small boats was maintained to carry cannons by water.

Finally, sieges of forts and cities were carried out by two allied corps: (1) the Miners (*Lağımcıyân*), who were in charge of digging subterranean mines and trenches to undermine enemy walls and cannon emplacements; and (2) the Mortar Men (*Humbaracıyân*), who were in charge of manufacturing, transporting, and firing the mortars, mines, grenades, and bombs that were propelled against enemy forts whether by land or sea. Organized under Murat II, the Miners were in two divisions according to their means of support. On the one hand, those who were salaried and part of the *kapıkulu,* serving to support Janissary attacks on fortified places, were attached to the *Cebeci* corps. On the other hand, those attached to timars were organized under the command of the provincial armies to support their campaigns. The Mortar corps also had two main sections, with those involved in the manufacture of weapons allied to the *Cebeci* corps and those charged with using them in battle and siege warfare being under the Artillery corps. In addition, a third section of the Mortar corps consisted of men who were permanently stationed in the forts around the empire and were supported by timars rather than salaries. Thus they were under the command of the fort commanders and feudal generals rather than their corps leaders even though they legally remained a part of the *kapıkulu* army.

(*c*) *The* Kapıkulu *Cavalry.* The *kapıkulu* also had a cavalry branch, the *Kapıkulu Süvarileri.* Occasionally, it is confused with the provincial cavalry but in fact was quite distinct, being maintained in Istanbul by salaries rather than timars and generally being called *Sipâh* (Horsemen), *Altı Bölük Halkı* (Men of the Six Regiments), or simply *Bölük Halkı* (Regiment Men) rather than *Sipahi,* which was applied to the feudal cavalry. Of the six divisions composing the *kapıkulu* cavalry the first two, called *Ulufeciyân* (Salaried Men) and divided into the right and the left were established by Kara Timurtaş Paşa, the *beylerbeyi* of Rumeli, during the reign of Murat I, out of the salaried cavalry then in his service. The third and fourth, named *Gureba* (Strangers, Foreigners), also divided into left and right, were organized soon afterward from among Muslim mercenaries entering Ottoman service from other parts of the Middle East. The final two regiments, named *Silâhtar*s (weapon bearers) and *Sipahi oğlan* (*Sipahi* children) were organized later, probably under Mehmet I, and were the elite of the entire force. In general, the men of the first four groups were known collectively as the "four regiments" (*Bölükât-ı Erba'a*) and operated on both sides of the sultan in battle, while the *Silâhtar*s and *Sipahi* children operated only on the right close to the sultan. All had higher salaries and more prestige than the *kapıkulu* infantry corps, so that positions in them were highly valued and sought. Members came from *Iç oğlan* graduates not considered quite capable enough for palace service; children of existing members of the six corps; Muslims from elsewhere in the Middle East, mostly Arabs, Persians, and Kurds; members of the Janissary corps who particularly distinguished themselves; and also, occasionally, abler members of the other *kapıkulu* corps. During campaigns, the *Sipahi* children and *Silâhtar*s were responsible for guarding the person of the sultan. The latter also had the job of clearing out and opening roads and bridges before the main army, leading and guarding the sultan's horses, and carrying his horsetails.

Since these corps were mounted forces, they were stationed mostly in the outskirts of Istanbul and the other major cities, with each of these groups being commanded by a *kethüda yeri* (local lieutenant) appointed by and responsible to the *ağa* of his own corps. They were salaried. For the same reasons as the provincial cavalrymen, they avoided heavy hand guns, instead using bows and arrows, scimitars, daggers, lances, and axes. Numbering about 6,000 men late in the sixteenth century, they rose to 20,844 in the late seventeenth century and 22,169 early in the eighteenth.

2. *The Provincial Forces.* The largest part of the Ottoman army was maintained in the provinces, including the landed *Sipahi* cavalry, the *akıncı* raiders, and various soldiers and other troops stationed at fortresses, passes, and other strategic locations. (a) *The* Timarlı Sipahi*s.* It was, of course, the timar system that nourished, sustained, and provided most of the cavalrymen who served in the sultan's campaigns. We have already examined the timar in its administrative and financial aspects. What was its military role? The timar holder, given the right to collect its tax revenues, held that position as a *dirlik,* or revenue granted as a "living," in return for performing other services to the state, mainly military ones. The timar thus was the equivalent of salary given the officers and soldiers of the army in return for continued performance of their military duty and for maintaining themselves and their retainers ready to join the fight, bringing whatever arms, supplies, and food were needed during the campaign without placing any further burden on the treasury.

The timars were classified into three groups according to the amount of their revenues and the importance of the service performed in return. The regular timars involved revenues of no more than 19,999 *akçe*s per year and were given to cavalrymen who distinguished themselves in battle or in other ways. Those producing from 20,000 to 99,999 *akçe*s annually were called *zeamet*s and were given to timar holders who demonstrated extraordinary ability or bravery in battle as well as to members of the Ruling Class who held high positions in the central government or permanent standing army. Those bringing more than 100,000 *akçe*s were the *hasse*s, originally set aside for the sultan and members of his family, but subsequently given also to the grand vezirs and other ministers who were particularly favored by the sultan.

For those required to provide military service in return, each holder had to maintain horses and provide arms, food, and other supplies for himself and for retainers (*cebeli*) in numbers proportional to his revenues. The basic revenue of the timar, called the *kılıç* (sword), or *iptida* (beginning), usually amounted to about 6000 *akçe*s annually in Rumeli and from 1500 to 3000 in Anatolia and Asia and was defined as being the amount needed for the holder to provide his own service and equipment to the army when required. For every 3000 *akçe*s of additional revenue accruing to the timar holder and 5000 *akçe*s to the *zeamet* holder, they were required to maintain, arm, and bring to campaigns an additional *cebeli* and his horse. Heroic and/or special service entitled the holders to bonuses (*terakki*) of from 3000 to 5000 *akçe*s annually added to their basic *iptida*s, which, of course, included the obligation to maintain additional *cebeli*s in return and automatically raised the timar of an individual to a *zeamet* or even a *hass* if the total rose to the appropriate amount.

Normally, if a timar holder died, the *iptida* portion of his holding would go to his eldest son if he was of age and qualified to perform the requisite service. But the *terakki* portions were supposed to return to the reserve pool held by the district *sancak* bey to provide similar rewards for other timar holders in the district. If the heir was not yet of age, he was allowed to send a *cebeli* in his place, often serving in fact as the latter's apprentice to learn his duties so that he could take over the timar. If the *Sipahi* was wounded or became too old to fight, he was retired to a portion of his *iptida*, which he was allowed to exploit as his *kılıç hakkı* (sword right), with the balance going to his son or other *Sipahi*s.

Younger sons usually received timars with slightly smaller *iptida*s than that of their father when they became available, but they were not entitled to hold the *iptida* and substitute a *cebeli* during their minority as was the eldest brother. If the timar holder died without leaving any male children, the holding went back to the *sancak* bey for redistribution to another competent horseman, often a man who had previously served as a *cebeli* in the district. When the *beylerbeyi* summoned the feudal contingents of his province to battle, the *sancak* beys were charged with calling up and commanding all the timar holders and *cebeli*s in their districts and also with canceling the holdings of those who failed to report or provide the required number of *cebeli*s.

The *Sipahi* lived in the village where the lands of his timar were located, collected the land tax from the peasants – usually in kind because of coin shortages and also the lack of accessible markets where the peasant could sell his crops – and then spent the revenues to maintain himself and his *cebeli*s. The peasants also had to give their timariots a certain amount of free labor as well as loads of fodder, hay, and wood; but the exact requirements varied according to the feudal customs in force before the Ottoman conquest. The peasant who worked the land had the right to continue to do so as long as he kept it under cultivation and paid his taxes, thus securing a kind of usufruct that even the timar holder did not possess. He could pass this right to his sons but could not sell it or give it away without special permission from his timar holder. Where the cultivator died or fled and left the land vacant, the timariot had the right to give it to another peasant who agreed to cultivate it in return for payment of a special tax. The timar holder also had the option of renting such vacated land to peasants who agreed to pay a certain annual rent in return for retaining the profits, like a sharecropper. Normally, in addition to the revenues received from the taxes paid by the cultivators, each timar holder was given one *çiftlik* of land for his personal use, usually farming it with hired labor as well as that which he was entitled to require from the cultivators in the timar. If the cultivator fled from his land but was found in an adjacent or neighboring district, the *Sipahi* could get the local kadi to issue a decree compelling him to return. Or if the cultivator in question had become an artisan and had income, the *Sipahi* could force him to pay instead compensation in the form of a tax called *çift bozan resmi* or "tax for disrupting cultivation."

The *Sipahi* was in charge not only of assuring cultivation and collecting taxes within his timar but also of keeping order in the villages, for the most part using his *cebeli*s for this purpose. When fines were levied for minor crimes, he kept half for himself and surrendered the other half to his *sancak* bey. When the authority of the kadi was needed to impose the fine, he also collected a share from both parties.

When the *Sipahi*s were called to service, the *sancak* beys of each district would arrange for 1 *Sipahi* in 10 to be left in the *sancak* to care for order and tax collection while his fellows were away. Only during campaigns did the *sancak* beys appoint subordinate officers to exercise their authority over the *Sipahi*s, with *alay* beys being appointed to command each 1000 *Sipahi*s. Usually, the *Sipahi*s returned home every winter to see to their duties, but when they had to stay away, those remaining from each *sancak* chose 5 to 10 of their number to return to the *sancak* as revenue collectors (*harçlıkçı*s), who secured the money and supplies needed to maintain them during the subsequent year's campaign. The *alay* beys normally were compensated for their services with *zeamet*s in the same or an adjacent district.

In 1527, immediately after Süleyman's accession, there were 37,521 timar holders in the empire, of whom 27,868 were regular *Sipahi*s, who with their *cebeli*s formed a cavalry force of some 70,000 to 80,000 men in all, as opposed to the *kapıkulu*, which still had, at best, no more than 27,900 men. In addition there were 9,653 timar holders who performed their service as members of fort garrisons: 6,620 in Europe, 2,614 in Anatolia, and 419 in the Arab world. At this time the timar holders absorbed 46 percent of the total land tax revenues in Rumeli, 56 percent in Anatolia, and 38 percent in the Arab world, with the remaining revenues going to the treasury through tax farms or to private properties or foundations.[3] In 1607 Ayn-i Âli Efendi reported that there were some 44,404 timars producing a mounted force of 105,339 men. It is clear, therefore, that Ottoman military supremacy was not achieved by superiority in numbers, as often was claimed by their defeated European enemies. Superiority in the quality of command, discipline, training, and tactics must, rather, have been the decisive factor.

(*b*) *Special Provincial Guards.* Special forces organized in the provinces provided particular service as guards. The most important of these were the fortress guards, the *derbent* guards, and the permanent advanced raiding forces.

(*i*) Fortress Guards. There were many forts around the empire, in and out of towns, not only to guard the frontiers but also to maintain authority over the feudatories. In many cases Janissary units were assigned to form the core of the fortress garrisons. There also were the *Azap*s, developed originally in the fourteenth century in the Menteşe and Ottoman principalities as naval marines, later becoming a light archery force serving in front of the artillery and Janissaries to keep the enemy away until the regular forces were fully prepared to attack. The *Azap*s began serving in the fortress garrisons late in the fourteenth century, normally as pickets and guards at night and when the remaining members of the garrisons were out of the forts to serve in the army, or to keep order and enforce tax collections in the districts under their supervision. The *Azap*s were a salaried force like the Janissaries but came mainly from among Anatolian Turkomans rather than *devşirme* Christians. They were, therefore, allowed to marry and leave their position to competent male heirs. Beginning in the sixteenth century the *Azap*s joining the imperial army from the forts began to help the other corps as sappers and bridge and road builders, largely supplanting the *Cebeci* corps in these functions once the latter was no longer provided with sufficient new members through the *devşirme* system. After this time, all Muslim males in the border areas were liable for conscription into the *Azap* corps, with every 20 to 30 households being forced to choose one of their young men to fulfill this obligation every year and the others providing food and provisions to the corps instead. In the mid-sixteenth century, the corps was officially divided into fortress (*Kale Azapları*) and naval (*Deniz Azapları*) forces, which remained in service until the reforms of Mahmut II early in the nineteenth century.

The other principal units manning the Ottoman forts were the *Gönüllüyan* (Volunteers), formed originally by enlistment from among the neighboring population, including Christians who were forced to convert to Islam as part of the process by which they entered this segment of the Ruling Class. This corps was divided into foot and cavalry units, and its men were usually paid by their own villages rather than by the treasury.

(*ii*) *Derbent* Guards. In considering the local forces that kept order, guarded the frontiers, and joined the war against the infidel across the borders, we must deal with a group of Ottomans that was in an intermediate stage between the Ruling and Subject classes. Composed largely of non-Muslim subjects – some converted, some not, and some born Muslims – this group derived a certain right to govern, and hence a limited privilege of tax exemption, through laws issued by the sultan by virtue of his "sovereign prerogative" (*örf*) to legislate. They were, therefore, included among the "people of the *örf*" law (*ehl-i örf*) (see p. 134). Most prominent among them, and by far the least known of the Ottoman armed forces, were those who guarded the *derbent*s, or fortified guardhouses, set up to command and guard military and trade roads, mountain passes, frontier strong points, as well as roads leading through villages. Developed essentially out of the Ilhanid *tutkavul* systems maintained to protect caravans and roads, the Ottoman *derbent* system spread widely as early as the fourteenth century, extending also into the lands of the Crimean Tatars and Golden Horde north of the Black Sea.

The first formal organization for the *derbent*s was developed in the mid-fifteenth century, with Muslim and Christian inhabitants alike being employed to guard their own villages and keep the adjacent roads and bridges in good order. As time went on, the *derbent*s often stimulated the development of villages whose entire population was devoted to serving and maintaining them, with their organization and numbers expanding in proportion to the weakening of the regular army in an age of social and economic discontent. In many cases *han*s and *kervansaray*s established originally to house merchants and other travelers became *derbent*s at least partly for self-protection if for no other reason. The name *martolos* was applied first to Christian soldiers, mainly fief holders under the Byzantines, Serbs, and Bulgarians, who entered Ottoman military service in return for retaining their holdings in the timar system. In the late fifteenth century these *martolos* performed garrison duties in most of the Ottoman forts established along the Danube and also in Hungary as it was added to the Ottoman domains by Süleyman the Magnificent. Süleyman used so many *martolos* to man the *derbent*s in his Christian provinces that the names *Derbentçi* and *martolos* were used interchangeably there. As time went on, in addition to the regular salaried men many local Christians were hired as auxiliaries in return for tax exemptions.

The *derbent*s in many places also were at least partly manned by the descendants of the Turkoman nomads, in Rumeli taking the name *yörük* (nomad) and in Anatolia *türkmen*. Usually formed into battalions of 25 to 30 men, their members served in campaigns in rotation, with no more than 5 going at any one time. The remainder stayed home and paid those who went 50 *akçe*s per campaign in lieu of service. Most members of these groups supported themselves by cultivating small pieces of land turned over to them, being excused from taxes in return – thus the origin of the word *müsellem* (exempted). There were 1294 *yörük*s, all Muslims, at the end of the sixteenth century, but many of the 1019 *müsellem*s of the same period were Christian, called *voynuk* when they were Bulgarians. They cared for the horses of high Ottoman officials or served as falconers (*doğancı*s) for the sultan and members of his family.

The *derbent* men were compensated either through timars in the vicinity or through tax exemptions. They often also collected fees from those whom they protected along the road but in some areas had to provide compensation to travelers who were robbed within the districts they were guarding. Typically, these positions were hereditary, for the timar posts at least. Sometimes entire villages were responsible for manning and maintaining the *derbent* posts and providing for their expenses, sending men out to serve in rotation and providing all necessary supplies. Such services were compensated through tax exemptions.[4]

(*iii*) The Raiding Forces. Through most of the sixteenth century much of the Ottomans' frontiers with the Christian infidel were guarded not by the regular garrisons but by the special raiding forces, the gazis, subsequently called *akıncı*s (raiders), who were organized in special frontier districts under the command of border princes (*uc* beys). Forming a kind of light cavalry, the *akıncı*s were in charge of raiding into enemy territory, capturing weapons, money, and slaves and also keeping the enemy forces too busy to attack the Ottomans or prepare defenses against the regular Ottoman army. The *akıncı* leaders and their followers were usually exempt from taxes, holding their districts as hereditary timars, with tax collections going to finance their operations and positions passing from father to son over the generations. The *akıncı*s continued to serve until 1595 when after a major rout in Wallachia they were dissolved by Grand Vezir Koca Sinan Paşa, their lands and men being annexed to the regular provinces in their vicinities. After this whatever raids were mounted into infidel territory were carried out by the *yörük*s as well as men sent especially for this purpose by the Crimean Tatars.

In addition there were the *deli*s, or "madmen," so called because of the ferocity of their attacks, although there are also indications that the name was simply a contraction from the term *delil* ("guide"), which was originally applied to the organization. Organized late in the fifteenth century, the *deli*s were mainly Croats, Serbs, and Bosnians converted to Islam so that they could carry arms in the service of the sultan, although apparently some Turks also were included.

Ottoman Campaign Organization and Strategy. The Ottomans depended on a well-organized spy system to plan their campaigns. Routes followed in earlier campaigns, sometimes a century old, usually provided the models. Geography determined the major bases and campaign routes. In Anatolia, Erzurum – reached through the Black Sea from Istanbul or overland via Diyarbekir – was the major base for campaigns northward into the Caucasus or east into Iran and Azerbaijan. Diyarbekir and Van were the bases for campaigns into Syria as well as Azerbaijan, with Mosul and Aleppo also being used at times. For campaigns north of the Dnieper and Dniester, the Danubian forts of Ochakov, Kilburun, Akkerman, and Kilia were especially important, with Ismail, Ibrail, Silistria, and Rusçuk also being used as bases for attack. Campaigns toward the middle reaches of the Danube went from Istanbul to Edirne, through the Balkan Mountains to Filibe and Sofia to Niş, then up the Morava valley to Belgrade. Across the Danube was Hungary, with the Tisza river valley giving access to Transylvania without the necessity of crossing the Carpathians from Wallachia. The Sava and Drava gave easy access to Bosnia, and from it the Ottoman army could pass through the mountain valleys into Montenegro, Herzegovina, and Dalmatia and along the Adriatic coast. Finally, Salonica was the main base for campaigns into Greece and Albania.

Because of the partly feudal nature of the army and the need for the sultan and his standing forces to return to Istanbul periodically, and also because of the extremely poor road conditions during the winter, campaigns were carried out mainly between April and September, with the army being demobilized during the winter months. Campaigns normally were planned soon after demobilization, in October and November. During the next two months – even while the timar holders were back home collecting taxes and supplies – orders were sent for them to gather for subsequent campaigns in April. As a rule, it was impossible for the entire army to gather together until early July, so that campaigns had to be carried out entirely in August and September, with the advance of winter and lessening supplies of food and fodder compelling the army to retire and disband before October was too far along. This situation made it virtually impossible for the sultan to mount a campaign extending beyond northern Hungary or eastern Anatolia in a single year.

Campaign preparations required the amassing of huge quantities of supplies and war matériel. Even more difficult was the supply of food and fodder for the men and animals. Herds of cattle and sheep were brought along with the army; cultivators living adjacent to the line of march also supplied animals, grain, and other food, sometimes with compensation. Although the government normally did not regulate agriculture and trade, it did encourage the cultivation of grain and rice along the main campaign routes so that these at least would be readily available. Oxen and buffalo were specially raised in Rumeli to pull the wagons and haul the cannon, while mules and draft horses from the lower Danube and camels from Anatolia and the Fertile Crescent also were used for lesser loads.

Campaigns were inaugurated with elaborate ceremonies and rituals. Two of the sultan's six horsetails, or one of the grand vezir's three if he was in charge of the campaign, were placed in the first courtyard of the palace in Istanbul to indicate that campaign preparations were underway. Thereafter, these horsetails were sent one day ahead of the main army to signify its impending arrival, with Istanbul's western suburb of Davut Paşa serving as the first night's camp when the army was going into Europe, and Üsküdar, across the Bosporus, performing the same function for marches into Anatolia. The forces leaving Istanbul were joined by a procession of contingents representing the various craft guilds that were sending members along to practice their trades in the service of the army. Then came the Janissary corps, the other corps, and the members of the Ruling Class, led by the sultan or the grand vezir, with ceremonies of farewell following for those left behind. It was customary for the sultan, the grand vezir, and all important officials to go with the army, along with their households, treasuries, and personal retainers. Substitutes (*kaimakam*) were left to perform their duties in Istanbul. This practice was gradually reversed after Süleyman's reign. The substitutes accompanied the army while the important officials stayed home.

Great care was taken to prepare the way for the army as it marched. Orders were sent ahead to repair roads and bridges; piles of rocks and stakes were set up to show the line of march when the regular roads were not followed. Through most of the sixteenth century, the sultans maintained very strict discipline among their men during the march, punishing anyone who damaged property along the way and providing full compensation to those who suffered. The army was composed of the advance forces of *akıncıs*, *delis*, and *yörüks* that prepared the way; a vanguard of special cavalry led by the *Çarhacıbaşı;* the Janissary infantry and the other corps; the sultan and other officials; and, finally, the feudal horsemen going on both sides and providing a rear guard.

Marches usually took place from the early hours of morning until about noontime, when the camp was established. At the center of the camp were the tents and retainers of the sultan and the other important members of the Ruling Class, which were surrounded by the Janissaries and the other palace troops forming the central force.

Then camped the provincial feudal forces and other standing corps from the non-feudal provinces, most often led by their governors or chief military officers. Strict discipline was enforced, with the soldiers being forbidden to drink and required to maintain cleanliness by regular barbering and washing, and with general quiet in force – all in considerable contrast to the situation existing in the armies of their Christian enemies at the time.

In battles the Janissaries and other palace corps were stationed around the sultan and the grand vezir and formed the central pivot of Ottoman tactics, although they were numerically small in relation to the other forces. They were protected by trenches and surrounded by cannons and wagons, with the *Sipahi* horsemen protecting their flanks and maneuvering to envelop or ambush the enemy as it attempted to reach the center.

The Naval Forces. It took some time before the structure and the organization of the navy were developed to a degree comparable to that of the land forces. As long as land warfare was the basis of the Ottoman strategies of conquest – with the navy doing no more than defending straits and coasts and transporting soldiers – the officers of the land forces held most of the positions and ranks of power and gained most of the financial fruits of victory. Nevertheless, a structure of naval organization and command gradually evolved based mainly on Venetian and Genoese models and often using Italian naval terminology or its Turkish equivalent. It became a fully developed system under the leadership of Hayruddin Paşa and his immediate successors in the late sixteenth century.

At the apex of the Ottoman naval structure was the *derya* bey (bey of the sea), called *kaptan* or *kapudan paşa* after the Italian *capitano,* and finally *kapudan-ı derya* or *kaptan-ı derya* (captain of the seas or grand admiral) beginning early in the sixteenth century. The first holder of this position was one Baltaoğlu Süleyman Bey, appointed by Mehmet II as a reward for his services in the Golden Horn during the capture of Constantinople. He and his immediate successors were given only the rank of *sancak* bey, receiving the revenues of the *sancak* of Gallipoli and the *kazas* of Galata (whose largely Genoese population was given certain trade and other tax concessions in return for helping with the navy) and Izmit (whose tax obligations were fulfilled in the form of lumber for the ships), to be used for building, maintaining, and manning the fleet. Only under Hayruddin did the leader of the fleet gain the title and rank of the *beylerbeyi,* with the right to sit in the Imperial Council. Various Aegean Islands were added to the original navy holdings to form the province of *al-Cezayir* (the Islands), which, with the province of Algiers, formed permanent timars to provide the commander of the navy with the necessary funds. Hayruddin's rank, however, was considered to be a personal reward for his success against Dorea, and his sixteenth- and seventeenth-century successors for the most part had the somewhat lower rank of vezir of two horsetails. It was only subsequently, as part of the general decline of Ottoman organization and titulary structure long after the power of the navy had declined, that the grand admirals definitively gained the rank and power of the three-horsetail vezir.

The affairs of the navy were centered in the Imperial Dockyard (*Tersane-i Âmire*), which coordinated several dockyards in different parts of the empire as well as the fleet and officers and men working in them. Both fighting and construction/maintenance activities were directed by the grand admiral, but the officers and men of the two services were kept relatively distinct. Each shipyard was operated by a hierarchy of officials led by the commissioner of the shipyard, assisted by the lieutenant of the shipyard, commander of the shipyard, port operations commanders, shipyard scribes, shipyard recordkeeper, and others. Fleet operations were less formally organized until Hayruddin's time. Each ship was commanded by a captain (*reis*), with those of the larger ships being called *kaptan* or *hassa reis,* the latter because they were given timars in the *sancak*s of the grand admiral to provide funds and men for their ships. After the mid-sixteenth century all ship captains were called *reis,* with the term *kaptan* being limited to the leaders of the flotillas into which they were organized. Between them and the grand admiral there was little formal organization until about a century later, when several ranks of admiral were provided.

Manning the ships, aside from the *Azap* marines, were men recruited from the adjacent coasts, including Turks, Greeks, Albanians, and Dalmatians, to whom the name *levent* was applied, probably a corruption of the Italian term *Levantino* then used for the sailors of most of the Mediterranean fleets. Sometimes they served in lieu of the taxes owed by their families or villages within the provinces of the grand admiral, sometimes in return for salaries paid by the shipyard treasury. In addition, there were the oarsmen (*kürekçiler*), including enslaved war captives and men sent as punishment for crimes, whose importance lessened as the fleet turned to sail power in the eighteenth century, and salaried seamen hired for expeditions. These were called *aylakçılar* in the sixteenth century and *kalyoncular* (galleon men) thereafter.[5]

The grand admiral maintained his own department and council at the shipyard, sending subordinates to administer the islands and districts under his jurisdiction, and himself directed the police responsible for keeping order in the areas adjacent to the shipyard, at Galata and Kasım Paşa in particular. As with the land army, the fleet's annual departure for the summer campaign was the occasion for elaborate ceremonies involving the sultan and other high officials. During the winter, the fleet was drydocked while its officers and men who had feudal revenues scattered to their timars to collect the money needed to maintain themselves and their ships. The salaried men spent the winter in barracks in Galata, largely outside navy jurisdiction, leading to increasingly boisterous conduct for which the name *levent* became synonymous beginning in the late sixteenth century.

The Learned Institution (Ilmiye)

Finally, those Ottomans who were expert in Islamic knowledge (*Ilim*) and were therefore called "learned men" (*ulema; sing. âlim*) and given the title *efendi* (gentleman) were grouped together in the Learned (*Ilmiye*) Institution, which was in charge of organizing and propagating the faith of Islam, maintaining a united community of Muslims, interpreting, applying and enforcing the religious law (*Şeriat*), expounding the religious sciences in the mosques and schools, and also maintaining standards and training new learned men.

The Educational System. Basic to the *Ilmiye* institution was the system of education organized around the elementary mosque schools (*mekteps*), which gave rudimentary religious instruction to the masses, and the higher institutions of learning (*medreses*), which trained new members of the *ulema* as well as others entering the Ruling Class. The first Ottoman *medrese* was built by Orhan in Iznik in 1331. There were hundreds of them throughout the empire by the end of the sixteenth century, capped by the eight (*medaris-i semaniye*) established by Mehmet the Conqueror in the environs of the great Istanbul mosque bearing his name. The latter were the top of a hierarchy of eight degrees or grades of education, commencing with the elementary *haşiye-i* *tecrit medrese*s in the smaller towns and going through the *miftah, kırklı, hariç, dahil,* and *sahn-ı seman* ranks, with each providing more advanced studies and additional subjects until those capable of it entered the higher stages of knowledge provided only in the *muhsıla-ı sahn* and the *sahn-ı seman medrese*s, which were part of the complex at the Fatih mosque. Those studying in the first seven ranks were called *suhte* or *softa* (religious student), while those who achieved the *sahn-ı seman* school were given the particularly honorable name of *danişman* (learned man).

Lessons were given in all branches of Islamic learning, including calligraphy, Arabic language and grammar (*sarf ü nahiv*), rhetoric (*belâgat*) and poetry (*şi'ir*), the sciences of reasoning such as logic (*mantık*), philosophy (*ilm-i hikmet*), and astronomy (*heyet*), and the religious sciences such as analysis of the Koran (*tefsir*), doctrines of the faith (*akait*), the traditions of the Prophet and his companions (*hadis*), the bases of the religious law (*usul-ü fıkıh*) and jurisprudence (*fıkıh*)', as well as theology and ethics.

In addition to the more traditional subjects studied in the *medrese*s developed through the early sixteenth century, the more exact sciences of medicine, mathematics, and some of the physical sciences were taught in a new complex of four *medrese*s built by Süleyman the Magnificent between 1550 and 1559 adjoining the mosque bearing his name. Here was provided a new, higher degree of study for those who passed beyond the *sahn-ı seman* degree and had the desire and ability to go on. Under Süleyman's new system the three lowest grades of the old system, which in any case provided only elementary education in the smaller towns, were lowered to the ranks of the elementary *mektep*s. The remaining five ranks, along with the four new ones in the Süleymaniye complex, were reorganized into a hierarchy of twelve ranks, which in turn were divided into four groups:

1. The *hâriç* (outside) *medrese*s provided elementary training in the most basic sciences, Arabic morphology and syntax, logic, geometry, theology, and rhetoric.

2. The *dahil* (inner), or intermediate, *medrese*s provided more exact training in the sciences already begun and added jurisprudence and analysis of the Koran.

3. The advanced schools included those previously forming the highest level in the complex of the Conqueror. The teachers received 50 *akçe*s daily, and a new higher grade was called *altmışlı* (those of the 60) because of the salaries paid to attract the very best.

4. The highest level, or *semaniye* (eight) *medrese*s, were located in the Süleymaniye complex, where students received the highest possible specialized training, particularly in jurisprudence, theology, and rhetoric, as well as the sciences related to them.

Individual *medrese*s were supported by religious endowments (*vakıf*) usually established to support the entire complex of buildings (including also hospitals, hotels, and other charitable institutions) established around great mosques. Each *medrese* usually was directed by a *müderris* (teacher) who used the funds turned over by the administrator of the *vakıf* to maintain the buildings, hire servants, and select and pay the students, with the best of the latter acting as his assistants to repeat and explain the lessons to the other students. Students were paid small stipends and also were given free food and lodging in the *medrese* or the adjacent buildings of the same complex. A few larger *medrese*s had as many as three teachers, with the senior one directing the other two and duties and salaries adjusted accordingly.

The remaining members of the ulema emerged from among the teachers and students of the *medrese*s. Those students who reached the rank of *danişman* were entitled to fill vacant positions within the *Ilmiye* hierarchy when available and sometimes outside as well, particularly in the Scribal Institution. Those students who left the *medrese*s before completing the full hierarchy of studies generally entered the service of the kadis as their assistants (*naip*) or became scribes in the treasury or other institutions maintained by the Scribal Institution or for private persons in the Ruling or Subject classes. Those who became *danışman*s generally remained in the system as *müderris*es in the most elementary schools, working up through the ranks according to ability and as vacancies became available. *Müderris*es in turn were allowed to apply for vacant positions as kadis, or for the positions of *nişancı* and *defterdar* in the Scribal Institution if they had the additional scribal qualifications. *Müderris*es in the more advanced *medrese*s, receiving 60 *akçe*s daily, could compete for positions as kadis of the major cities: Mecca, Medina, Jerusalem, Damascus, Aleppo, Cairo, Edirne, and Bursa, paying 500 *akçe*s daily, while those in the *medrese*s of the Süleymaniye complex could compete for these as well as those of kadi of Istanbul or *kazasker* of Rumeli or Anatolia. *Müderris*es in the old capitals of Istanbul, Edirne, and Bursa were given special preference in relation to those of equal rank in other schools when competing for positions. Finally, *müderris*es in the highest three groups could become candidates to become jurisconsults (muftis), but only those in the Süleymaniye group could be candidates or be chosen to be *şeyhulislam*, who was the chief mufti and leader of the *Ilmiye*. Appointments were made by the sultan and the grand vezir on the advice of the *şeyhulislam*, but the latter for the most part depended on the advice of councils of learned elders, which subjected candidates to oral and written examinations and questioned them on essays (*risale*) that had to be written on specified subjects.

The Legal System. In addition to the *müderris*es the ulema included those who applied the law in the courts as judges (kadis) and the jurisconsults (muftis), who studied and interpreted it. What was the Islamic legal system as it was developed in the Ottoman Empire? And how was the *Ilmiye* institution structured to apply and interpret it?

1. *The Law.* The idea of the law, as it evolved under the Ottomans, combined traditions from both the Persian and Turkish empires of the past as well as those of Islam as such. From the Persians came the idea – developed by the Abbasid caliphs – that the ruler was absolute and that all acts of law and justice were favors emanating from his absolute power. From the Turks, on the other hand, there came an idea of a supreme law (*yasa/yasak*) that the ruler had to enforce with justice regardless of his personal wishes. Paralleling these traditions was the Muslim idea of the religious law, or *Şeriat,* derived from the Koran and the early Muslim tradition. Whereas the *Şeriat* was highly developed in the fields of personal behavior and community life, it never was developed in detail for most matters of public law, particularly in regard to state organization and administration. At best it provided only principles, so that there was room for interpretation and legislation on specific matters by the ruler and his government. Most Muslim legal theorists recognized the right of the sultan, by "sovereign prerogative" (*örf*) to take the initiative and issue secular regulations (*kanun;* pl. *kavanin*) in matters not covered in the *Şeriat.* Thus the Ottoman Islamic community had two laws: the customary law of the sultan (*örf-i sultani*) and the religious law. Those charged with executing and enforcing the provisions of the former were called the *ehl-i örf,* while the ulema continued to enforce the latter throughout the empire and particularly in the Muslim *millet.* The *Şeriat* covered matters of personal status in the Muslim *millet* as well as providing principles of

public law for the government, while the religious laws of the non-Muslim *millets* were elaborated and enforced by their own religious leaders. Strictly speaking, members of the ulema had the right to invalidate any *kanun* that they felt to be in conflict with the *Şeriat,* but they rarely did this, since, as part of the Ruling Class, they were appointed and could be dismissed by the sultan. This left the latter free to legislate changes to meet the problems of the time, as long as such changes remained within the guidelines expressed in the *Şeriat.*

2. *The Kadis.* The principal interpreters of the religious law were members of the *ulema;* and the science of its study and interpretation was called *fıkıh.* There was a division between those who studied and interpreted the law, or jurisconsults (mufti), and those who enforced it in the law courts as judges (kadi), later also called arbiters (*hâkim;* pl. *hükkam*). The empire was divided into judicial districts (*kaza*), each with its own court (*mahkeme*) and judge as well as his lieutenant (*naip*) and other assistants. There were four orthodox schools of law in Islam, but that of Abu Hanifa was the only one that was accepted as official throughout the Ottoman Empire. Only Hanifi kadis then were appointed to courts. But since in some parts of the empire, especially Egypt and Syria, the native population and religious leaders accepted other legal schools, local officials were allowed to recognize leading local ulema of those schools as advisers and to recommend their decisions to the official Hanifi kadis of the districts concerned.

Each kadi had both judicial and administrative functions. As judge of the local Muslim court, he was charged with enforcing both the Islamic religious law and the sultan's *kanuns* for subjects and members of the Ruling Class alike. He had to make certain that the court was open to all Muslims seeking justice, that litigation was speedy and just and without the intervention of professional advocates, and that those unable to protect themselves, such as women, children, and orphans, were particularly protected. The people of his *kaza* accepted the fact that the *Şeriat,* represented by the kadi, guaranteed them (unlike the officials themselves) rights that no official of the sultan could take away. The officials, on the other hand, as slaves of the sultan were subject to his absolute will and could be executed and have their properties confiscated without any stated reason and without the right to secure the intervention and protection of the kadi.

The kadi used his own employees to investigate cases, summon witnesses, and punish the guilty, but he was assisted in these functions by the local *sancak* bey and the *subaşı* (police chief) under the supervision or at least in the presence of representatives of the Muslim community. The *sancak* beys and kadis were supposed to share authority locally, but because the former often were away on campaigns, the latter usually prevailed. Usually each city or town had its *subaşı,* who could and did apprehend offenders on his own authority as well as at the initiative of the kadi. When citizens wished to complain about illegal acts, they did so to the *muhtesip* in cases involving the market or to the *subaşı* in any other criminal act; but the *muhtesip* had to secure the help of the latter if market offenders refused to accept his authority. The *subaşıs* received their authority from the *sancak* beys and were responsible to them, but if they themselves violated the law, they were brought before the kadi for judgment and punishment. Thus it was the latter who once again predominated. The kadis were supposed to apply both the religious and secular law and were fairly autonomous in reaching their decisions. It was rare when the sultan or one of his officials, or even the kadi's superiors in Istanbul, actually intervened to influence or countermand a judgment once it had been given locally.

The highest allowable revenues for a kadi or a *kaza* was 150 *akçes* daily, while those in the lesser ranks received revenues down to 40 *akçes* supplemented by fees collected in court from the litigants or recipients of the certificates that they issued to certify births, marriages, divorces, deaths, and the like. In addition many kadis collected large sums from fines and the administrators of local foundations that they were supposed to supervise. Kadis normally also had the right to appoint the teachers and employees of the local *mekteps* and *medreses*, presumably also in return for fees from the successful candidates.

The kadis also had local administrative duties, mostly developed in Ottoman times. These included supervising the administrators in their districts, certifying tax assessment lists and collection accounts, mediating in conflicts of authority or jurisdiction, and sometimes authorizing and enforcing the dismissal of local officials who violated the law and acting in their places until substitutes arrived from Istanbul. Kadis supervised the actions of members of the Military Class in keeping order locally, handling cases of complaint involving arbitrary actions against the subjects. Kadis supervised the operations involved in seeding and harvesting crops and the assessment and collection of taxes. Mobilization of the local military forces, maintenance of the police and *derbent* garrisons, municipal functions such as the establishment of market regulations and price controls, and arrangements to build and maintain local streets and roads also were often supervised by the kadis. As Ottoman government tended to wither away in many localities beginning in the sixteenth century, the local kadis also tended to assume more and more administrative and financial duties in addition to their judicial and legal ones to the point where, in many areas, they were in fact the local government.

The Istanbul kadi received revenues of 500 *akçes* daily, making his position in many ways the most lucrative of all those available to members of the ulema. In addition to their normal duties the kadis of Istanbul, Eyüp, Galata, and Üsküdar attended the Wednesday meetings of the grand vezir's council to hear complaints concerning the decisions or actions of the kadis around the empire, thus forming a supreme judicial court. The Istanbul kadi also was in charge of supervising market and price controls in the city as well as building regulations, streetlighting and maintenance, water supply, and sanitation. He carried out these duties through assistants – the *ihtisap ağa* (in charge of markets), the *mimarbaşı* (buildings and streets), the *subaşı* (municipal policeman), the *çöplük subaşı* (in charge of cleaning streets and the like) and others – who together comprised what municipal government there was for the city outside functions performed by the *millets* and artisan and craft guilds.

The judiciary positions above the district level were given the rank of *mevleviyet,* and the holders were called *molla.* Since there were far more candidates for the various positions than there were openings, appointments were made for no more than a year for the highest-ranking judiciary appointments and for 20 months for the kadis of the *kazas,* after which the individuals in question left their posts and were included among the dismissed (*mezul*), with their names being placed at the bottom of lists of candidates for positions. While they waited, like other members of the Ruling Class without positions for one reason or another, they were given special pensions called *arpalık,* which were considered to be retirement pay for those whose idleness was from old age or illness, or simply unemployment compensation for others in between formal appointments. Some *arpalıks* for higher-ranking Ottomans consisted of *hasses* or timars, but most were simply cash payments from the treasury. *Mezul* members of the ulema also sometimes served as assistants (*mülazim*) in the offices of their own *kazaskers* or as adjudicators (*kassam*) of inheritances not falling within the normal jurisdiction of the local kadis, thus adding to their pensions. Kadis in the *mezul* category normally remained for two years before becoming eligible for new appointments to suitable positions.

In addition to regular kadi appointments there also were other positions available to suitable candidates in the *mezul* class. These included the *toprak* kadis (judges of the land), who served as traveling agents of the regular kadis, especially in the feudal provinces, going to investigate complaints of misrule or illegal actions on the part of local feudal or administrative officials, with the power to make summary judgments when warranted. Kadis also were sent as *mehayif müfettişleri* (injustice inspectors) to hear local complaints against established kadis and *naip*s, with the power to remove the latter when required or to transmit the complaints for action by the *kazasker*s or the Imperial Council. Kadis of high rank were appointed as army judges (*ordu kadıları*) to act in the place of the *kazaker*s when the latter was absent.

Equal in rank to the *molla*s were the members of the ulema employed in religious and/or cultural positions in the palace service of the sultan. These included the sultan's *hoca*, who was in charge of instructing and guiding him in the precepts of the faith and who in the fourteenth century at least served as leader of the ulema; two imperial imams, who led prayer in whatever mosque the sultan chose to attend for the official Friday prayer as well as in the mosque of the Topkapı Palace; the sultan's chief physician (*hekim başı*), who also served more or less as leader of the corporation of physicians throughout the empire; and his chief astrologer (*müneccim başı*), who advised him on the most propitious dates for important actions.

3. *The Muftis.* Since the Muslim law was not a fixed and immutable code, but rather the result of a great deal of study and discussion among legal experts over the centuries, the exact resolution of individual cases could not depend on mere reference to the law codes as such but had to rely also on study of all the available legal literature. The muftis, who applied general principles to specific cases, originally were called *muctahit*s (those who "strove" to acquire correct legal knowledge), and from their decisions there developed the different orthodox schools of Islamic law. But once the latter were accepted, this restricted the ability of individual *muctahit*s or other members of the ulema to interpret on the basis of their own examination of the sources. In consequence the "Gates of Interpretation were closed," and members of the ulema wishing to decide cases or interpret law had to adhere closely to the interpretations of the school to which they were attached. Those ulema who interpreted the law on the basis of these codes were called *fâkih*, while the science of commentary itself became known as *fıkıh* (jurisprudence). In Ottoman times the *fâkih*s were the muftis, who issued *fetva*s (statements on legal points) in response to problems submitted to them by kadis, officials, or private persons wishing legal authority to support their positions in particular cases. Strictly speaking, a mufti could not innovate or personally make a judgment on the basis of his own examination of the sources. He could only base his reply on the code of his particular branch of Islamic law and on precedent. In practice, of course, individual muftis could and did secure the answer that they wished by choosing appropriate parts of the code and precedents while ignoring others that countered their argument; then, too, kadis and others seeking particular interpretations referred to muftis whose interpretations would best support their own desires.

Unlike the kadis, who were appointed by the government, any member of the ulema who had the requisite qualifications could declare himself to be a mufti and practice this occupation if he was recognized as such by those wanting *fetva*s. Under Süleyman some efforts were made to establish an organization of muftis like that of the kadis. The new office of *şeyhulislam* (chief of Islam) was created largely for this purpose as grand mufti of the empire and mufti of Istanbul in addition to coordinating the work of the *kazaskers* and the kadis beneath them.

Official muftis, then, were appointed by the *şeyhulislam* for each of the major cities and also for many of the *kazas*, with the duty of issuing *fetvas* when needed by the kadis or the provincial and local authorities. These appointments were given to ulema who had passed through the complete course of *medrese* training in the case of major appointments and to those who had graduated at lower levels for the less important places. Since the Hanifite school was the officially accepted legal interpretation in the empire, most of the muftis, like the kadis, belonged to it. But in provinces where other schools were accepted – like that of Şafii in Egypt, Syria, and the Holy Cities – muftis of those schools were appointed at the request of local governors or religious leaders. Like the kadis, the muftis did not receive salaries and were dependent on fees charged in return for their *fetvas*, often levied in direct proportion to the wealth of the person requesting one or the profit that he could secure from its enforcement. Muftis appointed by the government received substantial fees from the treasury and also were appointed to profitable positions such as administrators of foundations and adjudicators of inheritances. There also were private muftis, issuing *fetvas* to individuals, sometimes in direct contradiction to those of the official muftis, with the relative ranking and prestige of the issuers finally determining which opinion should prevail.

Lesser Ulema. Hundreds of other ulema did not hold official jobs but retained their places in the Ruling Class by virtue of their possession of portions of *Ilim*. Educated only in the lower grades of the *medreses*, they served in mosques as *imams*, or leaders of public prayer, and, as such, more or less as directors of the mosques, and as *hatips*, in charge of the public oration (*hutbe*) recited in each mosque at the Friday public prayer. The *hatip* had the particularly important function of mentioning the name of the ruler who was recognized where the mosque was located. Below them other ulema served simply as *şeyhs*, or religious leaders in charge of instructing the populace in their religious obligations and duties, often in the form of sermons given to the assembled faithful in the mosques on weekdays. The *müezzins* were in charge of summoning the faithful to prayer from the minarets and reciting certain prayers during services, but they were normally selected more because of the quality of their voices than their learning and thus often were lower members of the ulema. Other ulema were hired to perform minor religious duties such as the care of cemeteries, prayer for the dead, upkeep of the holy places, particularly in the Holy Cities, and prayer for individuals. All ulema of this kind were appointed and paid by the supervisors of the religious endowments established to support their activities or by the persons whom they served. And as time went on, many of them were able to rise as endowment administrators, which in many cases gave them revenues and power considerably beyond that held by members of the ulema in the more prestigious educational and legal services.

Leadership of the Ilmiye *Institution.* While Muslim courts and kadis had existed from earliest times, it was only under Murat I that an effort was made to organize and control them by the creation of the position of kadi of the army (*kadıasker/kazasker*). Initially, the role of the *kazasker* involved the task of building up the ulema by importing learned men from the old centers of Islam, appointing them to judicial and other positions, and arranging for them to train Ottoman subjects to take their place by building up the *medrese* system. By the mid-fifteenth century this process had become so successful that the job of directing the ulema was too big for one man. Therefore, the *kazasker*ate was divided, with separate positions for Anatolia and Rumeli.

Beginning late in the fifteenth century leadership of the *Ilmiye* was shared by the *kazasker*s with the grand mufti of Istanbul, who, by virtue of his position as leader of the corporation of muftis around the empire as well as his prerogative of issuing *fetva*s legalizing the sultan's *kanun*s and reconciling them with the religious law, came to be given the official position of *şeyhulislam* (chief of Islam). Ebu us-Suud Efendi's long period of service as *şeyhulislam* during the reign of Süleyman the Magnificent altered the balance of power, since holders of the position received high incomes, as much as 750 *akçe*s daily in the late sixteenth century. Ebu us-Suud also secured the right to appoint all kadis, *müderrise*s, and muftis to the higher-paying positions of 40 *akçe*s daily and more, leaving the *kazasker*s with effective control only over the lesser ulema. However, the latter continued to have influence over the entire *Ilmiye* system by their membership on the Imperial Council. While the *fetva*s issued by the muftis had to be "respected" by the kadis, the latter were not legally obligated to accept them, but only *ferman*s issued by the sultan. The *şeyhulislam* lacked the authority to tell the kadis how to apply the law in their courts. This power was possessed, theoretically at least, only by the sultan (for whom the kadis administered the law), whose prerogatives in this respect were occasionally exercised by the grand vezir on the advice of the *kazasker*s rather than the *şeyhulislam*. On the other hand, though the administrative authorities legally did not have to accept the *fetva*s, because of the prestige of the muftis they often did defer to the wishes of important members of the *Ilmiye*.

Culture under the Ottomans. Since culture in the lands of Islam laid within the sphere of the institutions and individuals of the *Ilmiye* and since most of the great thinkers and writers of the time were members of the ulema, it is appropriate that we discuss Ottoman cultural life as part of our study of the latter. European observers have long maintained that Ottoman strength lay in military achievement and political organization, with little or no cultural contribution. Such observations have largely been products of European ignorance of and prejudice against Islam. They result from the lack of linguistic as well as aesthetic qualifications needed to discern and appreciate cultural developments outside the European sphere of experience and awareness. The Ottomans did in fact develop and maintain a very rich and diversified cultural life throughout the existence of their empire.

Ottoman Literature of the Classical Period. The basis of Ottoman cultural life, as laid in the Anatolia of the Seljuks of Rum from the eleventh to the fourteenth centuries, was largely that developed in the great Islamic caliphates. The Arabic language and culture predominated in the religious and legal spheres, and the rich Persian heritage, so well developed by the Seljuks of Baghdad, took the lead in literature and the arts. Officially, the Seljuks of Rum espoused orthodox Islam and brought orthodox teachers from the East to combat the influence of heterodoxy and assure that Sunni Islam would prevail, at least in the official institutions of state. And in Anatolia, as in the East, the *medrese* above all else became the institution through which the orthodox ulema and scribes emerged and dominated.

The highly stylized, elaborate, and formal style of expression that reflected the sophistication of High Islamic culture gave rise to classical Ottoman literature, patronized, practiced, and appreciated by the upper classes and the educated in the sultan's dominions. Poetry rather than prose was the main vehicle of expression in classical Ottoman literature, which was generally called *Divan* literature because of its characteristic manifestation in collections (*divan*s) of poems written by poets and others with literary ambition. Prose writing was developed only in certain limited areas such as the essay (*risâle*) and biographies of poets and saints and members of the Ruling Class, although there was also considerable prose literature in the areas of religion, law, and history. Other types of prose literature such as the novel, play, and short story were not to become significant elements of Turkish writing until they were brought in from the West during the nineteenth century.

Poetry, then, was the principal form of literary expression, composed in the *aruz vezni,* or prosodic meter, based on patterns of short and long syllables. Used by the Arabs and modified by the Persians, the *aruz* meter was an alien style and poorly suited to the sounds of Turkish; yet literary fashion and the identification of the Ruling Class with the Islamic heritage forced poets writing in Ottoman Turkish to contort their language to achieve poetic harmony while observing its rules. It was only in the late fifteenth century and afterward that the language and style were sufficiently reconciled for this meter to become an important and beautiful vehicle of literary expression. (Even then the means by which this was accomplished – the incorporation of large numbers of Arabic and Persian words and phrases into Ottoman Turkish – left the language little more than a skeleton for the expression of foreign ideas with foreign words.) Aside from the meter the principal forms of verse used in early Ottoman *Divan* poetry were: (1) the *kaside,* consisting of more than 15 rhymed distiches normally eulogizing a person or commemorating an important event; (2) the *gazel* (ode), with 4 to 15 couplets, the first in rhyme and all the summary lines rhyming with that of the first; (3) the *mesnevi,* a long poem, using a single meter throughout, but each couplet being of a different rhyme; and (4) the *rubai,* or quatrain, a verse of 4 lines used to express philosophical ideas.

Nevertheless, the concentration of Turkoman nomads in Anatolia encouraged the survival of practices and traditions of Central Asian Turks. Paralleling the *Divan* poetry of the Ruling Class was a literature of the people. Folk poets, usually traveling as itinerant troubadours and known as *saz şair*s (poets of the stringed instrument, so called because of their use of the one-stringed *saz* as accompaniment), continued to use the older syllabic meter as well as Turkish folk stories. Their language reflected the living, changing Turkish language as they developed folk literature (*Halk Edebiyatı*), which also came to be called the "literature of mystic devotion" or "minstral literature" (*Aşık Edebiyatı*) because of its close association with the wandering dervishes and the mystic religious ideas they espoused. While the *Divan* literature, with its alien accretions, came to impress many upper- and middle-class Muslim urban dwellers in Anatolia who were not members of the Ruling Class, the folk literature developed its grip on the mass of the peasants who formed the bulk of the Turkish population of the empire.

The bases of both *Divan* and folk literature were developed in the thirteenth century, in the late Seljuk and early Ottoman periods. *Divan* poetry had to struggle for some time to develop the content and structure of Ottoman Turkish as its principal vehicle of expression. Leading the way in this respect were the lyric poets. Writing for the Anatolian Seljuk ruler Alauddin Keykubad (1284–1307), Hoca Dehhâni wrote a series of lyric poems, *kaside*s and *gazel*s, in simple Turkish with just enough Arabic and Persian to form the meters and complete the verses. Unlike most other poets of the time, he did not emphasize religious or mystic themes but instead wrote poems of love and wine, themes that became common for his successors among the *Divan* poets, along with his ideas about the beauties of nature and praises of the ruler and other high officials. Out of this background rose later Ottoman *Divan* literature.

The *saz* folk poets entered Anatolia with the Turks following the Battle of Manzikert, spreading not only the messages from Central Asia but also describing the battles and praising the victories won over the enemy. These poets firmly established the syllabic meter as the basis of their craft. Their work is best exemplified and preserved in the 12 epic poems (*destans*) of Dede Korkuṭ as well as the works of Seyyit Battal Gazi and the *Denişmentnâme,* written by Danişment Ahmet Gazi, founder of one of the strongest Turkoman principalities in eastern Anatolia. The life and traditions of the people of the time and folk wisdom are best expressed in the collection of humorous short stories and anecdotes usually associated with Nasreddin Hoca, who probably lived in Anatolia during the time of Bayezit I and Tamerlane's invasion. The mystic element of Turkish folk literature was established first in the thirteenth century by Mevlana Celaluddin Rumi (1207–1272), whose major works were in Persian but whose lesser works influenced contemporary and subsequent Turkish folk literature both in content and form. The *Mevlevi* order, which he founded, carried his message throughout the Muslim world. His son Sultan Veled (1227–1312) spread his father's message in Turkish, though with considerably less originality in his poetry and philosophy, further instilling the *aruz* meter and *mesnevi* style into the emerging Anatolian literature of the time. This mystic literary movement, known as *Tasavvuf Edebiyatı,* culminated with the work of Yunus Emre (1238–1329), a Turkoman dervish in central Anatolia. His sensitive use of Turkish and the *hece* meter stimulated Anatolian folk literature, while his ideas of mystic union of the believer with God attracted many in the period of rapid social and political change.

The greatest folk product of the fourteenth century was the prose collection of Dede Korkut, the oldest surviving example of the Oğuz Turkoman epic. Dede Korkut relates the struggles of the Turkomans with the Georgians and Abaza Circassians in the Caucasus as well as with the Byzantines of Trabzon, adding stories of relationships and conflicts within the Turkoman tribes. We have no information at all about Dede Korkut's personality, and there is some question as to whether the stories did in fact have a single author. However, the form and the style indicate that some single hand must have had a role, although whether simply collecting scattered stories or originating them is not yet clear. In any case, the stories are a major source for both the history and the literature of the time, written in a pure and simple Turkish, displaying the basic music and style of the language uncontaminated by foreign intrusions as few other Turkish works are. Including many tribal epics, the work presents the basic traditions of tribal life, family relationships, morals, and the like, particularly in eastern Anatolia, where the White Sheep and Black Sheep dominated.

Divan literature also was now developing its own unique form, although it still did not equal folk literature in influence or popularity. Among the principal writers of the time whose works fell into both categories was Ahmet Gülşehri (d. 1317), who lived in Kırşehir. His *Mantık al-Tayr* (Logic of the Birds) was a free adaptation into Turkish of the Persian *mesnevi* of the same name written by Fariduddin Attar but was not merely a translation as has been commonly believed. Developing an allegory on the mystic idea of the unity of creation, Gülşehri related the story of a journey by a group of birds to their queen, of which only 30 reached their destination. Much of Gülşehri's additions reflected contemporary Anatolian society, including information on *fütüvvet,* the Muslim form of chivalry, spread by the *ahi* organizations, which developed and used its ideas for their own purpose. This work had a wide influence in spreading the idea that Turkish could indeed be a language equal to or even superior to Persian and Arabic.

The most important *Divan* writer of the Anatolian Turkish school in this formative period was the great Kütahya poet, Tacuddin Ibrahim Ahmedi (1335–1412), who served the Germiyan dynasty before entering Ottoman service, writing his famous *Iskendername*, a life of Alexander the Great in 8250 distiches, for Bayezit I's son Süleyman. Aside from providing information on his ostensible subject, Ahmedi developed an elegant style to discuss medicine, philosophy, and religion before concluding the work with one of the earliest contemporary descriptions of the Ottoman dynasty, giving us an important interpretation of Ottoman origins and rise to power. His rhymed work on medicine, *Tervih ul-Tervah,* began the development of Turkish into a language able to convey scientific information and at the same time stimulated the establishment of a school of medicine in the Ottoman court.

It was only really in the fifteenth century, following the Interregnum, that unified political power and stable institutions of government and society made possible a distinctly Ottoman cultural life, noticeable especially after the conquest of Edirne and its development as the new Ottoman capital, a center that had not been influenced by the Middle East. Gradually, a new school developed, whose foremost example was Şeyhi (d. 1429) of Kütahya. Born under Germiyan, he was trained as a physician and entered the Ottoman court under Mehmet I, treating members of the royal family before he finally retired to a life of solitude. He compiled a substantial *Divan* collection reproducing in Turkish poetry the lyrical style of the great Persian Hâfız, emphasizing that religion was more than formal rituals and that union with God could be achieved only by drinking the symbolic wine to complete the full mystical experience. He also introduced satire into classical Turkish *Divan* poetry with his *mesnevi,* the *Harname* (Book of the Donkey), in which animals personified his political enemies who, jealous over favors granted him by the sultan, had arranged for him to be beaten. The simple and straightforward style of the work gave it considerable influence on contemporary and later literature.

The greatest Ottoman poet of the later fifteenth century was Bursalı Ahmet Paşa, son of one of Murat II's *kazasker*s, who as kadi of Edirne became one of Mehmet II's principal teachers and confidential advisers before falling from favor due to his passion for one of the sultan's favorite boys. He was imprisoned and threatened with execution but finally won a pardon with an apologetic *kaside,* after which he served throughout the empire and continued to write until his death in 1497. The unusually beautiful *gazel*s and *kaside*s of his *Divan,* written with a great feast of style, enabled him to achieve wide popularity and to provide the main connection between the developing *Divan* style of the fifteenth century and its later classical forms.

Mehmet II's conquest of Istanbul and its establishment as the center of Ottoman administrative and commercial life was accompanied by a concerted effort to develop it as the focus of a reinvigorated and expanded cultural life. Learned men were brought to it from all parts of the empire, and state support was provided to encourage and promote their activities, with Bursa and Edirne losing their old prominence in this as well as other aspects of Ottoman life. As the Ottomans now achieved predominance in the Muslim world, a new wave of Muslim scholars flooded to the center of power. While Mehmet II spent much of his life in the field, he retained a keen interest in the arts and sciences and devoted every spare moment to encouraging scholars and participating in their work. He seems to have been a liberal and tolerant man who wished to learn as much as he could from all men, regardless of religion.

Byzantine and Serbian scholars, and others brought from Italy, were invited to participate in the cultural revival. The first Orthodox patriarch, Gennadius, is said to have taken part in religious discussions with the sultan as well as with his religious leaders. Amirutzes of Trabzon was commanded to compile a world map to guide the Conqueror in his advances. Italian scholars were ordered to write a history of the Roman Empire, which he hoped to re-create.

While encouraging contact with the Christian heritage, the promotion of Ottoman Muslim culture remained Mehmet II's primary aim. Thousands of abandoned and decayed Christian churches were rebuilt as mosques, and *medrese*s were built around them to serve as centers for the new enlightened ulema congregating in Istanbul. Great scholars of the time, such as Alauddin Tusi, Bursalı Hocazade Muslihiddin Mustafa Efendi, and Mevlana Abdülkerim Efendi rose to leading positions as *müderris*es. Preparatory *medrese*s also were built by the grand vezir and others in the capital and at key points around the empire to provide preliminary training for aspiring scholars. Istanbul, Edirne, and Bursa were the centers of the new culture. But poetry, literature and the sciences also flourished in the *sancak*s turned over to the Ottoman princes for their training and, as the empire expanded, in provincial centers such as Baghdad, Diyarbekir, and Konya in the East and Skopje (Üsküp), Sarajevo, and Buda in Europe.

Ottoman thinkers still accepted the orthodox Islamic tradition developed by al-Râzi and al-Ghazzali, which rejected the fanatical idea that the "sciences of thought" such as astronomy, logic, and mathematics violated the Islamic doctrine that the "gates of inquiry are closed." Ottoman scholars, therefore, achieved considerable distinction in these fields from early times. The first Turkish mathematician of note was Kadızade Musa Paşa, who founded a substantial school at the famous observatory built by Tamerlane's descendants at Samarcand, under the stimulus of the latter's grandson Uluğ Bey (1399–1449), and wrote a number of commentaries on Euclid. The leading Ottoman mathematician during Mehmet's reign was his pupil, Ali Kuşçu (d. 1474), whose brilliant career in the courts of the leading rulers of his time was a true mirror of the age. He rose originally as the falconer (and thus the name Kuşçu) of Uluğ Bey, who ruled Transoxania from his capital at Samarcand and assembled the greatest of the learned men from the centers of traditional Islamic culture. After Kadızade, Ali Kuşçu directed the Samarcand observatory until, following Uluğ Bey's death, he entered the service of the new lord of the area, the White Sheep ruler Uzun Hasan, who built his own cultural center in Tabriz. The latter sent him as ambassador to Mehmet II in Istanbul, where he was so lavishly received that he entered the sultan's service as *müderris* at the Ayasofya school and soon built his own school of mathematicians. Some of the leading ulema of the time received their mathematical and logical training from him. He also wrote a number of works on mathematics and astronomy that spread his fame throughout the empire. Among his students was the cosmographer Hafız Mehmet ibn Ali (d. 1543) and the famous admiral and geographer Seydi Ali Reis (d. 1562), who presented considerable mathematical information in his works on navigation and astronomy.

Medicine also developed rapidly in the fifteenth century, again under the impetus of scholars imported from Central Asia. Most important of the early Ottoman medical scholars was the chief doctor of the Amasya public hospital, Sabuncuoğlu Şerefeddin, whose study of surgery, *Cerrâhnâme-i Ilhan* (1465), based on his own medical experience, was the most original Ottoman medical work of its time. Sinoplu Mumin, trained under the Candar prince Ismail Bey and taken into Ottoman service by Murat II, wrote a detailed medical study, the *Zahire-i Muradiye* (1437), which combined the Arabic and Persian medical sources of the past with the latest practical experience and made it available in Turkish. Altuncuzâde (d. late fifteenth century) made important advances in the analysis and treatment of urinary problems and laid the bases for the science of surgery in the empire. Hekim Yakup, a Jewish convert to Islam, and the Persian Lârî became Murat II's personal physicians as well as leaders of the corporation of doctors that he established to train physicians and surgeons and establish and maintain standards of treatment.

In the religious sciences the fourteenth and fifteenth centuries witnessed a progression of major figures giving orthodox Islam the vigor it needed to withstand the threat posed by the popularity of heterodoxy among the masses. The transition between the older Arab traditions and those developed under the Ottomans was provided by Davud-u Keyseri (d. 1350) and Molla Fenari (1350–1431). They introduced the major Arabic works into Turkish while making Muhyiddin-i Arabi's ideas on the unity of existence the bases of the philosophical and religious systems then being created among the ulema being trained to staff the Learned Institution of the nascent Ottoman state. Another major religious writer of the fifteenth century was Şeyh Bedreddin Mahmud-i Simavni (see pp. 38–39). His works on mysticism and jurisprudence were particularly influential, along with his *Teshil* (Facilitation), which discussed the "unity of existence" concepts of the mystics, heaven and hell, and theories on angels, devils, and the perfect man, while evolving the ideas that led his followers to revolt against the sultan. The greatest fifteenth-century religious scholar was Hocazade Muslihuddin Mustafa Efendi, who began as one of Mehmet II's teachers and later used the sultan's favor to rise rapidly through the ulema. He suffered partial eclipse near the end of Mehmet's reign because of the jealousy of other scholars, who were supported by Grand Vezir Karamani Mehmet Paşa. But with Bayezit's accession he secured the major appointments of kadi of Bursa and *müderris* of its Sultaniye *medrese*, where he remained for the rest of his life teaching and writing. In encouraging Hocazade's scholastic theology, Mehmet II stimulated a resumption of the old Islamic quarrel over the connection between philosophy and religion begun in Seljuk times between Ibn Ruşd and al-Ghazzali, inviting Nasiruddin Tusi from Iran to debate the matter in court. Nasiruddin supported Ibn Ruşd's position that religion and philosophy could be reconciled and that man's logic was needed to secure full knowledge of the ominpresent God. Hocazade, on the other hand, took al-Ghazzali's position that reason could be applied to true sciences such as medicine and mathematics but that its application in religious matters could only lead to error; that the religious sciences, therefore, had to be defended against the claims of logic and philosophy. In the end with the sultan's support the Ottoman ulema accepted Hocazade's position and concentrated on an ever-narrowing scholastic approach to scholarship.

One of the greatest legal scholars of Mehmet II's time was Molla Husrev, called the "Abu Hanifa of our time" by the sultan, who after studying the school founded by Molla Fenari, rose as *müderris* in Bursa and kadi in Edirne before the sultan made him *kazasker* of Rumeli and kadi of Istanbul following the death of its first occupant, Hızır Bey (1458). After retiring to Bursa to establish his own *medrese*, he was recalled as the first *şeyhulislam* – more or less establishing it as the leading position among the ulema. He played a principal role in developing the latter into the *Ilmiye* hierarchy – and at the same time became a leading authority on Islamic law and jurisprudence. His work in this area was carried on by Zenbilli Ali Cemali Efendi (d. 1525), the best-known scholar among the masses of his time, who rose under Bayezit II and became a leading member of the ulema under Selim I and in Süleyman the

Magnificent's early years, using his position to save many scholars from the summary executions that were so common during Selim's reign.

Ottoman historiography had its real beginnings under Murat II and Mehmet II, who sponsored a number of historical works as a means of promoting the claim of the Ottoman family to rule over the various peoples of the empire. Ahmedi's *Destan-ı Tevarih-i Müluk-i Âl-ı Osman* (Epic of the Histories of the House of Osman) provides our earliest source for the study of Ottoman origins and their rise to power in the fourteenth century. Aşıkpaşazâde's *Tevarih-i Âl-ı Osman* (Histories of the House of Osman) transmits valuable contemporary information on Ottoman origins secured directly from Yahşi Fakih Efendi, imam of the mosque established in Bursa by Orhan. Writing in Mehmet II's early years, Kâşifi adds important information on Orhan's invasions of Rumeli in his *Gazânâme-i Rum* (Story of the *Gaza* in Rum), and Abdurrahman Bistami of Ankara provides material on the half-century following the rout at the Battle of Ankara. Enveri's *Düsturnâme,* presented to Grand Vezir Karamani Mehmet Paşa. Dursun Bey's *Tarih-i Ebul Feth,* Kritovolos's *Tarih-i Sultan Mehmet Han-ı Sani* (History of Sultan Mehmet II), written partly in Greek at the sultan's order, and Şehdi's *Tarih-i Âl-ı Osman* (History of the House of Osman), written in the style of the Persian *Şahname,* or epic of the ruler – all provide far more detailed information on the Conqueror's reign than that available for his predecessors while laying firm foundations for the historical school that was to follow.

Under Bayezit II Ottoman historiography continued to expand under the stimulus of dynastic encouragement. Aşıkpaşazâde's chronicle, begun under Mehmet II, was extended and completed, presenting personal descriptions of the events of the century since the Battle of Ankara. Neşri Mehmet Efendi wrote a similar history emphasizing Bayezit's reign. Idris-i Bitlisi, trained originally in the court of Uzun Hasan, wrote his Persian language *Heşt Behişt* at the order of Bayezit II, providing considerable information on events in Iran and eastern Anatolia during the previous century, much again the product of his own observations.

Probably the greatest historian of Bayezit's time was Ahmet Şemseddin Ibn-i Kemal (Kemalpaşazâde) (d. 1536), who also was a major scholar in Islamic law and literature. Coming from an old Ottoman family, with his grandfather Kemal Bey having been a governor and vezir for Mehmet II, he gained training in the military and scribal classes and thus had much more practical experience than most ulema of his time. He actually served as a *Sipahi* before he joined the ulema, becoming the kadi of Edirne (1515), *kazasker* of Anatolia (1516), and finally *şeyhulislam* during the last decade of his life. It was during this latter period that he produced major works on all the religious sciences as well as poetry, while his *Tarih-i Âl-ı Osman* (History of the House of Osman) provides the most original and important source material now extant on the reigns during which he himself lived.

The greatest literary man and scholar of Süleyman the Magnificent's reign was Taşköprülü zâde Ahmet Hüsamüddin Efendi (d. 1553), who wrote mainly in Arabic (with his works being translated into Turkish by his son and others), covering the entire range of the knowledge of his time with major works on biography, logic, the religious sciences, and grammar. His monumental *Şakayık-ı Nu'maniye* presents biographies of some 600 learned men of the previous century; and as it was translated into Turkish and supplemented by later writers under the title *Hadayık ul-hakayık fi tekmilet uş* Şakayık (Gardens of Truths of the Completion of the *Şakayık*), it became the principal source for the careers of the leading ulema almost to modern times. His *Nevâdir ul-Ahbar fi Menakıb ül-Ahyar* (Rarities of Information on the Exploits of the Virtuous) gives the same kind of information on leading Ottoman scientists, doctors, astronomers, and mathematicians as well as the leading Islamic doctors, saints, and disciples of the Prophet. And his *Miftah us-Sa'ade ve Misbah us-Siyâde,* translated into Turkish as *Mevzuat ul-Ulum* (Subjects of the Sciences), provides an encyclopedic compendium of the state of most of the religious and exact sciences as they had developed to his time, including chemistry, physics, botany, and zoology, summarizing all knowledge, as it was known in East and West, in the sixteenth century.

Ebu us-Suud Efendi (1490–1574), who was mentioned previously, served as *şeyhulislam* for 29 years during most of Süleyman's reign and was the greatest legal scholar of his time. Working to enforce the rule of the *Şeriat* throughout the sultan's dominions. Ebu us-Suud issued thousands of *fetvas* interpreting the law and applying it to conditions in his own time, often using political strategems to reconcile the sultan's secular law with the *Şeriat* while at the same time influencing leading statesmen in developing the former into a body of law applying to the whole empire. It was Ebu us-Suud who made the *şeyhulislam* into the director of the *Ilmiye* institution as well as the leading mufti of the empire, thus establishing a practice that lasted to modern times.

Ottoman historiography reached its peak in Süleyman's reign, with Ibn-i Kemal providing the connecting links with the historians of the previous century. Three chroniclers dominated the period. One was Hoca Saduddin Efendi (1536–1599), who taught quietly as a *müderris* during Süleyman's reign but then blossomed under Murat III, whom he had served as *hoca* while a prince, and Mehmet III, serving as *şeyhulislam* under the latter for two years before his death. Of his many works, his *Tac ut-Tevarih* (The Crown of Histories) provided a detailed history of the Ottoman dynasty from its origins to the death of Selim I, emphasizing the lives and careers of the leading political and learned men in each reign and including considerable original information on his own time and the immediately preceding reigns, presumably from interviews with aged contemporaries. His notes concerning Süleyman's reign, never formally compiled in his lifetime, were gathered together in a valuable volume by his son Mehmet Efendi along with his *Selimname,* or tribute to Selim I.

A second chronicler was Mustafa Âli (1541–1599), born in Gallipoli of a merchant family, who served as scribal and financial official in the provinces and in Istanbul. Although he wrote a number of major works of poetry, his greatest fame came as a historian. His most important work was *Kunh ul-Ahbar,* a universal history in four parts, the first constituting a geography of the world along with a history of mankind from Adam to Christ, the second describing classical Islam from the Prophet to the fall of the Abbasids, the third covering the Turks from ancient times to the rise of the Ottomans, and the fourth being a history of the Ottoman Empire to 1597, again including the lives of the learned men, ministers, poets, and the like. Among his other 40 historical works of note were his accounts of the Ottoman fine arts (*Menakıb-ı Hünerveran*); of Süleyman's Sigetvar campaign (*Heft Meclis*), presented to Grand Vezir Mehmet Sokullu Paşa; of the campaigns in the Caucasus (*Nusretnâme ve Firsatname*); of the conflicts between princes Selim and Bayezit late in Süleyman's reign (*Nadir ul-Meharib*); of Ottoman naval activities in the western Mediterranean under Süleyman; and particularly of the conquest of Rhodes (*Menakıb-ı Halil Paşa,* and *Fetihname-i Rodos*).

A third chronicler was Mustafa Selaniki (d. 1600). Also a scribe, he produced his *Tarih-i Selaniki,* extending from the last years of Süleyman's reign to the middle of that of Mehmet III (1563–1599), with the information on the latter seven years never being put together or published but forming the basis for the initial sections of the first official court chronicle, the seventeenth-century work of Mustafa Naima. Selaniki thus set the example and provided the basis for the position and function of official court historian, which was to begin with Naima and continue until the end of the empire.

The development of Ottoman geographic literature in the sixteenth century paralleled and was stimulated by that of Ottoman naval power, which provided the means for expanding Ottoman knowledge of the lands around them. Of course, the first Ottoman geographical works had to depend largely on the knowledge amassed by the Islamic writers of the previous centuries. It was only in the late sixteenth century that the first original Ottoman geographic works were written, appropriately enough by some of the empire's leading naval heroes. As early as 1513, Piri Reis (d. 1553) produced a map of the known world in two parts, of which the western portion alone has survived, which he presented to Selim I following the conquest of Cairo in 1517. He used as sources a number of European maps showing the Portuguese discoveries of the time and also a map showing the third voyage of Christopher Columbus to the New World, apparently received from a Spanish mariner captured at Valencia during a raid by Piri Reis's uncle, Kemal Reis. Piri Reis's most important geographical work was his *Kitab-ı Bahriye* (Book of the Sea) (1521), which incorporated all of the knowledge of the seas and navigation developed by Islamic seamen and writers during the previous eight centuries as well as his own experience and that of the Western seamen whose accomplishments came to his attention. The book was divided into 129 chapters, each with a map, in which he described the Mediterranean and the eastern seas, harbors, important points, dangerous and prominent rocks and natural features, the flow of tides, the imminence of storms, and the like. Added to an enlarged version subsequently presented to the sultan were 1200 verses on the lore of the sea.

Following Piri Reis in both the naval and literary aspects of his career was his successor as admiral of the Red Sea fleet, Seydi Ali Reis (d. 1562), who wrote voluminously on astronomy and mathematics but was best known for his geographical works. His *al-Muhit* (The Ocean), written while he was in exile in Ahmedabad, India, in 1554 (see page 107), was based on the experiences of Islamic sailors who had sailed the Persian Gulf and Indian Ocean during the previous centuries as well as those who had guided Vasco da Gama on his voyage to India at the beginning of his own century. It described the seas and lands bordering the Red Sea, the Indian Ocean, and the Persian Gulf in particular. His *Mirat ul-Memalik* (Mirror of the Lands) provided a more literary and personal account of his own travels back to the Ottoman Empire. Considerable geographical knowledge regarding Anatolia and the Balkans was also given in the many contemporary accounts compiled of the campaigns of Selim I and Süleyman the Magnificent and in the *Munşeat* of Feridun Bey.

As we saw earlier, the Ottoman sciences were given a major boost by the opening of the *medrese* complex of the Süleymaniye mosque, which emphasized mathematics and medicine rather than the religious sciences for the first time. While a number of scientific works were produced in the late sixteenth century, however, it was some time before a really original school could develop with major figures of the kind that stood out in the religious sciences.

The leading Ottoman mathematician of the early sixteenth century was Nasuh ul-Silâni ul-Matraki, also known as Matrakcı Nasuh, who also produced a detailed description of the towns and cities along the road from Istanbul to Baghdad in his *Beyan-ı menazil-i sefer-i Irakeyn* (Description of the Stopping Places of the Campaign to the Two Iraqs). But the first truly original scholar in the field was the Algerian Ali ibn Veli, whose *Tuhfet ul-adad* (The Rarities of the Numbers), a work on trigonometry, arithmetic, and algebra also included some ideas on logarithms, knowledge of which was only beginning to spread among European mathematicians under the leadership of Napier (1614).

Among a number of able sixteenth-century Ottoman astronomers, the most famous was Takiyuddin Mehmet (1521–1585), who served as the sultan's chief astronomer (*müneccim başı*) for many years, correcting the astronomical tables developed under Uluğ Bey in Samarcand and securing the construction of a new observatory (*rasadhane*) at the heights of the Tophane section of Istanbul. However, the objections of the *Şeyhulislam* Kadızâde Ahmet Şemseddin Efendi to such activity soon led the sultan to order its destruction (January 22, 1580), showing the difficulty that scientists encountered in developing their work in a culture where religious leaders predominated. Takiuddin's *Alât ur-Reşâdiye* (Instruments of the Observatory) described each astronomical instrument and its use and included an astronomical clock that could fix the locations of heavenly bodies far more exactly than ever before.

Medical knowledge was promoted more than any other science at the Süleymaniye complex, as indicated by the establishment of a large number of hospitals in Istanbul and around the empire during the latter quarter of the century. Leading this development was Ahi Ahmet Çelebi (1436–1523), chief doctor of the empire during the reign of Bayezit II and in Süleyman's early years. He used the considerable personal wealth inherited from his father to build small hospitals in the some 40 villages that he owned as well as elsewhere. He authored a work on kidney and bladder stones, their causes and treatment, and sponsored the work of a Jewish doctor, Musa Calinus ul-Israili, on the application of drugs and other medicines. He used his hospitals as schools to train physicians, whom he sent around the empire to treat the masses, and founded the first Ottoman medical school.

Ottoman *Divan* literature reached its peak in the mid-sixteenth century. The greatest classical Ottoman poet of the time was Muhammad Abd ul-Bâki (1526–1600), called "sultan of poets" by his contemporaries because of the perfection of structure and style he achieved. Son of a poor *müezzin*, he had some opportunity for contact with the ulema at an early age but subsequently was apprenticed to a saddle maker in his youth. Somehow, though, he secretly managed to enter a *medrese* while practicing his trade, gaining fame for the wisdom and lightness of his poems when he was only 19 years old. Learning the elements of the craft from the aged Zâtî and then selling his poems in the Bayezit mosque courtyard for whatever he could get to support himself, he finally won the attention of the great *müderris* of the Süleymaniye *medrese*, Kadızâde Ahmet Şemseddin Efendi, who gave him the financial support that enabled him to abandon his apprenticeship and poetic hawkings altogether. It was not long before he gained the favor of Ebu us-Suud Efendi and, through him, the sultan, whose close companion he now became, gaining a position and influence rarely achieved again by any other Ottoman poet. This earned him the jealousy of many men in court, however, even some of his patrons and friends, who began to fear the extent of his influence, finally easing him out of court late in Süleyman's reign shortly before the sultan's death. This event moved him to write his famous elegy, considered to be his greatest work. Though the last 40 years of his life he was involved in all the court intrigues of the time, rising and falling in court as well as gaining important *Ilmiye* positions culminating with those of *kazasker* but dying without achieving his life's ambition, the post of *şeyhulislam* largely because of the opposition of Hoca Saduddin and his friends in court. His death created tremendous mass passion throughout the empire, and he was given a magnificent state funeral in Istanbul, with the final prayer being read by Saduddin himself.

Bâkî wrote a few religious treatises, but it was his poetry that reflected his full talent as well as the life style of the Ottoman upper classes in Istanbul. Emphasizing the transitory nature of life in a rapidly changing world, he stressed the need for the individual to enjoy himself while he could, since pleasure was considered to be fleeting as the wind. Although he used mystic terminology at times, he was not really interested in religion. His mastery of the art of versification in the *aruz* system and achievement of unusually harmonious themes led to his reputation as the greatest *gazel* writer in Ottoman classical literature.

Mehmet ibn Süleyman Fuzuli (1480–1556) achieved repute second only to that of Bâkî among the poets of the classical age. Born a Shia in Iraq during the White Sheep rule, he had a complete *medrese* education without experiencing any of the tribulations that afflicted Bâkî in his early life, rising rapidly through the ulema at Baghdad and then gaining the patronage of the Safavid governors there until the Ottoman conquest in 1534. Fuzuli now managed to switch religions and patrons without too much difficulty, gaining Süleyman's favor with *kaside*s written in his honor and securing regular pensions from the governors of Baghdad thereafter. All of his work demonstrated an unusually wide knowledge and power of analysis, his typical themes being the unity of divine creation (*tevhid*), mystic love, and the tragic death of the Shia heroes Hasan and Hüseyin at Kerbela. His Persian verse never ranked him among its masters, but he was one of the greatest stylists of Turkish poetry.

While *Divan* literature won considerable popular favor as it achieved beauty of style in the sixteenth century, its continued tendency to favor themes of concern mainly to the upper classes left considerable scope for Turkish folk literature. The popular mystic poets of the sixteenth century were never able to achieve the heights of men such as Yunus Emre, but the various orders nourished and spread the words of a number of able mystic poets. Of these, the great Kızılbaş rebel and supporter of the Safavids, Pir Sultan Abdal, participated actively in the revolts against the sultan around Sivas before being executed for his crimes. The *saz* poets, or troubadours, remained foremost in popular literature. They developed the genre of Turkish popular poetry as singing poets very much in the tradition of the troubadours of medieval Europe, transforming the previous traditions of the heroic epic into a style called *hikâye,* literally "story," which carried on the old forms and themes while adding elements reflecting the social, economic, and religious movements of the time.

Among the leading troubadours and epic poets of the sixteenth century were Bahşi, who commemorated Selim I's conquest of Egypt; Öksüz Ali, who described the traditions and spirit of the Black Sea people as well as Ferhat Paşa's campaigns in Iran at the end of the century; and the greatest of all, Köroğlu, who participated in the Iranian expeditions of Özdemiroğlu Osman Paşa, taking his name from the great Celali rebel Köroğlu, causing some to think, incorrectly, that poet and rebel were the same. The *hikâye* epics of Köroğlu and others had a common stylistic pattern. The narrative and dialogues of individuals were in prose. Special recitatives were in verse, inserted into the prose texts, and sung with the music of the stringed *saz* by the troubadour himself. The sixteenth century also saw the development of the shadow play (*karagöz*), which provided a device for the troubadour to present his stories to the eye as well as the ear, considerably enhancing the effect and influence on his audience.

The Subject Class

All subjects of the sultan who were not members of his Ruling Class were considered to be his "protected flock" (rayas, Turkish *reaya*). In return for his care and protection they produced the wealth that the Ruling Class was to exploit and defend. All functions not assumed by the latter were left to the subjects to organize as they wished in numerous interlocking and overlapping groups based on religion, occupation, and residence, which together formed the substratum of Middle Eastern society. The status of each individual subject, then, like that of Ruling Class Ottomans, was determined by a combination of the groups with which he was associated. Through the regulation and protection of the subjects the Ruling Class coordinated their activities.

Divisions by Residence

There were two main groups among the subjects according to place of residence: (1) those living in the cities and rural towns and villages and (2) the nomads. Each group had distinct rights, privileges, and obligations, while official permission was needed for them to pass from one to another.

City Dwellers and Cultivators. The most privileged of the sultan's subjects were the city dwellers, since they were exempted from military service as well as many of the taxes and forced-labor requirements imposed on their rural counterparts. There was, therefore, constant pressure from the latter wishing to go and live in the cities. But since any migration of this kind would have disturbed the economy and inevitably cost the Ruling Class much of its tax revenue from agriculture – and probably would have deprived the city dwellers of many of their privileges – it was strictly controlled. Cultivators who left their lands and tried to settle in towns were forced to return to their old homes. They were allowed to become legal city dwellers only if they had managed to remain in the town for more than 10 years and had regular occupations so that they could live without public support. They were then required to pay a special tax (*çift bozan resmi*/tax on the breakers of the *çift*) in return for the privilege. Everyone's residence and situation were set down in the treasury's cadastral registers, which remained the basic records of tax obligations as well as individual status in the empire.

The Nomads. Largely outside the structure of urban and rural society were the nomads – those who lived in the mountains, steppes, and deserts – who remained as free as possible from the regulations of the central government. Living in the Dobruca, parts of Albania, and the Balkan Mountains in Europe and in eastern Anatolia and the southern Caucasus, they were grouped under the name *ulus* (nomadic people) and officially recognized in divisions as tribe (*boy* or *aşiret*), clan (*oymak* or *cemaat*), and tent (*oba* or *mahalle*). Their hereditary chiefs, called bey among the Turks and *şeyh* among the Arabs, were recognized by the state along with their principal assistants, the *kethuda*s (lieutenants), who were charged with caring for the tribes' internal problems and handling their relations with the officials of the state. Most of the tax revenues coming from tribal areas were gathered into large timars or *hasse*s and assigned to members of the imperial family or high officials of state. *Türkmen ağa*s were the principal state officials in contact with the tribes, confirming new chiefs, collecting taxes, and transmitting state orders, particularly in times when their services were required for the army. Special kadis also were appointed to the tribes to care for their religious and judicial needs during their long migrations. The tribes engaged mainly in animal raising during the summer and hunting and farming in the winter, and they provided the cities with most of the meat, oil, yogurt, butter, and cheese that they consumed. In addition, members of the more accessible tribes often were conscripted for military duty by the commanders of expeditions passing through their territory, and they also were used to guard crossroads and mountain passes, build and maintain roads, bridges, forts, and harbor facilities, transport goods and guard caravans, and to labor in the mines and transport their diggings. Those living near rivers and oceans had to build ships and provide supplies for the fleets.

Divisions by Religion

It was the Muslim religious law, the *Şeriat,* that determined the primary bases by which the subjects of the sultan were divided and organized to carry out their social functions.

The Millet *System.* Since the *Şeriat* was the Muslim religious law, it was not applicable to problems rising in the interrelations of non-Muslims except insofar as the latter came into litigation with Muslims or agreed to be judged by it in cases where their own religious laws were insufficient. It was left to the non-Muslims, therefore, to use their own laws and institutions to regulate behavior and conflicts under their leaders of religion. Similarly, Muslim subjects who were not members of the Ruling Class formed their own group around those who were charged with enforcing the *Şeriat,* the ulema. Division of society into communities along religious lines formed the *millet* (nation) system, with each individual or group belonging to one *millet* or another according to religious affiliation (see pp. 58–59). Subjects had status and position in society only through membership in such *millet*s. They normally dealt with the Ruling Class only through their *millet* leaders, while the latter in turn were responsible to the sultan and his officials for the behavior of their flock and the payment of tax and other obligations to the state.

The division of subjects into religiously oriented communities was not unique among the Ottomans. It was customary among the Romans and the medieval empires of Europe and in the great Middle Eastern empires, including those of the caliphs, for subjects to be allowed to apply their own laws under the jurisdiction of recognized authorities who were responsible to the leaders of the state. While the Ottomans added a few details to the system, their main contribution, as in other areas, was to institutionalize and regulate it, thus making it a part of the structure of state as well as society. Each *millet* established and maintained its own institutions to care for the functions not carried out by the Ruling Class and state, such as education, religion, justice, and social security. The separate schools, hospitals, and hotels, along with hospices for the poor and aged, have remained to modern times long after the *millet* courts and legal status were ended by the nation-states established in the nineteenth and twentieth centuries.

The Ottomans recognized three basic *millet*s in addition to that of the Muslims. At the end of the fifteenth century by far the largest *millet* was that of the Orthodox, which included Slavic subjects as well as those of Greek and Rumanian heritage. The Orthodox had been divided into a number of independent patriarchates before the Ottoman conquest, with the Bulgarian patriarchate being established at Ohrid and Tirnovo and those of the Serbs at Ipek in addition to the ecumenical Greek

Orthodox patriarchate of Constantinople. But their rites and doctrine were more or less the same except for language, so that Mehmet II was able to unify them under the leadership of the patriarch of Constantinople soon after the conquest, gaining the latter's support for Ottoman rule in return. The patriarch had to be confirmed by the sultan and was installed with as many of the Byzantine rituals as could be performed without the presence of the emperor. He was given the Ottoman rank of *paşa* with three horsetails, with the right to apply Orthodox law to his followers in secular as well as religious matters from his headquarters in the Fener district of Istanbul, thus adding important secular responsibilities to his extensive religious duties.

Soon afterward the Jews were allowed to form their own *millet,* led by the grand rabbi (*haham başı*) of Istanbul, who was given powers over his flock very similar to those of the patriarch, though apparently no legal charter was given until 1839. The Jews were allowed so much autonomy that their status improved markedly and large numbers of Jews emigrated to the Ottoman Empire from Spain at the time of the Christian reconquest and also from persecution in Poland, Austria, and Bohemia, bringing with them mercantile and other skills as well as capital. They soon prospered and gained considerable favor and influence among the sultans of the later sixteenth century. Within the Jewish *millet* there were several doctrinal and social divisions. Among the Jews who lived in the Middle East before the emigration of European Jews, there was a basic division between the Rabbinites, who accepted and revered the Talmud, and the Karaites, who were less strict. Most of the western European immigrants accepted the leadership of the former, who thus formed a considerable majority in the *millet*. Those coming from Spain and Portugal, however, turned toward the Karaites, at the same time grouping themselves into a distinct community of Sephardim, preserving the fifteenth-century Spanish dialect that they had brought along (which came to be called Ladino), while those coming from Germany and central Europe formed another separate group, the Ashkenazim. The Sephardic Jews emigrated in such large numbers that they soon dominated the Jewish community, its institutions, and traditions, while in the sixteenth century their most distinguished and wealthy members gained considerable influence in the courts of Selim II and Murat III.

The Armenian national church was monophysite in doctrine and so had been condemned as heretical by the Orthodox church. Its members were concentrated in the traditional center of the ancient Armenian kingdom in the easternmost reaches of Anatolia, in the Caucasus, and in areas of Cilicia where they had migrated following the absorption of their homeland first by the Byzantines and then the Turks. There also were many Armenians in Istanbul, since they had played a significant political and commercial role in the late Byzantine period. The catholicos of the Armenian church at the time of the conquest of Istanbul was at Echmiadzin, outside Ottoman territory in the Caucasus, and there was a rival see in Cilicia as well. When Mehmet II recognized the Armenian *millet* in 1461, he brought the archbishop of Bursa, the highest-ranking Armenian official, into his empire and made him Armenian patriarch, giving him the same authority over his followers as was possessed by the Greek patriarch and the grand rabbi. The Armenian *millet* also was given authority over all subjects not included in the two other *millets*, most numerous among which were the Gypsies (called *Kıbti,* or Copts, by the Arabs and Ottomans, apparently because of a mistaken identification of them with the original inhabitants of Egypt), the Assyrians, the Monophysites of Syria and Egypt, and the Bogomils of Bosnia, who were in fact doctrinally related to the Manicheans.

The sixteenth-century conquests brought considerable changes to the *millet*s. The conquest of the Arab world brought such an increase of Muslim subjects that they constituted a majority of the population for the first time, giving the Muslim *millet* a numerical dominance. However, the conquests brought sufficient numbers of new adherents to the non-Muslim *millet*s to enable them to withstand the resulting pressures as well as the problems created by the increasing political, economic, and social stresses of the time. Insofar as the Orthodox patriarch in particular was concerned, the conquests of the Arab world, and later of Cyprus and Crete, brought under its control major new areas of Orthodox persuasion including the ancient patriarchates of Jerusalem, Antioch, and Alexandria, which long had been sources of heresy in the church although they had been under Muslim rule since the seventh century. Bringing new patriarchates under the jurisdiction of the ecumenical patriarch inevitably increased his political problems in maintaining his primacy. But regulations issued by the sultan under the patriarch's influence prevented Arab and later Slavic natives from entering the higher ranks of the priesthood and began the process by which the Greek element emerged dominant. Insofar as the Armenians were concerned, they were particularly affected by Selim I's conquests of the great centers of Armenian life following the defeat of the Safavids at Çaldıran in 1514. The seat of the catholicos now was incorporated into the empire, but overall authority within the *millet* continued to be exercised by the patriarch of Istanbul. It was at this time also that the struggles began between the Armenians, who attempted to establish themselves in large sections of eastern Anatolia between Greater and Lesser Armenia, and their current occupants, the Kurds, who resisted strongly all efforts to remove them from their homes. This created tensions and problems that also were to survive to modern times.

One Roman Catholic group in the empire at the time were the Maronites of the Lebanon. Unlike the Orthodox, they believed that Christ had only one will, not one for each of his two natures, and they accepted the leadership of Rome in return for the right to continue their native rites under an autonomous clergy. Another group was the Latin Catholics of Hungary, Croatia, and northern Albania, later strengthened in numbers by the sixteenth-century conquests of the Aegean Islands and by the additions of Uniate Armenians in Cilicia and Palestine – all of whom were formally placed under the Armenian *millet,* albeit with considerable autonomy.

The Popular Religious Organizations. In addition to the official orthodox religious establishments, which determined and organized individual status and action in the Ottoman system, there also was a network of unofficial religious organizations that managed to capture the hearts and minds of a majority of the sultan's subjects, Muslim and non-Muslim alike. Insofar as the Muslims were concerned these unofficial religious groups were primarily products of the movement toward mystical union with the Creator, Sufism, which had converted most of the Turkish nomads to Islam even while they were camped in Central Asia preparing to invade the Middle East and whose practitioners, the dervishes, had established orders (*tarikat*s). Combined with the mystic tradition were the ideals of fighting for the faith against the infidel as gazis and an association of these mystic beliefs and warrior occupations with "knightly" traits of courage, generosity, and nobility, drawn from both the Persian and the Arab bedouin tradition, and brought together in special mystic, gazi, warrior groups known as *fütüvvet*. As the *fütüvvet* type of mystic organization predominated among both the gazis and the urban craft guilds during the fifteenth and sixteenth centuries, it gradually brought these extremes into close association, serving thus as a unifying factor within Muslim Ottoman society. The main change occurring in the mystic movement was a gradual diminution of the doctrinal differences among the groups through the influence of the *fütuvvet* movement, which brought the different groups together under the umbrella of the major mystic orders.

The orders, or *tarikat*s, referred literally to the "paths" of special action and behavior required of all adherents wishing to achieve a certain type of mystic union with God, as defined by the founders and leaders of each. Members were required to live lives of poverty, abstaining from the material life of the world, living in monasteries (*tekke*) maintained by the orders, or wandering between them while seeking the bare necessities of life in the form of alms (*zekat*) from their wealthier Muslim brothers. Mystic knowledge was stratified into levels. An apprentice (*mürit*) would attach himself to a full-fledged *derviş* to secure knowledge of the lowest levels, after which he would be initiated formally into the order by the head (called the *pir, şeyh,* or *baba*) of the *tekke*. He then could wear the particular cloak and cap of his order and join with his fellows in the rites, at the same time gaining additional knowledge of its beliefs and practices to rise into superior levels of knowledge – all toward the achievement of a kind of full union with God.

Dervish members considered themselves to be the spiritual descendants of the earlier mystic founders of their orders, which developed chains (*silsile*) of spiritual genealogy to connect them back through the ages of Islam, usually to the caliph Âli. The tomb of the order's founder was its main center. The founders of the orders thus were developed into Muslim saints, whose veneration led adherents at times to develop practices of ritual that differed very little from those of non-Muslim saint worshipers, often at the same places, providing continuity in tradition and encouraging association among subjects of different religions. Collectively, the mystic saints came to be known as the "friends" (*evliyâ*) of God. Included among them were all the prophets recognized by orthodox Islam from Adam, Abraham, Moses, and Solomon to the Prophet Muhammad and Ali up to the great Sufi leaders of Ottoman times.

Most important of the early Sufi orders that brought this kind of mysticism into Anatolia with the Turkish invasion following the Battle of Manzikert was that founded by Kalender, whose name has entered the Turkish language as the epitome of the wandering mendicant dervish and, by adaption, means any carefree person. Members of this order spread widely in the Muslim world during the twelfth century, dressing wildly, with unkempt hair and beards, beating drums and engaging in other kinds of "unsocial" behavior to attract attention and secure the gatherings needed to preach their message, and the alms that were their sole means of support. The popular and relatively crude message borne by their preachers induced most of the Turkoman tribesmen wandering in northern Iran and eastern Anatolia at the time to go to the frontiers of Islam and extend them against the infidels.

Once the empire was established and the orthodox Muslim establishment ulema were made basic elements of the Ruling Class, these *Kalenderi*s rose to lead the opposition to the new order of things, stimulating the fifteenth-century nomadic risings that culminated in the *Kızılbaş* movement and foundation of the Safavid Empire in Iran. The tendency of the state to suppress the kind of religious experience that the *Kalenderi*s supplied the uneducated masses led in turn to the development of a new order to fill the need within the bounds of orthodoxy. This was the *Bektaşi* order, founded by Hacı Bektaş Veli, probably in the thirteenth century, and three centuries later attached to the Janissary corps. While basically a heterodox mystic movement, because of its attachment to the Ottoman dynasty, it traced its descent back through the caliph Ali to Abu Bekir, the Prophet's most revered successor for orthodox Muslims, thus accepting orthodox interpretations more than any other Sufi order and becoming in turn more acceptable to the ulema. The order spread widely among the nomads in eastern Anatolia and Southeastern Europe. Active *Bektaşi* missionary work and their tendency to absorb both non-Muslim rituals and practices also led them to become the principal converters of Christian peasants in the Balkans, adding greatly to their strength. As the members of the Janissary corps entered the Ottoman populace as artisans and merchants in the age of decline, so too did the order extend its influence among the urban masses.

Another order of particular importance to the early Ottomans was that of the *Mevlevi*s, or "whirling dervishes." Their rites became better known in Europe than those of the other orders, but their use of music and dancing made them particularly abhorrent to orthodox Muslims. The founder and patron saint of the order was Mevlana ("our lord") Celaluddin Rumi (1207–1273), the great Seljuk mystic poet of the thirteenth century, whose doctrines attracted many Ruling Class as well as subject members and thus emphasized the order's urban and intellectual nature right from the beginning in opposition to the more fanatical and popular orders. It actually had no *tekke* during the founder's life, and it was only after his death that the order itself was founded in Konya and then spread throughout Anatolia. The doctrines of the *Mevlevi*s were far more sophisticated than those of the *Kalenderi*s and *Bektaşi*s. It never had any hold over the tribesmen, and because of its urban appeal it included members of the Ruling Class. It was even used by the government, at times, to play off the *Bektaşi*s.

The religious orders permeated Anatolian society in Ottoman times and provided refuge, protection, and religious fulfillment for the individual as well as means to express his interests and views in a society that otherwise was organized mainly to benefit the members of the Ruling Class.

Divisions by Occupation

The third primary determinant of division and organization among subjects of the sultan was their occupation, with the cultivators, craftsmen, and merchants being the primary groups aside from those involved in religion and education. Among the subjects who produced wealth, those who worked the soil and engaged in artisan crafts were particularly regulated and kept in their places, since they produced most of the goods that sustained life as well as the bulk of the treasury's revenues and were therefore considered the most basic elements of the Ottoman social and economic systems.

The Cultivators. We have already examined the system by which the members of the Ruling Class were given the authority to tax the cultivators. But what of the tillers of the soil themselves? How did they hold their positions? What property regulations were applied to them? What was their relation to the tax collectors? And to what extent could they retain the fruits of their labor?

From the rise of the empire until the seventeenth century the basic freehold ownership of agricultural lands was vested in the monarch as part of his sovereign attributes and was assigned by him to the state, as we have seen. According to the regulations imposed by the state in *kanuns*, the right to cultivate the land was leased to cultivators in units called *çiftlik*, each being defined as the extent of cultivable land that could be plowed by a pair (*çift*) of oxen, though the exact size varied according to the location, type, and fertility of the land. In most cases each *çiftlik* encompassed 60 to 150 *dönüm*s (each *dönüm* was about 1000 square meters). Such holdings were possessed by raya cultivators, Christian and Muslim alike, through deeds recorded in the cadastral registers and thus were a kind of property holding despite the sultan's ultimate ownership. Each year 22 *akçe*s had to be paid for each *çiftlik* regardless of how much the individual cultivated or kept for himself after the cultivation (*harac*) taxes were paid. Thus it was a land rather than an income tax.[6] Late in the sixteenth century, however, the constant inflation and insatiable demands of the sultan and his Ruling Class caused the tax to be raised to 33 and then 50 *akçe*s in Anatolia and Syria, but it remained at 22 *akçe*s in Europe most of the time. In addition, as the value of the *akçe* declined, the *çift resmi* lost much of its importance; thus it was gradually replaced by the *avarız* household tax imposed originally as an extraordinary tax, but later became a more or less regular state tax, which inevitably took much more of the crop from the cultivator than had the strongly regulated *çift resmi*, though it was supposed to be apportioned among the villagers according to their ability to pay (see pp. 120–121).

Cultivators were allowed to subdivide their *çift*s only under severe restrictions, since subdivision might hinder the efficient cultivation of the land and collection of taxes. But these regulations were often evaded, with the anticipated deleterious effects resulting. Rayas holding *çiftlik*s collectively were required to divide the burden of labor as well as taxes without actually splitting the holdings. Peasants could not normally transfer them to others or make them into foundations or private property. If the *çift*s were vacated or idle for three years, the *mukata'a* holder could sell the usufruct to other suitable cultivators willing to work the land and pay the taxes. But as long as the cultivator did what he was supposed to do, he could not be dispossessed and his rights could not be violated. The peasants thus were not particularly oppressed, especially in the first two centuries of Ottoman rule. The main agricultural problem of the Ottomans to the end of the sixteenth century was labor shortages. It was for this reason that peasants were forced to stay on the soil. Sometimes they were attracted to barren lands by encouragements such as tax exemptions for up to a decade and the right to sell surpluses on the free market. It was only the rapid increase of population in the late sixteenth century that produced such a surplus of labor that the cultivators could be and were subjected to increasingly harsh vexations without affecting cultivation, though this led ultimately to the rebel movements that spread through Anatolia.[7]

In addition to *çiftlik*s held by rayas, some lands were also assigned directly to soldiers or administrators as *zeamet*s or *hasse*s. Unlike the timars, these were held directly and farmed by them or by hired peasants, at least until the late sixteenth century when most of them were absorbed into the pool of raya *çiftlik*s and assigned as parts of timars, often to the same men who had held them previously as *çiftlik*s. In addition, whole villages or districts sometimes were granted by the sultan to relatives or individual members of the Ruling Class, again under the name *çiftlik*, which in this case was a kind of private estate, permanently alienated from the imperial possessions and transformed into private property while their lands were either leased to sharecroppers or subfarmed to tax farmers. Many barren lands were also brought into cultivation by awarding them as *çiftlik*s, with exemption from taxes until they were fully worked and then absorbed into the regular raya *çiftlik*s and handed out as timars.

The Craftsmen. In addition to dividing the subjects by religion and forming them into *millet*s to provide them with status in life, the corporative nature of Ottoman society also led most urban economic groups to establish their own guild organizations (*esnaf*) to regulate their affairs, promote group and individual interest, and care for their members as well as to represent them in the government and among individual members of the Ruling Class. The guilds performed all kinds of social functions, often in alliance with the religious orders or *millet*s. They enforced moral principles to supplement those imposed on the individual by his religion. Their primary purpose was to maintain the standards of each craft and limit the entry of new members, to maintain prices and profits, prevent cut-price competition, and handle members' relations with other guilds as well as with the government. Finally, the guilds performed social functions for the urban population. They built up funds out of fees to accumulate capital that was loaned at low interest to members, with the interest revenues in turn used for charitable activities such as distributing food to poor members and nonmembers, helping members who were ill and unable to practice their trades, and providing funerals for members whose families lacked sufficient money for the purpose. The guilds took the lead in organizing and participating in urban festivals and processions, such as those celebrating the births of princes, accessions of sultans, and the departure and arrivals of military expeditions and the annual pilgrims' caravans.

Guild membership varied considerably. Some of them were wholly Muslim or Christian or Jewish, while others banded together persons of different religions and classes for economic reasons. There were guilds of scribes and religious men as well as of artisans and craftsmen as such. Each guild was composed of master craftsmen (called *usta,* or *ustaz*). Leadership was entrusted to councils of elders, presided over by the guild leader, or *şeyh,* the spiritual and moral leader, while actual day-to-day executive authority was usually exercised by his lieutenant, the *kethüda,* or *kâhya.* Also on the council were the *yiğit başı,* responsible for enforcing guild regulations, fines, and the like; the *işçi başi,* who cared for standards; and two *ehl-i hibra* (men of experience), who were charged mainly with selecting and training new members before they were apprenticed. All members of the council were elected by the masters under the supervision of the local kadi, and the *kâhya* was charged with obtaining an authorization from the sultan certifying the results. Individual masters could select their own apprentices, but the latter's expertness had to be examined and certified by the council before they could be promoted to journeymen and then to masters, with the right to open their own shops. The council also advised the *şeyh* and *kâhya*s on their problems, investigated disputes among members and accusations of malpractice, and also cared for other matters of common concern, using the *ehl-i hibra* as agents and investigators.

The master's right to operate a shop, and thus pursue his occupation, was called the *gedik* (place, trade monopoly, license). A limited number of these were available to prevent excessive competition. The *gedik* was considered to be the private property of the master, who could sell it or leave it to heirs as long as the recipient was able to meet guild standards. Some *gedik*s authorized their holders to practice their crafts wherever they wished, while others were limited to specific localities.

In addition to serving their members and crafts, the guilds also performed a number of functions for the government and for the society as a whole. Their most important noneconomic function was as mediators between the Ruling Class and their members. The *kâhya* normally announced the sultan's *kanun*s to guild members and was responsible to the Ruling Class for seeing that they were carried out and that violators were punished. The *kâhya* also represented guild members in the government, complaining to the kadi or others when officials seriously violated their rights. In Egypt the guilds levied and collected the market taxes from members, but this was not the case elsewhere in the empire, where the *muhtesip* collected these charges while inspecting the markets (see p. 160–161). The guilds, however, were in charge of collecting customs duties from their members for goods shipped within or outside the empire. They were responsible for controlling the quality of products and the honesty of weights and measures as well as fixing wages and prices, although in this their authority was limited to denouncing violaters to the *muhtesip* and/or kadi rather than taking summary action themselves. The guilds also were responsible for providing the government and army with needed artisans and goods, particularly during military campaigns.

The Merchants. Whereas cultivators and craftsmen always were strictly regulated and their profits severely taxed, the merchants were largely exempt from such limitations, leaving them free to engage in the kind of enterprise that would enable them to accumulate capital and use it to gain more profit. Muslim law made it possible for merchants to form partnerships and other types of business corporations so that capital and enterprise could be brought together for profit. While the taking of interest was illegal, various devices allowed it in fact, encouraging wealthy men to invest. Turkish and Islamic tradition favored the merchant in society and encouraged the ruler to avoid measures that might hurt the former's ability to act for his own best interest. Those merchants whose product was money and were the moneylenders (*sarraf*) and bankers of Islamic society also were needed by all classes to finance their endeavors or to pay their taxes. Despite these traditions and needs, there was still a great deal of hostility toward merchants on the part of subjects. The very practices that had enabled the merchants to profit and build up capital – such as cornering the market on materials and bidding up their prices – made most guild members regard the merchants as bitter rivals. Accordingly, the guilds often tried to get the state to limit the merchants to the same profit margins that they allowed members, usually no more than 10 or 15 percent, but such efforts were usually defeated by subtle persuasion or, when that was not sufficient, by tactics such as withholding needed raw materials until the restrictive measures were removed.

So it was that native Ottoman merchants emerged in international trade in the fifteenth and sixteenth centuries, with Bursa, Istanbul, Cairo, Edirne, and Salonica being the major centers for the transit and sale of goods. Bursa was the way station for merchandise passing between Central Asia, India, Arabia, and India on one hand and Europe on the other, as well as being the center of a thriving silk industry. In return for the spices and coffee of the East, Bursa exported commodities such as silk, iron goods, hides, and timber, with the trade being handled by both native Ottoman and European merchants. The route from Bursa to Florence via Edirne and Ragusa was especially flourishing, with sizable groups of Muslim merchants forming their own trade organizations in the large northern Italian trade centers. Cairo and Alexandria were centers of trade in slaves, gold, ivory, and the like. Edirne's textile merchants traded extensively with Europe, sending the products of the looms of Istanbul, Anatolia, and even Dubrovnik to places like Paris, Florence, and London in return for special kinds of European cloths that were popular in the sultan's dominions. Cotton dealers brought their goods mainly from western Anatolia and also to a lesser extent from Egypt, the Yemen, and the Far East, selling them not only in Southeastern Europe, but also in the major centers to the north and west. Of course, Istanbul was also a major trade center, if for no other reason than its need for vast amounts of grain, white rice, and meat and oil, which led to large imports from the Balkans and the East. Its merchants included not only subjects but also many members of the Ruling Class, who sometimes used treasury funds or their own savings, as well as their authority derived from the sultan, to export the grains grown on their own timars or private estates, making huge profits because of the difference that existed between the regulated Ottoman prices and the vastly higher ones prevailing outside. The Sephardic Jews also brought large amounts of capital to Istanbul and Salonica, becoming bankers as well as merchants.

Very little of the profits earned by the great Ottoman merchants found its way into the state coffers as taxes. Therefore, merchants were able to amass considerable capital, which they invested in various internal enterprises, particularly the manufacture of cloths that were in special demand abroad, providing raw materials to weavers working at home or in small factories and then shipping the product to Southeastern Europe, southern Russia, and parts of western Europe. Merchant capital also was lent out at interest to other merchants and craftsmen as well as to the Ottoman government and members of the Ruling Class, often to enable the latter to gain higher positions with which they could reimburse their backers with money, tax farms, or monopolies over many of the necessities of life. Merchants were hired at times to organize factories to produce woolens and armaments for the army in larger quantities than the guilds could produce in a short time, but this only increased the unhappiness of the latter at the generally unbridled behavior of their rivals within the Ottoman economic system.

Women. In their household and personal roles in Ottomän society, Muslim women had a special and particular occupational position. This is not to say, however, that they were maintained in the servile and backward status that is generally supposed. Recent research has indicated that women in fact were able to hold property, including that brought as part of their dowry, and to manipulate its use without interference by their husbands, fathers, or other male relatives. Women had the full right to have direct recourse to the courts to enforce their rights when necessary, and they often did so. They could testify in the Muslim courts – although legally at least this testimony was supposed to be given only one-half the credence given to that of men – and also often held positions as executors of wills and participants in the legal process. Women could not be forced into marriage, although they were, of course, subject to social and other pressures. Though women's right to initiate divorce proceedings was limited to rare circumstances, they could leave their husbands and take their property along, maintaining themselves outside their husbands' control as long as they were able and willing to do so.[8]

Urban Organization

Since the guilds and corporations touched the urban population so widely and since their functions were deeply intertwined with those of the government agents assigned to regulate the cities, it is now pertinent for us to discuss the official urban structure shaped by guild and government.

Ottoman urban life was subjected to the independent authority of various officials assigned to regulate and control specific areas of life without being grouped into any real municipal organization as such. Foremost among the Ottoman municipal officials was the primary representative of the Ruling Class in each town or each quarter or district of the larger cities, the kadi. He was in charge of communicating all orders from the central government to the *millet*s, guilds, corporations, and others and of ensuring that they were carried out. The authority of the kadi of Istanbul extended only to the old city itself, while Galata and the other two principal cities in its environs (Üsküdar and Beyoğlu) were grouped as the "three cities" (*bilâd-i selase*), each with its own kadi performing the same functions. In Istanbul there was no single *subaşı* (police chief). The police authority was divided among the principal military corps, with the *ağa* of the Janissaries responsible for keeping order in most of the old city. Beneath the military officers there were lesser officers who performed the actual police duties and were in direct contact with the populace. The *muzhir ağa,* commanding a unit of Janissaries, was responsible for keeping order among the Janissaries and members of other corps whenever they violated civilian regulations in the capital. Civilians, on the other hand, were cared for by the *subaşı* (in this case a subordinate official), who was chief of the daytime police, and the *ases başı,* chief of the night police, who acted through the corps of night watchmen, or *bekçi*s, assigned to patrol the city when the regular policemen were off duty.

Municipal government as such was carried out by several officials who depended on the kadi and the police to enforce their desires. First there was the *şehir emini* (city prefect), a post created originally by Mehmet II to supervise the construction and/or repair of buildings in his new capital with the help of a subordinate called *mimar başı* (chief architect). By the sixteenth century the former was also charged with assuring the city's water supply, helped by the *su nazırı* (water inspector), and with keeping the city's streets and buildings clean and clear of refuse with the assistance of the *çöplük subaşısı* (trash policeman). No private building could be constructed without the authorization of the *mimar başı* and payment of a regular fee in return for his license. When public or religious buildings were to be constructed, the *mimar başı* was charged not only with inspecting and improving the plans but also with providing workers and materials, with funds coming from the treasury and the artisans supplied by the relevant guilds. The *mimar başı*'s agents walked the streets of the city to ensure that new buildings were being constructed according to plan and also to find buildings in disrepair and require their owners to repair or destroy them to assure public safety. The *mimar başı* worked with the *su nazırı* in building and maintaining the aqueducts needed to provide water for the city (built principally by Süleyman the Magnificent to bring water from the hills located between the Black Sea and the Golden Horn) and the fountains (called *sebil* or *çeşme*) located around the city to distribute fresh water to the populace.

Supervision and regulation of industry, trade, and commerce were mainly in the hands of the *muhtesip,* whose official task was to levy and collect all taxes imposed in the markets; as a result, he became the principal official in charge of policing and inspecting the markets and enforcing the sultan's price, profit, and quality regulations. As the subordinate of the kadi, he also supervised public behavior in the markets as well as in the public areas of mosques and other buildings, with particular attention to assuring respect for the performance of the rituals of Muslim prayer. In Istanbul the *muhtesip* also inspected caravans bringing goods from outside the city and apportioned the latter properly among the guilds and guild members entitled to receive them. The most important taxes that he levied on guild members were: (1) the *bac-ı pazar* (market tax), imposed on all goods coming from outside the city and sold in one of its markets; (2) the *damga resmi* (stamp tax), levied on precious metals and textiles to which the quality seal (*damga*) had to be applied to assure the buyer of its purity; (3) the *hakk-ı kapan* tax, paid in return for certifying the weight of sacks of cereals and dried vegetables; and (4) the *mizan* (scale) tax, paid for certifying the accuracy of scales and weights. Since so much money was involved, the *muhtesip*'s post normally was farmed out, with the holder paying a fixed annual sum to the treasury and keeping the remainder of his collections as profit.

The guilds were relatively autonomous, but the sultan's *kanuns* did give some of his urban officials a certain ability to supervise and control them to a greater extent than is apparent. The right of the sultan, on the advice of the kadi, to certify the *kâhya* of the guild of course included the right to decertify him if he refused to accept the wishes of the kadi or other local officials. The right of the *muhtesip* to determine whether the guild or its members were violating the law also enabled him to exercise much influence. Disputes within individual guilds or between guilds as well as mass deviations from the *kanun* on the part of guild members also led to interference by members of the Ruling Class. In general, however, the normal weight of government authority was exercised to enforce the control of the guild leaders over their followers, thus to stifle innovation and prevent change to preserve the status quo and keep order. The *muhtesip* and kadi suppressed artisans outside the guilds even though their products, and particularly their low prices, were greatly needed by the poorer elements of the population.

The Role of Endowments

The successful expansion of the frontiers of Islam was celebrated with the construction of mosques, *medreses*, baths, soup kitchens, fountains, and similar religious and charitable institutions. Such monuments added glory to the name of the sultan and served as the nuclei of Ottoman town and city life. Since the concept of government in the Middle East did not include public service, the running expenses of these institutions were met through the assignment of special revenues and regulations for their administration. The construction of such a socially beneficial structure and the assignment of a perpetual revenue for its proper functioning constituted an endowment (*vakıf;* pl. *evkaf*).

Aside from providing for religious institutions such as mosques, churches, synagogues, convents, and monasteries, endowments also supported educational institutions, the Islamic *mekteps* and *medreses*, equivalent Jewish and Christian schools, adult and children's libraries, help to the poor, such as food, payments of fines or debts, dowries, clothing, tuition, help to students, and medical aid. All the public hospitals, fountains, hostels and hotels, caravansarais, market and factory buildings and animal shelters provided around the empire were established and maintained as religious foundations rather than by the state treasury as such.

Even outside the cities and towns, endowments played important roles. The state encouraged trade and commerce by developing roads, protecting caravans, building ports, and granting privileges to foreigners to trade in the sultan's dominions. In addition, to facilitate land travel the government established military posts outside the cities and towns along the main roads, garrisoned by soldiers, to protect travelers. But beyond this most other services such as the maintenance of roads and bridges and the providing of caravansarais and inns to lodge travelers, merchants, and animals were supported by endowments. These were located at the more important road junctions, and around them there often arose new towns and cities that became centers of commerce, trade, and industry. Other endowments supported smaller foundations, prayer places, eating places, guesthouses, baths, toilets, and the like. Charitable functions sometimes were carried out at the headquarters of the mystic orders, which provided hospitality to those passing by, while revenue from adjacent lands was used to fund their social and religious activities.

Though imperial possessions legally could be set aside for religious endowments only by the sultan, members of the Ruling Class and private individuals also established endowments, and the state hesitated to reverse the process for fear of offending the public. Many of these endowments in fact were directed primarily to support the donor and his descendants, providing quite generously for family members appointed to administer them. Foundations thus became a convenient means for wealthy members of the Ruling and Subject classes to leave their wealth to heirs without being subjected to the regulations and taxes imposed on normal inheritances or to the threat of confiscation to which such property was subjected, particularly in the centuries of decline. With the imperial possessions also being illegally diverted in this way, it meant that large areas of wealth in the empire fell out of the hands of the state and into those of the foundations and their administrators, many of whom were associated with the ulema, which in consequence gained considerable economic power behind the scenes. Although this may have been harmful to the state and although large portions of the resulting revenues went to the administrators, the fact remains that a great deal was, indeed, devoted to supporting and maintaining the public institutions and services that greatly eased the lot of most subjects of the sultan.

The Structure of the Ottoman City

What of the physical structure of Istanbul and the other major cities of the empire? The basic local units in each city were the quarters (*mahalle*), which usually grew up around individual religious edifices or central markets (*bedestan*). Each *mahalle* comprised a separate and distinct community, often with its own rituals and way of life. Its inhabitants were linked by common religion, economic pursuit, or other factors that distinguished them from their neighbors. The place of worship or the market formed the community center, which was kept up and expanded when necessary by the cooperative activities of all the residents. The *mahalle,* therefore, can also be considered to have been the local unit of the *millet* or the guild or the dervish order of its inhabitants every bit as much as it was a physical center of urban life. It usually had its own fountain, school, and mosque or church; and if it was also a trade center, there were *han*s, factories, and the like, which were constructed and maintained by foundations contributed to or established by the local inhabitants as well as by the *millet*s or guilds to which they belonged. The inhabitants also normally organized and maintained their own police patrols, particularly at night when the city police and the *muhtesip* did not operate, hiring watchmen (*bekçi*s) who were considered to be the common servants of all. Individual *mahalle*s had to hire their own street cleaners and lamplighters and to organize volunteer fire fighters. Usually, it was the *mahalle*'s religious leader – whether he be imam, rabbi, or priest – who was its officially designated representative in the government, in charge of receiving the decrees of the sultan and sending out criers to proclaim them to inhabitants and also of receiving complaints whenever any *mahalle* residents violated the law. As time went on, neighboring *mahalle*s with common or similar religious and/or economic pursuits tended to group themselves into districts, particularly when non-Muslims were involved, and this was encouraged by the state to ease the task of supervising the diverse groups.

Common services were organized by the municipal officials in cooperation with the *mahalle* and district leaders, whose followers shared the cost in full or part. Street paving and repair, thus, were carried out by the guild of pavers under the supervision of the *şehir emini,* the *mimar başı,* and the *su nazırı,* with the cost of main streets being born by the Imperial Treasury, whereas the side streets were paved and cleaned at the expense of those whose homes and shops benefited. There was no public lighting in Istanbul and the other major cities until the nineteenth century, except what the *mahalle*s chose to provide for their own benefit.

Foreign Subjects in the Empire

Rather distinct from the Ottoman social system, yet in certain ways incorporated into its basic structure, were the foreigners living in the empire as official representatives, merchants, or simply as visitors for private purposes. The Ottomans followed the precepts of Islamic law and custom regarding the provision of protection (*aman*) by the community for those among them who came from outside their groups. The community as a whole and each Muslim within it had the right to give *aman* to any individual or small group who came from the "Land of War," that is, the lands outside Islam; but only the imam, or religious leader, could extend such protection to groups of unspecified size, such as all foreign representatives or traders. The individual protected in this way was given the right to pass through or dwell in Muslim territory without harm, while generally being assimilated into the category of all non-Muslim subjects in the domain. The individual in question had to request *aman* with a promise of peace and friendship, and it was granted in the form of an order (*berat*) conceded by the sultan or his representatives, who alone had the right to decide when the recipient had broken his pledges and thus made the right invalid.

In granting such orders the Ottoman government usually acted on the basis of considerations involving the acquisition of needed goods, such as tin, cloth, or iron, of maintaining friendship with certain European states, and of securing additional customs revenues, a major portion of the treasury's income over time, and particularly at the time when most revenues were assigned as timars. Treaties, generally called capitulations, were signed with individual nations specifying the conditions to be granted their subjects in *berat*s, which took precedence over all conflicting Ottoman laws and regulations. In such arrangements the Ottoman government usually specified reciprocal advantages, such as trade privileges for its merchants abroad, thus enabling such persons, Muslims as well as non-Muslims, to develop large-scale mercantile operations in southern and Southeastern Europe, at least in the fifteenth and sixteenth centuries.

All criminal cases and civil cases involving a dispute of a foreigner with an Ottoman subject had to be dealt with in the *Şeriat* court, just as were disputes among members of different *millet*s. But in such cases the foreign subject was entitled to the protection of his ambassador or consul, or the latter's representative, usually his translator. But cases involving sums above a certain amount could be and were appealed to the Imperial Council, where the representations of the foreign government in question usually had considerably more weight. Foreigners could and did appeal to the justice of the *Şeriat* courts in cases among themselves if they wished, and they often did so when the Muslim law seemed more favorable than their own or when the fees were less.

Foreigners had to secure permission for each trip outside their normal places, but this was no more than what was required of every subject and member of the Ruling Class. Ottoman officials could search the persons or houses or goods in transit of foreigners only when the latter were suspected of giving refuge to criminals or fugitive slaves or of shipping goods that could not be exported from the empire. Customs duties were specified in the Capitulations agreements, usually at rates of between 2 and 5 percent, invariably lower than those imposed on Ottoman subjects, But the rate varied according to the nationality of the shipper, the goods involved, and the place where the goods passed through the Ottoman customs establishments. Additional *bahşiş* fees also had to be paid to the customs officials, but the total still was substantially less than the dues paid by Ottoman subjects shipping the same goods. Thus foreigners had the advantage in international trade, which they used to gain dominance after the eighteenth century.

In sum, foreign subjects resident in the Ottoman Empire gained many of the advantages of *millet* status and an exemption from Ottoman laws that provided them with such a privileged position that they were, for all practical purposes, "nations within nations," an empire of their own, able to do what they pleased without interference by Ottoman authorities. The implications of this situation became apparent and affected Ottoman social and economic life more in the period of decline, and hence they will be discussed further in that context.[9]

The Sultan as the Center of the Ottoman System

Essentially, the preceding discussion shows the means by which the slaves and subjects of the sultan were organized and divided so that they could best fulfill their functions while, at the same time, avoiding contact and conflict. But how were they brought together into the unity of Ottoman society?

The principal cement of the Ottoman system was the sultan, who was its keystone, since he alone was the common focus of loyalty for the rulers and the ruled alike. There were particular means by which he appealed for and secured the loyalty of each element in the Ottoman system. To the members of the Ruling Class he was their master; they were his slaves, their lives and property entirely at his disposal. Unlike the members of the Ruling Class, the rayas, as the sultan's "protected flock" were safeguarded in their lives and properties as well as in their religions and traditions. To the non-Muslim Christian subjects the sultans were also able to claim a legal right to rule by assuming the position of *hünkâr,* or *hüdâvendigâr,* the "emperor," who had assumed the mantle of the emperors of Byzantium and were leading their state to world domination. They also could cite the marriages of the early Ottoman rulers and princes with the daughters of the pre-Ottoman Christian rulers in Southeastern Europe. The non-Muslim *millet* leaders' loyalty to the sultans was secured in consequence of their achievement of far greater power over their followers, in secular as well as religious matters, than was possible in Christian states.

To the Muslim subjects the Ottoman ruler also appealed for and secured loyalty on various grounds. As sultan he held the position that, since Seljuk times, had been accepted by the caliphs. In other words, he was granted the right to legislate in all matters not covered in the *Şeriat* in return for leading the fight to expand and defend the lands of Islam, particularly against the threat to orthodox Sunni Islam posed by Shiism, which, in Ottoman times, was supported by the Safavid Empire of Iran. To the non-Turkish Muslim subjects such as the Arabs and Kurds, the sultans further stressed their positions as imams, leaders and protectors of the religion of Islam, its holy places, pilgrimages, and other rituals, and as gazis, or "warriors of the faith." Finally, to the Turkish Muslims the sultans secured allegiance as beys, legal heirs to the Turkoman princes who had ruled thirteenth-century Anatolia by right of marriage and conquest; as *hans,* or successors to the rulers of the pre-Islamic Turkish empires of Central Asia; and even as *kagâns,* the great gods whom the pagan Turks worshiped in pre-Islamic days. The sultans achieved this last largely through the person of Osman's father, Ertuğrul, who by Ottoman tradition was said to have inherited leadership of the Turkomans through their elected leader, Oğuz Han. Thus as master of the Ruling Class members, as secular leader of all subjects and religious leader of all Muslims, and as secular and religious leader of the Turks in particular, the Ottoman sultans were able to lead the empire in all its aspects and bring it together as no other individual or group of leaders was able to do.

Exercising these rights the sultan alone had the right to legislate through decrees that were transcribed as if they were in his own words even when they were in fact drawn up through the delegated authority given in later times to the Imperial Council, the grand vezir, and others. The position of the sultan in regard to the state and the law continued both the Islamic–Middle Eastern and Turkic ideals of what the sovereign was and should be. His orders had to be obeyed without question by all members of the Ruling Class, including even the *ulema* in matters of the interpretation of the Holy Law by virtue of his position as imam, except where it could be very clearly demonstrated that members of the Ruling Class were in direct violation of that law. He was absolute commander of the army, although he could and sometimes did delegate this authority. He or his subordinates not only appointed members of the Ruling Class to all positions available to them but also confirmed the leaders of the *millet*s and could remove them. In theory, therefore, the sultan had almost absolute powers, certainly over members of the Ruling Class, and through them the government and also over his subjects.

In practice, however, the situation was quite different. The nature of the Ottoman system in fact left the sultan with very limited power. First of all, the scope of his authority was limited to functions involving the exploitation of the empire's wealth, promoting the institutions and practices of Islam and the other religions of his subjects, expanding and defending the territory of the empire, and keeping order within it. Therefore, significant aspects of Ottoman life were left to be dealt with autonomously, not only by *millet*s but also by the guilds, the corporations, the religious societies, and the other groups forming the corporative substructure of Ottoman society. Even within the Ruling Class the very complexity of the system made it extremely difficult for a single man – however autocratic he might have been in theory – to grasp the details sufficiently for him to require the bureaucrats to do what he wanted and ensure that they did so. It was more then as a symbol rather than as an active and all-powerful administrator that the sultan brought together the various elements of Ottoman society. And it was only in the nineteenth century, as the result of Western influence, that Ottoman government in fact secured the kind of autocracy and centralized power that Europe traditionally assumed it had.

What then brought and kept Ottoman society together, aside from the theoretical bonds provided by the sultan? The most concrete binding force of the system was the corporative substructure of society that brought together Muslims and non-Muslims alike as a result of common pursuits for union with God and common economic activities and interests. Products of the society that had evolved in the Middle East over the centuries to meet the needs of all its people, these institutions harmonized conflicting interests in a way that the Ottoman political structures never did nor aspired to do. One result of this was that decay within the political structures of empires such as that of the Ottomans had much less effect on the operation of the system than one might imagine, since the system itself was organized to accomplish almost all matters that were of interest or concern to the people.

The Bases of Personal Relations and Behavior in Ottoman Society

Within the confines of Ottoman society as dictated by tradition and law, how did the individual Ottoman regard himself and his relations with those around him? Individual behavior was closely bound by the concept of an individual *had,* or "boundary," which was determined by a combination of one's family, position, religion, class, rank, and wealth. Within this *had* the Ottoman was relatively free to act as he wished without any limit except that imposed by the dictates of traditional behavior and the law. But beyond it he could not go except at the peril of transgressing the *had* of another, an act that was considered not only boorish and ignorant but also criminal, punishable in varying degrees up to the loss of his position in Ottoman society. As applied to each government position, the concept of *had* meant that each official was autonomous within his own sphere. In addition, by the same standard, the individual bureaucrat had to limit his interests entirely to his own sphere and to ignore conditions and matters within the *had*s of his colleagues even when they were similar to or connected with his own activities. This was one reason why there were so few overviews of the Ottoman system written by Ottomans and also why it was so difficult to supervise and control violations.

According to the *had* of each Ruling Class Ottoman, the individual had his personal honor (*şeref*), which was a direct and vital indication of his status in life and position in the Ruling Class. Any encroachment on the rights defined by his *had* was an infringement of that honor and, therefore, was not only a personal insult but an attack on his status in life. It had to be avenged if that status was to be retained. Since the bounds of the individual *had*s were not written, if a particular right or power was absorbed by another, it was lost unless the act was in some way challenged. But in Ottoman society, unlike in the West, the reaction to such an infringement of personal honor depended very much on the relative rank and power of the violator and the man who had been attacked. When a man's honor was affronted by a higher-ranking person, society accepted the fact that revenge was impossible for the moment and agreed that a token protest was sufficient for the aggrieved party to retain his status. Ottoman society approved if the offended person smiled and then waited until his enemy was weak and vulnerable to avenge past humiliations.

Many of the dealings between individuals in the Ottoman system involved the practice of *intisap,* a tacit relationship established by mutual consent between a powerful individual and a weaker one. The weaker member put himself entirely at the disposition of the stronger to further the latter's wealth and position; and the stronger treated the weaker as a protégé, taking him along in the rise to power and wealth, although always in a subordinate position. When the stronger man lost his position or fell from the ranks of Ottoman society, he took his *intisap* supporters with him; and when revenge (*intikam*) had to be inflicted on or by one member, it involved all his associates as well. This bond of loyalty between individuals was a basic characteristic of Ottoman society and political life. Particularly after the Ottoman system began to decline and the *devşirme* rose to power in the mid-sixteenth century, most appointments to positions were determined by these personal attachments and loyalties rather than by considerations of ability or efficiency. It was considered to be in extremely bad taste – in fact a violation of one's personal honor – for either party to break the relationship or fail to live up to its obligations when required. The dictates of *intisap* influenced every administrative act and appointment, therefore, not only in traditional Ottoman society but up to modern times as well.

Notes to Chapter 5

1 L. V. Thomas, *A Study of Naima,* New York, 1972, p. 78; W. L. Wright, *Ottoman Statecraft,* Princeton, N.J., 1935, p. 119, n. 19.

2 Ata, I, 154, quoted in Gibb and Bowen, I/1, 337.

3 Ömer Lütfi Barkan, "Osmanlı Imparatorluğunda büyük nüfus ve arazi tahrirleri ve hakana mahsus istatistik defterleri," Istanbul Universitesi, *Iktisat Fakültesi Mecmuası,* 2 (1940), 20–59 (esp. 51), 214–247; and Barkan, "Timar," IA, XII 286–323 (esp. 288).

4 Cengiz Orhonlu, *Osmanlı Imparatorluğunda Derbend Teşkilatı,* Istanbul, 1967.

5 Ships powered by oars were generally called *çektiri* and classified according to the number of benches available for oarsmen. *Kırlangıç* frigates had between 10 and 17 benches, each seating 2 to 3 men manipulating each oar and carrying 70 to 80 additional *Levents* and officers. The somewhat larger brigantines *(Pergende)* usually had 18 benches and the galeotes *(kalite, kalyota)* between 19 and 24, with crews of up to 250 men. Oar-powered ships with 25 benches were known as galleys *(kadırga)*. They were between 36 and 40 meters long, had 190 to 200 oarsmen, and about 350 men in all. The larger galleys were called *bastarde,* having between 26 and 36 benches, with a length of 42 to 45 meters, and with 500 oarsmen and 300 cannoneers and sailors. In addition there were also some sail-powered ships in use, the two-masted *ağripar,* with about 40 cannon, the *barça* (bark), with two or three masts and 65 to 70 cannon, and various three-masted sail ships, including the *şalope,* about 20 meters long; the corvette *(korvet)*, 25 to 30 meters long with 175 to 200 men; the galleon *(kalyon)*, 33 to 50 meters and weighing 1500 to 2000 tons; the frigate *(firkateyn)*, 30 to 40 meters with 30 to 70 cannon; the *kapak,* or galleon, with at least two storerooms, with 69 to 80 cannon and up to 1000 men; and beginning in the seventeenth century the largest of Ottoman ships, called *üç anbarlı* (ships with three storerooms), about 50 meters long with 110 to 120 cannon and crews of from 800 to 1000 men.

6 Inalcık, "Çift Resmi," EI[2], II, 32–33.

7 O. L. Barkan, "The Social Consequences of Economic Crisis in Later Sixteenth Century Turkey," in *Social Aspects of Economic Development,* Istanbul, 1964; compare with M. A. Cook, *Population Pressure in Rural Anatolia, 1450–1600,* Oxford, 1972, who challenges the extent of population pressure.

8 R. C. Jennings, "Women in Early 17th Century Ottoman Judicial Records – The Sharia Court of Anatolian Kayseri," JESHO, 18 (1974), 53–114.

9 Halil Inalcık, "Imtiyazat," EI[2], III, 1185–1189.

PART TWO

DECENTRALIZATION AND TRADITIONAL REFORM IN RESPONSE TO CHALLENGE

Starting midway in the reign of Süleyman the Magnificent and continuing almost without pause until the end of the eighteenth century the complex structure of Ottoman government and society began to come apart in a process that gradually sapped the empire's strength and led to the loss of territories and increasing domination of European imperialism, which led to its being called the "sick man of Europe" as it entered the modern world during the nineteenth century.

6

Decentralization and Traditional Reform, 1566–1683

The process of decentralization and decline was as complicated as was the structure affected. Much was, indeed, internal, within the Ottoman body politic itself. But also at work were conditions and developments outside the empire, outside the ability of even the ablest sultans and ministers and most efficient of bureaucrats to control or remedy: the increasing power of the nation-states of Europe, whose political, economic, military, and cultural advances in particular left them far stronger than what the great fifteenth- and sixteenth-century sultans had faced, thus requiring the empire not only to regain what it had but to advance and develop if it was not to fall further behind.

Analysis of the decline must proceed on different levels. One must remember that the process was a gradual one, in which seeds of decay crept into the Ottoman body politic and society over many centuries; that because of the basic strength of the system, and in particular the internal substructure of Middle Eastern society, the trend was not noticeable within, and for long years Europe failed to recognize the decline or attempt to take advantage of it. Thus the empire was able to survive far longer than might otherwise have been the case. Ottoman decline in fact was not very apparent to Europe until well into the seventeenth century, leaving the sultans with a respite that could have been used to remedy the decay but that instead lulled them into a false sense of confidence, depriving them of the stimulus to reform until it was, indeed, too late.

The Political and Military Factors of Decline

It is often difficult to isolate one particular element as the principal cause of decline. But since the Ottoman system was so dependent on the sultan to stimulate and guide it and keep it together and since decline was, indeed, accompanied by serious elements of decay within the institution of the sultanate as well as the persons holding that office, one can assume that this was, indeed, the key to decline.

Even during the greatest days of the reign of Süleyman the Magnificent there was decline. Perhaps it was too much to expect that this or any dynasty could maintain a continuous series of able leaders such as those who had built the empire. On the other hand, because so much depended on the person of the sultan, one weak ruler was enough to open the gates to a series of incompetents and nonentities. The early sultans had been trained to rule and had risen to power by a process that assured the triumph of the ablest. They had been able to apply their ability to the problems of state by actively participating in the process of government and by leading their armies in battle. They had gained the power to control their followers by developing a slave class and playing it off against the older Turkish aristocracy. It should be noted, incidentally, that the old theory that Ottoman greatness was due to a system that made the slaves into the Ruling Class, to the complete exclusion of born Muslims, and that decline resulted from the entry of the latter into the system, while appealing to Christian Europe, is without foundation. The Ottoman rise to power had been led and sustained largely by elements from the old Turkish and Muslim aristocracies. It was only in the period of decline that the slaves achieved control, but this led not to triumph but to decay.

If the *devşirme* had been able to maintain its own unity once it won out over the old Turkish aristocracy in the sixteenth century, it might well have preserved the system that it now controlled, in self-interest if for no other reason. But without the stimulus of the competition previously provided by the aristocracy, and without the need to face the constant scrutiny and control of powerful sultans, the *devşirme* class itself broke up into conflicting political factions, each grouped around one or several ambitious political leaders as determined by the dictates of *intisap*. With no single political group able to dominate for very long, the Ruling Class fell into a maze of petty struggles, with the parties forming temporary coalitions and the revenue-producing positions of state becoming the rewards of victory. So that the sultans would not interfere with the struggles and their results, they were diverted to the more pleasant attractions of the harem. In addition, the process by which princes had been trained in governmental and military affairs by service in the provinces was abandoned. They were now kept in the private apartments of the palace, the so-called cage, and their education was limited to whatever its female and eunuch inhabitants could provide. Thus even when a well-intentioned and basically intelligent prince managed to gain the throne, he lacked the training and experience to reform the system in some way. At the same time, the process by which the brothers of the ruler were killed to avoid dynastic conflict was ended. The system providing succession to the ablest son of the sultan was replaced by one whereby the eldest living male relative or the member of the dynasty favored by the party with the most power at the moment was given the throne. The inevitable result was conflicts for power within the palace among brothers and sons of the sultan who formed their own harem political parties, usually led by their mothers or wives, to gain the throne for themselves. As time went on the most lasting triumphs went to coalitions formed by leading harem groups within the palace and *devşirme* groups without.

The corruption of the parties at the top soon spread throughout the system. The large gifts traditionally demanded by the sultans and other high officials from those appointed to important positions soon spread throughout the entire Ruling Class, with a corresponding increase in corruption and bribery. Every appointee to a position now had to pay for the privilege, and he in turn used it to recoup the payment, make a profit, and of course advance his own political fortunes and those of his party.

The situation was the same in all the institutions of the Ruling Class. While many individual scribes, ulema, and army officers still were extremely competent and honest, the situation was such that they had to fit in if they were to survive. Most members of the *kapıkulu* corps and the feudal *Sipahis* married, left the barracks, became merchants, artisans, or estate owners, abandoned military training altogether, and kept their corps memberships only for the revenues or privileges they received in return. They sent inferior substitutes when called to duty. A good part of the army, therefore, was composed of such men and anyone the officers could conscript in the course of expeditions, with the most effective force at times being those provided by the Crimean Tatars and other smaller vassal contingents. In the feudal provinces the timar holders did no more than the tax farmers, assessing and collecting taxes, while their former duties of keeping order and security were left to the *sancak* beys and governors, who had to build up their own military forces, most of whom were peasant boys and military deserters happy to use their official positions to their own advantage. In addition, as the timar army declined as a military and administrative organization, the *kapıkulu* corps that were left extended into the provinces to replace them as garrisons and security troops, becoming in turn privileged elites, particularly in Anatolia, where they joined the retinues of some *sancak* beys, kadis, and even tax farmers, using their position to dominate both rulers and subjects, appropriating more and more of the local tax revenues for their own benefit and exacting additional charges from the cultivators. Many local inhabitants, wishing to benefit from the privileged position of the Janissary corps, entered it, often by illegal means, causing it to expand to as many as 200,000 members by the mid-seventeenth century, a further drain on state and society alike.

Social and Economic Factors of Decline

Political decline was accompanied and aggravated by economic and social changes that were difficult for the Ruling Class to comprehend, let alone control.

Population Increases

Basic changes were taking place in Ottoman population as well as the financial and economic structures of the empire. The population of the empire almost doubled during the sixteenth century alone at the same time that similar population increases were occurring in lands bordering the Mediterranean. The Ottomans had, of course, experienced substantial population increases throughout their history from the influx of Turkoman tribesmen into Anatolia in flight from the conquering armies coming from Central Asia. But such immigrants were usually sent out once again as gazis or raiders, or through the process of mass deportations (*sürgün*). They were installed as settlers in the areas of Southeastern Europe or the islands of the Aegean and the Mediterranean that were especially difficult to subdue. During the sixteenth century, however, while the immigration of rootless Turkoman nomads declined, the problems of overpopulation resulted mainly from radical increases in the birth rate and declines in the death rate, a result most likely of the era of peace and security that the Ottoman Empire had brought and a decline in the frequency of the plague. Thus there were far too many people in relation to the land and jobs available in the empire. For a time peasants unable to find land in their own villages attempted to flee into the cities. Other landless peasants fled to the border areas, where they were employed as guards by the defense forces. Others served as irregulars in the fleet. Some joined the provincial guards formed by Ottoman officials as *segbans* and the like. But the population pressure kept growing. The last major deportation of landless peasants was to Cyprus, after its conquest in 1570. Though the rate of population growth eventually slowed down, the westward movement no longer acted as a safety valve, while the return of those who had participated in campaigns and were accustomed to the use of arms only added to the pressures.

Economic Disruptions

At the same time, the empire began to experience major internal problems resulting from international developments in trade, industry, and finance. The economic system of the Ottomans was based on the idea of imperial self-sufficiency. The powerful centralized structure developed in the fifteenth century enabled the sultans to develop the different areas of the empire to complement each other and to follow policies that were quite favorable to the prosperity of all.

But just as the ability of the government to enforce the system of self-sufficiency weakened, beginning in the late sixteenth century, so also did Europe develop a kind of economic and financial power that encouraged and enabled it to breach the system for its own advantage. This resulted largely from the establishment in western Europe of a new centralized mercantilist economy. European expansion to the Americas and Africa provided the wealth and means to extend its trade to the east through routes that bypassed customs and regulations imposed by those who controlled the Middle East. The injection of the resulting capital into Europe also created inflation there, further stimulating economic and social growth. But the Ottoman closed economy – supported by the restrictive attitudes of the guilds that controlled industry – resisted and prevented similar changes. As the demand for raw material increased in Europe, prices rose accordingly, and commodities such as wheat, wool, copper, and precious metals were sucked out of the Ottoman Empire, where the prices had remained relatively low. These materials in turn became scarce within the empire; and since guilds with their strictly regulated prices could not afford to compete with foreign merchants in securing raw material, their productivity fell, creating a vicious circle within the closed economic system.

Of course, sporadic efforts were made to meet these economic problems by stifling their manifestations. Regulations were issued again and again to prohibit the export of "strategic" grains and other commodities and to fix the prices charged for them in the empire. But the profits to be gained by the illegal export of such goods were so huge that those merchants who participated in this trade were at times able to bribe government officials to assure that their activities would continue. This trade in contraband goods provided many merchants with much more capital than they ever had before. Yet the continued restrictions under which the guilds operated made it impossible for them to invest it in the kinds of industry that could have met the new conditions and made it possible for the Ottomans to participate in the newly emerging European and Mediterranean economy.[1]

Another important effect of the rise of European capitalism and European-dominated trade was a steady decline of the traditional Ottoman craft industries. In Europe commercial expansion and the amassing of capital led to the creation of new industries, particularly in the areas of metallurgy and textiles, which had to find export markets to continue their expansion. Capitalist entrepreneurs developed their industries and markets by creating new techniques and new needs as well, in the process competing with traditional Ottoman industry even in its home territories. The traders of Europe purchased Ottoman raw materials, which they then manufactured in Europe and shipped back to the sultan's dominions, undercutting the traditional Ottoman goods in cost and occasionally in quality. Thus began the process that was to destroy the traditional Ottoman craft industry in the late eighteenth century and the first half of the nineteenth century. The trade imbalances that resulted drained the empire not only of its raw materials and native industries but also of much of the gold and silver on which the economy depended for much of its fluidity. The factors of inflation also multiplied, causing prices not only to double but to quadruple during the two centuries following Selim II's accession. The value of Ottoman coinage declined accordingly despite all government efforts to control prices and coin values. Prices of food and other materials increased rapidly, and those on fixed incomes, including most salaried members of the Ruling Class, suffered considerably, compensating for the situation by selling their services to the highest bidders and accepting bribes. In the end all the state could do was to devalue the coinage again and again, leading to new dislocations and one financial crisis after another.

One result of the inflation was to encourage the abandonment of the timar system as a base of military power. The smaller *Sipahi*-held timars in any case were too small to finance participation in campaigns due to the high prices now demanded for feed and arms. When their continued absence from campaigns ultimately led to state confiscation of their timars, the *Sipahi*s either ignored the confiscations and bribed the officials responsible for their enforcement or themselves joined or sometimes led the bandit forces rising in their areas. On the other hand, the price increases in agricultural commodities did make land a very lucrative source of investment, further enabling the large landholders to ignore their military obligations and to extend their holdings to maximize profits. Whether originating as timar holders or as the tax farmers to whom confiscated timars were given, there emerged a new class of rural notables owning very large estates (*çiftliks*). In many cases such individuals simply occupied land left barren and uncultivated as the result of the flight of their peasant cultivators, settling their slaves or salaried cultivators on them and appropriating them as private property. Many rayas fleeing from oppression and overtaxation on their own lands entered the employ of such estates as farm laborers, thus forming a new class of landless peasants exploited by their employers. Powerful members of the Ruling Class also were able to build large estates by taking timars or tax farms and illegally transforming them into religious foundations, under their own management and that of their descendants, or into life *mukata'as* known as *malikânes*, which for all practical purposes were private property, which could be bought and sold and left to heirs even though they nominally remained part of the imperial possessions. No longer accepting state control over their operations, these large estate owners kept the entire product of the land for themselves and used their wealth to bribe officials and to hire their own armies to protect their interests. The Janissaries, standing cavalry corps, and other *kapıkulu* forces that came to constitute the provincial garrisons as the timar system declined fought against disorder not as much to help the peasants as to share in the booty, in the process making themselves the dominant element in most towns and cities, often in alliance with, and sometimes as part of, the large estate owners. In many of the more distant provinces they came to form the dominant ruling class, developing their own Mamluk slave systems to provide themselves with a source of manpower independent of Istanbul, dominating political and economic life and appropriating most of the state revenues for themselves, while the central government stood by, almost helpless, unable to assert its power over those who were filling the political vacuum.

As provincial revenues declined, the treasury had to use all kinds of devices to meet its obligations. The coinage was debased regularly. *Mukata'a*s were confiscated when possible and given to the highest bidders along with the properties of those whose parties had temporarily lost political influence. In addition the state used the *avarız* system of household taxes, allowing governors to use the name as a cover for new taxes imposed to hire and pay the irregular forces needed to maintain order to the extent where it became the third major source of revenue, after the poll tax and land tax.

All these changes created a large group of Ottomans who benefited from the existing situation. They comprised a class with a vested interest in the abuses of the time, while the subjects lost most of the advantages that the Ottoman system originally had brought. Forced labor was again required, with the officials doing little to stop the practice and, actually, participating in it. In addition officials once again imposed their keep on villagers without limit of time. They began to requisition illegally the villagers' grain, livestock, and money without paying any compensation, a practice that came to be called *salgun* (epidemic).

To be sure, efforts were made to eliminate these abuses through "justice decrees" (*adaletnameler*) prohibiting such actions, which violated the law and were contrary to the justice inherent in the concept of the sultan. But the very fact that these decrees were issued and reissued throughout the seventeenth and eighteenth centuries indicates the degree to which the conditions that they were trying to remedy continued to be inflicted on the peasants regardless of the injunctions of a powerless central government.[2]

Uprisings and Revolts

Under these conditions it is not surprising that there were large-scale mass uprisings in the empire beginning in the late sixteenth century. We have already seen how unemployed peasants and soldiers formed *levent* bands that scoured the countryside in a flight from the land – which came to be known as the "Great Flight" (*Büyük Kaçgun*) – compounding the problems of inflation and famine. These formed a reserve of fighters ready to join official or unofficial armies at a moment's notice, hiring themselves out to the highest bidders or engaging in robbery on their own. Some fled into the large cities, greatly increasing urban populations and the problems of housing, employing, and feeding them. Many of them did find employment on the lowest levels of urban society, as servants, cleaners, and the like. In addition the Muslim school system was overwhelmed by poor boys who chose the educational career as the only outlet open to them. With falling standards in the cultural institution, largely unable to educate this mass of boys let alone control them, the schools became centers for idleness, immorality and disturbances, with the students (*softa*s) participating actively in urban social and political agitation whenever the opportunity presented itself.

Through all of this the observer is astonished not so much by the revolts and disturbances that became endemic in the empire during its age of decline but by the fact that the empire still managed to hold together for another three centuries and at times even to regain lost ground and so maintain itself as a major power in Europe to the dawn of modern times.

Traditionalistic Reform Efforts

In the face of apparent chaos the substratum of Middle Eastern society managed to cushion the mass of the people from the worst effects of the anarchy. In many cases the judges and religious leaders operated effectively as the principal instruments of local government. At times also, particularly when the results of internal decay became severe enough to threaten the destruction of the empire, individual sultans and ministers arose with reform programs that they thought would save it.

It is erroneous to believe that the Ruling Class faced the internal decline without making any efforts to remedy the situation. There were reformers and reforms at crucial times during the seventeenth and eighteenth centuries. But even the most intelligent and perceptive of Ottoman reformers at this time adhered to the basic premise that the Ottoman system was far superior to anything that the infidel might develop, an attitude that had considerable justification only when first evolved in the sixteenth century. According to this idea, the reason for Ottoman decline was a failure to apply the techniques and forms of organization that had achieved success at the peak of Ottoman power, normally equated with the reign of Süleyman the Magnificent. To the traditionalistic reformers of the seventeenth and eighteenth centuries, then, reform could be achieved by making the system work as it had previously, eliminating those who stole, ending bribery and corruption, making appointments only according to ability, reforming and revitalizing the traditional military corps, and throwing out all those who refused to perform the duties required of them. These reformers were often ruthless in their methods, but to a surprising extent they were successful, restoring things sufficiently well for the empire to recover from the worst effects of disorganization, so that it could repel foreign invaders and carry on. But as soon as the immediate dangers passed, the reforms were abandoned and the abuses tolerated. In the long run, then, the decline continued, resulting in the loss of territory and a situation in which the divisions among the European powers seeking to displace the Ottomans, rather than Ottoman strength, enabled the empire to survive as long as it did. Let us now discuss the age of decline and traditionalistic reform in more detail.

Manifestations of Decline, 1566–1623

The Ottoman age of decline fell into two distinct periods: (1) a century of decentralization, beginning with the reign of Selim II and lasting until 1683, when a revived Ottoman army failed in a second effort to take Vienna; and (2) a century of decomposition, comprising much of the eighteenth century, during which internal anarchy was combined with the loss of integral parts of the empire.

The Reign of Selim the Sot

Elements of decline as well as potential sources of strength that kept the Empire together for a long time manifested themselves during the relatively short reign of Selim II (1566–1574), called "Selim the Sallow" (*Sarı Selim*) and "Selim the

Drunkard" (*Sarhoş Selim*) in Turkish and "Selim the Sot" in the West. Selim was able to take the throne without opposition following the death of his father. His brother Bayezit and his four sons had been killed in Iran by Tahmasp (July 23, 1562) after the long civil war between the two, presumably as the result of an agreement by which Selim promised Kars and other eastern territories to the şah as well as a payment of some 400,000 gold pieces. Immediately after his accession Selim confirmed the territorial settlement. But the manner by which he had succeeded left him with many enemies. Most of his actions immediately after his accession, therefore, had to be devoted to conciliating the principal elements of power in the state. This was accomplished largely by distributing gifts and through bribes. Selim then joined the army, now led by Sokullu Mehmet, at Belgrade, resuming the old practice of paying "accession fees" (*culus bahşişi*) to each member of the Janissary corps and adding bonuses to their regular salaries to make sure that they would accept the new regime. Despite this generosity the Janissaries demanded more. While the sultan was returning to Istanbul in early December, they blocked the roads and forced him to provide additional payments of 1000 *akçe*s per man. The other *kapıkulu* soldiers who had helped Selim against Bayezit then insisted on an equal share, moving through Istanbul and attacking his friends and supporters to enforce their demands. On his return Selim had most of their leaders executed, but he still had to provide large salaries and fiefs to the rebels to quiet them. Thus was established the precedent by which the soldiers of the empire were involved directly in the struggles for succession and were able to secure such large bribes that they became major elements in the political spectrum and also further ruined the treasury.

At this time other important steps that weakened the sultanate came when Selim also paid similar bribes to the ulema and then allowed the grand vezir to run the state while the sultan retired to enjoy the pleasures of his harem. The process of decline was slow, however, and occasionally the empire still was able to bring together sufficient force to prevent the loss of important territories and even to add new ones.

Reconquest of the Yemen

Events in the Yemen demonstrated the new situation early in Selim's reign. The Ottomans had conquered most of southwestern Arabia a half-century earlier, but the Yemen never had been under firm control. The native Zeydis, who espoused a moderately heretical Shia doctrine involving the fifth imam, Zeyd ibn Ali, and thus called "the fivers," held out in the interior. Süleyman's effort to make Ottoman administration in the country more efficient by dividing it into two provinces had in fact led to a division of forces and conflicts of authority that weakened the Ottoman ability to resist. As a result the Zeydis were able to occupy most of the interior, culminating in the capture of Sana (August 16, 1567) shortly after Selim's accession. They then took most of the coast, including Aden, leaving only Zabid and its immediate environs to the Ottomans. Selim unified the two Yemen provinces (April 28, 1568) under the command of the able Circassian governor of Aleppo, Özdemir-oğlu Osman Paşa, who with the help of Sinan Paşa, governor of Egypt, managed to rout the Zeydis, retake Sana, and regain the allegiance of most of the local tribes. The Zeydis, however, retained their position in the mountains.

Northern Policies and the Don-Volga Canal Expedition

Soon after the Ottoman success in the Yemen, efforts were made to strengthen the sultan's position north of the Black Sea against the threat of new advances by

Muscovy. The Russian threat had not really been serious until Ivan IV the Terrible (1533–1584) expanded rapidly east and south, from the Urals to the Black Sea, overcoming the last major Tatar Khanates and using the Cossacks as guerrilla warriors against the Ottomans as well as the Crimean Tatars. Süleyman had been far too occupied against the Habsburgs to assist his friends north of the Black Sea, but soon after Selim II's accession Grand Vezir Sokullu Mehmet organized a major expedition in the hope of capturing Astrahan and using it as the center of a fortified defense system in the area and also of building a canal between the Volga and Don rivers, which would unite the Black Sea and the Caspian. The Russian advance southward would be blocked, and the sultan's forces would be in a position where they could drive the Persians out of the Caucasus and Azerbaijan. Communications with the anti-Safavid Uzbegs as well as with the Crimean Tatars would be facilitated, and the old Central Asian caravan routes between the east and the west might be restored. A sizable force sailed across the Black Sea to Kefe and thence northward during the summer of 1570, but it foundered due to the failure of the Ottoman commanders to provide adequate supplies and also to the withdrawal of the Crimean *han* at the last minute due to fears, apparently nourished by the Russians, that success would increase Ottoman control over him. The Tatars, however, were subsequently able to drive the Russians out of Kabarda (1570–1572) and actually raid all the way to the outskirts of Moscow, while Sokullu Mehmet increased the sultan's influence over the princes of Moldavia and Wallachia as well as Poland, thus blocking Russian expansion east and west of the Black Sea.

The French Capitulations Agreement

The Ottoman court now became a center of political intrigue. Mehmet Sokullu generally managed to dominate the government with funds provided by the wealthy Sephardic Jewish bankers led by Esther Kira and Doña Gracia and the latter's son Don Joseph. Opposed to him was a strong Venetian faction led by the sultan's wife Safiye Sultan, herself apparently of Venetian origin. The struggle itself was concerned mainly with questions of money and positions. Sokullu and his allies also sought to strengthen their position by supporting stronger ties with France and also by advocating an expedition against the last major Venetian possession in the eastern Mediterranean, Cyprus, which Don Joseph also hoped to make into a Jewish homeland for those of his coreligionists who were fleeing from persecution in Europe.

Sokullu's ascendancy enabled him to secure the first objective. The old Ottoman-French friendship, which had died out following the death of Francis I, was restored by a new Capitulations agreement (October 18, 1569); it allowed free passage for French ships into Ottoman waters and ports and required vessels from other western European states to fly the French flag to enjoy similar privileges, thus strengthening the position of the French consular representatives as leaders of the Frankish (European) community in the empire. French commercial and political preeminence in the Middle East, thus established, lasted into modern times, while the era of diplomatic cooperation between the two empires enabled the sultan and his ministers to undertake new efforts against Venice and the Habsburgs.

Naval Affairs and the Conquest of Cyprus

The Ottoman naval dominance left by Süleyman continued well into Selim's reign and made possible new adventures in the east and the west. Piyale Paşa captured

Sakız (Chios) from Genoa and gained much booty by raids throughout the Mediterranean. An Ottoman fleet was sent to help the Muslims of Sumatra against the Portuguese (1568). It did not take too much persuading for Don Joseph to convince Selim to undertake an expedition against Cyprus to enjoy its delectable wines. Piyale Paşa also was advocating its conquest to stop Christian pirates given refuge on Cyprus from mounting raids on Ottoman shipping in the eastern Mediterranean. Continued pirate attacks finally secured victory for the war party, now led by Nur Banu Sultan, mother of Prince Murat (later Murat III) and herself of Jewish origin. Venice appealed for European assistance, but France and Austria were anxious not to upset the new agreements they had just concluded with the sultan. The pope was able to secure the support only of Philip II of Spain and of Genoa for the Holy League he formed. Ottoman troops landed in Cyprus in mid-May 1570 and conquered it within a year. Regular Ottoman administration was introduced, and a large number of Turks from Anatolia were resettled there, thus laying the foundations for the large Turkish community that has remained on Cyprus to the present day. Some Greek Cypriotes were resettled in Anatolia, mainly near Antalya, as hostages for the good behavior of their compatriots, but the latter in fact warmly welcomed Ottoman rule, since it freed them from centuries of Catholic persecution under the aegis of Venice.

The Battle of Lepanto

The Holy League was able to organize and send a fleet to the eastern Mediterranean only after Cyprus had fallen. Its aim was to recapture not only the latter but all Christian lands that had been captured by the Turks. Led by Don Juan of Austria, bastard son of Charles V, it sailed into the Aegean in early October 1571 just as the Ottoman fleet that had taken Cyprus had retired to winter quarters at Lepanto (Inebahtı), a large bay on the Greek coast. The Ottoman fleet was hardly prepared for combat, since most of its sailors and officers had been sent home for the winter and the remaining officers had been seriously weakened by political quarrels between the followers of Piyale Paşa and Sokullu Mehmet. Eventually, the Ottomans sailed outside the harbor to engage the enemy. The two fought evenly for a time, but European numbers and command finally prevailed. The Ottoman fleet was routed and scattered, with most of its ships and men being lost (October 7, 1571).

The Battle of Lepanto was celebrated throughout Europe. The Ottomans had been defeated for the first time since the fifteenth century. The eastern Mediterranean was again under Christian control. It seemed only a matter of time before not only Cyprus but also the Holy Land would be taken from Muslim hands. For the first time Europe began to get an idea that the Ottomans were not as strong as they had been previously, and the taste of victory was in the air. In fact, however, Europe was to be disappointed. The Battle of Lepanto was not decisive. The Ottomans still were strong enough at this time to recoil from defeat and rebuild their forces. While Europe rejoiced during the winter of 1571–1572, Selim II rebuilt the entire fleet, adding eight of the largest capital ships ever seen in the Mediterranean. Within a short time internal divisions and Venice's need for peace caused the Holy League fleet to retire from the eastern Mediterranean, with Ottoman naval supremacy thus being restored.[3] Venice signed a new peace with the Ottomans (March 7, 1573) accepting the loss of Cyprus and increasing its annual tribute payments in return for continued commercial privileges in the sultan's domains, thus escaping rather cheaply from its involvement in the Holy League. That the Ottoman fleet still was supreme was demonstrated vividly later that same summer when it ravaged the coasts of Sicily and southern Italy and in 1574, when it captured Tunis from the Hafsids, who for some time had been supported by Spanish troops, thus restoring Ottoman domination of the western Mediterranean as well.

The Death of Selim II

The sultan occasionally intervened to manipulate politics or determine policy, but for the most part he spent the remaining years of his reign in his harem, leaving the actual working of affairs to Sokullu Mehmet. While he did, indeed, deserve the epithets of "the Sot" and "Selim the Yellow-Skinned," he also was a learned man, writing poems under the name Selimi and patronizing many scholars and poets of his time. It was during his reign, however, that the influence of the harem women reached its peak, establishing the "Sultanate of the Women," which was to last well into the next century. Selim also began the process by which the old custom of training Ottoman princes with administrative and military duties in the provinces was abandoned, beginning a tradition by which the princes spent their lives in the harem without gaining either the education or experience needed for them to rule effectively if they came to power. Selim died in mid-October 1574, apparently from injuries suffered from a fall in a Turkish bath, although some sources claim that this resulted from dizziness suffered when he tried to stop drinking.

Murat III, 1574–1595

Succession went automatically to Selim's eldest son, Murat III, already designated during his father's lifetime. He carried on one family tradition with ferocity – killing all five of his brothers on the day of his accession. Murat was the last of the sultans to have had some field experience before taking the throne, having served as a provincial administrator under both his grandfather Süleyman and his own father. But his unusually strenuous passion for women resulted in the presence of 40 concubines in his court who in all produced some 130 sons in addition to uncounted female children. As a result the "Sultanate of the Women" became stronger and more pervasive than ever, with two major parties, one led by his mother, Nur Banu Sultan, supported by Esma Han Sultan, daughter of Selim II and wife of Sokullu Mehmet, and the other by his wife Safiye Sultan, who as we have seen represented the pro-Venetian members of the Ottoman court. As Murat's reign opened, Sokullu managed to retain his dominance by alliance with Nur Banu Sultan, but Safiye Sultan intrigued against them. Like Selim II, Murat also resented the grand vezir's dominance, so that he was very susceptible to such intrigues. But in the process of weakening the latter by removing his men from key positions, Murat greatly increased the process of disintegration within the administration, appointing party hacks without ability or honesty. Sokullu, however, was to hang on to his position for some time, using his dominance to secure continued peace with the empire's principal enemies, renewing the peace and commercial treaties previously signed with Venice (August 8, 1575), Iran (1574), and the Habsburgs (January 1, 1577), although border strife continued because of the raids and counterraids mounted by the frontier defense organizations on all sides.

Ottoman Intervention in Poland

Even in this era of internal disintegration and political strife there still were some important diplomatic and military initiatives, beginning with Poland. During Süleyman's reign, common hostility with Russia and Austria had made the Ottomans and Poles friendly. But the Jagellonian dynasty, which had ruled Poland and Lithuania since 1386, came to an end just before Murat's accession (July 7, 1572), with all the major European states attempting to secure its replacement by a dynasty favorable to their interests. Sokullu feared that if the Russian or Austrian candidates were chosen, Poland would become a new base for infidel aggression from the north. Hence he worked to secure the succession of a Polish notable or, if the diet demanded, a foreign prince, a man who would at least keep the country from becoming hostile to the Ottomans. The French finally got Ottoman support for their candidate, Henri de Valois, whose promises to the non-Catholic nobles secured his election to the Polish throne (April 11, 1573). But the death of the French king Charles IX (June 18, 1574) led him to return suddenly to France, where he took the throne as Henri III, while leaving the Polish throne vacant and reopening the Polish question. Some of the great nobles elected Maximilian II, the Habsburg emperor, as king of Poland, but the Ottomans and French obtained majority support for Stefan Bathory, successor to Sigismund Janos as prince of Transylvania (from March 14, 1571) and, therefore, already a vassal of the sultan. The latter finally prevailed (April 23, 1576). Bathory now based his domestic and foreign policy on friendship with the Ottomans, securing the sultan's support against Habsburg influence in Transylvania, Hungary, and Poland and cooperating with the Crimean Tatars against Ivan IV's advances into Polish territory, although he apparently also secretly got papal support in Poland in return for promises to turn against his suzerain when the time was ripe.

Advances in North Africa

Meanwhile, important new advances were made in North Africa, particularly in Morocco, which since 1553 had been under the rule of a Shia dynasty. Murat used internal dynastic disputes to capture Fez in 1576. The sultan established the last remaining member of the old dynasty, Ahmet al-Mansur, as sultan of Fez, thus diminishing Portuguese imperial power. The Ottoman position in the western Mediterranean was considerably improved, and it seemed possible that Murat might try to restore Islamic rule to Spain as well.

Conquest of the Caucasus

Ottoman martial energies were, however, diverted to the East, where the death of Şah Tahmasp (1576) was followed by bitter internal divisions within the Safavid state. The *Kızılbaş* Turkomans who had formed the base of Safavid power were challenged by native Persian elements and also by various groups from the Caucasus that had entered Safavid service, all trying to end the centralized government established in Iran during the early years of the sixteenth century. This situation stimulated a number of Ottoman leaders, including third vezir Lala Mustafa Paşa and fourth vezir Sinan Paşa, to advocate a new attack in the hope of conquering those areas of the Caucasus and Azerbaijan that Süleyman had occupied but never retained. Sokullu led the antiwar party, remembering all too well the difficulties encountered during Süleyman's invasions and fearing that Europe would try to take advantage of any Ottoman preoccupation in the east. Murat finally accepted Sinan's proposals, not only because of his longstanding resentment of the grand vezir but also because of new pleas for a joint campaign from the Uzbegs, and from the ulema, who long had advocated a military effort to support the Sunni Muslims under Safavid rule in the Caucasus and to end Shiism in Iran entirely.

The war with Iran lasted five years until 1581, though most of the decisive battles were fought at the outset. Leading the Ottoman expeditionary force was its principal advocate, Lala Mustafa Paşa, helped by the famed conqueror of the Yemen, Özdemiroğlu Osman Paşa, who was his political ally against Sokullu Mehmet. Advancing via Ardahan, the Ottomans took Ahiska (August 9, 1576) and Tiflis (August 24, 1578), defeating several small Safavid forces. Most of the Georgian kings then surrendered without resistance in return for appointments as Ottoman governors of their provinces, providing needed supplies for further advances to the east. By the end of the summer Şirvan and most of the western Caspian coast were under Ottoman control. This opened the way for further advances north into Armenia and south into Azerbaijan the following year and provided the Istanbul treasury with considerable booty as well as revenues from several silk-producing areas, thus ameliorating the financial results of the decline.

Control of the Caucasus established direct land connections with the Crimean Hanate from that direction for the first time. Successful Safavid counterattacks, the massacre of thousands of Sunni Muslims with the assistance of the Georgian princes, who threw off Ottoman suzerainty just as soon as the sultan's military pressure was removed (1577–1579), and the continued political rivalries in Istanbul eventually reversed Ottoman fortunes. The Safavids were left in control of the southern part of the Caucasus, with the situation then remaining relatively stable for the next few years while the conflict was limited largely to raid and counterraid.

New Relations with England

The initial successes in the Caucasus undoubtedly dimmed the luster and influence of Sokullu Mehmet in Istanbul. But he attempted to fight back by basing his position on the maintenance of peace in Europe, attempting to enter the concert of nations and to manipulate European alliances and rivalries to Ottoman advantage. The Capitulations agreements with Venice and France had been a first step, the intervention in Poland another. Now he sought to gain the friendship and support of England by giving it a position similar to that of France in the trade of the Middle East. England had a more direct interest in Mediterranean affairs than previously due largely to its political and religious struggle against Catholic Spain. England was expanding its naval power and international commercial interests to challenge Spain's dominance in the New World as well as that of Portugal in the eastern seas. English merchants had already established the Moscow Company, which was developing trade in Russia along the Volga to the Caspian and also was attempting to develop trade relations with Iran. It obviously would be of advantage to its traders to send their goods and merchants through Ottoman territory as well as to enlarge their trade interests in the sultan's dominions. This kind of English penetration had been opposed for some time in Istanbul by both the Spanish and the French representatives, with the latter still insisting on France's right to collect fees from all Frankish merchants wishing to enter Ottoman territory. But in 1578 two London merchants, Richard Staper and Edward Osborne, in consequence of permission secured from Sokullu, sent William Harborne to Istanbul as their agent. In 1579 he negotiated a separate trade agreement giving England privileges in the Ottoman Empire formerly limited to France and Venice. Despite bitter French opposition, it was Harborne's promise to provide the sultan with iron, steel, tin, and brass, which would be used in the war with Iran, that finally persuaded the Ottomans. According to the new Capitulations agreement (May 3, 1590), English merchants were allowed to come to the Ottoman Empire with their merchandise by sea or land, under the protection of their own flag, and to buy and sell goods in the sultan's dominions without any hindrance. They also were allowed to live under the laws and customs of their own country as had the French and Venetians for some time. Soon afterward the same merchants who had sent Harborne joined others in forming the Levant Company and obtaining a charter for it to operate in Ottoman territory, thus breaking the Venetian and French monopoly and inaugurating the English commercial establishment in the Middle East.

The Execution of Sokullu Mehmet Paşa

The beginning of trade relations with England was not witnessed by the man who had begun the negotiations, however. The longstanding court politics, combined with the resentment of two sultans, finally led to Sokullu Mehmet's downfall. On October 12, 1579, an agent of the sultan stabbed and killed Sokullu while the grand vezir was walking through the palace to a meeting of the Imperial Council. Opinions differ on Sokullu's contribution to the empire. Some maintain, with considerable justice, that he was the main agent of the *devşirme* triumph and that it was through his influence that nepotism and corruption became endemic to the Ottoman system. Others point out that he used his power, however achieved, to keep the empire intact despite the declining ability of the sultans and the increased political and economic problems of the time and that it was he who secured the major territorial acquisitions made during his tenure. It should be noted, though, that the major wars of conquest were conducted in spite of his opposition and that his main contribution was the establishment of peaceful relations with the major European states. In any case, he did provide a major element of stability at the center of the Ottoman system, and his death further encouraged the decentralization within the Ottoman body politic that was to characterize most of the seventeenth century.

War with Iran, 1579-1590

The Iranian war that had been started by the Ottoman conquest of the Caucasus dragged on for over a decade following the death of its principal opponent, thus largely fulfilling his premonitions, though it did bring at least temporary financial gains to the empire. Ottoman success depended very much on the ability and willingness of the Crimean *han* to help the Ottoman forces in the east, while that of the Safavids was related to the şah's ability to bring his *Kızılbaş* and Persian supporters together in a common effort. The decisive point was the Ottoman victory at Vilasa, south of the Samur river in the Caucasus in the famous "Battle of the Torches" (May 7-11, 1583), so called because the struggles between the opposing forces went on night and day. Ottoman rule in the Caucasus as far as the Caspian was restored and direct rule in Şirvan and Dağistan established. The sultan's suzerainty over the Georgian kings was reasserted, with Ottoman garrisons assuring more constant loyalty than had been the case previously. The Safavids were so decisively defeated at this time that no further effort was made to drive the Ottomans out until a quarter-century later, during the regin of Şah Abbas. Özdemiroğlu Osman went on to occupy Erivan (Revan) and most of Armenia, securing rich new booty for Istanbul and establishing a strong defense line against possible Russian and Persian attacks.

Problems with the Crimea

Before returning to Istanbul, Osman Paşa had to deal with what amounted to open rebellion by the Crimean *han* Mehmet Giray. The Tatars had refrained from resuming their previous assistance, demanding first that they be given all the revenues of Kefe and Moldavia in return. Mehmet Giray in fact was interested in taking advantage of a recent Russian defeat along the Baltic to regain Kazan and Astrahan, and he did not wish to divert his forces to war in the Caucasus, which he felt would benefit only the Ottomans. Murat, therefore, deposed Mehmet Giray in favor of his brother Islam Giray and sent Osman to put the latter on the throne. Mehmet Giray put the Ottoman force under siege in Kefe (spring of 1584), but Ottoman agents managed to undermine his support among the Crimean notables. When a relief force from Istanbul reached Kefe, he was captured and killed (May 3, 1584). Osman Paşa then returned to Istanbul, where he was appointed grand vezir as a reward for his victories in the Yemen, the Caucasus, and the Crimea, despite the opposition of the harem-*devşirme* parties, which feared he would end their domination, while Murat hoped that he would be able to gain the military support necessary to capture the remainder of Iran.

Conclusion of the Iranian War

After the situation in Crimea had been put under control, Osman was ready to march into Azerbaijan with a large Tatar contingent and almost 300,000 men from Rumeli and Anatolia. Once again the Safavids retired with little resistance, enabling him to place Tabriz under Ottoman rule for the fourth time (the previous conquests were in 1514, 1534, and 1535). This time, however, the Ottomans did not retire immediately after their victory. They annexed Azerbaijan and put it under direct Ottoman administration. A substantial fleet was built on the Caspian that became strong enough to establish regular communications with the Uzbegs, leading the latter to attack the Safavids once again in Horasan during 1588. With the Ottomans pressing in from the west and the Uzbegs from the east, the new Safavid ruler Şah Abbas I (1587–1629) decided that his only recourse was to make peace, accepting whatever conditions his enemies chose to impose to give time to restore Iranian unity and rebuild the army. Since the Ottomans were now becoming involved with the Habsburgs once again, they agreed to a peace treaty with Iran (March 21, 1590) by which all their conquests were confirmed. Abbas agreed to end all Shia propaganda in Ottoman territory as well as the persecution of Sunni Muslims in his own. The Persian war of 1578–1590 thus brought major success to the Ottomans in the age of decline. The Caucasus, Kurdistan, and Azerbaijan were largely in the sultan's hands; huge amounts of booty and new tax revenues were filling the treasury. The prestige of the army had been restored. Yet glory was deceptive, and the social and economic problems facing the empire persisted.

Beginnings of the Habsburg War

The Habsburgs were not at all anxious for a war with the sultan. Thus the emperor signed the fourth and last renewal (November 29, 1590) of the treaty of 1547, adding tribute to high officials of the Porte to that previously paid to the sultan. Despite the wishes of both parties, however, war finally broke out between the Ottomans and the Habsburgs in 1593 due largely to large-scale border raids mounted into each other's territory in Hungary by the Ottoman *akıncı* raiders on one hand and by the Christian *Uskoks*, a group of refugees from Ottoman rule in Dalmatia, Croatia, Serbia, and Albania who were being used by the Habsburg governors to counter the Ottoman threat. Apparently, Venice too was encouraging and helping *Uskok* sea raids on the Ottoman shores in the Adriatic, but because of the bribes of the Venetian ambassador in Istanbul and the influence of Safiye Sultan, only the Austrians were blamed. The *Uskok* raids became so damaging that the Bosnian provincial forces replied with a savage raid across the Unna and Sava, capturing a number of major Habsburg forts and taking so much booty that the emperor renounced the peace treaty (October 1592) and sent a force that routed the Ottomans at Sissek/Şişka (June 20, 1593), with thousands being drowned in the Kulpa. Grand Vezir Sinan Paşa then declared war mainly because he was confident his army would win and also because he as well as the sultan and his other advisers had lost their annual Habsburg "gifts" as a result of the emperor's action (July 4, 1593).

The war that ensued lasted for 13 years (1593–1606), extending through the reign of Mehmet III (1595–1603) and into that of Ahmet I (1603–1617). Military activities during the first two years were indecisive, with the Ottomans making most of the gains, capturing a number of forts along the Croatian border. The Christians, however, were far more successful diplomatically. Pope Clement VIII (1592–1605) was not too successful in his efforts to raise a new Crusade army in Venice, Spain, Russia, and Poland, but with Habsburg assistance he secured the cooperation of Prince Michael of Wallachia, who was unhappy with the ever-increasing financial demands from Istanbul and who suddenly revolted against the sultan (November 1594), massacring all the Muslims he could find. This revolt was especially serious, since Wallachia provided much of the grains and meat used in Istanbul and also commanded the sea routes through the Black Sea and Danube that were used to send heavy equipment against the Austrians.

Mehmet III, 1595–1603

Murat III was replaced by his son Mehmet III, whose ferocity surpassed that of his predecessor. He killed off his relatives, assassinating not only his 19 brothers but over 20 sisters as well, all of who were strangled by his deaf-mutes. Otherwise the change was of little significance, since individual sultans no longer played a decisive role in Ottoman affairs. Mehmet's mother, Safiye Sultan, remained in control of affairs in the capital while the grand vezir was with his army on the Danube. Military influence continued to be manifested with the payment of heavy accession dues, but harem politics also was operative, with continually more damaging consequences. The aged Sinan Paşa, long a favorite of Murat, now was replaced by his lieutenant, the Albanian Ferhat Paşa.

Continuation of the Austrian War

Ferhat Paşa rose to lead the army as grand vezir more because of his political than his military qualifications, and under his leadership the relatively favorable position left by Sinan soon deteriorated. Ferhat spent most of his time attempting to organize his army while the Wallachians continued to revolt and the Habsburgs retook most of the recent Ottoman conquests in northern Croatia, capturing Gran (September 7, 1595), thus breaking the Danube defense line and threatening Bosnia. The sultan restored Sinan Paşa as grand vezir, but it really was too late. He did manage to occupy most of Wallachia, including Bucharest, during the summer, but a severe winter, combined with the Wallachians' guerrilla tactics, routed the Ottomans as winter came. Thousands perished as they attempted to cross the Danube (October 27, 1595). The Wallachian success encouraged the Moldavians to revolt. The sultan called for the assistance of the Crimean Tatars in suppressing the latter, leading Sigismund of Poland to intervene and occupy the province to keep the Tatars out. A clash between the two was threatened, but finally a settlement was reached, with all foreign troops retiring and a new Moldavian prince being appointed who was willing to accept Ottoman suzerainty in return for full autonomy. Sigismund then restored his friendship with the sultan to keep the Habsburgs from outflanking him.

The continued Ottoman defeats finally caused Mehmet III to take up leadership of the army, the first sultan to do so since Süleyman. He hoped to achieve a decisive and spectacular success by taking the fort of Erlau (Eğri). The latter controlled the communication routes between Habsburg Austria and Transylvania, which now also was beginning to revolt against Ottoman suzerainty. The sultan was very slow in organizing his army and marching it through the Balkans, so that by the time he besieged and eventually took Erlau (October 12, 1596), it was already very late in the season. Despite this the sultan pressed on in an effort to catch up with the Imperials. With a force of 100,000 men he finally reached them at the plain of Mezö Kerésztés (Haç Ova), where they were well entrenched. Though exhausted after the long siege and march, the Ottomans managed to push through several passes providing access across the swamp, and with a major contribution from their artillery they outflanked and routed the enemy (October 26, 1596). Habsburg determination to take advantage of presumed Ottoman weakness was shattered, and Ottoman stamina and morale were suddenly restored. The remaining decade of the war saw the Ottomans on the offensive against the Habsburgs in Hungary as well as the rebels in Wallachia, generally capturing fort after fort during the summer but losing many of them to the enemy after the sultan's army dispersed for the winter.

But internal Ottoman instability prevented army and government alike from taking advantage of military successes. The overall result was stalemate. By the end of 1597 most of the Ottoman border garrisons had lost all semblance of discipline, allowing the enemy to advance almost at will during the winter while the main army was dispersed. This enabled the Austrians to surprise and take Raab (March 29, 1598), again splitting the Ottoman defenses. In 1599 the rebel Prince Michael of Wallachia managed to take Transylvania with Habsburg assistance, while the Ottoman army was unable to march due to political disputes in Istanbul. Michael then captured Moldavia, but this caused him to split with the emperor, who had hoped to take it for himself. Taking advantage of the situation, a joint Ottoman-Polish campaign claimed both provinces in the name of the sultan (1601–1605). Native princes were restored in Wallachia and Moldavia, while Transylvania was put under the rule of Stefan Bocskay, who had been Sigismund Bathory's chief adviser; all three again accepted the sultan's suzerainty.

The Celali Revolts

Much of the reason for the Ottoman failure to push harder against the Habsburgs despite several successes was the rise of a series of major revolts against the sultan's authority in Anatolia, classified generally under the name Celali. It was in fact the stunning Ottoman victory over the Imperials at Haç Ova that inaugurated a series of events leading to the revolts. Cağalazâde Sinan Paşa (a Genoese convert), the new grand vezir appointed after the victory, attempted to remedy the serious disorder that had arisen in the army during the campaign by ordering that all men not assembled outside his tent after the battle be considered deserters; as such they were to be captured and executed as soon as possible, with their lands, properties, and possessions forfeited to the treasury. This order struck not only at those who fled out of cowardice, however, but also at thousands more who had become separated from their units simply because of the disorder then endemic in the army. The latter, numbering about 25,000 to 50,000 men, fled into Anatolia in fear of the grand vezir, giving new impetus and strength to the rebel bands that had been active there for some time.

All the economic and social difficulties that had been becoming more serious during the previous half-century now led large segments of the population to join or at least support the rebels; Turkish resentment against *devşirme* misrule from Istanbul again surfaced. In Istanbul these revolts were mirrored by increasing hostility between the Janissaries, the principal military arm of the *devşirme*, and the *Sipahi* cavalrymen in the capital, who were mostly Anatolian Turks. Behind the latter were members of the Turkish nobility who had lost their positions and a former *şeyhulislam*, Sunullah Efendi, who had been dismissed due to palace politics and who now led a massive popular revolt against the *devşirme* with the support of the *Sipahi*s and the religious students of Istanbul, the *softa*s (January 6, 1603). The sultan responded by giving in to the rebel demands, including restoring Sunullah Efendi's office. But the Janissaries, for the most part spending the winter in Belgrade, then started their own revolt and marched toward Istanbul, forcing the sultan to dismiss Sunullah Efendi and order the *Sipahi*s to lay down their arms. The Janissaries and Artillery corps entered Istanbul, besieged the *Sipahi*s at their barracks, and put it to the torch, with all the latter's goods and many men being burned. The rebel leaders were killed, the *Sipahi*s in Istanbul were suppressed, and the *devşirme* was back in power; but thousands of *Sipahi*s and other fugitives fled to Anatolia, joining the Celali movement. The revolts continued through much of the seventeenth century, cutting Istanbul off from much of its revenue and grain, although they did not constitute a serious enough military threat to divert the Ottoman armies in either the east or the west.

Ahmet I, 1603–1617

Four of Mehmet's sons, including the ablest one, Mahmut, were killed during his reign, mostly as a result of party politics. In consequence, following his death (October 21, 1603) of a heart attack, Mehmet was succeeded by his eldest surviving son, Ahmet I, aged 13, since his other son, Mustafa, was only 2. Abandoning the old tradition of killing his brothers, Ahmet sent Mustafa to live at the Old Palace at Bayezit along with their grandmother Safiye Sultan and her entourage, thus at long last breaking the hold she had exercised for so long and at the same time providing new opportunities for others. Since Ahmet was so young and since he came to the throne without any experience, he had to rely on those around him, first his mother, Handan (d. 1605) and then the eunuch Derviş Mehmet Ağa, who had been made *bostancı başı* by the queen mother a year earlier. Palace domination continued, nevertheless, though now led by the chief eunuch rather than the queen mother.

Conclusion of the Habsburg War

In the meantime, conditions on the Habsburg front had turned in favor of the Ottomans. Command was now given to the sultan's tutor, Lala Mehmet Paşa, a Bosnian who had gained considerable military and administrative experience as governor of Rumeli. Under his command the army regained Pest with little difficulty (September 25, 1604). In addition, in the Habsburg-occupied parts of Hungary and Transylvania the old problem of Catholic intolerance and the Habsburg determination to root out Protestantism led most natives to favor a restoration of Ottoman rule. Native opposition to Habsburgs rose under the leadership of Gabriel Bethlen, who had served in the court of Sigismond Bathory and now advocated some kind of autonomous rule of all Hungary and Transylvania under Bocskay, the only leader acceptable to all factions, Protestants and Catholics as well as the pro-Ottoman groups. In June 1605 Lala Mehmet sent arms and money to the rebels while he took Gran, key to northern Hungary (October 3, 1605), as well as Vişegrad, in Bosnia, placing the Imperials in a difficult position, and sending raiders through Styria into southern Austria. The Habsburgs evacuated Transylvania, and Bocskay gained general acceptance as its prince (July 26, 1605); he then signed an agreement with the prince of Wallachia assuring that all the Principalities would again support the sultan.

Military and Financial Changes

The long wars in the Caucasus and northern Hungary sapped Ottoman strength more than is generally realized. With the large-scale conquests at an end, garrison fortresses maintaining the boundaries were manned by infantrymen skilled in siege warfare rather than by the cavalrymen who had predominated for so long. Furthermore, to make full use of gunpowder, cannon, and rifles military action now demanded the kind of discipline, training, and tactics that only infantry forces could accept, leading to a further decline of the *Sipahi* cavalry as well as the feudal timar system originally established to support them. Many of the fiefs were now confiscated by the treasury and farmed out to produce as much revenue as possible, while many more were illegally transformed into foundations or private property by their holders. The decline of the feudal cavalry was accompanied, therefore, by a large increase in taxation to pay for the new standing corps, just at the time when many cavalrymen were left unemployed and quite willing to join whatever movements there were to express opposition to the regime in Istanbul. At the same time, the increasing need for infantry soldiers, combined with the tremendous casualties suffered during the long wars, made it impossible for the Ottomans to fill their manpower needs from the slaves and converts who had sufficed earlier for the *kapıkulu*. Since the timar system was also declining, it was inevitable that thousands of these warriors should be recruited into the *kapıkulu* and that the distinctions that had existed previously betwen the *devşirme* infantry and Muslim cavalry should break down. With the need for manpower thus largely satisfied in quantity, the *devşirme* system as such was abandoned as an instrument of recruiting and training soldiers as the seventeenth century progressed, leaving the army with far fewer well-trained and disciplined soldiers than had been the case in the past.

The Treaty of Sitva Torok

The tremendous financial and social difficulties resulting from the long years of war left the Ottomans more than ready for peace in 1606, particularly since the Principalities had been restored to obedience and the situation in Hungary settled and since there was renewed threat from Safavid Iran. Rebellions in Habsburg-occupied Hungary likewise impelled the emperor to seek peace so that he would be free to deal with his internal problems. The final Ottoman-Habsburg treaty (November 11, 1606) was signed at Sitva Torok, where the Sitva River flows into the Danube. The sultan's desire for peace was obvious. The longstanding Ottoman insistence on his precedence in rank over the emperor – as manifested by the latter's payment of tribute for his rule in northern Hungary – was ended, with the two rulers now being accepted as equal in rank. Peace in the west was thus secured, although by relinquishing his claim of supremacy the sultan opened European eyes even further to the extent of Ottoman decline. Indeed, the most important Ottoman gain came in addition to the treaty itself. Bocskay's death (December 29, 1606) was followed by some turmoil and a rapid succession of princes in Transylvania. But the sultan finally secured the rule of Gabriel Bethlen (1613–1629), who for many years accepted Ottoman protection and supported the princes of Wallachia and Moldavia in observing the bonds of vassalage and providing military assistance when required. The "Revolt of the Principalities" thus was ended, and the Ottoman position north of the Danube was restored at long last.

Resumption of the Iranian Wars and Suppression of the Celalis

At this point the Iranian wars once again came to the fore. Şah Abbas had used peace to centralize his government and build up a substantial army, well supplied with cannon and rifles brought by European technicians who stayed to train his men. Then he moved to regain the lost territory, first smashing the Uzbegs and capturing Herat, Meşhed, and Merv in Transoxania (1588) and, after negotiating with Spain and Portugal, recapturing Azerbaijan and the Caucasus from the Ottomans (1603–1604). The Ottoman efforts to resist the Safavid invasion were undermined by lack of discipline and poor leadership. Şah Abbas' rout of the defenders near Lake Urmiya (September 9, 1605) left him in a good position to move deeply in eastern Anatolia. The defeat also led to the defection of a number of local Turkoman and Kurdish chiefs and a new series of Celali revolts, of which the most serious were those led by the Kurdish Canbulat family in northern Syria and most of Cilicia and by the Kalenderoğlu in central Anatolia. The Celalis were finally crushed in the summer of 1608 by a force under the leadership of Kuyucu (the "gravedigger") Murat Paşa. All the Anatolian *sancak* beys were sent more soldiers, and a mass effort was made to hunt down the last of the rebels, with thousands of heads being sent to Istanbul as a demonstration of the new order being imposed. The Celalis thus had kept Anatolia in turmoil for a decade, but they were unable to maintain themselves because of a lack of coordination, the generally hostile reception given them by local populations, and an inability to compete against the organized Ottoman forces in open battles. The collapse of the Celali movement perhaps also shows that the Ottomans still had sufficient strength to meet the immediate danger arising from their internal problems while dealing with serious external dangers in both the east and the west.

Truce with the Persians

Şah Abbas' victory at Lake Urmiya and the ensuing Celali wars forced the Ottomans to move their eastern border defenses back to Van and Diyarbekir and allow the Safavids to take full control of the Kars area of eastern Anatolia as well as Tiflis, Gence, Derbend, and Baku. Once the Celalis were defeated, however, Kuyucu Murat moved against the Safavids, hoping to force Şah Abbas to evacuate these territories without open conflict. Murat was successful for a time, but his death at the age of 90

(August 5, 1610) disrupted the Ottoman offensive and led the sultan to agree to a new peace treaty with Iran (November 20, 1612), on the basis of the old Peace of Amasya of 1555. The Ottomans acknowledged Safavid rule in Azerbaijan and parts of the Caucasus, thus surrendering the conquests of 1590, and the Şah promised to cooperate in joint efforts against Russian pressure in the Caucasus. Boundary disputes and mutual raiding upset the peace for a time. But the dynastic quarrels that arose after the death of Ahmet I (October 22, 1617) and led to the accession of Osman II (1618–1622) following the short reign of Mustafa I (1617–1618) ended all fighting in the east and led to the signature of a new peace agreement (September 26, 1618) confirming the previous one.

Peace Agreements in Europe

During and after the struggles against the Celalis and Persians, the sultans' ministers managed to keep peace in Europe and settled whatever problems that arose without any resumption of hostilities. This effort was successful largely because the Habsburgs were enmeshed in the Thirty Years' War and wanted to avoid conflict with the Ottomans at all cost. A new agreement with Transylvania (July 17, 1614) assured its neutrality against both Habsburg and Ottoman pressure, although the sultan's right to confirm its prince assured him that it would not join any coalitions against him or interfere in the Principalities. This left Bethlen and his successor, George Rakoczy (1631–1648), free to develop centralized authority, establishing firm control over the nobles and burgers, enabling them to play important roles in Habsburg as well as Ottoman politics in central and eastern Europe. In the process Transylvania was made into a haven for the development of Hungarian national consciousness to a far greater extent than in those areas of Hungary that were under foreign control.

In addition, a new 20-year peace agreement with the Habsburgs (June 28, 1615) attempted to resolve problems that had arisen in regard to fulfilling the terms of Sitva Torok. The territory around Esztergom – which had been a particular point of dispute in the effort to establish a boundary – was given to Austria, but one-half of its tax revenues were to go to the Ottoman treasury. In addition the Ottomans allowed Austria to show interest in the free performance of Christian religious rites within the Ottoman Empire and to allow needed repairs to Christian churches, thus giving the Habsburgs a legal right to intervene in Ottoman internal affairs on the pretext of protecting the sultan's Christian subjects. The Capitulations rights previously given to France, Venice, and England also were extended to the merchants of the Habsburgs.

Finally, new agreements were signed (July 15, 1607) to end the strains that had arisen with Poland since the time of Sigismond Vasa, primarily over questions concerning Polish relations with the Habsburgs, their rivalry with the Crimean Tatars over the northern shores of the Black Sea, and their use of Cossack raiders against Tatar and Ottoman territory. The Poles and Ottomans now promised to keep the Tatars and Cossacks from raiding each other's territory and to give free trading privileges to the merchants of the other as long as they observed local laws and paid local taxes (thus *not* extending the Capitulations privileges to Poland). The king of Poland also agreed to pay a tribute to the *han* of the Crimea so that the latter would not cross Polish territory while on expeditions against the Russians or into the Principalities.

The treaty, however, did nothing to solve the difficulties. The Tatars began to raid into Poland and the Cossacks into the Crimea as well as down the Dnieper to the

Black Sea and by boat against Ottoman Black Sea shipping centers such as Sinop and Trabzon. Poland claimed that it could not control the Cossacks. But in fact after the Polish king Sigismund III failed in his effort to use the Russian "Time of Troubles" to capture Muscovy (1612), he secured help by a secret alliance with the Habsburgs (March 23, 1613), promising in return to encourage Cossack attacks on the Ottomans, although in this he was opposed by the Polish and Habsburg Protestants, who advocated some kind of Protestant union with the Ottomans against the Catholic rulers. Poland also continued to intervene in the Principalities, especially in their dynastic disputes. The governor of Bosnia, Iskender Paşa, led a large expeditionary force that restored princes favorable to the sultan and routed the Cossacks along with a large Polish force (April 17, 1616). His move to the Dniester the following summer threatened a major clash with the Poles, but an agreement was reached at Busza (Bose) on the Dniester (September 27, 1617) by which the Poles reiterated their previous promises and the Tatars again promised not to raid Polish territory. War thus was averted, and the Principalities were once again under firm Ottoman control.

Political Degeneration

As the *devşirme* system of recruiting came to an end, the great *devşirme* parties that had risen to dominate Ottoman affairs after the death of Süleyman the Magnificent broke into parties based on individual ambitions. The division between *devşirme* and Turk was no longer a significant factor in Ottoman political life. With Ahmet I's mother dying early in his reign – and his intriguing wife Kösem Sultan able to maintain her own political influence only during the reigns of their children, Osman II, Murat IV, and Sultan Ibrahim in the seventeenth century – the harem lost its longstanding power to influence affairs in Istanbul. Ahmet I relied on his tutor, Lala Mustafa Efendi, and the chief eunuch, Mustafa Ağa, but showed greater interest in directing state policies than had his immediate predecessors. Since only one brother was living when he took the throne (Prince Mustafa, later Mustafa I), Ahmet's abandonment of the tradition of killing the sultan's brothers established a new tradition of leaving the throne to the eldest member of the dynasty, usually the ruler's brother rather than his sons. This further complicated the intrigues that were to dominate the Ottoman court during much of the seventeenth century.

Like so many of the other later Ottoman sultans, Ahmet I was a distinguished poet, writing a number of political and lyrical poems of note under the name Bahti. He was also a deeply religious man, devoting much of his personal wealth to supporting the work of scholars and pious men and to building mosques and schools, especially in the Holy Cities and Istanbul, where the great Sultan Ahmet ("Blue") Mosque and the surrounding schools and hospitals were constructed under his personal supervision. He also attempted to enforce mass observance of the Islamic laws and traditions, restoring the old regulations that prohibited the consumption of intoxicating beverages (which had been abolished by Selim II); he established a wine bureau to enforce these laws as well as to ensure that his subjects observed their other religious duties, particularly those involving attendance at the Friday mosque prayers and paying alms to the poor in the proper way.

After Ahmet I's death from typhus (November 22, 1617) his brother Mustafa I (1591–1639) came to the throne with the support of Ahmet's wife Kösem Sultan. Kösem feared that if the throne went to one of the sultan's sons, it would go to the eldest, Osman, whose mother, Mahfiruz Sultan, was a bitter rival and might well induce Osman to kill Kösem Sultan's own sons, Murat (later Murat IV) and Ibrahim (later Sultan Ibrahim), who were much younger. If Grand Vezir Halil Paşa had been in Istanbul at the time, he might well have been able to secure the throne for Osman, whom he strongly supported despite the latter's youth (Osman was only 14). But since he was in the east fighting the Persians, Kösem Sultan prevailed and for her own political advantage secured the accession of the less capable candidate.

Mustafa proved feeble and incompetent. He was the first sultan to rise without any previous experience in governmental affairs. He had spent his entire life in the harem, learning only what the eunuchs and women could teach him, constantly fearing execution at the hands of each ruling sultan, with several palace officials, especially Chief Eunuch Mustafa Ağa, nourishing these fears to control him. Eventually, because he remained under Kösem Sultan's domination, the chief eunuch spread stories that he was insane and secured his deposition in favor of Osman II (February 26, 1618).

Osman II, 1618–1622

The new sultan, though very young, proved to be far from the incompetent cipher that his supporters expected. Trained in Latin, Greek, and Italian by his Greek mother as well as in Ottoman Turkish, Arabic, and Persian, and ably assisted by a number of advisers, Osman was an active leader, anxious to restore the power of the sultanate and to develop plans that placed him well ahead of his time among the Ottoman reformers of the seventeenth century.

Osman's first step was to eliminate from power not only Mustafa's supporters but also those who had secured his accession and expected to dominate him as a result. Kösem Sultan and her entourage were banished to the Old Palace at Bayezit. Grand vezirs and ministers were changed, and while *Şeyhulislam* Esat Efendi was not removed, his right to appoint and dismiss members of the ulema was transferred to the sultan's personal tutor, Ömer Efendi, leaving the *şeyhulislam* only with juridical powers and ending his authority over the ulema. As grand vezir he appointed Güzelce Ali Paşa, who had a successful naval career during the previous reign and who now eliminated most of Osman's early supporters, making sure that their confiscated properties enriched his own treasury rather than those of the sultan or the Porte. It was under the latter's influence that Osman resumed that old tradition of executing his brothers, at least one born of the same mother, Prince Mehmet (January 12, 1621), although his half-brothers Murat and Ibrahim were allowed to live and thus to remain in line to succeed him.

The Polish War

After quickly agreeing to the peace previously arranged with Iran, Osman's main military efforts were directed against Poland, which, continuing to support the Habsburgs in the Thirty Years' War (1618–1648), had violated its treaty promises. It had resumed its intervention in the Principalities and apparently did nothing to stop the Cossack raids. This brought the Ottomans and Poles into open conflict. An Ottoman army led by the governor of Oczakov (Özi) Iskender Paşa routed the Poles at Cecora on the Pruth (September 20, 1620) and sent Tatar raiders into southern Poland to gain vengeance for the years of Cossack depradations. While the Poles built a new army at Hotin (Khotzim) on the Dniester, Osman prepared to resume the traditions of his ancestors by leading a large force against them. But he marched ahead so slowly that the Poles were able to prepare; hence there was a stalemate, and a new peace agreement was reached (October 6, 1621), restoring the old borders and repeating the old promises, adding Hotin once again to the sultan's domains. Time alone would tell whether the Poles would live up to their promises any more faithfully than in the past. With Poland soon engaged in a long and unsuccessful war with Sweden (1617–1631), Osman could turn to internal reforms assured that he would not be attacked from the north.

The Reform Efforts of Osman II

Whether Osman II was a conscious reformer or whether conditions and problems simply led him to actions that can be called reforms is uncertain. The fact remains that his reign witnessed the first concentrated effort to change the Ottoman system with a view toward ending the decline.

His first effort involved a feeling on his part – most likely nourished by his mother and his teacher, Ömer Efendi – that it was the *devşirme* influence that had led to the nepotism, corruption, and decentralization that had infected the empire; he believed the sole remedy for these conditions was to "Turkify" both the palace and the Janissary corps. After his return from Hotin, Osman developed a plan to replace the Janissary and *Sipahi* corps, which he considered to be too heterogeneous, with a kind of national militia composed entirely of Muslim peasants from Anatolia and Syria. He also seems to have thought of moving the Ottoman government from the *devşirme* center of Istanbul to some place in Anatolia where Turkish traditions and values would prevail, perhaps to Bursa or Ankara, thus presaging the reforms of Mustafa Kemal Atatürk by some three centuries. Osman's reduction of the power of the *şeyhulislam* was only the first step in an effort to reduce the influence and power of the ulema generally and thereby heighten the power of the sultan to enable him to legislate to meet the needs of the time without restriction by the vested interests among the ulema and army leaders. But these plans soon brought the sultan into conflict with those groups that would be affected most. He had already incurred the wrath of the Janissaries and *Sipahi*s by criticizing their efforts during the Hotin campaign and by subjecting them to what they considered to be "humiliating" inspections. After returning to Istanbul he tried to curb military excesses by going incognito into the taverns and other "dens of iniquity," punishing those soldiers whom he found there by sending them to serve as galley slaves along with common criminals. He also gave them very limited accession gifts because of their performance in the campaign and prescribed regular drill for them to remedy their deficiencies.

While these acts, along with rumors of Osman's plan to create a new militia, had spread among the Janissaries for some time, it was only when they learned that he was planning to travel through Anatolia, ostensibly to go on the pilgrimage, that they were stirred to open action. With the support of most members of the bureaucracy and the ulema, the soldiers held a mass meeting at the Sultan Ahmet mosque (May 18, 1622) at which they demanded that Osman abandon his pilgrimage plans, on the pretext that this would remove his leadership at a time of great peril. Within a short time the meeting began to criticize him and make further demands. The *şeyhulislam* issued a *fetva* stating, in the form of a question and answer, "What must be done to persons who corrupt the sultan and raid the treasuries of Muslims, thus causing revolt and disturbances?" The Sultan was to be attacked, therefore, through his advisers. The *şeyhulislam's* answer was clear: "They must be executed." Osman's refusal to comply gave the soldiers just the opportunity they wanted. They spread through the streets of the capital, tearing apart the grand vezir and other officials found in their homes (May 18, 1622). When Osman saw that he lacked the force to stop the revolt, he gave in to its ostensible pretext, agreeing not to go on the pilgrimage. But success emboldened the rebels to further demands for the heads of all those considered to be ringleaders in developing the sultan's reform plans, although the demand for the surrender of each was cloaked in requests for punishment for other reasons. Thus the grand vezir was to be executed because some of the soldiers who raided his house the day before had been killed; the treasurer because some soldiers had received debased coins in their salary; and so forth.

At first the sultan refused. When the Janissaries broke into the palace (May 19, 1622), however, he executed Grand Vezir Dilâver Paşa in the hope of saving his throne. But each victory stimulated the rebels to demand more. The chief eunuch was also torn apart, and, after only brief hesitation, Osman was deposed and later assassinated and Mustafa I restored to the throne. The reign of Osman II ended without any of his goals being realized; moreover, the assassination of a ruling sultan set a new precedent that would be followed all too frequently in subsequent years.

Mustafa I, 1622–1623

Mustafa's second short term was even more brutish and disastrous than his first. While power initially went to the queen mother and Kösem Sultan, the Janissaries and others who had accomplished the revolt now reacted violently to the assassination of the sultan: They killed all those whom they considered responsible while at the same time attempting to protect the remaining sons of Ahmet I against the inevitable efforts of the queen mother to eliminate them to protect the reign of her son.

In an effort to build her own position, Kösem Sultan secured the appointment as grand vezir of the Albanian *devşirme* man Mere Hüseyin Paşa, who successfully presented himself as a kind of reformer, promising to move rapidly against the assassins. But Mere Hüseyin only used the situation for his own advantage, extorting widely under the pretext of punishing those responsible for Osman's death and raiding the state treasury for his own profit. The capital fell into anarchy. Groups of soldiers attacked private homes on various pretexts to enrich themselves. With the army largely dispersed, the Anatolian rebels once again resumed their uprisings. Inflation, insecurity, and famine were both cause and result. Taking advantage of this situation, the governor of Erzurum, Abaza Mehmet Paşa built a substantial army and took control of much of eastern Anatolia, gaining mass support by stressing the nature of *devşirme* misrule from Istanbul. Many of the governors and *sancak* beys, pressured by their own followers and populations, joined Abaza's army in what was becoming a general Anatolian revolt, with the local Janissary garrisons and the troops sent against them from Istanbul joining against the sultan.

Mere Hüseyin was unable to handle the situation. He tried to gain Janissary support by giving them almost everything that was left in the treasury, but his efforts to install his own men as commanders of the corps antagonized the latter despite the gifts. When he tried to secure payments from the ulema, they also began to support the Anatolian rebels, stimulating the Janissaries and *Sipahi*s in the capital to demand and secure his removal (August 30, 1623) and replacement by Kemankeş Ali Paşa, a Turk from Isparta.

But now the situation was completely out of hand, and all elements soon realized that only the replacement of the incompetent Mustafa with the harsh Prince Murat could restore some semblance of unity and save the empire from the Anatolian revolt. Abaza Mehmet and the other leading Anatolian rebels in fact sent their own agents to Istanbul to secure Murat's accession. Most governors refused to obey Mustafa's orders or to remit taxes on the grounds that it was illegal to have an insane sultan. The state was left in financial crisis, therefore, with no money to pay the salaries of the soldiers and others. The decisive moment came when the corps promised not to demand an "Accession Tax" if Mustafa was deposed for Murat. On September 10, 1623, Mustafa I was deposed and Murat IV installed by general agreement, thus bringing to the throne a sultan who was to lead the empire out of imminent disaster to firm rule and military success.

Rejuvenation Under Murat IV, 1623–1640

When Murat IV took the throne, the state was in political and financial anarchy. Most of Anatolia and Romeli had fallen under the control of provincial rebels. Foreign enemies were preparing to take advantage of Ottoman weakness. In the end Murat was able to restore the state and military power and provide the leadership needed to save the empire, but it took him nine years to assert himself. During the first part of his reign, until he reached puberty in 1632, he was under the domination of the political leaders who had brought him to power. After he took personal charge, he was ruthless in enforcing discipline and eliminating the elements of weakness in the state.

Internal Politics

Murat's accession signified the political triumph of his supporters, albeit there was some conflict among them as to who should prevail. Foremost among the victors was the new queen mother, Kösem Sultan, who had been banished to the Bayezit palace under his predecessors. Acting mainly through Grand Eunuch Mustafa Ağa the queen mother now exercised considerable influence in court, distributing much of the sultan's wealth to secure supporters throughout the Ruling Class. Her main opponents were: the Janissary and *Sipahi ağas*, who used their corps to maintain their power; the ulema, who worked to eradicate Osman's reform efforts completely and to increase their influence in the state; and the scribes and administrators, who sometimes cooperated with the *Sipahis* and ulema but most often worked through ministers and grand vezirs who were disgruntled with the queen mother's leadership. Soon after Murat's accession Kösem Sultan began to fight with Grand Vezir Kemankeş Ali Paşa, marrying her former slave Hafız Ahmet Paşa to Ahmet I's daughter Ayşe Sultan. Ali in turn bribed the soldiers and palace guard with coins made from melted-down objects taken from the palace and the treasury.

The Fall of Baghdad

Events in the East soon sealed Kemankeş Ali's doom. Abbas I took advantage of the Celali revolts in Anatolia, which effectively cut Istanbul off from its eastern provinces, and of a Janissary uprising in Baghdad to conquer the latter, entering to support the claims of one local faction against the other (January 12, 1624). The conquering army then slaughtered all the Sunni inhabitants of the city who could not escape. Abbas boiled in oil the Janissaries who had cooperated with him, on the grounds that if they had betrayed the sultan, they could just as easily betray him. The remainder of Iraq was soon occupied, and the Safavids pushed westward into Anatolia as far as Mardin, with only Mosul and Basra remaining in Ottoman hands.

The fall of Iraq produced a tremendous popular reaction in Istanbul, where Murat was able to save himself only by replacing Kemankeş Ali with the capable Çerkes Mehmet Paşa. In Anatolia the governor of Erzurum, Abaza Mehmet Paşa, again used popular discontent to raise a major rebellion against the sultan. Çerkes Mehmet defeated the rebels near Kayseri (September 5, 1624), but Abaza Mehmet was strong enough to force the grand vezir to restore him to his position in Erzurum, thus leaving him where he could strike again. In 1625 the Ottomans tried to regain Baghdad, but while they routed the Safavid army and put the Iraqi capital under siege, the arrival of the şah with a relief force compelled them to retire without success (March 26, 1626). Northern Iraq, however, was regained, putting the Ottomans in a position where they could threaten the Safavids in the Caucasus and Azerbaijan. Abaza Mehmet then reacted to the failure at Baghdad by starting his third revolt (July 1627), routing an Ottoman effort to besiege Erzurum (October 15–November 15, 1627) before a second major expedition finally forced him to surrender (September 22, 1628). Apparently, Murat always had considerable interest in the rebel leader, whom he recognized as an extremely able military commander; therefore, he pardoned Abaza Mehmet and his men and absorbed them into his army to take full advantage of their ability.

Grand Vezir Husrev Paşa was encouraged by Abaza Mehmet's defeat to attempt a new reconquest of Baghdad. As he marched through southern Anatolia toward Azerbaijan, he sought to deprive the Safavids of popular support by terrorizing the population between Konya and Aleppo, slaughtering thousands, including a number of Ottoman administrators who protested, further alienating the Anatolian Turks from the government. Husrev Paşa managed to get the support of most of the Kurdish tribal leaders during the winter and then moved into western Iran. Baghdad was put under siege soon afterward (October 6–November 14, 1630), but once again supply shortages, indiscipline in the attacking army, and successful Safavid forays forced Husrev to retire without success.

While Safavid successes in Iraq continued, there were numerous revolts against the sultan's authority throughout the Arab world, particularly in those areas whose geographic location made them difficult to reach. In Egypt it was the local military corps, increasingly controlled by the Mamluk slaves of the Ottoman officers, who gained power. Forming their own Mamluk houses, the slaves emerged as the dominant political force in the country, first using and then supplanting the Ottoman officials, absorbing more and more of the tax revenues supposed to be sent to Istanbul and the Holy Cities. In the Yemen, the Zeydis were able to limit the governor's authority to a very small part of the country around Zabid while taking Sana and most of the interior for themselves (1631). Finally, in Mount Lebanon, the Ma'nid prince Fahruddin II gradually extended his hegemony over most of the province, eliminating rival ruling families and extending his power into the Syrian hill areas as far as Hawran and Aclun, thus threatening the Ottoman governors of Damascus as well as gaining control of the land routes to the Hicaz.

Difficulties in the Crimea

Murat's weak position also affected the situation in the Crimea, where rival princes used the absence of strong Ottoman support for *Han* Canbay Giray to challenge him, sometimes getting the assistance of rival Ottoman factions in Istanbul. So it was that Canbay Giray's first term (1610–1623) was ended when his rivals, Mehmet Giray and Şahin Giray, came to Istanbul and obtained the support of Grand Vezir Mere Hüseyin Paşa for the appointment of the former in his place. The brothers then set out to massacre all their rivals in the Crimea, which did not bother Istanbul too much until the deposed *han,* with the support of the chief eunuch, spread the (false) story that the new rulers were about to attempt to capture Kefe in alliance with the Safavids. Murat sent an expedition to defend Kefe, but its arrival caused Mehmet and Şahin to besiege it with a huge army, compelling the Ottomans to confirm Mehmet Giray as *han* and to leave Kefe in his hands before returning to Istanbul by sea (1624). Canbay gained the support of Murat, however, and he was restored as *han* (June 3, 1628), while a joint land-sea expedition forced the brothers to flee to refuge in Poland. There they raised an army of some 50,000 Cossacks and Tatars, with the help of both the Poles and Russians; but when they returned to the Crimea, Canbay routed them in a battle of an intensity never before seen in the Black Sea area. The brothers were killed, and Canbay Giray now ruled without opposition once again, accepting Ottoman suzerainty and support (1628–1635).

Uprisings of the Soldiers

A series of military uprisings in Rumeli and Anatolia in turn enabled Murat to gain the personal power he had coveted since his accession. Increasing lack of discipline in the provincial military corps led to frequent revolts, sometimes to protest the government's failure to pay their salaries but more often simply to gain a share in the loot secured from the hapless populace. In 1629 when Husrev Paşa was dismissed as grand vezir because of his failure at Baghdad, he managed to obtain the support of both the Janissary and the *Sipahi* corps, leading to a whole series of military uprisings. While each was acting in its own area, there seems to have been some agreement also to join in an effort to restore Husrev as grand vezir. Much of Anatolia thus was in open revolt, for the most part under the leadership of men who only a short time before had been commanders of the Ottoman army in Istanbul.

However justified the reasons for the revolt, the reaction of the government defies understanding unless one assumes that leading political figures wanted the rebels to win. The new grand vezir, Hafız Ahmet Paşa, convinced the sultan and the Imperial Council that the way to solve the problem was to order the rebels, and in fact all the Janissary and *Sipahi* garrisons in the provinces, to come to Istanbul so that their grievances could be heard and solved (November 18, 1631). Within a short time thousands of undisciplined and riotous soldiers and bandits were flooding into the capital where they simply settled down, running through the streets, robbing and killing at will, pressuring the sultan to give in to all their demands. In a desperate effort to appease the bandits Murat dismissed 17 leading officials, including the grand vezir and *Şeyhulislam* Yahya Efendi, who were then torn apart by the soldiers immediately in front of the palace gates. The candidate of the rebels, Topal Recep Paşa (who had apparently convinced the sultan to invite them into his capital) became grand vezir; other positions were given to his associates; graft and corruption became far worse than before; taxes were raised enormously; the coinage was further debased; and food and other necessities were sold to the highest bidders. Groups of bandits entered the palace at will to demand and secure the head of this or that official. For a time some of the rebels advocated the deposition of Murat for one of his younger brothers, but in the end it turned out to be mainly a *Sipahi* plan not supported by the Janissaries – thus it was never carried out. In addition to the military bandits themselves, armed gangs of lower-class men took advantage of the situation to wander through Istanbul, exacting loot and tribute from the wealthy under the threat of setting fire to their houses and shops. All this occurred during the holy month of Ramazan, with not only looting and killing but also debauchery and drinking in public astonishing those who still believed in the faith and rituals of Islam.[4]

Sultan Murat Gains Control

In the end it was divisions among the rebels that saved Murat, his capital, and his people. Recep Paşa assassinated a number of rebel leaders to build his own power and wealth. Rival leaders began to emerge, organizing Janissary groups against him. New rebels entered Istanbul and clashed with those who had preceded them and regarded the pickings as their own. These divisions, combined with a general popular abhorrence of the excesses, finally enabled the sultan to use the situation for his own advantage. On May 18, 1632, he had Recep Paşa strangled and the body thrown in front of the palace gates. The new grand vezir Tabanı Yassı (flatfooted) Arnavut Mehmet Paşa, a close adviser of the sultan, directed the move to eliminate the rebels and gain direct power for the sultan. Murat had all the members of the military corps and Ruling Class remaining in Istanbul take an oath promising to support him against the bandits and to protect the revenues and subjects of the sultan, with the leaders of each group signing his name to a document of loyalty in support of Murat.[5]

The Reforms of Murat IV

With the major military corps behind him and with the lower and the upper classes alike exhausted by the excesses of the previous decade, Murat was in a good position to assert his own authority and to reform the Ottoman system, efforts that occupied much of the remainder of his reign. Murat set the pattern for all later "traditionalist" reformers by attempting to save the system by making the old institutions work, eliminating all those who had attempted to use them for personal advantage, more or less following the advice of his adviser Koçi Bey (see pp. 291–292). Accepting Koçi Bey's basic assumption that the traditional Ottoman institutions and ways were far superior to anything that had been developed in Europe, Murat and the reformers eliminated all those who refused to conform and attempted to appoint able and honest officials in their place.

The first step was to eliminate those who had led the military corps in banditry, and this was forcibly accomplished in a few months. Murat then ordered that the surviving bandits be cleansed out by a mass rising of the people who had suffered at their hands. There followed a general massacre of thousands who had participated, with the corps seeking them out and executing them on the spot. Throughout the provinces, Celali and *Sipahi* rebels also were ruthlessly eliminated in the same way, often by popular mass action in support of the Janissaries. The governors reorganized and reformed the timar system, dismissing all *Sipahi* holders unable or unwilling to perform active military service in return for their lands. The vacated holdings then were turned over to Janissaries and many members of the Celali rebel bands who had become bandits mainly because of the lack of military positions for them to fill. For the moment at least, the timar system once again was made into the financial and political basis for a strong army and administration throughout the empire. Within a short time firm control was established over all the remaining branches of the Ruling Class. Bribery and corruption were largely eliminated and order and security restored, with literally thousands of malefactors paying for their crimes with their lives. It seemed possible at least that Murat somehow had done the impossible and really restored the Ottoman system.

Nor did Murat stop with ending disorder and corruption. Efforts also were made to restore the kind of morality and adherence to duty that had made the institutions work a century earlier. These efforts were stimulated by a great fire that destroyed over a quarter of Istanbul, including at least 20,000 shops and houses, the barracks of the Janissary corps, and the government archives.[6] Murat declared that the fire was a sign of God that the people of the empire had strayed from godliness, which had to be restored if the empire was to be saved. Toward these ends the sultan prohibited the use of coffee and tobacco, which since their introduction (in 1555 and 1605 respectively) had become widespread, especially in coffeehouses, which Murat (correctly) felt had become centers for political intrigue and revolt. Everyone was ordered to wear only the clothing and headgear to which he was entitled by virtue of his *millet,* rank, class, occupation, and the like, and subjects of all religions were ordered to obey their leaders as well as their laws and traditions. At nights the sultan wandered incognito in the streets to uncover violators, administering summary executions on the spot and leaving the bodies of the victims to serve as object lessons to their fellows.[7] Murat stimulated cultural activity during his reign, but there was little room for intellectual deviation or the expression of divergent opinions. Many major literary figures met sudden and violent ends at the sultan's order, although much of this was due to their membership in the corps of ulema, which he was trying to reform. When Şeyhulislam Ahi zâde Hüseyin Efendi protested. Murat had him dismissed and then strangled (1633), doing away with ulema and bureaucrats alike whenever they resisted his orders or were accused of misdeeds. The sultan ordered the execution of Kara Çelebi zâde Abdul Aziz Efendi, one of the greatest scholars of the time, because as kadi of Istanbul he was held responsible for a shortage of butter in the city. Only the last-minute intercession of the queen mother saved him. Soon afterward the greatest poet of the time, Nef'i, was strangled by order of the sultan because of the satirical insults that he had inflicted on a number of high officials in his poems (January 27, 1635).

In order to enforce his regulations and end the indiscipline of previous reigns, Murat built a vast system of spies throughout the empire. Military discipline was restored. Governmental appointments again were made for ability; bribery was ended; and for the most part the regulations and law codes of the empire were observed. Murat also made a strong effort to protect the mass of subjects against official abuse, issuing a number of new regulations and beginning work to draw them together into a "Justice Book" (*Adaletname*), which was introduced and applied in subsequent reigns. Murat, however, tended to abuse more rights than he protected. He needed money to finance the reforms and pay for his campaigns, and to fill the treasury he largely restored the tax farm system, along with salaried tax collectors (*emins*) so that the treasury would secure the full product of their collections. In addition, however, as the need arose, he began to confiscate the properties of wealthy and not-so-wealthy subjects, the same kind of policies that had caused so much financial chaos in previous reigns.

Problems with Poland

Ottoman relations with Poland remained quiet through the remainder of the reign of Sigismund III (1587–1632), although the Cossacks continued their raids into the Crimea and the Principalities as well as through the Black Sea into the Bosporus. The Ottomans responded in kind, also building a major fortress at Oczakov (Özü) to prevent the Cossacks from reaching the Black Sea easily through the mouths of the

Dniester and renewing the old Polish peace agreement in 1630 in the hope of stabilizing their northern frontier. In 1633 a new campaign was undertaken against the Poles, largely due to the entreaties of Czar Michael Romanov (1613–1645), who was trying to drive the Poles from western Russia. A large force commanded by Abaza Mehmet crossed the Dniester and besieged Kamaniçe (August–September 1633) but was forced to withdraw without success due to insufficient siege equipment. Murat was preparing to lead a new campaign personally in 1634 when he accepted the peace overture of the new Polish king, Vladislav IV (1632–1648), so that he could concentrate on Iran. The Ottomans agreed to remove the Tatar tribes settled in the Bielgorod steppes and to allow Poland to annex the territories of the Zaporogian Cossacks in order to end the raids and counterraids that had been disrupting relations. Not trusting Polish promises, however, the sultan refused their demand for the destruction of the forts built by both sides along the frontiers; in this way he could defend his dominions by force if needed.

The Erivan Expedition

Murat devoted the remainder of his reign to two major campaigns against the Safavids. After reducing the Celalis and executing Abaza Mehmet (August 24, 1634), he executed Ahmet I's four sons to ensure that there would be no revolts while he was absent in the east. The campaigns into the Caucasus and Azerbaijan were initially quite successful, with Erivan (August 8, 1634) and Tabriz (September 15) being evacuated without resistance by the defenders and the sultan securing huge amounts of booty. Once again, however, as soon as he took his army back to Istanbul for the winter, the Safavids reoccupied both provinces – hence there was no permanent result. He was unable to mount a new eastern expedition in 1637 due to diversions in the north. Dynastic disputes in the Crimea enabled the Don Cossacks in Russian service to take Azov (June 18, 1637). In addition, the death of Bethlen Gabor (November 1629), vassal prince of Transylvania, led to disputes for power in which the Ottoman-backed candidate, Catherine of Brandenburg, was defeated by the candidate of the nationalist notables, Rakoczi George (October 6, 1636), who finally secured Ottoman approval by sending repeated assurances of his anti-Habsburg sentiments.

The Reconquest of Baghdad and the Treaty of Kasr-ı Şirin

The problems in the Crimea and Transylvania prevented Murat from moving to regain Baghdad from the Persians until 1638. This time the Safavid defenders put up a strong and prolonged defense (November 15–December 25, 1638), but the sultan ultimately prevailed, at the same time sending troops over much of Mesopotamia to restore Sunni Islam forcibly and drive out the Shia Mollas who had dominated during the previous half-century. Murat spent the winter in Mosul with the intention of campaigning into Azerbaijan the following summer. But when the şah offered to make peace and abandon his forts along the Iraqi and eastern Anatolian borders, the sultan abandoned his plans and returned to Istanbul. The final and definitive peace treaty between the Ottomans and Safavids – ending the long war that had gone on for over a century and a half and establishing the boundaries that were to survive with little change to modern times – was signed at the Ottoman camp in the plain of Zehab, near Kasr-ı Şirin, on May 17, 1639. Iraq was confirmed for the Ottomans while Erivan and the parts of the Caucasus then in Safavid hands were left to Iran, with the latter promising further to end its raids and missionary efforts in Ottoman territory and also to end the public condemnation of Sunnis that had been made previously throughout Iran. The sultan certainly had not secured everything he wanted, particularly in the Caucasus and Azerbaijan. But Iraq and the route to the Persian Gulf had been restored, the main foreign stimulus to revolt in Anatolia removed and the Persian threat in the East neutralized, thus greatly simplifying the situation of Murat's successors regarding internal reforms as well as wars in Europe.

Murat IV died soon afterward on February 8, 1640, just after his return from Baghdad, apparently of the gout or sciatica or as the result of excessive drinking. His reign had been a considerable success. He had come to the throne with the empire in disorder and declining rapidly. By the sheer force of his personality and by executing over 20,000 men, he managed to bring some stability and restore much of the empire's vigor, at least for the moment, thus delaying the results of the decline.

Resumption of Decline, 1640–1656

Murat's successes enabled the Ruling Class to replace him with the incompetent Ibrahim, during whose reign many of the old problems were revived.

Sultan Ibrahim, 1640–1648

The short and brutish reign of Kösem Sultan's son by Ahmet I, Sultan Ibrahim, so manifested and magnified the ills that had been creeping into the Ottoman system before Murat that no subsequent Ottoman ruler ever dared to take his name or give it to his children. Having spent much of his youth in fear of suffering the same fate as did his brothers at the hands of Murat, Ibrahim emerged on the throne without the education and experience to rule, depending entirely on those around him who used the situation to their own advantage. Leading the bureaucrats at this time was Grand Vezir Kemankeş Kara Mustafa Paşa, whose principal opponent was the most influential man among the ulema, the sultan's tutor and confidant, a young Turkish şeyh from Safranbolu named Hüseyin Efendi, known as Cinci Hoca. Intriguing against both from behind the scenes were the sultan's mother, Kösem Sultan, seeking to regain the power that Murat IV had denied her, often by alliance with Cinci Hoca, the sultan's seven wives and his sisters, and the commanders (ağas) of the military corps, who played off the competing political forces to regain the influence that the military had exercised during the previous century. Caught between the various aspirants for power and lacking the strength and courage needed to manipulate or control them, Ibrahim attempted to influence them by providing huge estates and lucrative revenues while spending most of his time enjoying the pleasures of his harem. Within a short time the treasury surpluses gained by Murat's successful campaigns, restoration of security, and the old tax system were gone, and Ibrahim's officers were compelled to resort to forced confiscations and debasement of the currency to satisfy the voracious demands of their master and those around him. Corruption again abounded; the treasury was empty most of the time; salaries and wages could not be paid; the soldiers and bureaucrats were restive; and only the bribes paid their leaders kept them from revolting to express their resentment.

The only stable period of Ibrahim's rule came at the beginning, when the government continued to be dominated by Murat IV's last grand vezir (1638–1644), Kemankeş Kara Mustafa Paşa, principal architect of the Treaty of Kasr-ı Şirin. For the moment Kara Mustafa continued Murat's reforming policies, stemming inflation by increasing the gold and silver content of the coinage and reducing government extravagance as well as the number of salaried Janissaries and *Sipahis*. New cadastres of taxable land were carried out for the first time in almost a half-century, with tax assessments again being made according to the current production of each parcel of land. Corrupt tax collectors were replaced, and tax revenues were largely restored to their old levels. The budget was balanced, with salaries being paid regularly once again and inflation put under control. The grand vezir maintained the newly established peace with Iran, efforts at provincial revolt were suppressed, and in cooperation with the Crimean Tatars the Cossacks were driven from Azov (1642), again frustrating Moscow's efforts to secure a place on the Black Sea. Relations with Venice were restored, while a new truce was signed with Poland to prevent a renewal of the old border conflicts. The grand vezir's dominating position, however, along with his reforms angered many in the Ottoman court. The sultan resented his own inability to control affairs. The queen mother began to intrigue against the grand vezir when she saw that she could not use or control him. All those whose salaries were reduced or eliminated by his budget reforms joined the opposition. At first they attempted to act by stimulating the revolt of one of his political rivals, Nasuh Paşa zâde Hüseyin Paşa, who had been sent to Aleppo as governor to get him out of the way. He soon built a sizable army there and threatened to march to Istanbul if his friends there were not given important positions and revenues. When the grand vezir refused, he led his army through Anatolia all the way to Izmit (Nicaea), but the grand vezir was equal to the occasion, leading the Istanbul garrison across the Bosporus and routing Nasuh Paşa's forces, thus for the moment suppressing the opposition (June 26, 1643).

With the sultan still weak and now ailing and the grand vezir pushing his budgetary reforms more strongly than ever, the opposition flocked around the sultan's tutor, Cinci Hoca, who used his influence to excite the sultan against Kara Mustafa, weakening the latter by eliminating his protégés from the positions of power. The grand vezir attempted to respond by getting the Janissaries to revolt outside the palace gates, but the sultan used this incident to have him caught and executed (January 31, 1644).

The Expedition to Crete

Kemankeş Kara Mustafa was followed by a series of grand vezirs who were puppets in the hands of Cinci Hoca. With the hope of replenishing the treasury, the queen mother and her associates convinced the sultan that an effort to take Crete from Venice would be a good idea, since it would end the pirate raids against Ottoman coasts and shipping. Venice actually opposed the pirate activities, but it was unwilling to close its ports to ships operating in the name of Christianity.

The war came in September 1644 when on the way to the pilgrimage a ship carrying many leading figures was captured by pirates, who brought their captives and booty to the island of Kerpe (Karpatos), northeast of Crete. Ibrahim assembled a huge fleet of some 400 ships, with over 100,000 soldiers, which after concealing its objectives with declarations that it was intended for Malta began landing on Crete on June 24, 1645. Considerable support was received from the local Greek populace, which long had chafed under the strict rule of the Venetians as well as the religious suppression of its Catholic clergy; within a short time the great port of Hanya (Canea) was taken (August 19) along with vast quantities of Venetian cannon and military supplies, a major victory indeed. However, the Ottoman fleet and most of the conquering army then left the island to return to their homes in Anatolia for the winter, leaving a relatively small garrison of 12,000 men to hold Hanya until the spring. Meanwhile, Venice reacted by getting the help of the pope in amassing a new Christian fleet. Soon afterward, most of the commanders who had achieved the victory were rewarded with execution apparently because of the dissatisfaction of the queen mother, Cinci Hoca, and even the sultan at what they considered to be insufficient booty.[8] As the new commander the sultan appointed an incompetent former grand vezir, Semin Mehmet Paşa, who while resuming the attack in July 1646, spent most of his time attempting to secure booty and positions for his own men. The effort to capture the rest of Crete, therefore, degenerated into a long and debilitating siege of Candia, capital of the island (beginning July 7, 1647), while subsequent commanders came and went according to the dictates of politics in Istanbul.

The siege of Candia in fact stretched on well beyond Ibrahim's reign into that of his successor, Mehmet IV. That both sides were able to carry on so long indicates that despite elements of decline both still had considerable wealth at their command. Venice had largely recovered from the depression caused by the closing of the Middle Eastern trade routes in the early sixteenth century. Whatever losses had been suffered had largely been compensated for through its expansion of trade into the Ottoman Empire. Not only was it able to hold out in most of Crete, but it was also to raid the Ottoman shores of the Adriatic and blockade the Dardanelles (April 24–May 26, 1648), throwing Istanbul into panic and leading to Ibrahim's fall after only eight years on the throne.

Further Internal Decline

In the meantime, conditions within the empire went from bad to worse following the death of Kemankeş Kara Mustafa, with the sultan's passions and crazes becoming public knowledge to such an extent that he came to be known among the masses as "Ibrahim the Mad" (*Deli Ibrahim*). Since he was the only surviving male member of the Ottoman line at the time of his accession, Ibrahim paid particular attention to a long series of concubines, whom he favored in return to such an extent that their influence was felt throughout the Ottoman state. Many well-paying positions and pensions were assigned to his favorite women, including the governorship of Damascus and the *sancak*s of Nicopolis and Hami.[9] He also married his daughters at early ages to important ministers, giving the latter huge estates and revenues to retain their loyalty and support. Several of his concubines and daughters formed their own political factions, adding to the confusion of the time.

Ibrahim had a particular passion for furs and silks, and his officials used every possible means to satisfy his whims. Heavy furs covered the walls and ceilings of the Topkapı Palace and the adjacent *köşk*s. Rich furs were given to important officials as they went to their posts, and they were expected to provide more furs and gifts in return, whose cost was, in the end, paid by the hapless subjects. Since most of the furs came from Russia, trade with Moscow became important for the first time, while much of the gold and silver of the empire found its way northward to pay for the sultan's fur collection. Bribery was the order of the day, with each official imposing as many illegal charges as possible to recoup his payments to superiors. Coins were again debased; provincial rebels rose to take most of the tax revenues; the revenues that reached the treasury went to pay for the sultan's extravagances; little was left to pay salaries; and bureaucrats and soldiers in turn imposed their own charges on the subjects. The siege of Candia was not pushed energetically because corrupt officials in Istanbul and officers on Crete were draining what little money was provided for the besieging army.

The situation did not bother the Janissaries and the ulema until Grand Vezir Ahmet Paşa demanded excessive furs and new bribes from them. They massed before the palace to demand his removal, and when the sultan refused, they secured his deposition for his son Prince Mehmet (born of Turhan Hadice Sultan, a Russian slave), much to the displeasure of Kösem Sultan, who at the last minute tried to keep Ibrahim on the throne by offering to give in to the leaders of the revolt if only she was left in a position of power (August 8, 1648). This time it was not to be, however. Ibrahim was imprisoned in his apartments in the palace, so disturbing his balance and causing him to rage that he finally was strangled by order of a *fetva* of the *şeyhulislam,* thus ending one of the most disgraceful reigns in Ottoman history.

The Accession of Mehmet IV, 1648–1687

Conditions certainly were not promising as Mehmet IV came to the throne. The son of a madman, himself only six years old, the new sultan seemed destined to be a puppet in the hands of those who brought him to power. Indeed the week following his accession witnessed a bitter struggle among the various political leaders, his mother, the Grand Vezir Sofu Mehmet Paşa, and the most powerful military corps in the capital, the Janissaries and the *Sipahis* of the Porte. Sofu Mehmet attempted to retain his power by reducing the extravagances for which he had been criticized late in Ibrahim's reign, ending the *devşirme* system of recruitment and dismissing most of the young palace slaves (*Iç oğlans*), who traditionally had served the sultans and satisfied their pleasures. Efforts also were made to increase treasury revenues by abolishing the monopolies established over the customs duties of the empire as well as salt and tobacco and by appointing salaried agents to collect their revenues for the treasury.[10] Sofu Mehmet sought to build his power by gaining the support of the Janissaries, who had united with the *Sipahis* against Sultan Ibrahim, dividing the two by turning 1000 positions formerly held by the latter over to the former. The result of the power struggle, however, benefited the Janissaries more than it did Sofu Mehmet, with their *ağas* using the situation to strengthen themselves. In return for suppressing the rebels they secured most of the principal state and palace positions as well as a monopoly over most of Istanbul's trade, gaining considerable wealth and power. Cinci Hoca was imprisoned and finally executed (October 29, 1648), with the Janissary corps dividing his wealth to use as accession fee. Sofu Mehmet then began to quarrel with his former allies. He freed a number of the *Sipahi* leaders in an attempt to redress the balance of power and invited the Anatolian Celalis to come to Istanbul to "rescue the sultan" from the Janissary tyrants. The Janissaries responded by using the Venetian siege of the Dardanelles (May 24, 1648–May 21, 1649) to secure his dismissal and replacement with their leader, Kara Murat Ağa (May 21, 1649), thus bringing to a climax the period that has come to be known in Ottoman history as the "Sultanate of the *Ağas.*"[11]

Sultanate of the Ağas, 1648–1651

While Istanbul was in the hands of the *ağas,* Anatolia fell to a new series of Celali leaders, stimulated and at times supported by the *Sipahis,* who now channeled general resentment against the misrule of the *ağas* to their own advantage. It was these Celalis who eventually shook the sultanate sufficiently to force the appointment of a dynasty of grand vezirs able to reform and save the state from its enemies. In the capital the oppression of the *ağas* increased in severity, as they divided into parties and began to ally with rival groups within the harem and even among the Celalis. Kösem Sultan generally supported Kara Murat, while her main harem rival, Mehmet's mother, Turhan Hatice Sultan, allied with his rivals in the Janissary corps led by its commander, Bektaş Ağa. The split soon spread throughout the empire, with the resulting divisions within the army further undermining the Ottoman forces in Crete. In the spring of 1650 the Venetians again blockaded the Dardanelles. When the Ottoman fleet was unable to break through, Kara Murat's opponents used this to force him to resign, replacing him with the far more malleable Abaza Melek Ahmet Paşa (August 5, 1650).[12] He was under the full control of the *ağas*, who formed the real cabinet of state, changing officials as rapidly as possible to secure bribes from each new appointee.

With this chaotic political situation at the top, the condition of the treasury worsened. The only way the government could continue at all was to debase the coinage even further and to collect "advance taxes" for two years and more into the future, further oppressing the taxpayers, while paying salaries according to the sums stated in the older more valuable coins. Inflation was rampant; food no longer came to the cities; starvation and famine spread; and the empire seemed ready for complete collapse through the winter of 1650–1651. To compound the difficulties an Ottoman fleet that managed to evade the Dardanelles blockade to bring supplies to the expeditionary forces in Crete was routed and scattered by the enemy off Naxos, causing a major popular rebellion in Istanbul (August 21, 1651).[13] Siyavuş Paşa, supported by Turhan Sultan, used the situation to replace Melek Ahmet Paşa as grand vezir, while Kösem Sultan and her allies tried to save themselves by plotting to poison the sultan and replacing him with a cousin, the mad prince Süleyman. But Turhan Sultan, supported by the palace black eunuchs and the sultan's personal servants, learned of the plot at the last minute and frustrated it by having Kösem Sultan strangled before her supporters could enter the palace (night of September 2–3, 1651), thus violently ending the latter's domination of the harem and the state, which had spanned the reigns of four sultans.[14] Sultan Mehmet, inspired by Turhan Sultan, now used the event to end the Sultanate of the *Ağas*, executing those directly involved but merely exiling the remaining leaders so that a bad example might not be set that subsequently could be used against him.

The Rise of Süleyman Ağa

Though the characters changed, the plot remained about the same. Turhan Sultan and her supporters now dominated the government in alliance with the chief eunuch of the Porte (*dar us-saade ağası*), Lala Süleyman Ağa, who had played an important role in ending the rule of the military *ağas*. The aged and weak Gürcü Mehmet Paşa was made the new grand vezir (November 30, 1651), but he was entirely under the control of the ruling *duumverate*. Inflation spread while the Celalis dominated the countryside. The Venetian blockade of the Dardanelles not only interrupted the dispatch of supplies to Crete but also prevented the shipment of badly needed grains to Istanbul from Egypt and Syria. Once again the mob of Istanbul was becoming restive, with the Janissaries again joining the *Sipahis* in resenting a situation in which their wages were worth less and came late. Süleyman Ağa and Turhan

Sultan realized that strong leadership was needed if the empire that supported them was to be saved. While they feared the resulting loss of political power, they finally agreed to replace Gürcü Mehmet with the former governor of Egypt, Tarhoncu Ahmet Paşa, who had shown himself to be an effective administrator and soldier with particular expertise in the very kind of financial problems that the empire was now experiencing.[15]

The Regime of Tarhoncu Ahmet Paşa, June 20, 1652–March 31, 1653

Tarhoncu Ahmet's short but highly effective term as grand vezir showed how much still could be done to save the empire under the proper leadership. He was given a relatively free hand to conquer Crete, restore the fleet, and secure the funds needed to meet the expenses of the state, with the promise that he could collect all the money owed the treasury by individuals, whether they were of the Ruling or Subject classes, and eliminate all unnecessary positions and salaries created for political reasons.

Like Murat IV, Tarhoncu Ahmet believed that only force and threats of force could secure the necessary results. But he realized also that his political position was tenuous. So instead of antagonizing one or another of the major political groups by killing some of their members, he secured the needed result by dragging in several hundred poor men found in the prisons of Istanbul and beheading them in the major public squares in order to impress high and low alike with his ferocity and determination to eliminate malefactors at all cost!

Tarhoncu Ahmet then went through the accounts of the Imperial Treasury as well as institutions such as the Dockyard, the Arsenal, the sultan's Kitchens, and the like, and managed to extort back all sums previously stolen by persons in high places, including even Turhan Sultan, while at the same time ruthlessly punishing instances of bribery and corruption. Large estates held by leading members of the palace and imperial services were confiscated along with hundreds of timars held by persons unable or unwilling to perform the military duties required in return. These were reissued as tax farms, with large segments of the revenues in question now coming to the treasury. Entire provinces and *sancaks* also were assigned as tax farms, just as Egypt and Syria had been since the early sixteenth century, with their chief officials bidding for their positions and being required to pay the treasury a considerable portion of their expected revenues even before they went to take up their assignments.

In addition Tarhoncu Ahmet was the first grand vezir to prepare an imperial budget in advance of the financial year, relating expenditures of the different departments to expected revenues and attempting to prevent all expenditures beyond these estimates, the basic structure of the modern state financial system. Of course, the Ottomans had prepared state budgets from early times, but these were only accounts of what had been accomplished during the previous financial years rather than guides to current and future operations. To balance the budget and obtain revenues for needed government activities, Tarhoncu Ahmet imposed heavy new taxes on officials and invented new mill (*değirmen*) and household (*hane*) taxes to be imposed on individuals so that they could share the burden.[16] The reforms were having considerable success when the grand vezir attempted to abolish one-third of all the positions assigned to members of the Ruling Class. This so threatened the heart of their privileged positions that they united against him, spread false rumors that he was planning to depose the sultan for his brother prince Süleyman, and finally secured his execution (March 21, 1653). Thus the second major Ottoman reform effort of the seventeenth century was aborted after it had only begun to secure results, but the policy, the method, and the results remained as examples when new crises arose soon afterward.

Resumed Political Chaos, 1653–1656

With Süleyman Ağa and Turhan Sultan again in control, the situation returned to what it had been before Tarhoncu Ahmet's short regime. There was a succession of corrupt and incompetent grand vezirs. Derviş Mehmet Paşa managed to balance the budget for a time by torturing and killing his predecessors' supporters and confiscating their properties.[17] His grand admiral, Kara Murat Paşa, also managed to assemble a fleet sent by the sultan's vassals in North Africa and to drive the Venetians from the Dardanelles, securing sufficient food from Egypt to stifle much of the popular discontent in Istanbul. Derviş Mehmet, however, was aged and suffering from palsy, and it was not long before the queen mother was plotting to replace him. The sultan's sister Ayşe Sultan joined with the chief eunuch to secure the appointment for her husband, Ibşir Mustafa Paşa, governor of Syria (October 28, 1654). But Ibşir Mustafa was the nephew of the old Celali rebel Abaza Mehmet Paşa, and he had built a sizable Celali army around Sivas before being sent to Syria in an effort to dilute his strength. Now he used his new appointment to get the support of the Anatolian *Sipahi*s and Celali leaders, promising them new revenues and positions in return for support against Janissary opposition in Istanbul. As soon as he took over the grand vezirate, his supporters ravaged the capital, and when he found the treasury did not have sufficient money to pay the *Sipahi*s in his personal army, he allowed them to collect their support directly from the people despite Janissary opposition. Kara Murat then used the situation to his own advantage, getting the Janissaries to behead Ibşir Mustafa and secure his own appointment as grand vezir (May 11, 1655) in return for promises that he would return all confiscated properties and have the *Sipahi*s return to Anatolia.[18]

Kara Murat's short term was, however, little better than those of his predecessors (May 11–August 19, 1655). He rewarded the Janissaries for their support by ending Tarhoncu Ahmet's restrictions on their numbers. This considerably increased their numerical strength but decreased their discipline and fighting ability while the salaries being paid by the treasury increased. The return to Anatolia of Ibşir Paşa's men led to a new upsurge of Celali and other revolts, not only in Anatolia, but also in Syria and Iran, sometimes with the connivance of the local Ottoman officials and military leaders.[19] Finally, the Janissaries and *Sipahi*s joined in a major revolt in Istanbul (March 4, 1656) to protest the payment of their salaries in base copper coins, forcing the sultan to turn over 30 key palace and government officials, hanging each one in front of the Sultan Ahmet Mosque, and forcing the entire populace of the city to close their shops and stay home in a kind of general strike in support of the military demands.[20]

The Kadizâdeler

While Ottoman officials had been hung or torn apart by dissidents in the past, nothing of this magnitude had ever occurred. But despite the tremendous difficulties the sultan and his entourage were not ready to act and adopt new measures. Part of the reason was the old belief in the superiority of Ottoman ways and institutions developed in the centuries of greatness and the feeling that the only solution was to restore them.

Another factor was increasing fanaticism among leading members of the ulema, at this time led by Kadizâde Mehmet Efendi (d. 1635) and his followers. They formed a group known as the *Kadizâdeler* (supporters of Kadizâde) ; in the guise of adhering to the strict dictates of the Koran and the traditions of the Prophet, they influenced the sultan and his subjects to adhere to a confining orthodoxy. Developing considerable wealth by controlling most of the religious foundations, the *Kadizâdeler* built and maintained their power by liberal distribution of bribes, at times intervening directly in state affairs to prevent modernization and secure laws and regulations to force the masses of the empire to accept their wishes. They gained influence in the palace, in particular through the gardeners and gatemen as well as the queen mother, the black eunuchs, and many harem residents.[21]

The old struggle between orthodox Islam and the sufi mystics, which had been resolved in the eleventh century by philosophers such as al-Gazzali, now rose again to plague Ottoman society. Kadizâde Mehmet and his successors, representing the orthodox ulema, took up the old dispute with the sufis, represented by Sivasi Efendi (d. 1640). The ideological struggle centered on 16 issues, with the followers of the two groups violently attacking one another in and out of the capital. Murat IV favored the *Kadizâdeler,* representing their influence in enforcing public morality, while they in turn became more and more intolerant to all those who refused to accept their kind of orthodoxy. The *Kadizâdeler* condemned all innovations introduced into Islam since the time of the Prophet and declared the sufis to be heretics of the worst kind.

Kadizâde's most influential successor was Ustuvani Efendi, who controlled many ulema appointments early in Mehmet IV's reign, often selling his influence to the highest bidders. At his initiative the mystic orders were suppressed despite the fact that their personal religion and extensive organization had provided a refuge for the mass of the people during periods of political anarchy. The *Kadizâdeler* spread a new mood of narrowness and intolerance, making it more difficult than ever for the sultan and those around him to seek out new solutions to their political problems. As the mystic *tekke*s were closed and their dervishes imprisoned, in desperation people accepted the leadership of the Celali rebels and others who were ready to use their discontent for their own advantage.

And so the situation became even worse. The Celali leader Abaza Hasan rose to control much of the East. Inflation led to famine. Peasants fled from the land. On June 26, 1656, a new Venetian fleet largely destroyed the Ottoman fleet at the mouth of the Dardanelles, capturing as many as 1000 Ottoman cannon with the loss of only 5 ships, thus subjecting the Ottomans to their worst naval defeat since Lepanto. The Dardanelles was again blockaded, the lines of communication being cut to both Crete and Egypt. Istanbul panicked as the populace began to fear that the enemy might sail in through the Sea of Marmara. Food became scarce, and prices began to mount. It was this crisis that finally compelled the sultan to raise as grand vezir a new reformer, Mehmet Köprülü, and to give him the power necessary to save the empire, thus beginning the rule of a dynasty of grand vezirs that was to dominate the state for the remainder of the century.

The Köprülü Years, 1656–1683

Mehmet Köprülü's rise in Ottoman bureaucracy illustrates the operation of the Ottoman system. Apparently born in the Albanian village of Rudnik, near Berat, probably of an Albanian Christian father, he reputedly entered the sultan's service as a *devşirme* youth, one of the last recruited. Entering the imperial palace service early in the seventeenth century, he worked first in the Imperial Kitchen (1623) and later in the Imperial Treasury and the offices of the palace chamberlain, Husrev Paşa. But he seems to have been unable to get along with his superiors and fellows due to his energy and honesty; so he "passed out" of the palace service with an appointment to the *Sipahi* corps in the provinces. He went to the village of Köprü, in the district of Rum, in central Anatolia, as part of its feudal garrison, taking over a timar, marrying the *sancak* bey's daughter, and thus beginning his rise to the top as well as gaining the name Köprülü (man from Köprü), which he was to use thereafter. Despite the circumstances of his departure from the palace, the young Köprülü retained his connection with his former protector, Husrev Paşa, rising with the latter, entering the Janissary corps when he became its *ağa,* and becoming a high official in the treasury when his master became grand vezir as Boşnak Husrev Paşa, thus following and illustrating the process of *intisap* within the Ruling Class.

Husrev was, however, assassinated. His household broke up, and his protégés scattered either into the services of other leading figures or as lesser officials in their own right, with Mehmet Köprülü returning to his adopted home of Köprü and to Amasya as *sancak* bey. He then built his own household with his own protégés, rising gradually to more important positions in Istanbul as head of the market police (*ihtisap ağa*), supervisor of the imperial arsenal (*tophane nazırı*), chief of the *Sipahi* corps, and head of the corps of armorers. He joined the siege of Baghdad as *sancak* bey of Çorum, attaching himself and his followers to the entourage of grand vezir Kemankeş Kara Mustafa Paşa, who as reward appointed him to the important palace positions of head gatekeeper of the Imperial Court and then head of the imperial stables. After Kara Mustafa's fall, Mehmet demonstrated his political skills by attaching himself to the new grand vezir, Sultan zâde Mehmet Paşa, who promoted him to the rank of vezir of two horsetails and made him governor of Trabzon.

When Mehmet Paşa fell, however, Köprülü Mehmet lost his position, remained for some time on his *sancak* in Köprü, and then through the intercession of friends in the palace became the tax collector in Damascus for Sultan Ibrahim's seventh wife when the entire province was given to her as a fief.[22] He later led a campaign against the Celali leader at Sivas, Vardar Ali, but was defeated and imprisoned and subsequently rescued (1648) by Ibşir Paşa, who was sent to fight the same rebels.[23] He then returned to Istanbul and became a supporter of Queen Mother Kösem Sultan early in Mehmet IV's reign,[24] gaining the high post of minister without portfolio (*kubbe veziri*) for a time until he was dismissed and banished to Köstendil by the grand vezir, who was jealous of the queen mother's power.[25] As the latter's influence waned, Köprülü held a few unimportant posts and at one point was even arrested because of debts owed to the treasury until he finally managed to attach himself to Ibşir Paşa in Kütahya (February 1655) as the latter was moving through Anatolia and building up his strength in preparation for becoming grand vezir. When Ibşir was defeated, Köprülü had to return once again to live in Köprü, apparently in final retirement, as his friends were unable to get anything for him from the new grand vezir Süleyman Paşa.[26] It was at this point that the new crisis engulfed the empire, and Köprülü's friends, led by the chief of scribes (*reis ul-küttap*) Mehmet Efendi and the chief architect (*mimar başı*), convinced the queen mother and the sultan that he was the man of the hour.[27]

The Grand Vezirate of Mehmet Köprülü

Through all his years of service Mehmet Köprülü had acquired the reputation of an honest and able administrator. He had served many masters in many positions; almost 80 years old, he apparently looked forward to retirement and an end to the ceaseless political struggles needed to maintain his position. But in the Ottoman system the slaves of the sultan were at his disposal as long as he wished. This did not mean, however, that he accepted the grand vezirate without considerable negotiation. Knowing how his predecessors, however capable they had been, had been frustrated by palace and military intervention, he knew that he could not correct the situation and drive the Venetians back unless he was certain that he could have a free hand. Therefore, he demanded and obtained the sultan's promise that he would decree only what his grand vezir wanted, allow him to make all appointments and dismissals, and refuse to hear or accept any malicious stories that might be spread about him (September 14, 1656).[28]

Mehmet Köprülü's first moves were directed toward solidifying his political position against those threatened by his rise to power. His predecessor was banished to Malkara, with his property confiscated and followers and protégés joined to the house of the new grand vezir. He then moved to confiscate the properties of the *Kadizâdeler;* when they responded by demanding his removal as well as the complete suppression of all the mystic orders and of "innovations" at the orthodox mosques – such as more than one minaret – he sent in his personal guard and the Janissary corps, which siezed Ustuvani and the other *kadizâde* leaders and banished them to Cyprus and then forced the rest of the ulema to approve these acts.[29] He summoned Abaza Ahmet to Istanbul and executed him on the spot, ostensibly for his failure to defend the island of Bozcaada adequately against the Venetians but in fact because he was close to the queen mother and her supporters, most of whom also were removed from office and banished to distant places (December 12, 1656).[30] When the *Sipahis* in Istanbul protested, he sent the Janissaries against them, using the occasion to slaughter all who resisted.[31] All the while he placed his own protégés and political allies in key positions, completing his rise to power by gaining the power to confirm new appointments to the leadership of the *millets* in order to assure himself of their support as well.[32]

It was not long before the grand vezir resumed the traditional style of reform developed by Murat IV, making the system work once again by dismissing and often executing those who abused it or refused to do his bidding. Once again the budget was balanced by eliminating unnecessary expenditures and assigning confiscated properties as tax farms or even *emanets* so that their revenues would come directly to the treasury. When former Grand Vezir Siyavuş Paşa attempted to resist Köprülü's order that he be displaced as governor of Damascus by raising a local rebellion, Köprülü asked the sultan to order his execution. Siyavuş's followers in the palace intervened to prevent the order from being issued, whereupon the grand vezir resigned on the grounds that the sultan had broken the agreement by which he had accepted the position. Since Köprülü was just about to lead an expedition against the Venetians, the sultan was forced to give him what he wanted. Siyavuş Paşa was executed, and his men were removed from their palace positions and replaced by the grand vezir's men, thus increasing his power even more (June 23, 1657).[33] Thus did Mehmet fully achieve his aim, gaining more authority than any other grand vezir since the early sixteenth century as he turned to meet the foreign threats that had forced the sultan to support him.

Breaking the Blockade of the Dardanelles

Once he had established his power in Istanbul, Mehmet Köprülü's plan was to end the debilitating war with Venice and the blockade of the Dardanelles with a successful conquest of Crete. The fleet was rebuilt and expanded under the new grand admiral Topal Mehmet Paşa while the grand vezir prepared a large new expeditionary force.

The fleet's initial efforts to drive the Venetians away from the Straits failed (July 17, 1657). Köprülü was so incensed that he executed the grand admiral and his principal officers on the spot,[34] including a number of his own supporters, whose appeals to the sultan were unavailing. In the end the Venetians were driven off when a chance explosion of the gunpowder magazine aboard the grand admiral's flagship so battered their ships that they had to scatter, finally ending the blockade.[35] A large new Ottoman fleet was built, largely with ships and men from North Africa, and it retook Bozca Ada and Limnos in 1657, thus assuring that the Straits would remain open and further enhancing the grand vezir's political prestige and power.

Suppression of Revolts in Transylvania

Mehmet Köprülü was not, however, able to follow up his naval victory by completing the conquest of Crete because new challenges arose in Transylvania and Anatolia. The prince of Transylvania, George Rakoczy (1648–1654), now aspired to use Ottoman weakness to build his state into a major power in central Europe. Declaring himself leader of Protestant resistance against the Catholics, he allied with the king of Sweden as well as the princes of Moldavia and Wallachia in the hope of conquering both Hungary and Poland, with the latter to be partitioned with Russia, Brandenburg, the Cossacks, and Sweden (December 6, 1656). Poland was invaded from all sides, and Mehmet Köprülü convinced the sultan to intervene to prevent Rakoczy from becoming strong enough to conquer all of Southeastern Europe. At first the Crimean Tatars were sent with a huge force that ravaged Transylvania, forcing Rakoczy to retire from Warsaw, and then defeated him on the Vistula late in the summer of 1657.[36] The princes of the other Principalities then attempted to recant their alliance with him but were displaced.[37]

When Rakoczy still refused to restore his obedience to the sultan, the grand vezir organized and led a large army into the province (June 23, 1658), while the Crimean Tatars ravaged widely, slaughtering thousands.[38] Rakoczy's capital of Fehervar was captured, but he managed to escape into Habsburg territory, while his treasurer, Barcsay Ekoş, was made the new prince in.return for promises to raise the annual tribute and recognize the sultan's suzerainty once again. In addition the key forts of Yanve (Yanova), Şebeş and Logos were garrisoned by Ottoman troops to prevent any further Transylvanian efforts toward independence.[39] When Rakoczy died in 1660,[40] his followers rallied around Kemény Janos, one of his generals, who gained considerable Habsburg support, was elected king by a diet of notables, and then managed to kill Barcsay and take over most of the country (January 1, 1661) before feudal contingents from Bosnia forced him to flee to Habsburg territory.[41] The Transylvanian nobles now were forced to elect another of their number, Apaffy Mihail, a pious and learned statesman, as the new king (September 4, 1661);[42] he in turn agreed to accept the sultan's suzerainty and to cooperate with the Ottoman forces in suppressing all further rebellions. By this time the population was tired of war, so when Kemény Janos returned in late December with a new force raised by the Habsburgs, he found little support and was routed and killed (January 22, 1662), leaving Apaffy in control for another 20 years.

Suppression of the Abaza Hasan Revolt

The conquest of Crete and the restoration of control in Transylvania were delayed because of threats of serious rebellion in Anatolia and Syria. Leading the revolt was

Abaza Hasan Paşa, who was not satisfied with his position as *sancak* bey. The conditions that had led to the Celali revolts earlier in the century now once again provided dry tinder for a conflagration, with all those Janissaries and *Sipahi*s who were suffering from the new regime in Istanbul fleeing to Anatolia, where they joined the robber bands and urged the populace to revolt against Istanbul.[43] In mid-May 1658 Abaza Hasan brought together a general assembly in Konya. Mehmet Köprülü attempted to forestall the revolt by ordering Abaza Hasan and his followers to join the campaign then in progress in Transylvania, while the latter held back their revolt, waiting until most of the army was busy in the west.[44] Finally, on July 8 Abaza Hasan openly declared his rebellion, demanding the grand vezir's head as price for his submission,[45] with his army getting larger by the day as thousands of Celalis, *levents*, peasants, and others flocked into his camp. Officials and troops sent to suppress the rebellion now joined it. Abaza Hasan was emboldened to declare his rule of Anatolia, leaving Rumeli to the sultan. There is some evidence that the grand vezir's efforts to suppress the revolt at this point were at least partly sabotaged by members of the sultan's entourage in the hope of causing his fall, thus restoring their power and wealth.[46]

When Abaza Hasan's horde approached the Bosporus, the capital panicked, hundreds fled, and the grand vezir was recalled from Transylvania,[47] reaching Edirne on October 12, 1658. Many court leaders advised compromise, but he finally convinced the sultan that only an open attack would save the empire as well as themselves.[48] As the army crossed the Bosporus to assemble at Üsküdar, its soldiers were given six months' wages in advance to assure their loyalty, while agents were sent around Anatolia to bribe as many supporters of the revolt as could be found. Abaza Hasan, feeling the pressure, withdrew from Bursa to Eskişehir while sending many of his men to join the Imperials to collect the salaries and attempt to assassinate the grand vezir at the same time. Mehmet Köprülü, however, managed to root out and execute them, some 6000 men in all, going on to march eastward with Abaza Hasan constantly retreating, losing followers, and suffering from severe shortages of food and supplies. When he offered a truce, the grand vezir lured him and his followers into his camp and then slaughtered them all during a banquet in Aleppo (February 16, 1659), thus breaking the heart of the revolt with a single stroke.[49] Mehmet Köprülü then sent his agents through Anatolia suppressing all those considered to be "suspicious," including Janissaries, *Sipahi*s, teachers, judges, and other members of the ulema, sending as many as 12,000 heads back to the capital and reestablishing order, but without remedying any of the problems that had contributed to Abaza's revolt.[50]

The Rise of Fazıl Ahmet Paşa

By this time the grand vezir, 85 years old, was too old to continue. He became more ferocious than ever, murdering some of his close friends on mere suspicion. When he learned that some Frenchmen had helped the Venetians defend Crete, he took severe measures against French subjects in Istanbul, for all practical purposes breaking relations with France despite its long friendship with the Porte. Finally, he agreed to retire after getting the sultan to replace him with his son Fazıl Ahmet Paşa, governor of Damascus, who reached Istanbul to take up his post on the day of his father's death (October 31, 1661).

Fazıl Ahmet held the grand vezirate for 15 years, until 1676, in the process building on his father's foundation to restore the state and army further while making the position more absolute and powerful than it ever had been in the sixteenth century. While his father always had betrayed his limited education, he had made certain that his son would have the best possible education and experience, enabling him in fact to rise as a member of the ulema to important positions in the *medreses* of Istanbul. Fazıl Ahmet seems to have been able enough to advance on his own, but his father, unable to restrain himself from interfering in his behalf, caused so much jealousy among his son's colleagues that the latter finally abandoned his preferred career to enter the bureaucracy, where he had considerable experience before replacing his father.[51] Fazıl Ahmet seems to have been a much more intelligent and supple administrator than his father. Though he was not hesitant to order executions when he had to, he gained what he wanted by political skill rather than force, thus eliminating much of the terror that his father's ruthless methods had spread throughout the empire. A learned man and a patron of scholars, Fazıl Ahmet's efforts were, however, seriously disrupted by the need to engage in almost continuous foreign campaigns, so that many of his ambitions remained unfulfilled, particularly since in his later years he appears to have succumbed to a passion for drink.

War with Austria

His first war was with Austria, brought about by continued Habsburg efforts to intervene in Transylvania. Fazıl Ahmet sent agents demanding an end to the Habsburg border raids, recognition of the sultan's suzerainty in Transylvania, and increased payments of tribute for northern Hungary. When these were refused (July 30, 1663), a campaign was prepared.[52] The same summer Tatar raiders were sent through Transylvania into Moravia and Silesia, stimulating a general European effort to support the Habsburgs in defense of Christendom. Fazıl Ahmet personally led the Ottoman army the following summer against an army commanded by Montecuccoli, who established himself on the right bank of the Raab to defend Austrian territory. The decisive battle took place near the village of Saint Gotthart, commanding the routes to Graz and Vienna (August 1, 1664). While neither side was in fact victorious, the Ottomans were prevented from advancing across the river. Europe, therefore, considered it a spectacular success. Indeed, the Ottomans had lost more than the Christians, including all their equipment and cannon, but the Ottoman army remained intact and ready to fight, as Montecuccoli well knew. When the sultan offered to negotiate peace, then, it was readily accepted, and the peace was concluded at Vasvar (Eisenburg) soon afterward (August 10, 1664). The Austrians agreed to evacuate all the territories that they had occupied in Transylvania and to recognize Apaffy, thus achieving Fazıl Ahmet's goals politically while allowing the Ottomans to retain the territories of northern Hungary and Transylvania. The emperor further agreed to provide a gift of money to the sultan, while his only consolation was an Ottoman promise to refrain from further raids into Habsburg territory if his border forces also abstained. To a Europe relishing what it thought was a major victory over the Turks, the treaty was a tremendous disappointment, but in fact it well reflected the military and political situation of the time and showed how much the Köprülüs had already restored Ottoman military power.[53]

The Conquest of Crete

Fazıl Ahmet now personally led his forces in a renewed siege of Candia, which ultimately led to its conquest as well as that of the rest of the island. The defenders had been securing large amounts of men and supplies from France, the pope, and Malta, but the Ottoman fleet was able to impose a complete blockade that assured victory. Finally, toward the end of August 1669 disagreements between the Venetian commander and the leaders of their European supporters led the latter to withdraw, forcing the Venetians to agree to a peace with the Ottomans that involved complete evacuation of the island in return for restoration of their trade privileges in the Ottoman Empire (September 5, 1669).[54] Fazıl Ahmet recognized the Ottoman interest in preserving good relations with France against the Habsburgs; thus despite French assistance to the Venetians, the conquest of Crete was followed by restoration of their trade privileges in return for promises to refrain from helping the sultan's enemies in the future.

The Polish Campaigns, 1672–1677

The expansion of the sultan's rule west of the Black Sea, along with the conquest of the Ukraine's southwestern province, Podolya – completing Ottoman control of the Black Sea littoral for the first time – demonstrated that the Ottoman Empire still had considerable power in the late seventeenth century. The situation that led to the war with the Poles began a decade earlier with the conclusion of peace between Poland and Sweden (May 3, 1660). The Polish king John Casimir then was free to turn his attention to the Ukraine, particularly against the Cossacks of the Dnieper, who since the sixteenth century had expanded from their island capital of Sech north and west while developing their democratic and militaristic society led by their elected *hetmans*. The Poles and Russians fought a series of battles over the Ukraine, with the Cossacks divided into pro-Russian and pro-Polish factions (1660–1665). Finally, out of the chaos emerged a new *hetman*, Peter Doroszenko, who attempted to ally with the Crimean Tatars and the sultan to secure Cossack independence from both Poland and Russia, promising to recognize Ottoman suzerainty if he succeeded. Moscow and Poland finally made peace, however (1667), dividing the Ukraine between them at the Dnieper. Ultimately, Cossack divisions and Russian weakness enabled the Poles to rout Doroszenko (October 1671) and occupy much of the Ukraine, and it was in response to this that the Ottomans were drawn into the conflict.

Mehmet IV's campaigns in Poland stretched over a five-year period, brought a number of territories under his rule, and finally led to a war with Russia (1678–1681) that was equally successful. His first Polish expedition (June 5–December 9, 1672) took Kaminiec/Kamenic (August 27) and most of the important forts of Podolya. The Poles were forced to accept the conquest, through the mediation of the Crimean *han*, in the peace treaty signed at Buczacz/Bucaş (October 18, 1672), recognizing Doroszenko as sole *hetman* of the Cossacks and accepting their vassalage to the sultan.[55] After the Polish king died (November 10, 1673), however, Jan Sobieski broke the peace by invading the Ukraine. His subsequent election as king (1674–1696) and his rise as leader of the European coalition was to stem the Ottoman tide at Vienna and then roll it back toward Istanbul as the century came to an end.

For the moment, however, Sobieski's involvement with the fractious Polish nobles enabled the sultan to send his armies back into the Ukraine during the summers of 1675 and 1676. But these were really nothing more than raids that, although they went deep into Poland, were defeated several times. Sobieski became involved in the west with a new war against Sweden, so that he agreed to a new treaty at Zoravno (October 27, 1676) by which the provisions of Buczacz were reconfirmed, with Podolya under direct Ottoman rule and the rest of the Ukraine under the sultan's suzerainty. This marked the high point of Ottoman expansion into eastern Europe, although provisions allowing the Poles to retain their garrisons in the north left them in a position to intervene later once the Ottomans' ability to resist was weakened.[56]

The Grand Vezirate of Kara Mustafa Paşa

Fazıl Ahmet's death of dropsy (November 3, 1676) was followed by the appointment as grand vezir of his foster brother, Kara Mustafa Paşa (b. 1634), who was to bring the Ottomans to the gates of Vienna once again.

The First Russian War

Even before Kara Mustafa's ambitions led to the attack on Vienna, he had to face a war with Russia in the Ukraine over the question of who would rule the Cossacks. Although the Cossack *hetman* Doroszenko had accepted the sultan's suzerainty after 1669, after the Russian-Polish peace of Zoravno he had succumbed to the urgings of Czar Alexis "the Quiet" (1645–1676) to join a general attack on the Ottomans from the north, leading Kara Mustafa to replace him with his bitter enemy George Chmiel-nicki, former *hetman* of the Zaporojni Cossacks. But several Ottoman campaigns against the Russians sent to enforce his rule in the area between the Dnieper and Bug were unsuccessful, compelling the grand vezir to accept peace at Bahçesaray (January 8, 1681), by which Ottoman claims to the area were abandoned and the Dnieper was recognized as the northernmost boundary of the sultan's dominions, thus leaving the Russians in a position to make further advances in the area in the not-too-distant future.[57]

War with the Habsburgs

Kara Mustafa's willingness to accept an unfavorable peace with Russia stemmed mainly from new difficulties in Hungary that were leading to war with the Habsburgs. The Ottomans were seduced into the war by the rise of a Hungarian nationalist movement nourished strongly by anti-Habsburg, anti-Catholic, and anti-nobility sentiments that hoped to establish an independent Hungarian kingdom. The nationalists' most important leaders, Nicholas Zrinyi and Count Imre Thököly, sought Ottoman assistance in return for promises to accept the sultan's suzerainty, an effort that was supported by France in the hope of diverting its Habsburg enemy. Hoping to use the Hungarian revolt as a means of driving the Habsburgs back, the sultan recognized Thököly as king of Hungary[58] and conquered all of upper Hungary during the late summer of 1682. The Habsburgs had in fact held back in the hope of avoiding an open war with the Ottomans while they were fighting the French in the west, but Kara Mustafa was convinced by French agents that the time had come to take Vienna and thus achieve what the great sultans of the past could not.[59]

While a vast army was being brought together at Edirne, the emperor formed a new European coalition to resist the threat. His most important ally was Jan Sobieski of Poland. Pope Innocent XI appealed widely for a new Christian Crusade against the infidel, going so far as to ask for help from the şah of Iran, and while French opposition partly nullified the effects of the appeal, he still managed to secure men and money for the Habsburgs from Portugal and Spain as well as from Poland and various princes in Germany. The Ottoman advance on Vienna began in late June 1683, and the Habsburg capital was put under siege in July; but heavy fortifications and a staunch defense of the city – greatly assisted by Sobieski's last-minute arrival – finally compelled the Ottomans to retire in September 1683. Although huge amounts of booty were taken by a series of raids throughout the remainder of Austria, no territorial gains were made. The Ottoman army retreated, leaving behind all its heavy

equipment and supplies. When the Ottomans tried to make a stand at Gran (No\
ber 1) they were overwhelmed by Sobieski and the Imperials. The Ottoman def\
system thus was smashed and the way opened for a major European effort to dr\
the Ottomans out.[60] Kara Mustafa sought to pull his forces together once again to
stop the enemy, but his opponents at court were able to convince the sultan that he
was entirely responsible for the failure at Vienna as well as for the rout that followed.
Thus he was dismissed and executed at Belgrade (December 15, 1683), leaving the
army even more disorganized than before.[61]

Notes to Chapter 6

1 Ömer Lütfi Barkan, "The Price Revolution of the Sixteenth Century: A Turning
Point in the Economic History of the Near East," IJMES, 6 (1975), 3–28.

2 Halil Inalcık, "Adaletnameler," *Belgeler,* II, 3–4 (1965), 49–145; Yücel Özkaya,
"XVIIIinci Yüzyılda Çıkarılan Adalet-nâmelere göre Türkiye'nin İç Durumu," *Belleten,*
38 (1974), 445–491.

3 Andrew C. Hess, "The Battle of Lepanto and Its Place in Mediterranean History,"
Past and Present, 52 (1972), 53–73.

4 Described in Naima, III, 101–108; Mehmet Halife, *Tarih-i Gilmani,* p. 42.

5 Naima, III, 113–119; Kâtip Çelebi, *Fezleke,* II, 143.

6 Kâtip Çelebi, *Fezleke,* II, 154.

7 Mehmet Halife, *Tarih-i Gilmani;* Naima, III, 162–164; BVA, Mühimme, vol. 85, pp.
134–135.

8 Naima, IV, 174–178.

9 Naima, IV, 243, 250, 270, 280.

10 Naima, IV, 350.

11 Naima, IV, 400.

12 Naima, V, 12.

13 Naima, V, 98–102.

14 Naima, V, 108–109, 115; Kâtip Çelebi, *Fezleke,* II, 376.

15 Naima, V, 203–216, 223.

16 Naima, V, 278.

17 Naima, V, 300.

18 Naima, VI, 74, 91.

19 Naima, VI, 174.

20 Naima, VI, 148–154; Uzunçarşılı, OT, III[1], 296–298.

21 Naima, VI, 232–234.

22 Silahdar, I, 225; Naima, IV, 243.

23 Evliya Çelebi, II, 452.

24 Naima, IV, 459.

25 Naima, V, 178.

26 Naima, VI, 22, 125, 142.

27 Naima, VI, 220–221; Silahdar, I, 57.

28 Mehmet Halife, *Tarih-i Gilmani,* p. 44.

29 Naima, VI, 228; Silahdar, I, 58; Thomas, *Naima,* p. 108.

30 Naima, VI, 249; Silahdar, I, 23.

31 Naima, VI, 247–254; Silahdar, I, 64; Mehmet Halife, *Tarih-i Gilmani,* p. 44.

32 Naima, VI, 252, 264; Silahdar, I, 68.

33 Naima, VI, 248.

34 Naima, VI, 271, 280.

35 Mehmet Halife, *Tarih-i Gilmani,* p. 44; Naima, VI, 279.

36 Naima, VI, 302–303; Silahdar, I, 105.

37 Naima, VI, 325.

38 Naima, VI, 354.

39 Ismail Hakkı Uzunçarşılı, "Eroş Barçay'ın Erdel kırallığına tayini hakkında bir kaç vesika," *Belleten,* 7 (1943), 361–377, and "Barçay Eroş'un Erdel kırallığına ait bazı orijinal vesika," *Tarih Dergisi,* 1953, no. 7.

40 Silahdar, I, 203.

41 Silahdar, I, 213.

42 Witnessed by Evliya Çelebi, VI, 56.

43 Naima, VI, 342.

44 Naima, VI, 345; Silahdar, I, 135.

45 Naima, VI, 347–349.

46 Naima, VI, 339.

47 Naima, VI, 352.

48 Naima, VI, 371.

49 Naima, VI, 378; Silahdar, I, 132, 157; Mehmet Halife, *Tarih-i Gilmani,* pp. 57 and *passim.*

50 Naima, VI, 402–405.

51 Silahdar, I, 214.

52 Raşit, I, 24; Katip Mustafa Zühdi, *Tarih-i Uyvar,* Istanbul University Library, TY 2488.

53 De Testa, IX, 50; Raşit, I, 78–80; Silahdar, I, 361; Mehmet Halife, *Tarih-i Gilmani,* pp. 90–93; *Muahedat Mecmuası,* III, 89–92; Noradounghian, I, 51, 121–124.

54 Raşit, I, 240–242, *Muahedat Mecmuası,* I, 141–143; Noradounghian, I, 132.

55 Noradounghian, I, 52; Raşit, I, 284; Silahdar, I, 613.

56 Noradounghian, I, 53.

57 Silahdar, I, 737; Noradounghian, I, 54.

58 Silahdar, I, 74–75.

59 Silahdar, I, 757; Raşit, I, 387.

60 Silahdar, II, 88–111; Thomas Barker, *Double Eagle and Crescent: Vienna's Second Turkish Siege and Its Historical Setting,* Albany, N.Y., 1967.

61 Silahdar, II, 124.

7

New Challenges and Responses, 1683–1808

The collapse of the Ottoman army following its failure to take Vienna opened a new era in Ottoman relations with Europe. Aware of how weak the Ottoman Empire had become, Europe took the offensive. In a century and a half of nearly continuous warfare the Ottomans lost major territories in spite of continued efforts at traditional reform and attempts to modernize elements of the Ottoman army.

The War of the Holy League and the Peace of Karlowitz, 1683–1699

Louis XIV used the Ottoman attack on Vienna to invade the Spanish Netherlands, so that the Habsburgs were unable to follow up the Ottoman rout of 1683. If the French had continued their attack, the Ottomans might have been able to recover from the defeat. But as was to happen many times in their dealings with Europe, as soon as their ally achieved what it wanted in the West it made a separate peace, abandoning the Ottomans. Within a short time the Imperials were reinforced by contingents from Venice, Poland, Malta, Tuscany, and the papacy, with Russia joining soon afterward in return for Polish promises of concessions in the Ukraine. In the next two decades what armies the Porte could pull together fought on several fronts simultaneously: against the Habsburgs in Hungary, in Bosnia, and Serbia; against Poland in the Ukraine; against Venice in Dalmatia, Albania, and the Morea; and, finally, against the Russians in the Crimea and the Principalities.

The Austrian Front

Austrian advances into Hungary, the great landmark of Ottoman penetration of Europe, shattered Ottoman morale and organization. Pest and most of northern Hungary fell with little resistance during the summers of 1684 and 1685, followed by Buda in June 1686. During the winter of 1686–1687, shortages of food and other supplies and arrears of payments led to revolts among the Ottoman troops, forcing the grand vezir and other high officials to flee to Belgrade. The army in Transylvania and the rest of southern Hungary was left without command or the ability to resist. Within a short time the lands north of the Danube were lost, and Belgrade itself was in danger. Thousands of feudal *Sipahi*s who had lost their estates fled across the Danube determined to find new wealth and positions and to avenge themselves against those responsible for the collapse.

The Polish and Venetian Fronts

Despite the chaos that prevailed on the Austrian front and the heavy losses, the Ottomans still were able to resist the European advance when there was proper organization and command, as was shown very clearly on the Polish front. While the Austrians were advancing, Sobieski's efforts to regain Podolya and also conquer Moldavia were beaten back. Part of the reason was the emperor's refusal to allow him to bargain with Thököly and Apaffy to get their support against the Ottomans in return for promises of autonomy. The Habsburgs had their own plans for the area. Also the Ottomans here had substantial military assistance from the Tatars. Thus between 1684 and 1687 Polish efforts to cross the Dniester into Moldavia with Cossack assistance were routed by a combination of a scorched-earth policy, Tatar raids, and Ottoman resistance. A Polish-Russian treaty signed at Lvov (December 22, 1686) – by which the former acknowledged Russian control of the parts of the Ukraine that it had conquered (including Kiev, Smolensk, and Poltava) and its rule over the Cossacks in return for help against the sultan – failed to secure results. Ottomans also had to contend with Venice, which attacked Bosnia, Dalmatia, Greece, and the Morea. But it was only in the latter that they were successful, and then because of a native revolt stimulated by papal and Venetian agents and confusion caused by rapid changes in the Ottoman command (1685–1686). On the other hand, a major Venetian land push into Bosnia was routed (April 1685), and Venetian landings at Cattaro (Kotor) and other points along the Dalmatian coast were beaten back for two years (1685–1687). At the end, however, only the hinterland remained in Ottoman hands. In 1687 the Venetians moved north from the Morea into mainland Greece, capturing Athens (September 25) after a siege in which they inflicted major damage on the Parthenon, and then moved west to take Lepanto. The news reached the sultan just as he learned of the new disasters inflicted on him by the Austrians.

Internal Disintegration Following the Failure at Vienna, 1683–1687

The disaster at Vienna, the loss of major territories in Hungary and Transylvania, the influx of thousands of refugees, and the Venetian attacks in the western Balkans produced severe internal problems. Given the background of internal disintegration that the Köprülüs had stemmed but not corrected – combined with rulers content to leave the government in the hands of yet more incompetent ministers – it is not surprising that the years after 1683 saw the empire reach a low point internally as well as externally. For instance, the agriculture of the empire had been severely damaged by Kara Mustafa's conscription of men for the army, which depopulated large parts of Anatolia and Rumelia alike, leaving only the very old and the very young to care for the crops and animals and leading to serious shortages of food and supplies in town and country. And just as had occurred a century earlier, discontent was fanned by thousands of soldiers fleeing from the European fronts. New bandit forces arose strengthened by the successive waves of soldiers fleeing their own generals as well as the enemy. The financial condition of the state became increasingly serious. The loss of the revenues of Hungary and Transylvania would have been serious enough, but now the new notables were diverting even more of the treasury's tax revenues, causing salaries to fall into arrears by one year and then two years.[1] Battles were lost when ammunition and supplies could no longer be secured from the government or when soldiers refused to obey their officers until their own salaries were paid. In desperation the central government decreed a new special "campaign tax" (*imdad-ı seferiyye*), which was imposed on all officials and subjects regardless of their income or actual ability to pay.[2] Even members of the ulema were not exempted, and when they protested, many were banished to Cyprus and elsewhere.

Inflation accompanied food shortages, famine, and plague, particularly in 1685 and

1686. The price of bread doubled and then doubled again, leaving the masses in panic. Throughout 1687 thousands in Anatolia were forced to survive by eating grass, oak nuts, and walnut shells³ Thousands more starved to death. The coinage was debased several times, and decrees were issued to force merchants and salary recipients to accept coins at their legal rate rather than their actual market value.

The Deposition of Mehmet IV

Despite these difficulties the sultan spent most of his time hunting and enjoying the pleasures of his harem,⁴ leading most of his own palace retinue, the ulema, and the mass of the populace to share the rebellious feelings of the military. When soldiers marching from the Danube reached the outskirts of Istanbul, they were joined by the mass of notables and ulema, who had been brought together at the Aya Sofya Mosque by Köprülü zâde Fazıl Mustafa Paşa, son of former Grand Vezir Mehmet Köprülü. It was simple, therefore, for the *şeyhulislam* to issue a *fetva* deposing Mehmet IV on the grounds that he was no longer fulfilling his duties.⁵ He and his son were retired to the secluded apartment in the rear of the palace, and in his place the second child of Sultan Ibrahim, Süleyman II (b. April 15, 1642) was brought to the throne.

Süleyman II, 1687–1691

Süleyman had spent most of his 40 years in seclusion, always afraid that someone might kill him. It was inevitable, therefore, that he should be under the control of those who had brought him to power and that the troops of the capital should use his accession to ravage the capital, with their *ağas* becoming the real rulers for the moment.⁶ Troops fanned out throughout the city, occupying private buildings, tearing officials apart, burning and stealing at will. Whenever the men thought of a new demand, they enforced it by new uprisings until the grand vezir obeyed their wishes. For five months the terror continued. Then the sultan surprised everyone by intervening. He used the pretext of the Habsburg threat to Belgrade to call a meeting of the Ruling Class in Istanbul (March 1, 1688) and declared that the troops should gather under the banner of the Prophet to march against the infidels threatening the empire. Since many of the Janissaries were artisans and merchants and their homes, shops, and families had been threatened by the disorder, they responded to the sultan's call to march not against the Habsburgs but against those soldiers who were continuing the rebellion. Süleyman took personal command of his troops as they went through the city, hunting out and slaughtering the rebels as well as anyone else they disliked.⁷ Süleyman then went on to end the onerous campaign taxes, which had so oppressed the mass of the people, and efforts were made to restore the value of the coinage. But beyond that little was done. The endemic food shortages, famine, and inflation continued to sap the Ottoman body politic.

New Collapse on the Austrian Front

The Venetians and Poles remained relatively quiet during Süleyman's reign, since they were diverted by internal problems. The Habsburgs, however, were able to move ahead rapidly, taking advantage of the chaos in Istanbul following Süleyman's accession to advance from Mohaç to Peterwaradin and then to Belgrade, while the Ottoman defenses in Croatia and Slovenia panicked and dispersed.⁸ The Hungarian notables had to elect the Habsburg prince Joseph as their king (December 9, 1687) and surrender much of their autonomous power to him, after which a highly centralized government was imposed throughout the country. During the summer of 1688, the Habsburgs crossed the Danube and took Belgrade (September 8, 1688), thus breaking the Danube defense line and opening the way to the Balkans.[9] The news led to a series of Balkan revolts against the Ottomans in support of the advancing Imperials, often in conjunction with local Orthodox churchmen in Serbia and Bulgaria. The prince of Wallachia sent agents to Vienna to convey his recognition of the emperor's suzerainty and promises of help against the sultan.

In response to this new menace Süleyman sent agents to Vienna to secure peace on the basis of the status quo, offering to recognize all the conquests already made by the western allies if only the war was ended. The Habsburgs were, indeed, anxious for peace as Louis XIV had attempted to use their preoccupation to advance to the Rhine and into Bavaria, areas that had supplied large numbers of troops to the army advancing across the Danube. But while Leopold was willing to give up the conquests south of the Danube to obtain peace, his allies, not feeling the French threat so directly, wanted to continue the struggle until their ambitions were fulfilled. The negotiations foundered (June 11, 1689), therefore, and the Habsburg troops marched into Bosnia and up the Morava toward Niş.[10] Süleyman organized a new army, proclaiming a general amnesty for all those who had previously taken up arms against the central government.[11] But before he could move, the revolt of thousands of Serbs and the rapid Habsburg conquest of Niş. Vidin, Skopje, and Prizren (July–November 1689) seemed to presage the end of Ottoman rule in Europe. Another Habsburg army crossed into Transylvania and Wallachia, making an agreement with the nobles to recognize their autonomy and religious freedom in return for recognition of the emperor's suzerainty and help against the Ottomans.[12]

The Ottoman Counteroffensive

In fact, however, the Habsburg advance had reached its peak. In one of the most surprising and astonishing turnabouts in the long history of the house of Osman, Süleyman II's forces managed to regroup and reorganize during the winter of 1689–1690 and to mount a counteroffensive that drove the Habsburgs all the way back across the Danube. Once again a member of the Köprülü family, Fazıl Ahmet's younger brother Fazıl Mustafa Paşa (October 25, 1689) came to power. Acting like his illustrious predecessors, he moved quickly to appoint able and honest men to key positions in government and army, to stamp out corruption and to balance the treasury budget. At least 30,000 members of the Janissary corps unable to perform their duties were stricken from the rolls, thus greatly reducing the treasury's expenditures while helping its officers to restore order and discipline.[13] Those who had illegally acquired wealth during the previous disorders were executed and their properties confiscated. Inducements were offered to get the Turkish and Kurdish tribesmen of the east to join with the forces being assembled at Edirne. A general overturn of the provincial governors also brought renewed efficiency in tax collection as well as in the command of the provincial contingents that arrived to join the army. New coins at full value were issued to replace the debased coins, and price regulations were enforced.

While the Ottoman army massed in Edirne, good news came from the Slavic provinces under Habsburg occupation. The strictness of the Catholic priests in the emperor's army soon reminded the Orthodox population why their ancestors had welcomed the Ottomans centuries earlier. From Serbia, Wallachia, and especially

Transylvania came appeals to the sultan for help to restore their political and religious freedom. Thököly Imre once again took the lead in organizing resistance to the Habsburgs.

In mid-July 1690 the reorganized and revived army moved under the grand vezir's leadership against the Habsburgs, who – weakened by the need to withdraw most of their troops to fight France – soon were forced into a rapid retreat. Thököly's revolt in Transylvania was gaining the support of thousands of Hungarians, seriously impeding the emperor's efforts to supply the troops remaining in the south. It was not long before the Habsburg troops simply folded. The Ottomans took Niş (September 9, 1690), Semendria, and Belgrade (October 14, 1690) after only a six-day siege.[14] Many Serbs had assisted the Austrian advance, but many more, bitterly disappointed by Habsburg rule, helped the Ottomans with renewed enthusiasm, with Fazıl Mustafa making a special effort to win back their loyalty rather than punishing their previous treason. Other Serbs crossed the Danube with the retiring Imperials in fear of punishment, and while many of these settled permanently under Habsburg rule in southern Hungary, many also returned to their homes once their fears were allayed by the Ottomans. Special decrees were issued to make sure that none of the local Muslims would seek vengeance and that the returning Serbian refugees would regain their houses and property, at times at the expense of the treasury. Thus the Austrian appeals for a Christian uprising against the sultan were forgotten, and efforts were made to restore that just regime that had attracted so many Balkan peasants to Ottoman rule in the past. Those Serbs who did remain under Habsburg rule in southern Hungary were placed under the religious authority of a new patriarchate established at Karlowitz, which now became the center for subsequent Habsburg efforts to stir the kind of Serbian nationalism that would in the long run undermine Ottoman rule south of the Danube.

Following the capture of Belgrade the Danube defense line was fully restored.[15] Fazıl Mustafa reinstituted the reforms he had begun earlier, showing sincere concern for the feelings of the subjects and seeking to create conditions that would inspire loyalty. In this, however, he stimulated Muslim opposition to reform by limiting its effect mainly to the non-Muslim provinces, thus making many feel that reform really was an effort to turn the state over to the Christians. The grand vezir also attempted to restore efficient administration, abolishing the payment of gifts by high officials to the sultan in the hope that this would encourage them, in turn, to end their own demands for gifts from their subordinates. He worked to rebuild the power of the grand vezirate by limiting the number and power of the other ministers and by requiring them to communicate with the sultan only through him. He attempted to curb the local notables by establishing powerful provincial garrisons and also councils of notables in the major cities and towns to provide means through which the notables could exercise their influence without actually having to take over the government or oppress the people.

In general, the Ottoman systems of justice and administration began to operate more efficiently and effectively than they had done for over a century. In the end however, these reforms were undermined by the grand vezir's failures in the economic sphere. Seeing that price controls had failed to end the inflation and famine, he concluded that artificial government restraints were in fact the cause of the trouble, stating that if the cultivators were allowed to charge what they could, they would be encouraged to grow more. This would bring an increased food supply, which would, finally, lead to a fall of prices far more generally than that achieved by price controls. But with the large-scale disruptions of the time, particularly in

Serbia and the Principalities, the shortages of food continued, and the immediate result of his measures was an even more rapid price increase.

Fazıl Mustafa continued his predecessor's work of restoring the Ottoman army and, in particular, the timar system. Capable young soldiers were appointed to the timars and required to drill regularly. Special provincial schools were established to train their officers. Inspectors were sent to ensure that they performed their tax and administrative duties fairly and without overburdening the peasants. Significantly, he constructed new Imperial Gunpowder Works (*Baruthane-i Âmire*) in the Istanbul suburb of Bakırköy, on the Sea of Marmara, and provincial works at Salonica, Gallipoli, Baghdad, Cairo, Belgrade, and Izmir, running them through tax farmers who were given the task of producing the empire's gunpowder and who kept as personal income whatever profits remained.

Stalemate in Central Europe

Süleyman II died of hydropsy (June 22, 1691) and was replaced by Ibrahim's third son, Ahmet II (1691–1695), just as Fazıl Mustafa set out on his second Austrian campaign. He moved from Belgrade across the Danube before the arrival of the Tatars in the hope of surprising the enemy near Peterwaradin. Instead, he was ambushed and routed at Slankamen, 26 kilometers southeast of Karlowitz (August 20, 1691), with his army dispersing after he was shot in the forehead and killed.[16]

The loss of Fazıl Mutsafa and disaster at Slankamen effectively ended the Ottoman counteroffensive and with the Habsburgs busy in the west resulted in a stalemate; the Danube emerged as the new permanent boundary between the two empires. Ahmet II soon proved to be as susceptible to the intrigues of his confidants as were some of his predecessors. Grand vezirs, ministers, and commanders again rose and fell rapidly, and the heart went out of Fazıl Mustafa's reforms, with all the old problems returning. England and the Netherlands now worked in Istanbul to mediate a peace. But the emperor continued to insist on Ottoman cession of Transylvania, Temesvar, Wallachia, Moldavia, and Bessarabia for himself, Morea to the Venetians and Podolya to the Poles, while Ahmet II, equally intransigent, demanded the return of most of Hungary as well as the old Habsburg tribute payments. Thus hostilities dragged on even though both sides realized that the stalemate was only draining strength that might be used more effectively elsewhere.

Nor was the stalemate limited to central Europe. Venice's effort to take Crete was beaten off after a long siege (July 18, 1692). The Venetians did take Chios (Sakız) in September 1694, but the occupying soldiers and priests were so oppressive that a general popular uprising early the next year forced them to abandon the island, thus endangering continued Venetian rule of the Morea.[17] Poland was sapped by the decline of Jan Sobieski's health, and it made only a few weak raids in the direction of Kamanice during the summers of 1692 and 1694.[18]

Internal conditions, however, continued to worsen. Central control weakened, and notables ruled almost everywhere, including the Arab provinces. In North Africa the local Ottoman garrisons formed their own pirate republics, living on the fruits of raids against European and Ottoman shipping alike, at times attacking Ottoman shores. Lacking any education or experience the sultan was content to assuage his problems through immersion in the harem while leaving real power to the chief eunuch and the palace parties. His death (February 6, 1695) passed with little notice or effect on the general run of affairs in the empire.

Mustafa II, 1695–1703

Rule now went to the eldest living male member of the Ottoman house, Mehmet IV's son Mustafa, who twice before had been passed over for the throne in favor of his more maleable brothers. His reign epitomized all the glories and disasters of the Ottoman Empire in its age of disintegration. The pattern was a quick recovery from disaster followed shortly by a stalemate and subsequent collapses, which when they did come, were sudden and disastrous.

Born in 1664 in the midst of his father's long reign, Mustafa received no more than the traditional harem and religious educations reserved for princes of the imperial line in the age of decline. But in his years of puberty he lived in a far freer environment than most princes before him. He was left to roam the palace with little restraint, joining with his brother Ahmet (later Ahmet III) in pastimes of horsemanship, poetry, and music as well as drinking – hardly the kind of education to fit them for the cares of state but at least without the debilitating effects of the complete confinement imposed on most Ottoman princes during the previous century.

Mustafa's principal adviser and agent was Seyyit Feyzullah Efendi (1638–1703), long his tutor, who was appointed şeyhulislam (April 30, 1695) with the task of reforming the ulema and mobilizing them in his support while at the same time serving as Mustafa's executive assistant in his effort to dominate and direct the remainder of the Ruling Class.[19] Feyzullah Efendi soon settled in as the real power in the state. He came to dominate the Ottoman system the way the Köprülü ministers had done in the past, working through members of the sultan's party who were placed in key positions in the army and administration.

The Austrian Campaigns

Feyzullah Efendi was able to rule as much as he did by diverting his master, either to the old pleasures of the harem or to his new passion for action against the Habsburgs. While the Venetian front remained in stalemate, Mustafa led three major campaigns against the Austrians (1695–1697). He earned the title of gazi while defending Temesvar, last Ottoman possession north of the Danube, but as in the campaigns of Mustafa Köprülü, victory ultimately enticed him to a culminating disaster, this time at Zenta at the hands of the greatest military genius of the time, Prince Eugene of Savoy (September 11, 1697). Suddenly the entire Ottoman army was gone, the empire defenseless.

The Northern Front

At the same time, Russia was becoming more threatening under the leadership of Peter the Great (1689–1725), who was reorganizing and modernizing his army and government while developing a plan to gain control of the Black Sea as the first step toward the open sea, through the Straits to the Mediterranean. After failing in a premature effort in 1695, he captured Azov in August 1696. This was the beginning of a campaign that, within a century, would change the Black Sea from an Ottoman to a Russian lake and threaten the empire from an entirely new direction.

The Peace of Karlowitz

Unable to pursue the war, the Ottomans were ready for peace. The sultan left the army and returned to Edirne, and a fourth member of the Köprülü dynasty, Amcazâde Hüseyin Paşa, was made grand vezir in the hope that he could use the family magic to secure the best possible terms. The empire now was in desperate straits. Its villages were stripped of their men, and without result. Famine, disease, inflation, and disorder abounded. The Austrians were poised on the Danube, the Russians had established a claim to the Black Sea. The French had just accepted the Peace of Ryswick (1697), which removed them as a serious diversion for Austria although the two powers soon were to be embroiled again in the War for the Spanish Succession (1701–1714). Leopold also wanted peace with the Porte so that he could prepare himself for the new conflict. He was satisfied with the removal of the Ottoman army as a serious threat to his rear. Peter the Great wanted to continue the war to secure the Straits of Kerch, which connected the Sea of Azov with the Black Sea, but Austria's withdrawal forced him to go along as well.

Negotiations were concluded at Karlowitz, on the right bank of the Danube near Peterwaradin, basically on the principle of uti possidetis, with each party retaining all territories held at the time. Transylvania remained in Habsburg hands while Temesvar was to be Ottoman, with the Tisza, the Sava, and the Unna rivers forming the new boundaries between the two empires. The sultan confirmed freedom of worship to Catholics in his dominions, thus enabling the emperor to intervene in internal Ottoman affairs in the guise of protecting the Catholics, while clauses guaranteeing the merchants of both sides free trade in the territory of the other assured the Austrians in particular of means to exploit the empire commercially while stirring its Christian subjects against the sultan. The Ottomans accepted full Polish control of Podolya and the Ukraine, giving up claims to suzerainty over the Cossacks and ending their short-lived rule northwest of the Black Sea, and promised to restrain the Tatars from further raids. Venice kept the Morea and its conquests in Dalmatia, but gave up Lepanto and the island of Aynamavra to the Porte in return for a restoration of Venetian trade privileges in the Ottoman Empire. Negotiations with Russia stalled over how much of a foothold the Russians would be able to retain on the Black Sea, but a separate treaty was finally signed in Istanbul (July 15, 1700). It allowed the Russians to retain their conquests on the Sea of Azov and along the Dniester. In return, however, they had to promise to destroy all the forts that they had built in those areas, thus leaving them in position for new advances from both ends of the Black Sea as soon as the Ottoman guard was lowered. Russian participation in the European concert was assured, and Ottoman promises to end the Tatar raids left Peter free to strengthen his army and state until he was ready to resume the attack under more favorable circumstances.[20]

The Treaty of Karlowitz was the first of many agreements between the Ottomans and coalitions of European powers allied against them, and it represented the Ottoman transition from the offensive to the defensive. The sultan accepted the mediation of powers that were ostensibly neutral but in fact manipulating events in their own favor. The legal acknowledgment of the loss of integral parts of the empire – Hungary and Transylvania to the Habsburgs; Dalmatia, the Morea, and important Aegean Islands to Venice; Podolya and the southern Ukraine to Poland; Azov and the lands north to the Dniester to Russia – marked the real beginning of the Ottoman withdrawal from Europe. Russia and Austria had been put in positions to intervene in Ottoman affairs for their own advantage. The western approaches to the Aegean were back in Venetian hands, enabling Venice to threaten the Straits and Istanbul once again if it wished. The Danube had replaced northern Hungary as the outpost of Austrian aggression. And Poland also was in position to attack the Crimea and Principalities from the north. The Ottomans still might deal with one of these enemies alone, except perhaps with the Habsburgs, but in concert they were now shown to be far too strong, changing the equality established with the rulers of western Europe at the beginning of the century into a position of ever-increasing inferiority. More was to come.

The New Age of Decline and Traditional Reform, 1683–1808

Not only did the Treaty of Karlowitz mark a watershed in Ottoman relations with Europe, but it also marked the culmination of the era of internal disintegration and the beginning of rapid decline. The long years of war drained the empire of much of the strength and spirit that remained from the early centuries of Ottoman greatness. The loss of territories long considered integral parts of the empire also shook Ottoman morale to the point where, to many people, any kind of effort to save the empire seemed impossible. For the first time a few Ottomans began to see that reform was possible if only the empire could discover what Europe had done to achieve its new supremacy and incorporate what was best into the Ottoman system. Reformers now began to accept the possibility that Europe might have developed certain specific techniques that might be used to strengthen and preserve the traditional ways, particularly new forms of military organization and weapons. Traditionalistic reform, therefore, became a combination of old and new, creating an amalgam that, while not successful in itself, opened the way for a new style of modern reform during the nineteenth century. Even this limited change was to develop only hesitantly and gradually in response to new challenges and in the face of continued opposition from those who felt that any "innovations" would only weaken the entire Ottoman structure. Therefore, reform had its ups and downs during the eighteenth century; temporary successes usually led to disaster for the reformers, but enough traces of them remained to provide models and experience for those who followed.

The Reforms of Amca zâde Hüseyin Paşa

It was perhaps appropriate that the new trend should be begun by the fourth member of the Köprülü dynasty, Amca zâde Hüseyin Paşa (1644–1702), son of Mehmet Köprülü's oldest brother, who served as grand vezir for three years following the disaster at Karlowitz (1699–1702). A member of the Mevlevi *derviş* order. Hüseyin Paşa, far more than his Köprülü predecessors, sought to meet the needs of the common people as well as those of the army and government by emphasizing economic and financial solutions. The excise taxes on tobacco and coffee – which had been doubled and then doubled again during the war to provide the treasury with ready cash – were substantially reduced along with impositions on essentials such as oil and soap.[21] Efforts again were made to restore the value of coinage by replacing the debased wartime issues with coins of full value.[22] Back taxes owed the treasury for all special wartime impositions were excused without penalty,[23] and the impositions themselves were abolished, while the traditional taxes were geared more to the ability to pay. Tax concessions were given to induce cultivators to return to their fields and merchants to their trades. In places such as Cyprus, Urfa, Malatya, and Antalya, where new cultivators were particularly needed, nomadic tribes were encouraged to settle.[24] Efforts were made to develop factories to compete with European manufactured imports that had devastated the traditional Ottoman craft industries.[25]

Hüseyin Paşa also took steps to make the Ottoman army effective and reliable. The salary rolls of the *kapıkulu* corps were inspected. Members no longer performing their duties were dismissed and replaced by Turkish peasants from Anatolia, who were required to remain under discipline and training at all times. The previous practice of taking artisans into the corps to serve on a part-time basis was abolished.[26] By such measures the Janissary corps – which had ballooned to 70,000 men before Karlowitz (with no more than 10,000 members actually serving) – now was reduced to 34,000 fighting men, all ready and able to serve, while the Artillery corps was similarly reduced from 6,000 to 1,250 men. The feudal cavalry was also replenished and revitalized with nomadic tribesmen brought from eastern Anatolia as well as the abler *Sipahis* who had fled from Hungary. All *Sipahis* were again required to maintain sufficient retainers, train and arm them under the supervision of their *sancak* beys, and bring them to the army when called. Particular care was taken to ensure that the *Sipahis* were not dismissed without cause by superiors seeking bribes, a practice that had become quite common during the previous century.[27]

Efforts also were made to revive the Ottoman navy under the command of Mezamorto (Half-Dead) Hüseyin Paşa, who had gained considerable prestige from several successful encounters with the Venetians in the Aegean and off the Dardanelles (1695–1698). It was only now that the Ottomans followed the seventeenth-century European naval innovations involved in the change from oar-powered to sail-powered vessels, building a new fleet of galleons and developing a new naval structure to man them. The fleet was divided into squadrons, each under a *derya* bey (bey of the sea), who had to supervise the captains and their ships and ensure that each man was paid and trained and that each ship had sufficient ammunition and supplies, thus eliminating major problems encountered during the previous decade. A general staff, between the grand admiral and his captains, was created, including three main assistants of the grand admiral, the *kapudane* (rear admiral), the *patrona,* (vice admiral) and the *riyale* (staff admiral). Beneath them the naval service was arranged in a hierarchy of command, with the sale of posts ended and all vacancies filled according to ability and experience from among men in the next lower ranks. Sailors and officers now were to be paid full wages and allowed to retire on pension when no longer able to serve because of old age or injury contracted in service. A special artillery corps also was established to end the navy's dependence on the *kapıkulu* artillery and enable it to develop a service more responsive to its own needs.[28]

Finally, the grand vezir instituted reforms in the scribal service and the palace. Incompetent scribes were retired on half-pay and replaced by young Ottomans trained in the scribal schools. Efforts were renewed to end bribery and reimpose the standards of efficiency that had prevailed in the sixteenth century. And for the first time, to increase efficiency, all officials and scribes were required to enter the dates on official documents and to preserve them.[29]

The Fall of Amca zâde Hüseyin Paşa

But as was to be the case so often in the last century of traditional Ottoman reform, the grand vezir's efforts to make the old system work soon ran into the opposition of those with a vested interest in abuse, the members of the Ruling Class, now led by *Şeyhulislam* Feyzullah Efendi, who as the confidant of the sultan remained the strongest single power in the state. As had been the case in the seventeenth century, the Ruling Class allowed reform only as long as it was needed to save the empire from its enemies. But as soon as the danger was past, it worked to undermine the reforms. Hence as soon as the immediate effects of Karlowitz were over, Feyzullah began to intrigue against the grand vezir. He placed relatives and allies in key positions and secured the appointment of his son Fethullah Efendi as the heir apparent to the post of *şeyhulislam*. The creation of a dynasty of leaders within the ulema was something unheard of previously in Islamic or Ottoman history.[30] Feyzullah also began to intervene in affairs of state, often contravening the grand vezir's orders whenever they hurt his interests. Grand Admiral Mezamorto Hüseyin attempted to mediate between the two, but with his death the balance was upset (July 1701). Hüseyin Paşa became so frustrated that he became ill and finally retired in September 1702, dying soon afterward. Thus was the most important reformer of the time driven from office.

The Edirne Event

With Hüseyin Paşa out of the way Feyzullah Efendi was more dominant than ever, controlling the grand vezirs and extending his power to all areas of government. Bribes came to him and his men from most members of the Ruling Class and holders of tax farms and fiefs. He even was able to secure a large portion of the funds set aside for the wages and supplies of the army. The sultan's tendency to retire to his palace at Edirne and allow Feyzullah to do what the wished further antagonized the the soldiers as well as the powerful merchants and artisans of Istanbul, who began to fear that the sultan was planning to transfer the empire's center of power to Edirne, thus harming their economic interests. Hüseyin Paşa's son-in-law, Sührablı Ahmet Paşa, and other relatives magnified these fears and sought to use the discontent to restore their political fortunes.

Added to Feyzullah's domination, the sultan's impotence, and the politicking of their opponents were serious financial and economic difficulties. The long war and the series of imperial accessions had drained the treasury, so that arrears now mounted to three or four years and the payments that were made were in new debased coins. Inflation continued. The regular systems of assigning and collecting taxes broke down almost completely. Many of the *mukata'a*s of the treasury, both tax farms and fiefs, were transformed into life holdings called *malikâne* (possession), for which only token payments were required to the treasury, while the holders could sell or will them to heirs with only minimal interference from the state. *Malikâne* holders gathered together hundreds of *mukata'a*s in vast estates with tremendous private revenues, often subfarming them to secure their maximum exploitation, all at the expense of the artisans and cultivators who paid the taxes. Once again, therefore, thousands of peasants began to flee from their lands, cultivation fell off even more, the cities became overcrowded, and town and country alike became tinderboxes, waiting for only a spark to catch.

The soldiers provided the spark for rebellion. Four companies of Janissaries assigned to the Georgia expedition refused to go unless their back wages were paid in full (July 18, 1703). They complained that the sultan and *şeyhulislam* were enjoying themselves in Edirne while the empire's problems remained unsolved. As they marched before the Sultan Ahmet Mosque in Istanbul to vent their rage, they were joined by thousands of other soldiers, artisans, merchants, and others. Feyzullah ordered the grand vezir to pay two years' back salaries to the soldiers in the hope of appeasing them. But it was too late: Each concession was followed by new demands. The rebels marched before the gates of the palace, where they were joined by the ulema, led by the religious students (*softa*s), who had long resented the domination and misrule of the *şeyhulislam*. With the sultan and Feyzullah in Edirne it was easy for the rebels to take the palace. Within a short time all Istanbul was in their hands (July 21, 1703). Members of the government in the capital were torn apart and replaced by the appointees of the rebels, who then issued a decree demanding that Feyzullah and his associates be returned from Edirne for trial.

For some time both the sultan and his adviser remained oblivious to the events in Istanbul, spending their time hunting in Edirne. When the sultan finally learned of the affair, he attempted to save himself by dismissing Feyzullah and his sons and ordering them exiled to Erzurum (July 30). When the sacrifice of Feyzullah did not end the revolt, Mustafa attempted to summon the feudal army to defend Edirne and march to Istanbul as the only way of saving his throne. But the rebels anticipated him, gained the support of most of the feudal soldiers, and left the sultan with only a few thousand men. The sultan ordered his troops to prepare to march to Istanbul to suppress the rebellion, but the rebels responded by sending their own forces toward Edirne, including several thousand ulema and members of the Istanbul guilds (August 13, 1703). The rebels proceeded slowly, gathering the support of thousands of subjects in the towns through which they passed. The sultan attempted to negotiate a settlement, maintaining that with Feyzullah gone, the reason for revolt was ended and that the rebels should return to their homes. On August 21 the two armies approached Babaeski, and it seemed certain that there would be a clash, the first major conflict between Ottoman forces since the fifteenth century. But the sultan's soldiers went over to the rebels; Mustafa was deposed; and his brother Ahmet III was proclaimed sultan (August 22, 1703). The crisis ended without much bloodshed. Feyzullah and his entourage were caught and killed just before they reached Varna (September 3, 1703). Mustafa spent the rest of his life in seclusion in the palace.

Ahmet III, 1703–1730

The new sultan, like his predecessor, had grown up in the palace, but he had enjoyed some freedom and education. He was interested in poetry, painting, and calligraphy. Ahmet showed interest in state affairs, regularly changing his grand vezirs and ministers to control them and their parties, and tried to remedy some of the difficulties that had led to the Edirne Event. It took him about a decade to free himself from the pressure of those who had brought him to the throne.

To the soldiers who had brought him to power Ahmet was forced to distribute the largest accession tax ever paid, mainly from the proceeds of the confiscated properties of Feyzullah Efendi and his associates. Other soldiers who had not participated in the revolt then began to demand equal accession payments and influence. They gathered at Silivri with the intention of overthrowing the Ottoman family and replacing it with a prince from the house of the Crimean *han*s or, perhaps, a descendant of the marriage between Sokullu Mehmet and the daughter of Selim II, a line that continued well into the eighteenth century. When they found they lacked sufficient support, they began to ravage eastern Thrace, developing into another provincial rebel band.

The sultan gradually achieved personal power by adapting the age-old political weapon of divide and conquer, appointing members of one party and then another to key positions and ultimately placing his own men as grand vezir and *ağa* of the Janissary corps. The latter again became a weapon of the sultan against his political opponents as well as the provincial rebels, particularly those in Thrace and western

Anatolia. Once his authority was recognized, Ahmet was content to retire and leave the affairs of the state in the hands of his chosen ministers.

The first of these, Çorlulu Ali Paşa (1670–1711), was an example of how the old Ottoman success story of a lower-class boy with ability rising to the top still was possible in the eighteenth century. Coming from a raya family – either a cultivator or a barber according to different historians – Çorlulu Ali had risen through the Palace Institution, eventually coming to the attention of the new sultan during the Edirne Event. He served as governor of Syria, married Mustafa's daughter Emine Sultan (1708) as a particular mark of favor, and then served as grand vezir until 1710. Çorlulu Ali avoided the kind of wars that had drained the empire's resources in the seventeenth century. He devoted his attention to balancing the treasury's budget by increasing revenues and decreasing expenses, in the latter respect going so far as to reduce the extravagances of the palace kitchens, the first "traditional reformer" who dared suggest that the sultan and his family should join the effort. Çorlulu Ali willingly supported Ahmet's effort to eliminate his opponents, executing thousands while confiscating their properties to increase treasury revenues and transforming timar fiefs into tax farms to provide the treasury with cash revenue. The Janissary corps again was reorganized, with those having even the remotest connection with the Edirne Event being removed. Mezomorto Hüseyin's naval reforms also were continued; the number of new ships and large-caliber cannons were increased. The new naval hierarchy was extended, unfit officers and men were weeded out, and naval ammunition and supply warehouses were filled to capacity. The feudal and *kapıkulu* forces were strengthened, with the armed forces being restored at least to the peak achieved under the early Köprülüs.

The Pruth Campaign

While reforming the government and the army, Çorlulu Ali kept the empire out of the War of the Spanish Succession (1701–1714) and the Great Northern War (1700–1721) despite the efforts of France and Sweden to get the sultan's cooperation against Austria and Russia and the agitation of the new Crimean *han,* Devlet Giray, who wanted support to resist the Russian advances north of the Black Sea. This left Peter the Great free to defeat the Swedish king Charles XII at Poltava (July 8, 1709). This event fundamentally altered the balance of power in eastern Europe in favor of Russia and forced Ali to grant refuge to Charles and the Cossack *hetman* Mazepa when they fled across Poland into Ottoman territory in mid-July 1709.[31] The Ottoman court then became a center of intrigue, with the partisans of the Crimean *han* and opponents of the grand vezir supporting Charles, who liberally spread his own inducements with the financial help of the French ambassador, while the British and Russian ambassadors supported the peace party.[32] Ultimately, however, the war party prevailed, securing the appointment as grand vezir of the governor of Aleppo, Baltacı Mehmet (August 18, 1710–November 20, 1711).[33]

The party struggles and foreign intrigues now increased, with the war partisans being divided between those advocating alliance with Sweden and Poland against Russia and those who wanted instead a new campaign to regain the Morea and other losses to Venice in the Treaty of Karlowitz. Charles continued to have the support of Devlet Giray, who as *han* attended the meetings of the Imperial Council, and also of Stanislas Poniatowski, who exercised considerable influence in the harem through the sultan's mother and Swedish doctor. This party also gained the support of Mazepa's successor as Cossack *hetman,* Phillip Orlik, who tried to use the situation in the

Ukraine to build an independent Cossack kingdom, much to the unhappiness of both Poland and Russia. Peter's efforts to stir up the sultan's Orthodox subjects for a general uprising as well as the news that he was building forts along the Dnieper and at Azov further justified the position of the war party. Recent reforms inspired an unfounded confidence, and the ulema, who had deeply felt the loss of Muslim territories to the infidel, were strongly susceptible to any plan to regain these losses. The tide shifted, therefore, in favor of those who wanted a new move against Russia. By this time, however, it mattered little whether the partisans of peace or war dominated in Istanbul. Peter had resolved that the time was ripe for the attack. Gaining promises of support from the princes of Moldavia and Wallachia and expecting a general uprising of the sultan's Christian subjects in response, Peter decided to strike, using as pretext the continued presence of Charles XII on Ottoman territory. The arrival of Peter's ultimatum enabled the partisans of war to prevail, with the Imperial Council declaring war the same day (December 20, 1710). Thus began the conflict between Ottomans and Russians that was to become the central element of the Eastern Question during the next two centuries.

Yet Peter's fear that without Habsburg assistance he might lose both Poland and the Ukraine as well as the general prestige gained by his victory at Poltava caused him to delay war and attempt to make peace. But since the Ottomans ignored his overtures, Peter prepared a campaign through Moldavia and Bulgaria to Istanbul. Even as he prepared to march, however, he suffered a major diplomatic defeat when an agreement was signed between the Tatars and the Cossacks (February 5, 1711) for joint action against the Russians, with the resulting raids further upsetting Peter's campaign plans and preventing him from bringing his army together as rapidly as he might otherwise have done.

While the Ottomans left Istanbul on May 24, the Russians marched through Poland, already suffering severe distress as a result of Cossack and Tatar raids and resulting shortages of supplies. They crossed the Pruth into Moldavia (July 1) but were astonished to find popular reluctance to provide the support promised by their prince along with shortages resulting from a general famine and the flight of thousands of villagers into the hills. When Baltacı Mehmet led his army through Wallachia into Moldavia, therefore, Peter decided to retreat but was caught and surrounded as he attempted to recross the Pruth (July 20). Here was one of the great crises in modern history. The builder of modern Russia and his army were completely surrounded and at the mercy of the Ottomans. While the Ottoman artillery peppered the czar's camp, causing severe casualties, the Russians also were suffering from a lack of food and other supplies. With the Russians at his mercy it appeared that the grand vezir could have demanded and obtained unconditional surrender and major territorial and other concessions. But he too was facing severe problems. His army lacked sufficient supplies to carry on much longer, and he was uncertain whether or not the Tatars would remain loyal or whether the Russians might be bringing replacements from the north. Therefore, when Peter offered peace on the basis of returning all territories taken from the Ottomans, Baltacı Mehmet was more than ready to listen, demanding only that the Russians surrender their cannons but not their arms as a prerequisite for talks.

The negotiations were long and complicated, with the Ottomans abandoning a number of points because of the grand vezir's feeling that his army would fall apart and he would lose everything if the Russians did not retire soon. The final Treaty of the Pruth (July 23, 1711) provided that the Russians return all conquered areas to the Ottomans. They had to destroy all their frontier forts and promise to abstain from further intervention in Ottoman internal affairs. The sultan in return agreed to allow free trade in his dominions for Russian merchants and to attempt mediation for a peace between Russia and Sweden.[34]

There were a number of important ramifications to the treaty both within and outside the empire. The help promised the Russians by the native princes of Wallachia and Moldavia led the Ottomans to supplant them with rulers appointed from among the Greek Phanariote mercantile families of Istanbul, who had already come to monopolize the position of grand dragoman of the Porte, which controlled the sultan's foreign relations. The Principalities thus lost their native leadership while resenting the increased presence of Greek language and culture in their political and religious administration. Another important result was a split between the Balkan Christian nationalists and the Russians, with the former disappointed with Peter's failure to provide concrete assistance, and the latter unhappy with the absence of popular support for the invasion. The Russians slackened their efforts to raise a Balkan revolt against the sultan. Austria subsequently took the lead in attempting to stir nationalist agitation.

In Istanbul the news of the victory was received enthusiastically. It now appeared that the threats of a Russian attack and a Balkan revolt were only myths and that the Ottoman army could be turned to gain revenge from the Habsburgs. However, there were many who wanted to renew the war with Russia, led still by Charles XII, the Crimean *han,* and the ambassadors of Sweden, Poland, and Venice. Others, including Baltacı Mehmet, the queen mother, and the Phanariotes, advocated war with Venice to regain the Morea and Greece, the latter at least in the hope of securing a monopoly of the trade and taxes of these areas, the former simply to regain the losses at Karlowitz. At first the advocates of war with Russia again prevailed, largely because of rumors spread that Baltacı Mehmet had accepted Russian bribes in return for the peace settlement; the sultan gradually edged away from supporting someone accused of betraying Islam and finally dismissed him (November 20, 1711) in fear of a military revolt.[35] Ahmet then went to Edirne to prepare a new campaign against the Russians. But the Russian ambassador, joined by the advocates of war with Venice and the English and Dutch ambassadors, spread sufficient bribes to secure a reversal of policy and a new Ottoman-Russian agreement (April 17, 1712), incorporating several provisions left ambiguous at the Pruth, including Russian evacuation of the fort at Azov.[36] The ambassadors of France, Sweden, Poland, and Venice intervened to renew Ottoman war fervor against the Russians, using Peter's slowness in removing his troops from Poland to get the sultan to resume his war preparations and, after a Swedish success against the Russians in the west, to declare war once again (April 30, 1713).[37] Further intrigues to secure an immediate campaign, however, soured the sultan toward his quarrelsome and constantly intriguing Swedish royal guest as well as his Crimean supporter Devlet Giray. The latter was displaced and exiled to Chios, the former put under house arrest in Edirne, and a new and definitive peace treaty was concluded with Russia (June 5, 1713) providing for the latter to evacuate Poland at once and allow Charles XII to return home in addition to giving up all territory along the Black Sea coast.[38] The problem of the northern frontier thus was settled, although Peter was free to rebuild his army.

War with Venice and Austria

Signature of the peace treaty with Russia signified a new triumph of the advocates of war with Venice in the Ottoman court, with their leader Silahtar Damat Ali Paşa assuming the grand vezirate (August 27, 1713–August 6, 1716). Internal pressure on the sultan to attempt to regain the Morea was supported not only by the Phanariotes but also by appeals from its Orthodox inhabitants for help against the Catholic domination under Venetian rule. War finally was declared (December 8, 1714) when Venice stirred a large-scale uprising against the Ottomans in Montenegro[39] and sent its ships to raid Ottoman merchant and pilgrimage vessels sailing between Egypt and Istanbul – all in violation of its obligations under the Treaty of Karlowitz. The grand vezir was able to reconquer the Morea with little difficulty with a land-sea expedition (summer 1715). Spanish and other Western interests dictated continued Habsburg peace with the Ottomans, but the sultan's threat to Dalmatia and Croatia finally led the Austrians to renew their alliance with Venice (April 13, 1716) and demand full Ottoman withdrawal from their latest conquests as well as the provision of compensation to Venice.[40] A number of Ottoman ministers, remembering their previous defeats at the hands of Eugene of Savoy, urged caution, but the grand vezir convinced the sultan that the Ottomans were now strong enough to defeat the Habsburgs and regain Hungary.[41] War soon led to new disasters. Rakoczi Ferencz II, who had fled to Paris following the Habsburg occupation of Hungary and Transylvania, now joined the sultan in the hope of regaining his rule following the expected victory (May 23, 1716). The easy victory in the Morea seems to have made the grand vezir overconfident, for as he marched northward, he left the Crimean Tatars at home to guard against a possible Russian attack and sent sizable forces to Albania to join an expected attack on Corfu. This reduced his own force to little over 100,000 men, who were easily routed by Eugene at Peterwaradin, on the Danube (August 5, 1715). Once again the Ottoman camp fell to the Imperials and Serbia was opened to easy conquest. The campaigns of 1717 witnessed one disaster after another. The Austrians took Temesvar and then Belgrade (August 20), in the process capturing all the Ottoman artillery and ammunition as well as thousands of prisoners.[42] The Bosnian defense forces held out along the Drina and the Una, but the Venetians, supported by ships from the pope and the Knights of Malta, attacked the Ottoman rear by capturing Preveze and landing troops in Dalmatia, although the Ottomans were able to defeat a contingent off Cape Matapan (July 1717) and frustrate an enemy effort to regain the Morea.[43]

The terrible defeats to the north led to the collapse of the prowar faction and its replacement in power by a peace party led by the sultan's slave and close adviser, Nevşehirli Damat Ibrahim Paşa (August 26, 1717), who as grand vezir became the sultan's chief agent to end the war. Damat Ibrahim even gained the support of the war elements who feared Russia might use the defeats as an occasion to occupy the Principalities ahead of the Austrians. The emperor was impelled toward peace by disappointment over the Venetian failure to use Austrian successes to recoup their losses as well as by Spanish attacks against his position in Italy. Thus with the help of the British and Dutch ambassadors[44] peace was reached at Passarowitz (July 21, 1718), with all sides keeping what they had conquered.

As a result, the Habsburgs were left in control of Belgrade and Semendria as well as the lands between the Timok and the Una, leaving the Sava and Drina as the new boundary and a substantial part of Serbia in Austrian hands. Catholic priests in Ottoman territory were to regain their old privileges, once again making the Habsburgs their champions, able in intervene in Ottoman affairs on their behalf. A separate agreement provided free trade for the merchants of the signatories, with Austria being allowed also to protect foreign merchants within the sultan's borders and to station its consuls wherever it wished around the empire, thus providing further means for stirring up the sultan's subjects. The Habsburgs virtually abandoned Venice for whom they had ostensibly entered the war, allowing the Ottomans to remain in the Morea while Venice kept only Dalmatia and the Ionian Islands as well as the forts it had captured in Herzegovina and at Preveze. The defeat was not as bad as it might have been; yet it was substantial. The Ottomans suffered not only losses of territory and men but also of prestige and morale. The defeats had demonstrated to both the Ottomans and the Europeans that however much individual Ottoman reformers could restore the army and government, they were no match for the new infantry and artillery of Europe. Thereafter, the Ottomans were much more cautious about new involvement in European wars, and they were also much more willing to accept the new era of peace and diversion that was to be offered during the long 12-year regime of Grand Vezir Damat Ibrahim Paşa (1718–1730).

Ibrahim Paşa the Politician

Ibrahim used the power available to him as grand vezir first to secure the Peace of Passarowitz and then to maintain it to provide a respite from the ravages of the conflicts that had gone on since 1683. He assured Peter the Great that he would never intervene in the renewed Russo-Swedish war, consented to modifications in the agreements with Poland and Austria to guarantee that the Tatars would end their raids into Polish territory,[45] and pressured the Tatars to avoid any hostility that might lead to war with Russia. Ibrahim was the first Ottoman minister of any importance to believe that knowledge of Europe was important to Ottoman foreign policy. Accordingly, he entered into regular contact with the European ambassadors in Istanbul and began sending Ottoman ambassadors abroad for the first time, to Paris and Vienna at least, not only to sign diplomatic and trade agreements and arrange for the fulfillment of previous treaties but also to secure information about European diplomacy and military power. Yirmisekiz Çelebi zâde Mehmet Efendi thus went to Paris (1720–1721), the second treasurer Ibrahim Paşa to Vienna (1719), Nişli Mehmet Ağa to Moscow (1722–1723), Mustafa Efendi to Vienna (1730), and Mehmet Efendi to Poland (1730) – all of whom sent back reports to keep the grand vezir informed. This was the first breach in the Ottoman iron curtain, a concession to the reality that the Ottomans could no longer afford to ignore internal developments in Europe.[46]

Ibrahim stayed in power and maintained a consistent peace policy because he kept the sultan's confidence. He was a master of palace politics. During the early years of his grand vezirate, he was opposed by most of the palace courtiers as well as the treasurer, the *bostancı başı,* and others. But he built his own political party in alliance with the sultan's chief scribe (*reis ul-küttap*), with whose help he divided and then eliminated his opponents, replacing them with his own men. Beyond this he was the consummate statesman:

> He did not dictate, he diverted Achmet III's attention and lulled him into inactivity. Ibrahim's methods were not simple, direct and consistent; they were a combination of contrasting characteristics. At times he showed tremendous energy, holding official conferences and secret consultations with a few, convening divans, ordering preparations for war, visiting the arsenal, launching ships, supervising the construction of buildings, planning amusements; then if the occasion warranted procrastination, he became as passive as he had been active and appeared interested only in diversions. He assumed a suave or a severe, a cordial or an indifferent manner, catered to or neglected a diplomat, announced or withheld news from the public as he saw fit. He could be out-

wardly gracious, though he maintained independence. He used rumors, secrecy, dissimulation, artifices, and intrigue, playing the Persians against the Russians and Persians against Persians; yet he practised watchful waiting, caution and prudence. A lover of power and wealth, he brooked no rivals and collected a huge fortune; without doubt these factors influenced his adoption of a peace policy and made him unwilling to give up the known for the unknown. With more than average astuteness he knew when to dismiss a council to avoid a hasty decision and when to substitute generosity for a more natural avarice.[47]

The Tulip Period

The grand vezir's schemes to divert his fun-loving master set the tone for a new life style for the palace as well as the upper classes. To provide a center for the sultan's entertainments Ibrahim personally supervised the construction of a large new pleasure palace named, appropriately, *Sa'dabat* (Place of Happiness). It was located as far away from the palace as possible, at one of the most beautiful places in Istanbul, at the Sweet Waters of Europe (Kâğıthane), on the right tip of the Golden Horn. With sketches of Fontainbleau brought from Paris by Yirmisekiz Çelebi Mehmet used as models, the main building was surrounded by luxurious pavilions as well as statues, baths, gardens, and fountains – all intended to emulate the same kind of life style as that of the French king and those around him.[48] The sultan's example was mirrored by ministers and members of the Ruling Class who, as in other ways, sought to copy their master as part of the process by which they retained their privileged positions in Ottoman society. Similar palaces, pavilions, gardens, and fountains were built privately throughout the capital in direct imitation of *Sa'dabat*. Ibrahim Paşa's own palace went up at Kandilli, on the Anatolian shore of the Bosporus. Plots of land along the Bosporus and the Golden Horn were distributed by the sultan to relatives and members of the Ruling Class, turning those areas into residential centers for the wealthy. In the gardens surrounding the palaces and pavilions, the Ottomans of the time competed with one another in designing lavish and extravagant gardens, ornate fountains, and especially cultivating tulips. Interest in this bulb was so pervasive that the age came to be known as the Tulip Period (*Lâle Devri*). Rare strains of tulips were among the most coveted possessions and were used as a means of securing high offices. Horticultural secrets were most carefully guarded. The sultan, members of the Ruling Class, wealthy subjects, resident diplomats, and foreigners shared this interest, and fortunes were spent on tulips as well as garden parties and festivals where entertainment was provided by poets, musicians, and dancers. At night turtles carrying candles on their backs walked around the tulip beds. Singing birds and parrots provided further diversion. In the summertime exhibitions of fireworks, cannonry, and naval warfare were arranged by the imperial navy. Along with a new appreciation of the out-of-doors, echoed in the works of the famous court poet Nedim, there was an open assertion of joys to be derived from the senses and from nature. The general loosening of upper-class behavior found its counterpart among the lower classes in the increased number of coffeehouses and taverns that became centers of popular entertainment.[49]

In addition to the palaces and entertainments, the Tulip Period manifested a wild period of extravagance on the part of the sultan as well as everyone else who had money to spend. In contrast to the previous Ottoman reluctance to be affected by European customs and manners, it now became the mode for the wealthy to import articles considered representative of Western life. Sofas and chairs replaced the low divans traditionally used. Trousers and gowns also became the rage. Western artists were imported to paint murals on the walls, not only of the new palaces but also to cover the mosaics that had adorned the Topkapı Palace for centuries. For the first time since the Seljuks, the old tradition barring representation of the human form was ignored, as Western painters produced portraits of Ottomans wealthy enough to pay for their services.

Nor was construction limited only to pleasure palaces. Ibrahim Paşa busied himself with rebuilding the ancient capital, providing it with palaces, fountains, aqueducts, and gardens. Many governmental and ministerial buildings, which had been neglected during the previous century, were repaired along with mosques and *medreses*, which had suffered from the tendency of their administrators to divert their endowment revenues. Ministers also competed with each other and with the grand vezir to build the new mosques, *medreses*, and fountains. They often embellished the environs of their pleasure palaces, with the Bosporus area in particular benefiting in this respect.[50]

The Tulip Period also marked the beginning of the Ottoman intellectual awakening that was eventually to blossom a century later in the Tanzimat period, partly within the classical confines of traditional Ottoman literature, but partly also breaking new ground in style, content, and interest. The sultan, the grand vezir, and others competed in promoting and subsidizing the work of Ottoman poets, primarily of course to embellish their palaces and entertainments. Damat Ibrahim formed groups of learned men to translate the great Arabic and Persian works of the past into Ottoman Turkish, thus putting them forth as models for his own scholars. With the court and pleasure palaces as centers of life, it was inevitable that patronage should concentrate on court poets to the extent that this particular genre of Ottoman literature reached its peak. Innumerable works extolled wine and love as well as the munificence and magnificence of the sultan and those around him. The secular nature of the themes furthered an acceptance of secular interests and pleasures, preparing the way for the acceptance of new ways and ideas. The poets' willingness to deviate from the Persian style and experiment with new forms and increased Turkish vocabulary made their contributions far more readable and widely felt than had been the case in the past.

It appears that the translation groups formed by the grand vezir translated a few Western works on history, philosophy, and astronomy as well as the more traditional subjects acceptable to conservative Muslim tradition. To the Ottoman mind still content in the traditional belief of Ottoman supremacy something more concrete was needed than these translations and the works of the court poets. This was provided by those Ottomans who contacted the new might of Europe on the battlefield or were sent to its capitals as ambassadors or agents. They communicated their impressions in the form of reports that could not have failed to impress those who read them. For instance, Yirmisekiz Çelebi Mehmet was sent to Paris by Damat Ibrahim "to visit the fortresses, factories and works of French civilization generally and report on those which might be applicable" in the Ottoman Empire.[51] He wrote the grand vezir not only about such things but also about what he saw in the streets and shops, hospitals, zoos, and gardens, with particular attention to French military schools and training grounds and those aspects of French society and ways of doing things that differed most markedly from those of the Ottomans, such as the position and status of women, the manner in which the king and other high officials passed quietly through the streets of Paris, and, most important, the wide use of the printing press.

Other reports, less elaborate but still original and enlightening, came from Damat Ibrahim's other emissaries. These reports must certainly have had some influence on the grand vezir and others in his entourage, but it is questionable whether more than a few Ottomans ever read them, and it is very likely that comments and descriptions most alien to the Ottoman ways of life and thought were probably interpreted in Ottoman terms to such an extent that their impact was limited. Much more influential was the work of Çelebi Mehmet's son Mehmet Sait, who circulated far more widely in the French capital than did his father, making numerous friends, going to plays, entertainments, and soirees, and becoming the first Ottoman Turk to become somewhat conversant in the French language. He brought back to Istanbul books, costumes, and items of furniture that influenced and stimulated the passion for Western ways.

Even more significant was the enthusiasm brought back by father and son alike for use of the printing press. Works in Hebrew, Greek, Armenian, and Latin had been printed in the Ottoman Empire, but the printing press had not been used for Ottoman Turkish, To build and operate it they chose a Hungarian convert named Ibrahim Müteferrika (1674–1745), first of a group of European "renegades" to convert to Islam during the eighteenth century but who, unlike the *devşirme* converts, transmitted many of the artifacts and ideas of the West into the empire as part of the process by which the old iron curtain of the past was being broken down.

Born in Kolozsvár, Transylvania, of a Calvinist or Unitarian Hungarian family, the young Müteferrika (his original name is not known) suffered from the Catholic religious oppression that overwhelmed his homeland following the restoration of Habsburg rule and apparently participated in Imre Thököly's independence movement while attending a religious school. He was captured by an Ottoman raiding party (1692) and enslaved and converted to Islam, indicating that while the *devşirme* system as such had been abandoned, the old process of training and conversion still remained as a matter of private initiative. Once he was accepted as a full Ottoman, Ibrahim entered the *Müteferrika* corps, acquiring its name. He used his knowledge of European languages to assist the *reis ul-küttap* in the negotiations with the Habsburgs in Vienna in 1715, attracting the attention of Damat Ibrahim. He went on to serve as Ottoman agent with Rákoczi in the latter's effort to stir a Hungarian revolt against the Habsburgs. When Sait Mehmet Paşa returned from Europe, Ibrahim Müteferrika joined him in promoting the establishment of a Turkish printing press in Istanbul.

There was considerable opposition to the plan from the scribes, who feared the loss of their jobs and position in the Ruling Class. But through the influence of the grand vezir the plan was approved through a compromise, with the *şeyhulislam* agreeing to allow the printing of books on all but the traditional religious subjects, thus preserving for the scribes their most lucrative source of income and leaving Müteferrika free to print whatever he wanted on history, languages, mathematics, geography, and the sciences.

The press itself was installed in Ibrahim's own house in the Sultan Selim quarter of Istanbul, immediately beneath the Sublime Porte toward the Golden Horn. Damat Ibrahim quickly perceived how the press could be used to help the armed forces, and at his insistance the very first works printed were maps of the Sea of Marmara (*Marmara Deniz Haritası*, 1132/1720) and of the Black Sea (*Bahriye-i Bahr-ı Siyah*, 1137/1724–1725). Beginning with the publication of the *Van Kulu* dictionary (January 31, 1728), a total of 16 works (in 20 volumes) were published until Ibrahim Müteferrika's death in 1745, with Sait Mehmet largely dropping out of the operation as he rose in the Ottoman hierarchy. Six of the works were on the exact sciences, and the remainder on history and geography. In advocating the establishment of the press, Ibrahim had emphasized how printing would help Islam by facilitating the revival of learning among Muslims – both by providing copies to all wishing to read and by making them cheap enough for anyone to buy – thus enabling the Ottomans to regain their former role as leaders of learning throughout the world.

Yet the result hardly achieved these hopes. In many ways it was in his *Usul ul-Hikam fi Nizam al-Umam,* which he himself wrote and published in 1731, that the possibilities of the press were most suitably used in a kind of "Mirror for Princes" presented to the ruler. Describing the governments and military systems of Europe, Müteferrika told his sultan that the Ottomans could survive only if they borrowed not only the military sciences but also the geographic knowledge and governmental techniques developed in the modern world. Stressing the importance of geography, he published Kâtip Çelebi's *Cihannumâ,* adding a later description of Anatolia and Arabia written by Ebu Bekir ibn Behram ud-Dimişki as well as an introductory section on geometry and the work of Copernicus, although in such a way as to not upset the ulema, who were not inclined to accept such modern theories. Maps and other useful geographic information also were incorporated into his printing of Kâtip Çelebi's *Tuhfat ul-Kibar fi Asfar al-Bihar* (1141/1728) (translated and published in London in 1831 as *History of the Maritime Wars of the Turks*) and in his own *Tarih al-Hind al-Garbi al musamma bi Hadis-i Nav* (History of Western India, Known as the New World), describing the geography and history of the Americas, information previously unknown to even the most educated Ottomans at the time.

Ibrahim Müteferrika's publications in the field of history were even more traditional in nature and content, designed to avoid any possible accusation of disloyalty to the sultans and ministers. His first history, *Tarih-i Timur Gurgan* (1142/1729), discussed the great world conqueror Tamerlane. Then came a Turkish translation of an Arabic history of Egypt before and after the Ottoman conquest, written by Süheyli Efendi, *Tarih-i Misir al-Cadid vel-Kadim* (1142/1729). Under Mahmut I he published Kâtip Çelebi's *Takvim al-Tevarih,* a chronology of the great dynasties of the world, including that of the Ottomans until 1648 (1146/1733–4), and a major series of Ottoman chronicles of previous reigns, by Mustafa Naima for the years from 1591 until 1660 (1147/1734–5), Mehmet Raşit for 1660 to 1722 (1153/1740–1), and Küçük Çelebi zâde Ismail Asım Efendi, from 1722 to 1729. Müteferrika added his own history of the Ottoman conquest of Bosnia (1154/1741), but aside from the work of Naima, which concerned considerably earlier times, none of the others was in any way a critical assessment of the events and personalities treated.

Perhaps most daring and enlightening of all his publications were those in the sciences, to which Ibrahim Müteferrika contributed liberally through the years. Already in the *Cihannuma* he used a Latin work by Edmund Pourchot (1651–1734) as a basis for discussing the theories of Descartes on vortexes and those of Galileo on physics, magnetism, and the compass. In 1732 he brought together translations of several English and Latin works under the title *Fuyuzat-i miknatisiye* (The Enlightenment of Magnetism), adding information on the use of the compass. He translated the work of the seventeenth-century Dutch geographer and astronomer Andrea Keller as *Mecmua-i Heyet-i Kadime ve Cedide,* originally published in Holland in 1665, including all available astronomical and cosmographical data; but this was not printed and remained only for the information of the palace. There also was an unpublished treatise on Islam, *Risâle-i Islamiye,* cautiously describing his entire religious experience and conversion to Islam.[52]

The influence of Müteferrika's press in opening Ottoman eyes to the modern world cannot be measured. But the fact that this awakening continued, that the press eventually published more works later in the century, and that in fact an Ottoman enlightenment continued to emerge leads us to the conclusion that his work was perhaps the most outstanding legacy of the Tulip Period.

Ibrahim Paşa's Financial Policies

The grand vezir was responsible for financing the sultan's extravagances. The Janissary corps and bureaucrats and scribes were reduced in number, ostensibly to improve discipline and efficiency but in fact to reduce their drain on the treasury.[53] The value of coins was manipulated for the treasury's profit, with salaries being paid at the unrealistically high rate of three silver *akçes* for each *para* of salary listed in the registers rather than at the previously used market rate of four.[54] Efforts were made to eliminate the *malikâne* holdings which had diverted much of the treasury's traditional revenues as well as the timars of those unwilling to serve in return. These areas were now assigned to salaried *emins* or to tax farmers who delivered their collections to the treasury.[55] Since most of the illegal taxes previously imposed to support the middlemen used by the *malikâne* and timar holders now were incorporated into the regular tax structure, the changes were intended to help the treasury rather than relieve the overburdened rayas. For the first time in over a century extensive cadastral surveys were made of revenue sources in town and country alike so that those not entered in the previous surveys could be taxed legally and fully.[56] The annual payments required from the holders of the principal treasury positions also were increased considerably, requiring them in turn to raise the fees they charged in return for the performance of their official duties.[57] An annual capital tax was imposed on the property and stock of urban artisans and merchants, and the emergency "campaign assistance tax" (*imdad-ı seferiye*) was imposed on a regular basis and used as a major source of revenue. Efforts also were made to water the currency, although these were mostly abandoned when they were met with strenuous protests from the guilds.[58]

Those affected by the oppressive measures – soldiers, bureaucrats, urban dwellers, and cultivators alike – contrasted their own misery with the opulence of the sultan and those around him. While the sultan and the Ruling Class played, the empire was entering a new era of rampant inflation, famine, and plague, with the government doing nothing to remedy the situation. Occasional uprisings began to disturb the empire again. Bandits, peasants, and military rebels, known now collectively as *levents* (adventurers) began to raid and ravage large areas of Anatolia and parts of Rumeli as well.[59]

The Iranian Wars (I)

Though there was mounting social and economic tension, it was Ottoman involvement in Iran that precipitated the end of the Tulip Period. Iran's internal weakness enticed Ibrahim Paşa into a war that he hoped would solve the Ottomans' financial problems and lessen the burden on the sultan's subjects. Iran, indeed, seemed ripe for conquest in the late years of the long and dissolute reign of Şah Hüseyin (1694–1723). last of the Safavids. An Afghan tribe based in Kandahar first killed the local Safavid governor (1712) and then invaded and conquered Iran (1723), forcing Şah Hüseyin to surrender his rank and titles to his conquerors. While the Afghans went on to ravage the north and west of the country, the remainder of Iran decomposed politically. Şah Hüseyin's son Tahmasp fled to Tabriz, where he declared himself Şah Tahmasp II. Supported by the Sunni Muslims of the Caucasus, who were being persecuted by both the Iranian Shias and the Georgian Christians, he appealed for Ottoman help. Peter the Great took advantage of the situation by moving his army into the Caucasus from the north, occupying Derbent and Baku in the fall of 1723. The Ottomans too feared a Russian occupation of Iran as well as the Caucasus. Damat Ibrahim felt that he had to act at once to assure an Ottoman share of the declining Iranian state. (April 1723).[60] A three-pronged invasion followed between 1723 and 1725. In the Caucasus, forces from Kars and Diyarbekir captured Tiflis and Kuri relatively easily and after the Russians entered Baku, Ottoman forces took Erivan, Nahcivan, and Gence (August, September 1725).[61] In western Iran Ottoman forces from Baghdad and Van took Kirmanşah and Luristan with the help of the local Sunnis,[62] and then took Hamadan and Maraga the following summer.[63] Tabriz and most of Azerbaijan were occupied during the summers of 1724 and 1725 along with the Shia holy city of Ardabil.[64] Thus all the major objectives were secured, and Istanbul was in rapture.

This in turn raised the possibility of a new conflict with Russia, with the Crimean *han* again using his political influence toward this end to regain his territories north of the Black Sea. His intrigues were successfully countered, however, by the efforts of the Russian and French ambassadors, supported behind the scenes by the sultan and the queen mother, who were even more desirous for continued peace than was the grand vezir.[65] As a result a new Ottoman-Russian agreement (June 24, 1724) provided for Ottoman control of Georgia, Şirvan, and Azerbaijan, and the sultan confirmed Russian presence in the Caspian provinces of the Caucasus, Gilan, Mazanderan, and Esterabad. Both parties recognized Tahmasp II as the Persian ruler, and the Ottomans agreed to allow Russian help against the Afghans. But if the latter attacked Ottoman territory, then the sultan could join in the move to push them out of Iran altogether.[66]

Both Ottomans and Russians seemed content with an arrangement that satisfied their ambitions at the expense of Iran. In Istanbul the populace forgot its troubles when deluged with the news that the Sunni Muslims of the east had been saved. But events in Iran soon upset the settlement and led to the fall of both the sultan and the grand vezir. Tahmasp II proved unable to stop the Afghans, who gained control of much of the country. He had to flee to Horasan. There he was joined by a number of Turkoman nomadic tribes led by the Kajars, commanded by Feth Ali Han, and the Afşars, whose leader Nadir Han soon drove the Afghans not only out of Iran but also out of Afghanistan, setting Tahmasp II on the Persian throne under his protection (1730). Tahmasp then demanded Russian and Ottoman evacuation of Persian territories. To avoid war the grand vezir consented, giving up Kirmanşah, Tabriz, Hamadan, and Luristan in return for Persian recognition of continued Ottoman rule in Tiflis, Erivan, and Şirvan.[67] Nadir Han followed up the Ottoman evacuation by going on to capture Ferahan, routing the Ottoman army near Tabriz. The grand vezir ordered a new campaign in response, but even as preparations were being made, the news from the east finally ignited the revolt that had been smoldering for so long.

The Patrona Revolt

With most of the army camping in Üsküdar to prepare for the expedition to Iran, Damat Ibrahim had little power to resist his enemies in the capital. Taking the lead in the rebellion was one Patrona Halil, an Albanian Janissary who had joined the Anatolian *levent*s during the Iranian war and now used the surrender of territory to Iran to stimulate a revolt. On September 28, 1730, he and five friends came before the Bayezit Mosque, declaring that the sultan and the grand vezir had violated the *Şeriat* by surrendering Sunni territory to infidels. After attracting a crowd, they went to the new Janissary barracks at Et Meydan shouting their message, with hundreds of civilians and soldiers joining them as they went. The ulema and others alienated by the grand vezir supported the revolt and demanded the heads of Damat Ibrahim and his associates. The sultan, fearing for his own life, had the latter dismissed and strangled to save them from the mob and perhaps save his throne (September 29, 1730). But the events so strongly affected him that he soon abdicated and accepted the will of the leading ulema that the throne should pass to the eldest prince in the palace, Mustafa II's son, who was raised to the throne as Mahmut I (October 1, 1730). Patrona Halil and his men ran through the streets of the city, ravaging and burning the palaces of the wealthy and killing many, creating a mass terror almost unequaled in Ottoman history. The glory of the Tulip Period was extinguished along with the results of its excesses. But with or without the palaces and tulips the general awakening that accompanied the period had spread too far for it to be completely suppressed.

Mahmut I, 1730–1754

Mahmut was brought to the throne by Patrona Halil's rebels, but he did not actually share their desire to suppress reform and return to the ways of the past. Most of his first year was spent in a prolonged effort to put out the flames of the lower-class uprisings that had spread in Istanbul and much of the empire. Patrona Halil proved to be a better rebel than a statesman in victory, perpetuating the revolt to secure booty for his men. Eventually, the sultan satisfied the rebel soldiers with assurances that they would not be punished for their crimes, and the revolt subsided (October 1730).[68] Yet none of the problems underlying the rebellion had been removed, and Patrona Halil continued his campaign in the streets of Istanbul, collecting protection money from house and shopowners and burning the properties of those who resisted. Within a short time he was able to force the sultan to give him a voice in state affairs, particularly in new appointments. Some of his men took state positions and used them to oppress rich and poor alike. It was only at the end of November that the uprising finally was ended when the sultan invited Patrona Halil and his friends to the palace to discuss a new campaign against the Persians and then had them strangled (November 24, 1731). Their followers scattered, and Istanbul was once again left in peace.

New Military Reforms

With the suppression of the Patrona revolt, Mahmut was free to rule as he willed, maintaining his power by the old Ottoman game of balancing off palace parties and rapidly shifting the major offices to keep all in line. The policy of traditionalistic reform adopted by Mahmut I seems to have been influenced by Ibrahim Müteferrika, whose "Rational Bases for the Policies of Nations" stressed the importance of the kind of monarchy in which "the people obey a just and wise sovereign and follow his opinions and measures in all of their affairs" and urged technical reforms in the new military sciences.[69] Since there were no Ottomans schooled well enough in European military ways, Mahmut decided to bring in a European adviser, the first of many technical experts who were to link the Ottomans with the contemporary world during the next two centuries. The adviser was a French nobleman, Claude-Alexandre Comte de Bonneval (1675-1747), who having served his king with distinction during the War of the Spanish Succession, had fallen out with Louis XIV, and had joined Eugene of Savoy in several campaigns against France and the pope as well as the Ottomans at Peterwaradin.

Being a tempestuous young man, he could not get along with Prince Eugene either, so he turned elsewhere. Finding no ready response in Venice, he traveled to Sarajevo to place himself at the disposal of the sultan to gain vengeance against both the king of France and the emperor. The Ottomans still were not ready to accept the services of an unconverted Christian, especially in the era of religious fervor following the Patrona Revolt; Bonneval converted to Islam and took the name Ahmet. He went to Istanbul, where, after several attempts, he attracted the attention of Grand Vezir Topal Osman Paşa (September 10, 1731-March 12, 1732), himself a military man who had already tried to interest the sultan in some kind of modern rifle force using European tactics, discipline, and weapons. Ahmet was assigned to revive the old Bombardier (*Humbaracı*) corps, which, with the decline of the timar system, had fallen into disuse. Thus was introduced another pattern copied by later traditionalistic reformers, that of introducing new organizations under the guise of the old structure so as not to excite conservative opposition. Bonneval actually presented the sultan with a plan to restructure the entire military establishment on French and Austrian lines, emphasizing the need to make military service a real career again by providing adequate and regular salaries and pensions. He proposed that the Janissary regiments be made more efficient and disciplined by breaking them into small units commanded by young officers whom he would train. Janissary opposition, however, prevented the execution of this project, so that he concentrated his efforts on the Bombardier corps, whose name he now took as Humbaracı Ahmet Paşa.

Within a short time the grand vezir provided him with training grounds, barracks, and a workshop for the new corps at Ayazma Sarayı, near Üsküdar. Three young French officers, also converts to Islam, came to help along with Irish and Scottish mercenaries and men recruited among former timar soldiers from Bosnia. The corps was organized and trained according to the methods that Bonneval had learned in French and Austrian service; the uniforms resembled those worn in Hungary, and the Bosnian cap was adapted as headgear.[70] Bonneval attempted to advise the sultan on foreign affairs, urging him to base his defense on the empire's economic as well as military strength. He was active also in helping the Porte modernize its technical services, the cannon foundry, powder works, and musket factory, and also apparently had some role in introducing new weapons into the Mining and Cannon-Wagon corps.

But when Topal Osman fell from the grand vezirate (March 1732), Bonneval's influence in court also vanished. He was not removed from his corps, but very little attention or money was devoted to it by the new grand vezir, Hekimoğlu Ali Paşa (March 12, 1732-July 12, 1735), an Italian convert. Late in 1734 Bonneval was allowed to open a new barracks and drill field for the corps at Toptaşı, also in Üsküdar, along with a military engineering school (*Hendesehane*) devoted to geometry and the other sciences needed as the basis for a successful modern artillery service.[71] Hekimoğlu Ali's fall again cost Bonneval most of his influence for a time, but the school continued to function. Most of its students came from, the *Bostancı* corps, which guarded the palace, thereby avoiding the anger that the older corps would have expressed had their men been taken. Bonneval continued to train his bombardiers and brought them into the Ottoman campaign against Austria in 1736. But the strong protests of the Janissaries, aware of their own technological obsolescence, combined with a bitter dispute between Bonneval and Grand Vezir Silahdar Mehmet Paşa led the latter to banish Bonneval to Kastamonu and to cut off wages to the corps and school. Subsequent grand vezirs recalled Bonneval, and he remained in his position until his death in 1747, with the corps carrying on for a time under his adopted son (a convert to Islam named Süleyman Ağa) before it finally was dispersed and the school closed (1750) due to continued Janissary opposition.

Mahmut's military reform efforts were not limited to the Bombardier corps, however unique and interesting an experiment that might have been. The Sultan understood that efforts would have to be made to reform the older corps, since they formed the bulk of the army. Soon after the Patrona Halil revolt had been suppressed, new laws were issued to reorganize and stabilize the timar system (January 29, 1732).[72] The sultan appointed his own man as Janissary *ağa,* and while no strong reform efforts were made here for fear of a new revolt, salary payments were regularized in return for promises that the corps would at least perform its traditional duties and accept traditional training. New forts were built along the Habsburg and Russian borders, and border garrisons established, much on the model of the fourteenth-century *uc* principalities, with the commanders having wide authority over the neighboring lands and towns and their garrisons bound to keep order and collect taxes in the countryside.[73] But though these traditionalistic reforms may have restored the army to what it had been in 1717, they did little to inspire a spirit of progress.

Other Changes

Mahmut I did not consider it his duty nor that of his state to promote the welfare of his people. But since it was the sultan's duty to care for his "flock" and keep it secure, he sent the army into Anatolia to suppress the worst of the *levent*s, although in the light of the continued famine, inflation, and plagues this gave little help or comfort to the mass of his people.

Mahmut continued the cultural development begun during the Tulip Period, subsidizing Ibrahim Müteferrika's press as well as the work of poets and writers. He also built a number of public libraries in Istanbul and sent agents around the empire to gather collections of books and manuscripts of note. To meet the need for paper created by the intellectual awakening of the time, he built the first Ottoman paper factory at Yalova, on the Anatolian shores of the Sea of Marmara, bringing masters from Poland to operate the plant, and supplemented its product with increased imports from France, Venice, and Poland.

Finally, he acted to meet a serious water supply problem in Istanbul caused by its rapid expansion of population as well as the decay of the old Byzantine aqueducts and cisterns. Istanbul's natural water supply had always been inadequate; the Byzantines had arranged to bring water from distant places, gathering it in reservoirs during the winter and then conveying it by aqueducts to Istanbul, where it was stored in large underground cisterns and distributed as needed from water division stations (*taksim*) to public fountains, mosques, baths, and a few private houses. This system prevailed for the old city, with an aqueduct built by Constantine the Great and improved by Valens passing near the city walls at Edirne Kapı, bringing water from Thrace and the Belgrade forest via Kâğıthane to the western part of the city, and another system bringing water from the Belgrade forest to the heights of Eyüp to a *taksim* at Eğri Kapı, from where it was distributed throughout old Istanbul. Galata,

Pera, and the northern side of the Golden Horn had no such system and had to depend on wells and rain water until the beginning of the eighteenth century. Ahmet III started to build a new water system to bring supplies from Bahçe Köyü, near Büyükdere on the Bosporus, but he lost interest in it in later years and it was finished by Mahmut I, who built an aqueduct to carry the water to a major new distribution center established at the heights of Beyoğlu (the present-day Taksim). From here water was distributed to the major population centers along the Golden Horn and the Bosporus as well as to Galata and Beyoğlu, thus completing the water system (1732), which remained unchanged until it was modernized by Abdulhamit II at the end of the nineteenth century.

The Iranian Wars (II)

Most of the rest of Mahmut's reign was devoted to a series of wars with Iran as well as another disastrous encounter with Austria and Russia. Of course, the conflict with Nadir Han's army had not been ended by the Patrona revolt; only the Ottoman response had been postponed. The first phase of hostilities ended with a peace agreement (January 1732) that left the Caucasus under Ottoman control and western Iran and Azerbaijan to the Persians, thus making the Aras River the boundary between the two states in the north while the Kasr-ı Şirin boundaries remained unaltered in the south.[74]

There was peace, but neither side was satisfied. The sultan had not authorized his envoy to surrender Azerbaijan, and the Persians were unhappy with the territory that had been left to the sultan. Nadir had been in Herat fighting the Afghans. But when he heard of the şah's surrender, he returned to dethrone Tahmasp and replace him with his year-old son, Abbas, with Nadir having real power as chief minister (July 7, 1732), declaring the reconquest of the territories lost to the Ottomans as his primary aim.[75] The following summer while the Ottomans prepared for a new Iranian push into Iraq, he surprised them by moving into the Caucasus, capturing Şirvan and Dagistan with Russian help and getting Georgian help in putting Tiflis under siege.[76] He routed an Ottoman relief force at Bogaverd (June 14, 1735) and took Georgia and Armenia during the summer, again against only limited Ottoman resistance.[77] By the summer of 1735 Nadir had taken everything he wanted, including Kerkuk, Derne, Şehrizor, as well as areas in the Caucasus. Then he proposed peace, which the Ottomans accepted because of the imminence of a new war with Russia. The victory over the Ottomans enabled Nadir to take advantage of the death of the young Şah Abbas III (1736) to assemble the representatives of the major elements of the Persian population who declared him şah, thus establishing the new Afşar dynasty in place of the Safavids (March 6, 1736). He also developed a new religious policy that favored Sunnism as a means of undermining the power of the Shia religious clergy. Insofar as the Ottomans were concerned, this meant that orthodox Islam had come to Iran, making it much easier for the sultan to sign an agreement ceding lands than it had been in the past. Nadir also was anxious for peace so that he could carry out plans to invade India, where he could and eventually did find wealth far greater than anything that he could possibly have gained from the Ottomans.

War with Russia and Austria, 1736–1739

In regard to the Ottoman Empire, Russia's immediate aim was to make the Black Sea into a Russian lake by expanding its power in the Crimea and the basins of the major rivers emptying into the Black Sea, ending the Tatar attacks that had disrupted Russian society for so long. With Sweden now defeated and Poland ruled by the pro-Russian Augustus III following the War of the Polish Succession (1733–1735), the new Russian empress, Anne (1730–1740) was able to attack the Ottomans without fear of diversion, setting a pattern that was crystallized at the end of the century under the leadership of Catherine the Great. The cooperation of Russia and Austria in Poland led to the conclusion of a secret agreement, with the emperor promising to join any Russo-Ottoman war and the spoils to be divided equally. Nor were the Ottomans particularly reluctant to accept the challenge. They had almost attacked when Augustus had been put on the Polish throne instead of the French candidate whom they had supported (summer 1734),[78] but they had not done so because of the continuing war with Iran. Now the French urged them to attack both Austria and Russia, while the Russian ambassador's reports of Ottoman weakness encouraged the czarina to prepare for a surprise attack. The way for war was paved by a territorial agreement between Russia and Austria, with the former to get the Crimea and Azov and the latter Bosnia and Herzegovina as the first step toward even greater advances in the western Balkans. Russia then sent an ultimatum to the sultan denouncing him for a long series of violations of the Treaty of the Pruth – for the most part Tatar raids that he could not control – and demanding the kind of satisfaction that was certain to be rejected, thus providing a pretext for war.[79] While the British and Dutch advised peace as preferable to what might be a cataclysmic conflict, the bellicose advice of the French ambassador coincided with the wishes of both the sultan and the grand vezir; war was declared (May 2, 1736).[80]

At first the Ottomans suffered a series of disasters, since the Russians were poised for the attack, whereas the sultan's army had not even been mobilized. The sultan sent large Tatar contingents to defend the Danube until the Imperial army took over, but the Russians, led by Marshall Münnich, invaded the Crimea, ravaging, slaughtering, and destroying as they went and capturing Azov after a siege of three months (July 13, 1736). It was the very extent of their victory that defeated the Russians here, however. Advancing farther and farther from their own sources of supply and unable to live off the devastated land, they succumbed to such famine and illness that they were forced to evacuate the entire peninsula.

The Russians intended to push across the Dniester into Moldavia during the summer of 1737, but heavy Ottoman reinforcements pushed them back at Bender, and confusion in the Russian army prevented further efforts. The Austrians made a more concentrated attack, with their main force marching up the Vardar toward Niş while smaller units invaded Bosnia and Wallachia. With supplies and men provided by the Serbian population, the invading army took Niş (August 1, 1737) and then fanned out in southern Serbia. The Austrians used Montenegrin help to take much of Bosnia, including Sarajevo.[81] At the end of the summer, however, the Ottomans, once organized, fought back, retaking Niş (October 20, 1737) and blocking further enemy advances into Macedonia or Bulgaria; they routed the Austrians near Bucharest, forcing them to retire back to Transylvania for the winter. In Bosnia the former Hungarian timariots fought with particular vigor because of their memories of what happened to their families north of the Danube; thus the major forts held out against the invaders. The Austrians were routed near Banjaluka (August 1737). These victories emboldened the Ottomans to reject French mediation efforts made during the winter.

The Ottoman campaigns against the Austrians during the summers of 1738 and 1739 were largely successful. The key forts of Belgrade, Semendria, and Irsova were retaken, thus reestablishing the Danubian defense line despite internal weaknesses caused by disputes between the grand vezirs and their principal commanders.[82] The Austrians then feared that continuation of the war would only help the Russians on their front; hence a peace treaty was signed at Belgrade (September 18, 1739) by which the Austrians surrendered all their gains at Passarowitz, thereby establishing the Sava and Danube once again as the boundary between the two empires. But emphasis on Austria had left the Principalities almost undefended against the Russians. Münnich wasted the summer of 1738 trying to secure a revolt of the Balkan Christians to assist his advance, and it was only the following summer that he moved ahead. By agreement with Poland he marched through Polish territory to attack and take Hotin and Bender, thus shattering the Danubian defense line here. He subsequently moved on into Moldavia, took Jassy, and prepared to move on into Wallachia (September 1739). Russian victory seemed assured, therefore, when the news of the Treaty of Belgrade arrived.

Münnich now feared a full-scale Ottoman counteroffensive the following spring. As assistance expected from the Moldavians had not come, the Russians were also beginning to suffer from the same kind of supply problems that had led to disaster in the Crimea. Thus Münnich accepted French offers to mediate a peace (October 3, 1739) by which the Russians essentially gave up their ambitions. They would return Azov and withdraw all their trade and warships from the Sea of Azov and the Black Sea. The Tatars would have to end their raids on Russian territory only when the Cossacks ceased their attacks. Russians were permitted to trade and visit the Christian holy places in Ottoman territory but without any tax exemptions or other concessions such as those allowed to other foreigners in the sultan's dominions. Russians would ship their goods through the Black Sea only in Ottoman ships and abandon all their conquests in Moldavia. Thus the Ottomans recouped their fortunes in east as well as west. But the Russians emerged with more than appears on the surface: Though they had lost Azov, they did compel the sultan to take responsibility for future Tatar raids. In addition, the Russians allowed to trade and go on pilgrimages soon would be able to stir up the Christian subjects as they had in the past. And their military victories left them with a considerable reputation in Europe, showing that Peter's initial modernization of the Russian army had, indeed, been carried to successful fruition by his successors. The basis was laid, then, for further advances against the Ottomans at a later time.

The Ottoman victories and resumption of rule in Bosnia and Serbia in particular also had important internal repercussions. The supporters of traditionalistic reform began to claim that the innovations had made possible the defeat of Russia and Austria. In the countryside three years of campaigns had once again raised taxes and forced many villagers to flee the lands, again forming robber bands or crowding into towns and cities. Some local notables used the available manpower to form private armies and to dominate entire districts, becoming the first *ayan*s (notables) or *derebey*s (lords of the valley). Istanbul, overcrowded, suffered from shortages of food, and mobs broke into shops and stores to take and distribute supplies. It was only under Nişancı Hacı Ahmet Paşa (June 23, 1740–April 21, 1742) that the towns and large areas of the country were brought under control once again.

The Iranian Wars (III)

Nadir Şah had been diverted in India for four years (1737–1741), but he had not given up his ambitions in the Ottoman Empire. First he made an unsuccessful effort to get the support of the Sunnis of Dağistan (May 1741) and then demanded an equal share in the right to rule and maintain the Holy Cities (April 1742), something the Sunni ulema would not approve and the sultan could not grant. Mahmut replied by declaring war, supporting the Safavid prince Şah Safi as ruler of Iran in place of Nadir Şah.[83] The war that followed was fitful and bloody. At first Nadir attacked Kerkuk, Mosul, and Baghdad but was beaten back with heavy losses[84] (summer 1743). He was more successful in the Caucasus, particularly after the Anatolian *levent*s and notables disrupted the sultan's effort to mobilize his army.[85] The desultory nature of the war finally convinced both sides that they could not win a decisive victory, and an agreement was reached (September 4, 1746) whereby the Kasr-ı Şirin boundaries were again restored.

The Interval of Peace, 1747–1768

The last years of Mahmut I's reign as well as the inconsequential reign of Mustafa II's son Osman III (1754–1757) and of Ahmet III's son Mustafa III (1757–1774) provided the Ottoman Empire with the longest continuous period of peace in its history. This peace came about because Europe was diverted by the War of the Austrian Succession (1740–1748) and then by the Seven Years' War (1756–1763), while the sultans and grand vezirs worked to keep the empire out of conflicts. In Iran, for example, though there were numerous opportunities for new adventures following the assassination of Nadir Şah (1747), the Ottomans resisted the entreaties of their frontier governors to regain lost territories and remained faithful to the last agreement signed with Nadir.[86] They also avoided efforts to entangle the empire in the European wars, with the sultan supporting the peace party at court with the help of the English ambassador. Of all the belligerents, Prussia came closest to securing an alliance with the Ottomans, but in the end nothing more than a trade and friendship treaty was signed (July 1761).

Throughout this period the sultans retained power by playing off political rivals and rapidly changing the occupants of the principal offices. Without the challenge of foreign attack, however, most of the reforms made during the previous three decades gradually and silently disappeared and the old abuses reappeared: Offices were again sold, nepotism practiced, and bribes demanded. Ibrahim Müteferrika's printing press and Bonneval's corps disappeared, and the Ruling Class settled into its stupor, again assuming that the supremacy of Ottoman ways was keeping the enemy at bay. The old problems of inflation, the plague, shortages of food, overcrowded cities, unemployment, bandits, and insubordinate notables prevailed throughout the empire, while in Egypt, Syria, Iraq, and North Africa the local military corps seized control and made themselves mostly independent. Since members of the Ruling Class continued to benefit from the abuses, they opposed all change or reform that might threaten their vested interests. Occasional efforts to solve urban problems by fixing prices and sending recent immigrants back to the lands, accompanied by attempts to suppress the worst of the provincial notables, were sporadic and of limited success.

The only grand vezirate of any consequence during the period was that of Koca Mehmet Ragıp Paşa (1699–1763), a learned and distinguished poet and an able administrator, although even he was not able to achieve permanent results. He was appointed grand vezir by Osman III in the hope that he could establish the same order and security throughout the empire that he had accomplished earlier as governor of Baghdad, Egypt, Damascus, and Aleppo. But since Osman was accustomed to controlling his vezirs, he gave Ragıp little initiative, and it was only under Mustafa III that the grand vezir could work with some independence. Both Mustafa and Ragıp shared similar views of the empire, realizing that, despite external appearances, it was weak. They avoided external ties that might bring its downfall before it could be strengthened. Ragıp kept the peace with the support of the sultan against the constant pressure of various war parties in and out of court, which were encouraged and supported by the foreign ambassadors stationed in the capital. He so gained the confidence of the sultan that he married the latter's widowed sister, Saliha Sultan, giving him a kind of prestige and security that few other grand vezirs, after Damat Ibrahim Paşa, had during the eighteenth century.

Ragıp Paşa made a strong effort to improve the lot of the people, introducing a process by which the scope of Ottoman government was extended. Codes of justice were issued again, and the local kadis were made the principal protectors of the people against the exactions of the government officials, *levents*, and *ayans*, using their moral authority to assuage the worst effects of the lack of strong governmental organization. Timar and *mukata'a* holders were required to pay their obligations in full and on time and were prohibited from levying extralegal taxes on the rayas; inspectors were sent out to enforce obedience. The wealth of the sultan and the grand vezir and other high officials was devoted to building libraries, mosques, and other institutions to make the lives of the subjects a little easier. Supervisors (*nazır*) were appointed to check the work of the administrators of religious endowments to ensure that the revenues were spent for their pious objectives. Troops were sent to suppress *levents* who attacked the cultivators, and notables who became too powerful. But without solving the basic economic problems that gave them power, his efforts were of little avail and, as we shall see, in the war with Russia that followed, the *ayans* gained major importance.

As much as Ragıp's early life had been spent in the scribal service, it is not surprising that he devoted considerable effort to regularizing the finances of the treasury and balancing its budget. A new corps of agents was organized to enforce the laws and regulations concerning the tax farmers and timar holders. The latter also were forced to renew their grants (*berat*) at the accession of each new sultan, giving Ragıp the money he needed to pay the accession taxes demanded by the troops as well as the salaries of many members of the Ruling Class. Efforts again were made to restore the value of the coinage to facilitate trade and commerce, and the grand vezir used all his influence to reduce palace expenditures. Ragıp was successful in his efforts to raise revenues and balance the budget, but his lasting contribution was the improvement of the navy. The arsenal was reorganized and a number of ships were built to continue the shift from oar to sail power. His aim of protecting the rayas, however, was never achieved. Overtaxation and misrule continued to exist in most of the provinces, and bad coins continued to crowd out the good; and after Ragıp's death even his limited accomplishments were forgotten, a story typical of the era of traditionalistic reform.

New Struggles with Russia and Austria, 1768–1774

The new war with Russia was the direct result of the aggressive imperialist policies followed by Catherine the Great (1762–1796), who took up Peter the Great's old ambitions. In 1764, following the death of August III, Catherine sent her troops into Poland and arranged for the election of her former lover, Stanislas Poniatowski (1764–1795), as king. Poniatowski proved to be an able ruler, but his effort to provide religious equality for non-Catholics stimulated the formation of a Polish national resistance confederation at Bar, in Podolya (1768), which requested Ottoman assistance. This – combined with the agitation of the Crimean *han* and the French for war against Russia – finally led the sultan into the conflict (October 4, 1768).[87] His request for immediate Russian evacuation of Poland was rejected by Catherine, and war ensued.[88]

The war proved to be far wider in scope and more devastating to the Ottomans than the previous one, despite the fact that Austria stayed out at first in the hope that Ottoman attacks would prevent the Russians from building their Balkan empire. Ottoman participation seems to have been ill omened from the outset. When the grand vezir attempted to bring together an army at Edirne, the Tatars were unable to provide their usual help because of internal divisions, fomented by the Russians, who had arranged for the assassination of the able Kirim Giray (January 1769) and his replacement by the incompetent Devlet Giray IV, leaving the Tatars hardly able to defend themselves, let alone help the sultan.[89] In addition, Grand Vezir Mehmet Emin Paşa, who had obtained his position through the usual political intrigue and was incompetent militarily, was unable to organize his army or arrange for a rational plan to meet the expected Russian push. Poor supply arrangements left the army without sufficient food, and failure to pay wages on time caused indiscipline within the ranks. That the Ottomans were able to hold out as long as they did was due less to their own strength than to weaknesses within the Russian army, which was hampered by a divided command and political interference from the court.

Nevertheless, the Russians were far better prepared than the Ottomans, with armies poised in the Ukraine, at Azov, and north of the Caucasus ready to attack the sultan from three directions. Russian agents were also organizing uprisings in Montenegro, Serbia, and the Principalities, where the large landowning *boyar*s supported Russian occupation in the hope of gaining more autocratic and oligarchical rule than was possible under the Ottomans, and with a native instead of a Greek prince at their head. As the Russians pushed across the Danube into Moldavia during the winter of 1769–1770, the Ottoman garrisons were able to offer only token resistance, particularly after the populace rose in support of the invaders, slaughtering thousands of Muslims without mercy.[90] The Russians moved into Wallachia, occupying Bucharest (February 2, 1770) and fanning out through the principality. When the grand vezir finally was able to bring an army to meet the invaders, it was routed and utterly destroyed at Kartal (August 1, 1770), with one-third of the defenders being wiped out in the battle and another one-third drowning in a desperate attempt to cross the Danube following the defeat. This enabled the Russians to complete their occupation of the Principalities, taking the Danube forts and putting themselves in position to advance through Bulgaria toward Istanbul the following spring. The empire seemed helpless to stop the enemy.

Naval Warfare in the Mediterranean

In the meantime things were going no better for the sultan in the Mediterranean. With no fleet in the Black Sea to attack the Ottomans, Catherine sent a squadron from her Baltic fleet through the Atlantic into the Mediterranean to beard the sultan in his "soft underbelly." In this she was supported by England, which needed her help in Europe and also hoped to use the Russians to end the long French preponderance in the Levant. The fleet was refitted and supplied at Portsmouth, with a number of English officers accompanying it into the Mediterranean to assist Admiral Alexis Orlov, who joined it at Leghorn. Russian agents went to Morea to stir it to revolt against the sultan in anticipation of large-scale assistance from the fleet when it arrived. The rebellion was launched early in March 1771.

Soon afterward the Russians landed some uniforms and arms to help the rebels, with thousands of Muslims being slaughtered in the Maina and adjacent areas. Greeks on the islands of Zanta and Cephalonia also joined the revolt by attacking their Ottoman garrisons as well as the local Muslim populations. The rebellion at first seemed promising for Greek and Russian interests, but the Russians failed to provide really significant assistance in the form of men and arms; thus the Ottomans were able to suppress most of its manifestations by the spring, leaving the Greeks as mistrustful of Russian promises as the Serbs and Moldavians had become as the result of previous experiences.

The response of the Ottoman fleet to the Russian incursion was slow and indecisive. When the two fleets came together near Chios, the grand admiral and his officers were so incapable of matching the enemy's tactics that the entire Ottoman fleet fled into the harbor of Çeşme, where it was set aflame and destroyed by an enemy fire ship, with a tremendous loss of lives (July 6/7, 1770). The entire eastern Mediterranean was exposed to Russian attack. Only continued disputes between Orlov and the English negated the advantage. Orlov could do no more than unsuccessfully attempt to take the islands of Rhodes and Eğriboz, partly disrupting Ottoman trade in the Aegean and providing some assistance to the Mamluk rebels against the sultan in Egypt and Syria, hardly the type of massive attack that Catherine had in mind.[91]

The Crimean Front

By far the most spectacular Russian war success came in the Crimea, which was completely separated from Ottoman suzerainty. Kirim Giray's devastating foray into southern Russia in January 1769 had attracted Catherine to this front, with a rapid shift of *hans* in 1769 and 1770 and Kaplan Giray's participation in the campaigns in the Principalities leaving the Crimea vulnerable during most of the war. Catherine prepared the way for invasion by stimulating disputes between the Tatars and the Nogays, who lived between the Danube and the Dniester, and also by stirring the Crimeans to seek full independence from the sultan. While she did gain influence over the Nogays, Tatar resistance finally led her to undertake a full-scale invasion during the summer of 1771. Since the main Tatar army was still in the Principalities and since most of the Crimean princes joined the Russians as soon as they saw that the latter would win, there was no organized resistance. The Russians installed their own man, Sahip Giray, as *han* and established an autonomous Tatar state under Russian suzerainty. However, Crimean demands for suzerainty over the Nogays and other Turkic tribes north of the Black Sea, combined with their resistance to Russian demands for garrison rights in the Crimea and ulema-inspired popular resentment against any dealings with the infidels, led to a series of revolts against the occupiers. The Crimean notables who had fled to Istanbul elected their own candidate, Maksud Giray, as the new *han* in exile.[92] They and their supporters settled at Rusçuk under Ottoman protection to wait for the day when they could return to the Crimea under the dominion of the sultan.

The War Winds Down

Though the war went on for another two years, in fact it reached its culmination in 1772 with the Russian occupation of the Principalities and the Crimea. Catherine hesitated to press ahead due to resistance from both Austria and Prussia. Their fears of Russian predominance in the area led to the First Partition of Poland in 1772, with Frederick securing Polish Prussia, except for Danzig and Thorn, in compensation for Russian acquisition of White Russia and the territory south to the Dnieper, while Austria took Galicia and western Podolya, including Lvov and Krakow. Thus, paradoxically, the war that had begun with Ottoman intervention to save Poland from the Russians enabled the latter to gain victories over the Ottomans, but both Prussia and Austria had to be compensated at Polish rather than Ottoman expense so that a balance of strength could be preserved.

Though Catherine might have wished to acquire additional territory from the Ottomans, Austria and Prussia had no desire to encourage further Russian expansion. In addition, Catherine was soon immersed in internal difficulties, as demonstrated by the Pugachev Rebellion (1773–1775), in which the involvement of peasants in the valleys of the Ural and Volga rivers and the Cossacks made it extremely difficult for campaigns against the Ottomans to be continued. The Ottomans generally were willing to accept the Russian demands for territory on the Black Sea and new rights for Russian merchants and consuls in the empire in return for evacuation of the Principalities; but negotiations broke down over the sultan's insistence on maintaining his suzerainty over the Crimea. Catherine then decided to force the Ottomans to accept her conditions by resuming the offensive. Russian forces once again moved forward in the Principalities, and new attacks were made in the Caucasus during 1773. But there was little success until command of their armies was given to one of the great military geniuses of the time, Alexander Suvorov, who in 1774 marched toward Şumna, cut the road to Varna, and routed the Ottomans at Kozluca. The grand vezir was forced to ask for peace negotiations, which took place at the Russian camp at Küçük Kaynarca, about four hours south of the Danube in Bulgaria.

The Treaty of Küçük Kaynarca

The settlement signed on July 21, 1774, was one of the most fateful documents of Ottoman history, although its territorial provisions were limited. The Crimea's independence was recognized by both sides, but the Russians agreed to allow the sultan to act as supreme religious leader of its Muslim inhabitants, with the title of caliph, long since fallen into disuse, resurrected to express the new arrangement. In return for this, however, Russia was allowed to occupy the territory between the Dnieper and the Bug as well as the ports of Azov and Kinburun, which controlled the mouth of the Dnieper, thus giving it a far firmer foothold on the Black Sea than ever before. Russia would evacuate the Principalities and the Caucasus as well as Orlov's conquests in the Aegean Islands. But in return the sultan had to give the czarina the right to build and protect an Orthodox church in Istanbul – which was subsequently interpreted to signify Russian protection over all Orthodox Christians in the empire as well as the population of the Principalities – thus enabling Russia to intervene in Ottoman internal affairs for its own advantage during the century that followed. And, finally, the sultan agreed to pay a substantial war indemnity of 7.5 million *akçes* over a three-year period, a substantial sum indeed for the impoverished treasury. With the longstanding Crimean military assistance gone and with the Russians put in a position to extend their power, it seemed very likely to many, including the fearful Austrians, that it would not be long before Catherine or her successors would take advantage of their new gains to advance even further at Ottoman expense.[93]

Resumption of Reforms under Abdulhamit I, 1774–1789

Although he had spent most of his 50 years in the seclusion of the palace, particularly during the reign of his brother Mustafa III, Abdulhamit I emerged on the throne with a clear understanding of the need to reform the empire in order to save it, and he left his mark as one of the strongest reforming sultans of the eighteenth century. While he resorted to the old Ottoman game of playing off parties and changing ministers to keep power in his hands, he promoted traditionalistic reform, seeking to introduce only those new military techniques and weapons that were absolutely necessary to meet the armies of Europe. He went much further than his predecessors in one important respect, however. He was the first sultan to import large numbers of foreign military advisers and to use them without the requirements of conversion and adoption of Ottoman dress and ways, thus inaugurating a transition to the new style of reform that was to dominate through the nineteenth century. While maintaining personal direction of reforms, he operated through two grand vezirs, Kara Vezir Seyyit Mehmet Paşa (August 21, 1779–February 20, 1781) and Halil Hamit Paşa (January 31, 1782–March 31, 1785), with the latter especially becoming one of the great Ottoman reformers in the course of his relatively brief term of office.

Baron de Tott and the Rapid-Fire Artillery Corps

One of the most influential foreign advisers to serve the Ottoman army in the late eighteenth century was Baron François de Tott (1730–1793), a Hungarian nobleman and soldier who had fled to France during the Rakoczi revolt, rising in the artillery service of the French army. He was sent to Istanbul in 1755 with ambassador Vergennes to learn Turkish – a task that he accomplished so well that for almost a decade he acted as agent of the French embassy and inspector of French commercial establishments throughout the Levant. His embassy to the Crimean *han* (1767) to counteract Russian influence was so successful that he came to the attention of Mustafa III, who hired him as adviser on military reforms, assigning him to create a modern artillery corps and an attached geometry school, which occupied him until 1776 when he returned to France and served the king until driven out by the French Revolution (1790).

During the war with Russia, de Tott busied himself with studying the existing Ottoman military establishment and recommending changes. He also built new defenses for the Dardanelles and devised pontoon systems to enable the army to cross streams without disasters such as those that had occurred during crossings in the past. In 1774 he established a new Rapid-Fire (*Süratçi*) Artillery corps for the sultan at Kâğithane, near the old Sa'dabat palace, with 250 recruits and officers. With money and some light cannon supplied by the French embassy, de Tott drilled his men in modern cannon techniques, assisted principally by a Scottish officer named Campbell (who, unlike most of his colleagues, converted to Islam and took the name Mustafa, becoming known, inappropriately enough, as Ingiliz Mustafa, "Mustafa the Englishman") and a Frenchman named Aubert. De Tott also built a modern cannon foundary at Hasköy, on the Golden Horn, and a new mathematics school (*Hendesehane*) next to the Artillery corps barracks, more or less a reincarnation of the Engineering School of the Tulip Period and the forerunner of the Army Engineering School later established by Selim III. Following de Tott's departure the Rapid-Fire corps and school continued operating under Aubert and Campbell respectively, and while they were disbanded for a time under Janissary pressure, they were rescued and continued their work during the grand vezirate of Halil Hamit Paşa, largely under the protection and encouragement of Gazi Hasan Paşa, who by now had emerged as the leading naval reformer of the time.

Gazi Hasan Paşa and the Revival of the Ottoman Navy

A survivor of the disaster suffered by the navy at Çeşme, Gazi Hasan Paşa was appointed grand admiral in July 1774. Since the navy establishment had been wiped out, he was able to proceed with rapid modernization of the naval service without internal opposition of the kind that slowed and frustrated attempts to reform the land army. He understood that while modern ships were needed, they would not be enough unless they were manned by able officers and men trained in the new techniques of naval warfare. Hence his reforms proceeded on two fronts: Firstly, new shipyards were built in the Golden Horn, the Black Sea, and the Aegean. Two French naval engineers, Le Roi and Durest, came to direct their operations along with a number of French artisans who trained Ottoman workers in the new techniques. Ships were built on the lines of those of the British and French navies, with a lighter draft than those previously used at the Porte and with more attention paid to the placement of cannon to improve maneuverability. Efforts also were made to build smaller ships better able to operate in the inlets and narrow channels of the Aegean Islands and Anatolian coast.

Secondly, Gazi Hasan also worked to build a career naval service. Sailors were enrolled from villages along the coasts of the Aegean and eastern mediterranean, but the old system of allowing them to live unsupervised in bachelor quarters in Kasımpaşa and Galata was replaced with barracks at the naval arsenal itself, at Sinop on the Black Sea, and on Midilli Island in the Aegean, where they were subjected to constant discipline and training. To provide officers for the fleet he developed de Tott's mathematics school into a full-fledged Naval Engineering School (*Mühendishane-i Bahri-i Hümayun*), with instruction provided by de Tott, Campbell, and foreign and Ottoman specialists in geometry, navigation, and the like.

Gazi Hasan was quite successful in modernizing the fleet. By 1784, the sultan's fleet had 22 new ships of the line and 15 smaller frigates. But he was less successful in improving the quality of his officers and men. Only a small number of officers came from his school, since appointments continued to be made because of bribery and politics and often in complete disregard of ability. Conditions aboard the ships remained as anarchical as they had been before, and the few able officers whom he did place in command were frustrated by their inability to alter the situation. Nevertheless, Gazi Hasan's efforts continued and provided a nucleus for the more substantive reforms carried out in the nineteenth century.[94]

Reform of the Older Corps

Of course, the base of the Ottoman army remained the Janissary corps and *Sipahi* cavalry, particularly after the loss of the Crimea. In addition to the artillery and naval reforms, though, the sultan strongly felt the need to restore his regular army. To a surprising extent he was successful. The timar holders returned to their lands; the Janissary corps was restored; and within a short time the corps were as they had been before the war with Russia – no better but at least no worse.

Provincial Difficulties

Abdulhamit, however, had little repose to concentrate on his military reforms. His primary internal problem involved the government's loss of provincial authority to the notables. They used the government's dependence on their military assistance during the war with Russia to build their own treasuries, armies, and administrations, making themselves virtually independent and acknowledging the sultan's continued suzerainty as a formality.

In Anatolia the most powerful notables were the Karaosmanoğlu, who dominated large areas of the southwest, the Çapanoğlu, who ruled much of the central plateau, and the Canikli Ali Paşaoğlu, who ruled the northeast. In Egypt, Syria, Iraq, and Arabia the political vacuum left by the Ottomans was filled less by local notables with popular support than by Ottoman officials themselves helped by their Mamluk slaves and sometimes by bedouin tribes who used the situation to develop their own power independent of central or provincial authority; the urban natives were no more than passive observers of the struggles, neither participating in nor benefiting from them. In Egypt the Mamluks filled most of the administrative and military positions after 1681, with the leader of their dominant faction occupying the extralegal position of *şeyh ul-beled* (chief of the city), the real ruler of the country, while the Ottoman governor did what he could to play them off in the prescribed manner. When one Mamluk faction was able to secure full control and eliminate the opposition – such as under Ali Bey ul-Kebir (1760–1773) and later under Murat and Ibrahim Beys after 1783 – Ottoman rule ceased altogether. It was only under such circumstances that direct intervention was attempted, like the expedition led by Gazi Hasan himself in 1786, which did not displace the Mamluks because of the beginning of a new war with Russia but at least divided them and restored them to obedience.[95]

In Syria the outstanding Mamluk leader of the time was Ahmet Cezzar Paşa (d. 1804), originally a Mamluk of Ali Bey ul-Kebir, who subsequently had fled to Ottoman service in Istanbul. He had risen as governor of Damascus and Acre, suppressing local revolts and extending his authority through much of Syria, Lebanon, and Palestine, with his domination being opposed successfully only by the autonomous notables of Mount Lebanon. The Mamluks of Iraq also maintained their autonomy under the leadership of Umar Paşa (1764–1780) and Süleyman Paşa the Great (1780–1802), both of whom drove the bedouins out and ruled without opposition, sending little revenue to Istanbul and defying all the efforts of the sultan to remove them.

In the Arabian peninsula the conditions of revolt were different, involving not Ottoman governors or slaves but the puritanical native Wahhabi religious movement and the armies of the Sa'ud family, who joined in a religious-political movement that came to dominate the Necd and much of the northern part of the peninsula by the end of the century, sending destructive raids into Iraq as well as against the Holy Cities, which seriously threatened the sultan's prestige and rule in the remainder of the peninsula.

Finally, in the Balkans Abdulhamit I did not have to face the kind of powerful notables then ruling in the east, but they were beginning to spread between the Danube, the Balkan range, and the Adriatic and along the Maritsa, laying the basis for similar large-scale revolts later in the century. The most powerful of these were Dağdevirenoğlu, who dominated the area of Edirne; Tirsiniklioğlu Ismail Ağa, who controlled the regions of Nicopolis, Sistova, and Rusçuk along the Danube; Ali Paşa of Janina, who was just beginning his rise to power in central Albania; the Buşatlı family of northern Albania; and Vladika (Prince-Bishop) Peter I Niegos Petrovich of Montenegro, who used the help of both Austria and Russia to develop his autonomy.[96]

In the face of such a general dissolution of central power, the sultan struggled vainly to keep the notables in line, at times appointing them to official positions or simply bribing them to gain some kind of loyalty, playing them off or sending military expeditions against them. The latter efforts usually resulted only in large numbers of soldiers going over to the notables, who gave them better pay and conditions. With the notables in control of the most productive areas of the empire, treasury revenues dropped steadily, Istanbul and the major cities were deprived of important sources of food, and conditions of life became worse and worse; the sultan and those around him were able to do very little to remedy the situation.

Difficulties with Iran

Nor was there real peace in foreign relations. The anarchy in Iran that had followed Nadir Şah's assassination (1747) was ended by Kerim Han, leader of the Zand tribe, who unified the country under his own military rule and established the short-lived Zand dynasty (1751–1794). Once he controlled Iran he pursued an aggressive policy against the Ottomans, raiding into eastern Anatolia (March 1774, March 1775) and then attempting to mix into internecine Mamluk politics in Iraq by capturing Basra (April 1776) and putting up his own candidate as Mamluk leader in Baghdad.[97] Abdulhamit responded by sending raiders from Iraq into Iran but failed to dislodge the Persians from Basra. It was only when Süleyman Paşa had restored Mamluk rule in Iraq that he was able to eliminate the latter and to rule the entire province, at least nominally, in the name of the sultan. The danger from Iran was ended for a century, enabling him and his successors to attempt to control the bedouins. But these efforts were never very successful, and the incursions of the Wahhabis from Arabia added to the difficulty. In the end, therefore, it was the inhabitants of the deserts rather than the Persians who posed the major threat to Ottoman rule in Iraq.[98]

Russian Annexation of the Crimea

Catherine's undisguised appetite for additional Ottoman territory and the determination of the other powers to gain compensation for any new Russian advances strained relations with Europe. At first Catherine limited her direct intervention to the Nogays, whom she made vassals, while at the same time working to secure the Hanate of the Crimea for those susceptible to her influence. It was at this time that hundreds of Crimeans, high and low, began to migrate to Anatolia, thus beginning a refugee movement from lost provinces that was to mount into the millions in the nineteenth century, creating major social and economic problems that the empire was ill equipped to handle. The immediate problem came from the wealthier refugees who financed the rise of a war party in Istanbul, demanding a resumption of the conflict with Russia in order to restore the Crimea to the sultan's suzerainty. But while they had some political success, the war with Iran prevented them from translating their influence into action.

The conclusion of the Pugachev Rebellion freed Catherine for more direct military action to achieve her ends in the Crimea. This was an opportune time for her, since the Ottomans were occupied in Iran and their main European friend, France, was diverted in North America. A Russian invasion of the Crimea put their puppet Şahin Giray on the throne, while the sultan's protégé Devlet Giray had to flee to Istanbul. The rule of Şahin Giray as *han* was not as subservient as the Russians expected. Since he no longer was able to rule in the traditional way – by using Ottoman subsidies to influence the heads of the major Tatar clans – he attempted to establish Russian-style centralized government, eliminating the influence of the ulema and all but the most important clans, placing his own men in key administrative positions, and building a standing army to replace the one dominated by the clans and tribes. Resentment against Şahin's rule led to a revolt, with the Ottomans sending Selim Giray and his supporters back to the Crimea in the hope of using the situation to restore the sultan's rule (January 2, 1778). The Russians moved in at once, however, slaughtered the rebels, and occupied most of the peninsula before the Ottomans could react. Şahim Giray was installed once again but now without any local support and entirely dependent on the Russian army (February 1778). Since the Ottomans despaired at driving the Russians out, they attempted a compromise, recognizing Şahin Giray as *han* for his lifetime, specifying that future *han*s would require confirmation by the sultan in his capacity as caliph, and in return asking the Russians to evacuate once again. The Russians agreed, and Crimean independence was restored; but Şahin Giray was able to maintain himself only with Russian financial and military assistance. Thus it did not take long for Catherine to move toward open and direct annexation (January 1779).[99]

France, involved with the British in North America, discouraged Ottoman reaction to the Russian attack. A strong and liberal grand vezir, Halil Hamit, had just come to power in Istanbul, with the intention of inaugurating major reforms, and neither he nor the sultan was anxious to be tied down in a new Russian war that could only result in further losses before the army was revived. Only Gazi Hasan advocated forceful reaction to the Russian advances, realizing what a tremendous strategic advantage had been gained by the czarina. But the sultan, lacking effective power, reluctantly conceded the annexation in an agreement signed at Aynalı Kavak (January 9, 1784). It confirmed the Treaty of Küçük Kaynarca with the exception of those sections concerning the Crimea, which were eliminated except for the provisions allowing the sultan the right to act as religious leader of its Muslims.[100] The Crimean Hanate now was supplanted by direct Russian rule; thousands more Muslim refugees began to flee into Ottoman territory; and it was not long before Catherine transformed the Crimea into a major military base for further expansion against the Ottomans.[101]

The Politics of Traditional Ottoman Reform

Halil Hamit's type of reform had considerable support among members of the Ruling Class, led by the sultan and those who found it to their political advantage to support him against the conservatives. He also had the backing of the officers and men of Bonneval's and de Tott's military corps and schools as well as those few Ottomans who perceived the importance of what they were doing. Leading the conservatives were, of course, those whose interests were most immediately threatened by the innovations, members of the old military corps, whose revenues and positions were threatened by any change that threatened to make them obsolete and useless. Since many members earned a living as merchants and artisans, with substantial resources and family interests, they were able to involve their guilds and families in support of the old ways. They were supported most vehemently by the majority of the ulema, those who lacked both the ability and the will to maintain the old standards or to carry out their functions. Those with vested interests were joined by others for political reasons, as, for example, by Gazi Hasan and the officers of his new navy, who opposed Halil Hamit largely because he was a rival for the favor of the sultan. Perhaps the greatest strength of the conservatives was their ability to gain the support of the mass of the people by appeals to Islamic and Ottoman tradition, while the reformers, being an elite, were still traditional enough not to wish to involve the subjects in the process of rule or even to develop a middle class that might identify its interest with their own. The greatest support reformers had was crisis, threats to the existence of the empire, which compelled even the most reactionary conservatives to allow some change to save the empire. When the crises were over, however, the conservatives were able to combine mass support with the power of the army to drive the reformers out and eliminate their reforms.

Mixing into this imbroglio were the foreign representatives in Istanbul. Acting in support of the policies of their own governments, the enemies of the sultan, particularly Austria and Russia, supported the opponents of reform in the hope of further undermining the Ottoman system and making it easier prey to the armies of their masters, while the British, Dutch, and French generally supported the reformers in the hope of saving the empire and through it the European balance of power. This is not to say that even French assistance came from any deep-seated support among the French nobility or intelligentsia. Even through the long years of official Ottoman-French friendship, this was based on the French commercial interests in the Levant and religious interests in the Holy Places, while the French popular mind shared the violent hostility and anti-Muslim propaganda spawned since the Crusades. Compounding the traditional Christian bigotry toward Muslims was the new enthusiasm of the eighteenth-century French intelligentsia for the "enlightened despots" of Russia, who ostensibly were modernizing the Russian state and society in the face of continued "Muslim barbarity and ignorance." Others defended Ottoman integrity against Russia, but only to give France the time to take over when the time was ripe. With such intentions often publicly expressed in Europe, it was not difficult for the Ottoman conservatives to identify reformers such as Halil Hamit, who depended on and accepted French assistance, with the effort to supplant Ottoman with Christian rule in the Middle East, an association that was utilized by the opponents of reform throughout much of the nineteenth century.

The Reforms of Halil Hamit

Like Mehmet Ragıp, Halil Hamit was a Turkish Muslim whose experience was shaped largely by long years of service in the Scribal Institution, particularly in the office of the *reis ul-küttap,* in charge of the Sultan's correspondence with foreign ambassadors and governments. He gained a wider view of the Ottoman system only after 1781, when he was appointed lieutenant (*kethüda*) of the grand vezir.[102]

During the conflict with Russia over the Crimea, Halil Hamit attempted to strengthen the existing Ottoman forces against the war that he thought would follow. Soldiers were mobilized and sent with supplies and ammunition to the major border forts, which were repaired and, in a few instances, entirely reconstructed under his supervision. Systematic efforts were made to establish standing reserves of supplies and men at major rear-guard posts at Edirne, Sofia, and Isakçi to provide reinforcements to whichever front first met the enemy attack and to enable the army to regroup in case the enemy broke through front line positions.[103]

The grand vezir very quickly realized, however, that such efforts were doomed to failure as long as the Ottoman army as a whole was not modernized and reinforced. He attempted to end the old–new dualism by coordinating the two groups and giving the older corps the organization, discipline, and weapons associated with the new corps and schools. To be sure, his first reform efforts were no different from those of his reforming predecessors, except in extent and degree. De Tott's Rapid-Fire Artillery corps was revived and enlarged along with the mathematics school with the help of French technicians; Gazi Hasan and the navy participated despite his bitter political opposition to the author of these reforms. French technicians largely manned the Engineering School. French fortification experts modernized the major frontier forts, published Turkish translations of French textbooks, and built a fortification school that became the basis for the later Army Engineering School.[104]

Efforts also were made to restore the traditional institutions. Inspectors were sent to the provinces to force the *timar* holders to live on their lands, train, and come to the army when called.[105] Those of their officers found to be condoning violations or concealing vacancies were subjected to instant execution.[106] Members of the Janissary corps refusing to accept training and discipline were dismissed. Children of members were not allowed to enroll in the corps unless they were found to have particular ability and interest in the service.[107] Halil Hamit dismissed as many as two-thirds of the men listed on the Janissary rolls, raising the salaries of the balance to make them cooperate in modernizing the corps. He also established groups of Janissaries and *Sipahis* to be trained in the new weapons and tactics of the European-style infantry and artillery.[108] New regulations were introduced to institutionalize all the changes made in naval organization, manpower, and tactics under Gazi Hasan.

Halil Hamit devoted considerable attention to the empire's economic problems. Though orders to restore the value of the currency and to control prices were traditional, he encouraged the revival of Ottoman craft industries, which had been overwhelmed by European competition during the previous century. In order to lessen conflict among the different social and religious groups, he ordered all subjects to wear the garments traditionally required according to their class and rank rather than the Indian and European robes that had become the mode since the Tulip Period. The cloth-manufacturing guilds also were encouraged to increase production in order to meet the current need.[109] Ibrahim Müteferrika's old printing press, which had long since fallen into disuse, resumed printing, and treasury funds were used to begin publication with the official chronicles of Suphi and Izzi, who described the development of the empire in the two decades after the Patrona Revolt.

Eventually, however, Halil Hamit fell to the intrigues of his political enemies, now led by Gazi Hasan Paşa, who resented the prestige gained by the grand vezir. A story was spread that the grand vezir was involved in a plot to displace Abdulhamit with his nephew, young prince Selim, who appeared more receptive to modern reform and less susceptible to political pressure. Halil Hamit was dismissed and soon after executed by order of the sultan (April 27, 1785). Without his encouragement and stimulus the impetus for reform was lost. In 1787 the French technicians were withdrawn because Louis XVI was seduced away from his friendship for the Porte by his father-in-law in Vienna. But as had been the case with the efforts of Bonneval and de Tott, an even larger number of Ottomans were left with the knowledge and desire to carry on the reforms when political conditions made it possible.[110]

Background to War

In the meantime, Catherine II's ambitions for Ottoman territory had been only whetted by the annexation of the Crimea. Realizing she could go no further without compensating the other powers, she developed her famous "Greek Scheme," embodied in a secret agreement concluded with the emperor of Austria. The basis of the plan was the expulsion of the Ottomans from Europe and division of the spoils in such a way as to retain the balance of power. The Principalities would be united in a new and independent Orthodox state called Dacia, with Russian influence over it assured by the appointment of Potemkin as its first prince. Even more important in Catherine's eyes, Istanbul would be united with Thrace, Macedonia, Bulgaria, and northern Greece in a revived Byzantine Empire, with the capital at Istanbul, under the rule of Catherine's grandson (b. 1779), who had been named Constantine and trained especially for this role. In compensation Austria would get the western Balkans – Serbia, Bosnia, Herzegovina, and the parts of Dalmatia held by Venice. The latter in return would get the Morea and the strategic islands of Crete and Cyprus. Even France, long the Porte's chief defender in Europe, was involved as a result of its turn toward Russia and Austria since the accession of Louis XVI and his Austrian queen Marie Antoinette, would be compensated with Syria and Egypt, thus giving it a stranglehold on the Levant trade, to be shared, perhaps, only by England if it went along.

Against this alignment Austria's rival in Germany, the rising state of Prussia, moved closer to England, which was beginning to see how much Ottoman territorial integrity was necessary to its own interests as both a barrier to Russia and a market for English goods. The English and Prussian ambassadors encouraged the sultan to resume his reforms and resist Russian expansion as much as possible.

The Russian danger was, indeed, becoming ever more menacing. Potemkin transformed the Crimea into a base for expansion throughout the Black Sea area, with Sevastopol in the Crimea, and Kherson, at the mouth of the Dnieper, built as homes for the new Russian Black Sea fleet. Russian agents established in the Balkans by the terms of the Treaty of Küçük Kaynarca began to fan the flames of dissatisfaction and revolt as well as to encourage Greek pirates in the Aegean to attack Ottoman shipping. The Ottoman reaction was general hatred of the infidel, a desire for revenge, and the determination to regain the Crimea in particular, by force if necessary. Only Gazi Hasan held out against the advocates of war, pointing out that Britain and Prussia had offered only advice, not concrete financial and military support. But as Catherine's ambitions became more apparent, the partisans of immediate war – led by the governor of the Morea, a Georgian convert named Koca Yusuf Paşa – rose toward ascendancy in the sultan's court, leading to his assumption of the grand vezirate for a long three-year term (January 24, 1786–June 7, 1789). Russia and Austria were not yet ready for war because of internal discontent in their empires. But when Gazi Hasan was sent at the head of an expedition to curb the rebellious Mamluk beys in Egypt, the Porte was left entirely in the hands of those wanting war. Koca Yusuf pushed the sultan and the Imperial Council to a war declaration (August 14, 1787), to be rescinded only if Russia evacuated both the Crimea and the Caucasus. When mediation was attempted but failed, Russia responded with its own war declaration soon afterward (September 15), leaving Austria to enter when ready at a time calculated to force the sultan to make peace on the terms set by the allies.

War with Russia and Austria, 1787–1792

The war that followed went through several quite distinct phases, before and after the Austrian entry (February 19, 1788) and well into the reign of Selim III, who ascended the throne on August 6, 1789. With neither side really prepared to attack, the early campaigns were brief and indecisive. Both sides were diverted from offensive action until 1788: the Ottomans by the return of Gazi Hasan from Egypt and his bitter quarrel with the grand vezir over the management of the war; the Russians by Potemkin's military incompetence in preparing a new offensive and also by quarrels for command in the Black Sea between the German prince Charles of Nassau-Siegen and the American Revolutionary hero John Paul Jones, both seduced into Russian service by the personal attentions of the empress. In addition, both Russia and Austria were driven to caution by the formation of the new Triple Alliance among Great Britain, Prussia, and the Netherlands (June 13, 1788) and by a Swedish effort to use Catherine's diversion in the south to retake Finland. The Austrians, waiting to move across the Danube and Sava against the Ottomans, were frustrated by Russia's failure to divert the Ottomans in the east.

Both sides, therefore, had over a year of relative quiet to prepare for the more active phases of the war. It was only in the spring of 1788 that the deadlock was broken when the Imperials occupied Bosnia and northern Moldavia, the latter with the help of its Greek prince, Alexander Ipsilanti, who deserted the grand vezir at a critical moment. Koca Yusuf's successful campaigns through the Carpathians into Transylvania in the spring of 1789 were disrupted by Abdulhamit's death and the efforts of the new sultan, Selim III, to remove the principal opponents of reform, Koca Yusuf and Gazi Hasan. This left the Ottoman armies disorganized and enabled the enemy to recoup and seize the initiative. The Russians went on the offensive, moving through Moldavia into Wallachia and routing the Ottomans. This news in turn caused the defending armies in Serbia and Bosnia to break up as well. The Austrians, therefore, were able to take Belgrade (October 8, 1789) and move rapidly through Serbia to Niş while Potemkin occupied Bucharest and the remainder of Wallachia, thus ending one of the most disastrous campaigns in Ottoman history and opening the way for a joint push toward Istanbul the following spring.

During the winter of 1789–1790, all sides in Europe wanted peace. Catherine was diverted by Sweden's invasion of Finland, Joseph II of Austria by nationalist uprisings in the Netherlands and Hungary. In addition, the outbreak of the French Revolution caused the Triple Alliance to advocate an end to the war in the east so that Austria could join against revolution in Europe while Poland would be restored as a bulwark against further Russian advances to the west. Selim, however, now supported by Gazi Hasan, refused the overtures, feeling that he could force the Russians and Austrians to return all their past conquests in return for peace. Gazi Hasan revived the Ottoman army once again, organized a new supply system, and seemed to be successfully restoring the empire's military power when he died suddenly of fever (March 29, 1790), leaving the army to fall apart once again. Despite Selim's intransigence, the Triple Alliance got Austria to sign a separate agreement at Reichenbach (August 5, 1790) by which it agreed to abandon all its Ottoman conquests in return for peace. The sultan at first was extremely unhappy at what he considered to be betrayal by Prussia in negotiating for him without the presence of his representatives, but he finally accepted the arrangement and signed a peace with Austria at Sistova (August 4, 1791) which confirmed the arrangement. Austria surrendered its conquests in Bosnia, Serbia, and the Principalities in return for the sultan's promises to treat his Christian subjects well and to allow them to be protected by the Austrians. Thus once again Austria had deserted Russia in the heat of a joint campaign against Istanbul.

Selim now restored Koca Yusuf to the grand vezirate (February 27, 1791–May 4, 1792) in the hope that he could repeat his earlier successes, but the Ottoman army by now was too far gone for him to do anything. Although he brought a large number of men together, they lacked discipline, morale, and training. Hence it was not difficult for the Russians to rout and destroy them at Maçin, southwest of Ibrail (April 4, 1791), again leaving the empire defenseless. Selim therefore was forced to accept Triple Alliance mediation, resulting in a peace agreement with Russia signed at Jassy (January 8, 1792). The Treaty of Küçük Kaynarca was the basis for the new agreement, as amended by the treaty of 1784, with Ottoman acknowledgment of the Russian annexation of the Crimea as well as its suzerainty over Georgia. Catherine agreed to evacuate the Principalities and the major ports at the mouth of the Danube, but Selim accepted the Dniester as the new boundary between the two empires. Russia obtained the port of Oczakov as well as the land between the Bug and the Dniester, on which the port of Odessa soon would be built as the new center of Russian naval power on the Black Sea. Russia thus was left in position to dominate the Principalities as well as the Black Sea. But the European concert at least had rescued the Ottomans from more severe losses in Serbia and Bosnia. The empire still survived. Thus Selim was given an opportunity to reform and revive what was left before it was too late.

The Turning Point in Ottoman Reform: The New Order of Selim III, 1789–1807

Selim had been introduced to traditional reform by his father, Mustafa III, who allowed him to witness the new artillery and musket corps training under Baron de Tott and others. Following the accession of his uncle he had been confined to the palace, but he continued to learn of the world around him through his slaves and friends as well as his Venetian doctor, who was in the pay of both the French and the Austrian embassies. Through these influences he had come to see the need for reform, but his concept was mainly traditionalistic. As far as he was concerned, the empire was in difficulty because the traditional institutions were not being operated properly. Abuses and inefficiency had to be ended and discipline and service restored. Only when military necessity required the acceptance of modern weapons and techniques could new military units be created to use them, but they had to be isolated from the old so that the equilibrium of Ottoman society would not be upset.

Even while he was a prince incarcerated in the palace, Selim corresponded with Louis XVI, the model of the enlightened monarch he hoped to be, asking for French help in rebuilding the Ottoman army and regaining the territories previously lost to Russia. Following his accession, for three years he was prevented from instituting any significant reforms by the need to prosecute a difficult war. But he did raise many of his childhood companions to positions of importance, building a new cadre of reforming administrators and soldiers waiting only for peace to put their ideas into practice. There were others who joined the reform movement on the sultan's initiative and prepared a series of reports on the condition of the empire and what should be done to save it. In many cases the scope of the reports went far beyond what the sultan intended. Many of them advised that reform include not just military modernization but also social and economic changes, that it be devised in consultation with the people whom it would affect, not only the Ruling Class, and that efforts be made to develop the empire's economic base to provide the resources needed for the other reforms. Most of the reports did, however, concentrate on the military, emphasizing that the Janissaries and other corps be restored to their original forms and operation, that they be given modern weapons and techniques to enable them to defeat the armies of Europe, and that new corps be created to fill specfic needs. A few reports went on to express the more modern idea of reform that was not, in fact, to be implemented for another half-century, namely, that the older military institutions could not possibly be reformed and therefore had to be abolished and replaced by new ones.[111]

Military Reforms

As soon as the peace of Jassy permitted, Selim and his reform cadre were able to proceed with the task of carrying out those proposals they chose to accept. While all aspects of Ottoman life were in some way affected, the emphasis was, indeed, on the military, for it was there that the war had made the decay most apparent and the cure most essential. Decrees were issued to reform all the existing military corps, including the Janissaries. The basic principle of organizational reform was the separation of the administrative and military functions in each corps, with a separate supervisor (*nazır*) being appointed to handle the former, while the formerly all-powerful commanders, the *ağa*s, were left with military duties. New organizations and hierarchies were established to assure the maximum efficiency of each corps. Officers and men were subjected to examinations, and those found wanting in ability, efficiency, or honesty were replaced. Efforts were made to assure that appointments were made only according to ability, but promotions were generally made by seniority to lessen the effect of influence and bribery. Pools of apprentice soldiers were created, usually from children of existing officers and soldiers but also from irregulars who performed well in battle, providing a source of replacements when vacancies occurred at the bottom. The barracks of the corps were enlarged and modernized. All members were required to drill regularly. Wages were raised and paid monthly, and care was taken to ensure that only those who fulfilled their duties were paid.

In addition to the general reforms applied to all the corps, there also were specific ones for the special needs of each. In the case of the feudal *Sipahis*, inspection boards were set up locally to weed out inactive or incapable members, with pools of apprentices established in each district to help them in peace and war and to provide replacements as needed. Timar holders were allowed to will their fiefs to the ablest of their sons, but only if the latter could perform their duties. Otherwise, they joined their younger brothers in the corps of apprentices, waiting until they became old and experienced enough and until vacancies were available. To end the old system that caused the Ottoman army to disband each winter so that the timar holders could return to exploit their holdings, a new rotational system was devised: One of each 10 *Sipahis* from the same district was sent home to administer the holdings of the others, while the rest stayed in the field, at advanced bases along the frontiers, or in the service of the provincial governors. Finally, the old practice of awarding fiefs to palace favorites was abandoned so that they would be held only by fighting men.

The reforms applied to the other corps were even more radical. The Janissary rolls were halved, to about 30,000 men, to improve their ability and discipline. The provincial governors were ordered to train youths in their own entourages to provide replacements as needed. Sons of members were allowed to enter the corps only if they had ability. Efforts were made to issue new European-type rifles and ammunition to the Janissaries, with each regiment being given eight trained riflemen to provide leadership and instruction in their use. To conciliate the Janissaries in the face of such changes, their arrears were paid and salaries increased and paid on time. Their barracks were rebuilt and enlarged, and their officers were won over with special gifts and tax farms.

The efforts to reform the *Sipahi*s and Janissaries were not overly successful, as might be imagined. The inspectors sent to the provinces tended to rely on information provided by the corps officers, who managed to conceal most of the abuses. While some fiefs were in fact confiscated, most remained in the hands of their former owners, and the *Sipahi* force remained ineffective. All efforts to reduce the size of both forces were bitterly opposed, so that by the end of Selim's reign they remained in about the same low state as they had been when he first came to power.

Reforms were far more successful in the older Artillery (*Topçu*), Mortar (*Humbaracı*), Mine-Laying (*Lağımcı*), and Cannon-Wagon (*Top Arabacı*) corps, already influenced by the work of de Tott and others. They were completely reorganized and manned and put under the command of able young Ottoman officers trained by de Tott, assisted by French advisers brought in after 1794. Discipline was restored; the men were not allowed to marry and had to remain in their barracks; and high wages were provided to attract the best youths into their service. By the end of Selim's reign these corps were by far the most efficient part of the traditional army.

But with the Janissaries and *Sipahi*s resisting reform, the main fighting forces of the empire remained as ill prepared for modern warfare as before. Selim finally developed an entirely new infantry force to supplement them, the *Nizam-ı Cedit* or "New Order," created as an entirely separate institution so as not to alarm or annoy the older corps more than necessary. The corps was organized, trained, and clothed in the European manner, with European tactics, discipline, and weapons applied under the direction of experts brought not only from France but also from England and Germany. To finance the corps, an independent treasury was created, the *Irad-ı Cedit*, or "New Revenue," with funds from new sources like lands brought into cultivation since the old cadastres were compiled, fiefs seized for the treasury from incompetent or absent holders, and the like. Here again, the new institution was created to supply revenues not previously collected by the treasury, leaving the latter intact and unreformed.

Soldiers for the new corps came mainly from among Turkish peasant boys from Anatolia sent by the provincial governors and notables. Barracks were provided for it outside Istanbul, at Levend Çiftlik, overlooking the Bosporus, to remove it from the sight of the older corps as much as possible (September 1794). A second regiment based on Üsküdar was created later, during the French expedition to Egypt (November 1799), and a third soon afterward back at Levend Çiftlik, so that the corps expanded from 2,536 men and 27 officers in May 1797 to 9,263 men, still with 27 officers, in July 1801. Beginning in 1802 a system of conscription was introduced in Anatolia. Each official and notable was required to send men to Istanbul for training, after which many were returned to form local trained militias. As a result of these efforts, at the end of 1806 the new corps had 22,685 men and 1,590 officers, approximately one-half of these in Anatolia and the remainder in Istanbul. Efforts to establish a similar system in the Balkans were frustrated, however, by the strong opposition of the local notables, who, as we shall see, were by this time much more powerful than those in Anatolia. By the end of Selim's reign, then, the *Nizam-ı Cedit* army had a large number of men armed with new weapons and trained and commanded by European officers, and they were praised for their efficiency and good bearing by almost all the Europeans who saw them. Together with the reformed Artillery corps it should have provided the sultan with an effective military force, able to meet the enemy on equal terms.[112]

Technical Reforms

Technical reforms were introduced into the empire to provide the sultan's armies with modern weapons. The cannon foundries and rifle works were modernized by officers brought from Great Britain and France, although rivalries among the foreign contingents, incompetence of many of their members, and political intrigues within the Ottoman army and palace ultimately frustrated much of their work.

More useful and long lasting were the technical schools established to train young Ottomans in the sciences and techniques of the West. The only technical schools that survived to the Peace of Jassy were Gazi Hasan's Naval Engineering School and the small *Mühendishane-i Sultani* (Engineering School of the Sultan), established during the war by Selim to train some of his young servants and companions in the elements of arithmetic and geometry so that they could advance to the higher technical schools that he intended to open once the war was over. After 1792, however, Selim was very slow in expanding these schools because he concentrated on the reform of the army and particularly the *Nizam-ı Cedit*. It was only in 1795 that he established the new *Mühendishane-i Berri-i Hümayun* (Land Engineering School) out of the defunct artillery school as a parallel to the Navy Engineering School, to train army officers in the theoretical and practical aspects of artillery, fortification, mine laying, and engineering. All graduates who did not stay to teach or assist were assured of positions as officers in the Cannon, Mortar, and Mine-Laying corps, and all the officers of these corps, in turn, were required to go to the school at regular intervals for refresher courses. As far as can be made out, none of its foreign teachers or Turkish graduates were allowed to serve with the Janissaries, but they did take most of the posts of the *Nizam-ı Cedit* army and the Artillery and associated corps, providing a nucleus of well-trained, modern, and reforming officers to help Selim and his successors in their efforts.

Naval Reforms

As we have seen, Gazi Hasan was able to build 22 modern ships of the line by Selim's accession, though he was much less successful in creating a cadre of able officers and men. Nevertheless, he did provide the plan and cadre for further reforms undertaken by Selim's boyhood companion Küçük Hüseyin Paşa, who was grand admiral through most of the sultan's reign (March 11, 1792–January 7, 1803). Laws were passed and enforced to attract and retain able officers, with promotions based on ability rather than bribery and a hierarchy of promotion maintained to assure that the best men would rise to the top. Inspectors were sent out to prevent the captains from diverting the food, equipment, and money assigned to their ships to their own profit. The navy took over the responsibility for feeding its men aboard ship in place of the old system by which groups of men maintained and used their own kitchens. To man the fleet a kind of conscription was restored to the Aegean coastal provinces, which traditionally had contributed men for the navy, and high salaries, regular training, and a system of discipline and control were adopted to encourage the development of sailors into a professional and permanent force. The Imperial Naval Arsenal (*Tersane*) was enlarged under the direction of French naval architects. New provincial arsenals were opened. The old ships in the fleet were modernized, and a large number of modern ships were built according to the latest standards of naval architecture. The naval school at Hasköy was enlarged and modernized; lessons in geometry and arithmetic were now accompanied by more practical subjects in seamanship and navigation; and a separate division was created to provide training in naval architecture geography, and cartography.

The age-old struggle for power between the grand admiral and the chief of the Arsenal was ended with a reorganization that replaced the latter with a superintendent of naval affairs (*umur-u bahriye nazırı*) in charge of an Admiralty department with its own treasury (*Tersane Hazinesi*). Under him separate military and administrative departments were organized, with the grand admiral in charge of naval organization, arrangement, equipment, training, and military command as well as the assignment, promotion, and demotion of men and the maintenance and administration of ships; the director of the Naval Treasury was responsible for all matters regarding provisions, supplies, and weapons of the arsenal and fleet. A separate naval medical service was established, with a medical school to train doctors, and doctors and surgeons were assigned to care for the men of each ship. European medical books were translated into Turkish by members of the staff; instruments and books were purchased from Europe; and each of the medical students was required to gain practical experience by serving periodically in the public hospital of Istanbul as well as the hospital of the arsenal, which was built in an isolated section so as to be useful for the treatment of infectious diseases, particularly the plague. Thus the idea of quarantine was introduced into an empire that till then had accepted the plague's ravages without any organized effort to resist. Thus as part of the process by which the navy was modernized, the empire was given its first regular state medical service, again demonstrating how closely modern reform was associated with the military.[113]

Administrative, Economic, and Social Reforms

Selim was a true heir of the eighteenth-century Ottoman reformers in devoting most of his attention and energy to the military. Neither he nor his advisers understood how much Europe's technological reforms were products of the social, economic, and political revolutions that had been going on since the Reformation. There were no general efforts at governmental, economic, or social modernization, only piecemeal attempts to meet the old problems in the old ways. Much of the financial troubles had come from the treasury's traditional systems, with specified revenues assigned to particular expenditures and promissory notes issued to care for additional obligations, to be paid from the first available revenues. There was no overall budget, and the result was periodic financial chaos. Government officials always had been relatively independent in their posts and were allowed to spend as much as they wanted without either administrative or financial supervision. Selim responded to the problem, not by trying to establish a budgetary system but simply by making the old system work, reorganizing the scribal service into an expanded administrative department of the grand vezir, called *Bab-ı Âsafi*, subjecting the scribes to new standards of honesty and efficiency, and dismissing those unable or unwilling to comply. Nepotism and bribery were ended; scribes were appointed and promoted once again according to ability; and the *reis ul-küttap*, now administrative assistant to the grand vezir, was put in charge of making the system work. Selim's only other important administrative reforms involved a reduction of the number of Ottomans holding the rank of vezir to no more than the number of positions available for persons of that rank – so as not to leave any of them unemployed and subject to the political intrigues of the time – and an effort to reduce the appointment gifts paid to the sultan by Ottomans appointed to administrative positions in the hope that they in turn would no longer be forced to demand and accept bribes and extralegal taxes to recoup the expense of obtaining and maintaining their positions.

Selim's social and economic reforms were not innovative, either. The urban and rural problems were met with regulations attempting to suppress their most serious results. Peasants who fled from the countryside were compelled to return to their homes, whether or not there were land and jobs waiting for them there. Decrees were issued closing hotels, taverns, and coffeehouses to prevent transients from finding lodging and food in the cities, thus forcing them to leave, and also to eliminate "centers of dissension," as though closing meeting places would solve the causes of the discontent. Increased tension among different religious and economic groups, largely consequent on the economic difficulties of the time, were "solved" with regulations requiring persons to wear only the traditional clothing allowed them according to their class and rank, assuming that if everyone knew the position and place of every other person, there would be fewer conflicts. And to get the money needed to pay the soldiers and bureaucrats as well as the foreign advisers, Selim resorted to the traditionally disastrous methods of debasing the coinage, confiscating the property of wealthy merchants, and increasing taxes. His most important economic successes came in his efforts to regulate the provision of grain, coffee, and other food to the cities, thus partly counteracting the worst effects of overpopulation and inflation, though these continued to be endemic to the end of his reign.

Window to the West

Although most of Selim's reforms were only partly successful, they were opening wedges and guides for his successors. Perhaps even more influential in the long run was the concurrent introduction of an awareness of the West among the mass of Ottomans, continuing the process begun in the Tulip Period of breaking down the old iron curtain. Now the old isolation was pierced, though not entirely destroyed, and into the world of the Ottomans flowed not only the military and technical achievements of Europe but also many of the ideas that had made them possible. To be sure, in an introspective society based on a religion that provided a close-fitting cloak of protection for the traditions of the past, such an opening could only have a slight effect. Yet it did lay the groundwork for the more widespread and significant penetration that followed in later decades when the real foundations of modern Turkey were laid.

The channels through which knowledge of the West and its ways penetrated the empire were many and varied, and different levels of Ottoman society were affected in different ways. By far most important was the process by which military techniques and weapons were introduced to young Ottomans in the new corps and schools by European officers and technicians. The latter comprised the first Western social group ever thrust into Ottoman society without special arrangements to limit their contact with Ottomans. And while they were providing only technical instruction, inevitably young Ottomans under their tutelage were exposed to European patterns of thought and behavior. These technical advisers also influenced a wider segment of Ottoman society. Unlike the European advisers who had preceded them, they were not isolated. They roamed openly in the streets. They gave parties to which some Ottomans were invited, thus enabling the latter to observe their homes and ways of life. Western merchants, technicians, and soldiers met the subjects of the sultan in the streets, bazaars, and coffeehouses of the capital. Selim himself is said to have invited European actors to perform in his palace, attempted imitations of Western music and poetry, and imported Western paintings with human representations for his personal use.

Europeans of all nationalities were instrumental in introducing new ways, but the French had a special impact. The Ottoman Empire at this time was one of the few neutral places left in Europe. Therefore, it provided a unique place where friend and foe of the French Revolution could dwell in uncomfortable proximity, attempting to gain Ottoman support. So it was that the supporters of the revolution went into the coffeehouses and distributed Turkish and French-language pamphlets speaking of the rights of man and of liberty, equality and fraternity, with opposing messages being spread with equal vigor with the support of the ambassadors of France's enemies in Europe. It is difficult to assess the extent to which these ideas were really understood by the Ottomans. Translators of both sides complained that Ottoman Turkish lacked words in which they could express either the new revolutionary ideas or their refutations. The fact that Selim at times supported revolutionary France certainly must indicate that he did not understand the implications of its message for royalty or the Ottoman social system. Nevertheless, this was another means of contact, another crack in the old isolation. By the end of his reign, there were, indeed, enough Ottomans who understood the revolution's real significance to criticize it vigorously as being inimical to the Ottoman system.

Other influences came through Ottoman representatives stationed permanently in the great capitals of Europe for the first time and in particular in the reports they were encouraged to provide about all aspects of European civilization. For the most part the same factors that limited the effectiveness of Europeans in Istanbul also limited Selim's representatives abroad. They were Ottomans brought up in the Ottoman tradition and limited by Ottoman attitudes. As few were trained in Western languages or the new sciences being taught in the military schools, they really did not understand what they saw. The reports that did get through were read by only a handful of Ottomans in the palace, and it is questionable how much the limited kind of information they contained was understood by their readers.

It is difficult, then, to assess the extent to which these Western influences and ideas took root among the Ottomans of Selim's time. Though the sultan and those around him tried to imitate Europe in some respects, this should not be overstressed. All Selim's reforms, even the *Nizam-ı Cedit,* followed patterns of reform developed prior to the establishment of sustained and regular contacts with Europe. They were traditional Ottoman responses to the needs of the time. The relative ease with which Selim was deposed and his reforms abolished in 1807 would seem to indicate that he lacked any deep-seated support among his followers. A really modern school of literature failed to appear at this time, suggesting that the contacts at best merely opened the way for understanding, that European ideas took no root at this time, but only left the seeds for a real flowering that came later.[114]

Disintegration of the Empire, 1792–1798

Limited as they were, Selim's reforms were further hindered by serious internal and foreign problems, which occupied much of his attention. For one thing, the notables of Anatolia and the Arab world were now joined by even more powerful counterparts in the European provinces, costing the central government heavily in revenue and prestige and forcing the sultan to send what armies he had in expeditions against them. The tremendous demands of the war of 1787–1792 had in fact forced the government to rely more and more on these notables for men and armies, in return granting them official positions that enabled them to strengthen and extend their power. Thus once the war was over, it was virtually impossible for the sultan to gain any significant control over them.

Ali Paşa of Janina now controlled most of central and southern Albania and northern Greece from Elbasan to the Gulf of Corinth, with his expansion limited only by the efforts of the Venetians based in the Ionian Islands to raise revolts against him as well as the sultan and by efforts of the Ottoman governors to play him off against the Buşatlıs of northern Albania. Each at times served the sultan against other notables and brigands in the Balkans, but in the end these expeditions only increased the money and men supporting their virtually independent rule. Pasvanoğlu Osman Paşa also rose around Vidin to be one of the most powerful notables of the time, spreading his direct rule through much of northwestern Bulgaria, raiding widely into Serbia and Wallachia, and attracting into his service thousands of bandits as well as Janissaries and other notables who opposed Selim's reform in fear of its consequences. Unlike Ali Paşa of Janina and the other notables, Pasvanoğlu was usually in open revolt against the sultan, refusing to pay taxes or recognize the authority of the latter's governors. It was in reaction largely to him that Selim tried to conciliate the Serbs following the Peace of Sistova, not punishing those who had helped the Austrians and also attempting to end Janissary misrule in the province and establish a regime of security, tolerance, and justice, perhaps as a model for subsequent reforms elsewhere in the empire. Pasvanoğlu led the opposition to these reforms, receiving the Belgrade Janissaries as refugees and cooperating with their counterparts in Bosnia to prevent the spread of those measures that would restrict their ability to oppress the population. For a time the governor of Rumeli, Hakkı Paşa (1796–1798), was able to beat Pasvanoğlu and his friends and restore order and security in much of Rumeli. But his efforts were frustrated by the political opponents of reform in Istanbul as well as by the beginning of the new war with France in 1798, which forced Selim to make peace with the notables and give them almost unlimited power to secure their military support against the empire's enemies.[115]

European Diplomatic Alignments, 1792–1798

Selim benefited from six years of peace with Europe following the Peace of Jassy, with the powers being diverted by the second and third partitions of Poland (in 1793 and 1795 respectively) and by the beginning of the French Revolution. The Ottoman attitude toward the revolution was a curious combination of self-interest and ignorance of European conditions. Selim was disturbed by the death of the monarch whom he considered to be a friend and model, but he and his colleagues did not dread the ideals of the revolution, since they did not understand them. Selim in fact welcomed the revolution because of the very conflicts it spawned. He sympathized with France in its war with his enemies, Russia and Austria, but he preferred to stand aside, avoiding alignment with either side and playing off the ambitions of both to secure their continued help for his reforms. Britain subordinated its interests in the Middle East at this time to those of Russia to assure its cooperation against France in Europe, leaving the Russians free to work to disrupt the Ottoman Empire, in the Balkans in particular, and to agitate for a removal of the French advisers from Istanbul. Ottoman relations with Austria were cool as a result of troubles along the borders, but since the emperor was too busy with France to engage in open hostilities, raid and counterraid did not lead to war.

But in October 1797 Habsburg Austria was forced to sign a separate peace with

France at Campo Formio, by which the emperor abandoned his allies and recognized French conquests in western Europe in return for territorial acquisitions in the east. The Republic of Venice was brought to an end, with its territories divided to satisfy the ambitions of both. Austria obtained the Istrian Peninsula and Dalmatia, while Franc got the Ionian Islands as well as the Albanian ports of Parga, Preveze, and Butrinto, thus making the latter an immediate neighbor of the Ottomans for the first time. Bonaparte immediately denied having ambitions in Ottoman territory, but Selim's attitude toward France and its adversaries necessarily changed. This change was helped by Catherine's death (November 1796), which dissipated much of the antagonism toward Russia left by her wars. Her son and successor, Czar Paul, abandoned the aggressive attitude of the past and began to press for a rapprochement with the Porte based on mutual advantage, hoping to gain the right for his warships to use the Straits to counter the French advances into the Adriatic and eastern Mediterranean. When reports came of French agents active in the Balkans, Selim began negotiations for a new alliance with Russia and Britain, but he still held back from consummating the arrangement until he was forced to do it by the news of the French invasion of Egypt.

The French Expedition to Egypt and the War of the Triple Alliance

Selim's fears were in fact well founded. Bonaparte had abandoned any hope of the sultan's holding together his empire and now merely wanted to ensure that France could get its share. At one point he hoped to set Ali Paşa on the Ottoman throne; but when he finally decided that the latter was too attached to Britain, he attempted to work through Pasvanoğlu, who would be set up as sultan under French protection and control. Bonaparte also planned to strike back at Britain by getting control of Egypt, which could then be used as a base for further penetration of the Levant and also for an expedition to drive the British from India as well. After evading a British fleet under Lord Nelson sent to watch his preparations in Toulon, Bonaparte led his expedition onto the shores of Alexandria (July 1, 1798), thus triggering a fundamental alteration in the diplomatic alignments of the Ottoman Empire.

The French expedition to Egypt has been the subject of numerous detailed studies and need only be summarized here. The original landings were not opposed by the Mamluks, who had no idea of what was going on in Europe and in any case lacked the modern weapons needed to face the French on equal terms. Most of them fled to Upper Egypt without offering any resistance, while those who stayed to fight were routed at Rahmaniye (July 13) and again at the Battle of Giza (July 21). Cairo was occupied by the French without resistance (July 25), and Bonaparte consolidated his control of the Delta within a short time. But he was unable to catch and destroy the Mamluks before they could flee up the Nile; thus they organized a new resistance in the south, largely in cooperation with the major bedouin tribes of the area. As a result, while several French expeditions reached Aswan, Bonaparte never gained firm control of Upper Egypt, nor could he conquer its Red Sea littoral. His effort to consolidate his flanks by conquering Syria culminated in a startling failure to take Acre, competently defended by Ahmet Cezzar Paşa with the help of Ottoman and British ships and a large contingent of *Nizam-ı Cedit* soldiers sent from Istanbul (March 23–May 21, 1799). Thus cut off from the East, Bonaparte was isolated from France by Nelson's destruction of his fleet off Abukir (August 1, 1798). With the expedition doomed to slow strangulation, Bonaparte and his chief aides abandoned it in search of greater glory in France (August 22, 1798), leaving its final liquidation to subordinates. His immediate successor, General Kléber, made an evacuation agreement with the grand vezir at al-Ariş (January 24, 1800), but this was overturned by Britain and Russia, which preferred to save Egypt for a grateful sultan through their own efforts. Though the French subsequently routed the Ottoman army at Heliopolis (March 20, 1800) and managed to gain control of Upper Egypt by agreement with the Mamluk leader Murat Bey, Kléber was assassinated (June 14, 1800), and his successor, Abdullah Jacques Menou, who converted to Islam, attempted to establish a permanent French colony in the country. In the end, however, a combined Ottoman-British expeditionary force obtained their surrender and evacuation (August 31, 1801).

What did the French accomplish during their short stay in Egypt? Their policy was a curious combination of timid conservatism and radical innovation and change, of professed respect for Muslim tradition and complete disregard of it in practice. Bonaparte and his successors declared time and again that the laws and customs of the Egyptians had to be respected. Yet whenever the latter conflicted with the basic need to exploit Egypt to support the French expeditionary force, they were abandoned. Basically, the French revolutionized both government and society in Egypt by removing its old ruling class and substituting French and native officials for the Ottomans and Mamluks. For the first time since the sixteenth century Egyptians were called on to participate directly in their own rule as assistants to the French military officers. A few native mercantile and religious leaders also were brought into the advisory councils, which served to mediate between the occupiers and the native population. While at first the Ottoman tax system was preserved, in the end its inefficiencies, combined with the flight of the officials who knew how to operate it, led Bonaparte to substitute a new direct tax system, with French methods of assessment and collection replacing those previously used. Removal of obsolete institutions thus left Egypt in a position to move ahead far more rapidly and with far more experience than was the case with other parts of the Ottoman Empire.

The most immediate result of the expedition was the disruption of Ottoman-French relations and Selim's signing of an alliance with France's enemies, Britain and Russia, in September 1798. This was accompanied by the imprisonment of the pro-French ministers in the council and the confiscation of French commercial property around the empire, thus depriving France of its Middle Eastern position built over the centuries. Russia's Black Sea fleet was allowed to pass through the Straits, and it joined the Ottoman fleet for joint campaigns against the French in the Adriatic. Within a short time the latter were driven from the Ionian Islands, with the less-than-willing cooperation of Ali Paşa of Janina, who wanted to displace the French himself (November 1798). Success, however, led to conflicts among the allies, with the Ottomans resisting Russian desires to establish themselves in the Adriatic and particularly in the Ionian Islands. In the end an Ottoman-Russian convention (March 21, 1800) organized the latter into the new Septinsular Republic, which was made independent under Ottoman suzerainty, with protection provided jointly by Ottoman and Russian garrisons. The coastal ports were returned to direct Ottoman rule but under a special administration to guarantee local rights and protect them from the claims of Ali Paşa, with local officials taken from the native Christian population. In compensation Ali was made governor of Rumelia, leaving him in a position to expand his power in other directions as soon as possible.

The Conclusion of Peace

The end of the French occupation of Ottoman territories in Egypt and the Adriatic opened the way for a renewal of the old alignments, with the British and Russians desperately intervening in an effort to prevent an Ottoman-French peace that might harm their interests. The main obstacle to peace came from the continued maintenance in Egypt of the British troops that had helped the Ottomans drive the French out and were trying to support one Mamluk faction in the hope of securing British influence in a future Mamluk state. The Ottoman forces, soon to be led by Muhammad Ali, were struggling to restore direct Ottoman rule as it had existed before the rise of the Mamluks. Within the Ottoman court Grand Admiral Küçük Hüseyin led a faction that, alienated from Britain by its actions in Egypt, wanted peace and alliance with France against both Russia and England. On the other hand, Grand Vezir Yusuf Ziya Paşa led those who felt that British friendship had to be preserved as a bulwark against both Russian and French ambitions.

Selim played the factions off as usual to retain his own power and freedom of action. However much he wanted French friendship, he hesitated to be dragged into war through an open alliance until continued British occupation of Egypt and the strong agitation of French agents in Istanbul led to the signature of the Peace of Amiens (June 25, 1802), which provided for peace and friendship between France and the Ottomans as well as mutual assistance in case of war. All prewar treaties and Capitulations agreements were renewed, French properties restored, and the French predominance in the Levant reestablished. Thus the diplomatic revolution caused by the French occupation of Ottoman territories was, indeed, reversed soon after the evacuation was accomplished. Selim regained his lost territories and escaped from involvement in the wars of Europe. Once again the empire had a short respite in which reform might be undertaken, with the setbacks experienced during the war providing a new impetus for change.

Further Internal Disintegration, 1799–1806

Peace, however, was illusory indeed, as Selim became embroiled in a series of internal and foreign entanglements. The major notables in western and central Anatolia supported and helped the *Nizam-ı Cedit,* using its men to develop their own armies and maintain order in their areas. But some notables in the east – particularly the Canikli family, now led by Tayyar Paşa – succumbed to the lure of Russian arms and money and established independent regimes between Trabzon and Bursa, thus leaving much of Anatolia detached from the influence and the tax collectors of Istanbul. In the Arab provinces the local notables were more powerful than before the war, but the sultan's suzerainty continued to be recognized everywhere except in Arabia, where the Wahhabis threw off all pretense of loyalty and mounted a series of raids against the Holy Cities and into Iraq, seriously threatening the sultan's claim to be protector of Islam. In Egypt the uneasy balance among Ottoman, Mamluk, and British forces was broken by the evacuation of the latter (March 14, 1803) to restore good relations with the Porte, with the subsequent rise of the commander of the Ottoman forces, Muhammad Ali, to dominate the country, for the moment assuring recognition of the sultan's suzerainty and the payment of tribute. In Syria the Wahhabi menace led Selim to appoint Ahmet Cezzar Paşa, the victor of Acre, as governor of Damascus (October 1803), leading to the creation of a major Mamluk state with considerable potential for trouble. But his death (April 23, 1804) precipitated struggles for power that enabled the sultan to restore his authority.

Much of the reason for Selim's failure to take more decisive action against the separatist movements in Anatolia and the Arab provinces lay in his preoccupation with superficially similar but actually far more dangerous threats in the Balkans. Ali

Paşa of Janina used the War of the Triple Alliance to build an empire of major proportions stretching from northern Albania to the Gulf of Corinth and from Ohrid to the Adriatic, with a lavish capital and court, direct diplomatic relations with the powers of Europe, and foreign experts training his soldiers in the European style. Pasvanoğlu also extended his power from western Bulgaria into Serbia and the Principalities. Tirsiniklioğlu Ismail Ağa of Silistria and Rusçuk and his lieutenant and (after 1806) successor, Bayraktar Mustafa Paşa, occupied eastern Bulgaria, advanced through the Balkan Mountains, and gained considerable influence over Thrace. The only governor able to control the notables, Hakkı Mehmet Paşa, was in the end undermined by the Istanbul politicians, many of whom were in the pay of the notables. Finally, Janissary misrule in Serbia led the local chiefs to unite behind one of their number, Kara George. At first the movement supported the sultan's suzerainty against his rebellious subordinates, but it was not long before it developed into a full-scale Serbian revolution against Ottoman rule (1803–1805).

The Eastern Question, 1802–1807

The most salient characteristic of Ottoman diplomacy in this period was a reversal of the alliances molded by Bonaparte's invasion of Egypt and a return to the more traditional bonds forged by longstanding considerations of national self-interest, particularly after Britain and France renewed their war (May 1803) and Russia and Austria joined the former in the Third Coalition. French agents in turn attempted not only to gain Ottoman support but also to spread French influence among the sultan's Catholic subjects and to spread French influence from the Levant into Danubian Europe. Russia now had considerable naval power in the eastern Mediterranean as a result of its hard-won right to send ships through the Straits and its continued protectorate over the Ionian Islands. While it avoided involvement in the Franco-British war at first, it tried to use the situation to advance its position in the Ottoman Empire, encouraging revolt among the sultan's Balkan subjects.

Aware of the danger posed by Russian expansion in the Middle East, but unable to act openly against Russia because of the need for Russian support against France in Europe, Britain worked to frustrate Russian ambitions while encouraging Selim to strengthen his empire internally. Selim disliked having to accept Russian protection and advice, since he was aware of the czar's ambitions and activities in the Balkans. Yet he avoided an open break, since he felt this would mean a rupture with Britain, which seemed to be the principal bulwark against both French and Russian ambitions. He worked, rather, to keep a delicate balance among these interests, avoiding extreme actions that might lead to open warfare.

It was very difficult, however, to avoid the Russian embrace. A new agreement in 1802 strengthened the czar's position in the Principalities and gave him the right to intervene in Istanbul on their behalf, resulting in the appointment of Russophile princes in both Wallachia and Moldavia in 1803. The real test came in 1804 when Selim was faced with the issue of whether or not to accept Bonaparte's declaration of himself as emperor. When Selim finally refused to do so because of British and Austrian influence, Bonaparte broke relations (December 22, 1805), forcing the sultan to accept a new alliance with Russia that further strengthened the czar's influence in his dominions. Selim agreed to cooperate in the war against France, facilitate the passage of Russian ships through the Straits, and allow the czar to intervene in Istanbul regarding Ottoman rule in Albania, thus opening a new field for Russian expansion. However, Bonaparte's victories over the armies of Austria and Russia at Ulm

(October 17, 1805) and Austerlitz (December 2, 1805) caused Selim to feel that the Triple Alliance was dead and that he would have to gain Bonaparte's favor if he was to preserve the Ottoman Empire. Hence he recognized Bonaparte as emperor (February 1806) and with French encouragement and support from Dalmatia planned to move against the Serbs from both the east and the west. The Russians responded by blockading the Adriatic coast of Dalmatia and sending help to the Serbs. But while the French sent help to the Ottomans by land from Venice, Selim still hesitated to join an open alliance, not only because of his fears of French ambitions in the Balkans but also because of the realization that Bonaparte lacked sufficient men and supplies in the area to provide significant assistance in any war with Russia. With the Serbs almost independent and under Russian protection, with the French in Dalmatia, with the Balkan notables in control of much of the countryside, and with the British, the French, and the Russians all combining professions of friendship with threats of attack, Selim was in a quandary.

The Edirne Incident

To add to the sultan's difficulties, a dangerous new threat rose within the empire during the summer of 1806, making it impossible for him to deal adequately with any of these problems. Early in 1805 Selim issued an order for the establishment of a new *Nizam-ı Cedit* corps in Edirne, with men secured by general conscription in the Balkans. Fearing that they would lose their best men and also that the Ottoman army might become strong enough to end their independence, the notables, led by Tirsinikli Ismail Paşa, revolted. Ismail entered into an alliance with the Istanbul conservatives led by Grand Vezir Hafız Ismail Ağa, who plotted to have Ismail march to Istanbul and eliminate both the sultan and the *Nizam-ı Cedit*. When a *Nizam-ı Cedit* force was sent to Edirne to recruit and train men (June 20, 1806), the notables boycotted it, refusing to provide any supplies and threatening to march to Istanbul unless it was withdrawn. As was to happen frequently in the last year of his reign, Selim caved in under pressure, ordered the *Nizam-ı Cedit* force to return to Istanbul, and dismissed the commanders who in fact had only been carrying out his orders. The sultan's capitulation further encouraged the notables. When Ismail Ağa died, Selim did not even intervene in the struggles for powers among his lieutenants, allowing one of them, Bayraktar Mustafa, to gain as much power as his master had. Furthermore, in reaction to the threats of the notables, Selim placed command of the *Nizam-ı Cedit* in the hands of its enemies, hoping thereby to satisfy the conservatives, but in the process depriving himself of the means of defending himself. Emboldened by these developments, his opponents proceeded to plan for the sultan's eventual overthrow.[116]

War with Russia and Britain

Further complicating the situation was a new war with Russia and its British ally, which was forced to abandon its neutral position regarding the Porte because of Russian nervousness about French advances in the Balkans. Still hoping to retain the Ottoman-Russian peace, the British ambassador demanded that the sultan end French influence in the empire and allow Russian warships to pass through the Straits to drive the French away (September 22, 1806). Selim at first gave in to these demands but recanted following Bonaparte's victory over the Prussians at Jena (October 14, 1806). This led the Russians to invade the Principalities and forced Britain to enter the war in support of its ally. The Russians occupied Moldavia quickly (December 1806), declaring that they had only come to protect their friend the sultan from Bonaparte and that they would leave as soon as Selim fulfilled his treaty obligations. The only effective Ottoman resistance came from Bayraktar Mustafa. He kept southern Moldavia and the Dobruca out of Russian hands with the help of Pasvanoğlu, whose independent position also was threatened by the Russian advance. But the notables were no match for the Russians in open conflict; the latter finally prevailed, going on to take Wallachia and Bessarabia in a six-week campaign.

Meanwhile, the British Mediterranean fleet sailed through the Dardanelles and anchored before Istanbul in the hope of forcing the sultan to give in to the Russian demands and thus be spared from further Russian advances. Largely under the influence of Bonaparte's agent in Istanbul, Horace Sebastiani, Selim only pretended to negotiate while secretly mobilizing the people and troops in Istanbul for a fight to the death against the British. When the defenses were ready, Selim openly rejected the allied proposals and requested a formal alliance with France as soon as possible. With Istanbul fortified and negotiations ended, the British fleet was in a dangerous position. Therefore, it sailed back into the Mediterranean before the Ottomans could blockade it at the Dardanelles and landed in Egypt in a final effort to secure rule for the Mamluks under British influence (March 16, 1807). By this time, however, the Mamluks had been routed and destroyed by Muhammad Ali in the name of the sultan. Since the British lacked sufficient men and supplies to conquer Egypt, they quietly evacuated their forces by negotiation, with nothing accomplished except, perhaps, turning the country over to the man who soon was to develop his own rule and found his own dynasty (September 17, 1807).

Still under French influence, Selim continued to prepare campaigns to resist both the Russians and the Serbs in cooperation with Bayraktar and the other Balkan notables. With only the Montenegrins rising in support of the Russians, the Ottoman position seemed far more favorable than it had the previous winter.

The Fall of Selim III

At this point, however, a revolt in Istanbul overthrew Selim and upset the Ottoman defense preparations. Opposition to the sultan had been building for a long time. The Janissaries and others threatened by his reforms had been agitating since early in his reign. Opposition also came from the ulema, most of whom considered every innovation to be a violation of Islamic law and tradition. There were many other Ottomans, including some reformers, who now began to understand how destructive to the Ottoman system the new secularist ideas could be and who therefore demanded that the iron curtain be lowered again before it was too late. Selim's seizure of timars and efforts to reform the older corps only added to the resentment. And the reforms had been carried out without any rational financial policy, with the debasement of the currency and tremendous government expenditures resulting in a new inflation, leaving the people deeply resentful of the sultan and the reforms that they considered responsible for all their difficulties. Finally, Selim's policy of splitting the reformers into rival factions and playing them off against each other and the conservatives secured him momentary power but at the same time deprived supporters of reform of the political strength needed to back the sultan in a crisis.

The revolt broke out in late May 1807 when the Janissary auxiliaries (*yamaks*) guarding the Bosporus forts at Büyükdere, led by on Kabakçı Mustafa, assassinated a *Nizam-ı Cedit* officer who had attempted to get them to accept the new uniforms and training (May 25, 1807). At this point Selim might have stifled the revolt, but he was convinced by the conservatives among his advisers, led by the reactionary *Şeyhulislam*

Ataullah Efendi, that it would be better to negotiate and conciliate. So he ordered the *Nizam-ı Cedit* troops back to their barracks as a sign of good faith while sending negotiators to the rebels. This gave the conservatives in Istanbul time to use the incident to ignite a general conflagration. On May 27 the *yamak*s threw off the guise of negotiating and began marching along the Bosporus into Istanbul, joined as they went by thousands of Janissaries, ulema, religious students, and others who opposed the sultan. When they reached the palace, Selim tried to appease them by disbanding the *Nizam-ı Cedit,* sending some of his officials out to the vengeance of the crowd, and by appointing conservatives to key positions (May 28, 1807). But as happened so many times previously, surrender only emboldened the rebels to demand more and, eventually, to secure a *fetva* declaring Selim's reforms illegal violations of religion and tradition and authorizing his deposition. Selim quietly accepted his fate and retired to the palace "cage," while his cousin Mustafa IV ascended the throne as the candidate of the conservatives (May 29, 1807). Thus the reign of the most liberal of the traditionalistic reformers ended in ultimate defeat and failure, although, as we shall see, in the failure lay the elements by which more significant reforms were to be introduced later in the century.

Mustafa IV and the Ottoman Reaction

The new sultan was only a puppet in the hands of those who had put him on the throne. Within a short time, decrees were issued eliminating the *Nizam-ı Cedit* and all the institutions, schools, and other reforms associated with it. Stating that the reforms had been created by evil associates of the sultan to secure power and money for themselves, Mustafa declared that they had destroyed order, violated law and tradition, and caused all the anarchy and defeats that had torn the empire asunder during Selim's reign. Thereafter, the traditional laws and institutions would prevail. All the taxes introduced during Selim's reign were supplanted by those that had preceded them. The confiscated timars were given back; all those dismissed from the corps were given new memberships. *Nizam-ı Cedit* officers and men were hunted out and killed throughout the empire, and a general reign of terror followed against those who in any way had supported Selim and others, with the *yamak*s' in particular terrorizing the capital.

The new regime did not last very long, however. At first, the main rebel groups coordinated their efforts and tried to share the fruits of victory evenly. The Janissary elders promised to end their intervention in state affairs in return for assurances that the reforms, indeed, would be ended and their wages increased. To get the *yamak*s away from the capital Kabakçı Mustafa was made commander of the Bosporus forts in Rumeli; thus he and his men left, leaving power in the hands of the leading court figures and ulema who had planned and carried out the revolt. But it was not long before the latter were fighting among themselves, with the struggles between *Şeyhul-islam* Ataullah Efendi and the grand vezir leaving the government almost powerless to develop any kind of policy. Adding to the problems was the situation in the Balkans. As soon as Selim had been overthrown, the grand vezir and his main officers were killed by Janissary supporters of the revolt and the army fell into chaos. Bayraktar Mustafa then moved in to drive the rebels out and restore discipline in the army (June 8, 1807), expecting to be named grand vezir in return. When the rebels in Istanbul named one of their own to that post, however, Bayraktar Mustafa reacted violently. He left the army to its own devices and took his men back to Rusçuk, which he now made a center of opposition to the new regime, attracting all those who were fleeing from Istanbul.

The Treaty of Tilsit

Events in Europe, however, saved the Ottomans once again from the consequences of their own weakness. Bonaparte's victory over the Russians at Friedland (June 14, 1807) ended his need for an Ottoman alliance and led him to negotiate with Czar Alexander, who was ready to desert Britain not only because of the defeat but also because of food and supply problems in his own army. The resulting Treaty of Tilsit (July 7, 1807) involved French agreement to abandon the alliance with the Ottomans and to force them to make a settlement satisfactory to the czar, who in turn would mediate peace between France and Britain. But Bonaparte also agreed that if the negotiations failed, he then would join the war against the Porte and make arrangements to divide the sultan's dominions with his new ally. In return for this Russia recognized all his conquests, agreed to return the Principalities, and left the Ionian Islands and Cattaro to France. It was a major French victory, secured by sacrificing the Ottomans. The Russians had been kept out of the Balkans and the Straits. France had achieved control in the Adriatic regardless of what might happen in the negotiations that would follow.

At first the Ottomans were furious when they learned that Bonaparte had violated his treaty obligations by making peace without consulting or involving them. But on reflection Istanbul decided to accept the settlement, since Russia agreed to abandon its conquests in the Principalities and end its help to the Serbian rebels. Politically, Tilsit also would be a new blow at Selim, since it was he who had inaugurated the policy of relying on France only a short time before. The new regime, therefore, entered into negotiations with the Russians at Paris, under French mediation, with an armistice being signed at Slobosia (March 21, 1808). Within a month Russian troops would leave Moldavia and Wallachia, while the Ottomans would move south of the Danube with the right to leave garrisons only at Ismail, Ibrail, and Galatz to police the area. And the Russian ships in the Mediterranean would be allowed back through the Straits into the Black Sea.

But only the Ottomans lived up to the treaty's provisions. The Russians did temporarily sever connections with the Serbs, but they remained in Moldavia and refused to move without direct orders from the czar, which did not come, ostensibly on the pretext that the Ottomans were not maintaining security in the parts of Wallachia they were reoccupying. As soon as the czar returned to Petersburg from Tilsit, he refused to ratify the armistice at all on the pretext that his representative lacked the authority to sign it. Apparently relying on an oral promise from Bonaparte that he would not oppose continued Russian occupation of the Principalities, Alexander left his troops there to pressure the Porte to accept his conditions concerning Serbia, trade, and other matters in the peace negotiations then going on. The Ottomans, however, reacted by ending the negotiations; the war continued, albeit sporadically, for another five years, with both sides diverted by internal and foreign difficulties, until the Treaty of Bucharest (1812) finally ended it.

The Rusçuk Committee and the Deposition of Mustafa IV

On the Ottoman side the main diversion came from Selim's supporters, who wanted to put him back on the throne. Leadership of the movement was assumed by Bayraktar Mustafa Paşa, hardly a strong partisan of reform at first, but a strong advocate of autonomy for the notables against whoever was in power in Istanbul. His master, Ismail Ağa, had joined the other notables in opposing Selim's reforms as threats to their autonomy and power. But now it was the reactionaries who ruled in Istanbul and who once in power disliked the notables' insubordination as much as Selim had. It was natural therefore for Bayraktar Mustafa and his friends to provide asylum to Selim's supporters and to promote their efforts to regain power, thus forming what came to be known as the Rusçuk Committee. The committee members decided right at the beginning that the only way to regain power and restore Selim was to bring Bayraktar's army to Istanbul to overcome their enemies by force. But Selim was in the hands of his successor. Such an effort might well cost his life as well as that of Prince Mahmut, who was with him in the seclusion of the palace. The committee therefore followed a much more devious plan. Openly they broke up in disputes. Many members returned to Istanbul, declared their loyalty to the new sultan, and entered the service of a regime desperate for experienced administrators willing to serve it. Once this was accomplished, they used their positions to guard Selim from possible assassination while at the same time exploiting latent divisions between the Grand Vezir Çelebi Mustafa Paşa, the *şeyhulislam,* and Kabakçı Mustafa. There were, indeed, rivalries developing over how to share the fruits of victory. Added to them was the sultan's resentment over the domination of those who brought him to power. During the summer of 1808 the now secret members of the Rusçuk Committee convinced the sultan that Bayraktar Mustafa was a loyal subject whose only aim was to rescue him and the empire from the tyranny of the Janissaries and the *yamak*s. The grand vezir was equally satisfied that the triumph of the sultan would end the involvement of Kabakçı Mustafa and Ataullah Efendi in affairs of state and leave him supreme. So Bayraktar Mustafa was ordered to bring his army to Istanbul, on the pretext of congratulating the sultan on his accession, but in fact to act against his enemies (July 1, 1808).

Soon after Bayraktar entered Istanbul with his army (July 19), he sent agents who assassinated Kabakçı Mustafa, while the grand vezir cooperated by displacing Ataullah with his own man. Most of those who had played important roles in Selim's deposition and the destruction of the *Nizam-ı Cedit* were dismissed and exiled. Bayraktar Mustafa's men went around Istanbul putting down the Janissaries and *yamak*s, and within a week all opposition was ended (July 26, 1808). At this point both the sultan and the grand vezir felt that the army of Rusçuk had done its work and asked it to return to the Danube to protect the empire against a possible Russian attack while they turned to ruling at home.

It was at this point, when Bayraktar Mustafa presented various pretexts to retain both himself and his army in Istanbul, that the die was cast, that a movement that was ostensibly helping the sultan turned into a revolution against him. Çelebi Mustafa managed to learn of Bayraktar Mustafa's true intention, warned the sultan, and when the latter failed to act, sent agents to assassinate Selim as well as the Rusçuk Committee members (July 27). When Bayraktar Mustafa learned of this from his own spies, he moved his army before the palace, got the ulema to agree to restore Selim, and then demanded that Mustafa IV surrender. This was a fatal delay. It gave the cowering sultan time to send his own agents to kill both Selim and Mahmut so that he would be left safe as the sole surviving member of the Ottoman line. Selim was, indeed, caught in his apartment and killed after a short struggle. But Prince Mahmut managed to escape over the palace roofs to Bayraktar Mustafa, who immediately placed him on the throne as soon as he learned of Selim's fate (July 28, 1808). The rebels thus were successful, but now they had to work to restore the *Nizam-ı Cedit* through the person of an unknown and untried prince rather than the sultan whom they had championed. In fact, as we shall see, they had unwittingly set on the throne a far stronger man, the man who was, eventually, to be successful in ending their power and setting Ottoman reform on the road toward modernization that was to characterize it through the last century of the empire's existence. The era of traditionalistic reform was at an end, and radically new approaches were to follow in the effort to save the empire.

Notes to Chapter 7

1 Silahdar, II, 262, 270.
2 Silahdar, II, 270.
3 Silahdar, II, 243.
4 Silahdar, II, 245–246.
5 Raşit, II, 2; Silahdar, II, 281–295.
6 Silahdar, II, 296–303.
7 Silahdar, II, 329–340.
8 Silahdar, II, 354, 359, 364.
9 Raşit, II, 55, 58; Silahdar, II, 368.
10 Silahdar, II, 652–668; Uzunçarşılı, OT, III, 526.
11 Silahdar, II, 378.
12 Silahdar, II, 472; Raşit, II, 95.
13 Silahdar, II, 489; Raşit, II, 99.
14 Silahdar, II, 501–536; Raşit, II, 131.
15 Silahdar, II, 548.
16 Raşit, II, 161–162; Silahdar, II, 583–589; Uzunçarşılı, OT, III[1], 547–550.
17 Silahdar, II, 787.
18 Raşit, II, 169, 269.
19 Silahdar, II, 29, 31; Sabra Meservey, *Feyzullah Efendi: An Ottoman Şeyhulislam*, unpublished Ph.D. dissertation, Princeton University, 1966.
20 *Mecmua-i Muahedat*, III, 209–219; Noradounghian, I, 197–203; Rifat Abou El-Haj, "Ottoman Diplomacy at Karlowitz," JAOS, 87 (1967), 498–512.
21 Raşit, II, 377.
22 Raşit, II, 383, 393.
23 Raşit, II, 477.
24 BVA, Mühimme 108, p. 142; 112, p. 121; 141, p. 127.
25 Raşit, II, 587.
26 BVA, Mühimme 111, p. 617.
27 BVA, Mühimme 111, pp. 616, 682; 114, pp. 113, 172.
28 BVA, Mühimme 112, pp. 1–6, 16, 17, 442; Uzunçarşılı, *Osmanlı Devletinin Merkez ve Bahriye Teşkilatı*, Ankara, 1948, pp. 432–436.
29 Orhan Köprülü, "Hüseyin Paşa, Amca Zâde," IA, V, 646–650; Silahdar, II, 615, 619.
30 Raşit, II, 526.
31 Raşit, III, 295–296, 301; BVA, Name Defteri, VI, 174, 183.
32 Raşit, III, 303, 311–312, 314; BVA, Name Defteri, VI, 181; Mühimme 116, pp. 296, 328.
33 BVA, Mühimme 115, pp. 503, 508, 518, 535, 543, 551; 116, p. 261.
34 The Pruth campaign and peace have been brilliantly studied by Akdes Nimet Kurat, *Prut Seferi ve Barışı*, 2 vols., Ankara, 1951, summarized in "Der Pruthfeldzug und der Prutfrieden von 1711," *Jahrbücher für Geschichte Osteuropas,* 10 (1962) 13–66.
35 Raşit, III, 368–369, 374.
36 BVA, Mühimme 119, p. 139.
37 BVA, Mühimme 119, pp. 139, 247, 269; Raşit, IV, 3.
38 Raşit, IV, 8; BVA, Mühimme 120, p. 5; Uzunçarşılı, OT, IV/2, 97n; Kurat, *Prut Seferi*, II, 701.
39 BVA, Mühimme 119, p. 127; 122, p. 40.
40 Raşit, IV, 197, 199, 201, 204.
41 Raşit, IV, 195, 266, 268; Uzunçarşılı, OT, IV/1, 111–113.

42 BVA, Mühimme 116, pp. 73, 93, 96, 111, 114; Uzunçarşılı, OT, IV/1, pp. 132–136.
43 BVA, Mühimme 125, pp. 77–82; 126, pp. 189–190, 196, 216, 225, 249; 127, pp. 146–153, 179, 181, 184, 193.
44 Raşit, V, 21–26.
45 Raşit, V, 181–184.
46 Faik Reşit Unat, *Osmanlı Sefirleri ve Sefaretnâmeleri,* Ankara, 1968, pp. 52–70.
47 Report of the Venetian consul, tr. in Mary Lucille Shay, *The Ottoman Empire from 1720 to 1734 as Revealed in Despatches of the Venetian Baili,* Urbana, Ill., 1944, pp. 17–18.
48 Raşit, V, 443–446; Yirmisekiz Çelebi Mehmet, *Sefaretname,* Paris, 1872, pp. 28–29; *Nedim Divanı,* ed. Gölpnarli, p. 337; Aktepe, *Patrona Isyanı,* pp. 50–54.
49 Lady Mary Wortley Montagu, *Letters,* New York, 1906; Ahmet Refik, *Lale Devri,* Istanbul, 1928; Raşit, V, 19, 29, 45, 88, 134, 177, 233, 247, 267, 366, 401, 424, 439, 527–528, 205–217, 420–444; Küçük Çelebizade Ismail Asım. *Divan,* Istanbul, 1851, pp. 377–378, 555–561, 610–611.
50 Aktepe, *Patrona Isyanı,* pp. 48–50.
51 Translated by Berkes, p. 33, from Çelebi Mehmet, *Sefaretname,* London, 1872.
52 Analyzed in detail by Berkes, pp. 37–39.
53 Raşit, IV, 53; V, 185–186.
54 Raşit, V, 272–273.
55 Raşit, IV, 176.
56 Raşit, V, 146, 177.
57 Raşit, V, 311–315.
58 Raşit, V, 172, 175–176.
59 BVA, Mühimme 125, pp. 110, 158.
60 BVA, Mühimme 131, p. 17; 130, p. 396.
61 Mühimme 131, p. 190.
62 Çelebizâde Asım, pp. 79–81.
63 BVA, Mühimme 132, pp. 92, 117; Çelebizâde Asım, pp. 180–189.
64 BVA, Mühimme 132, p. 345.
65 Aktepe, *Patrona Isyanı,* pp. 73–85.
66 BVA, Name Defteri, VII, 78; Uzunçarşılı, OT IV/1, pp. 193–194.
67 BVA, Mühimme 136, p. 189.
68 Suphi, I, fol. 12.
69 Berkes, pp. 42, 45.
70 Suphi, 58b, 59a–b; Benedikt, pp. 114–115.
71 Suphi, fol. 58b; Ata, I, 158; Ergin, *Maarif,* I, 49–50; Adıvar, *Ilim,* pp. 161–162.
72 Uzunçarşılı, OT, IV/1, 325n.
73 BVA, Mühimme 116, p. 17; 132, p. 50.
74 Suphi, I, 39–41.
75 BVA, Mühimme 138, pp. 258, 388, 410.
76 BVA, Mühimme 140, p. 300.
77 Mühimme 140, pp. 410, 418–419, 422.
78 BVA, Name Defteri, VII, 359.
79 BVA, Name Defteri, VII, 460.
80 Suphi, II, fol. 79–80; BVA, Name Defteri, VII, 428, 499.
81 BVA, Mühimme 142, p. 275; Suphi, 100b.
82 BVA, Mühimme 145, p. 198.
83 BVA, Mühimme 148, pp. 226, 243.
84 Suphi, II, 235.
85 BVA, Mühimme 152, p. 66.
86 BVA, Mühimme 153, p. 278.
87 Vasıf, I, 266, 281, 315.
88 BVA, Mühimme 166, p. 170; Cevdet Hariciye 5218, 5288, 6076.
89 Cevdet[1], I, 81; Resmi Ahmet Efendi, *Hulasat ul-Itibar,* Istanbul 1286, p. 3.
90 BVA, Mühimme 168, p. 3.

91 Fevzu Kurdoğlu, *Rus Harbinde Akdeniz Harekatı,* Ankara, 1942; R. C. Anderson, *Naval Wars in the Levant,* Princeton, 1952, pp. 277–304.

92 Fisher, pp. 44–51; Vasıf, II, 100, 114.

93 Hurewitz, *Diplomacy,* pp. 54–161; Fisher, pp. 51–56; Uzunçarşılı, OT, IV/1, pp. 422–425.

94 Shaw, *Between Old and New,* p. 154.

95 S. J. Shaw, *The Financial and Administrative Organization and Development of Ottoman Egypt, 1517–1798,* Princeton, N.J., 1962.

96 Shaw, *Between Old and New,* pp. 211–237.

97 BVA, Name-i Hümayun IX, 90; Mühimme 166, pp. 371, 373, 427.

98 Holt, *Egypt and the Fertile Crescent,* pp. 146–148.

99 Fisher, pp. 108–109; Cevdet[1], I, 179–180, 320–327; Noradounghian, I, 338–342; Uzunçarşılı, OT, IV/1, p. 451.

100 Cevdet[1], II, 219–221; Uzunçarşılı, OT, IV/1, 494; Fisher, pp. 135–139.

101 Fisher, pp. 139–150.

102 Ismail Hakkı Uzunçarşılı, "Sadrazam Halil Hamid Paşa," TM, 5 (1935), 213–267; Cevdet[2], II, 132–133, 158, 159, 355; III, 134.

103 BVA, Mühimme 181, pp. 127, 135, 148, 252–253; Uzunçarşılı, "Halil Hamid," pp. 223–224.

104 Uzunçarşılı, "Halil Hamid," pp. 225–227, 233–238; Enveri, fol. 294–295, 304; Cevdet[2], II, 261, 357; III, 85; Auguste Boppe, "La France et le 'militaire turc' au XVIIIe siècle," *Feuilles d'Histoire,* 1912, pp. 386–402, 490–501; Adıvar, *Ilim,* pp. 183–185.

105 Cevdet, II, 84.

106 BVA, Mühimme 182, fol. 9.

107 BVA, Mühimme 181, p. 144.

108 Uzunçarşılı, "Halil Hamid," pp. 231–232; BVA, Cevdet Askeri, 7834, 9081.

109 Cevdet[2], II, 359; Enveri, fol. 296–297.

110 Uzunçarşılı, "Halil Hamid," pp. 239–258.

111 Shaw, *Between Old and New,* pp. 72–75.

112 Shaw, *Between Old and New,* pp. 71–210.

113 Shaw, *Between Old and New,* pp. 71–210.

114 Shaw, *Between Old and New,* pp. 180–199.

115 Shaw, *Between Old and New,* pp. 211–246.

116 Shaw, *Between Old and New,* pp. 345–351.

8

Ottoman Society, Administration, and Culture in the Age of Decentralization and Traditionalistic Reform, 1566–1808

Before looking into the process by which modern reform transformed the Ottoman system, we must first conclude our examination of the era of decentralization and traditionalistic reform with a study of the means by which society adjusted itself to the problems that the empire faced from the reign of Süleyman the Magnificent to the beginning of the nineteenth century.

Administration and Society

In spite of economic mismanagement, administrative inefficiency, political corruption, and policies based on group rather than state interest, state and society survived with much less disruption than one might imagine. How was this accomplished?

The process of adjustment was characterized at the center by an expansion in the numbers and functions of the corps of scribes (*küttap*), who extended their power to all branches of the Ruling Class, forming a permanent substructure of career bureaucrats who continued to administer the law and carry out the functions of administration almost oblivious to the shifts and starts as well as the incompetence and corruption of those nominally above them. Coordinating their operations and influence was the scribal guild itself, training, maintaining, providing, and commanding the scribes who carried out every function according to their own traditions and systems with only nominal reference to the officials supposedly directing them. Thus it was that the *reis ul-küttap* (chief of scribes) – officially only head of the Chancery of the Imperial Council beneath the orders of the grand vezir and equal to the chief treasurer and the *ağas* of the military corps – in fact exceeded them in power through his parallel position as leader of the scribal corporation. It was formed into a complex hierarchy of command and service under his direction, existing parallel to but apart from the administrative hierarchies in the offices of the Imperial Council, the treasury, and other branches of government. In its training functions it assigned new members as unpaid apprentices or as students or assistants to subordinate positions (*mülazim*) in the government. Thus they were supported at government expense while assisting the scribes, who, as full members of the guild, trained them in calligraphy, composition, counting, and accounting as well as in the functions of their particular offices. Apprentices and students were graduated into the ranks of the scribes and thus entitled to fill scribal positions in the government once they had sufficient training and ability, as signified by graduation ceremonies carried out by the guild whenever there were vacancies. Above the rank of scribe (*kâtip*), members could rise, as vacancies became available, to the ranks (*paye*) of clerk (*halife*), chief clerk (*ser halife*), keeper of the purse (*kisedar*), and, finally, bureau chief (*hâce*); the latter position placed one among the senior guild members, called *hacegân,* to whom the highest permanent scribal and secretarial positions were given, thus making them equal to or above the *reis ul-küttap* in the official hierarchy while sharing power and influence with him in the guild.[1]

The scribal guild exercised power through the positions held by members throughout the Ruling Class under the direction of the *reis ul-küttap,* who – though under the nominal command of his chief, the grand vezir – controlled the offices of government determining all appointments and dismissals. His multifarious duties and powers were reflected by the different offices that came under his personal direction. The oldest of these was his original office, director of Chancery of the Imperial Council (*Divan-ı Hümayun Kalemi*), itself divided into three functions: (1) the *Beylik* office, which issued and recorded decrees and other documents concerning nonfinancial activities of government, including relations with foreign countries and the *Mühimme* records of council decisions; (2) the *Tahvil* (transfer) office, which issued, recorded, and thus controlled appointment documents (*berat*) for the more important offices; the *Ru'üs* department, which did the same for lesser positions; and (3) the *Âmedi* (Correspondence) office, which acted as the private secretariat of the *reis ul-küttap,* handling his personal correspondence, including that with foreign countries, thus being the closest equivalent to a foreign office.

In addition, the grand vezir's office – which originally cared for no more than executing the orders of the Imperial Council and handling minor matters for which the council had no time – eventually developed such executive functions of its own that beginning in 1654 it had its own buildings, at different locations outside the palace until late in the eighteenth century, when it was provided with its own compound of offices, to which the names *Bab-ı Âli* (Sublime Porte) or *Bab-ı Âsafi* were applied. During the age of decline, it drew more and more power and functions away from the Imperial Council and the treasury. This culminated in 1794 when the *reis ul-küttap* was transferred from the council to direct the activities at the *Bab-ı Âli,* bringing with him the *Beylik* and *Âmedi* offices, while the Imperial Council retained only the duty of keeping the *Mühimme* records. To handle his new functions at the Porte the *reis ul-küttap* established a new office under his direction, the Office of the Grand Vezir's Letter Writer (*Mektubî-i Sadaret Odası*), which was in charge of the grand vezir's correspondence with all other departments of government and as such helped the *reis ul-küttap* in both his clerical and administrative functions. The *Âmedi* office, still the latter's personal secretariat, now prepared all his reports and communications with the sultan, kept records of meetings and negotiations with foreign representatives, and collected the fees paid the *reis ul-küttap* by all those receiving *berat*s of appointment. The Sublime Porte thus became the principal executive and administrative department of the government, with the grand vezir exercising general supervision, while the *reis ul-küttap,* representing the scribal corporation, held real power in his hands. The *Mektubî* office in particular became the most prized of all departments open to the scribes.

The final important office directed by the *reis ul-küttap* – nominally under the Imperial Council but in fact quite independent from it – was that of the translator of the Imperial Council (*Divan-ı Hümayun Tercümanı*), the legendary grand dragoman; until this time, composed as it was entirely of non-Muslims, mainly Greeks, this office had remained outside the scribal corporation although it did exercise considerable influence over foreign policy and, through its role of interceding on behalf of foreign representatives, over internal affairs as well. It gained considerably more importance in scribal affairs when after 1826 it was purged of its non-Muslim members as a result of the Greek Revolution and a new corps of Muslim scribes and translators was trained for its service in a new office established especially to direct and control their work, the Translation Office (*Tercüme Odası*).[2]

Beyond the Sublime Porte and Imperial Council, whose chanceries were controlled directly by the *reis ul-küttap* in his official capacity, the scribal corporation extended its influence well into the other institutions of the Ruling Class. The Imperial Treasury (*Hazine-i Âmire*) lost many of its functions to the grand vezirate and was left as the *Bab-ı Defteri* (Registry), to indicate its major function, with most of its scribal positions being staffed by the scribal guild. Scribal power also extended into the military institution through members acting as secretaries and treasurers of the corps, controlling the distribution of wages and supplies and more and more limiting the *ağas* to purely military functions. Other scribes often passed into the Imperial Institution, becoming vezirs and rising to be governors, ministers, and even grand vezirs – all the while remaining under the influence of the group that had nourished and sustained them.

This is not to say that the other institutions of the Ruling Class were without power and influence. The ministers of the Imperial Institution continued to rule the state but were seriously weakened by the political and factional struggles as well as their relatively short terms of office. The military institution maintained a powerful position through intimidation and violence as well as the placement of many members in high positions, but it also lost power due to its internal anarchy and the decline of its corps as an important military instrument. The only institution of the Ruling Class that was at all able to compete with the scribes was the *Ilmiye,* the religious and cultural organization of ulema. Religious training was, of course, a basic part of the education of every Ottoman regardless of his institution, and members of the ulema continued to influence the other institutions as teachers, tutors, and advisers of high officials. The ulema's right to declare invalid any order or administrative action gave them considerable authority and power in the day-by-day course of affairs. Their monopoly of education within the Muslim *millet* gave them a hold over the minds of the masses as well as many members of the Ruling Class. Their ability to bring thousands of students into the streets gave the ulema an instrument of force second only to that of the Janissary corps. Their control of over one-half the wealth of the empire through the religious foundations gave them tremendous financial power, with ample funds to reward and maintain not only their own members but also others who adopted their desires and goals.

But the ulema, more like the military than the scribes, were weakened considerably by internal decay. Ever since the early years of the seventeenth century fanaticism and obscurantism had triumphed over reason, and the avenues of thought and logic that had given the ulema the ability to react to new conditions in previous times had been lost. Standards of learning, training, and efficiency built in the age of greatness declined considerably because appointments and promotions were made as the result of bribery, personal relationships, and party politics. As a result, while the ulema remained influential, they lost the cohesiveness and ability to act in pursuit of common objectives and policies that had enabled them to be an element of strength and balance in earlier times. Even its financial power derived from the control of religious foundations was largely dissipated as the ulema used these resources for individual or party advantage rather than for the political or religious advantage of the group. A few ulema actually supported the eighteenth-century reforms in the hope of restoring their own institution, but few reformers dared to approach an institution so covered with the sanctity of religion, however corrupt it might be. For the most part, then, it remained little changed until the twentieth century, a powerful but disunited and dissolute rival to the ability of the scribes to penetrate most of the institutions of Ottoman government.

How did society respond in the provinces when power shifted from agents of the government to private estate owners and notables? Security was provided in feudal and tax farm provinces alike by the armies of the new elements of power, those who had the greatest stake in maintaining resources, the great estate owners, the notables, and the governors. There were now four main factors that provided some protection to the mass of the subjects. The first was the self-interest of the governors and estate owners. They could not be so oppressive as to drive away all the revenue producers. Those who were unchallenged within their domains did gain a vested interest in the continued productivity of the cultivators and provided reasonably good rule, in many cases far better than that provided by the regular Ottoman officials themselves. The difficulty came when there were competing notables and estate owners struggling among themselves with no one strong enough to prevail. Such situations were encouraged by the governors, since they then could play them off to secure continued revenues for themselves and the treasury. But in such cases the competing forces had little time to worry about the long-range productivity; each imposed itself on the towns and villages under dispute; and oppression was at its worst.

The second element of stability and protection in the empire in the age of decline was provided by the Janissary garrisons, extended from the tax farm provinces into the feudal ones as the timar forces declined. While nominally under the control of the provincial governors, these garrisons in fact were relatively independent elements of power, with their commanders the equivalents of the provincial governors and played off against them by the Porte to secure the garrisons' services in an age when the government's ability to enforce obedience was very limited. The Janissaries often were very exploitative, enforcing their maintenance on the hapless inhabitants of the towns and areas where they were stationed. But in many places they also acquired vested interests in local society and property. As in many cities, they married into the local populations, became merchants and artisans with independent incomes, and began using the corps to support the local establishments. As time went on, then, the Janissaries often became instruments of military protection for the local populations against the exactions of the notables and *levent* forces.

Closely associated with the decline of Ottoman government on the local level was the rise of the ulema as the principal administrators of the empire. Only the ulema had an empire-wide organization of judicial districts (*kazas*) manned by kadis and *naips* able to assume the duties of the agents of the imperial and financial classes. Thus in the age of decomposition the functions assumed by the kadis in the sixteenth century became indispensable. They became the principal agents of authority acting to protect the mass of the people against the worst effects of the disintegration of Ottoman government, acting also to organize and provide all the services needed by members of the Muslim *millet* that were provided for the non-Muslims by their own *millet*s.

It was, in fact, this substructure of traditional Middle Eastern society that rose with the kadis to fill the gap left by the receding Ottoman system and to constitute the fourth factor of stability in the declining empire. The scope of government always had left much to the *millet*s, and they continued to provide schools, justice, social services, and the like. But in this they did what they always had done – the only difference being the increased importance of their actions for the well-being of the subjects. The area that did expand most was that of the guilds. This was natural enough, since they had always included many members of the Ruling Class and had cooperated with the government in the economic sphere. Now the guilds acted as administrative links between the government and the urban population, enforcing government regulations, assessing and collecting taxes, cooperating with government efforts to enforce price and wage regulations in vain efforts to control inflation, and providing the government with necessary services. The guilds thus in themselves and in cooperation with the *millets* provided the autonomous nuclei of local governance that was otherwise lacking in late Ottoman society.[3]

Of course, the ability of the guilds to accomplish their functions was weakened by the gradual decline of Ottoman trade and industry. Control of the eastern seas passed from the hands of the Portuguese to the much stronger navies of England and the Netherlands; and with the help of the Safavids it was not long before the goods of India and China were passing through Iran and the Caucasus and across the territories of Muscovy to Europe, or all the way around southern Africa, completely ending trade between the East and the West through the Middle East. The merchant fleets of Europe now dominated the Mediterranean as well, gaining control of Ottoman trade to and from Europe and so reducing Ottoman communications with Egypt and North Africa that they became autonomous, almost independent. Russia, now in control of the Volga basin and the northern Caucasus, took over the role formerly exercised by Ottoman merchants of acting as intermediaries for trade between Europe and Central Asia. The Ottoman Empire thus was left in almost complete economic isolation, subject to the expanding commercial power of Europe, whose merchants used the Capitulations to squeeze out the Ottoman merchants and drain the empire of raw material essential to manufacturers. But the response of the Ottoman guilds was to become ever more restrictive in their regulations, using their connection with the government to preserve what native trade and industry remained for their own members and their children, preventing the influx of new labor and techniques that might have enabled them to fight back and compete with the manufactures of Europe. Thus while they helped organize and protect urban society, they discouraged the growth of a competitive spirit and prevented the Ottoman Empire from following Europe in adjusting to the new international economic conditions of the time.

Cultural Developments

Political and economic disintegration was not paralleled by a decline in most areas of culture. On the contrary, with the sultans now concentrating their attentions on matters that they could promote and practice in their palace without the diversion of military and political activities, and with ministers and governors as always striving to emulate their masters, there rose many leading cultural figures during the long centuries of disintegration, although the vitality of the classical age did, perhaps, lessen as the increasing disorder affected all classes of society.

The Seventeenth Century

The patronage of the great and powerful brought forth an abundance of court poetry and prose. The schools founded by Bâkî and Fuzuli a century earlier continued to dominate during the seventeenth century, emphasizing distinct traditions based on Persian and Turkish influence as time went on, with the latter gradually triumphing over the former. As a result there was a decline in the romantic *mesnevi* style, which was limited mainly to shorter works of ethical, didactic, and anecdotal content, while the Turkish *kaside* became the supreme vehicle of poetic expression.

The dominant seventeenth-century poet was Nef'i (1582–1636), who while continuing the tradition brought about by Persian influence perfected the *kaside* form. We know little of his childhood other than that he was born near Erzurum of a Sunni family, although in a territory that was mainly Shia or heterodox at the time. Entering the service of Kuyucu Murat Paşa during his campaign against the Celalis, he returned with his patron to Istanbul, serving him as an accountant while striving rather unsuccessfully to get his poetry patronized by three successive sultans, Ahmet I, Osman II, and Murat IV. Finally, the latter accepted and promoted his work, in return for which he eulogized the sultan in a series of magnificent *kaside*s. Nef'i was also a satirist, subjecting many of the great figures of his time to bitter and pungent ridicule and exposing prevalent corruption and nepotism. As a result he was subjected to alternate periods of exile and recall until he finally was strangled by orders of Grand Vezir Bayram Paşa.

Leading the opposition to Nef'i's school was the three-term *Şeyhulislam* (1622–1623, 1625–1632, 1634–1644) Zekeriyya zâde Yahya Efendi (1552–1644), who attempted to lead Ottoman poetry away from the restrictions and forms imposed by the Persian school and to develop originality of subject and feeling, while sharing the effort to develop the *kaside* as the main vehicle of Ottoman poetic expression. Himself the son of a *şeyhulislam*, Zekeriyya Efendi (d. 1593), he was "upright in an age when corruption was the rule, gifted with a far-seeing sagacity, learned as a jurist, accomplished as a scholar and poet, and endowed with an irresistible charm of manner."[4] Accompanying Murat IV on his expedition to Baghdad, he wrote some of his most beautiful verses to entertain the sultan, thus gaining the favor that was to last for the rest of his life. His poetry contained images inspired by his own observations of life and nature in place of the traditional metaphors used by his predecessors and contemporaries, thus forming a link with later writers, particularly in developing the *gazel* into a graceful, subjective, and delicate form.

The writer who brought Persian influence in Ottoman court poetry to both culmination and conclusion was Yusuf Nabi (1642–1712), who rose in the scribal service of one of Mehmet IV's favorite ministers, Musahip Mustafa Efendi. Deeply learned in Arabic and Persian literature and in the religious sciences, Nabi demonstrated his unusual depth of learning in his poems, which were models of technique as well as style regardless of the form he used. Touching all the traditional subjects – religion, philosophy, romance, love, wine, and mysticism – he also extended into biography, history (*Tarih-i Kamınça*, an account of Köprülü Ahmet's capture of Podolya in 1672), prose style (*Munşeat*, his collected letters), and geography and travel literature (*Tuhfet ul-Harameyn*, an account of his pilgrimage to the Holy Cities in 1683), developing a reputation as a master of his craft.

In the field of prose literature the seventeenth-century Ottoman Empire produced two of its greatest stylists, Kâtip Çelebi and Evliya Çelebi. Perhaps the greatest of all Ottoman secular writers, at least in the variety of his interests and depth of knowledge and research was the encyclopedist Mustafa Ibn Abdullah, known as Kâtip Çelebi or Hacı Halife (1609–1657). While some believe his father's name, Abdullah, indicated that he was a non-Muslim, there is firm historical evidence that the father was in fact a Muslim soldier in Murat IV's army. The young Mustafa received much of his early education and experience in his father's company, going with him on expeditions to Baghdad and Erzurum, acquiring the taste for military affairs as well as travel and geography manifested in many of his later works. After his father's death he rose in Murat IV's service as a scribe (*kâtip*), then to the rank of *kalfa* (*halife*), hence acquiring the epithets under which his works came to be known. A bibliophile, he consulted all the books and manuscripts he could find during his travels and assembled the mass of information that was to make him the most learned man of his time. His love of books was manifested in his greatest work, the *Keşf uz-Zunûn an-Esâmî ul-Kütüb vel-Fünun* (Survey of Thoughts of Names of Books and Sciences), a presentation of the biographies of the most important writers in the Eastern world at that time along with lists and descriptions of over 1500 books that they produced in Turkish, Persian, and Arabic – certainly an exhaustive record of Islamic cultural accomplishment.

Similarly, his *Cihannumâ* (View of the World) was an all-encompassing compilation of the geographical knowledge of his time obtained not only from Muslim travelers and geographers but also from European writers such as G. Mercator and L. Hondius and from the works of Ortelius and Cluverius. In the field of history Kâtip Çelebi's *Fezleke* (Compendium) provides a detailed account of Ottoman history from 1591 to 1655, including biographies of leading figures, often based on personal knowledge and experience. His *Tuhfat ul-Kibâr fi Asfâr al-Bihâr* (Gift of the Greats on Naval Expeditions) describes the Mediterranean and the islands under Ottoman rule as well as the main Ottoman naval campaigns until 1651; it contains biographies of the great Ottoman naval heroes and descriptions of the Ottoman fleet and arsenals of his own time. His *Takvim ul-Tevarih* (Calendar of Dates) serves almost as an index to his other works, containing a chronology of the principal events of world history from the Creation to the time of the Prophet and then to the year 1648, adding the names and dates of the main dynasties of the world and the great sultans, grand vezirs, and other principal officeholders of the Ottoman Empire to the reign of Mehmet IV. Kâtip Çelebi was one of the first Ottoman writers to have a significant awareness of Europe. And unlike his contemporaries he seems to have received this knowledge with appreciation and esteem, indicating a desire that his own world incorporate what was best in the knowledge and advances of others.

The seventeenth century also produced by far the greatest Islamic travel epic, the *Seyahatname* (Book of Travels) of Evliya Çelebi (1614–1682). Born in Istanbul in 1614, Evliya later said that his family had settled in Kütahya even before the Ottoman period, moving to Istanbul as part of Mehmet II's effort to resettle the city following its conquest but always retaining considerable wealth through land holdings in Anatolia. His father, Derviş Mehmet Zilli Efendi, was chief gold maker (*kuyumcu başı*) in the Topkapı Palace and leader of the gold makers' guild, which with its sufi connections was the center for artisans coming to Istanbul from all over the Islamic world; thus the young Evliya was instilled with a thirst for seeking out the unknown, a thirst that was to dominate his life. His mother was an Abaza woman brought to the palace by Ahmet I and given to his chief gold maker as a reward for his services. She seems to have been related to Grand Vezir Melek Ahmet Paşa and Ibşir Mustafa Paşa, in whose service the young Evliya later rose and undertook many of his trips. He received the traditional Muslim *medrese* education, became an excellent poet and singer, and entered the sultan's service as a page through the intercession of his relatives. But since he seems to have felt restrained and frustrated by palace service, after four years he obtained Murat IV's permission to join the *Sipahi* corps, shortly before the sultan's expedition to Baghdad, thus at long last gaining the opportunity to go out into the world as he had long dreamed of doing.

In accompanying Evliya Çelebi, one participates not only in his travels but also in the vicissitudes of his time. Beginning in 1639 the young *Sipahi* made several trips into Anatolia on official missions, making short trips to places such as Kütahya, Manisa, Bursa, and Izmit. His first major trip was in the suite of his father's adopted son, Ketenci Ömer Paşa, going with him to Trabzon, where Ömer had been appointed governor, sailing through the Black Sea and then traveling widely in eastern Anatolia. At times Evliya left his master, going on his own to Anapa (ostensibly to collect taxes) and then to the fort of Azov, where he participated in the Ottoman siege (April 1641) against the Russians. He returned with the army to the Crimea, participated in the second siege of Azov with the Crimean *han,* spending the winter with him in Bahçesaray before returning to Istanbul by sea. He suffered so much from storms that when he later was assigned to accompany Yusuf Paşa on the expedition to Crete (1645), he used various pretexts to remain home, subsequently describing the expedition in his *Seyahatname* on the basis of information supplied by others. Evliya accompanied his uncle Defterdâr zâde Mehmet Paşa when the latter was made governor of Erzurum, serving as his *müezzin* and later also as collector of customs in Erzurum itself. Again he used the occasion to travel extensively, this time through central Anatolia on his way to Erzurum. He also went with his master on many missions in eastern Anatolia, joining the campaigns against several Celalis and falling into the hands of one, Kara Haydar oğlu, before returning to Istanbul in 1648.

Evliya remained in Istanbul for two years, apparently dealing with family obligations following the death of his father. But his wanderlust continued, and when Murteza Paşa was appointed governor of Damascus, Evliya joined his suite as tax collector and messenger, traveling widely in Syria and Palestine as well as parts of central Anatolia before returning to Istanbul when Murteza was dismissed. He spent the next 20 years in the service of another uncle, Melek Ahmet Paşa, while the latter was governor at Oczakov (Özü), Rumeli, Van, Diyarbekir, and again Oczakov, as well as during a short term as grand vezir (1650–1651). He again traveled extensively through the Balkans as well as Anatolia to see places he had not seen before, participating also in Mehmet IV's tour through Bursa, Gallipoli, and Çanakkale. In 1668 he accompanied the new prince of Moldavia from Istanbul to Jassy, witnessing his battle with the prince of Wallachia and riding with the Crimean Tatars who were supporting the former in the name of the sultan. In 1669 and 1670 he traveled in Bosnia while Melek Ahmet was its governor. He then accompanied Fazıl Ahmet Paşa on his Austrian expedition, going with Kara Mehmet Paşa, who was sent as ambassador to Vienna following the Treaty of Vasvar. Evliya relates that while in Vienna he met Montecuccoli as well as Emperor Leopold I and from them secured a passport that enabled him to travel in Spain, the Netherlands, Brandenburg, Denmark, and elsewhere; but he gave no information on this trip, leading one to treat the claim with some doubt. He traveled extensively through Hungary as a census taker, through the Principalities to the Crimea to witness Mehmet Giray's struggles with the Cossacks, through the Caucasus to the shores of the Caspian in Dağistan, then back down the Volga to the Crimea, where he spent some time before returning to Istanbul.

The last years of Evliya's life were spent seeing those parts of the empire that he had missed earlier. Late in 1669 he went through Thrace and Macedonia, then into Thessaly and the Morea, sailing to Crete and witnessing the siege and conquest of Candia before returning to Istanbul via Albania and the Adriatic coasts (January 1670). Finally, he went on his first and only pilgrimage to the Holy Cities, going through western Anatolia, then sailing through the eastern Aegean and eastern Mediterranean, visiting Sakız, Sisam (Samos), Istanköy, and Rhodes, landing in Cilicia and going through Adana, Maraş, Ayntap, and Kilis on his way to Syria. Joining the Syrian pilgrimage caravan, he went to Mecca, returning with the Egyptian pilgrims' caravan to Cairo, where he remained for 8 years, visiting extensively in the Sudan and Abyssinia as well as all parts of Egypt. He returned to Istanbul in

1680 and then spent the last three years of his life bringing together all his notes and observations.

The *Seyahatname* itself, left to us in 10 complete volumes (published in Istanbul between 1897 and 1938), presents in great detail Evliya's observations of men, buildings, cities, and events in the lands that he visited throughout his life. His accounts of urban life and organization and of Ottoman monuments long since destroyed are unique records of a civilization whose traditions and ways of life are otherwise rather poorly recorded. Using many Arabic and Turkish works as well as the observations of friends and relatives to supplement his own observations, Evliya sometimes has been accused of inventing trips that he himself never made, especially those in the Balkans and western Europe. But aside from the instances mentioned, careful comparison of the details provided in the *Seyahatname* with other sources, many found only in the Ottoman state archives, indicates a kind of depth and accuracy that could only have been gained by personal presence and participation.[5]

Ottoman historiography manifested three distinct aspects during the seventeenth century. The first, or traditional one, consisted of chronicles compiled by Ottoman officials or private writers patronized by officials, who brought together the events of their time as best they could, helped occasionally by oral information, documents, and other sources, a tradition begun in the previous century by Hoca Saduddin and Idris Bitlisi. One of the best chroniclers of this genre, Ibrahim Peçevi (1574–1650), a relative of Sokullu Mehmet and a scribe in various parts of the Balkans, compiled a detailed account of the empire's history and life from the accession of Süleyman the Magnificent to that of Mehmet IV (1520–1648), giving particularly important information derived from his own experience in Istanbul and the Balkans. Kara Çelebi zâde Abdülaziz Efendi (1591–1653), *kazasker* of Rumeli (1648–1650) and *şeyhulislam* for a short time (1650) before spending many years in exile due to his criticism of the sultan regarding problems of state, left a vast history of Islam, *Ravzat ul-Abrar,* with considerable information on his own time from the accession of Mehmet IV until the year preceding his own death (1648–1657), including a history of Murad IV's Baghdad campaign. There were many other works of general and particular interest as well as biographies of members of the Ottoman Ruling Class.

Ottoman historiography in the seventeenth century was enriched by the establishment of a position of official court chronicler (*vakanüvislik*), initiated by Grand Vezir Amcazâde Hüseyin Köprülü Paşa, who held office from 1697 to 1702. The court chronicler was, in concept, not really a true historian, who selects, appraises, and evaluates information, but rather simply a recorder of the activities of the sultan and the events of interest to him and those around him in the form of a "daybook" or diary (*ceride-i yevmiye*), as a convenient guide to past events for those in power.[6] The *vakanüvislik* was established as a separate division of the Chancery of the Imperial Council so that the court chronicler would have direct, immediate, and continuous access to the *Mühimme* registers of council decisions as well as other important state papers, and he could set them down or summarize them before they were lost or scattered.[7]

This very limited concept of the position was, however, soon surpassed. Its first occupant was Mustafa Naima Efendi (1665–1716), one of the greatest of a line of court historians that was to continue, with some gaps, right into the twentieth century. Born in Aleppo of a father who was the commander of the local Janissary garrison and a powerful political and military figure in the area, the young Mustafa spent his early years in affluence, receiving a good *medrese* education before going to Istanbul as a young adult (1688). He used his father's influence to enter the palace service and served as one of the secretaries to the chief eunuch, helping him administer the revenues of the pious foundations of the Holy Cities and also participating in the party alliances and disputes of the time. Mustafa also acted as an apprentice scribe and continued his Islamic studies at the nearby Bayezit Mosque, where he specialized in literature, astrology, and history, so that he finally was able to enter the *Kalemiye* Institution, becoming a scribe in the Chancery of the Imperial Council. He rose as the protégé of Amca zâde Hüseyin Köprülü Paşa, who was maintaining his prestige by, among other things, promoting learned men. Included among these were the famous poet and *Reis ul-Küttap* Rami Efendi (later Paşa) and the *kazasker* of Rumeli, Yahya Çelebi. Members of such households cared for each other by the normal dictates of *intisap* or "association," and Rami Efendi's influence soon enabled Naima to rise in the scribal corporation, gaining important scribal positions and finally being appointed as the first *vakanüvis*. After Hüseyin Paşa fell from the grand vezirate, Naima retained his position for a time, since the next two grand vezirs had connections with the same household. But with the rise of Baltacı Mehmet Paşa as grand vezir early in the reign of Ahmet III (1704–1706), a new household came to power. Mehmet Raşit was thus made *vakanüvis,* and Naima, like his followers in the house of Hüseyin Paşa, fell from favor and was exiled to Bursa for a time. He did manage to maintain his position in the scribal corporation, however, because of the influence of other friends and associates; thus during the last 12 years of his life he achieved the rank of *hacegân* and occupied many of the important positions open to them while abandoning the historical activity that earned him eternal fame.

Perhaps the main reason that his work, the *Ravzat al-Hüseyin fi Hulasat Ahbar al-Hafikayn,* was such a landmark in Ottoman historiography was that while Naima did fulfill his master's wish for him to keep a day book of events, he also wrote about events from before his own time, from 1591 to 1660. Unhampered by current sensitivities, his work analyzed and explained important events on the basis of information secured from all the sources he could find, whether previously written chronicles, the state archives, or his own experience and observations and those of his friends. That this was not mere accident is shown by his detailed exegesis on the science of history and role of the historian:

> They must be reliable in what they say and must not make foolish statements or write spurious tales. If they do not know the truth about any particular question they should address themselves to those who have fathomed it, and only then put down whatever they have ascertained to be the fact. . . . They should disregard the disquieting rumors which are gossiped about among the common people. Instead they must prefer the reliable, documented statements of men who knew how to record what actually did happen. . . . Historians ought first to inform themselves, from those who have proper information concerning the question in hand, of what was the divinely ordained condition of any age in history, what it was that men thought and what it was they believed to be the best course in the conduct of war and in making terms with the foe, what were the causes and the weaknesses which were then bringing triumph or entailing destruction. . . . Historians should speak frankly and fairly . . . , they should not exaggerate . . . , and if, to attain their end, they must criticize and censure great men of praiseworthy works, they should never be unjust. In any case, they must

take care to present the real nature of the question, regardless of what it may be. . . .[8]

Naima drew liberally from Kâtip Çelebi to analyze the causes of Ottoman decline and present methods and means of reform, concluding that the Ottoman structure could be preserved with a balance between the men of the sword and his own class of the pen, stressing that administrators must act to prevent expenditures from exceeding revenues and to restore the army and the state to their pristine efficiency.[9] Naima always emphasized his belief in the need for strong and effective leadership such as that provided by the Köprülüs, for the exercise of influence on the sultan for the best interests of the state rather than for selfish personal and party interests, and for the sultan himself to guard against the advice and influence of men acting for their own interest. Honestly describing the effect of numerous salaries and pensions paid in return for no service to the state, Naima at the same time pointed out the practical impossibility of abolishing them all, which would throw a large portion of the Ruling Class into the streets; instead he advised that they be confiscated as vacancies occurred by death and that such practices be avoided in the future.[10]

Very closely associated with Naima's analysis and similar in genre to "mirror of princes" in the West were the "letters of advice" (*nasihatnames*) submitted to the Ottoman rulers and ministers beginning in the sixteenth century and continuing well into the seventeenth century. The first of these was the *Asafname* (The Book of Asaf, who was the lengendary wise minister of King Solomon), written for Süleyman the Magnificent by his grand vezir Lütfi Paşa (1488–1563) in an effort to apply the latter's long years of experience and historical study to the problems of the empire. For Lütfi Paşa the wise minister had to be without greed or private interest and had to persuade the sultan of the importance of protecting the property rights of the subjects. Lütfi advised that the grand vezir should be open in his dealings with the sultan, regardless of the consequences, and that he should above all avoid gifts of any kind. Appointments should be made only on the basis of ability without regard to politics or personal relationships, and complaints against officials should be investigated carefully and dealt with honestly to preserve the integrity of the state. He singled out the financial system as the basis of the state and said it had to be maintained if the state was to survive. Expenditures should be limited to available revenues. Taxes should be collected through salaried agents (*emins*) rather than tax farmers, since the latter kept most of their collections for themselves, and steps should be taken to eliminate as many of the burdensome supplementary taxes as possible so that the cultivators would remain and till their lands.

The *nasihatname* was further developed by Gelibolulu Mustafa Âli Efendi (1541–1599), also a distinguished historian, who presented his *Mevâ'id un-Nefâis fi Kava'id il-Mecâlis* (Rare Items on the Regulations of Assemblies) to Murat III, describing Ottoman society and government, how people lived and worked and how the members of the Ruling Class conducted their affairs, recommending essentially that everyone keep his place and follow the traditional ways. Ayn-i Âli Efendi, a treasury scribe and provincial treasurer (in Egypt) early in the seventeenth century, presented Ahmet I with a series of surveys on different aspects of the Ruling Class institutions, the *Kavanin-i Âl-i Osman der hulâsa-ı mazâmin-i defter-i Divan* (Essay on the Duties and Ranks of the Servants of the House of Osman), describing the institutions of the government and army, with particular attention to the salary and wage systems; the *Risâle-i Asâkir-i Osman* (Essay on the Soldiers of Osman), discussing the organization and state of the *kapıkulu* army; the *Kanun-u Osmaniye* (The Ottoman Law) summarizing traditional Ottoman criminal law, the tax system, and the status and problems of the rayas; and, finally, his *Kanun-u Mali-i Mısır* (The Financial Law of Egypt), describing the operation of Egypt's financial system during his tenure there as treasurer, all at the instigation of the reforming grand vezir Kuyucu Murat Paşa (1606–1611).

Perhaps the best-known and most perceptive of the genre was the *Risâle* (Treatise), presented to Murat IV in 1631 by his close adviser, Mustafa Koçi Bey, an Albanian *devşirme* convert who also presented a similar essay to Murat's successor. In essence Koçi Bey was the founder of the ideology of traditional Ottoman reform, emphasizing the power and grandeur of the empire in the time of Süleyman and then describing the causes and manifestations of decline since that time. According to Koçi Bey, four interdependent variables contributed to the decline: (1) the withdrawal of the sultans from personal participation in governmental and military affairs, (2) the decreasing authority of the office of grand vezir, (3) the rise of the palace and ministerial factions and parties, and (4) the consequent spread of corruption into every part of the Ottoman system. Corruption in the palace, above all else, had contaminated the rest of the system. The decline of the timar system, manifested by the passing of many timars into the hands of women, children, and others unfit to serve, had caused the breakdown of the army, the agricultural system, and also the system of provincial government. The efficiency of the *kapıkulu* had also deteriorated, with the corps filled with nonserving parasites, leading to defeat and the loss of territory. Even the ulema were beginning to decline as appointments were no longer being made in accordance with ability, knowledge, or seniority, and many judges, therefore, were using their offices to benefit themselves rather than the subjects. The revenues formerly derived by the treasury from tax farms were being lost, while imperial lands were being permanently alienated as foundations or private property, largely to benefit members of the Ruling Class. The resulting decline of revenues relative to expenditures had been met by increasing taxes on the peasants, who in the face of such oppression had fled the land, causing further losses of food and money for the empire. In the face of all of this the empire and its institutions could be restored if only the sultan acted firmly and decisively.

Koçi Bey's warnings were reiterated in the *Düstur ül-'Amel fi Islah ul-Halal* (The Code of Practice for the Reform of Defects), written in 1656 by Kâtip Çelebi in response to a request of Mehmet IV for the reasons for the continued deficits in imperial finances. For Kâtip Çelebi the Ottoman Empire, like other states, was subject to a normal process of vigorous development, stationary peak, and slow decline, but the actual time of each stage varied according to the wisdom and action of its leaders. The Ottoman Empire was in the second stage and appeared to be ready to pass on to the third; but because of its basic strength the Ottoman system was still powerful, and remedies could be found to avoid the final stage for many centuries to come.

The strength of the Ottoman system lay in three bodies, the cultivators, the military, and the treasury, each reflecting the different phases of the state's development. In the first stage the peasants had been protected from oppression, so that cultivation and resulting taxes were high and everyone prospered. The second phase had begun when overtaxation and disturbances had caused many peasants to flee their lands into the cities, leaving the countryside barren and the cities overcrowded. This had been caused mainly by the system of payment (*bahşiş*) to senior officials in return for appointments; that is, each officeholder had been forced to extort extra taxes and other levies from the peasants to recoup his payments and make a profit, while the offices were administered from this point of view rather than for the welfare of state and subject. The result was a decline in treasury revenues, which debilitated the army. The solution was to end the sale of offices, reestablish just and equitable taxes, restore obedience to the law, and then restore efficiency to the army. The number of men in the army had to be reduced to balance the budget. But this could be done only by a man of the sword, since members of the other three institutions of the Ruling Class were too interested in their own benefit to acquiesce and too weak to do what was necessary. Such a reformer would end the sale of offices, reform the financial system, reduce expenditures, and revive the army as well as the countryside.

Finally, there was Sarı Mehmet Paşa, a scribe who rose into the Imperial Class late in the seventeenth century. After writing a substantial history of the quarter-century of events that led to Karlowitz, he developed his conclusions in a separate essay, *Nesayih ul-vüzera vel-ümera* (Advice to ministers and princes), adding the knowledge gained from a lifetime of service in the treasury to elaborate on the conditions of decline developed by his predecessors. Thus came the conclusion of a century of traditional criticism in which the manifestations rather than causes of decline were described. But in their willingness to examine and question the system and to propose remedies, the critics marked a major step forward over those who revered the system as it was and opposed any effort to remedy its difficulties.[11]

The seventeenth century also was a golden age for Turkish popular literature, with poetry and stories exhibiting particular vitality. The mystic *tekke* poets continued to be popular and a number of new poets writing and singing in the style of Yunus Emre emerged, the most renowned of whom was Mehmet Niyazi-i Misri (d. 1693), a member of the Halvetiye order, who as part of the continuing government efforts to suppress the dervish orders was banished several times but still retained a wide popularity. Often living among the Janissaries, *Sipahi*s – and even among the *Levent*s, who so often were scourging the countryside – these poets reflected these groups, intermingling with the local population, singing their poems in army encampments, coffeehouses, fairs, and other places where the masses gathered. The popular poets filled the need for information as well as consolation in an age of uncertainty and sometimes despair. The principal form used was the *mani*, a short verse of four lines, each of seven syllables, with the first, second, and fourth lines rhymed while the third was free. Contests of *mani* recitation were common, with people often responding with *mani* verses of their own on the same or related themes, often playing on similar-sounding words to achieve particular effects. Far freer in form was the *koşma,* almost free form, composed either of 6 + 5 or 4 + 4 + 3 meters each. The *destan* (epic) now was composed of *koşma* verses, which continued for considerable lengths, relating heroic tales of past glories, traditions, or conditions. It formed an important tradition of oral history reflecting the language of the people. The *türkü* (folk song) also was in the *koşma* form but with a fifth or even sixth line added to the basic unit of four; it was used to recite tales of love, perceptions of nature, or the daily events of ordinary life in the village or among the nomads; the listeners adding lines of their own to express their particular experiences and interests. The *semaî* was recited by minstrels while singing, apparently in imitation of the rhythm of the whirling dervish dance, the *sema,* performed during the *Mevlevi* mystic services.

There were many popular practitioners of the art, but the most famous were: Âşık, who accompanied the Ottoman army in many of its seventeenth-century campaigns, particularly in Crete; Âşık Ömer (d. 1707), who visited the border fortresses and was present at many battles fought with the Russians, Austrians, and Venetians during the reign of Mehmet IV, leaving tales of the lives of common people as well as of the long marches and battles; and, finally, the best known of all the Turkish folk poets, Karacaoğlan, who described the social and natural environment in Anatolia with more understanding and detail than any other writer, presenting the customs of the people with a vigor and enthusiasm that has kept his verses fresh throughout the ages and in a clear and vital reflection of the popular language that has provided for the development of the modern Turkish literary language.

The Eighteenth Century

The openings toward natural and national forms and themes developed during the seventeenth century continued to expand their influence and to infiltrate Ottoman court literature during the eighteenth century. While the influence of Iran was not yet wholly forgotten and the *gazel*, the *kaside*, and the *mesnevi* continued to be used, their themes were now more Turkish and less Persian, more practical and direct and less dreamy and mystic, better reflecting local life, customs, and ways, with Turkish vocabulary beginning to be used with greater frequency, displacing the Persian words and idioms that had predominated for so long. The typical Turkish form of *şarkı* (song), with its rhythmic pattern of 13 beats, was used to provide lyrics to songs that expressed the feelings, moods, and vocabulary of the people to whom it was addressed. In many ways the eighteenth century was the most Turkish of all the literary periods for the Ottomans, since while the Eastern influence was largely cast off, the dominance of European ways that was to characterize the modernizing period of the nineteenth and twentieth centuries had not yet set in. This was truly a Turkish literature, based on Turkish aesthetic appreciation, reflecting Turkish ideas, Turkish ways of doing things, and Turkish costumes and customs, with a feeling for local color not achieved to such a full extent either before or after except in folk literature as such.

The transition came in the work of Alauddin Sabit (d. 1713), a member of the ulema, whose purely Turkish vocabulary and natural humor distinguished him from his predecessors and left a clear model for his successors. Sabit brought humor into a genre previously far too dignified and formal for such efforts, introducing with it the Turkish vocabulary and themes that ultimately were to prevail. Turkish proverbs now entered the *Divan* literature. Plays on Turkish words, puns, and jokes prevailed throughout his writing, even when he used the classic forms and themes. Sabit, however, was to continue to produce too many works in the traditional way for him to be fully characterized as the true author of the new era.

That honor falls to Ahmet Nedim (1681–1730), boon companion of Ahmet III during the most frivolous activities of the Tulip Period, who emerged as one of the greatest of all Ottoman *Divan* poets. Born in Istanbul of an ulema family, the young Ahmet received a *medrese* education from some of the most learned scholars of his time and rose as a *müderris* until, as a result of his early poems, he received the patronage first of Grand Vezir Silahtar Ali Paşa (1713–1716) and then of Damat Ibrahim Paşa. The latter appointed him as librarian and then sent him to divert and entertain the sultan at Saadabat and Çırağan and stimulated him to reflect and record the period in verse and song. His work was to stand out in classical Ottoman literature not only as a model of its kind but also as a model of form and theme for subsequent generations.

Never was there a court poet who better reflected the court life of his day, the passion for pleasure and beauty of the Tulip Period, in verses characterized by sheer joy and exuberance and, at the same time, grace and delicacy achieved by few in any language. Nedim wrote his poems largely on the spur of the moment to entertain those around him in court, preserving the harmony of the spoken language and avoiding awkward constructions dictated by the complexities of the *aruz* meter. Singing of the pleasures of wine and love, he reflected the natural human emotions of joy rather than the mystic dreams of the classical writers on the subject. But more than a mere court poet, Nedim was a true child of the great city of Istanbul and of the "beautiful people" of the Tulip Period. In his poems there came alive the palaces and gardens, the illuminated boats and fireworks displays, the tulips and musical instruments, the essence of the joy that was characteristic of upper-class life at the time.

This is not to say that the older traditions were entirely dead. The greatest of the eighteenth-century Ottoman *mesnevi* writers was Nevizâde Atâ'i (1683–1734), son of the poet Nevi, who served as kadi in many parts of the empire during his short life. Skilled also in the religious sciences and biography, his skill is best demonstrated by the *mesnevi*s in his *Divan*. Of these, his *Hamsa* (The Five) contains subtle and passionate verses with the third, his *Sâkinâme* (Song of the Cup Bearer) being most popular among his contemporaries. Atâ'i was the last Ottoman writer to challenge the great Persian writers in their own style and verse. After him the Ottoman *mesnevi* died out. He also provided a transition between the new and the old, bringing in popular Turkish proverbs and sayings, thus in his own way attempting to reconcile the form with the mood of the time.

Other poets in the early part of the century carried on Nabi's tradition. Mustafa Sami Bey (d. 1734), a career scribe and *vakanüvis* under Mahmut I, developed the classical forms to new heights of form and technique, even while avoiding almost entirely the local color and vocabulary of the new-style poets and emphasizing the traditional philosophical meditations of the past, albeit in a very sincere and meaningful manner. Another *vakanüvis*, Mehmet Raşit Efendi (d. 1735), whose historical work is the most important chronicle of the Tulip Period, left a collection of didactic *gazel*s. Raşit's immediate successor, Ismail Âsım Efendi, a scribe and *şeyhulislam* just before his death in 1760, was the leading traditionalist poet of the Tulip Period, leaving well-developed *gazel*s and *kaside*s reflecting the age that was past. The eminent *mesnevi* writer, Süleyman Nahifi (d. 1739), a scribe specializing in fine calligraphy and accounting, made his mark with a brilliant and emotional Turkish translation of Celaluddin Rumi's *Mesnevi*, preserving far more of the original meter and phraseology of the original than ever had been thought possible in Turkish. The last and greatest of Nabi's followers was Koca Mehmet Ragıp Paşa (1699–1763), grand vezir of Osman III and Mustafa III. Leader and promoter of a major school of writers, Ragıp was trained as a scribe and a member of the ulema, was learned in the old ways, but was at the same time open to new ideas in the best Ottoman sense. Himself a master of the traditional Persian forms and themes, Ragıp was also far too learned and intelligent to entirely ignore the new ways developed by Nedim. While preserving the old forms and aiming at the perfection of the craft as Nabi had, he was direct and forceful in his language, using a Turkish vocabulary and style far closer to Nedim than to Nabi and including local and current stories and traditions to illustrate his philosophical points. Integrity and common sense pervade his verses, thus making him the true unifier of the schools, pointing the way for those who would remain with tradition to develop their work in a Turkish rather than a Persian context.

It was, then, the new natural school of Nedim that prevailed through the remainder of the eighteenth century. Though none of his successors quite achieved the distinction of their master in form, many carried his example of broadening poetic themes to include different aspects of life, treating the life and ways of the common people as well as of the court and thereby providing the direct models for the new Turkish literature of the nineteenth century. Seyyiy Hüseyin Vehbi (d. 1737), a Molla and court poet to Ahmet III, wrote *gazels* and *kasides* in honor of the sultan and his close associates as well as many of the buildings that the sultan had constructed during his long reign. Mehmet Emin Beliğ (d. 1758), a judge in the provinces – thus removed somewhat from the court orientation of most of his colleagues – devoted his style to the common people around him. Beliğ developed a delicate and direct language to describe popular themes, the tavern and its habitués, the public bath, the shops of artisans such as the shoemaker, the tailor, and the barber. He visited and described the public bazaars where the people congregated most often in the course of their daily lives, presenting the human dramas of the individuals whom he saw as examples of their types.

The last of the great eighteenth-century *Divan* poets, and in fact the last *Divan* poet of any real merit, was Mehmet Esat Efendi, known as Galip Dede or Şeyh Galip (1757–1799), who during his relatively short life rose to be head of the *Mevlevi* monastery of Galata during Selim III's early years, restoring it from ruins and making it into one of the most important religious and cultural centers of his time. Even while in Konya, before going to Istanbul, Şeyh Galip's poems attracted the attention of Selim while he still was prince. Soon after his accession, the latter chose to cultivate the dervish-poet, perhaps as a means of securing ulema acquiescence for his reforms by personally contributing to the restoration of this as well as other *Mevlevi tekkes* around the empire as well as to the copying and wide distribution of Şeyh Galip's poems, making of the Galata *tekke* a true cultural and religious center. Şeyh Galip regularly came to the palace to recite and sing for the sultan and for his mother and sisters, for whom some of his best poems were written. Many of his poems were written when he was young, before he came to Istanbul, but his *Hüsn ü Aşk* (Beauty and Love), written in the environment of Selim's court, is the work that gives him a place in the history of modern Turkish poetry as well as in the vibrant cultural life of his own time, being the epitome and peak of the *mesnevi* style in its modern Turkish form. Developing new and fresh metaphors and similes, Şeyh Galip made the *mesnevi* into a living vehicle for the transmission of religious and mystic ideas and themes.

It should be noted that while Selim can be said to have been a modernizer in certain ways – just as his *Nizam-ı Cedit* was no more than the culmination of the traditional modes of reform – so also was his literary patronage largely devoted to preserving what was at best a modernized form of the traditional forms and themes. Despite the greatly increased number of Europeans in the empire, Western literary trends had no impact on eighteenth-century Ottoman literature.

Of those who followed in the path of Nedim probably the most original was Fazıl Bey (d. 1810), grandson of the great Syrian notable of Acre and Safed, Zahir ul-Ömer. After the latter was killed by Gazi Hasan Paşa (1776), Fazıl was sent to Istanbul to be trained in the palace service of Abdulhamit I. He remained as a page until 1783, learning the arts of scribesmanship, which would enable him to leave the palace and enter the *Kalemiye* guild, serving as scribe in various parts of the empire during the remainder of his life, and rising to the rank of the *hacegân* in his later years. His observations of the life of the common people formed the basis for many of his poems, and his works remain a treasury of insights into the society of time, covering the manners and customs of the peoples of the empire before the impact of Western ways and ideas, as well as providing accounts of the late eighteenth-century Ottoman court life that he observed in his early years in the palace.

Ottoman historiography during the eighteenth century wavered back and forth between the traditional chronicle-type account and the type of interpretation and evaluation encouraged by Naima. The institution of *vakanüvis* largely lapsed into the kind of "daybookkeeper" envisaged originally by its creator, with the vagaries of eighteenth-century political life, the rapid shifts of grand vezirs, and the relatively rapid rises and falls of *vakanüvis*es leaving the latter without the kind of strength and independence that might have enabled them to develop their work along Naima's lines. This was also prevented by the tendency to limit their chronicles to their own times, making it almost impossible for them to include their own opinions and impressions under the gaze of their master as well as those of their political enemies.

The difficulties of the post were very well illustrated in the career of Naima's immediate successor as *vakanüvis*, Mehmet Raşit Efendi (d. 1735), himself a member of the ulema rather than a scribe, thus perhaps adding to the difference in approach between the two writers. Raşit was maintained in the position by Damat Ibrahim for a decade (1714–1724), also serving as *hoca* and religious adviser to the grand vezir during his campaigns to the Morea and Peterwaradin (1715–1716) and then as a *müderris* in Istanbul before leaving the *vakanüvislik* altogether to serve as kadi of Aleppo. Raşit continued the chronicle of Naima while serving in all these positions, commencing his account with the events of the year 1660 and continuing to his own time to 1722. Raşit's successor, Küçük Çelebi zâde Ismail Âsım Efendi (d. 1759), was the last member of the ulema to hold the post, serving as *müderris* as well as *vakanüvis* like Raşit between 1723 and 1730, producing a chronicle that completed the former's account of the Tulip Period before leaving imperial service because of the political turmoil following the overthrow of Ahmet III. Raşit and Âsım were the last court chroniclers having any kind of position of independence in or out of the court. The position fell to an even lower state during the remainder of the century, being assigned for relatively short terms to low-ranking scribes, who could do no more than record events without analysis, although their works did provide information for the more substantive efforts of the great nineteenth-century court historians.[12]

The long period of service of Ahmet Vasıf Efendi (1739–1807) as *vakanüvis* stretched from 1783 to his death in 1807. A member of the Scribal Class who also served as *reis ul-küttap*, Vasıf brought together the works of his immediate predecessors and added his own interpretation in his *Mahasin al-Âsâr ve Hakayık al-Ahbar* (The Most Beautiful of Relics and Truths of Events), covering the years from Abdulhamit I's accession in 1774 until early 1805, just before the end of Selim's reign, giving considerable analysis and evaluation of divergent sources, particularly of course for the years before Selim's reign. Vasıf was followed by three major figures who developed the *vakanüvislik* into a major office, writing history rather than mere chronicles. The first of these, Ahmet Âsım Efendi (1755–1819), rose originally as a translator, rendering the famous Arabic dictionary *Burhan-i Kati'* into Turkish. He served as historian from 1807 to 1808, producing a chronicle covering the years from 1791 to the enthronement of Mahmut II in 1808, including considerable inside information on the momentous events that took place after Selim's deposition and the destruction of the *Nizam-ı Cedit*. Âsım not only read and critically compared and evaluated the written and oral sources available to him in Ottoman Turkish but apparently knew some French as well. He was the first Ottoman historian to incorporate some of the methodology and information found in the works of the Western historians into his own narrative, thus opening a new direction in both method and content.

Let us go briefly into the nineteenth century to complete our story of the official chroniclers. Âsım was succeeded by Mehmet Ataullah Şanizade (d. 1827), a member of the ulema, whose work covered the years from 1808 to 1822 and applied considerable criticism and interpretation, even to events of his own time, though with a far more conservative approach than that of Âsım. Mehmet Esat Efendi (1789–1848) continued the chronicle for 20 years (1826–1848) after having gained lasting fame by describing and justifying the destruction of the Janissaries in 1826. And, finally, all the work of the previous half-century of chroniclers was compiled and analyzed in the monumental history of Ahmet Cevdet Paşa (1822–1894), which covered the years from 1774 to 1825 and brought the critical style of Naima to its logical culmination.

While poetry and prose literature reached new heights in certain areas, the traditional Islamic sciences suffered along with the institutions that produced them, leaving a few derivative works that are of little interest to us here. Thus we leave the Ottoman Empire in a halfway stage, still seriously threatened from within and without but moving toward the development of a new system of reform that was to revive and reinvigorate it during the next century, beginning with the reign of Mahmut II. It is to this reform period and to the Turkish Republic that we will turn in the second and concluding volume of this work, *Reform, Revolution, and Republic: The Rise of Modern Turkey, 1808–1975*.

Notes to Chapter 8

1 Joel Shinder, "Career Line Formation in the Ottoman Bureaucracy, 1648–1750; A New Perspective," JESHO, 16 (1973), 217–237; N. Itzkowitz, "Eighteenth Century Ottoman Realities," *Studia Islamica,* 16 (1962), 73–94; L. V. Thomas, *Naima,* pp. 22–24; Uzunçarşılı, *Merkez,* pp. 63–69, 260–265.

2 Uzunçarşılı, *Merkez Teşkilatı,* pp. 1–110; Inalcık, "Reis ül-Küttâb," IA, IX, 671–683; Bernard A. Lalor, "Promotion Patterns of Ottoman Bureaucratic Statesmen from the Lale Devri Until the Tanzimat," *Güney-Doğu Avrupa Araştırmaları Dergisi,* I, 77–92; C. V. Findley, "The Legacy of Tradition to Reform: Origins of the Ottoman Foreign Ministry," IJMES, I (1970), 334–357.

3 G. Baer, "The Structure of Turkish Guilds and Its Significance for Ottoman Social History," *Proceedings of the Israel Academy of Sciences and Humanities,* IV/10, pp. 176–196; idem, "The Administrative, Economic and Social Functions of Turkish Guilds," IJMES, I (1970), 28–50.

4 Gibb, *Ottoman Poetry,* III, 273.

5 The best monographic studies of Evliya Çelebi are Meşkure Eren, *Evliya Çelebi Seyahatnâmesi Birinci Cildinin Kaynakları Üzerinde bir Araştırma* (A Study of the Sources of the First Volume of the Book of Travels of Evliya Çelebi), Istanbul, 1960, and M. Cavid Baysun, "Evliya Çelebi," IA, IV, 400–412; F. Taeschner, "Osmanlılarda Cografya," *Türkiyat Mecmuası,* 2 (1928), 301–306.

6 Raşit, III, 7; V, 449.

7 Thomas, *Naima,* pp. 36–42.

8 Thomas, *Naima,* pp. 110–115, from Naima, I, 4–8.

9 Thomas, *Naima,* pp. 73–83.

10 Thomas, *Naima,* p. 104.

11 The *nasihatname*s are discussed in detail in a brilliant essay by Bernard Lewis, "Ottoman Observers of Ottoman Decline," *Islamic Studies,* 1 (1962), 71–87.

12 Âsım was succeeded, then, by Mustafa Sami Efendi (d. 1733), who chronicled the three years from 1730 until his death; Hüseyin Şakir Efendi, who served from 1733 to 1740, but whose notes were never put together in his own time; Mehmet Suphi Efendi (d. 1769), *vakanüvis* from 1739 to 1744, who produced a chronicle covering the years from the Patrona Revolt (1739) to 1743, thus using the materials left by his predecessor; Süleyman Izzi Efendi (d. 1754), who served twice as *vakanüvis,* from 1743 to 1745 and again from 1746 to 1753, producing a work covering the years from 1744 to 1752; Mehmet Hakim Efendi (d. 1770), chronicler from 1753 to 1770, during which he held a number of high posts in the scribal service of the treasury, producing a chronicle for 1747 to 1766; Çeşmi zâde Mustafa Reşit Efendi (d. 1770), Hakim's *kalfa* and successor between 1766 and 1768; Musa zâde Mehmet Abdullah Efendi (1718–1782), *vakanüvis* from 1770 to 1775; Hafız Süleyman Efendi, from 1775 to 1776; Sadullah Enveri Efendi (d. 1794), a high scribal official who served as *vakanüvis* several times while continuing to work in the treasury and as a substitute in Istanbul for the regular chroniclers who accompanied the army to battle between 1768 and 1774, in 1777, and between 1779 and 1794, producing a chronicle covering the years from 1769 to the Peace of Jassy in 1792; Edip Efendi (d. 1798), also in the scribal service of the treasury, who acted as Enveri's substitute in Istanbul during the war years from 1787 to 1792; and Halil Nuri Efendi (d. 1799), Enveri's successor in the treasury as well as *vakanüvis* from 1792 to 1798, whose written chronicle, however, covered only 1794 to 1799.

50°N

10°E   15°E   20°E   25°E

Danube   Boundary 1683   **Vinnits.**
Vienna   **PODOLI**
1683 ✕   *Dniester*   to Poland
AUSTRIA   Chernovtsy   1699

BUKOVINA   Jassy

Budapest   MOLDAVIA
Milan   **HUNGARY**   Grosswardein   1829   Galati   Ismai
to Austria 1699   **TRANSYLVANIA**   Ibrail
Venice   Trieste   to Austria 1699   1829
Agram   *Drava*   **Mohacs**   R U M A N I A
45°N   Po   *Sava*   **Temesvar** BANAT   to Austria   *Created 1861*   1878
Carlowitz   to Austria   1718-39   Constan.
CROATIA   1718   1829   **Bucharest**
BOSNIA   **Belgrade**   Craiova
to Austria-Hungary   Passarowitz   1878   Silistria   Küçük
1878   SERBIA   Kaynarca
DALMATIA   Sarajevo   to Austria   Vidin   Plevna   Sistova   Varna
to Venice 1699–1797   HERZE-   1817   1718-39   Niš   BULGARIA   1878   1908
to Austria 1797&1816   GOVINA   1878   Burgas
to Italy 1805–9   EAST RUMELIA
to France 1809–16   1718 Ragusa   Üsküp   1878   Filibe (Plovdiv)   to Bulgaria
Cattaro   (Skopje)   Sofia   1913
1878   Scutari   to   Edirne   Bosporu
(Shkodra)   Serbia   to Greece   Istanb
ROME   to Serbia   1913   to Bulgaria
1913   1913   Kavala   1913   Üsküdar (Scutari)
ALBANIA   MACEDONIA   Salonica   *Marmara Sea*
1913   EPIRUS   to Greece   Thasos   Mudanya
Janina   1913   Gallipoli
Corfu   Larisa   Lemnos   Dardanelles   Izm.
THESSALY   Mytilene   to Greece
Ionian Is.   to Greece 1881   1920–22
to Venice 1797   Negroponte   Chios   Menderes   A.
France 1797-9 & 180745   (Euboea)   Samos   Muğla
Br. Prot. 1815–63   GREECE   Athens
to Greece 1863   1830   MOREA   Argos
Missolonghi   to Venice   Dodecanese
1685–99   to Italy 1912
Navarino   1715–18   Rhodes

35°N   Tunis   Candia Spinalonga
Canea   CRETE   Turkey 1718
TUNIS   Turkey 1718   to Greece 1908
Nominally Subject   Cerigo
until 1881

Tripoli
T R I P O L I
Ottoman Vassal until 1835   **C Y R E N A I C A**   E   G   Y
Ottoman Province 1835–1912   Bengazi   Ottoman Vassal until 1835   1811
to Italy 1912   Ottoman Province 1835–1912   Br. Occupation 1882
L   I   B   20°E   Y   A   Br. Protectorate 1914
10°E   15°E   1922
25°E

■	Losses 1683–99 (*Treaty of Karlowitz*)	▨	Turkey in 1923
▦	Losses 1700–18 (*Treaty of Passarowitz*)	1878	Date or period of autonomy
▥	Losses 1719–74 *Treaty of Küçük Kaynarca*	1830	Date of independence
▨	Losses 1775–1812 *Treaty of Bucharest*	—·—·	Boundaries of spheres of influence in Anatolia after the 1914–18 War
⬚	Losses 1813–29/30 *Treaty of Edirne*	········	Boundary after Treaty of Sèvres 1920
▦	Losses 1830–78 *Treaty of Berlin*	——	Boundary after Treaty of Lausanne 1923
▨	Losses 1879–1915 *Treaties of London & Bucharest*		miles 300
▨	Losses 1916–23 *Treaty of Lausanne*		km 500

DECLINE OF THE
OTTOMAN EMPIRE
AND RISE OF THE TURKISH REPUBLIC
1683–1975

Bibliography: Ottoman History to 1808

I. General Histories

The most authoritative work is that of Halil Inalcık, *The Ottoman Empire: The Classical Age 1300–1600,* London and New York, 1973, which, however, is rather short and limited mainly to institutional, social, and economic history. L. S. Stavrianos, *The Balkans Since 1453,* New York, 1958, is excellent on the Ottoman conquests and rule in Southeastern Europe but is out of date on internal Ottoman history and devotes a great deal of space to the Balkan states after they secured their independence from the Ottomans. By far the best account available in Turkish is Mustafa Cezar, Midhat Sertoğlu and others, *Resimli-Haritalı Mufassal Osmanlı Tarihi* (Detailed Ottoman History, with Illustrations and Maps), 6 vol., Istanbul, 1957–1963, which makes judicious use of Ottoman and Western source materials. Also useful, and based almost entirely on Ottoman chronicle and archival sources, is the series of volumes published by the Turkish Historical Society (*Türk Tarih Kurumu*) under the authorship of Ismail Hakkı Uzunçarşılı, *Osmanlı Tarihi* (Ottoman History): vol. I, *Anadolu Selçukluları ve Anadolu Beylikleri hakkında bir mukaddime ile Osmanlı Devletinin kuruluşundan Istanbul'un fethine kadar* (From the Foundation of the Ottoman State Until the Conquest of Istanbul, with an Introduction on the Anatolian Seljuks and the Anatolian Principalities), Ankara, 1947; 2nd ed., 1961; vol. II, *Istanbul'un Fethinden Kanuni Sultan Süleyman'in Ölümüne kadar* (From the Conquest of Istanbul to the Death of Sultan Süleyman Kanuni), Ankara, 1949; vol. III/1, *II. Selim'in Tahta Çıkışından 1699 Karlofça Andlaşmasına kadar* (From the Accession of Selim II to the Karlowitz Agreement of 1699), Ankara, 1951; vol. III/2, *XVI. Yüzyıl Ortalarından XVII. Yüzyıl Sonuna Kadar* (From the Middle of the Sixteenth Century to the End of the Seventeenth Century), Ankara, 1954; vol. IV/1 *Karlofça Anlaşmasından XVIII. Yüzyılın Sonlarına Kadar* (From the Treaty of Karlowitz Until the End of the Eighteenth Century), Ankara, 1956; vol. IV/2, *XVIII. Yüzyıl* (The Eighteenth Century), Ankara, 1959. Ismail Hami Danişmend, *Izahlı Osmanlı Tarihi Kronolojisi* (Expanded Chronology of Ottoman History), 4 vols., Istanbul, 1947–1955 (2nd ed., 5 vols.), Istanbul, 1971–1972, is particularly good on settling disputed dates and presenting a chronological account of Ottoman history. Joseph von Hammer-Purgstall, *Geschichte des Osmanischen Reiches,* 10 vols., Pest, 1827–1835 (repr. Graz, 1963), is a rather uncritical but still very useful collection of information derived from Ottoman chronicle sources. Johann Wilhelm Zinkeisen, *Geschichte des Osmanischen Reiches in Europa,* 7 vols., Hamburg, 1840, Gotha, 1854–1863 (repr. Darmstadt, 1963), is a more analytical work, using European diplomatic reports as well as Ottoman sources, but emphasizing mainly diplomacy, military affairs, and the European portion of the empire. N. Iorga, *Geschichte des Osmanischen Reiches,* 5 vols., Gotha, 1908–1913 (repr. 1963), is more general, much more biased, and less critical.

II. Bibliographies

The most comprehensive bibliography of Ottoman history is Hans-Jürgen Kornrumpf, *Osmanische Bibliographie mit Besonderer Berücksichtigung der Türkei in Europa, Leiden/ Köln,* 1973. The best available listing of works published in Turkish is Enver Koray, *Türkiye Tarih Yayınları Bibliyografyası* (Bibliography of Turkish History Publications), 2 vols., Istanbul, 1959–1971. Also useful is Fehmi Edhem Karatay, *Istanbul Üniversitesi Kütüphanesi. Türkçe Basmalar. Alfabe Kataloğu. Memleketimizde ilk Türk matbasının kuruluşundan yeni harflerin kabulüne kadar* (The Istanbul University Library, Turkish

Printed Works. Alphabetical Catalog. From the establishment of the first Turkish press in our country until the acceptance of new letters, 1729–1928), 2 vols., Istanbul, 1956. For currently published works, see J. D. Pearson, *Index Islamicus, 1906–1955,* Cambridge, 1958, and supplements, and *Türkiye Bibliyografyası,* Ankara, Milli Kütüphane, 1949 to date. N. V. Mihov (Michoff), *Sources bibliographiques sur l'histoire de la Turquie et de la Bulgarie,* 4 vols., Sofia, 1914–1934, is a useful collection of the accounts of Western travelers and specialists concerning the European portions of the empire, particularly Bulgaria. The same author's *La Population de la Turquie et de la Bulgarie au XVIIIᵉ et au XIXᵉ siècles,* 4 vols., Sofia, 1915–1935, gives those works that bear particularly on the empire's social and demographic situation. Mihov also has left a *Bibliographie des articles de périodiques allemands, anglais, et italiens sur la Turquie et la Bulgarie,* Sofia, 1938. The most useful dictionary of Ottoman technical terms is Mehmet Zeki Pakalın, *Osmanlı Tarih Deyimleri ve Terimleri Sözlüğü* (Dictionary of Ottoman Historical Terms and Expressions), 3 vols., Istanbul, 1946–1956. See also Midhat Sertoğlu, *Resimli Osmanlı Tarihi Ansiklopedisi* (Illustrated Encyclopaedia of Ottoman History) Istanbul, 1958; and Kâmil Kepeci, *Tarih Lûgatı* (Dictionary of History), Istanbul, 1952. On travelers and travel in the empire, see S. H. Weber, *Voyages and Travels in Greece, the Near East and Adjacent Regions Made Previous to the Year 1801,* Princeton, 1953: Carl Göllner, *Turcica, Die europäischen Turkendrucke des XVI Jahrhunderts,* vol. I, *1501–1550,* Bucharest-Berlin, 1961; vol. II, *1551–1600,* Bucharest-Baden, 1968; Selçuk Trak, *Türkiye hakkında yazılan coğrafya eserleri genel bibliyoğrafyası* (General Bibliography of Geographical Works Written on Turkey), Ankara, 1942; T. C. Maarif Vekâleti, *Istanbul Kütüphanelerinde Osmanlı devrine ait Türkçe-Arapça-Farsça yazma ve basma coğrafya eserleri bibliyoğrafyası* (Bibilography of Manuscript and Printed Works in Istanbul Libraries Concerning the Ottoman Period), Istanbul, 1958. See also Berna Moran, *A Bibliography of the Publications in English Concerning the Turks, XV–XVIIIth Centuries,* Istanbul, 1964.

III. General Reference Works

The best available biographical dictionary of Ottoman soldiers, administrators, and writers is Mehmed Süreyya, *Sicill-i Osmani* (The Ottoman Register), 4 vols., Istanbul, 1890–1893, continued by Gültekin Oransay, *Osmanlı Devletinde Kim Kimdi?* I, *Osmanoğulları* (Who's Who in the Ottoman State? vol. I, The Ottoman Dynasty), Ankara, 1969. Biographies and bibliographies of most Ottoman authors are found in Bursalı Mehmed Tahir, *Osmanlı Müellifleri* (Ottoman Authors), 3 vols., Istanbul, 1915–1928, with index by Ahmet Ramzi, *Miftah ul-Kutup ve Esami-i Müellifin Fihristi* (The Key to Books and Index to the Names of Authors), Istanbul, 1928; republished in Latin letters by A. Fikri Yavuz and Ismail Özen, *Osmanlı Müellifleri* (Ottoman Authors), Istanbul, 2 vols., 1972. The most comprehensive biographies of Ottoman historians along with lists of their manuscript and published works and their locations are found in T. C. Maarif Vekâleti, *Istanbul Kütüphaneleri Tarih-Coğrafya Yazmaları Kataloğu,* I, *Türkçe Tarih Yazmaları* (Catalog of History and Geography Manuscripts in Istanbul Libraries, vol. I, Turkish Historical Manuscripts), 10 parts, Istanbul, 1943–1951; Fehmi Edhem Karatay, *Topkapı Sarayı Müzesi Kütüphanesi Türkçe Yazmaları Kataloğu* (Catalog of the Turkish Manuscripts in the Topkapı Palace Museum Library), 2 vols., Istanbul, 1961, and *Topkapı Sarayı Müzesi Kütüphanesi, Farsça Yazmaları Kataloğu* (Catalog of Persian Manuscripts in the Library of the Topkapı Palace Museum Library), Istanbul, 1961. The most comprehensive account of Ottoman archival materials in Istanbul is Midhat Sertoğlu, *Muhteva Bakımından Başvekâlet Arşivi* (The Contents of the Prime Minister's Archives), Ankara, 1955. See also S. J. Shaw, "Archival Sources for Ottoman History: The Archives of Turkey," *JAOS,* 80 (1960), 1–12; Tahsin Öz, *Arşiv Kılavuzu* (Archives Dictionary), 2 vols., Istanbul, 1938–1940, an index to the documents in the Topkapı Palace archives; Bernard Lewis, "The Ottoman Archives, A Source for European History," in *Report on Current Research,* Washington, D.C., 1956, pp. 17–25; Bernard Lewis, "The Ottoman Archives as a Source of History for the Arab Lands," *JRAS* (1951), 139–155; S. J. Shaw, "Cairo's

Archives and the History of Ottoman Egypt," in *Report on Current Research, Spring, 1956,* Washington, 1956, pp. 59–72; Jean Deny, *Sommaire des Archives Turques du Caire,* Cairo, 1930; and S. J. Shaw, "Turkish Source Materials for Egyptian History," in *Political and Social Change in Modern Egypt,* ed. P. J. Holt, London, 1968, pp. 28–48. Ottoman archival materials in European collections are described in J. Reychman and A. Zajaczkowski, *Handbook of Ottoman-Turkish Diplomatics,* tr. A. S. Ehrenkreutz, ed. Tibor Halasi-Kun, The Hague/Paris, 1968.

The best available account of Ottoman geography is Franz Taeschner, *Das Anatolische Wegenetz nach osmanischen Quellen,* 2 vols., Leipzig, 1924–1926. Place names and their various equilavents in different languages are partly presented in C. Mostras, *Dictionnaire Géographique de l'Empire Ottoman,* Saint Petersbourg, 1873, and in the indexes to Danişmend, *Izahlı Osmanlı Tarihi Kronolojisi.* See also D. E. Pitcher, *An Historical Geography of the Ottoman Empire,* Leiden, 1972; Kâtip Çelebi, *Cihannüma,* Istanbul, 1732 (including sections on Anatolia from the description by Abu Bakr al-Dimaşki); and C. Jirecek, *Die Heerstrasse von Belgrad nach Constantinopel und die Balkanpasse,* Prague, 1877. Mehmed Eşref (Albatı), *Tarih-i Umumi ve Osmanlı Atlası* (General History and Ottoman Atlas), 2nd ed., Istanbul, 1329/1911, presents 139 maps of the empire. Ibn ul-Cevat Efdaluddin (Tekiner), *Tarih-i Osmani Haritaları* (Maps of Ottoman History), Istanbul, 1329/1911 provides a detailed collection. Faik Reşit Unat, *Tarih Atlası* (Atlas of History), Istanbul, 1952, and later printings, is more general. W. M. Ramsay, *Historical Geography of Asia Minor* (London, 1890), concerns Anatolia in the Byzantine period. G. Le Strange, *The Lands of the Eastern Caliphate,* Cambridge, England, 1930, is useful for the pre-Ottoman centuries. See also F. Taeschner, "Anadolu," EI[2], I, 461–480 and V. Cuinet, *La Turquie d'Asie,* 4 vols., Paris, 1892–1894.

IV. The Turks in History to 1280 A.D.

The best general account of Central Asian history is R. Grousset, *The Empire of the Steppes,* New York, 1970. More authoritative but also considerably more detailed is W. Barthold, *Turkestan down to the Mongol Invasion,* translated from the original Russian and revised by the author with the assistance of H. A. R. Gibb, 3rd ed., with an additional chapter, translated by Mrs. T. Minorsky and edited by C. E. Bosworth, London, 1968. See also Zeki Velidi Togan, *Umumi Türk Tarihine Giriş, Cild I.En Eski Devirlerden 16. Asra Kadar* (Introduction to General Turkish History, Vol. I, From the Oldest Ages to the Sixteenth Century), Istanbul, 1946. The earliest Turkish peoples are described by Faruk Sumer, *Oğuzlar (Türkmenler),* (The Oğuz Turkomans), Ankara, 1967, and "Oğuzlar," IA, IX, 378–386. On the assimilation of the Turks to Islamic civilization and their entry into the Middle East see Claude Cahen, "The Turkish Invasion: The Selchükides," in *History of the Crusades,* ed. K. M. Setton, vol. I, *The First Hundred Years* (Philadelphia, Pa., 1955, 2nd ed., Madison, Wis., 1967), pp. 135–176; C. E. Bosworth, "The Political and Dynastic History of the Iranian World (A.D. 1000–1217)", *Cambridge History of Iran,* vol. V., *The Saljuq and Mongol Periods,* ed. J. A. Boyle, Cambridge, England, 1968, pp. 1–202; and B. Spuler, "The Disintegration of the Caliphate in the East," *Cambridge History of Islam,* ed. P. Holt, A. K. S. Lambton, and B. Lewis, vol. I, *The Central Islamic Lands,* Cambridge, 1970, pp. 143–174. On the individual Muslim Turkish dynasties see Omeljan Pritsak, "Die Karachaniden," *Der Islam,* XXXI (1953), 17–68 (tr. as "Kara-Hanlılar" in IA, VI, 251–273); C. E. Bosworth, *The Ghaznevids: Their Empire in Afghanistan and Eastern Iran,* Edinburgh, 1963; Ibrahim Kafesoğlu, *Harezmşahlar Devleti Tarihi* (History of the State of the Harezmşahs), Ankara, 1956; Heribert Horst, *Die Staatsverwaltung der Grosselǧugen und Horazmşahs, 1039–1231,* Wiesbaden, 1964. The Great Seljuk Empire as well as that of the Seljuks of Anatolia are discussed extensively in Osman Turan, *Selçuklular Tarihi ve Türk Islam Medeniyeti* (Seljuk History and Turko-Islamic Civilization), Ankara, 1965; Claude Cahen, "The Turks in Iran and Anatolia Before the Mongol Invasions," in *History of the Crusades,* ed. K. M. Setton, vol. II, *The Later Crusades 1189–1311,* ed. R. L. Wolff, Philadelphia,

Pa., 1962, 2nd ed., Madison, Wis., 1967, pp. 661–692; Mehmed Altay Köymen, *Selçuklu Devri Türk Tarihi* (Turkish History in the Seljuk Period), Ankara, 1963; and Ibrahim Kafesoğlu, "Selçuklular" (The Seljuks), IA, X, 353–416. Also Ibrahim Kafesoğlu, *Sultan Melikşah devrinde büyük Selçuklu imparatorluğu* (The Great Seljuk Empire in the Age of Sultan Melikşah), Ankara, 1953. M. A. Köymen, *Büyük Selçuk Imparatorluğu tarihi, Ikinci imparatorluk devri* (History of the Great Seljuks, The Age of the Second Empire), Ankara, 1954, and F. Sanaullah, *The Decline of the Saljuqid Empire*, London, 1938, discuss Seljuk decline. The Mongol Middle Eastern Empire (Ilhanid Empire) is described in Bertold Spuler, *History of the Mongols*, Berkeley and Los Angeles, 1972, and the same author's *Die Mongolen in Iran : Politik, Verwaltung und Kultur der Ilchanzeit, 1220–1335,* 3rd ed., Berlin, 1968; Claude Cahen, "The Mongols and the Near East," in *History of the Crusades,* vol. II, pp. 715–734; J. A. Boyle, "Dynastic and Political History of the Il-Khans," in *Cambridge History of Iran,* vol. V, pp. 303–421; and I. P. Petrushevsky, "The Socio-Economic Condition of Iran Under the Il-Khans," in *Cambridge History of Iran,* vol. V, 483–537.

Anatolia in the thirteenth and fourteenth centuries is discussed in three major studies: Claude Cahen, *Pre-Ottoman Turkey,* London and New York, 1968; Speros Vryonis, Jr., *The Decline of Medieval Hellenism in Asia Minor and the Process of Islamization from the Eleventh Through the Fifteenth Century,* Berkeley and Los Angeles, 1971; and Osman Turan, *Selçuklular Zamanında Türkiye* (Turkey in the Time of the Seljuks), Istanbul, 1971. The most useful general account of Byzantine history is G. Ostrogorsky, *History of the Byzantine State,* London, 1956. There are a number of important monographs on early Turkish society in Anatolia, including: Claude Cahen, "La Première pénétration turque en Asie Mineure," *Byzantion* (1948); Mukrimin Halil Yinanç, *Türkiye Tarihi, Selçuk Devri* (History of Turkey, The Seljuk Period), Istanbul, 1944; P. Wittek, "Von der byzantinischen zur türkischen Toponymie," *Byzantion* (1935); Barbara Flemming, *Landschaftsgeschichte von Pamphylien, Pisidien und Lydien im Spätmittelalter,* Wiesbaden, 1964; W. C. Bryce, "The Turkish Colonization of Anatolia," *Bulletin of the John Rylands Library,* 38 (1955), 18–44; Paul Wittek, *Das Fürstentum Mentesche. Studien zur Geschichte Westkleinasiens im 13.–15. Jh,* Istanbul, 1934 (repr. Amsterdam, 1967); Ismail Hakkı Uzunçarşılı, *Anadolu Beylikleri ve Akkoyunlu, Karakoyunlu devirleri* (The Anatolian Principalities and the White Sheep and Black Sheep Periods), Istanbul, 1937, 2nd ed., Ankara, 1969; Paul Lemerle, *L'Emirat d'Aydin: Byzance et l'Occident. Recherches sur "La Geste d'Umur Pacha,"* Paris, 1953; Mustafa Akdağ, *Türkiye'nin Iktisadi ve Ictimai Tarihi,* (The Economic and Social History of Turkey), vol. I, 1243–1453, Ankara, 1959; Osman Turan, "Le droit terrien sous les Seldjoukides de Turquie," REI (1948); Claude Cahen, "Le Régime de la Terre et l'occupation turque en Anatolie," *Cahiers d'Histoire Mondiale* 2 (1955), 347–362; Franz Taeschner, "Beiträge zur Geschichte der Achis in Anatolien, 14–15. Jahrhundert," ZDMG, 12 (1933), 6–49; Franz Taeschner, "Akhi," EI², I, 321–323; Franz Taeschner, "Futuwwa," EI², II, 961–969.

V. Ottoman Origins to 1324

The two classic studies of Ottoman origins are Paul Wittek, *The Rise of the Ottoman Empire,* London, 1938, which stresses their gazi connections, and Fuat Köprülü, *Les Origines de l'Empire Ottoman,* Paris, 1935, which emphasizes the essentially Turkish origins of Ottoman institutions. The latter was translated into Turkish and published as *Osmanlı Devleti'nin Kuruluşu* (The Foundation of the Ottoman State) Ankara, 1959, with an introduction and commentaries on later studies on the subject by the author. Ernst Werner, *Die Geburt einer grossmacht – Die Osmanen, 1300–1481,* Berlin, 1966, provides a comprehensive but rather Marxist-oriented study of the period. Fuad Köprülü, *Türk Edebiyatında Ilk Mutasavvıflar* (The First Mystics in Turkish Literature), 2nd ed., Ankara, 1966, discusses the role of the mystic leaders in the development of Turkish culture and civilization in Anatolia. Mukrimin Halil Yinanç, "Ertuğrul Gazi," IA, IV, 328–337, provides an exhaustive study of Osman's father, Ertuğrul. M. Tayyip Gökbilgin, "Osman I," IA, IX,

431–443, brings together all available information on Osman I himself. See also Fuad Köprülü, "Osmanlı Imparatorluğu'nun Etnik Menşei Meseleleri" (Problems of the Ethnic Origins of the Ottoman Empire), *Belleten,* 7 (1944), 219–313. Problems associated with the Kayı tribe, out of which the Ottomans emerged, are discussed by Fuad Köprülü, "Kayı kabilesi hakkında yeni notlar" (New notes on the Kayı Tribe), *Belleten,* 8 (1944), 421–452; Faruk Sumer, "Kayı," IA, VI, 459–462; Faruk Sumer, "Osmanlı Devletinde Kayılar" (The Kayıs in the Age of the Ottomans), *Belleten,* 12 (1948), 576–615; Faruk Sumer, "Anadolu'ya yalnız Göçebe Türkler mi geldi?" (Did Only Nomadic Turks Come to Anatolia?), *Belleten,* 24 (1960), 567–594; F. Demirdaş, "Osmanlı Devrinde Anadoluda Kayılar" (The Kayis in Anatolia in the Age of the Ottomans), *Belleten,* 12 (1948), 576–615; Paul Wittek, "Deux Chapitres de l'Histoire des Turcs de Roum," *Byzantion,* 11 (1936), 85–319; and Ismail Hakkı Uzunçarşılı, "Osmanlı Tarihi'nin Ilk Devreleri'ne Aid Bazı Yanlışlıkların Tāshihi" (Correction of Some Mistakes Concerning the First Ages of Ottoman History), *Belleten,* 21 (1957), 173–188.

VI. The First Ottoman Empire, 1324–1413

The reign of Orhan Gazi is exhaustively studied by M. Tayyıp Gökbilgin, "Orhan," IA, 9 (1962), 399–408 and Irene Beldiceanu-Steinherr, *Recherches sur les actes des règnes des Sultans Osman Orkhan et Murad I,* Monachii, 1967. The roles of Orhan's brother Alauddin and his minister Alauddin are differentiated by Ismail Hakkı Uzunçarşılı, "Alauddin Paşa," IA, I, 282–285. On the initial Ottoman relations with the Byzantines see M. Münir Aktepe, "Osmanlıların Rumelide Ilk Fetihleri: Çimpe Kalesi" (The First Conquests of the Ottomans in Rumeli: the Fortress of Çimpe), *Tarih Dergisi,* 2 (1950), 283–307; G. G. Arnakis, "Gregory Palamas Among the Turks and Documents of His Captivity as Historical Sources," *Speculum,* 25 (1951), 104–118, and "Gregory Palamas, the Khiones and the Fall of Gallipoli," *Byzantion,* 22 (1952), 305–312; V. Mirmiroğlu, "Orhan Bey ile Bizans Imparatoru III. Andronikos arasındaki Pelekanon Muharebesi" (The Battle of Pelecanon Between Orhan Bey and the Byzantine Emperor Andronicos III), *Belleten,* 13 (1949) 309–320; Johannes Dräseke, *Der Übergang der Osmanen nach Europa im XIV. Jahrhundert,* Berlin, 1913; and M. M. Alexandrescu-Dersca, "L'Expédition d'Umur Beg d'Aydın aux bouches du Danube (1337 ou 1338)," *Studia et Acta Orientalia,* 2 (1959), 3–23. On the problem of Orhan's accession see Ismail Hakkı Uzunçarşılı, "Gazi Orhan Beyin Hükümdar olduğu tarih ve ilk sikkesi" (The Date That Gazi Orhan Bey Became Ruler, and His First Coin), *Belleten,* 8 (1945), 207–211. European involvement in Ottoman and Byzantine affairs in the first half of the fourteenth century is discussed by J. Gay, *Le Pape Clément VI et les affaires d'Orient, 1342–1352,* Paris, 1904; W. Miller, *The Latins in the Levant: A History of Frankish Greece, 1204–1566,* London, 1908; and J. Delaville le Roulx, *La France en Orient au XIV siècle,* 2 vols., Paris, 1908. H. A. Gibbons, *The Foundation of the Ottoman Empire,* New York, 1916, is outdated and obsolete. G. G. Arnakis, *Hoi Protoi Othomanoi: Symbole eis to problema tes ptoseos ou Hellenisme tes Mikras Asias, 1282–1337* (The Early Ottomans: A Contribution to the Problem of the Fall of Hellenism in Asia Minor, 1282–1337), Athens, 1947, is useful but exaggerates the Greek role in the development of Ottoman institutions.

Murad I's reign (1359–1389) is discussed generally by Ismail Hakkı Uzunçarşılı, "Murad I," IA, 8 (1960), 587–598. The same author also considers the rise of the Turkish nobility, led by the Çandarlı, in Ottoman service in *Çandarlı Vezir Ailesi,* (The Çandarlı ministerial family) Ankara, 1974. The same subject is also discussed by Franz Taeschner and Paul Wittek, "Die Vezirfamilie der Gandarlyzade (14.15 Jh.) und ihre Denkmäler," *Der Islam,* 18 (1929). Murad's relationship with the *ahi* orders is studied by F. Taeschner, "War Murad I. Grossmeister oder Mitglied des Achibundes?" *Oriens,* 6 (1953), 23–31. His conquests in Rumeli are described by Apostolos E. Vacalopoulos, *Origins of the Greek Nation, 1204–1461,* New Brunswick, N.J., 1970; Alexandre Burmov, "Türkler Edirne'yi ne vakit aldılar?" (When Did the Turks Capture Edirne?), *Belleten,* 13 (1949), 97–106;

M. Münir Aktepe, "XIV ve XV asırlarda Rumeli'nin Türkler tarafından iskânına dair" (On the Settlement of Rumelia by the Turks in the Fourteenth and Fifteenth Centuries), *Türkiyat Mecmuası*, 10 (1953), 299–313; P. Charanis, "On the Date of the Occupation of Gallipoli by the Turks," *Byzantinoslavica*, 16 (1955), 113–117; Halil Inalcık, "Edirne'nin Fethi (1361)," in *Edirne*, Ankara, 1965, pp. 137–159; English tr. in *Archivum Ottomanicum*, 1971; P. Charanis, "The Strife Among the Palaeologi and the Ottoman Turks, 1370–1402," *Byzantion*, 16 (1942–1943), 286–314; 17 (1949), 104–118. By far the best single study of Ottoman conquests is that of Halil Inalcık, "Ottoman Methods of Conquest," *Studia Islamica*, II, 103–129. See also D. Angelov, "Certains aspects de la conquête des peuples balkaniques par les Turcs," *Byzantinoslavica*, 17 (1956), 220–275. The Battle of Kosova is analyzed in M. Braun, *Kosovo*, Leipzig, 1937; A. d'Avril, *La Bataille de Kossovo, Rhapsodie Serbe*, Paris, 1968; Ali Haydar, *Kosova Meydan Muharebesi* (The Battle of Kosova), Istanbul, 1328/1910; and Mukerrem, *Kosova, 1389*, Istanbul, 1931.

By far the most exhaustive and useful study of the reign of Bayezit I (1389–1402) is Mukrimin Halil Yinanç, "Bâyezid I," IA, II, 369–392; that of Halil Inalcık, "Bâyezid I," EI², I, 1117–1119 is short but authoritative. Bayezit's relationships with the Byzantines are described in P. Charanis, "The Strife among the Palaeologi and the Ottoman Turks, 1370–1402," *Byzantion*, 16 (1942), 286–314. The Battle of Nicopolis has been the subject of numerous studies of which the most useful are Aziz Suryal Atiya, *The Crusade of Nicopolis*, London, 1934, and E. Gling, *Die Schlacht bei Nicopolis in 1396*, Berlin, 1906. Bayezit's other European conquests are discussed in R. J. Loenertz, "Pour l'histoire du Peloponèse au XIV siècle," REB, I, 152–186; A. Zakythinos, *Le Despotat Grec de Morée*, Paris, 1932; A. Gegaj, *Albanie et l'invasion turque*, Paris, 1937; Max Silberschmidt, *Das Orientalische Problem zur Zeit der Entstehung des Türkischen Reiches nach Venezianischen Quellen*, Leipzig, 1923; Franz Babinger, *Beiträge zur Frühgeschichte der Türkenherrschaft in Rumelien*, Munich, 1944; and G. Beckmann, *Der Kampf Kaiser Sigmunds gegen die werdende Weltmacht der Osmanen, 1392–1437*, Gotha, 1902.

Bayezit's invasion of Anatolia is described in M. Yaşar Yücel, "Kastamonu'nun ilk fethine kadar Osmanlı-Candar Münasebetleri, 1361–1392" (Ottoman Relations with the Candar Principality Until the First Conquest of Kastamonu), *Tarih Araştırmaları Dergisi*, I (1963), 133–144; and B. P. Saxena, *Memoirs of Bayezid*, Allahabad, 1939. Tamerlane's resulting invasion is followed in M. M. Alexandrescu-Dersca, *La Campagne de Timur en Anatolie*, Bucharest, 1942. His relationships with the Ottomans' enemies in eastern Europe are studied by Zeki Velidi Togan, "Timur's Osteuropapolitik," ZDMG, 108 (1959), 279–298. The Battle of Ankara (1402) is studied by T. Yılmaz Öztuna, *1402 Ankara Muharebesi* (The 1402 Battle of Ankara), Istanbul, 1946, and Gustav Roloff, "Die Schlacht bei Angora," *Historische Zeitschrift*, 161 (1943), 244–262. The problems involved in Bayezit's imprisonment and subsequent death are resolved by Fuad Köprülü, "Yıldırım Bâyezid'in Esâreti ve Intihârı" (The Imprisonment and Suicide of Lightning Bayezit), *Belleten*, 1 (1937), 591–603, and the same author's "Yıldırım Bâyezid'in Intiharı Meselesi" (The Problem of Bayezit's Suicide), *Belleten*, 7 (1943), 591–599. See also Jean Aubin, "Comment Tamerlan prenait les villes," *Studia Islamica*, 19 (1963), 83–122.

The definitive article on the Interregnum (1402–1413) is Paul Wittek, "De la défaite d'Ankara à la prise de Constantinople," REI, 12 (1938), 1–34. More recent research has been incorporated into studies of the individual Ottoman participants: M. C. Şehâbeddin Tekindağ, "Mûsâ Çelebi," IA, VIII, 661–666; Ismail Hakkı Uzunçarşılı, "Mehmed I," IA, VII, 496–506; M. C. Şehâbeddin Tekindağ, "Mustafa Çelebi," IA, VIII, 687–689; and M. Tayyib Gökbilgin, "Süleyman Çelebi," IA, XI, 179–182. In addition, for the subsequent reign of Mehmet I (1413–1420), see Ismail Hakkı Uzunçarşılı, "Çelebi Sultan Mehmed'in kızı Selçuk Hatun," *Belleten* 21 (1957), 253–260; Franz Babinger, "Schejch Bedr ed-Din, der Sohn des Richtern von Simâvs . . . ," *Der Islam*, 11 (1921), 1–106; Mehmed Şerefeddin, *Simavna Kadısı-Oğlu Şeyh Bedreddin*, Istanbul, 1340/1924; Hans J. Kissling, "Badr al-Dîn b. Kâdi Samâwnâ," EI², vol. 1, p. 869; Şerif Baştav, "Les Sources d'une Histoire de l'Empire Ottomane rédigée par un auteur anonyme Grec," *Belleten*, 21, pp. 161–172; J. W. Barker, *Manuel II Palaeologus, 1391–1425*, New Brunswick, N.J., 1969; and H. J.

Kissling, "Das Menâqybnâme Scheich Bedr ed-dîns, des Sohnes des Richters von Samavna," ZDMG, 100 (1950), 112–176.

VII. Restoration of the Empire, 1413–1451

The reign of Murat II (1421–1451) is brilliantly studied by Halil Inalcık, "Murad II," IA, VIII, 598–615. See also Ducas, *Istoria Turco-Bizantina (1341–1462)*, ed. Vasile Grecu, Bucharest, 1958; G. Beckmann, *Der Kampf Kaiser Sigmunds gegen die werdende Weltmacht der Osmanen, 1392–1437*, Gotha, 1902; Mehmed Cemil, *Çandarlı Halil Paşa*, Istanbul, 1933; Ismail Hakkı Uzunçarşılı, "Çandarlı," IA, III, 351–357 and *Çandarlı Vezir Ailesi* (The Çandarlı Ministerial Family), Istanbul, 1974, describe the power exercised by the nobility through the Çandarlı family. Murat's relations with the Mamluks of Egypt and Syria are included in A. Darag, *L'Egypte sous le Règne de Barsbay, 1422–1438*, Damascus, 1961. On European relations leading up to the Crusade of Varna see Halil Inalcık, "1444 Buhranı" (The Crisis of 1444), in his *Fatih Devri Üzerinde Tetkikler ve Vesikalar, I* (Studies and Documents on the Period of Mehmet II the Conqueror), Ankara, 1954, pp. 1–53; and David Angyal, "Le Traité de Paix de Szeged avec les Turcs (1444)," *Revue de Hongrie* (1911), 233–268, 374–392. On the Crusade of Varna itself and the Ottoman victory (1444) see Nicholas Iorga, *Notices et Extraits pour Servir à l'Histoire des Croisades au XVe Siècle*, 6 vols., Bucharest, 1899–1915, and the same author's *La Campagne des Croisés sur le Danube*, Paris, 1927. Also Oskar Halecki, *The Crusade of Varna: A Discussion of Controversial Problems*, New York, 1943, to be used with the review of J. Bromberg, *Speculum*, 20 (1945). Franz Babinger, "Von Amurath zu Amurath. Vor- und Nachspiel der Schlacht bei Varna (1444)," *Oriens*, 3 (1950), 229–265, 4 (1951), 80. J. Dabroski, "La Pologne et l'expédition de Varna en 1444," *Revue des Etudes Slaves*, 10 (1930), 37–75; Huber, "Die Kriege zwischen Ungarn und die Türken (1440–1444)," *Archiv für Österreichen Geschichte*, 68 (1886), 159–207. Necâti Salim (Tacan), *Türk Ordusu'nun Eski Seferleri'nden bir Imhâ Muhârebesi, Varna 1444*" (Among the Old Battles of the Turkish Army, A Battle of Annihilation, Varna, 1944), Istanbul, 1931; and Adnan Erzi, "II Murad'ın Varna muharebesi hakkında fethnamesi" (A Bulletin of Victory of Murat II Concerning the Battle of Varna), *Belleten*, 14 (1950), 595–647.

Ottoman efforts to conquer Albania, and the resistance led by Scanderbeg, are described in A. Gégaj, *L'Albanie et l'Invasion Turque au XVe Siècle*, Paris, 1937; Halil Inalcık, "Timariotes Chrétiens en Albanie au XVe Siècle," *Mitteilungen des Österreichischen Staatsarchiv*, 4 (1952), "Arnavutlukta Osmanlı Hâkimiyeti'nin Yerleşmesi ve Iskender Bey Isyânı'nın Menşei" (The Establishment of Ottoman Rule in Albania, and the Origins of the Revolt of Scanderbeg), *Fatih ve Istanbul Mecmuası*, I, 153–191, and "Iskender Bey," IA, V, 1079–1082; F. S. Noli, *George Castrioti Scanderbeg, 1405–1468*, New York, 1947; and C. Marinesco, *Alphonse V, Roi d'Aragon et de Naples et de l'Albanie de Scanderbeg*, Paris, 1923. The second Battle of Kosova is described in Necati Sâlim (Tacan), *Ikinci Kosova Meydan Muharebesi* (1448), Istanbul, 1932. On Murat's subsequent effort to besiege Constantinople, see Zafer Taşlıklıoğlu, "II Murad'ın Istanbul muḥasarası hakkında bir eser" (A Work on Murat II's Siege of Istanbul), *Tarih Dergisi*, VIII, 209–226. His initial efforts to establish contacts with the Tatar *hans* of the Crimea are presented in Fevzi Kurtoğlu, "Ilk Kırım Hanlarının Mektupları" (The Letters of the First Crimean *Hans*), *Belleten*, 1 (1937), 641–655. Europe's reaction to the Turkish Question is discussed by Hans J. Kissling, "Die Türkenfrage als europaisches Problem," *Südostdeutsches Archiv*, 7 (1964), 39–57, and the same author's "Militärische-politische Problematiken zur Türkenfrage im 15. Jahrhundert," *Bohemia: Jahrbuch des Collegium Carolinum*, 5 (1964), 108–136.

VIII. The Apogee of Ottoman Power, 1451–1566

The definitive studies of the reign of Mehmet II the Conqueror have been made by Halil Inalcık, "Mehmed II," IA, VII, 506–535, and *Fatih Devri Üzerinde tetkikler ve vesikalar*

(Studies and Documents on the Period of the Conqueror), Ankara, 1954. Salahaddin Tansel, *Osmanlı Kaynaklarına göre Fâtih Sultan Mehmed'in Siyasî ve Askeri Faaliyeti* (The Political and Military Activities of Sultan Mehmet the Conqueror According to Ottoman Sources), Ankara, 1953 (repr. Istanbul, 1971), provides detailed information on his military activities. Franz Babinger's immense work, *Mehmed II. der Eroberer und Seine Zeit. Weltenstürmer einer Zeitenwende,* Munich, 1953 (2nd ed., Munich, 1959) (transalted into French as *Mahomet Le Conquérant et son Temps. Une peur du Monde au tournant de l'Histoire,* Paris, 1954, and into Italian as *Maometto il Conquistatore e il suo Tempo,* Turin, 1957; English tr. by W. Hickman in preparation), must be used with caution due to the author's overreliance on European sources and failure to use information in some Ottoman sources. (See the review by Halil Inalcık, "Mehmed the Conqueror and His Time," *Speculum,* 25 (1960), 408–427; a complete list of reviews of this work is found in F. Babinger, *Aufsätze und Abhandlungen zur Geschichte Südosteuropas und der Levante,* 2 vols., Munich, 1962–1966, I, 37–39 and *passim*). A detailed chronological study of the reign is provided by Ismail Hami Dânişmend, *Fâtih'in Hayâtı ve Fetih Takvimi* (The Life of the Conqueror and Calendar of Conquest), 2 parts, Istanbul, 1953–1955. His conquests in the Mediterranean, Aegean, and Black Sea are studied in I. H. Ertaylan, *Fâtih ve Fütuhatı* (The Conqueror and His Conquests), 2 vols., Istanbul, 1953, Ankara, 1966. The conquest of Constantinople is discussed in Sir Stephen Runciman, *The Fall of Constantinople,* Cambridge, 1965; B. Lewis, R. Betts, N. Rubenstein, and P. Wittek, *The Fall of Constantinople,* London, 1955; A. D. Mordtmann, *Belagerung und Eroberung Constantinopels durch die Türken in Jahre 1453 nach Originalquellen Bearbeitet,* Stuttgart, 1858; and Feridun Dirimtekin, *Istanbul'un Fethi* (The Conquest of Istanbul), Istanbul, 1949. Also G. Schlumberger, *La Siège, La Prise et le Sac de Constantinople par les Turcs en 1453,* Paris, 1914, and later printings; and Sir Edwin Pears, *The Destruction of the Greek Empire and the Story of the Capture of Constantinople by the Turks,* London, 1903; but these are prejudiced and one sided. See the contemporary description by Kritovoulos, *History of Mehmed the Conqueror,* tr. Charles Riggs, Princeton, 1964. Mehmet's effort to rebuild and repopulate the city is described by Halil Inalcık, "The Policy of Mehmed II Toward the Greek Population of Istanbul and the Byzantine Buildings of the City," *Dumbarton Oaks Papers,* no. 23 (1970), pp. 213–249; and A. M. Schneider, "Die Bevölkerung Konstantinopels im XV Jahrhundert," *Nachr. der Akad. der Wiss. in Göttingen,* 1949.

The cultural and scientific development of the empire during Mehmet II's reign is described in Süheyl Ünver, *Fatih, Külliyesi ve zamanı ilim hayatı* (The Conqueror, His College, and the Scientific Life of His Time), Istanbul, 1946; Emil Jacobs, "Mehemmed II. der Eroberer, Seine Beziehungen Renaissance und Seine Büchersammling," *Oriens,* 2 (1949), 6–30; L. Thuasne, *Gentile Bellini et le Sultan Mohammed II,* Paris, 1888; Ahmed Refik, *Fatih Sultan Mehmet ve Ressam Bellini, 1470–1480,* Istanbul, 1325/1909; and J. von Karabacek, "Abendländische Künstler zu Konstantinople im XV, und XVI. Jahrhundert. 1. Italienische Künstler am Hofe Muhammeds II des Eroberers," *Denkschriften der Akad. der Wissenschaften in Wien, Philos.-Hist. Klasse,* 92 (1918).

The Conqueror's administrative and economic policies are discussed in Ömer Lütfi Barkan, "Les déportations comme méthode de peuplement et de colonisation dans l'Empire Ottoman," *Revue de la Faculté des Sciences Economiques de l'Université d'Istanbul,* 9 (1949–1950), 67–131; Halil Inalcık, "15. asır Türkiye iktisadi ve içtimai tarih kaynakları" (Sources on Turkey's Economic and Social History in the Fifteenth Century), Istanbul University, *Iktisat Fakültesi Mecmuası,* 15 (1955), 51–75; N. Beldiceanu, "Recherches sur la réforme fonciere de Mehmed II," *Acta Historica,* 4 (1965), 27–39; Bistra A. Cvetkova, "Sur certains réformes du régime foncier du temps de Mehmed II," *JESHO,* 6 (1963), 104–120; and Mustafa A. Mehmet, "De certains aspects de la société ottomane à la lumière de la législation (Kanunname) du sultan Mahomet II (1451–1481)", *Studia et acta Orientalia,* 2 (1959), 127–160. Source collections concerning his legislation are: Franz Babinger, *Sultanische Urkunden zur Geschichte der Osmanischen Wirtschaft und Staatsverwaltung am Ausgang der Herrschaft Mehmeds II., des Eroberers. I. Teil, Das Qânûn-*

nâme-i Sultanî ber Müdscheb-i Örf-i Osmanî, Munich, 1955; N. Beldiceanu, ed., Les Actes des Premiers Sultans conservés dans les Manuscrits Turcs de la Bibliothèque Nationale à Paris, vol. I, Actes de Mehmed II et de Bayezid II du MS. fonds Turc Ancien 39 (Paris and the Hague, 1960) ; vol. II, Réglements Miniers 1390–1512, Paris and the Hague, 1964. Dr. Halil Inalcık, Dr. Robert Anhegger, eds., Kânûnnâme-i Sultânî ber Mûceb-i Örf-i Osmânî: II. Mehmed ve II. Bayezid Devirlerine ait yasakname ve Kanunnameler (Prohibition Regulations and Laws Concerning the Periods of Mehmet II and Bayezit II), Ankara, 1956; Ömer Lütfi Barkan, XV ve XVIinci asırlarda Osmanlı Imparatorluğunda ziraî ekonominin hukukî ve malî esasları. Kanunnameler, I (The Legal and Financial Bases of the Agricultural Economy of the Ottoman Empire in the Fifteenth and Sixteenth centuries. The Law Codes), Istanbul, 1945; and Nicoara Beldiceanu, Code de lois coutumières de Mehmed II. Kitab-i Qavanîn-i Örfiyye-i Osmani, Paris, 1967.

Ottoman relations with the White Sheep and Black Sheep are described in Mukrimin Halil Yinanç, "Akkoyunlular" (The White Sheep), IA, I, 251–270; Faruk Sümer, "Kara Koyunlular" (The Black Sheep), IA, VI, 292–305; V. Minorsky, La Perse au XV siècle entre la Turquie et Venise, Paris, 1933; Walther Hinz, Irans Aufsteig zum Nationalstaat im XV Jahrhundert, Leipzig, 1936; and Faruk Sümer, Kara Koyunlular (The Black Sheep), Ankara, 1967. On relations with Uzun Hasan and Venice, see Şerafeddin Turan, "Fatih Mehmed-Uzun Hasan mücadelesi ve Venedik" (The Struggle Between Mehmet the Conqueror and Uzun Hasan and Venice), Ankara Universitesi, Tarih Araştırmalar Dergisi, 3 (1966), 63–138.

On the political struggles that preceded the Conqueror's death, and the problems involved with the death itself, see Ismail Hakkı Uzunçarşılı, "Fatih Sultan Mehmed'in Veziri âzamlarından Mahmud Paşa ile Şehzade Mustafa'nin araları neden açılmıştı," (Why Was There a Quarrel Between one of Sultan Mehmet the Conqueror's Grand Vezirs, Mahmud Paşa, and Prince Mustafa?), Belleten, 28 (1964), 719–728; Şehabeddin Tekindağ, "Fatih'in ölümü meselesi" (The Problem of the Conqueror's Death), Tarih Dergisi 16 (1966), 95–108; Ismail Hakkı Uzunçarşılı, "Fatih Sultan Mehmed'in Ölümü" (The Death of Sultan Mehmet the Conqueror), Belleten, 34 (1970), 231–234.

The definitive study of the political and military sides of the reign of Sultan Bayezit II is provided by Selahattin Tansel, Sultan II. Bayezid'in Siyasi Hayatı (The Political Life of Sultan Bayezit II), Istanbul, 1966. The reign is also discussed generally by V. J. Parry, "Bayezid II," EI², I, 1119–1121; and Ismail Hakkı Uzunçarşılı, "II Bayezid," IA, II, 392–398.

Regarding the revolt of Cem Sultan, see E. H. Ertaylan, Sultan Cem, Istanbul, 1951; L. Thuasne, Djem Sultan, Paris, 1892; M. Cavid Baysun, "Cem," IA, III, 69–81; C. S. Tekindağ, "II. Bayezid'in Tahta çıkışı sırasında Istanbul'da vukua gelen hadiseler" (Events That Took Place in Istanbul While Bayezit II Took the Throne), Tarih Dergisi, 14 (1959), 85–96; S. Tansel, "Yeni Vesikalar Karşısında Sultan II. Bayezid" (Bayezit II in the Light of New Documents), Belleten, 27 (1963), 195–236; Sidney N. Fisher, "Civil Strife in the Ottoman Empire, 1481–1503," Journal of Modern History, 13 (1941), 448–466; Şerafeddin Turan, "Barak Reis'in Şehzade Cem Meselesi ile Ilgili olarak Savoi'ya gönderilmesi" (The Sending of Barak Reis to Savoy Regarding the Problem of Sultan Cem), Belleten, 26 (1962), 529–555; and Ismail Hakkı Uzunçarşılı, "Cem Sultan'a dair beş orijinal vesika" (Five Original Documents concerning Cem Sultan), Belleten, 24 (1960), 457–483.

Bayezit's relations with Europe and the Mamluks are studied in Sidney N. Fisher, The Foreign Relations of Turkey, 1481–1512, Urbana, Ill., 1948; R. S. Schwoebel, The Shadow of the Crescent: The Renaissance Image of the Turk, 1453–1517, New York, 1967; H. Pfefferman, Die Zusammenarbeit der Renaissancepäpste mit den Turken, Winterthur, 1946; Hans S. Kissling, Sultan Bayezid II's Beziehungen zu Markgraf Francesco von Gonzaga, Munich, 1965; V. J. Parry, "The Ottoman Empire (1481–1520)," New Cambridge Modern History, 1 (1957), 395–410; Tayyip Gökbilgin, "Korvin Mathias (Mátyás) in Bayezid II ile mektupları tercümeleri ve 1503 (909) Osmanlı Macar Muahedesinin Türkçe metni" (Translations of the Letters Between Mathias Corvinus and Bayezit II, and the Turkish

Text of the 1503 Turkish-Hungarian treaty), *Belleten,* 22 (1958), 369–390; V. Coroviç, "Der Friedensvertrag zwischen dem Sultan Bayazid II und dem König Ladislasi," ZDMG, 90 (1936, N.F. 15), 52–59; C. Cogo, *La Guerra di Venezia contro i Turchi (1499–1501),* Venice, 1888; Victor Ménage, "The Mission of an Ottoman Secret Agent in France in 1486," JRAS (1965), 112–132; M. C. Şehabeddin Tekindağ, "II. Bayezid Devrinde Çukurova'da Nüfuz Mücadelesi, Ilk Osmanlı Memlûklu Savaşları, 1485–1491" (The Struggle for Influence in Cilicia During the Time of Bayezit II – Ottoman-Mamluk Battles, 1485–1491), *Belleten,* 21 (1967), 345–373, *Berkuk Devrinde Memluk Sultanlık* (The Mamluk Sultanate During the Time of Barkuk), Istanbul, 1961, "Son Osmanlı-Karaman Münasebetleri" (The Last Relationships Between the Ottomans and Karaman), *Tarih Dergisi,* 17–18 (1963). H. A. von Burski, *Kemâl Re'is: ein Beitrag zur Geschichte des Türkischen Flotte,* Bonn, 1928; Ali Rızâ Seyfî, *Kemal Reis ve Baba Oruç,* Istanbul, 1326/1907; and F. Kurdoğlu, *Gelibolu ve Yöresi Tarihi* (The History of Gallipoli and Its Environs), Istanbul, 1938, study Ottoman naval development during Bayezit's reign.

The reign of Selim I (1512–1520) is studied in detail by Şelâhattin Tansel, *Yavuz Sultan Selim* (Sultan Selim the Grim), Ankara, 1969: and Şinasi Altındağ, "Selim I," IA, X, 423–434. The events surrounding his accession are described by M. Çağatay Uluçay, "Yavuz Sultan Selim Nasıl Padişah Oldu?" (How Did Sultan Selim the Grim Become Ruler?) *Tarih Dergisi,* 6 (1954), 53–90; 7 (1954), 117–142; 8 (1955) 185–200. The best general account of his Eastern relations is G. W. F. Stripling, *The Ottoman Turks and the Arabs, 1511–1574,* Urbana, Ill., 1942 (repr. 1968). His relations and struggles with the Safavids are described by E. Eberhard, *Osmanische Polemik gegen die Safeviden im 16. Jahr. nach arabischen Handschriften,* Freiburg, 1970; H. Sohrweide, "Der Sieg der Safeviden in Persien und seine Rückwirkungen auf die Schiiten Anatoliens im 16. Jahrhundert," *Der Islam,* 41 (1965), 95–223; V. Minorsky, *La Perse au XVe siècle entre la Turquie et Venise,* Paris, 1933; R. M. Savory, "The Principal Offices of the Safewid State during the Reign of Ismail I (1501–1524)," BSOAS, 23 (1960), 91–105; Tahsin Yazıcı, "Şah Ismail," IA, XI, 275–279; Jean Aubin, "Etudes Safavides, I. Sâh Ismâ'il et les notables de l'Iraq persan," JESHO, II (1959), 37–81; L. Lockhart, "The Persian army in the Safavi period," *Der Islam,* 24 (1959), 89–98; Zeki Velidi Togan, "Sur l'origine des Safavides," *Melanges Louis Massignon,* 3 (1957), 345–357; A. J. Toynbee, "The Schism in the Iranic World and the Incorporation of the Arabic Society into the Iranic," *A Study of History,* I (1934), 347–402; and W. Hinz, "Das Steuerwesen Ostanatoliens im 15. und 16. Jahrhundert," ZDMG, 100 (1950), 177–204. Relations with the Dulgadir state are studied in J. H. Mordtmann and M. H. Yinanç, "Dulkadırlılar," IA, III, 654–662. The Battle of Çaldiran and its results are analyzed in M. Tayyip Gökbilgin, "Çaldıran," IA, III, 329–331; J. R. Walsh, "Câldırân," EI, II, 7–8; and Tahsin Yazıcı, "Safeviler" (The Safevids), IA, IX, 53–59.

Selim's conquest of the Arab world is described by H. Jansky "Beitrage zur Osmanische Geschichtschreibung über Agypten," *Der Islam,* 21 (1933) pp. 269–278; and the same author's "Die Eroberung Syrien durch Sultan Selim I," *Mitteilungen zur Osmanischen Geschichte,* 2 (1926), 173–231, and "Die Chronik des Ibn Tulun als Geschichtes-quelle über den Feldzüg Sultan Selim's I gegen die Mamluken," *Der Islam,* 18 (1929), 24–33; W. H. Salmon, *An Account of the Ottoman Conquest of Egypt,* London, 1939; Marie-Therese Speiser, *Das Selimnâme des Sa'di b. 'Abd al-Mute'âl,* Zürich, 1946; H. Massé, "Selim Ier en Syrie, d'après le Sélim Nâme," *Mélanges René Dussaud,* 2 (1939), 779–782; Halil Edhem, *Sultan Selim's aegyptischer Feldzug,* Weimar, 1916; Stanford J. Shaw, *The Financial and Administrative Organization and Development of Ottoman Egypt, 1517–1798,* Princeton, N.J., 1962; and Stanford J. Shaw, "The Land Law of Ottoman Egypt (960/1553): A Contribution to the Study of Landholding in the Early Years of Ottoman Rule in Egypt," *Der Islam,* 38 (1962), 106–137. On the question of whether the caliphate was transferred to the sultan, see C. A. Nallino, *Notes sur la nature du 'Califat' en général et sur la prétendu 'Califat Ottoman,'* Rome, 1919; and Carl H. Becker, "Barthold's Studien über Kalif und Sultan," *Der Islam,* 6 (1915), 386–412.

The most authoritative study of the reign of Süleyman I the Magnificent is M. Tayyip

Gökbilgin, "Süleyman I," IA, XI, 99–155. This can be supplemented by V. J. Parry, "The Ottoman Empire, 1520–1566," *New Cambridge Modern History,* 2 (1958), 510–533, and Halil Inalcık, "The Heyday and Decline of the Ottoman Empire," *Cambridge History of Islam,* vol. I, pp. 324–353, for military and political affairs. Unfortunately, the old biographies of Süleyman – R. B. Merriman, *Suleiman the Magnificent,* Cambridge, Mass., 1944; Harold Lamb, *Suleiman the Magnificent,* New York, 1951, F. Downy, *The Grande Turke,* New York, 1929 – and of his chief minister – H. D. Jenkins, *Ibrahim Pasha: Grand Vizir of Suleiman the Magnificent,* New York, 1911 – are extremely inaccurate and of little value. A number of articles on Süleyman are collected in *Kanuni Armağanı,* Ankara, 1970.

Süleyman's early campaigns are detailed in Hüseyin G. Yurdaydın, *Kanûnî'nin cülûsu ve ilk seferleri* (Süleyman's Accession and His First Campaigns), Ankara, 1961. Some of his European campaigns are described in L. Forrer, *Die osmanische Chronik des Rüstem Pascha,* Leipzig, 1923; F. Tauer, *Histoire de la campagne du Sultan Suleyman Ier contre Belgrade en 1521,* Prague, 1924; J. H. Mordtmann, *Zur Kapitulation vom Buda im Jahre 1526,* Budapest-Istanbul, 1918; M. Pavet de Courteille, *Histoire de la compagne de Mohacz par Kemal Pacha Zâdeh,* Paris, 1859; Ettori Rossi, *Assedio e Conquiste Turca di Rodi nel 1522 secondo le Relazioni edite e inedite del Turchi, con un cenno sulla Bibliotheca Hâfiz di Rodi,* Rome, 1927; Binbaşı Eşref, *Mohac Meydan Muharebesi, 1526* (The Battle of Mohacs, 1526), Istanbul, 1930; and E. Brockman, *The Two Sieges of Rhodes, 1480–1522,* London, 1969. The first Ottoman siege of Vienna and Austrian campaign (1529) has an immense bibliography: See W. Sturminger, *Bibliographie und Ikonographie der Türkenbelagerungen Wiens 1529 und 1683,* Graz-Köln, 1955. In particular, see Felix Tauer, "Solimans Wiener Feldzug," *Archiv Orientalni,* 24 (1956), 507–563. On the European results see Dorothy Vaughan, *Europe and the Turk: A Pattern of Alliances, 1350–1700,* Liverpool, 1954; S. Fischer-Galati, *Ottoman Imperialism and German Protestantism, 1521–1555,* Cambridge, Mass., 1959; and Kenneth Setton, "Lutheranism and the Turkish Peril," *Balkan Studies,* 3 (1962), 133–168. The Habsburg defense system against the Turks is studied by G. E. Rothenberg, *The Austrian Military Border in Croatia, 1522–1747,* Urbana, Ill., 1960; that of the Ottomans by Cengiz Orhonlu, *Osmanlı Imparatorluğunda Derbend Teşkilâtı* (Guardhouse Organization in the Ottoman Empire), Istanbul, 1967. Ottoman relations with the Habsburgs in Hungary are studied by A. Géray, *Urkunden und Aktenstücke zur Geschichte der Verhältnisse Zwischen Österreich, Ungarn und der Pforte im XVI. und XVII. Jahrhundert,* 3 vols., Vienna, 1840–1842; L. Kupelwieser, *Die Kämpfe Oesterreichs mit den Osmanen vom Jahre 1526 bis 1537,* Vienna, 1899; and F. Salamon, *Ungarn im Zeitalter der Türkenherrschaft,* Leipzig, 1887. Ottoman relations with France at this time are outlined in J. Ursu, *La Politique Orientale de François I,* Paris, 1908; E. Charière, *Négociations de la France dans le Levant, 1515–1580,* Paris, 2 vols., 1848–1853; G. Tongas, *Les Relations de la France avec l'Empire Ottoman,* Toulouse, 1942; C. D. Rouillard, *The Turk in French History, Thought and Literature, 1520–1660,* Paris, 1938; and Ismail Soysal, "Türk-Fransız Diploması münasebetleri'nin Ilk Devresi" (The First Period of Ottoman-French Diplomatic Relations), *Tarih Dergisi,* 3 (1953), 63–94. See also M. Mignet, *Rivalité de François Ier et de Charles-Quint,* 2 vols., Paris, 1875, and Lajos Tölgyes, *Ungarn, Bollwerk der Christienheit zur Zeit der Europaeischen Türkenkriege, 1360–1790,* Cologne, 1957.

The 1540 peace with Venice is discussed in L. Bonelli, "Il trattatto turco-veneto del 1540," *Centenario della nascitá di Michele Amari,* 2 (1910), 332–363; and W. Lehmann, *Der Friedensvertrag zwischen Venedig und der Türkei am 2 Okt. 1540,* Bohn, 1936; also Alessio Bombaci, "Ancora sul trattato turco-veneto del 2 ottobre 1540," *Rivista dei Studi Orientali,* 20 (1943), 373–383, and M. Tayyip Gökbilgin, "Venedik devlet arşivindeki vesikalar külliyatında Kanuni Sultan Süleyman devri belgeler" (Sources on the Reign of Sultan Süleyman the Magnificent in the Collection of the Venetian State Archives), *Belgeler,* I/2 (1965), 119–220.

The sixteenth-century maritime wars are studied in J. de la Gravière, *Doria et Barberousse,* Paris, 1886; Enver Ziya Karal, "Barbaros Hayreddin Paşa," IA, II, 311–315; Ali Riza Seyfi, *Barbaros Hayreddin,* Istanbul, 1910; Fevzi Kurdoğlu, *Turgut Paşa,* Istanbul, 1935; Şerafeddin Turan, "Piyâle Paşa," IA, IX, 566–569; R. C. Anderson, *Naval Wars in the Levant, 1558–1853,* Princeton, N.J., 1952; Aziz Samih Ilter, *Şimali Afrika'da Türkler* (The Turks in North Africa), 2 vols., Istanbul, 1935; Ekkehard Eickoff, *Seekreig und Seepolitik zwischen Islam und Abendland,* Berlin, 1966; E. Rossi, *L'Assedio di Malta nel 1565 secondo gli Storici Ottomani,* Malta, 1926; Fevzi Kurdoğlu, *Malta Muhâsarası* (The Siege of Malta), Istanbul, 1936; and Jaime Salva, *La Orden de Malta y les Acciones navales Espanoles contra Turcos y Berberiscos en los Sigalos XVI y XVII,* Madrid, 1944. The naval expeditions in the eastern seas are described by M. Longworth Dames, "The Portugese and Turks in the Sixteenth Century," JRAS, 1 (1921) 1–28; R. B. Serjeant, *The Portugese off the South Arabian Coast,* Oxford, 1963; Cengiz Orhonlu, "XVI Asrın Ilk Yarısında Kızıldeniz Sahillerinde Osmanlılar" (The Ottomans Along the Shores of the Red Sea in the First Half of the Sixteenth Century), *Tarihi Dergisi,* 12 (1962), 1–24; H. Melzig, *Hadım Süleyman Paşa'nın Hind Seferi* (The Indian Expedition of Hadım Süleyman Paşa), Istanbul, 1943; Afet Inan, *Türk Amirali Piri Reis'in Hayat ve Eserleri* (The Life and Works of the Turkish Admiral Piri Reis), Ankara, 1954; F. Ezgu, "Piri Reis," IA, IX, 561–565; Cengiz Orhonlu, "Hint Kaptanlığı ve Piri Reis" (The Captainship of India and Piri Reis), *Belleten,* 34 (1970), 235–254; Z. P. Pachi, "The Shifting of International Trade Routes in the 15th–17th Centuries," *Acta Historica,* 14 (1968), 287–321; and A. Hess, "The Evolution of the Ottoman Seaborne Empire in the Age of the Oceanic Discoveries," *AHR,* 75 (1970), 1892–1919, and "The Battle of Lepanto and Its Place in Mediterranean History," *Past and Present,* 52 (1972), 53–73.

The economic and financial situation of the Ottoman Empire in the sixteenth century studied in F. Braudel, *The Mediterranean and the Mediterranean World in the Age of Philip II,* 2 vols., New York and London, 1972; Ömer Lütfi Barkan, "Quelques observations sur l'organisation économique et sociale des villes ottomanes, des XVIᵉ siècles," *Recueil Soc. Jean Bodin,* 7 (1955), 289–311; N. Beldiceanu, "La crise monétaire ottomane au XVI siècle et son influence sur les princípautés roumaines," *Südost-Forschungen,* 15 (1957), 70–86; Mustafa Akdağ, "Osmanlı imparatorluğunun kuruluş ve inkişafı devrinde Türkiye'nin iktisadi vaziyeti" (The Economic Situation of Turkey in the Age of the Foundation and Expansion of the Ottoman Empire), *Belleten,* 13 (1949) 497–571, 14 (1950) 319–418; Halil Inalcık, "Osmanlı Imparatorluğunun kuruluş ve inkişafı devrinde Türkiye'nin iktisadi vaziyeti üzerinde bir tetkik münasebetiyle" (Regarding the Study Concerning Turkey's Economic Situation in the Age of the Foundation and Expansion of the Ottoman Empire), *Belleten* 15 (1951), 629–690; Lütfi Güçer, "Le Commerce Interieur des Céreals dans l'Empire Ottoman pendant la second moitié du XVIème siècle," *Revue de la Faculte des Sciences Economiques de l'Université d'Istanbul,* 11 (1953), 1–26; W. Heyd, *Histoire du Commerce du Levant,* 2 vols., Leipzig, 1936 (repr. Amsterdam, 1959); Gino Luzzatto, *Storia Economica di Venezia dall'XI al XVI secolo,* Venice, 1961.

The rise to power of the sultan's harem, led by Hürrem Sultan (Roxelana), is discussed in M. Tayyib Gökbilgin, "Hürrem Sultan," IA, V, 593–596; Michel Sokolnicki, "La Sultane Ruthène: Roksolanes," *Belleten* 23 (1959), 229–239; and Ahmed Refik, *Kadınlar Saltanatı* (The Sultanate of the Women), Istanbul, 1332. Internal politics and the execution of Prince Mustafa are described in J. von Karabacek, *Geschichte Suleimans des Grossen, Verfasst und Eigenhändig Geschrieben von seinem Sohne Mustafa,* Vienna, 1917; Yarbay Tahsin Ünal, "Şehzade Mustafa'nın Eregli'de Idam Edilmesi" (The Execution of Prince Mustafa in Eregli), *Anıt,* no. 28 (1961), 9–22; Çagatay Uluçay, "Mustafa Sultan," IA, VIII, 690–692. On the struggles between princes Selim and Bayezit and the triumph of the former, see Şerafettin Turan, *Kanuni'nin oğlu Şehzade Bayezid vakası* (The Event of Süleyman the Magnificent's Son Prince Bayezit), Ankara, 1961; Ahmed Refik, "Konya Muharebesinden sonra Şehzade Sultan Bayezid'in Irana firarı," (The flight of Prince Bayezid to Iran following the Battle of Konya), TOEM, no. 36 (1331), 705–727; Şerafettin Turan, "Şehzâde Bayezid'in babası Kanuni Sultan Süleyman'a gönderdiği mektuplar" (Letters Sent by Prince Bayezit to His Father Süleyman the Magnificent), *Tarih Vesikaları,* I (1955), 118–127; and by the same author, "Lala Mustafa Paşa hakkında Notlar ve Vesikalar" (Notes and Documents About Lala Mustafa Paşa), *Belleten,* 22 (1958), 551–

593; Ismail Hakkı Uzunçarşılı, "Iran Şahı'na iltica Etmiş Olan Şehzâde Bâyezid'in Teslimi" (The Surrender of Prince Bayezit, Who Had Fled to the Şah of Iran), *Belleten*, 25 (1960), 103–110. On the principal political figures of Süleyman's time, see M. Tayyib Gökbilgin, "Ibrâhim Paşa," IA, V, 908–915; M. Tayyib Gökbilgin, "Lütfi Paşa," IA, VII, 96–101; H. A. R. Gibb, "Lutfi Paşa on the Ottoman Empire," *Oriens*, 15 (1962), 287–295; Şinasi Altındağ and Şerafettin Turan, "Rüstem Paşa," IA, IX, 800–802; Cavid Baysun, "Ahmad Paşa," IA, I, 193; Cavid Baysun, "Cemâli Ali Efendi," IA, III, 85–88; Ismet Parmaksızoğlu, "Kemal Paşa zâde," IA, VI, 561–566; Cavid Baysun, "Ebussuud Efendi," IA, IV, 92–99; and Faruk Sümer, "Kasim Paşa," IA, VI, 386–388.

The internal revolts in the empire that began late in Süleyman's reign have been studied by Mustafa Akdağ, *Celâli Isyanları, 1550–1603* (The Celali Revolts, 1550–1603), Ankara, 1963, and the same author's *Büyük Celâli Karışıklıklarının Başlaması* (The Beginnings of the Great Celali Disturbances), Erzurum, 1963.

IX. The Dynamics of Ottoman Society and Administration

The most useful general studies of Ottoman society and administration are H. A. R. Gibb and Harold Bowen, *Islamic Society and the West*, vol. I. *Islamic Society in the Eighteenth Century*, 2 parts, London and New York, 1950–1957; Ismail Hakkı Uzunçarşılı, *Osmanlı Devletinin Merkez ve Bahriye Teşkilâtı* (The Central and Naval Organization of the Ottoman State), Ankara, 1948, based on exhaustive research in the Ottoman Archives; and Joseph von Hammer-Purgstall, *Das Osmanischen Reichs Staatsverfassung und Stattsverwaltung*, 2 vols., Vienna, 1815. See also S. J. Shaw, "The Ottoman View of the Balkans," *The Balkans in Transition*, ed. G. and B. Jelavich, Berkeley and Los Angeles, 1963, pp. 56–80, and Halil Inalcık, *The Ottoman Empire: The Classical Age, 1300–1600*, New York and London, 1973, pp. 55–202. The accounts of P. Rycaut, *Present State of the Ottoman Empire*, London, 1670; M. A. Grassi, *Charte Turque ou Organization religieuse, civile et militaire de l'Empire Ottoman*, 2 vols, Paris, 1925, and Mouradgea d'Ohsson, *Tableau Général de l'Empire Ottoman*, 7 vols., Paris, 1788–1824, also are useful.

Provincial and military organization, the timar fiefs, tax farms, and the like, are described in Gibb and Bowen, I/1, pp. 45–173, 314–362; Ismail Hakkı Uzunçarşılı, *Osmanlı Devleti teşkilâtından Kapukulu Ocakları* (The Kapıkulu Corps Within the Organization of the Ottoman State), 2 vols., Ankara, 1943–1944; F. A. Belin, *Du régime des fiefs militaires dans l'islamisme et principalement en Turquie*, Paris, 1870; Ömer Lütfi Barkan, "Timar," IA, XII, 287–333; and his "Türk-Islam toprak hukuku tatbikatının Osmanlı Imparatorluğunda aldığı şekiller. I. Malikâne-divâni sistemi" (The Forms Taken by the Turko-Islamic Land Laws Within the Ottoman Empire – the *Malikâne-divani* system), *Türk Hukuk ve Iktisat Tarihi Mecmuası*, no. 2 (1939), 119–137; V. P. Mutafchieva-Str. A. Dimitrov, *Sur l'Etat du système des Timar des XVIIe–XVIIIe*, Sofia, 1968; Halil Sahillioğlu, "Bir mültezim zimem defterine göre XV. yüzyıl sonunda Osmanlı Darphane Mukataaları" (Ottoman Mint *Mukata'as* at the End of the Fifteenth Century According to a Tax Farmer's Account Book), *Istanbul Üniversitesi Iktisat Fakültesi Mecmuası*, 23 (1963), 145–218; V. P. Mutafcieva, "Les catégories de population dépendante dans les terres bulgares sous domination Turque au XVe–XVIe siècle," *Izvestia na Instituta za Istoriya*, 9 (1960), 57–93; Cengiz Orhonlu, *Osmanlı Imparatorluğunda Derbend Teşkilatı* (Guardhouse Organization in the Ottoman Empire), Istanbul, 1967; T. C. Genkur. Bak. Harb Tarihi Dairesi, *Türk Silahlı Kuvvetleri Tarihi* (History of the Turkish Armed Forces), Ankara, 1964; N. Filipovic, "A Study of Some Questions of the Earlier History of the Ottoman Timar," *Radovi*, 1 (1963), 61–118; Bistra Cvetkova, "Recherches sur le système d'affermage (Iltizam) dans l'Empire Ottoman au cours du XVIe–XVIIIe siècles par rapport aux countrées Bulgares," *Revista Orientalni*, 27 (1964), 111–132; and Halil Inalcık, "Eyâlet," EI², II, 721–724. The Ottoman navy is described in Uzunçarşılı, *Merkez ve Bahriye Teşkilatı*, pp. 389–528 and Gibb and Bowen, I/1, 88–107.

The systems by which Ottomans were recruited and trained for service to the sultan are studied in Victor Ménage, "Devshirme," EI², II, 210–213; Basilike D. Papoulia, *Ursprung und Wesen der 'Knabenlese' im osmanischen Reich,* Munich, 1963; Barnette Miller, *The Palace School of Mohammad the Conqueror,* Cambridge, Mass., 1941; J. A. B. Palmer, "The Origins of the Janissaries," *Bulletin of the John Rylands Library,* 25 (1953), 448–481; S. Vryonis, "Isidore Glabas and the Turkish Devshirme," *Speculum,* 21 (1956), 433–443; and Halil Inalcık, "Ghulam," EI², II, 1085–1091. The Palace Institution is studied exhaustively, on the basis of archival materials, by Ismail Hakkı Uzunçarşılı, *Osmanlı devletinin Saray teşkilâtı* (The Palace Organization of the Ottoman State), Ankara, 1945. See also A. D. Alderson, *The Structure of the Ottoman Dynasty,* Oxford, 1956; N. M. Penzer, *The Harem: An Account of the Institution as It Existed in the Palace of the Turkish Sultans with a History of the Grand Seraglio from Its Foundation to the Present Time,* Philadelphia and London, 1936; Gibb and Bowen, I/1, 29–63; Gültekin Oransay, *Osmanlı Devletinde Kim Kimdi? Osmanoğulları* (Who's Who in the Ottoman State? The Ottoman Imperial Family), Ankara, 1969; and Halil Inalcık, "Osmanlılarda Saltanat Veraseti Usulu ve Türk Hakimiyet Telakkisi ile Ilgisi" (The System of Succession and Concept of Rule Among the Ottomans), *Siyasal Bilgiler Fakültesi Dergisi,* 14 (1959), 69–94, and "Osmanlı Padişahı" (The Ottoman Sultan), *Siyasal Bilgiler Mecmuası,* 13 (1958), 68–71. The ceremonial of the court is studied by Konrad Dilger, *Untersuchungen zur Geschichte des Osmanischen Hofzeremoniells im 15. and 16. Jahrhundert,* Munich, 1967; Serif Baştav, *Ordo Portae. Description grecque de la Porte et de l'Armée du Sultan Mehmed II,* Budapest, 1947; J. Ebersolt, *Le grand palais de Constantinople et le livre des cérémonies,* Paris, 1910; F. Giese, "Das Seniorat im osmanischen Herrscherhaus," *Mitteilungen zur osmanischen Geschichte,* 2 (1923–1926), 248–256, and Barnette Miller, *Beyond the Sublime Porte: The Grand Seraglio of Stambul,* New Haven, Conn. 1941.

The scribal system, the treasury, and the financial and tax structures are presented in Uzunçarşılı, *Merkez ve Bahriye Teşkilatı,* pp. 325–388; S. J. Shaw, *The Financial and Administrative Organization and Development of Ottoman Egypt,* Princeton, N.J., 1962; Ömer Lütfi Barkan, "Osmanlı Imparatorluğu Bütçelerine dair Notlar" (Notes on the Budgets of the Ottoman Empire), Istanbul Üniversitesi, *Iktisat Fakültesi Mecmuası,* 18 (1955–1956), 193–224, and "Kanunname," IA, VI, 185–196; S. J. Shaw, *The Budget of Ottoman Egypt, 1005–1006/1596–1597,* The Hague/Paris, 1968, *Ottoman Egypt in the Eighteenth Century,* Cambridge, Mass., 1962, *Ottoman Egypt in the Age of the French Revolution,* Cambridge, Mass., 1966; R. Mantran et J. Sauvaget, *Règlements fiscaux ottomans,* Beirut, 1951; Walther Hinz, "Das Steuerwesen Ostanatoliens im. 15. und 16. Jh.," ZDMG, 100 (1950), 177–204; Halil Inalcık, "Dariba (3) Ottoman Empire," EI², II, 146–148, and "Osmanlılarda Raiyyet Rüsumu," *Belleten,* 17 (1959), 575–610; and Gibb and Bowen, *Islamic Society and the West,* I/2, pp. 1–49.

The Learned Institution is studied in Ismail Hakkı Uzunçarşılı, *Osmanlı devletinin Ilmiye Teşkilâtı* (The Learned Institution of the Ottoman State), Ankara, 1965; the legal system in Uriel Heyd, *Studies in Old Ottoman Criminal Law,* ed. V. L. Ménage, Oxford, 1973; Halil Inalcık, "Örf" (Customary Law), IA, IX, 480; "Mahkeme: Osmanlılarda" (Courts in the Ottoman Empire), IA, VII, 149–151; "Süleyman the Lawgiver and Ottoman Law," *Archivum Ottomanicum,* 1 (1969), 105–138; "Osmanlı hukukuna giriş" (Introduction to Ottoman Law), *Siyasal Bilgiler Fakültesi Dergisi,* 13 (1958), 102–126; and "Adâletnâmeler (Justice Decrees), *Belgeler,* 2 (1965), 49–145. Also see Ebul Ula Mardin, "Kadi" (The Judge) IA, VI, 42–46; Ömer Lütfi Barkan, "Kanunname" (Law Code), IA, VI, 185–195; Dr. Abdulkadir Altunsu, *Osmanlı Şeyhülislâmları* (Ottoman Şeyhulislams), Ankara, 1972; Gibb and Bowen, I/2, 70–206; and Halil Inalcık, "Kadi," EI², IV, 373–375.

The *millet* organizations of the Ottoman subject classes are described in Gibb and Bowen, I/2, pp. 179–261; Ahmet Refik Altınay, *16 asırda Istanbul hayatı* (Life in Istanbul in the Sixteenth Century), 2nd ed., Istanbul, 1935; Ömer Lütfi Barkan, "Osmanlı Imparatorluğunda bir iskan ve kolonizasyon metodu olarak vakıflar ve temlikler" (Religious Foundations and Land Grants as a Method of Settlement and Colonization in the Ottoman Empire), *Vakıflar Dergisi,* 2 (1942), 279–386; Avram Galanté, *Histoire des Juifs d'Istanbul,* Istanbul, 2 vols., 1941–1942; Avram Galanté, *Histoire des Juifs d'Anatolie,* Istanbul, 1939;

U. Heyd, "The Jewish Communities of Istanbul in the XVIIth Century," *Oriens,* 6 (1953), 299–314; Esat Uras, *Tarihte Ermeniler ve Ermeni meselesi* (The Armenians in History and the Armenian Problem), Ankara, 1950; A. E. Vacalopoulos, *Origins of the Greek Nation, 1204–1461,* New Brunswick, N. J., 1970; Sir S. Runciman, *The Great Church in Captivity,* Cambridge, 1971; N. J. Pantazopoulos, *Church and Law in the Balkan Peninsula During the Ottoman Rule,* Salonica, 1967; L. Arpée, *A History of Armenian Christianity from the Beginning to Our Own Time,* New York, 1946; L. Hadrovics, *Le peuple serbe et son église sous la domination turque,* Paris, 1947; B. Homsy, *Les capitulations et la protection des chrétiens au Proche-Orient aux XVIe, XVIIe et XVIIIe ss,* Paris, 1956; J. Mécérian, *Histoire et institutions de l'église arménienne,* Beirut, 1965; Stavro Skendi, "Religion in Albania During the Ottoman Rule," *Sudost Forschungen,* 15 (1956), 311–327; and T. Ware, *Eustratius Argenti: A Study of the Greek Church Under Turkish Rule,* Oxford, 1964.

Urban, social, and economic life are described in Robert Mantran, *Istanbul dans la Seconde Moitié du XVIIe Siècle,* Paris, 1962; Halil Inalcık, "Capital Formation in the Ottoman Empire," *Journal of Economic History,* 29 (1969), 97–140; and Robert Mantran, *La vie quotidienne à Constantinople au temps de Soliman le Magnifique et de ses successeurs,* Paris 1965. An extremely comprehensive and understanding study is Raphaela Lewis, *Everyday Life in Ottoman Turkey,* London and New York, 1971. Also see N. Todorov, ed., *La ville balkanique, XVe–XIXe Siècles,* Sofia, 1970; Gabriel Baer, "The Administrative, Economic and Social Functions of Turkish Guilds," *IJMES,* 1 (1970), 28–50; Bernard Lewis, *Istanbul and the Civilization of the Ottoman Empire,* Norman, Okla., 1963; Halil Inalcık, "Bursa and the Commerce of the Levant," *JESHO,* 3 (1960), 131–147; "Imtiyâzât: Ottoman," *EI²,* IV; W. Behrnauer, "Mémoire sur les institutions de police chez les Arabes, les Persans et les Turcs," *Journal Asiatique,* Ve Serie, 15 (1861), 347–392; Franz Taeschner, *Alt-Stambuler Hof und Volksleben,* Hanover, 1925; Osman Nuri (Ergin), *Mecelle-i Umur-u Belediye* (Journal of Municipal Affairs), vol. I, Istanbul, 1338/1922; and Halil Inalcık, "Bursa: XV. asır sanayi ve ticaret tarihine dair vesikalar" (Documents Concerning the History of Industry and Trade in Fifteenth-Century Bursa), *Belleten,* 24 (1960), 45–102. The most monumental description of Ottoman state organization and popular life and culture is that of the seventeenth-century traveler Evliyâ Çelebi, *Seyahatnâme* (Travels), 10 vols., Istanbul, 1896–1938. The first two volumes, concerning Istanbul, have been partially translated by Joseph von Hammer, *Narrative of Travels in Europe, Asia and Africa,* London, 1834, and this in turn was used as a source for A. A. Pallis, *In the Days of the Janissaries,* London, 1951. An excellent study of business practices in the empire is Ronald C. Jennings, "Loans and Credit in Early 17th Century Ottoman Judicial Records: The Sharia Court of Anatolian Kayseri," *JESHO,* 16 (1973), 168–216.

Information on the classic Ottoman literature can be found in E. J. W. Gibb, *History of Ottoman Poetry,* 6 vols., London, 1900–1909; Nihat Sami Banarlı, *Resimli Türk Edebiyatı Tarihi* (Illustrated History of Turkish Literature), Istanbul, 1950; Alessio Bombaci, *Storia della letteratura turca,* Milan, 1956 (English tr. by Kathleen Burrill, Leiden, 1975); Abdül Baki Gölpinarlı, *Divan Şiiri, XV–XVI yüzyıllar* (Court Poetry, Fifteenth-Sixteenth Centuries), Istanbul, 1954; *Divan Şiiri, XVII yüzyıli* (Court Poetry, Seventeenth Century), Istanbul, 1955; and *Divan Şiiri, XVIII yüzyılı* (Court Poetry, Eighteenth Century), Istanbul, 1955; J. von Hammer-Purgstall, *Geschichte der osmanischen Dichtkunst bis auf unsere Zeit,* 4 vols., Pesth, 1836–1838; Fuat Köprülü, *Türk Edebiyatı Tarihi* (History of Turkish Literature), Istanbul, 1926–1928; J. H. Kramers, "Historiography Among the Osmanli Turks," *Analecta Orientalia,* 1 (1954), 3–21; Franz Babinger, *Die Geschichts-Schreiber der Osmanen und ihre Werke,* Leipzig, 1927; Franz Taeschner, "Die geographische Literatur der Osmanen," *ZDMG,* 77 (1923), 31–80; Bursalı Mehmed Tahir, *Osmanlı Muellifleri* (Ottoman Authors), 3 vols., Istanbul, 1919–1927; Walther Björkman, "Die Altosmanische Literatur," *Philologiae Turcicae Fundamenta,* vol. II (Wiesbaden, 1964), pp. 403–465.

The most complete account of Ottoman scientific development is in Abdulhak Adnan

Adıvar, *La Science Chez les Turcs Ottomanes,* Paris, 1939, later expanded and translated into Turkish as *Osmanlı Türklerinde Ilim* (Science Among the Ottoman Turks), Istanbul, 1943. On Ottoman miniature painting see E. Esin, *Turkish Miniature Painting,* Tokyo, Japan, 1960; I. Stchoukine, *La peinture turque d'après les manuscrits illustrées. I ere partie, de Süleyman I à Osman II, 1520–1622,* Paris, 1966; C. E. Arseven, *L'art turque depuis son origine jusqu'à nos jours,* Istanbul, 1939; and F. Öğütmen, *Miniature Art from the XIIth to the XVIIth Century,* Istanbul, 1966. On Ottoman architecture see Godfrey Goodwin, *History of Turkish Architecture,* London, 1972; Oktay Aslanapa, *Turkish Art and Architecture,* London and New York, 1971; Kurt Erdman, *Zur türkischen Baukunst seldschukischer und osmanischer Zeit,* Istanbul, 1958; Abdullah Kuran, *The Mosque in Early Ottoman Architecture,* Chicago and London, n.d.; Metin And, *A History of Theater and Popular Entertainment in Turkey,* Ankara, 1972.

On popular Turkish literature and religious movements see Hellmut Ritter, *Karagöz, türkische Schattenspiele,* 3 vols, Hanover, Istanbul, and Wiesbaden, 1924–1953; John Kingsley Birge, *The Bektashi Order of Dervishes,* London, 1937; and F. W. Hasluck, *Christianity and Islam Under the Sultans,* 2 vols., Oxford, 1929.

X. *Decentralization and Traditional Reform, 1566–1683*

The best general discussions of the era of decentralization are Halil Inalcık, "The Heyday and Decline of the Ottoman Empire," *Cambridge History of Islam,* vol. I, pp. 324–353; and Bernard Lewis, "The Decline of the Ottoman Empire," *Emergence of Modern Turkey,* pp. 21–39, and "Ottoman Observers of Ottoman Decline," *Islamic Studies,* 1 (1962), 71–87. Its political aspects are described in Ahmed Refik (Altınay), *Kadınlar Saltanatı* (The Sultanate of the Women), 3 vols., Istanbul, 1923, and the same author's *Ocak Ağaları* (The Commanders of the Corps), Istanbul, 1931. Its financial aspects are discussed by Mustafa Akdağ, "Osmanlı imparatorluğunun kuruluş ve inkişafı devrinde Türkiye'nin iktisadi" (The Economic Situation of Turkey in the Age of the Foundation and Expansion of the Ottoman Empire), *Belleten,* 13 (1949), 497–571, 14 (1950), 319–418, which in turn is analyzed and criticized by Halil Inalcık, *Belleten,* 15 (1951), 629–690. The general population situation is studied in Fernand Braudel, *The Mediterranean and the Mediterranean World in the Age of Philip II,* 2 vols., London and New York, 1972. The provincial uprisings have been described by Mustafa Akdağ, *Celâlî Isyanları, 1550–1603* (The Celali Revolts, 1550–1603), Ankara, 1963; Mustafa Cezar, *Osmanlı Tarihinde Levendler* (The Levents in Ottoman History), Istanbul, 1965; M. Çağatay Uluçay, *Saruhan'da Eşkiyalık ve Halk Hareketleri: XVII. Asırda* (Banditry and Popular Movements in Saruhan: The Seventeenth Century), Istanbul, 1944; Nejat Göyünç, *XVI Yüzyılda Mardin Sancağı* (The Sancak of Mardin in the Sixteenth Century), Istanbul, 1969; Mustafa Akdağ, "Celâlî Isyanlarında Büyük Kaçgunluk (1603–1606)" (The Great Flight in the Celali Rebellions [1603–1606]), *Tarih Araştırmalar Dergisi,* 2 (1966), 1–49; Cengiz Orhonlu, *Osmanlı Imparatorluğunda aşiretleri iskân teşebbüsü, 1691–1696* (Efforts to Settle the Tribes in the Ottoman Empire, 1691–1696), Istanbul, 1963; and Şerafeddin Turan, "XVII. yüzyılda Osmanlı Imparatorluğunun idari taksimatı" (The Administrative Division of the Ottoman Empire in the Seventeenth Century), *Atatürk Universitesi 1961 Yıllığı,* Erzurum, 1962, pp. 201–232. Ottoman population problems are described by Ömer Lütfi Barkan, "Contribution à l'étude démographique des villes balkaniques au cours des XVe–XVIe siècles," *La Ville Balkanique,* Sofia, 1970, pp. 181–207; "Essai sur les données statistiques des régistres de recensement dans l'Empire ottoman aux XVe et XVIe siècles," *JESHO,* 1 (1958), 9–36; "Osmanlı Imparatorluğunda büyük nüfus ve arazi tahrirleri ve Hakana mahsus istatistik defterleri" (The Great Census and Land Surveys in the Ottoman Empire and the Statistical Registers Prepared for the Ruler), *Istanbul Üniversitesi Iktisat Fakültesi Mecmuası,* 2 (1940), 20–59, 214–257. The gradual degeneration of the Ottoman administrative and tax systems are studied in Ahmet Mumcu, *Osmanlı Devletinde Siyaseten Katl* (Political Executions in the Ottoman State), Ankara, 1963, and the same author's *Osmanlı Devletinde Rüşvet* (Bribery in the Ottoman State), Ankara, 1969. Documents elaborating on these problems are presented in Ahmet Refik, *On Altıncı Asırda Istanbul Hayatı, 1553–1591* (Life in Istanbul in the Sixteenth Century), Istanbul, 1935; Edip Âli Baki, *Şer'iye Sicillerine Göre: Afyonkarahisar'da XVII, XVIIIinci Asırlarda Meçhul Halk Tarihinden* (Previously Unknown Popular History in the Seventeenth and Eighteenth Centuries in Afyonkarahisar, According to the Registers of the Religious Courts), Afyon, 1951; Ali Faik Bey, *Volkswirtschaftspolitik der Türkei im 16. und 17. Jahrhundert, Agrarverfassung, Lehnsystem, Finanzpolitik unter dem Lehnsystem und Geldpolitik,* (Ph.D. dissertation), Kiel, 1920; Lütfi Güçer, *XVI–XVII Asırlarda Osmanlı Imparatorluğunda Hububat Meselesi ve Hububattan Alınan Vergiler* (The Grain Problem in the Ottoman Empire in the Sixteenth and Seventeenth Centuries and Taxes Taken from Grains), Istanbul, 1964.

The reign of Selim II (1566–1574) is discussed by Şerafeddin Turan, "Selim II," IA, X, 434–441. The policies and politics of Sokullu Mehmet, his grand vezir, are analyzed by M. Tayyib Gökbilgin, "Mehmet Paşa Sokullu," IA, VII, 595–605; M. Brosch, *Geschichte aus den Leben dreier Grosswesire,* Gotha, 1899; Ahmed Refik (Altınay), *Sokullu,* Istanbul, 1924; and T. Y. Öztuna, *Sokullu Mehmed Paşa, Tarihten Sesler,* Istanbul, 1945. The influence of Don Joseph of Naxos is described by Cecil Roth, *The House of Nasi: Dona Gracia,* London, 1947, and the same author's *The House of Nasi: The Duke of Naxos,* London, 1948. Also Avram Galante, *Don Joseph Nassi,* Istanbul, n.d.; Miralayı Safvet Bey, "Nakşa Dukalığı ve Kiklad Adaları" (The Dukedom of Naxos and the Ciciliad Islands), TOEM, 4 (1329), 1444–1457, and the same author's "Yasef Nasi," TOEM, 3 (1328), 982–993; C. Sathas, *Joseph Nassy,* Athens 1867. The war in Cyprus is discussed in P. Herre, *Europaeische Politik in Cyprischen Krieg (1570–1573),* Leipzig, 1902; Jurien de la Gravière, *La guerre de Chypre et la bataille de Lépante,* 2 vols., Paris, 1888; R. C. Anderson, *Naval Wars in the Levant, 1559–1853,* Princeton, N.J., 1952; Ismail Hakkı Uzunçarşılı, "Kibris fethi ile Lepant (Inebahti) Muharebesi sırasında Türk devletile Venedik ve Müttefiklerinin faaliyetine dâir bazi Hazine-i Evrak Kayıtlar" (Some Archival Documents Concerning the Activities of the Turkish State, Venice and Its Allies During the Conquest of Cyprus and the Battle of Lepanto), *Türkiyat Mecmuası,* III, 257–292; Halil Fikret Alasya, *Kıbrıs Tarihi ve Kıbrısta Türk Eserleri* (The History of Cyprus and Turkish Works in Cyprus), Ankara, 1964. The Battle of Lepanto is studied by E. von Normann-Griedenfels, *Don Juan de Austria als Admiral der Heiligen Liga und die Schlacht bei Lepanto,* Pola, 1902; Henri Cambon, *Don Juan d'Autriche le vainqueur de Lépante,* Paris, 1952; Angelo Tomborra, *Gli Stati Italiani l'Europa e il Problema Turco dopo Lepanto,* Florence, 1961; Ali Haydar Emir (Alpagut), *Kılıç Ali ve Lepanto,* Istanbul, 1931; L. Serrano, *La Liga de Lepanto entre Espana, Venecia y la Santa Sedo (1570–1573),* Madrid, 1918–1920. The Ottoman effort to construct a canal between the Don and Volga rivers is the subject of a vigorous scholarly debate between Halil Inalcık in "Osmanlı-Rus Rekabetinin Menşei ve Don-Volga Kanalı Teşebbüsü (1569)," *Belleten,* 12 (1948), 349–402, translated as "The origins of the Ottoman-Russian Rivalry and the Don-Volga Canal," *Annals of the University of Ankara,* 1 (1946–1947), 47–106, and Akdes Nimet Kurat, *Türkiye ve Idil Boyu. 1569 Astarhan seferi, Ten-Idil Kanalı ve XVI–XVII yüzyıl Osmanlı Rus münasebetleri* (Turkey and the Banks of the Volga. The 1569 Astrakhan Campaign. The Don-Volga Canal and Ottoman-Russian Relations in the Sixteenth and Seventeenth Centuries), Ankara, 1966, summarized in the same author's "The Turkish Expedition to Astrakhan in 1569 and the Problem of the Don-Volga Canal," *Slavonic and East European Review,* 40 (1961), 7–23. See also C. Max Kortepeter, *Ottoman Imperialism During the Reformation. Europe and the Caucasus,* New York, 1972; W. E. D. Allen, *Problems of Turkish power in the Sixteenth Century,* London, 1963; W. H. McNeill, *Europe's Steppe Frontier, 1500–1800,* Chicago, 1964; and A. Benningsen, "L'expédition Turque contre Astrakhan en 1569 d'après les Registres des 'affaires importantes' des archives ottomanes," *Cahiers du Monde Russe et Sovietique,* 8 (1967), 427–446.

The conquest of the Yemen and the Ottoman naval expeditions to India and Sumatra are discussed by Şerafeddin Turan, "Lala Mustafa Paşa hakkında notlar ve vesikalar" (Notes and Documents Concerning Lala Mustafa Paşa), *Belleten,* 22 (1958), 551–593;

Safvet Bey, "Bir Osmanlı filosunun Sumatra Seferi" (The Sumatra Expedition of an Ottoman fleet), TOEM, 1 (1327), 604–614, 678–683; Safvet Bey, "Şark Levendleri: Osmanlı Bahr-ı Ahmer Filosunun Sumatra seferi üzerine vesikalar" (The Sailors of the East: Documents on the Expedition of the Ottoman Red Sea Fleet to Sumatra), TOEM, 4 (1329), 1521–1540; Şerafettin Turan, "Süleyman Paşa (Hadim)," IA, XII, 194–197; Anon., *Viaggio et impresa che fece Solyman Bassa del 1538 Contra Portoghesi pe aracgui la città del Diu in India,* Venice, 1545, tr. as "Particular Relation of the Expedition of Solymen Pacha from Suez to India Against the Portugese at Diu"; R. Kerr and F. A. S. Eden, *A General History and Collection of Voyages and Travels,* vol. VI (1812), pp. 258–287; I. Longworth Dames, "The Portugese and Turks in the Sixteenth Century," JRAS, (1921), pp. 1–28; Fevzi Kurtoğlu, "Hadim Süleyman Paşa'nın mektupları ve Belgradın muhasara planı" (The Letters of Hadim Süleyman Paşa and the Plan to Besiege Belgrade), *Belleten,* 4 (1940), 53–56; Cengiz Orhonlu, "XVI asrın ilk yarısında Kızıldeniz sahillerinde Osmanlılar" (The Ottomans Along the Shores of the Red Sea in the First Half of the Sixteenth Century), *Tarih Dergisi,* XII/16, 1–24; Herbert Melziğ, *Büyük Türk Hindistan kapılarında, Kanuni Sultan Süleyman devrinde Amiral Hadım Süleyman Paşa'nın Hind seferi, Istanbul,* 1943.; and A. Hess, "The Evolution of the Ottoman Seaborne Empire in the Age of the Oceanic Discoveries, 1453–1525," AHR, 75 (1970), 1892–1919.

Turkish advances against Poland and relations with the Crimean Tatars are studied by C. Max Kortepeter, *Ottoman Imperialism During the Reformation: Europe and the Caucasus,* New York and London, 1972; Ahmed Refik (Altınay), "Lehistanda Türk Hakimiyeti" (Turkish Rule in Poland), TTEM, 14 (1340), 227–243; and Jonuzs Pajewski, *Projekt Przymierza Polsko-Tureckiego za Zygmunta Augusta,* Warsaw, 1935.

The reign of Murat III (1574–1595) is outlined by Bekir Kütükoğlu, "III Murad," IA, VIII, 615–625. Ottoman-Safavid relations during this time are the subject of a detailed monograph by the same author, *Osmanlı-Safevi Siyasi Münasebetleri,* (Ottoman-Safavid Political Relationships), Istanbul, 1962. The beginnings of Ottoman-English relations are studied in G. H. Rosedale, *Queen Elizabeth and the Levant Company,* London, 1904; J. J. Podea, "A Contribution to the Study of Queen Elizabeth's Eastern Policy," *Mélanges d'Histoire Générale,* II (Cluj, 1938), pp. 423–476; Arthur Leon Horniker, "Anglo-French Rivalry in the Levant from 1583 to 1612," *Journal of Modern History,* 18 (1946), 289–305, and the same author's "William Harborne and the Beginning of Anglo-Turkish Diplomatic and Commercial Relations," *Journal of Modern History,* 14 (1942), 189–316; see also Hamid Dereli, *Kıraliçe Elizabeth devrinde Türkler ve Ingilizler* (The Turks and the English in the Age of Queen Elizabeth), Istanbul, 1932; Akdes Nimet Kurat, *Türk-Ingiliz Münasebetlerinin Başlaması ve Gelişmesi, 1553–1610* (The Beginnings and Expansion of Turko-English Relations, 1553–1610), Ankara, 1953; Orhan Burian, "Türkiye hakkında dört Ingiliz seyahatnamesi" (Four English Travel Reports on Turkey), *Belleten,* 15 (1951), 223–245; A. C. Wood, *A History of the Levant Company,* London, 1935. See also N. H. Biegman, *The Turco-Ragusan Relationship According to the Firmans of Murad III (1575–1595),* Istanbul, 1968. On internal decline and court politics see Mustafa Akdağ, "Yeniçeri Ocak Nizâmının Bozulması" (The Breaking up of the Organization of the Janissary Corps), Ankara University, *Dil ve Tarih-Coğrafya Fakültesi Dergisi,* 5 (1947), 291–313, and Ettore Rossi, "La Sultana Nûr Bânû Maglie di Selim II et Madri di Murad III," *Oriente Moderno,* 33 (1953), 433–441.

The reign of Mehmet III (1595–1603) is described by M. Tayyıp Gökbilgin, "III Mehmet," IA, VII, 535–547, and Mehmed Celâl, *Sultan Mehmed-i Salis* (Sultan Mehmed the Third), Istanbul, 1308/1891. Court politics is discussed by Ismail Hakkı Uzunçarşılı, "III Mehmed'in oğlu Şehzâde Mahmûd'un Ölümü" (The Death of Prince Mahmut, Son of Mehmed III), *Belleten,* 24 (1960), 264–267. In addition to the works previously cited on the internal revolts, see A. Tveritinova, *Vosstaniye Kara Yazıdjı-Deli Chasana ve Turtsii, 1599–1603* (The Revolt of Kara Yazıcı and Deli Hasan in Turkey), Moscow, 1946. On the leading political figures of the period refer to Şerafeddin Turan, "Sâdeddin Efendi," IA, IX, 27–32; Ismet Parmaksızoğlu, "Ibrahim Paşa, Damad," IA, VII, 915–919; Şerafeddin Turan, "Sinan Paşa," IA, IX, 670–675; M. Tayyip Gökbilgin, "Hasan Paşa, Sokullu zâde," IA, VI, 325–329; Şerafeddin Tekindağ, "Mehmed Paşa Lala," IA, VI, 591–594. The most important chronicle source of the period is the *Tarih* (History) of Mustafa Naima (1655–1716), partly translated by Charles Fraser as *Annals of the Turkish Empire from 1591 to 1659,* 2 vols., London, 1832–1836. See L. V. Thomas, *A Study of Naima,* New York, 1972. On the Ottoman-Austrian war, see Alfred Loebl, *Zur Geschichte des Türkenkriegen von 1593–1606,* 2 vols., Prague, 1899–1904.

Ottoman decline in the seventeenth century is analyzed by Mustafa Akdağ, "Genel Çizgileriyle XVII yüzyıl Türkiye Tarihi" (Turkish History in the Seventeenth Century Along General Lines), *Tarih Araştırmaları Dergisi,* 4 (1966), 201–247. See also the contemporary analyses of Mustafa Koçi Bey, *Risale,* Istanbul, 1277/1860 and 1303/1886; Ayn-i Ali Efendi, *Kevanin-i âl-i Osman der hulâsa-i defter-i Divan,* Istanbul, 1280/1863–4; and Gelibolulu Mustafa Âli, *Mevâ'idü'n Nefâ'is fi Kavâ'ii'l-Mecâlis,* Istanbul, 1956. The reign of Ahmet I (1603–1617) is discussed by M. Cavit Baysun, "Ahmed I," IA, I, 161–164; Cengiz Orhonlu, "Murad Paşa Kuyucu," IA, VIII, 651–654; Şinasi Tekindağ, "Mehmed Paşa Damad Öküz," IA, VII, 581–583; Orhan Burian, *The Report of Lello, Third English Ambassador to the Sublime Porte,* Ankara, 1952; and Hrand D. Andreasyan, "Ermeni Seyyahi Polonyalı Simeon'un seyahatnamesi (1608–1619)" (The Travel Report of the Armenian traveler Simeon of Poland, 1608–1619), *Türkiyat Mecmuası,* X, 269–276. The short reigns of Mustafa I (1617–1618) and Osman II (1618–1622) are described by Münir Aktepe, "Mustafa I," IA, VIII, 692–695; Şinasi Altındağ, "Osman II," IA, IX, 443–448; A. Danon, "Contributions à l'histoire des sultans Osman II et Mouctafâ I," *Journal Asiatique,* 11th ser., 14 (1919), 69–139, 243–310; Madame de Gomez (Madaleine Angélique Poisson), *Histoire d'Osman,* 2 vols., Paris, 1734, tr. by J. Williams as *The Life of Osman the Great,* 2 vols., London, 1735. Political affairs are also discussed by Tayyip Gökbilgin "Dilâver Paşa," IA, III, 587–588; Fahri Derin, "Mehmed Paşa Gürcü," IA, VII, 585–587; Münir Aktepe, "Esad Efendi," IA, IV, 358–359; and Cavid Baysun, "Hasan Beyzâde Ahmed Paşa," *Türkiyat Mecmuası,* X, 321–340. The Anatolian revolts during these reigns are studied by William J. Griswold, "Political Unrest and Rebellion in Anatolia, 1605–1609" (unpublished Ph.D. dissertation), University of California, Los Angeles, 1966 as well as the works of Mustafa Akdağ on the Celalis, cited earlier.

The eventful reign of Murat IV (1623–1640) has been described by M. Cavid Baysun, "Murad IV," IA, VIII, 625–647; Sir Paul Rycaut, *The History of the Turkish Empire from the Year 1623 to the year 1677,* 2 vols., London, 1680, and D. Cantemir, *The History of the Growth and Decay of the Othman Empire,* London, 1756. Also *The Negotiations of Sir Thomas Roe in His Embassy to the Ottoman Porte from the Year 1621 to 1628 Inclusive,* London, 1740, and Gerard Tongas, *Les relations de la France avec l'Empire Ottoman durant la première moitie du XVIIe siècle,* Toulouse, 1942. On his eastern expeditions, see Halil Sahillioğlu, "Dördüncü Murad'in Bağdad Seferi Menzilnamesi-Bağdad seferi Harptunali" (The Stopping-Station Book of Murat IV's Baghdad Expedition), *Belgeler,* 2 (1965), 1–36; and Süheyl Ünver, "Dördüncü Sultan Murad'in Revan seferi Kronolojisi" (Chronology of Murat IV's Expedition to Erivan), *Belleten,* 6 (1942), 547–576. See also F. Marich, *Aufstandsversuche der Christlichen Voelker der Türkei im den Jahren 1625–1648,* Innsbruck, 1882; Halil Inalcik, "Hüsrev Paşa," IA, VI, 606–609; Hayriye Aydınalp, "Filibeli Hâfiz Ahmed Paşa" (unpublished thesis), Istanbul University Edebiyat Fakültesi library no. 398 (1947), and Ahmed Refik, "Sultan Murad-i Rabinin Hatt-ı Hümayunları," TOEM, 3 (1332), 129–141.

The reaction to Murat IV's reforms under Sultan Ibrahim (1640–1648) is described by Tayyip Gökbilgin, "Ibrahim I," IA, V, 880–885. On the influence of the harem, led by Kösem Sultan during this period, see Cavid Baysun, "Kösem Sultan," IA, VI, 915–923; Ahmed Refik (Altınay), *Samur Devri, 1049–1059* (The Period of Furs), Istanbul, 1927. The question of the sultan's sanity is discussed by Çağatay Uluçay, "Sultan Ibrahim Deli mi, Hasta mi idi?" (Was Sultan Ibrahim Mad or Sick?), *Tarih Dünyası,* no. 6/24. The political figures of his reign are studied in Ismet Parmaksızoğlu, "Hüseyin Paşa Deli,"

IA, VI, 650–654; Münir· Aktepe, "Mehmed Paşa Civankapıcıbaşı," IA, VII, 605–607; Münir Aktepe, "Mustafa Paşa Kemankeş," IA, VIII, 730–732.

The long reign of Mehmet IV (1648–1687) is presented in Cavid Baysun, "Mehmed IV," IA, VII, 547–557. The policies and programs of the Köprülü ministers are also discussed in Tayip Gökbilgin, "Köprülüler," IA, VI, 892–908; Ahmed Refik Altınay, *Köprülüler*, 2 vols., Istanbul, 1331/1913; Franz Babinger, "Köprülü," EI[1], II, 1059–1062; M. Kunt, "The Köprülü Years, 1656–1661" (unpublished Ph.D. dissertation), Princeton University, 1972; and M. Brosch, *Geschichte aus dem Leben dreier Grossvesire*, Gotha, 1899. On the state of the empire in the late seventeenth century, see Sieur de la Croix, *Mémoires, contenans diverses relations très curieuses de l'Empire Othoman*, Paris, 1684; Pétis de la Croix, *Etat géneral de l'Empire Othoman*, Paris, 1695; P. Rycaut, *The Present State of the Ottoman Empire*, London, 1686; Heidrun Wurm, *Der osmanische Historiker Ḥüseyn b. Ga'fer, genannt Hezârfean, und die Istanbuler Gesellschaft in der zweiten Hälfte des 17. Jahrhunderts*, Freiburg, 1971; Ahmed Refik, *Felâket seneleri* (The Disaster Years), Istanbul, 1332; and A. Galland, *Journal d'Antoine Galland, Orientaliste 1646–1715, pendant son sejour à Constantinople, 1672–1673*, ed. C. Shefer, 2 vols., 1881 (repr. 1971). The principal chronicle of the late seventeenth century is the *Tarih* (History) of Mehmet Raşit, 5 vols., Istanbul, 1865. On Transylvania see Ismail Hakkı Uzunçarşılı, "Barcsay Akos-un Erdel Kırallığına ait bazi orijinal vesikalar" (Some Original Documents on the Kingship in Transylvania of Barcsay), *Tarih Dergisi*, V, 51–68, and the same author's "Ekos Barçkay'in Erdel Kralliğına tayini hakkında bir kaç vesika" (Some Documents on the Appointment of Barcsay as King of Transylvania), *Belleten*, 7 (1943), 361–377. The Crete expedition is the subject of Kur. Yzb. Ziya ve Kur. Yazb. Rahmi, *Girit Seferi, 1645–1669* (The Crete Expedition, 1645–1669), Istanbul, 1933; and W. Bigge, *Der Kampf von Candia in den Jahren 1667–1669*, Berlin, 1899. The Battle of Saint Gotthard is described by Ferik Ahmed Muhtar Paşa, *Sengotarda Osmanlı Ordusu* (The Ottoman Army at Saint Gotthard), Istanbul, 1326/1908; and Kur. Yzb. Raif ve Kur. Yzb. Ekren, *Sengotar Seferi, 1662–1664* (The Saint Gotthard Expedition, 1662–1664), Istanbul, 1934. The diplomatic background to the Ottoman siege of Vienna (1683), and the siege itself, is studied in Thomas M. Barker, *Double Eagle and Crescent: Vienna's Second Turkish Siege and Its Historical Setting*, Albany, New York, 1967. Also see Gerit, "The Warning of Ibrahim Pasha of Buda," JRCAS, 21 (1934), 621–670; C. B. O'Brien, "Russia and Turkey, 1677–1681: The Treaty of Bakhchisaray," *Russian Review*, 11 (1953), 259–268; Kurt Koehler, *Die orientalische Politik Ludwigs XIV., ihr Verhältnis zum Türkenkrieg von 1683*, Leipzig, 1907; Kur. Alb. Necati Salim Tacan, *Ikinci Viyana Seferi, 1683* (The Second Vienna Expedition, 1683), Istanbul, 1945; Richard F. Kreutel, *Kara Mustafa vor Wien*, Vienna, 1955, Cologne, 1959; and John Stoye, *Siege of Vienna*, London, 1964.

The reign of Süleyman II (1687–1691) is studied by Bekir Kütükoğlu, "Süleyman II," IA, XI, 155–170. The War of the Holy League between the Ottomans and much of Europe is described in J. B. Wolf, *The Emergence of the Great Powers, 1685–1715*, New York, 1951; Akdes Nimet Kurat, "The Retreat of the Turks 1683–1730," *The New Cambridge Modern History*, 6 (1970), 608–647; V. L. Tapié, *Les Relations entre la France et l'Europe Centrale de 1661 à 1715*, 2 vols., Paris, 1958; P. Argenti, ed., *The Occupation of Chios by the Venetians, 1694*, London, 1953; M. Braubach, *Prinz Eugen von Savoyen, Eine Biographie*, 5 vols, Vienna, 1963–1965. Also see Bruzzo, *Francesco Morosini e la Conquesta della Morea*, Venice, 1890; Necati Salim Tacan, *Niş-Belgrad-Salankamen-Petrovaradin-Lugo Timişvar Kuşatma ve Meydan Muharebeleri, 1690–1696* (The Ambushes and Battles of Niş, Belgrade, Salankamen, Peterwaradin, Lugoş, and Temeşvar), Istanbul, 1939; Cavid Baysun, "Ahmed II," IA, I, 164–165, and Cengiz Orhonlu, "I Mustafa," IA, VIII, 695–700, describe the reigns of the sultans of the period, Ahmet II (1691–1695) and Mustafa II (1695–1703). Efforts to settle the tribes in eastern Anatolia during the same time are studied by Cengiz Orhonlu, *Osmanlı Imparatorluğunda Aşiretleri Iskân Teşebbüsü, 1691–1696*, Istanbul, 1963. On the Peace of Karlowitz see Ismet Parmaksızoğlu, "Karlofça," IA, VI, 346–350; Rifat A. Abou El-Haj, "Ottoman Diplomacy at Karlowitz,"

JAOS, 87 (1967), 498–512; and M. R. Popovic, *Der Friede von Carlowitz,* Leipzig, 1893.
Some of the political figures of the period are studied by Cengiz Orhonlu, "Mezomorta
Hüseyin Paşa," IA, VIII, 205–208; Orhon Köprülü, "Hüseyin Paşa Amca zâde," IA, V,
646–650; Cengiz Orhonlu, "Mehmed Paşa Elmas," IA, VII, 583–585; Sâdeddin Nüzhet
Ergun, *Râmî Paşa. Hayatı ve Eserleri,* Istanbul, 1934; Fahri Perin, "Şeyhulislâm Fey-
zullah Efendi'nin nesebi," *Tarih Dergisi,* 4 (1959), 97–104; Huriye Gerçek, "Feyzullah
Efendi, Ailesi, Evlâda, Akrabâsı" (Feyzullah Efendi, His Family, His Children, His
Relatives), Istanbul University, Edebiyat Fakültesi, history thesis no. 1970 (1950); and
Orhon Köprülü, "Feyzullah Efendi," IA, IV, 592–600.

XI. New Challenges and Responses, 1699–1826

The Edirne Event, which brought Ahmet III to the throne, is described in an unpublished
Istanbul University history thesis by Ömer Aziz, "Edirne Vakası," Istanbul Universitesi,
Edebiyat Fakültesi tarih tezi 193. Ahmet III's reign is generally described by Enver Ziya
Karal, "Ahmed III," IA, I, 165–168, and Harold Bowen, "Ahmad III," EI², I, 268–271.
On the Russian war and the Pruth campaign, see Akdes Nimet Kurat, *Prut Seferi ve
Barışı, 1123/1171* (The Pruth Campaign and Peace), 2 vols., Ankara, 1951; B. H. Sum-
ner, *Peter the Great and the Ottoman Empire,* Oxford, 1949; and Akdes Nimet Kurat, ed.,
The Dispatches of Sir Robert Sutton, Ambassador in Constantinople (1710–1714), London, 1953. Charles XII's sojourn in the Ottoman Empire and his pressure on the Porte
are discussed by Akdes Nimet Kurat, *İsveç Kiralı XII Karl'ın Türkiyede Kalışı ve bu
sıralarda Osmanlı Imparatorluğu,* (The Swedish King Charles XII's Stay in Turkey and
the Ottoman Empire at This Time), Istanbul, 1943; R. M. Hatton, "Charles XII in
Turkey. 'Narrative of the King of Sweden's movements, 1709–1714,' " *Tarih Araştırmaları,*
1 (1957), 83–142. On the subsequent diplomatic relations and wars in Europe, see Lavender
Cassels, *The Struggle for the Ottoman Empire, 1717–1740,* London, 1966; A. Vandal,
Une Ambassade Française en Orient sous Louis XV, Paris, 1887; M. le Comte de Saint-
Priest, *Memoires sur l'ambassade de France en Turquie et sur le commerce les Français
dans le Levant,* Paris, 1877; Marquis de Bonnac, *Memoire historique sur l'ambassade de
France à Constantinople,* Paris, 1884; P. Masson, *Histoire du commerce français dans le
Levant au dix huitième siècle,* Paris, 1911; Ilse Jacob, *Beziehungen Englands zu Russland
und zur Türkei in den Jahren 1718–1727,* Basel, 1945; C. Lemercier-Quelquejay, "Les
Kalmuks de la Volga entre l'Empire Russe et l'Empire Ottoman dans le règne de Pierre
le Grand," *Cahiers du Monde Russe et Sovietique,* 7 (1966), 63–76.

The Tulip Period (1717–1730) is described by Ismet Parmaksızoğlu, "İbrâhim Paşa,
Dâmâd," IA, V, 915–919; Ahmed Refik, *Lâle Devri* (The Tulip Period), Istanbul, 1928;
M. Münir Aktepe, "Damad Ibrahim Paşa Devrinde Lâle" (Tulips in the Period of Damad
Ibrahim Paşa), *Tarih Dergisi,* 4 (1952), 85–106; 5 (1953), 85–104; 6 (1954), 23–38;
Muzaffer Erdoğan, "Osmanlı devrinde Istanbul bahçeleri" (Istanbul Gardens in the Otto-
man Age), *Vakıflar Dergisi,* 4 (1958), 149–192; Ahmed Refik, *On Ikinci Asri Hicride
Osmanlı Hayatı* (Ottoman Life in the Twelfth Century of the Hicra), Istanbul, 1930; M.
L. Shay, *The Ottoman Empire from 1720 to 1734 as Revealed in Despatches of the Vene-
tian Baili,* Urbana, Ill., 1944; and Lady Mary Wortley Montagu, *Letters,* ed. Robert
Halshand, 2 vols., Oxford, 1965–1966. The printing press and cultural developments are
presented by G. Toderini, *Letteratura turchesca,* 3 vols., Venice, 1787; Franz Babinger,
Stambuler Buchwesen im 18 Jahrhundert, Leipzig, 1919; Tibor Halasi-Kun, "Ibrahim
Müteferrika," IA, V, 896–900; E. J. W. Gibb, *A History of Ottoman Poetry,* vol. IV,
London, 1905, pp. 3–57; Niyazi Berkes, "Ilk Türk matbaası kurucusunun dini ve fikri
kimliği" (The religious and philosophical personality of the founder of the first Turkish
press), *Belleten,* 26 (1962), 716–737; Osman Erensoy, *Türkiyeye matbaanın girişi ve ilk
basılan eserler* (The entry of the press into Turkey and the first published works), Istanbul, 1959.

The Iranian wars and the Caucasus campaigns are discussed by M. Münir Aktepe,
*1720–1724 Osmanlı Iran Münâsebetleri ve Şilâhşör Kemânî Mustafa Ağa'nın Revân
Fetihnamesi* (Ottoman-Iranian Relations, 1720–1724, and the Bulletin of Conquest of Eri-

van of Şilahşör Kemâni Mustafa Ağa), Istanbul, 1970; Mohammad Ali Hekmat, *Essai sur l'histoire des relations politiques Irano-Ottomanes de 1722 à 1747*, Paris, 1937; André de Claustre, *Histoire de Tomas Kuli Kan Roi de Perse*, published in Paris in 1743; Münir Aktepe, "Dürri Ahmed Efendi'nin Iran Sefâreti" (The Iranian Embassy of Dürri Ahmed Efendi), *Belgelerle Türk Tarihi Dargisi*, nos. 1–6 (1967–1968); *Relation de Dourry Efendy, Ambassadeur de la Porte Othomane aupres du roi de Pers*, Paris, 1910.

The revolution that overthrew Ahmet III and ended the Tulip Period is studied in M. Münir Aktepe, *Patrona Isyanı (1730)* (The Patrona Revolt [1730]), Istanbul, 1958, which also provides extensive information on the social and economic background to the revolt. See also Abdi, *1730 Patrona ihtilali hakkında bir eser* (A Work on the 1730 Patrona Revolt), Ankara, 1943; and de Crouzenac, *Histoire de la dernière revolution arrivée dans l'Empire Ottoman*, Paris, 1740.

The reign of Mahmut I (1730–1754) is studied in some detail by M. Munir Aktepe, "Mahmud I," *IA*, VII, 154–165. On the work of Bonneval see Heinrich Benedikt, *Der Pascha-Graf Alexander von Bonneval, 1675–1747*, Graz-Cologne, 1959; Comte de Bonneval, *Mémoires sur M. Le Comte de Bonneval*, Paris, 1802; Albert Vandal, *Le Pacha Bonneval*, Paris, 1885; Septima Gorceix, *Bonneval Pacha*, Paris, 1953; "Bonneval und Prinz Eugen," *Mitteilungen des Instituts für österreichische Geschichts-forschung*, 18 (1950), 470–502. The most authoritative study of Eugene of Savoy is M. Braubach, *Prinz Eugen von Savoyen, Eine Biographie*, 5 vols., Vienna, 1963–1965, although the old study of A. Arneth, *Prinz Eugen von Savoyen*, 3 vols., Vienna, 1858, is still useful on his campaigns against the Ottomans. The Ottoman victories after his death are described in M. E. von Angeli, *Der Krieg mit der Pforte, 1736–1739*, Vienna, 1880; and Albert Vandal, *Une ambassade française en Orient sous Louis XV. La mission du Marquis de Villeneuve, 1728–1741*, Paris, 1887; Salahuddin Tansel, "Büyük Friedrich devrinde Osmanlı Prusya münasebetleri hakkında" (On Ottoman-Prussian Relations During the Time of Frederick the Great), *Belleten*, X, 133–165; and Theodor Tupetz, "Der Turkenfeldzug von 1739 und der Friede von Belgrade," *Historische Zeitschrift*, 40 (1878). The short reign of Osman III is described by Şinasi Altındağ, "Osman III," *IA*, 448–450.

On the reign of Mustafa III (1757–1774) see Bekir Sidki Baykal, "Mustafa III," *IA*, VII, 700–708, and the same author's "Ragib Paşa," *IA*, IX, 594–596. The latter is the subject of an unpublished Ph.D. dissertation at Princeton University by Norman Itzkowitz, "Mehmed Raghib Pasha: The Making of an Ottoman Grand Vezir" (1959), summarized in Itzkowitz, "Eighteenth Century Ottoman Realities," *Studia Islamica*, 16 (1962), 73–94. On the war of 1768–1774 see Iu. R. Klokman, *Feldmarshal Rumiantsev v period russko-turetskoi voiny 1768–1774 gg*, Moscow, 1951; Selaheddin Tansel, "1768 Seferi hakkında bir Araştırma" (A Study of the 1768 Campaign), Ankara Universitesi, *Dil ve Tarih-Coğrafya Fakültesi Bulteni*, VII, 477–537; M. S. Anderson, "Great Britain and the Russo-Turkish War of 1768–1774," *English Historical Review*, 64 (1954), 39–58; G. S. Thomson, *Catherine the Great and the Expansion of Russia*, New York, 1950; Boris Nolde, *La formation de l'empire russe*, 2 vols., Paris, 1953; and Alan W. Fisher, *The Prussian Annexation of the Crimea, 1772–1783*, Cambridge, 1970. Military reforms during the reign are described by Baron de Tott, *Mémoires sur les Turcs et Tartares*, 3 vols., Amsterdam, 1784. Relations with Iran are included in Lawrence Lockhart, *Nadir Shah: A Critical Study Based Mainly upon Contemporary Sources*, London, 1938. The most authoritative study of European diplomatic relations concerning the Ottoman Empire from this time forward is M. S. Anderson, *The Eastern Question, 1774–1923*, London and New York, 1966. A. Sorel, *La question d'Orient au XVIIIe siècle. Le partage de la Pologne et le traité de Kainardji*, Paris, 1889, tr. as *The Eastern Question in the Eighteenth Century*, London, 1898, is still useful for presenting the French point of view. Neither book is accurate on Ottoman internal affairs and diplomatic policies. A useful general account of the empire's internal situation and the eighteenth-century reform efforts is Dr. Yücel Özkaya, "XVIIIinci yüzyilda çıkarılan adalet-nâmelere göre Türkiye'nın iç durumu" (The internal situation of Turkey According to the Justice Orders Issued in the Eighteenth Century), *Belleten*, 38 (1974), 445–491.

The important reign of Abdulhamit I (1774–1789) has not yet received any kind of definitive treatment. The short summaries by Cavid Baysun, "Abdülhamid I," IA, I, 73–76, and " 'Abd al-Hamid I," EI², 62–63, are inadequate. The most useful information on internal reforms and modernization is found in Ismail Hakkı Uzunçarşılı, "Sadrazam Halil Hamid Paşa" (Grand Vezir Halil Hamid Paşa), *Türkiyat Mecmuası,* 5 (1936), 213–267, and the same author's "Cezayirli Gazi Hasan Paşa'ya dâir" (On Cezayirli Gazi Hasan Paşa), *Türkiyat Mecmuası,* VII–VIII, 17–40, the latter emphasizing naval reforms following the Battle of Çeşme. See also Abdulhak Adnan (Adıvar), *Osmanlı Türklerinde Ilim,* Istanbul, 1943; Auguste Boppe, "La France et le 'militaire turc' au XVIIIe siècle," in *Feuilles d'Histoire,* 1912, pp. 386–402, 390–501; Bekir Kütükoğlu, "Müverrih Vâsıfın kaynaklarindan Hâkim Tarihi" (The History of Hakim, one of the Sources of the Historian Vâsıf), *Tarih Dergisi,* V, 69–76, VI, 91–122; VII, 79–192; and Baron de Tott, *Mémoires du Baron de Tott sur les Turcs,* 4 vols., Amsterdam, 1785.

On the war of 1787–1792 see S. J. Shaw, *Between Old and New: The Ottoman Empire Under Sultan Selim III, 1789–1807,* Cambridge, Mass., 1971, pp. 21–68; also A. Beer, *Die orientalische Politik Oesterreichs seit 1774,* Prague, 1883; Jean Lemoine, "The Reversal of Alliances and the Family Compact," *Cambridge Modern History,* vol. VI, pp. 329–360; Allen Fisher, *The Russian Annexation of the Crimea, 1772–1783,* Cambridge, England, 1970; and Anderson, *The Eastern Question,* pp. 1–27.

The reign of Selim III has been studied exhaustively in Shaw, *Between Old and New,* and A. Cevat Eren, "Selim III," IA, X, 441–457, both of which have extensive bibliographies. See also Uriel Heyd, "The Ottoman 'Ulema and Westernization in the Time of Selim III and Mahmud II," *Studies in Islamic History and Civilization. Scripta Hierosolymitana,* 9 (1961), 63–96; J. C. Hurowitz, "Russia and the Turkish Straits: A Reevaluation of the Origins of the Problem," *World Politics,* 14 (1962), 606–632; the same author's "The Background of Russia's Claims to the Turkish Straits: A Reassessment," *Belleten,* 28 (1964), 459–503; Bernard Lewis, "The Impact of the French Revolution on Turkey," *Journal of World History,* 1 (1953), 105–125; and the following articles and books by S. J. Shaw: "The Established Ottoman Army Corps Under Selim III (1789–1807)," *Der Islam* 40 (1965), 142–184; "The Origins of Ottoman Military Reform: The Nizam-i Cedid Army of Sultan Selim III," *Journal of Modern History,* 37 (1965), 291–306; "Selim III and the Ottoman Navy," *Turcica: Revue d'Etudes Turques,* 1 (1969), 212–241; *Ottoman Egypt in the Age of the French Revolution,* Cambridge, Mass., 1964; and *Ottoman Egypt in the Eighteenth Century,* Cambridge, Mass., 1962. A daybook account of Selim's reign is transcribed into Latin letters by Fahri Ç. Derin, "Tüfengçi-başı Arif Efendi Tarihçesi," *Belleten,* 38 (1974), 379–443; while one of the most important Anatolian notable families is described in Ismail Hakkı Uzunçarşılı, "Çapan oğulları," *Belleten,* 38 (1974), 215–261. The rise of Bayraktar Mustafa Paşa and his role in Selim's deposition is discussed in A. F. Miller, *Mustafa Pasha Bayraktar,* Moscow-Leningrad, 1947; and Ismail Hakkı Uzunçarşılı, *Meşhur Rumeli Ayanlarından Tirsinikli Ismail, Yılık oğlu Süleyman Ağalar ve Alemdar Mustafa Paşa* (Some of the Famous Rumeli Notables, Tirsinikli Ismail and Yılık oglu Suleyman Ağas and Alemdar Mustafa Paşa (Istanbul, 1942).

Index

This index has been formulated to serve also as a glossary. Parentheses are used to indicate alternate names, exact translations, and dates; definitions and explanations follow colons. Muslim names are alphabetized by first name except for individuals whose fame by other epithets justifies their being listed first.

Bosporus (Boğaziçi), 7, 11, 34, 56, 59, 75, 198, 201, 211, 234, 235, 243, 273, 274
bostancı başı (Chief of Gardeners), *Bostancı Ocağı* (Corps of Gardeners): guardians of gates and environs of imperial palaces, 114, 117, 186, 233, 241
Bozca Ada, 210
Brankoviç, George (1398–1456): king of Serbia (ruled 1427–1456), 29, 37, 48, 49, 50, 51, 52, 53, 63
Brankoviç, Vuk: Serbian prince, 21, 29
bribery, bribes, 98, 101, 171, 173, 175, 176, 202, 204, 205, 226, 227, 231, 246, 252, 263, 264, 265
bridges, 59, 125, 130, 151
Bucharest, 185, 244, 248, 259
Treaty of (1812), 275
Buczacz (Bucaş), Treaty of (1672), 213
Buda: city, and province of central Hungary, 33, 53, 93, 94, 102, 143
budget, budgetary regulations, 101, 119, 205, 209, 201, 229, 247, 264
Bug river, 214, 250, 260
Bulgaria, Bulgars, 12, 16, 17, 18, 19, 20, 21, 22, 24, 31, 34, 43–48, 49, 51, 52, 53, 64, 65, 72, 128, 220, 230, 244, 248, 253, 258, 267, 271
Bulgarian Patriarchate, 151
bureaucracy, bureaucrats, 5–6, 23, 66, 83, 85, 87, 101, 118–120, 136, 166, 171, 202, 207, 238, 280–283
Burhaneddin, Kadi (1344–1398), 20–21, 28–35
Bursa, 14, 16, 20, 26, 32–38, 42, 45, 60, 71, 78, 80, 83, 113, 134, 142–145, 158, 192, 211, 270, 286, 287
Byzantium, 1–3, 6–67, 113, 141, 143, 152, 164, 258

cadastre, 92, 104, 150, 156, 201, 238
Cairo, 39, 84, 134, 147, 158, 222, 268, 287
caliph, caliphate, 4, 5, 8, 39–40, 62, 78, 85, 96, 164, 250, 255
Cambrai, Treaty of (1529), 93
campaign tax (*imdad-ı seferiyye*), 218, 238
Campbell (Ingiliz Mustafa); Scottish military expert in Ottoman service, early 19th century, 251, 252
Campo Formio, Treaty of (1797), 268
Canbay (Canibek) Giray: Crimean han (ruled 1610–1623, 1624, 1627–1635), 195, 196
Canberdi al-Gazzâli: 16th-century Mamluk and Ottoman provincial governor, 88
Canbulat, Syrian rebel family, 188
Candar: Anatolian Turkoman notable family, 11, 41, 42, 43, 45, 64

Candia, 202, 203, 212, 287
Canik (Canit, Müslüman Samsun), 11
Canikli: Anatolian Turkoman notable family, 253, 270
cannons, cannon foundries, cannon corps, 21, 46, 56, 58, 123, 124, 187, 229, 241, 251, 262, 263
capitulations agreements: grants of special privileges to Europeans resident and trading in the Ottoman Empire, 29–30, 62, 97–98, 163, 177, 182, 181, 189, 270, 284
caravans, 3, 4, 83, 108, 160, 177
caravansarays, 161
Carpathian mountains, 2, 129, 259
Casimir IV: king of Poland (ruled 1447–1492), 68, 213
Caspian sea, 7, 177, 181, 182, 183, 239, 287
Cateau-Cambresis, Treaty of (1559), 106
Catherine II The Great: Empress of Russia (ruled 1762–1796), 244, 247–250, 254–255, 257, 258, 259, 260, 268
Catholicos: head of Armenian church, 152, 153
Catholics, 153, 178, 181, 201, 210, 220, 224, 232, 271
Caucasus, 2, 5, 32, 33, 46, 81, 83, 96, 104, 109, 129, 141, 146, 150, 152, 177, 180–183, 187, 188, 189, 195, 199, 200, 239, 243, 248, 250, 258, 284, 287
cavalry, 17, 25, 26, 41, 46, 49, 94, 108, 123, 124, 125, 127, 129, 130, 173, 187, 226
Cebeci (Armorer Corps), 123, 124
cebeli: military retainer, 125–127
Cecora, Battle of (1620), 191
Celali revolts, 86, 90, 92, 149, 185–186, 188, 194, 197, 199, 203, 204, 206, 207, 208, 211, 285, 287
Celaluddin Rumi (1207–1272): Turkish mystic leader, 141, 155, 294
Cem Sultan (1459–1495): rebel Ottoman prince, son of Mehmet II, 66, 67, 70–71, 73, 75, 76, 80
cemaat (clan), 150
census, 61, 287; *see also* cadastre
Central Asia, 9, 10, 13, 23, 28, 33, 61, 107, 140, 141, 143, 153, 158, 164, 171, 284, 304
Cephalonia (Kefalonya), 69
Cerbe, 111
cerrah başı (chief surgeon), 117
Cevdet Paşa, Ahmet (1822–1894): 19th-century Ottoman administrator and historian, 297
al-Cezayir: Aegean island province, attached to grand admiral, 131
charity, charitable institutions, 89, 161; *see also* social services and *evkaf*

329

Cüneyt Bey, Izmir oğlu: Anatolian notable, 42, 44, 45, 47

Çağatay (Chagatay) Mongols, 9, 11, 32

Çaldıran, Battle of (1514), 81, 82, 83, 95

Çanakkale, 10, 15, 16, 287

Çandarlı family of grand vezirs, 27, 28, 33, 37, 38, 39, 41, 45, 46, 49, 50, 52, 53, 56, 58

Çankırı (Gangra), 11

Çapanoğlu: Anatolian notable family, 253

çarhacıbaşı: chief of skirmishers corps, 130

Çarşamba, 11

Çarşamba suyu river, 30

Çavuşan, Çavuşlar: corps of palace messengers, guards, sergeants; *çavuş başı:* chief of the corps, 117

çektiri: oar powered ship, 50

çelebi: title of Ottoman prince, 167

Çeşme, Battle of (1770), 249, 252

Çetince, 69

Çırağan, 293

çift: pair (of oxen) ; *çiftlik:* agricultural plot of land, theoretically cultivated by a pair of oxen or a single plot, equalling 20 to 30 acres, 120, 126, 150, 155, 156, 173

çift bozan resmi: tax paid by cultivator for permission to abandon his plot, 126, 150

çift resmi: plow tax, 51, 67, 120, 156

Çimpe (Tzympe), 16

Çirmen, 20

Çobanoğulları : Turkoman notable family, and principality, 12

çohadar ağası: director of the Sultan's palace pages, 115

çöplük subaşısı: officer in charge of garbage and trash collections, 160

çorbacı: battalion commander, 123

Çorlu, 16, 86

Çorum, 208

Çubuk, 35

Dacia: reconstituted Byzantine state proposed by Catherine the Great, 258

Dağdevirenoğlu: 18th-century Balkan notable, 253

Dağistan: province in the Caucasus, 182, 243, 246, 287

dahil: intermediate-ranked *medrese,* 133

Dalmatia, 18, 31, 63, 68, 69, 72, 75, 99, 129, 184, 218, 224, 232, 233, 258, 268, 272

Damascus (Şam), 35, 84, 88, 122, 134, 195, 202, 208, 209, 211, 253, 270, 287

damga resmi; stamp tax ; tax charged in return for hallmark indicating quality of precious metal, 160

danişment, danışman: highly ranked Muslim religious student, learned man, 133

Danişment Ahmet Gazi: 13th century Anatolian poet and Turkoman prince, 141

Danube (Tuna) river, 12, 18, 21, 29, 32, 33, 42, 46, 48, 50, 52, 53, 54, 61, 63, 67, 68, 72, 73, 87, 91, 94, 102, 120, 128, 129, 130, 184, 185, 220, 221, 223, 232, 244, 245, 248, 249, 253, 259, 260, 275

dar üs-saade ağası (Ağa of the Abode of Felicity) : chief black eunuch of the palace of the Sultan, 115, 204

Dardanelles (Çanakkale Boğazı), 10, 12, 15, 19, 56, 65, 111, 202, 203, 204, 206, 207, 209, 226, 251, 273

Darphane-i Âmire (Imperial Mint), *darphane emini* (commissioner of the Mint), 117

Davut Paşa: grand vezir (1482–1497), 72

Davut-u Kayseri (d. 1350): Anatolian religious writer, 144

debasement of currency, 107, 108, 174, 200, 219, 224, 227, 238, 265, 273

Dede Korkut: 14th-century Anatolian folk poet, 141

defter emini: commissioner of registers of landed property, 119

defterdar: treasurer, minister of finances, director of provincial finances, 58, 119, 122, 134

Defterhane: Treasury, Registry of landed property, 119

deli: raider, lunatic, heroic man, 25, 129, 130

Deliorman, 43

depositions, 191, 193, 194, 203, 219, 228, 240

derbent: mountain pass, fort guarding a pass or strategic road, 94, 127, 128–129, 136

derebeys: lords of the valley, Anatolian notables, 245

dervish (*derviş*), 153, 154, 155, 162, 207, 225, 292, 295; *see also* mystic orders

derya bey: admiral, naval supervisor, 131, 226

Despina, Maria: Serbian wife of Bayezit I, 24, 29

destan (epic, ballad), 141, 292

Devlet Giray II: Crimean *han* (ruled 1699–1702, 1708–1713), 229, 231

Devlet Giray IV: Crimean *han* (ruled 1769–1770, 1775–1777), 248, 255

devşirme (collection): conscription of non-Muslim youths for conversion and service to the Ottoman sultan: 27, 29, 46, 57, 58, 85, 113–114, 115, 123, 127, 187, 190, 236, 291, 314–315

Elbistan, 34, 42, 73, 92

emanet: commission type of *mukata'a;*
  emin: commissioner, holder of *emanet,*
  121, 198, 209, 238, 290
Emine Sultan (1696–1738): daughter of
  Mustafa II, 229
emir: prince, chief, commander, 9, 15
emir of the marches: 12, 16, 36
emir-i ahor: chief of the Imperial stables,
  117
emir-i âlem: bearer of the Sultan's standard; pasha of lowest rank, 117
Emir oğulları: Anatolian Turkoman principality, 11
endowments, *see evkaf*
Enez (Aynos), 63
engineering schools, 241, 251, 252, 257, 263
England, 33, 91, 96, 107, 181–182, 189, 222,
  229, 231, 244, 248, 258, 259, 262, 263,
  267, 268, 269, 270, 271, 272–273, 275,
  284
Enveri Efendi, Sadullah (d. 1794): 18th-
  century Ottoman chronicler, 145, 298
Epirus, 18, 49, 64
Ereğli, 109
Eretna: Anatolian Turkoman principality,
  20
Erivan (Revan), 183, 199, 239
Erminak Giray: Crimean *han,* 68
Erzincan (Erez), 21, 35, 42, 43, 64, 81, 82
Erzurum, 6, 35, 43, 66, 81, 82, 95, 129, 193,
  195, 285, 287
Esat Efendi, Mehmet (1789–1848), 19th-
  century Ottoman chronicler, 297
Esat Efendi: *şeyhulislam* (1623–1625), 191
Eskihisar, 15
Eskişehir, 14, 16, 42, 211
Esma Han Sultan (1545–1585): daughter
  of Selim II, 110, 179
esnaf, see craft guilds
Esther Kira, 177
Eşref: Anatolian Turkoman principality,
  11, 42
Eugene of Savoy (1663–1736): Habsburg
  general, 223, 232, 241
eunuchs, 115, 204, 289
Euphrates river, 13, 35, 61, 65, 66, 81, 82, 84
evkâf, pl. of *vakıf* (Ar. *waqf*): endowments,
  pious foundations, estates in mortmain,
  15, 27, 60, 67, 89, 104, 120, 121, 133, 136,
  138, 156, 161–162, 187, 247, 282, 289, 291
Evliya: mystic friends of God, saints, 154
Evliya Çelebi (1614–1682): Ottoman
  traveller, 286–288
Evrenos Bey: Byzantine convert to Islam
  in service of early Ottomans, 16, 20, 31

eyalet (province), 26; *see also* provincial
  organization
Eyüp, 136, 242

factories, 59, 159, 161, 162, 225
Fahruddin II: Ma'nid ruler of the Lebanon,
  195
famine, 73, 204, 207, 218, 219, 221, 224, 242
Fatih mosque, 60, 133
Fazıl Bey (d. 1810): Ottoman folk poet, 295
Fazıl Ahmet Paşa, Köprülüzade: grand
  vezir (1661–1676), 211–214, 285, 287
Ferdinand I: Austrian Archduke, Emperor
  (1558–1564), 91, 93, 94, 101–102, 105
Ferhad Paşa, 92, 149, 184–185
fetva: Muslim legal opinion supplied by
  müfti, 30, 103, 137, 138, 139, 146, 203, 219
feudal organization, leaders, fiefs, 7, 18, 23,
  25, 26, 27, 36, 41, 46, 51, 52, 61, 71, 76,
  79, 88–89, 93, 108–110, 121, 124, 126,
  131, 171, 173, 187, 226–227, 261–262, 283
Feyzullah Efendi, Seyyit: *şeyhulislam*
  (1695–1703), 223, 226, 227, 228
Filibe (Plovdiv, Philippopolis), 18, 19, 27,
  39, 43, 129
finance
  organization, 23–26, 77, 89–90, 101, 104,
    115, 118, 119–121, 181, 290, 291, 313, 315
  problems, 51, 60, 66, 67, 71, 107–108, 172–
    174, 187, 200, 204, 218, 227, 264, 273, 291
  programs and reforms, 67, 100, 198, 203,
    205, 220, 225, 229, 238, 247, 257, 264–265
firefighting, 123, 162
Foça (Phocaea), 45
folk literature, poetry, 28, 140, 141, 149, 292–
  293
food provision, shortages, 28, 104, 108, 117,
  130, 204, 221, 222, 246, 254, 263, 265
forced labor, corvée, 104, 126, 150, 174
foreign affairs offices, 102, 119, 231, 256, 281
foreigners in Ottoman Empire, *see* Capitulations
fortresses, fortifications, 120, 124, 125, 126,
  127, 151, 187, 242, 256, 257, 263
fountains, 27, 60, 160, 161, 162, 235, 242
France, Ottoman relations with, 71, 75, 86,
  91, 92, 96, 97, 98, 102–103, 106, 177, 178,
  180, 181, 182, 189, 211–214, 217, 220,
  224, 229, 241, 242, 244, 248, 254, 266,
  267, 271, 272, 273, 275
Francis I: king of France (ruled 1515–
  1547), 91, 93, 103, 106, 177
fratricide, 44, 56, 80, 179, 184, 186, 190, 191,
  199
French Revolution, influence on Ottoman
  Empire, 251, 259, 266, 267, 268–269

frigate (*firkateyn, kırlangıç*), 167

frontier organization, fortresses, operations, 3, 9–11, 14, 16, 19–20, 25, 29, 34, 36, 38, 41, 58, 64, 72, 74, 82, 91, 94, 100, 102, 105, 121, 128, 129, 179, 185, 187, 199, 230, 242

furs, 202

Fuzuli (1480–1556), classic Ottoman poet, 149

fütuvvet, Ar. *futuwwah:* Muslim chivalric brotherhoods, 8, 141, 153, 154

Galata, 57, 85, 131, 136, 160, 243, 252, 295

Galata Saray school, 85

Galatz, 275

galeote (*kalyota*), 167

Galip Dede (1757–1799) : dervish leader and poet, 295

galleon (*kalyon, kapak*), 167, 226

galley (*kadirga, bastarde*), 167

Gallipoli peninsula (Gelibolu), 15, 16, 17, 19, 20, 42, 44, 52, 56, 86, 97, 105, 109, 131, 146, 222, 287

garrisons, 43, 61, 90, 91, 100, 104, 108, 120, 124, 125, 126, 128–130, 136, 171, 173, 182, 185, 187, 210, 221, 222, 283, 288

gazel (ode) : lyric poem of 4 to 15 couplets, with first couplet rhyming, and second hemstiches rhyming with hemstiches of first couplet, 140, 142, 293–295

gazi: fighter for Islam against the infidel, frontier raider into non-Muslim lands, outstanding Muslim warrior ; *gazis,* *gazi* tradition, *gazi* leaders, 3, 9, 10, 12, 13, 15, 24, 25, 27, 28, 29, 30, 31, 33, 34, 35, 36, 37, 38, 41, 44, 45, 46, 49, 52, 56, 58, 62, 72, 74, 76, 79, 85, 121, 129, 145, 153, 164, 171, 223

Gebze, 15

gedik: occupational license, established place in a particular service, 157

Gediz (Hermon) river, 10

Gence, 188, 239

Genefe, Battle of (1527), 92

Genghis Han, 8, 32, 81

Gennadious Scolarious: first Patriarch of Greek Orthodox *millet,* 59, 143

Genoa, Genoese, 10, 16, 17, 29, 31, 34, 41, 42, 45, 47, 48, 53, 57, 62, 63, 64, 68, 97, 98, 99, 110, 131, 178

geographic literature, travels, 107, 118, 143, 146, 147, 237, 264, 285–288

Gerede, 17

Germiyan: Anatolian Turkoman principality, 10, 17, 21, 29, 30, 34, 36, 37, 40, 42, 44, 45, 47, 142

al-Ghazzali, 112, 144

Giresun, 11

gold, gold mines, 88, 107, 114, 120, 158, 172, 173, 201, 286

Golden Horde, 11, 62, 128

Golden Horn (Haliç), 31, 57, 59, 68, 86, 131, 160, 234, 236, 251, 252

Goletta (Halk ul-Vad), 96

governors, 24, 26, 79, 121–122, 283

Göktürk Empire, 2–4, 10

Gönüllüyan corps, 127

Göynük, 11, 15, 34

grain, grain trade, 18, 75, 88, 117, 130, 159, 172, 204

Gran, 94, 185, 187, 215

grand admiral (*kapudan paşa, kapudan-ı derya,* 97, 105, 107, 131, 132, 226, 252, 264

grand dragoman, *see baş tercüman*

grand vezir (*sadr-ı azam, sadrazam, vezir-ı azam*), 25, 27, 40, 58, 90, 94, 100, 101, 115, 118, 119, 121, 130, 134, 136, 164, 176, 204, 209, 221, 264, 281, 282, 290, 291

Greece, 12, 17, 22, 25, 31, 47, 51, 53, 65, 97, 129, 218, 231, 249, 258, 259, 267

Greek Orthodox *millet,* church, people, 19, 50, 58–59, 67, 84, 151–152, 153, 201, 231, 250, 281

Greek Revolution, 281

Greek Scheme, 258

Grosswardein (Varadin), 101, 105

Gucerat, 100

gulam: child male slave, foreign youth, 27, 114, 115

gunpowder, 123, 187, 222, 241

Gülbahar Sultan: wife of Süleyman I The Magnificent (d. 1581), 104

Gümülcine, 20

Habsburg Empire, Habsburgs, 72–75, 86–87, 91–99, 100–102, 105, 106, 111, 177, 179, 180, 183, 186–190, 210, 212, 213, 217–222, 230, 231–233, 236, 267–268

Haç Ova, Battle of (1596), 185, 186

hace (pl. *hacegân*), head of scribal department, senior clerk, 118, 280, 289, 295

had: boundary of individual Ottoman status and behavior, 166

hafiye-i tecrid: rank of *medrese*s, 133

Hafsa (Hafise) Hatun (d. 1534): mother of Süleyman I The Magnificent, 90, 98

Hafsid dynasty, 96, 179

haham başı: grand rabbi, head of Jewish *millet,* 152

Hakim Efendi, Mehmet (d. 1770): Ottoman chronicler, 298

hünkâr imamı: Ottoman palace religious ritual leader, 117
Hürrem Sultan (Roxelana, 1500–1558): wife of Süleyman I the Magnificent (1520–1558), 90, 98, 104, 108–110, 115
Hüsamuddin Çoban, 12
Hüseyin Paşa, Abaza, 193
Hüseyin Paşa, Amcazâde: grand vezir (1697–1702), 224–227, 288, 289
Hüseyin Paşa, Küçük (d. 1803): friend of Selim III and grand admiral (1792–1803), 263–264, 270
Hüseyin Paşa, Mere: grand vezir (1622, 1623), 193, 195
Hüseyin Paşa, Mezamorto: grand admiral (1695–1701, 1690), 226, 227, 229
Hüseyin Paşa, Nasuh Paşa zâde, 201
Hüseyin Şakir Efendi: 18th-century chronicler, 298
Hüseyin Vehbi; Seyyit (d. 1737), 295

Ibrahim (1615–1648): Ottoman sultan (ruled 1640–1648), 190, 200–203, 208, 320–321
Ibrahim Bey: late 18th-century Egyptian Mamluk leader, 253
Ibrahim Bey: prince of Karaman (ruled 1426–1464), 47, 49, 51, 56
Ibrahim Müteferrika (1674–1745): founder of Ottoman printing press, 236–238, 240, 242, 246, 257
Ibrahim Paşa, Çandarlı: grand vezir (1421–1429), 38
Ibrahim Paşa, Damat: grand vezir (1523–1536), 89, 90, 95, 98, 100
Ibrahim Paşa, Nevşehirli, Damat: grand vezir (1717–1730), leader of Tulip Period, 232–235, 239, 240, 293, 296
Ibrahim Paşa: Ottoman ambassador to Vienna (1719), 233
Ibrahim Peçevi (1574–1650): Ottoman chronicler, 288
Ibrail (Brailia), 67, 129, 260, 275
Ibşir Paşa, 208
icmal: summary register of treasury revenues and expenditures, 119
İç Hazine: Inner Treasury of Imperial Palace, 115
İç Oğlan: Inner Service boys of Imperial Palace, slaves of Sultan, pages, 113, 114, 117, 125, 203
Içel, 71
Idris Bitlisi: 15th-century Ottoman governor and historian, 76, 82, 145, 288
ihtisap ağa: regulator of markets, 208
ihtisap resmi: municipal market tax, 120

ikta: assignment of revenue-producing unit to agent of Sultan for administration and tax collection, 5, 23, 26, 121; *see also mukata'a*
Ilhanid Empire (1256–1349), 9, 11, 12, 14, 30, 32, 33, 36, 66
Ilmiye: Learned/Cultural/Religious Institution of Ottoman Ruling Class, 85, 103, 132–149, 174, 191, 282–283, 291, 315
iltizam: tax farm, 121; *see also* tax farms
imam: leader of prayer, 138
imdad-ı seferiyye: military assistance tax, 218, 238
Imperials: soldiers of Habsburg Empire, Austria, 215, 217, 221, 259
Imperial Council, *see Divan-ı Hümayun*
Imperial Treasury, *see Hazine-i Âmire*
Imroz (Imbros) island, 63, 65
India, 33, 34, 83, 99, 100, 107, 147, 158, 268, 284
Indian Ocean, 83, 107, 147
industry, manufacturing, 60, 112, 114, 160, 172, 173, 225, 257, 284; *see also* artisans
Inegöl, 14
infantry, 17, 25, 26, 46, 123, 130, 187; *see also* Janissaries
inflation, 107, 108, 156, 173, 201, 204, 207, 219, 221, 224, 227, 242, 246, 265, 273, 284
inheritance, 104, 136, 162
Inner Service (*Enderun*) of Imperial Palace, 114, 115–117
Interregnum (*Fetret,* 1402–1413), 12, 28, 35–40, 42, 45, 142, 307–308
intikam (revenge), 166
intisap: patronage/vassal-client relationship between strong and weak individuals, 166, 170, 208, 289
Ionian Islands, 99, 233, 267, 268, 269, 271, 275
Ipsilanti, Alexander (1725–1807): Phanariote notable, *hospodar* of Wallachia (1774–1784, 1796–1797) and Moldavia (1786–1788, 1807), 259
iptida: basic starting revenue of a timar or salaried position, 125–126
Iran (Persia), 2–6, 9, 13, 21, 32, 33, 40, 48, 61, 64, 81, 83, 85, 87, 95, 107, 129, 145, 149, 154, 176, 177, 181, 183, 187, 195, 199–201, 206, 214, 238–239, 284
wars with, 77–78, 80–83, 103–105, 109, 177, 180–183, 188–189, 199–200, 238–239, 243, 245–246, 254
Iraq (Mesopotamia), 3–9, 13, 23, 32–33, 35, 64, 85, 95–96, 97, 100, 107, 109, 149, 194–195, 199, 200, 243, 246, 253, 254, 270
iron, 158, 182

Lüleburgaz, 16

Lütfi Paşa (1488–1563): grand vezir (1539–1541) and chronicler, 100–101, 290

mâbeyin (the inbetween): apartments between the inner Harem and outer quarters of the Imperial palace where the Sultan usually received vezirs, 115

Macedonia, 12, 16, 17, 20, 29, 31, 33, 37, 39, 47, 48, 53, 65, 109, 244, 258, 287

maden resmi (mines tax), 120

mahalle: district of town or city, 162 nomadic tent section, 150

Mahdiye, 106

Mahmut I (1696–1754): Ottoman sultan (ruled 1730–1754), 237, 240–246, 323

Mahmut II (1785–1839): Ottoman sultan (ruled 1808–1839), 127, 276, 296

Mahmut Çelebi (1413–1429): son of Mehmet I, 44

Makri, Gulf of, 11

Maksut Giray: Crimean Han (ruled 1767–1768, 1771–1772), 249

mal defterdarı: provincial treasurer, 122

Malatya (Melitene), 34, 35, 42, 84, 225

malikâne: Imperial properties held as property by private persons, 227, 238

Malikşah: Seljuk sultan (ruled 1072–1092), 7, 8

Malkara (Malgara), 16

Malta, 89, 97, 106, 201, 212, 217, 232

Maltepe (Pelecanon), Battle of (1328), 15

mamluk, memluk (slave), mamluks, 5, 7, 80–81, 82, 83, 89, 90, 174, 195, 249, 253, 254, 268, 269, 270, 272

Mamluk Empire of Egypt and Syria (1250–1517), 8, 9, 21, 32, 34, 35, 39, 42, 47, 49, 60, 64, 65, 66, 71, 74, 78, 79, 80, 82, 83, 84, 87, 99, 100, 123, 258, 310–311

Mangat Çay, 21

mani: verse style, 292

Manisa (Magnesia), 10, 79, 80, 110, 286

Manual II Palaeologus: Byzantine emperor (ruled 1391–1425), 31, 33, 37, 39–41, 42, 44

Manzikert, Battle (1071), 6, 7, 11, 13, 141, 154

Mara (Tamara): Serbian wife of Murat II, 52, 56, 63

Maraş (Marasim), 34, 42, 73, 287

Marc Dabik, Battle of (1516), 84

Mardin (Marde), 33, 82

Maritsa (Meriç) river, 17, 18, 19, 20, 51, 72, 253

market taxes, 158, 160

markets, 59, 72, 120, 121, 135, 136, 158, 160, 161, 162

Marmara, Sea of, 10, 11, 14, 15, 37, 56, 57, 59, 86, 117, 207, 222, 242

Maronite Catholics, 153

Martinuzzi, Bishop (d. 1551), 105

martolos soldiers, 128

Maskat, 107

massacres, 32, 33, 35, 36, 42, 51, 78, 95, 181, 194, 195, 196, 197, 244, 248, 249, 255

Matbah-i Âmire (Imperial kitchen), *matbah-ı âmire emini* (commissioner of the Imperial kitchen), 117

Matrakcı Nasuh: 16th-century mathematician, 147

Maximilian I: Holy Roman Emperor (ruled 1493–1519), 73–74

Maximilian II, 180

Mazeppa: *hetman* of Cossacks, 229

Mecca, 84, 109, 134, 287; *see also* Holy Cities

medaris-i semaniye: the eight highest ranking *medrese*s in the Ottoman Empire, 132

medicine, medical schools, 117, 133, 137, 142, 143–144, 146, 147, 148, 264

Medina, 84, 109, 134

Mediterranean sea, 7, 21, 36, 57, 69, 75, 76, 86, 89, 95, 96, 97, 99, 102–103, 105–106, 111, 132, 146, 171, 178, 179, 180, 181, 223, 248, 249, 271, 273, 275, 284, 285, 287

medrese: advanced Muslim school, theological school, 5, 72, 85, 132–133, 136, 138, 139, 143, 144, 147, 148, 149, 160, 161, 212, 235, 286, 289, 293

Mehmet I (1389–1421): Ottoman sultan (ruled 1413–1421), 36–39, 41–44, 124, 142

Mehmet II (1432–1481): Ottoman sultan (ruled 1444, 1451–1481), 44, 49, 51, 52, 55–70, 77, 79, 85, 100, 103, 113, 123, 131, 132, 142, 143, 144, 145, 152, 160, 308–309

Mehmet II: prince of Karaman (ruled 1423–1426), 47

Mehmet III (1566–1603): Ottoman sultan (ruled 1595–1603), 146, 184–186, 319–320

Mehmet IV (1642–1693): Ottoman sultan (ruled 1648–1687), 202–215, 219, 285, 286, 287, 288, 291, 292, 321

Mehmet Abdullah Efendi, Musa zâde (1718–1782), Ottoman chronicler, 298

Mehmet Ağa, Derviş, 186

Mehmet Ağa, Nişli: Ottoman ambassador to Moscow (1722–1723), 233

Monastir (Manastir), 20
moneylenders (*sarraf*), 108
Mongols, Mongol Empire, 8, 9, 10, 11, 12, 13, 23, 32, 39
Monophysites, 152
monopolies, 60, 67, 120, 159, 203
Montecuccoli, Count Raimond: 17th century Habsburg general, 212, 287
Montenegro (Crnagora, Karadağ), 25, 69, 75, 129, 232, 244, 248, 254, 273
Morava river, 18, 20, 51, 129, 220
Morea (Mora, Peloponnesus), 17, 31, 37, 42, 49, 51, 52, 53, 63, 65, 69, 75, 76, 99, 218, 222, 224, 229, 231, 232, 233, 248–249, 258, 287, 296
Morean despots, 51, 52, 53, 63, 67
Morocco, 96, 180
Moscow (Muscovy), 177, 202, 233
mosques, 29, 36, 60, 72, 85, 132, 133, 138, 161, 162, 235, 247
Mosul (Musul), 33, 129, 199, 246
Mudanya (Modrenae), 14
Mudurnu, 11
mufassal: detailed registers of revenues and expenditures, 119
mufti (*müfti*): jurisconsult, 134, 135, 137–138, 139, 146
Muhammad Abd ul-Bâki (1526–1600): Ottoman poet, 148
Muhammad Ali (Mehmet Ali): Ottoman governor of Egypt (1808–1849), 270, 273
muhasebe: accounting offices, 119
muhtesip: market inspector, regulator, 120, 135, 158, 160, 161
mukata'a (*mukataa*), assignment of revenue-producing part of Imperial Possessions to agent of Sultan for administration and tax collection; unit of finance and administration, 26, 120, 121, 156, 174, 227, 247
murakebe: auditing offices, 119
Murat I (1326–1389): Ottoman sultan (ruled 1360–1389), 17–22, 23, 24, 25, 26, 28, 30, 124, 306–307
Murat II (1404–1451): Ottoman sultan (ruled 1421–1451), 43, 44–54, 77, 113, 124, 142, 143, 144, 145, 308
Murat III (1546–1595): Ottoman sultan (ruled 1574–1595), 146, 152, 178, 179–184, 319
Murat IV (1609–1640): Ottoman sultan (ruled 1623–1640), 190, 194–200, 201, 205, 207, 209, 285, 288, 291, 320
Murat Bey al-Kazduğli (d. 1801): Egyptian Mamluk leader, 253

Murat Paşa, Kuyucu: grand vezir (1606–1611), 188, 285, 291
Murat Su river, 6
Musa Calinus: 15th-century doctor, 148
Musa Çelebi (d. 1413): son of Bayezit I, 36–39, 41, 42, 43
Musa Paşa, Kadızade, 143
muskets, 21, 46, 58, 241
Muslihuddin Mustafa Efendi, 143, 144
Muslims, Muslim *millet,* 4, 9, 59, 60, 61, 66, 67, 85, 88, 120, 134, 151, 153, 164, 170, 192, 282, 283
Mustafa, Düzme revolt (1555), 109, 110
Mustafa I (1591–1639): Ottoman sultan (ruled 1617–1618, 1622–1623), 189–194
Mustafa II (1664–1703): Ottoman sultan (ruled 1695–1703), 223
Mustafa III (1717–1774): Ottoman sultan · (ruled 1757–1774), 246, 251, 260, 323
Mustafa IV (1779–1807): Ottoman sultan (ruled 1807–1808), 274–277
Mustafa Ağa: Chief Eunuch of Mustafa I and Murat IV, 190, 194
Mustafa Ağa, Kabakçı (d. 1808): leader of revolt against Selim III, 273–274, 276
Mustafa Âli Efendi, Gelibolulu (1541–1599): chronicler and minister, 146, 290
Mustafa Çelebi (1515–1553): son of Süleyman I the Magnificent, 104, 108–109, 186
Mustafa Çelebi: son of Mehmet I, 44
Mustafa Çelebi (Düzme Mustafa): claimed son of Bayezit I, 36, 43, 44–45, 47
Mustafa Efendi: Ottoman ambassador to Vienna (1730), 233
Mustafa Efendi, Lala, 180, 181, 190
Mustafa Efendi, Musahip: *vezir* under Mehmet IV, 285
Mustafa Paşa (Svilengrad), 20
Mustafa Paşa, Bayraktar (1765–1806): notable of Rusçuk, leader of Rusçuk committee to rescue Selim III, first grand vezir of Mahmut II (1808), 271–276
Mustafa Paşa, Çelebi: grand vezir (1807–1808), 276
Mustafa Paşa, Fazıl, Köprülüzade: grand vezir (1689–1691), 219–223
Mustafa Paşa, İbşir: grand vezir (1654–1655), 206, 286
Mustafa Reşit Efendi: 18th-century chronicler, 298
Mustafa Sami Bey (d. 1734): 18th-century chronicler, 294, 298
Mustafa Selâniki (d. 1600): 16th-century chronicler, 146–147

orphans, 135
Orsova (Irşeve, Orşova), 33, 52
orta (batallion), 123
Osman I (1258–1324): founder of Ottoman dynasty (ruled 1280–1324), 10, 13–14, 15, 16, 22, 24, 163, 305–306
Osman II (1604–1622): Ottoman sultan (ruled 1618–1622), 189, 190, 191–193, 285
Osman III (1699–1757): Ottoman sultan (ruled 1754–1757), 246
Osman Çelebi: revolt in 1444, 53
Osman Paşa, Özdemiroğlu: grand vezir (1584–1585), military leader, 149, 176, 183
Osman Paşa, Pasvanoğlu (Pasbantoglu) (1758–1807): rebel Bulgarian notable, 267, 268, 271, 273
Osman Paşa, Topal: grand vezir (1731–1732), 241
Otluk Beli, Battle of (1472), 66
Otranto, Ottoman invasion of, 69, 70
Ottoman origins, 10–11, 12–13
Ottoman Ruling Class, 9, 17, 24–26, 32, 60, 62, 82, 87, 90, 104, 112, 113–149, 159, 161, 162, 164, 165, 166, 170, 174, 175, 194, 197, 200, 205, 219, 226, 227, 234, 246, 247, 255–256, 280–283, 288, 290, 291, 314–316
Ottoman vassals, vassal troops, 19, 20, 21, 24, 26, 27, 28, 29, 30, 31, 34, 35, 37, 38, 43, 44, 45, 47, 48, 49, 50, 53, 54, 55, 61, 62, 64, 67, 68, 72, 73, 75, 82, 91, 94, 99, 100, 102, 103, 105, 171, 178, 182, 185, 189, 249
Outer Service (*Birun*) of Imperial Palace, 117–118, 115
Oxus river, 2, 4
oymak: Turkish tribal clan, 150
Öksüz Ali: 16th-century Turkish poet, 149
örf: sovereign prerogative, customary law, common usage, 120, 127, 134
örfi: customary taxes, 120

painting, 235, 266
pages, 117
palace schools, 85, 113–114
palace service, 113–118, 119, 125, 137, 208, 226, 229, 282, 289, 295
palaces, 59, 117, 234, 235
Palestine, 9, 153, 253
paper, paper manufacture, 242
Paris, 158, 233
Pasinler, 35
Passarowitz, Treaty of (1718), 232–233, 245
paşa: highest title of rank, 122, 152
Paşa Yiğit Bey, 29

Paşakapısı, 119
patriarchate, patriarchs, 59, 143, 152, 153
patrona (vice admiral), 226
Patrona Halil: leader of Patrona revolt against Ahmet III, 240, 242
Patrona Revolt (1730), 239–240, 241, 243, 257, 298, 323
pençik (one fifth): right of military leader to one fifth of booty, 23, 26, 46, 113, 119
Peñon island, 96, 97
pensions, 136, 149, 226, 241, 290
pergende (brigantine), 167
Persians, 5, 112, 125, 180, 182, 183, 199, 200; *see also* Iran
Persian Gulf (Arab Gulf), 83, 95, 99, 107, 109, 147, 200
Persian language and literature, 5, 41, 114, 139, 140, 141, 142, 144, 145
Pest, 102, 187
Peter I of Montenegro, 254
Peter I the Great (1672–1725): czar of Russia (ruled 1689–1725), 223, 224, 229–231, 232, 233, 239
Peterwaradin (Varadin), 219, 222, 224, 232, 241, 296
Phanariote (Fener) Greeks, 231, 232
Philip II of Spain: Habsburg emperor (ruled 1558–1569), 106, 178
philosophy, 133, 142, 143, 235
physical sciences, physics, 133, 146
pilgrimage, pilgrims, 61, 79, 88, 89, 157, 164, 232, 285, 287
pir: head of dervish lodge, patron saint, spiritual teacher, 154
Pir Ahmet: ruler of Karaman, 65
Pir Sultan Abdal: 16th-century mystic poet, 149
pirates, 42, 69, 72, 75, 76, 88, 96, 106, 107, 178, 201, 222, 258
Piri Mehmet Paşa: grand vezir (1518–1523), 90
Piri Reis (1465–1554): Ottoman admiral, naval hero, and writer, 107, 147
Piyale Paşa: grand admiral (1554–1568), 106, 177, 178
plague, 73, 218, 242, 246, 264
Ploşnik, Battle of (1388), 20
Podolya (Podolia), 213, 218, 222, 224, 248, 250, 285
poetry, 76, 133, 140–149, 190, 235, 284–285, 292–293, 293–296
Poland, 20, 33, 52, 62, 68, 74, 75, 80, 92, 94, 102, 105, 152, 177, 180, 181, 198, 199, 201, 210, 213, 214, 217, 218, 219, 222, 224, 229, 230, 242, 244, 245, 247, 250, 259, 267

police, 26, 61, 87, 108, 117, 122, 123, 135, 136, 160, 162; *see also subaşı*

politics, political parties, disputes in Ottoman Empire, 36–39, 44–45, 46, 49–50, 52, 53, 55–56, 58, 66–67, 70–72, 74, 76, 77, 78, 79, 80, 90, 98, 101, 104, 108–110, 148, 166, 170–171, 174–179, 190–194, 195–197, 200, 201, 203, 204, 206, 208, 209, 211, 219, 222, 223, 227, 228, 229, 230, 231, 232, 233–234, 240–241, 246, 252, 255–256, 257, 270, 271, 273–274, 282, 291

Poniatowski, Stanislas: king of Poland (ruled 1764–1795), 229, 247

popes, 19, 21, 51, 52, 63, 65, 69, 71, 74, 75, 86, 91, 93, 98, 99, 178, 180, 184, 212, 232, 241

population, population problems, 59–60, 77, 104, 107, 108, 171–172, 246, 265

port facilities, 69, 75, 120, 151, 161

Portugal, Portuguese, 83, 86, 95, 99–100, 107, 111, 147, 152, 178, 180, 181, 188, 214, 284

Potemkin, 258, 259

potor: Bosnians taken in Devşirme conscription, 114

Preveze, 99, 232, 233, 268

prices, price controls, 60, 67, 104, 108, 136, 157, 158, 159, 160, 172, 173, 219, 220, 221, 222, 257, 284

Prilep, 20

Principalities of Rumania, 19, 22, 64, 122, 187, 189, 190, 191, 198, 210, 217, 222, 224, 231, 232, 245, 248, 249, 258–260, 271, 272, 273, 275, 287; *see also* Moldavia, Wallachia, and Transylvania

printing press, 239–242, 246, 257

prisoners, 5, 46, 101, 109, 113, 123

Priştina, 21, 29

Prizren, 220

property, 23, 27, 50, 60, 104, 121, 126, 156, 159, 173, 187, 238

protestants, protestantism, 91, 102, 105, 106, 187, 190, 210; *see also* Reformation

provincial organization, provincial government, governors, 24, 25, 26, 27, 32, 34, 50, 79, 82–83, 89–90, 94, 96, 97, 101, 102, 107, 118, 121–122, 125–129, 171, 172, 174

Prussia, 250, 258, 259

Pruth river, 100, 191
    Treaty of (1711), 229–231, 244

public services, 27, 59, 60

Raab river, 94, 185, 212

Rabbinite Jews, 152

Radu IV the Handsome: prince of Wallachia (ruled 1462–1479), 64, 67

Ragıp Paşa, Koca Mehmet (1699–1763): grand vezir (1756–1763), 246–247, 256, 294

Ragusa (Dubrovnik), 18, 29, 48, 72, 91, 158

Rahmaniye, Battle of (1798), 268

raids, raiding forces, 10, 16, 17, 25, 29, 31, 33, 38, 39, 41, 43, 46, 47, 48, 49, 50, 54, 63, 64, 65, 67, 68, 69, 72, 73, 74, 75, 86, 91, 93, 94, 96, 97, 98, 101, 102, 111, 125, 129, 171, 178, 184, 187, 189, 191, 199, 212, 214, 244, 245, 254, 267, 268

Rakoczi Ferencz II: prince of Transylvania, 232

Rakoczy, George I: prince of Transylvania (ruled 1631–1648), 189, 199, 210

Rakovitza, Battle of (1475), 68

rapid-fire artillery corps, 251, 257

Rareş, Peter, prince of Moldavia, 100

Râşit Mehmet Efendi (d. 1735): Ottoman chronicler, 237, 294, 296

rayas (*re'âyâ*): subjects, protected flock of the Sultan, 19, 60, 61, 62, 112, 113, 114, 150–163, 164, 173, 174, 229, 238, 247, 283–284, 290

Recep Paşa, Topal: grand vezir (1632), 196, 197

Red Sea, 86, 99, 100, 107, 147, 268

reform in Ottoman Empire, 175, 192–193, 197–198, 203, 205–206, 209, 220, 221, 222, 225–226, 229, 240–242, 246, 247, 251–252, 256–257, 260–266, 269, 273, 291

Reformation, the: relationship to Ottoman Empire, 92, 93, 94, 106

refugees to Ottoman territory, 69, 218, 254

registers, 119

Reichenbach, Treaty of (1790), 259

reis: naval captain, 132

reis ul-küttap: executive secretary to the Grand Vezir; chief of the scribal guild, 118, 119, 208, 233, 264, 280–283, 289, 296

religious conversion, 4, 15, 19, 20, 24, 28, 46, 61, 113, 114, 127, 129, 155, 237, 241

religious/cultural class, *see* Ilmiye

religious movements, orders (*tarikat*), and institutions, 25, 27, 28, 34–35, 40, 72, 75, 77, 78, 123, 141, 153–155, 207, 295

religious persecution, 95, 96, 178, 183, 239

religious sciences, 144–146, 147

resettlement, 19, 59, 61, 66, 81, 87, 171, 172, 178

revolts, 43–45, 47, 71–72, 80, 86, 88, 89, 92, 95, 109, 122, 149, 173, 174–175, 184, 185, 186, 187, 188, 192–194, 195, 196–197, 202, 206, 210, 211, 217, 219, 220, 227–228, 232, 238, 239–240, 248–249, 270–273, 314

Rhodes (Rodos), 17, 69, 70, 71, 86, 88, 89, 111, 146, 287
Rhodope mountains, 17, 20
rice, rice trade, 18, 130
Ridaniye, Battle of (1517), 84
rifles, rifle factories, 263
rikâb ağaları: high ranking *ağa*s around the Sultan, 117
riyale: staff captain, 226
roads, 114, 125, 128, 129, 130, 136, 151, 161
Romanov, Michael: czar of Russia (ruled 1613–1645), 199
Romanus IV Diogenus: Byzantine emperor (ruled 1068–1071), 6
Rome, 50, 69, 71, 102, 153
Rumeli (Rumelia) province, 34, 38, 40, 43, 46, 49, 51, 52, 58, 79, 105, 111, 119, 120, 121, 124, 134, 145, 150, 151, 155, 156, 157, 194, 211, 218, 238, 267, 287, 288
Rumeli Hisarı: Bosporus fortress, 56
Rusçuk (Ruse), 129, 249, 253, 271, 274
Russia, 67–68, 74, 75, 80, 85, 90, 159, 176–177, 180, 181, 183, 184, 189, 190, 199, 202, 210, 213, 214, 217, 218, 220, 221, 222, 224, 225, 229, 231, 239, 243–245, 247–250, 254, 255, 256, 258, 259, 260, 267, 268, 270, 271, 272–273, 273–274, 275, 291
ruzname: register of daily revenues and expenditures in Imperial Treasury, 119
Rüstem Paşa, Damat: grand vezir (1555–1561), 104, 105, 108, 110
rüsum taxes: authorized by decrees of the Imperial Council, 77, 120
Rüus Kalemi: Appointments Department in Imperial Council, 119, 281

Sabatz, 91
Sabit, Alauddin (d. 1713): Ottoman humorist and writer, 293
Sabuncuoğlu, Şerefeddin: 15th-century doctor, 143
Sa'dabat palace, 234, 251, 293
Safavid dynasty of Iran, 77–78, 79, 80–83, 85, 86, 87, 92, 95, 96, 104, 105, 108–109, 149, 154, 164, 177, 180, 181, 182, 183, 195, 196, 199, 238, 243, 246, 284
Safiye Sultan: wife of Murat III, 177, 179, 184, 186
Safranbolu, 43, 200
Sahip Giray II: Crimean Tatar *han* (ruled 1772–1775), 249
sailors, 75, 86, 96, 132, 252
Sakarya river, 13, 14
salaries and wages, 5, 25, 46, 51, 70, 90, 119,

121, 122, 125, 127, 128, 200, 202, 204, 218, 226, 238, 241, 242, 247, 261, 290
salgun: illegal requisition, 174
Saliha Sultan (1715–1778): sister of Mustafa III, 247
Salonica (Selanik, Thessaloniki), 16, 17, 20, 27, 33, 37, 41, 47, 48, 52, 60, 69, 129, 159, 222
salt, 120, 203
Samakov, 20, 39
Samarcand, 32, 143, 148
Samsun, 11, 34, 42, 43, 47
Sana, 106, 107, 176, 195
sancak (banner): provincial district, 26, 49, 61, 94, 100, 121, 122, 126, 127, 131, 132, 143, 202, 205, 208, 211
sancak bey: commander of district, military commander, 26, 50, 92, 126, 131, 135, 171, 226
Sancar: last Seljuk sultan (ruled 1118–1157), 8
Sarajevo (Saray Bosna, Bosna Sarayı), 143, 241, 244
sarraf: money lender, 158
Saruhan: Turkoman Anatolian principality, 10, 21, 29, 30, 38, 42, 44
satire, 142
Saudi family, 253
Sava river, 129, 184, 224, 232, 245, 258
saz şair: folk poet, troubador, 140, 141, 149
Scanderbeg (Iskender Bey, George Castriotis; d. 1468): Albanian resistance leader, 49, 51, 53, 63, 64, 65, 68, 308
schools, 29, 36, 60, 132, 133, 151, 161, 174, 162, 190, 251, 252, 263, 265, 283; *see also* education
Scribal Institution (*Kalemiye*), scribes, scribal guild, 27, 86, 101, 118–134, 139, 146, 157, 171, 194, 226, 236, 238, 247, 256, 264, 280–283, 285, 289, 290, 294, 295, 315
Sébastiani, General Horace (1772–1851): French agent to Selim III (1801–1803, 1806–1808), 273
security and order, 26, 122, 123, 160, 171, 197, 283
Seferli Odası: Campaign Chamber of Topkapı Palace, 117
Segban (Seymen) corps: personal guard of the Sultan, 123, 172
Selim I (1470–1512): Ottoman sultan (ruled 1512–1520), 79–86, 87, 90, 96, 101, 107, 123, 144, 146, 147, 149, 153, 311
Selim II (1524–1574): Ottoman sultan (ruled 1566–1574), 98, 104, 110, 111, 152, 173, 175–179, 228, 318

346

Selim III (1761–1808): Ottoman sultan
(ruled 1789–1807), 251, 259, 260–274,
295, 324
Seljuks, Great Seljuk Empire (1038–1157),
4–8, 10, 23, 25, 27, 62, 304
Seljuks of Rum, 7, 8, 10, 12, 13, 14, 21, 24,
25, 139, 140, 155, 304
Selman Reis: 16th-century Mamluk and
Ottoman admiral, 86
semaî: minstral verse form with three beats,
292,
semaniye: highest ranked *medrese*s, 133
Semendria (Smederovo, Semendire), 49,
50, 68, 74, 221, 232, 244
Sephardic Jews, 152, 159
Septinsular Republic (Ionian Islands), 269
Serbia, Serbs, 12, 16, 17, 18, 19, 20, 21, 22,
29, 30, 31, 33, 35, 36, 37, 38, 39, 45, 47,
48, 49, 50, 51, 52, 53, 56, 63, 65, 68, 69,
72, 79, 91, 107, 129, 143, 151, 184, 220,
221, 222, 244, 248, 258, 259, 260, 267,
271
Serbian church, 151
Serbian Revolution (1803–1805), 271–275
Severin, 50
Seydi Ali Reis (d. 1562): 16th-century
Ottoman admiral, astronomer and
mathematician, 107, 143, 147
Seydişehir, 11
Seyfiye: Military Institution, *see* military
organization
Seyyit Battal Gazi: 13th-century poet, 141
Shamanism, 1, 3, 4, 28
Shia, Shiism, 5, 7, 9, 77–78, 80, 95, 104, 109,
149, 164, 176, 180, 181, 183, 239
ships, 75, 167, 226, 252
shipyards, 65, 75, 83, 86, 97, 100, 131–132,
205, 252, 263
Shiraz, 32
Sibiu (Hermanstadt), 50
Sicily, 97, 179
Sigetvar, 111, 146
Sigismund: king of Hungary (ruled 1386–
1437), 31, 33, 36, 42, 46, 48, 50
Sigismund I: king of Poland (ruled 1506–
1548), 92, 102, 105
Sigismund II August: king of Poland
(ruled 1548–1572), 105
Sigismund III Vasa: king of Poland (ruled
1587–1632), 185, 189, 190, 198
Sigismund Janos (1540–1571): son of John
Zapolya and prince of Transylvania,
102, 105, 180
silahtar ağa: swordkeeper and secretary of
the Sultan, 115

Silahtar cavalry, 114, 124, 125
Sile, 15
Silistria (Silistre), 34, 129, 271
Silivri, 228
silk, silk trade, 60, 83, 158, 181, 202
silver, silver mines, 39, 63, 107, 114, 120,
172, 173, 201
Sinai peninsula, 6, 84
Sinan Paşa, Cağalazâde: grand vezir
(1596), 186
Sinan Paşa, Koca: grand vezir (1550–
1554), 105, 106, 176
Sinan Paşa, Koca: grand vezir (1580–1582,
1589–1591, 1593–1595), 129, 181, 184,
185
Sinop (Sinope) 11, 31, 190, 252
Sipah cavalry, 114, 124
Sipahi Ocağı, Sipahiyân: cavalry corps, 26,
46, 60, 81, 94, 100, 108, 124–127, 131,
145, 171, 173, 186, 192, 193, 194, 196,
197, 201, 204, 206, 208, 209, 211, 217,
226, 252, 257, 286, 292
Siroz, Serez, 18, 20, 48
Sisam (Samos), 287
Sissek (Şişka), Battle of (1593), 184
Sistova, 253, 259
Treaty of (1791), 259, 267
Sitva Torok, Treaty of (1606), 187–188,
189
Sivas (Sebastea), 20, 30, 34, 35, 37, 42, 66,
70, 82, 149, 206, 208
Sivasi Efendi (d. 1640): liberal member of
Ulema, 207
Siyavuş Paşa: grand vezir (1651, 1656),
204, 209
sır kâtibi: personal scribe of the Sultan, 115
Sırp Sındığı, Battle of (1364), 18, 19
Skopje (Üsküp), 17, 21, 27, 29, 39, 143, 220
Slankamen, Battle of (1691), 222
slaves, slavery, 4, 5, 30, 36, 46, 58, 83, 88,
101, 104, 114, 115, 129, 132, 135, 158,
164, 170, 209, 253
Slaves of the Porte, *see Kapıkulu*
Sliven, 18, 39
Slovenia, 18, 94, 102, 219
soap, 120, 225
Sobieski, Jan III: king of Poland (ruled
1674–1696), 213, 214, 215, 218, 222
social services, 135, 151, 157, 161, 190, 283
Sofia (Sofya), 17, 20, 27, 39, 51, 74, 129, 256
softa (suhte): Muslim religious student,
133, 174, 186, 228
Sokullu Mehmet Paşa (1505–1579): grand
vezir (1565–1579), 105, 110, 111, 146,
177, 178, 179, 180, 181, 182, 228, 288

Tokay, 92

Top Arabacı Ocağı (Cannon Wagon Corps), 124, 262

Topçu Ocağı (Cannon Corps), 46, 58, 124, 262; *see also* Artillery corps

Tophane Naziri: Superintendent of Imperial Arsenal, 208

Tophane-i Âmire (Imperial Foundry, Arsenal), 124, 148

Topkapı Sarayı: Topkapı Palace, Imperial Palace, 59, 85, 86, 115, 116, 137, 202, 286

de Tott, Baron François (1730–1793), 251–252, 255, 257, 260, 262

Trabzon (Trebizond), 6, 7, 11, 15, 17, 34, 36, 42, 63, 64, 81, 141, 143, 190, 208, 270, 287

trade, trade concessions, 3, 6, 7, 26, 27, 57, 60, 69, 73, 75, 76, 80, 83, 87, 88, 91, 95, 97, 99, 100, 103, 107, 112, 114, 120, 130, 158–159, 160, 161, 162, 163, 172, 173, 177, 181–182, 202, 213, 224, 231, 232, 233, 245, 246, 247, 250, 258, 256, 269, 270, 284

Translation Office (*Tercüme Odası*), 282

translations, 235, 257, 264, 266, 281, 282

Translator of the Porte, *see Baş Tercüman*

Transoxania, 2, 3, 4, 8, 32, 33, 78, 85, 143, 187, 189

Transylvania (Erdel), 18, 42, 50, 52, 74, 91, 92, 100, 102, 105, 111, 122, 129, 180, 185, 187, 199, 211, 212, 217, 218, 220, 221, 222, 224, 232, 244, 259

travellers, 128, 129, 161

treasurer, *see defterdar*

treasuries, 115, 119, 281; *see also Hazine-i Âmire* and *Hazine-i Hassa*

Tripoli of Libya (Trablus Garp), 97, 106, 111

Tripoli of Syria (Trablus), 99, 122

Triple Alliance, 259, 260, 268, 271–272

Tuğrul Bey: founder of the Seljuk dynasty, 4, 6

Tulip Period (*Lâle Devri*, 1718–1730), 234–238, 242, 257, 265, 293–294, 296

Tuman Bay: Mamluk sultan (ruled 1516–1517), 84

Tunis, 96, 106, 179

Turgut Reis (Dragut): 16th-century Ottoman admiral, 105, 106

Turkish notables, Turkish aristocracy, 22, 24–25, 27–28, 30, 33, 36–39, 41, 45, 46, 49–50, 52, 53, 55, 58, 67, 70–71, 76, 79, 90, 92, 110, 113, 170, 186

Turkoman principalities, princes, beys, 1, 10–11, 20–21, 22, 24, 28, 29, 30, 32, 35,

36, 37, 38, 39, 41, 44, 45, 48, 55, 61, 64, 66, 71, 113, 164

Turkomans, Turkoman nomads, 1, 2, 5, 6, 7, 8, 9, 10, 11, 12, 13, 15, 17, 19, 21, 22, 23, 25, 27, 28, 29, 30, 31, 33, 35, 37, 41, 43, 47, 65, 66, 71, 75, 77–78, 80, 86, 92, 95, 108, 110, 120, 127, 128, 140, 141, 150, 151, 154, 188, 195, 220, 226

settlement of, 29, 43, 53, 61, 225

Turks, pre-Ottoman, 1–11, 23, 164, 192

Turna Dağ, Battle of (1515), 82

türkmen ağa: state representative with nomadic tribes, 150

türkü: folk song, 292

uc (march), *uc bey* (frontier commander), 9, 13, 121, 129, 242

Ukraine, 62, 68, 213, 217, 218, 224, 230, 248

ulema: members of Muslim learned/ religious/cultural institution (*Ilmiye*); possessors of Muslim knowledge (*ilim*), 30, 41, 76, 78, 79, 103, 104, 109, 117, 118, 132–149, 151, 162, 164, 171, 181, 191, 192, 194, 202, 207, 209, 218, 228, 230, 237, 240, 246, 255, 273, 282–283, 291, 293, 295

Ulubat, Battle of (1422), 45

Ulufeciyân cavalry corps, 124

Uluğ Bey: Timurid ruler, 143, 148

ulus: nomadic people, tribe, 150

Umar Paşa: Iraki Mamluk leader (1764–1780), 253

Umur Bey: prince of Turkoman principality of Aydın, 10, 16

umur-u bahriye nazırı (superintendent of naval affairs), 264

Una river, 184, 224, 232,

unemployment, 104, 172, 246

Urfa (Edessa), 33, 225

Urmiya, Lake, 82, 188

Uruc Reis: 16th-century Turkish sea *gazi,* 96

Uskoks, 184

usta: master craftsman, 157

Ustuvani Efendi: leader of conservative 17th-century Ulema, 207, 209

Uzbeg empire, 78, 80, 109, 177, 181, 183, 188

Uzun Hasan (1433–1478); ruler of White Sheep Turkomans (ruled 1453–1478), 61, 64, 65, 66, 67, 73, 77, 82, 143, 145

Üsküdar (Scutari), 15, 130, 136, 160, 211, 239, 241

vakanüvis: official Ottoman court chronicler, 288–290, 294, 296–298; *see also* historiography

vali (governor), 121–122